MW00484442

Abraham Kuyper was not only an outstanding political leader but a deep diver into the complexities of the human heart. Every week for nearly fifty years he shared his reflections on the challenges and blessings of the Christian life with the readers of his Sunday journal. Thanks to the superb work of James A. De Jong, we now have a collection of two hundred of these meditations available in a clear, lively English translation. Deeply rooted in Scripture, refracted through experiences both rare and commonplace, enlivened by Kuyper's lively imagination, these meditations lead us along the confrontation between a most holy God and our various spiritual aspirations—from hope to doubt, trial to repentance, pride to joy. The good news of the Gospel, Kuyper points out again and again, is that the last word in these encounters always belongs to God's mercy. This is a bracing piety that can well serve Christians today, and every day.

—**JAMES D. BRATT**
Professor of History emeritus, Calvin College

Imagine opening a collection of meditations by the young Augustine, a young Martin Luther or John Calvin. In this new volume we find a collection of meditations by the young Abraham Kuyper, never before published in English translation. Here are the devotional thoughts of one of the most significant Protestant thinkers of the last 150 years and from the most formative period of his influential life. This treasure is both timeless and timely.

—**R. ALBERT MOHLER JR.**
President, The Southern Baptist Theological Seminary

I have been reading Kuyper's *Near Unto God* collection of meditations for decades—so much so that I wore out my first copy. He is my favorite devotional writer. And now this wonderful collection of 200 more. I hope all who have come to appreciate Kuyper's writings on politics and culture in recent years will now taste the spiritual sweetness of *Honey from the Rock*!

—**RICHARD J. MOUW**
President emeritus, Fuller Theological Seminary

All too often piety and doctrine are held in tension and even contrast. The same is true for practical, Christian discipleship and theological acumen. ... This set of devotions from Abraham Kuyper should definitively overturn the idea that doctrinal fidelity and practical piety are necessarily in competition. ... This collection of spiritual insights promises to help us understand Kuyper better, and more importantly, to understand Scripture and the will of God better, and thereby to be better subjects of his (and our) Lord and Savior.

—**JORDAN J. BALLOR**
General editor *Abraham Kuyper Collected Works in Public Theology*;
Senior research fellow, Acton Institute for the Study of Religion & Liberty

Was Kuyper a Kuyperian, a doctrinalist, or a pietist? In the best sense of this standard taxonomy he was all three. These pastoral meditations on Scripture by the relatively young Kuyper, intended for a broad readership, are consistently edifying with often striking and unexpected insights. They also reveal that the transformationalist ("Kuyperian"!) aspects of his thought which have received so much attention, are not properly appropriated apart from appreciating that they plainly stem from his heart—a heart that in embracing sound doctrine, true to the Reformed confessions, overflows with genuine piety devoted to the worship and service of the Triune God of Scripture.

—**RICHARD B. GAFFIN JR.**
Professor of Biblical and Systematic Theology emeritus, Westminster Theological Seminary

HONEY FROM THE ROCK

ABRAHAM KUYPER

HONEY FROM THE ROCK

DAILY DEVOTIONS
FROM YOUNG KUYPER

TRANSLATED BY

JAMES A. DE JONG

LEXHAM PRESS

Honey From the Rock: Daily Devotions from Young Kuyper

Copyright 2018 Dutch Reformed Translation Society

Lexham Press, 1313 Commercial St., Bellingham, WA 98225
LexhamPress.com

All rights reserved. You may use brief quotations from this resource in presentations, articles, and books. For all other uses, please write Lexham Press for permission. Email us at permissions@ lexhampress.com.

Original Dutch edition: *Honig uit den Rotssteen*, 2 vols. (Amsterdam: Wormser, 1880; Amsterdam & Pretoria: Höveker & Wormser, 1883).

Print ISBN 9781683592341
Digital ISBN 9781683592358

Lexham Editorial Team: Claire Brubaker, Todd Hains, and Christy Callahan
Cover Design: Brittany Schrock
Typesetting: ProjectLuz.com

CONTENTS

VOLUME II

TRANSLATOR'S PREFACE

Writing a weekly meditation on Sunday was sacrosanct for Abraham Kuyper (1837–1920). He tolerated no compromise of that commitment even during his harried years as prime minister of the Netherlands (1901–1905). While he often delayed or interrupted other writing projects, he never did so with respect to writing his weekly meditation. That pattern prevailed from the early 1870s until several days before his death in November 1920. In fact, in the weeks just preceding the high Christian holidays, he consistently wrote two devotionals. The size of this body of material is enormous. It consists of over twenty-two hundred pieces.

Kuyper's religious rigor in writing biblically based meditations must be understood as the profoundly spiritual experience it was for him. Sitting alone while quietly reflecting deeply, often imaginatively, on a biblical passage, was an act of communing with God. Such intimate fellowship with his Creator and Redeemer replenished his spirit. It fortified, invigorated, inspired, instructed, and directed him. These benefits of his precious time alone with the Lord flowed from his heart and soul through his gifted pen. They become ours through his meditations.

UNDERSTANDING KUYPER FULLY

One cannot understand Abraham Kuyper apart from his meditations. The more one delves into them, the better one comes to know Abraham Kuyper. Kuyper is famous for his initiatives in Christian journalism. He began a Christian daily newspaper in the early 1870s. He founded and edited an eight-page religious weekly. He was a rigorous advocate for government funding for Christian schools. His vision of a Christian scientific mind compelled him to establish a Christian university. Politics and justice were such important arenas needing faith-based guidance that he exchanged his pastoral office for a political one.

Urbanization, industrialization, and colonialism all presented new challenges in a rapidly changing world order that begged for Christlike solutions. So he galvanized the Anti-Revolutionary Party into a passionately dedicated political movement. As a theological professor, he produced major theological works, many now being translated into English for the first time. Kuyper's amazing stamina and productivity, seen in these initiatives, were nurtured by the spirituality so transparent in his meditations. Kuyper did not wear his heart on his sleeve, but his meditations are the lens through which we are privileged to look into his soul.

A great deal of fine scholarship has been directed recently to Kuyper's many accomplishments. Much of it has focused on the younger Kuyper during the formative years of his public career—when he began publishing his weekly meditations. They first appeared in the Sunday weekly inserted into his daily newspaper, *De Standaard* (*The Standard*). After a few years, that insert became the separately printed religious weekly known as *De Heraut* (*The Herald*); it began appearing in December 1877. Remarkably, despite scouring Kuyper's meditations in these two sources, one looks in vain for Editor Kuyper reprinting one of them there under the duress of a heavy schedule. Over the years, he might produce a meditation on the same text several times, even five or six times. But in such cases, each meditation was the product of a new spiritual encounter with the Lord. Despite the originality of each of Kuyper's meditations, despite their paramount importance in the weekly rhythm of his life, and despite the convictions and biblical insights they convey, modern scholarship has given Kuyper's meditations largely only casual acknowledgment. This includes studies on Kuyper during the formative stage of his emerging public career. Fortunately, that is beginning to change.

ABOUT THE *HONEY FROM THE ROCK* MEDITATIONS

These meditations—originally published as two volumes, in 1880 and 1883 respectively—reflect the younger Kuyper's spirituality. Volume 1 consists of one hundred meditations written from December 1877 to late 1880. Kuyper reprinted them in the same sequence in which they originally appeared in *De Heraut*. Volume 2 includes another one hundred meditations that first appeared between May 1879 and mid-1882. For unspecified reasons, he did not reprint them in the same sequence in which they were published in that paper. The two-volume collection was republished only once in the Dutch language, in 1896 (volume 1) and 1897 (volume 2).

The title *Honey from the Rock* is based on Psalm 81:16: "But you will be fed with the finest of wheat. I will satisfy you with honey from the rock."[1] While Kuyper never did write a meditation on this verse, it perfectly captures how he felt about meditating on Scripture. Communion with the Lord is sweet. It feeds the deepest hungers of the human spirit. Spiritual nourishment comes from all parts of the Bible. This collection draws heavily from the Gospels, Psalms, New Testament Letters, and Old Testament Latter Prophets. But it also includes meditations based on passages from the Pentateuch, Former Prophets, and wisdom literature.

The themes and topics in this collection are rather wide ranging. Emphasis on personal assurance based on God's covenant promises is prominent. So is God's patience and long-suffering with his often-indifferent people. The power and glory of the Christian life are frequent motifs. Endurance and perseverance in the face of hardship appear consistently. The responsibilities of Christian parenting are regularly treated, as are the sad consequences of neglecting them. Formal, empty, powerless religious practice is often denounced, as are hypocrisy and religious practice for social recognition. The meditations are equally emphatic against cultivating subjective religious experience as the basis for assurance; Kuyper unmasks the spiritual peril of such piety. He is graphic and candid about the power of sin in the lives of Christians as well as among unbelievers. For him, the Devil, sin, and hell are looming realities regularly referenced in his material. He emphasized the ministering power of angels in Christian experience. He stressed the urgency of vibrant Christian community, the Sabbath as a time of sacred refuge and renewal, and the centrality of worship and preaching and sacraments in the ministration of grace. Worldly diversion and the pursuit of material gain and human recognition elicit his warnings. Kuyper does employ theological terms in these meditations: calling, election, adoption, regeneration, sanctification, atonement, and others. But he does so not to teach doctrine; he assumes that readers understand this vocabulary. He uses these terms only to stress the riches of fellowship with God. Kuyper's handling of his chosen themes and topics, and his occasional use of theological terms, occur in a surprisingly fresh, creative style. His meditations are spiritually gripping and memorable.

---

1. Following the policy of the Dutch Reformed Translation Society, I translated Kuyper's Dutch quotation of this verse. In doing this, I usually consult several English translations, but am dependent on none.

Equally important about this collection of meditations is what it does not include. Not found here are urgent calls to Kuyper's political and social agendas. As he stresses from time to time, meditating and Christian public worship are essential spiritual exercises, in which we leave external preoccupations at the door. Here we enter the sacred space where we consciously stand in the presence of God. Here we search our hearts and souls in the light of his Word. Here we are spiritually renewed, restored, and replenished for returning to our daily callings.

This two-volume set appears here in English translation for the first time. Several meditations in it did find their way into other topical collections of Kuyper meditations that he subsequently published and that have been translated into English. But this involves no more than a half dozen of the two hundred in this set. And their appearance in later Dutch collections and in arcane pre–World War II English translations was not acknowledged as coming from *Honey from the Rock*.

Because the original two volumes appear here in one volume, original placement is designated in the upper left corner on each meditation's opening page.

KUYPER'S MEDITATIONS IN CONTEXT

This translation attempts to be completely faithful to the Kuyper text. No attempt is made here to hide the social biases that mark him as a man of his time. It also presents him in readable, contemporary prose. This required breaking apart his inordinately long and intricate sentences, adding an occasional clarifying footnote, and infrequently substituting a contemporary equivalent idiom or term for an arcane Dutch one.

Only one other republished collection of Kuyper meditations is as wide ranging thematically and scripturally as this one. Entitled *To Be Near to God*, it appeared in 1908 and is a collection of mediations written while and shortly after he was prime minister. They also first appeared in *De Heraut* and were then republished in book form. Unlike *Honey from the Rock,* they were soon translated into English and reflect the spirituality of the mature Kuyper.

Six other collections of Kuyper meditations that first appeared in *De Heraut* and were then republished in book form are shorter and topically focused. They deal with pastoral issues like sickness and death, family life and marriage, Christ's sufferings and death, and the Christian high holidays. But *Honey from the Rock* and *To Be Near to God* are the wide-ranging bookends that bracket all these other more focused collections. While Kuyper continued writing meditations after 1908, none of them were ever gathered and reprinted as collections in book form. Some of the earlier collections were reprinted in the Dutch language, and most of these were eventually translated into English. But by the end of World War II, Abraham Kuyper's meditations were largely disregarded by readers in both the Dutch and English languages.

The board of the Dutch Reformed Translation Society is grateful to Lexham Press for its collaboration in printing this collection. Its appearance in print now makes Kuyper's spiritual writing available in addition to his other material now appearing in modern translation.

Special thanks is due to Mr. Paulus Heule for generously underwriting this translation project; he is a former board member of the Dutch Reformed Translation Society and the Honorary Consul of the Netherlands for Western Michigan.

James A. De Jong
Advent 2017

VOLUME I

LIKE A WEANED CHILD

Quiet like a weaned child with its mother. Psalm 131:2

A child nursing at its mother's breast is still living in the initial luxury of its young life. But even in that luxury it's still unsettled. It always wants the breast again because the breast never fails to provide in abundance. That child feels intensely how much it cherishes the breast, especially when its thirst for its mother's milk returns.

But now consider the same child after it has gone through the process of being weaned. I'm not thinking about it during the process of being weaned, but after it has been weaned. The time of always crying to be fed has passed. That little child has learned to take a more measured approach to eating. If you set it on its mother's lap now, it's no longer drawn to her breast, but it sits there blissfully, simply basking in its mother's presence!

And isn't this the way it is for the soul in its transition from the turbulent conversion experience to the sense of peace that follows? Isn't this similar to the experience of a weaned child? Isn't the recent convert like a nursing child in always dreaming about the bounty of divine love? By drinking deeply, isn't it refreshed by its new source of life? Doesn't it take in more than weak, infant faith can possibly swallow? And in its restless and intense prayer life, isn't it always asking for an even fuller stream of divine grace?

But then the soul that was initially satiated by such bounty goes through a disillusioning experience. It is weaned from being overly excited, from the excess it enjoyed, and from what is too wonderful for this world. It still focuses on divine love, but it is now a love tempered by Golgotha and the sobering reality of the cross. It now takes the measure of things more dispassionately. A spirit of longer-term expectation replaces one of urgent immediacy. Now it imbibes a sense of what the soul needs to endure. Former unsettledness is replaced by a growing sense of peace. This is like the peace of a child that first drank milk but that has now been weaned from it and asks for its mother as mother. The maturing believer now looks to God as God, and prays with humble entreaty, knowing how very small one's soul really is.

What we have here is an example of deep dependence. An even greater dependence than that of the little child nursing at the breast is that of one who has been weaned. The little child on the breast is willful. That breast belongs to it! That breast is there for it! The mother's warm breast is its little kingdom! With its own tongue and little lips it sucks the lukewarm milk! It's very different for the weaned child. That child has nothing. It discovers that nothing has been prepared. It eats right along with what others eat. And it even lacks the ability to bring to its mouth by itself the food that has been set before it. Its dependence is total!

And is this also how it is for you who have been weaned from the bounty of your first love? Don't you now feel small and dependent in your heart? You first thought so much was possible! You were so satisfied in your own little kingdom! You were always ready to express yourself on everything. Your lips were always ready to sing God's praises!

But if you're honest with yourself, haven't you now developed appreciation for what's small? Don't you take pleasure in the lowly state of God's servants? In the fact that you encounter opposition? That you're denied honor and status? That your plans and aspirations fail, so that you now come to enjoy with a joyful heart all with which God has favored you? With a measure of resignation, haven't you learned to testify with David: "O Lord, my heart is not proud. I will not concern myself with things that are too great and wonderful for me. I'm like a weaned child with its mother, and my soul is like a weaned child within me. Israel, hope in the Lord!"

Let me say this yet. A mother's milk is also bread, as Augustine so beautifully put it. But it's bread that has passed through a mother's veins and become milk. Bread, therefore, but by derivation. Bread, therefore, but bread first enjoyed by someone else so that the suckling could also enjoy it. Sweetened, weakened, and broken down!

But as soon as the small child is weaned, it gets solid food and it eats actual bread. This is bread that is softened and broken into small pieces. But it is nevertheless bread, bread with all its nourishing elements that make a person strong.

And now isn't that just the way it happened with you when you were brought to your Savior, who is your Bread of Life? Initially you had more desire for that Bread when it had passed through another person and become for you like "mother's milk for a newborn child." People fed you from Christ, but Christ himself still remained distant to you. The Word was still too difficult for you, too demanding, and too indigestible. Then you had no desire for the Word other than as blended with a sweet little song and as reworked into a very light meal with all the seeds and pits and removed.

But now that you've been weaned from the bounty of your first love and have developed a desire for what's much more modest, you have an appetite for the Bread of Life himself. That's because you are no longer a "newborn child in Christ." Now the hard crust that covers the Word that inside is soft and chewable no longer deters you. Now you patiently bring to your lips the bread of the Word that has such a heavenly, life-giving aroma. And what's now missing is the mammoth pretense of thinking that you already know everything. All your knowledge in fact fails you! You really know nothing! And crying out from your blindness of soul, you wait for the light from your Only True Love. And in that waiting you sit like a weaned child with its mother, quietly content in the presence of your Lord!

THE FOXES HAVE HOLES

The foxes have holes and the birds of the heavens have nests,
but the Son of Man has nowhere to lay his head. Luke 9:58

Isn't this soul-piercing verse breathtakingly beautiful and deeply moving? The foxes still have their dens, and the birds still have their nests high up in the trees, but I, your Lord Jesus, don't have a spot where I can rest here on earth! It's especially beautiful when you note what precedes it and pay attention to what follows it. Then you live into the thought world reflected by this heart-wrenching complaint on Jesus' lips.

The transfiguration of Jesus on Mount Tabor, the heavenly radiance flooding that scene, and Peter's question about building three tabernacles—one for Moses, one for Elijah, but also one for Jesus (Luke 9:33)—all precede this verse. So does the refusal of the Samaritans to provide lodging for Jesus as he continued his journey to Jerusalem. The result is that he had to spend the night on the cold, hard ground.

Even the fox could dig a den in that ground and find shelter in the heart of the earth. Even the bird could flutter upward, high above that ground, and take refuge there in its nest. But for the Son of Man there was no resting place for his weary head. No resting place, even if a palace opened its gates to him or Peter put up a tabernacle for him. As things were, the earth was definitely suited for the fox and its claws or for the swallow and her wings, but not for Jesus. Not for the Son of Man! He belonged to a higher world, a world whose radiance had enveloped him on Tabor. It is a more perfect world, where no fox can dig his hole and no meadowlark can fly. It is a world where your Lord Jesus offers you what he would win by his soul-absorbing work when once seated on his glorious throne, namely, heartfelt peace and rest with the Father.

It's not possible for a permanent tabernacle worthy of the Son of Man to exist here on this earth that lies under a curse. When Peter suggested erecting one, says the evangelist, he had no idea what he was saying. Jesus belongs to an order that is too high for this impoverished world. It's too high not only by virtue of him being God but also because he is the Son of Man. People, like the fox, eventually dig a dark hole in the ground for others. They do this when a person dies, descends into the pit of death, and is carried off to a grave. But now listen to what Jesus says to another inquirer immediately after our verse. He says that for whoever would follow him there is no grave: "Let the dead bury their dead, but you go out and proclaim the kingdom of God!" Similarly, a person undertakes building a place to live like a bird undertakes the building of its nest. But that house can never be one's eternal home. Look at how Jesus insistently rejects the following plea: "Lord, give me permission first to return and say goodbye to those in my house."

No, no! Remaining here on earth is even less permissible for those redeemed by Jesus than for their Savior himself. They grow into one plant with their Lord and are thus cut off at the root from this world. To live in him is to live outside the world. Like pilgrims on a pilgrimage, they are no longer at home on earth but are on a journey to their real homeland. Whoever finds what they are looking for here below lowers themself beneath their true calling as a human being. They have no fellowship with God's holy angels, but merely with the foxes, birds, and animals of the forest.

True glory lies in living out the prophetic vow of the Rechabites found in Jeremiah 35:7: "We will build no houses for our dwellings, but we will live in tents before the face of the Lord!" And the letter to the Hebrews praises the patriarchs for wandering around and living in tents. The apostle advocates a break with this world when he urges "wandering in the heavens" and "leaving behind" what is here.

Accordingly, whoever follows Jesus turns his back on the world. She repeatedly finds its charms fading. In her heart and soul she crucifies its glories. She does so not because she relinquishes a desire for happiness, but because she yearns for a greater, higher, richer, and more brilliant glory. In hope, he desires a glory through which already now his quieted heart finds itself swelling with a holy joy. This is joy in the divine splendor and pure luster of God's kingdom.

When that brilliance once breaks through and the celebrated day finally arrives for which your soul has been longing day and night, O elect child of God, then it will not be the foxes that crawl into their dens. According to the word of the prophet in Isaiah 2:19, it will be those who have not honored the King of Glory here on earth. It will be those who flee into "the caves and holes in the ground." Then "pain and anguish like that of a woman in childbirth" will overcome those who, like the birds of the air, have been driven by haughtiness but who have in fact lowered themselves because "they have made their home on the heights of Lebanon and built their nests on the cedar's branches" (Jer 22:23). But for you, for all of you who regarded the world as nothing and were mocked and driven out of it, you will live "in the home of the seraphim." The precious word spoken by the Lord himself is for all of you who have suffered pain in your pilgrim wanderings: "In the home that is above are many rooms, and a place has been prepared for you there in my Father's house."

3

VOLUME I

FOR HE IS SO SMALL

*Lord, Lord, please forgive! How can Jacob possibly
survive, for he is so small? Amos 7:2*

The Lord's favor rests on whoever is small, on whoever is despised and discouraged, on whoever is laid low in the dust. "O save us, O God!" the prophet implores in his anguish, "for we no longer amount to anything. We've been completely beaten down. Jacob is so small!"

That's the way it is!

The Lord's anger turns against whatever is exalted. His power is directed against what is haughty and pompous, against all that is lofty. It will all be laid low—every high tower, every solid wall—until people's pride is broken and their arrogance is trampled!

He has no patience for anyone who takes a spot alongside him or against him. He alone, the Lord our God, will be exalted.

That's why he shows favor to those who want to be small, make themselves small, and enter his presence as those who are small.

Look at Mary! Didn't she sing: "He has noted the lowly state of his servant"? Also consider the tiny baby Jesus himself. It's even clearer here. He made himself of no account; he humbled himself to the point of dying, even dying on a cross. And for that reason, says the apostle, because he willingly became like a worm in the ground—and only for that reason—his Father was able to comfort him with a surpassing sense of well-being and exalted him highly, giving him a name that is above all names in heaven and on earth.

Is that the controlling principle of your life, my brother and sister? To deny yourself? To willingly become less and less in order that your exalted Head might increase in your life? Listen to the psalmist as he announces: "I am small and despised, O Lord!" Listen to what Jehovah announces to his people Israel through the multitude of prophets: "I will make you small among the nations, O my people; and afterwards I will take pity on you!" Note carefully how he produces something glorious out of what is lowly: "O Bethlehem Ephrata! You were small among the thousands in Judah." But also note how he ties the promise of consolation to his Exalted One: "When the sword is unsheathed against my Shepherd, then I will extend my hand to those who are small."

And as always, God's elect echo their "Amen" to all of this! When first made small, they experienced a sense of well-being as well. As long as they remained humble, that sense of well-being was undiminished. It ebbed when their hearts swelled; but it flowed in full measure once they were shattered again.

"Become like one of these little children," Jesus said to his disciples in words that ring true, jot and tittle, for you as well as for me. You have to lose your life, not keep it. "Self-denial" is the marching order that gives you the right to follow him. "I am nothing, but you are everything, O Lord," becomes the theme song of a person's soul.

It's a source of comfort to you, isn't it, that you are not counted among the high and mighty or considered as great? Or that you are forgotten here on earth because of your smallness, but that you are highly valued by God because of it. He knows! "You have very little power!" But, the promise "Don't be afraid, my little flock!" is spoken by his divine lips. Oh, everyone who suffers and is oppressed, everyone who is miserable and poor, everyone who is naked or blind, everyone who is helpless and is wandering around abandoned—you have the assurance that your appeal will be heard. "Lord, don't abandon me," Isaiah cries out, "for we are so few!" The entreaties rising from your heavy heart and oppressed soul, as well as your own piercing cries, you may be sure, will register your complaints before the throne of grace: "Lord, God, show me mercy ... for I am small!"

That infant child lying in a crib was made small in order to make you with your dry, cold, and empty heart great in the kingdom that is above. This Immanuel, lowly and humble, has the power to penetrate your heart ever more frequently and with ever greater depth. He can do this until finally the flame of your own unbelief that still sometimes flares up within you is completely extinguished. On the other hand, he also has the power over the smothered heart "not to quench the smoldering wick" but to gently blow on it until it bursts into the flame that is "a light in the valley" of this earth. This is a light of comfort and reassurance.

May the All-Merciful One show you mercy, so that you in turn may show mercy to people who are destitute and oppressed!

May you choose, by examining and discerning your own condition, to show your love to those who are small here on earth! May you open your own heart to those who are despised and rejected! May you be merciful to those who are oppressed and humble! And may you be inclined to listen when people look to you in their lowly circumstances, crying: "Help me, my brother or sister, for I am so small!"

VOLUME I

FOR ALL THESE MANY YEARS

I have been serving you now for all these many years. Luke 15:29

Stop for a minute as you begin reading this. Think about something. Before you start a new year, think about how you are living your life before the face of the living God.

You serve him. You are numbered among those who confess his name. You have a personal knowledge of how the Spirit works. And whenever there is talk about the flock that he has chosen, you definitely think of yourself as one of those people who seek his face.

People would do you an injustice if they regarded you as unconverted or grieved over you as an unbeliever. That's because sometimes you have even been zealous in testifying verbally for the Lord. The Lord's testimony through the prophet Isaiah can rightly be applied to you: "Daily they search me out and desire to know my ways, whether I belong to a people that do what is right and will not forsake God's righteous ways" (Isa 58:2).

But in all of this there is no free pass for you any more than for all the best of your brothers and sisters in the Lord. The question is not whether you serve him, but whether there is any vitality in that service, any faith in that vitality, and any increase in being filled with the Spirit in that faith.

So look deep inside yourself!

For so many years now, you have acted as a doorkeeper in God's outer courts. Think back on the five, ten, twenty, or even more years that have gone by since you first saw the light in your heart. What a long and broad experience you have had in your life! What an opportunity this has presented for you to reflect with greater urgency on the length and breadth of Christ's love for you. How your faith could have been deepened through all those years. How your knowledge of the eternal and true God could have been clarified. How a greater nobility of spirit could have flowed from above and into your soul. For so many years now you have sat down beside the Fountain of Salvation. How often you drank the refreshing drafts from that soul-refreshing source. How often it became a spring of water leading to eternal life for you.

For so many years now, you have become accustomed to serving him. And yet, what has happened to the remnants of your old nature that have been crucified by the power of Christ's cross, put to death, and buried?

For so many years now, you have been involved in his service. But where is the blessing that you spread all around you? Where is the grace for which you have wrestled in prayer on behalf of your home, your friends, and your subordinates? Where is the grace that you wanted to call down from Immanuel on behalf of this spiritually darkened world?

For so many years now, you have followed the Man of Sorrows. But how much progress have you made in denying yourself? In humbling yourself? In willingly bearing the cross assigned to you? Has the shoot on your vine set a bud yet? Has the bud blossomed? After the budding was there blossoming, and after the blossoming was fruit produced? Has there been a lot of fruit as a guarantee that you are worth keeping as a branch on the vine? Has this been the fruit of a cooling ardor for the sensuous and what appeals to the eye? Has it been the fruit of becoming disentangled from wealth and material possessions so that you now treasure giving to the poor more than you do a hefty bank account or stock portfolio? Is it fruit in the more excellent sense of "the fruit of the Spirit," namely, gentleness, patience, and tenderheartedness toward God and others? Above all, is it the greatest fruit of all, namely, the complete and pure love that flows from God into you? And does this love enable you to love and serve him not from a sense of obligation but from the adoration of your heart?

What more needs to be said? Your conscience already accuses you!

You drop your eyes in quiet shame and lament in your lonely bitterness: "How can I make up for those many long years of living in his temple and bearing fruit hardly worth mentioning? Of making so little progress? How can I make up for the fact that while there may not have been regression since I experienced my first love, there has not been much progression in cooling toward the things of this world either?" And in that inner self-awareness, you cry out, hands covering your face: "O God, be merciful to me, a poor sinner, an ineffective witness, and a miserable example of a Christian!"

Where would you be now, if during all those many years there had been consistent growth and fruit bearing in the eternal and invisible things of God? How fully you could have participated in the light, in confident trust, in strength of soul and a lively faith life, in an understanding of the mysteries of God, in a precious prayer life, and especially in tender fellowship and intimate communion with God. What heartfelt love you could have shared. For all those years!

This is the terrible power of sin, the world, and Satan that has impeded you in the course of your life. They have crippled in you what is noble. They have deadened for you what is precious.

If only you had realized this! Then the pride would never have stealthily entered that let you think: "I have served him for all these many years; it will certainly go well for me!" Then you would never have imagined ascending an angels' ladder, but you would have appreciated walking further down the sinner's staircase in order to receive greater grace. Then you would have been more fully aware, contended for your God, and received all you needed from above. To him, not to you, may all praise be given! But now, may you find the strength in your soul to give thanks for the grace of learning that truth. Forget about what you have gambled away for all these years. Extol what he has accomplished in you over many years. Be washed in the blood of the Lamb and reach out for quiet fellowship with him.

All those many years!

How many years still lie ahead for you? Will they be as many as you've already had, or will they be fewer? Do you have only a few left—or maybe only months? Will they be marked by the same old routine, the same deadness of heart, and the same putting of self above the living God?

That would definitely block his compassionate love! Then in judgment on your soul even the smoldering wick would be snuffed out.

THE EXTENSION OF YOUR TRANQUILITY

And it may be that your tranquility will be extended. Daniel 4:27

There can be moments in a person's life when they feel like something bad is about to happen. They shudder apprehensively about some unseen and impending ruin being forced on them. They feel like a whirlwind is churning up a cloud of debris all around them. As a godly minister once put it, all of heaven and earth seemed to have overwhelmed him. Shaken to the core of his being, he felt that he was being forced to experience "how terrible it is to fall into the hands of the living God."[1]

Pray that a terrible day like that never comes, even if it seems that God is approaching you only from a distance. For more than a mere rebuke is involved in this kind of disturbance of your tranquility. God's rage and anger are involved here. We're talking about God opposing you with conflict and oppression. Even if you are tied to him with cords of everlasting divine love and even if you reach out to cling to God's mercy, you find that his love no longer comforts you. You first have to endure the opposite of that love. Your shattered heart has to buckle with each blow he sends daily, knowing that more are coming tomorrow.

---

1. Kuyper's footnote: "Stated by F. N. de Waal, a student of Voetius and minister in 's-Hertogenbosch."

This applies to the person who wants to walk with the Lord. He can't escape it. If this is what it's like in personal life, what will these days be like for the church? Jesus described them when he said: "If those days are not been shortened, even the elect will be weakened." These are days of judging and sentencing when Almighty God works out his sovereign counsel and pursues it in contrast with your best-laid plans. It is a time when his Word prevails over your own mutterings. It is a time for his will to be done rather than yours. For your efforts are expressions of flesh and blood, of what's in your heart, and finally of what the inner recesses of your soul contrive and pursue. But he is always the Conqueror, and the one conquered is the one saved, but saved like grasping a piece of burning firewood and forcibly pulling it out of the fire.

If you were to be thrown into a fiery furnace, only God would be able to discern your inner reaction. No person other than you could do so, not even your closest brother. That's because what is terrible about that kind of day is not the external distress it brings, but what cuts to the chase of your heart. Two people could be walking around in the same furnace, and one of them might perish, while not a hair on the other might be so much as singed. A person might be burned like a bramble bush in the eyes of the world, but nevertheless not be consumed. Like Daniel in the lions' den, their tranquility is undisturbed. The situation about which we are warning you here is this. It's like flames searing your skin terribly. It's like a lion pouncing on you. It's the hand of the spotlessly holy and long-suffering God falling heavily on you.

With the prophet, we appeal to you to "examine yourselves closely, O people who have not yet been seized by a desire to give yourselves to him, lest his decision is revealed and the heat of his wrath overwhelms you."

The Lord is in no hurry to show his fierce anger. On the contrary, your God readily shows you his mercy and is slow to anger. Even when you no longer pray and when you attempt to cover your faithlessness toward him with hypocrisy, he preserves your tranquility. Long-suffering and gracious, he allows it to continue.

Our merciful Father has again averted calamity during the year that lies just behind you.[2] You can judge in your own hearts how the balance tilts between his benevolence and your own coolness toward him. Even though there was no tender fellowship between the two of you, your tranquility remained undisturbed.

---

2. Kuyper first published this meditation in *De Heraut*, no. 5 (January 4, 1878). It was written shortly after his recuperation from a nervous breakdown.

But what about now? Have things reached a turning point? Does the last drop need to fall that will make the cup of his wrath overflow? Hasn't the measure by which he measures now been filled?

O my friend, pray, pray hard that tranquility might be extended for you and your house. Wake up, finally, before destruction falls on you like a raging storm and God comes like a mighty wind that annihilates everything before it. Take heart. Get a grip on yourself in the light of God's everlasting pity. Turn and avert the rupture of your tranquility by confessing and repenting.

God wants to extend your tranquility indefinitely, so that it might become an enduring and eternal tranquility that assures you of your election. He has no delight in seeing your heart cower. But he does delight in seeing it pray triumphantly in the blood of the Lamb and in watching it breathe the air of sacred tranquility. Don't force him, then, to visit you with the flaming sword of his righteous anger.

It depends on you. What do you want? Do you prefer to meet your God in the howling wind of a storm, or would you rather meet him in the cool touch of a gentle breeze?

If you prefer in the gentle breeze, if you really want to remain in his love, and if you want your tranquility to be extended, pray that your prayers to God are genuine. Let them be marked by an earnestness that distinguishes your entire life. Offer them in contriteness and brokenheartedness. Offer them daring to plead on the basis of what Jesus wants. Offer them in dismay about yourself and without any personal claims. Offer them pleading only on the mercy of God.

YET, BECAUSE HE IS PERSISTENT

Yet, because he is persistent he will get up and
give him as much as he needs. Luke 11:8

Luke repeatedly has Jesus using words—three times as a matter of fact—in the context of ordinary human activities that are exemplary for the spiritual life of God's children. In chapter 16, they occur in connection with the shrewd manager. In Luke 18, they appear in the story of the widow who persisted in making life difficult for her landlord. And in the chapter here, they apply to the persistent friend.

At first appearance, the Lord's words in each case seem shocking. One often wishes that he had never said such unexpected things. And you become uncomfortable with them when you consider how they sound to someone who mocks the gospel—or even to you when you do! What is still worse, when they are misunderstood or mishandled, these loaded words often profane the practice of prayer.

It is considered a mark of greater holiness in some circles when people speak with the living God crudely and with an indecent familiarity that mimics how the persistent friend addressed his neighbor. This produces the kind of praying that is weaned from all reverence for the holy God. It is praying more reminiscent of the insistence of a willful child than of the approach made by a mere creature to their Lord and Creator.

See to it that no one ever misleads you by dragging you down that ungodly path! Rather, lead such a person back from the error of their ways. What is appropriate for the believer to experience in their heart is the kind of presumption that Abraham showed when he approached God's holy throne with a pleading spirit.

What Jesus says about the persistent friend is also relevant in this connection. Here our Savior is teaching us to pray only on the basis of honoring God's name, not by putting pressure on God by appealing to our friendship with the Father.

A stranger had dropped in on the persistent questioner. So he knocked on the door to ask for bread for this nighttime traveler. When his sleepy-eyed neighbor hesitated in giving him that bread, he appealed to the sacred principle of hospitality. He sided with the stranger and through him with every stranger from a far country when they are treated gruffly and heartlessly, since that kind of thing shouldn't happen. His good name wouldn't allow it. That's the reality that confronted him. And so, when his friend dared to wake him up by banging on his door, the neighbor didn't dare simply to brush off his request. He gave him the bread requested for the sake of his own good name.

There is no indication at all that this persistent friend asked in a crude or uncivil tone of voice when he made his urgent plea. Rather, one gets the impression that he imposed on his neighbor in an apologetic and friendly way. His persistence rested not in what he was asking, but his asking depended on this expectation: "If I knock on his door, he certainly can't refuse, if only for the sake of honoring his good name."

Doesn't all of Scripture show that that's how God's children should always pray? It is according to the Lord's own explanation, when he says: "I do this not because of you, O Israel, but because of my holy name that you have defiled." And when today's Israel believes this and has the courage to act on it, tell me this: Doesn't it seem that she is being persistent, then, in daring to plead on the basis of that name that she had once defiled? It dares to plead like Moses did when he pointed out that he was doing so, "so that your enemies, O Lord, may not slander your name." It dares to be persistent like Daniel, when he prayed "because your name is merciful, O Lord." Then it dares to pray like all God's saints in the Old and New Testaments have done when, with inner stammering, they exclaim: "Lord, depart from me, for I am a sinner!" But even then they approach the throne of grace with the appeal: "O God, be merciful to me, a sinner, for the sake of your holy name."

The mistake lies in the fact that you don't comprehend that actually all your praying, as long as you are focused on yourself, is actually one continuous expression of persistence.

People caress their soul with the notion that as long as they are praying, they are engaged in a God-pleasing activity. They think they are spiritual because they pray a lot. They think that their praying props up their chances of being heard. They amble around in Rome's bramble patch, where folks think that their praying has merit.

And this Jesus rejects totally out of hand.

Meritorious? God pleasing? Spiritual? O my brother and sister, it's shameful when we treat our troubles in such a shallow way! Our lack of holiness so superficially! Our standing with the Almighty with such insensitivity! It's shameful that we think we are the kind of people who can simply run to the Lord like this with our needs. Do we really dare to pray on any other basis than on our Immanuel? Then the One who hears our prayers simply whispers to us: "For the honor of his name!"

UNMARKED GRAVES

You are like unmarked graves that people walk
over without knowing it. Luke 11:44

The image that Jesus uses here of our human hearts is both deeply somber and disturbingly beautiful: "an unmarked grave beside which people walk without suspecting what it contains."

Use that picture to test the hidden depths of your own heart!

I understand clearly that Jesus is applying this to the Pharisees. But does that exempt you? Are you free from being pharisaical? Can you escape the penetrating brightness of the eternal Light that fully reveals even the darkest recesses of your own heart? Do you have such a strong grip on the truth, and does the truth have the same on you so that you can't really distinguish any longer between what's on the inside and what's on the outside? Have all the walls of separation toppled? Have all the curtains separating them been ripped in half, so that what you say with the tongue and what lies hidden in your soul are completely one and the same for you? Is that the case in your own conscience as well as for the One who judges you?

"Don't steal!" is what you profess. But does this mean nothing more than that you don't make off with something in a way that would make you a thief? In God's sight it has a more precise meaning. It means that you don't have anything in your house or vault that God himself hasn't put there.

And applying that approach to all God's commandments is how you keep the person honest who feels no guilt because they haven't blatantly transgressed the law.

So why, I ask, would you stop with a condemnation of crass Pharisees? Why would you have in mind only those secret hypocrites and outwardly pious frauds? Meanwhile, isn't your own crafty heart also caught in the snares set for holier-than-thou Pharisees by the even craftier Satan?

Or don't you believe that Pharisaic behavior is really a plague that in its most basic form can have its deadly effect in your soul too? Do you think that Jesus would have warned you about this in such a soul-searching way if playing along with it produces no collateral damage? Or if doing so is not unbelievably harmful? Don't you understand that the smallest involvement with anything Pharisaic makes the most beautiful flower wilt?

An unmarked grave! People notice you. They walk beside you. They stare at you. Then they even study the beautifully carved headstone and its pious inscription. But they know nothing of what is roiling and churning in the depths of your heart.

Oh, you had better believe there's a seductiveness involved with being pious. But when piety is all about being pious and not about God in his holiness, then it's only cold ashes. It throws off the stench of decay. It banishes all true piety from your life.

Being Pharisaic is when people pray aloud in the presence of or along with others while fostering the impression of never thinking about other people but only about God!

It's being holy more in appearance than in actuality. It's doing or refraining from something because another pious individual is close by, an individual who, like you do, is in turn paying more attention to you than to God. The reward for such behavior is empty.

It's when what's on the outside is different from what's on the inside. It's when the heart concentrates on its own importance, while the lips never give a hint of this. It's mumbling with the tongue a prayer that doesn't come from the soul.

It's giving the appearance that you have it all together with God and other people. It's appearing to have visibly broken with the world, when in fact you've left the back door of your soul open to it and resumed a steady conversation with it.

Even worse, it's giving the appearance that you have it all together between God and yourself. It's misleading yourself just as badly by often seeming to take up a cross that still lies undisturbed on the ground. By thinking that you've brought a sacrifice that is still actually walking around and grazing in the pastures of your self-love! Or by already ascribing to yourself sweet mysteries of the faith that your impure, malicious, and contentious heart never gives the first appearance of encountering.

And then we have to identify yet what is the most atrocious of all that's lodged within. It's the most accursed and most disgraceful of all. O may God still be gracious to your soul! It is secretly caressed and cherished within. It still coddles and fondles the deadly worm that has been gnawing at you from the time of your youth. It's the evil that extends to the depths of wickedness in your soul. It clings to you all the time. It is the most tempting of all your bosom sins, as they rightly deserve to be called. It's a cancer on the work of God's grace in your soul. It joins right in with "all the little sheep of the only Good Shepherd." It's involved with whatever occupies God's elect. It assures you that you're always becoming more holy.

So tell me now, do you still not get the point about the "unmarked graves"? Will the headstone finally shed light on what is churning and swirling around inside them? Will it do this in a way that produces deep revulsion?

O the danger of beginning to think that none of this applies to you!

Whoever wants to make any progress and develop a walk with the Lord (thus live in the light of eternity) will readily conclude that they are far from finding any peace.

But whoever goes into these matters more deeply at length sees that what they once thought was their uprightness is nothing but darkness. With this new insight, they implore God: "Be merciful to me, a sinner! Especially to the Pharisee living within me!"

PROPER PORTIONS AT JUST THE RIGHT TIME

*Who, then, is the loyal and prudent manager that the
master will place over his servants in order to give them their
proper portion of food at just the right time? Luke 12:42*

Christ, our Immanuel, is the caretaker of our inner selves!
Our souls are alive. That's why they need to be nourished and fed with
food that they can handle. As our Savior, he's the one who offers our souls that
kind of life-giving food. In fact, he himself is that life-giving food. He is bread
for the soul, the life in our lives. All strength that our souls ever received came
to us by virtue of his resurrection.

But it is exceptional for Jesus himself to convey that soul food directly to
and for our hearts. In fact, that's such a rare exception that it is experienced
only occasionally by even the most sanctified among God's people. This is a special grace reserved almost exclusively for those who are "fathers in Christ." As
a rule, Christ distributes that life-giving bread through the service of others,
whether through angels or humans. He assigns one the responsibility for distributing it to others. To use the comparison employed by Jesus in this parable,

he appoints managers over his household in order to provide his servants with their proper portions of food at just the right time.

In every Christian family, the father is just that sort of Jesus-appointed provider. And the guilt falls on your heads, you fathers, when those in your house languish for lack of food, whether that is your wife, your offspring, or your servants. It's on you if they suffer from spiritual anemia and hunger. You are charged by Jesus to nourish them with the Word, through prayer, with warnings, and by Christian example.

But the mother, in turn, is also that kind of provider. And woe to you mothers if the Mary in your hearts is eclipsed by the Martha in your lives. Don't be so preoccupied with cleanliness and appearance or with food and clothing for the body that you have no heart or eye for the souls of your children and maids. Extend to them what Jesus has entrusted to you for sharing with others rather than hoarding it for yourselves. He has given you different gifts than he has given fathers. Share these tenderly with others.

Yes, Jesus gives something to everyone for the purpose of distributing it to others. He gives something to older brothers and sisters to distribute to their younger siblings. He gives something to friends to distribute to others at school and to younger playmates. However that might go, they get something from you and appropriate something for themselves. And you are responsible for what is transmitted from you to their souls, whether that is a taste of Jesus' bread of life or a slice of evil from your own heart.

More than people might imagine, this applies also to our service people, particularly those who work with children. Those impressionable youngsters eagerly drink in everything, especially where heaven is involved. So pay close attention to your own soul so that you never cause those tender young plants to wilt and shrivel. They want to appropriate something from you. They want to take it to heart. They crowd around you with wide-open mouths, as it were. For the love of God then, give them something of what Jesus has given you. Don't let the gift of his grace, his life-giving bread, get moldy from neglect in your own heart of hearts.

But first and foremost what I am saying applies to pastors, managers in the household of Jesus. They are the shepherds who have to feed us. They need to do so not just by delivering a sermon, or by answering our questions, or by visiting church members in their homes. But they need to do so by feeding our souls in and through all these activities. They need to distribute spiritual food. It has to be food first given them by Jesus, food that continues to taste good to them, food then redistributed by them. It needs to be a gift of food that enlivens the soul. It must foster grace and life-giving power. It must truly refresh the soul and make the heart beat faster. It must replenish the strength of eternal life. If only there were such a preacher of righteousness in every village and ten so anointed by the Lord in every city! Then true knowledge would increase, sin would retreat, and God would be greatly praised.

Similarly, if the teachers in our schools faced our children each morning in a way that made the children feel that they were being given something from Jesus himself, what a blessing that would be! It would have to be more than mere platitudes. It would have to be something that overwhelms their hearts and renews their strength. It would have to really feed their souls. Then blessings would be poured out over our national life from both church and school, and Jesus would be highly exalted among us.

Eventually the day of reckoning is coming for all these providers: parents for their homes, sisters for their brothers, caregivers for children entrusted to them, but especially pastors for their congregations and teachers for their students. They will be asked whether they have been loyal and prudent in dispersing to hungry souls every morning and evening what Jesus has entrusted to them.

Who can measure the enormous level of guilt incurred in these matters? God's righteous anger will definitely be poured out on it!

And yet, your Savior sincerely desires not just that you don't let the life-giving bread he has entrusted to you for feeding others spoil because of your neglect. He wants you to distribute their proper portion to them. They are entitled to it. Be ready to give it in a way that each soul can digest and in the proper amount. Do it in a way uniquely suited to each individual. In addition, do it faithfully and prudently, with a sense of good timing. Don't do it haphazardly or inconsistently—now giving too much, then distributing nothing at all. Do it daily. Do it when the person is open to it and the heart is hungry for it.

Distributing food for the soul in this way shows great sensitivity. Doing it faithfully is a privilege that has glorious rewards, both for you and for the person to whom you serve it. Pay attention to this: "Blessed is the servant whom his master, when he returns, finds faithful."

9

VOLUME I

COME TO BRING FIRE ON THE EARTH

I have come to bring fire on the earth. Luke 12:49[1]

No, that's indisputable!

Jesus said it. It's totally understandable. There's no double meaning here. To put it as bluntly as possible, he didn't come to bring peace on earth. He came to do just the opposite. He came to create division, not peace. He came to cause discontent and rifts even in the heart of family life. He doesn't even spare the bond between mother and child.

Jesus came to earth not to bless with joy and happiness, but to baptize with fire. And whoever says otherwise doesn't understand the gospel but is simply being arbitrary and spouting weak ideals.

Oh, we definitely know that Jesus is also associated with the promise of everlasting peace. He bears the honorable title of "Prince of Peace." The heavenly hosts sang "peace on earth" when he was born. "He is our peace!" He assured his discouraged disciples: "Peace I leave with you; my peace I give to you." But this glorious prospect is definitely not what is meant by the syrupy, tepid, predictable peaceableness offered by false prophets at the expense of

---

1. Both in the original entry in *De Heraut*, no. 9 (February 3, 1878) and in *Honig uit de Rotssteen* the biblical reference is erroneously given as Luke 11:49.

any honor, obligation, truth, or conviction—even when that is offered in the name of our Lord Jesus.

Peace that is offered through Jesus is something far more glorious. It is something enduring, richer, and higher. It is peace in the deepest sense of the word. It is peace of the highest order, the broadest scope, and uninterrupted duration. It is not superficial, but it is lodged in our hearts. It doesn't come at the expense of truth, but as its fruit. It is peace with God and therefore peace from God. It is wrought in us by the Holy Spirit through baptism by suffering and by oppression of our souls so that we may one day be exalted in glory and honor. It will be fully realized when the Lord comes "on the clouds of heaven."

But in order to give us that sacred peace then—his peace—he must intentionally dare to shatter any existing peace, since it really has no right to exist at all.

For example, consider what an immigrant does when he tries to create a peaceful existence for his family in a place that he has never visited before. All that he sees around him is forest, primeval woods where the solemn stillness has the semblance of peace for him. But he does not embrace that kind of purposeless peace at all. Far from it! In order to create the sort of peaceful habitation he wants, he has to disturb the existing solitude of the forest. He has to dare to set fire to the dead vegetation. He has to cut down trees so that they fall creaking to the ground with a huge thud, one that sends the frightened animals running off in loud protest. He has to transform everything around him in a great drama of destruction. Even then the desired peace doesn't come. The bare ground must first be turned over, the tree stumps and their roots burned, trenches dug for foundations, and pits scooped out to yield their lime. Eventually the walls of a dwelling are erected, and the floors are laid. A shelter from the seasonal winds appears. And only after all this do the welcoming living quarters that offer him the desired peace and quiet eventually emerge.

So why shouldn't Jesus take the same approach?

Why should he have to honor the semblance of peace found among humanity that is similar to that in the primeval forest? Why shouldn't he first burn off the nettles and thistles of envy and greed? Why would you think that it conflicts with his calling if he first has to swing his axe against the roots of the towering tree trunks of pride and self-righteousness? Why would it contradict any of our sacred ideals that he first has to scare off demons or grab "the roaring lion" by his snout? What strikes you as unnatural, I therefore ask you, if our Savior first has to uproot the stubbornly rooted stumps of sin, turn over the ground of our hearts, and lay new foundations for state and society as well as for nations and families? Why would it be remarkable if before true peace can come either around us or within us, the walls of the Lord's house need to be erected and our new habitation has to be completed?

Or don't you recognize heavenly signs?

When a cloud first emerges, Jesus asks, don't you expect rain? And then, when the south wind drives the clouds off, don't you anticipate the warmth of sunlight once again? So then, wasn't Jesus' appearance initially like the appearance of a rain-laden cloud that promised to refresh with its gentle raindrops our poor world, withering in prolonged drought? Can it be any different that when those clouds come, it gets darker, and the wind begins to howl? It begins pouring until the clouds are emptied and the ground that has been plowed up is saturated. And only then does the bright light of "the Sun of Righteousness" break through.

So take careful note of the Lord's ways! In the land of Goshen the sun is always shining. That's why peace needs to be disrupted when it exists as satisfaction with your own flesh, your inflated egos, the world, Satan, hypocrisy, compromising Christians, and all kinds of other ungodliness. Even so, there is already a peace on earth that you can savor. That's true at least if you long for peace with God. That's a peace that comes through ever-deepening self-denial. It's your peace when he's the center of your life and you're willing to bleed for him on your own cross!

10
VOLUME I

SET FREE ON
THE SABBATH

*Should not this woman, who is a daughter of Abraham but
who has been bound by Satan for eighteen years now, be
set free from these bonds on the Sabbath? Luke 13:16*

According to Jesus' own words, mustn't the Sabbath be a day for "breaking the bonds"?

I tell you that the superspiritual enthusiasts are out of touch with life's realities. They are out of touch with the burdens and troubles experienced by the vast majority of people and weigh them down to the ground. They simply can't comprehend why every day of the week couldn't be a conduit of divine power to our souls, just like the Lord's Day is.

For what is the reality of daily life for thousands upon thousands of people except one continuous, entangling bondage? It amounts to being bound in many ways and to various degrees. This causes the wings of our souls to flap first in this direction and then in that, and it severely restricts the free and exhilarating spreading of our wings of faith.

A person can offer a quick little prayer. Sometimes part of a Bible verse can be just as strengthening for you as an entire chapter. And even when your head is spinning and the clutter of the day's responsibilities is wearing you out, right in the heat of dealing with them you can get a jolt of strength from on high, like an electric shock. By the same token, doing nothing for an entire

Sunday can sometimes leave you cold and spiritually lifeless. Just remember that the miracle worked by that quick prayer, by that bit of Scripture, or by that jolt of faith comes only when ordinary living is laced with a life of prayer, of living into Scripture, and of walking with the Lord. But those tender and blessed experiences of the soul elude not just a few people but the vast majority of them. They never put such things into practice. They are always preoccupied with getting ahead. They have never once stood still and alone in the presence of their God.

That's exactly why there is a Sabbath to which God calls his people, saying: "Shake off your dust; rise up; sit on your thrones, O Jerusalem! Free yourself from the chains around your neck!" (Isa 52:2). That's when the bonds are loosened. These can be the bonds of daily labor that can choke and oppress us. They can be the bonds of busy and turbulent living. Or they can be the bonds of being upset and restless. That's when those who can bring praises bring them. That's when those who know the way to God make their way to the "appointed place of their salvation." That's when those unfettered from their bonds rejoice. That's when they feel tremendously exalted, regal, and liberated. It's on the Sabbath!

At least that's what happens when they give God all the glory on the Sabbath. That's what happens when they turn out for it in righteousness. I can't turn Sunday into a Sabbath by doing nothing. I can't do it by behaving properly. I can't do it by doing my duty. I can't even do it by simply praying and meditating. The Sabbath is a gift from God. I always only succeed in making my bonds tighter, but he's the only one who can loosen them. My determined efforts and attempts to turn Sunday into a Sabbath only produce a hollow day that is nothing more than pretense and empty forms. The Sabbath only comes alive when he's pleased to hear our humble prayers. That's when sap starts flowing into dry branches. That's when divine abundance pours into empty lives. That's when he blows warmth and a glow back into the cold coals of my heart.

And if this is what happens in your experience, sisters and brothers, then the loosening of the bonds of your daily labor becomes the glorious prophecy of an entirely different loosening. It indicates that your Sunday is definitely a day of resurrection. It signifies that your Savior has loosened the shackles of death and hell and that he shattered Satan's work.

What a glorious experience, then, to be transported far beyond yourself in sacred joy. On the Sabbath the word of the Lord directed at Israel's seducers is fulfilled for you and your family: "I will set free the people that you would ensnare like birds in your garden" (Ezek 13:20). And how glorious it is when those who have been set free from the bonds of this world's vanity and passion are also given a deep desire for "the courts of the Lord." There, in that everlasting day, fruit ripens on the Tree of Life.

But aren't there even worse things than the bonds of daily work and the shackles of vanity? Aren't there also cords of injustice in your life? Doesn't the Lord hold you accountable for them when he says: "This is the sort of fasting that I prescribe, that you loosen the bonds of injustice"? (Isa 58:6). So tell me now, is it at all strange just how often on the Sabbath your heart is set free from these bonds of death? He achieves this by addressing these matters with the cutting edge of his Word and through the sheer power of his inner appeal.

I am well aware that the bonds of death remain in force until the day we die. But sometimes it's as though God Almighty, the All-Merciful, tenderly takes friendly pity on us on the Sabbath and releases us for a while from our bonds. He does so that our souls might be filled with the joy of his salvation.

This is a moment of tender mercy. Then the Sabbath becomes a time when we once again experience the blessed moment of our conversion. Then that holy love is once again aroused that first compelled us to rejoice, saying: "O Lord, I am surely your servant. You have loosened my bonds!" Or it may be that by the light of the Spirit we see that the bonds of death still bind our old, perishable selves but no longer oppress our new selves because we have been set free in Christ. "We are hid with God in Christ Jesus."

In truth, the person who can talk about being set free on the Sabbath like this can hardly oppress either a brother or a stranger by holding them in bondage on the Sabbath. Such a person in turn sets others free. Free from daily labor. Probably free from even more terrible kinds of bondage! At least, if God wants to use them for that purpose. Preachers, what are you doing?

WALLETS THAT NEVER WEAR OUT

Use wallets that never wear out and acquire treasure
that is not diminished in heaven. Luke 12:33

Don't people get it? Can't they see how foolish and ridiculous they look to God's holy angels when they chase after money and follow Jesus at the same time?

It's very obvious to these good spirits how "pious Christians" here on earth while kneeling before the crude, unsightly cross and reaching out to it for support are jubilantly proclaiming something to each other and the world. They are saying that they are "pilgrims on the way to a better place." "We don't feel at home in this world!" they say. "Each morning and every evening we look to the Savior for comfort and support. We find no relief on this faithless earth where everything is parched and dead, fit only for burning."

They see and understand perfectly well, those ministering spirits that have been sent on behalf of those who will inherit salvation, that this language of faith is neither excessive nor exaggerated. They know that it is simply the weak expression of the full, glorious reality that they have been privileged to see. They witness the contrast between the dry, dead world to which they have been sent to minister and the lush glories of heaven, where they dwell.

They see and understand above all, because it happens so consistently in our earthly existence that no one ever keeps any of their personal goods and treasures. They know that everyone must leave it all behind—even the least significant individual. They witness how someone who works slavishly to acquire what he has is given only a few short years to enjoy it, and even then he is riddled with anxiety, and he's often contested and disrupted in his pursuits. Even if there are no thieves to break in and steal, moth and rust consume what he has. Or he may receive an adverse legal judgment through which he loses what he considered secure.

So then, is it putting it too strongly to talk about how foolish and ridiculous the angels regard all this? They notice how none of these pious pilgrims who talk so jubilantly about a better homeland hold back from acquiring this world's goods and fortunes, even though they know that their journey is short and that they can't take as much as a thin dime with them into that new home. They see how people in both the higher and lower classes of society remain focused on piling up more money and goods. They see how people are unable to disentangle themselves from always striving to acquire more possessions and being lured by earthly things.

There's a tremendous irony in Jesus' powerful words: "Use wallets that never wear out and acquire treasure that is not diminished in heaven."

Jesus doesn't spare you here, either.

It is accepted and customary for people, also among Christian friends and in press reports, to celebrate one another's generosity, to acknowledge the good deeds of friends, and to sing the praises of generous contributors.

But Jesus loves you too much to accept that kind of empty flattery. As your Lord he knows how these visible bonds bind you with chains harsher than iron and ropes stronger than steel. He understands how every flattering compliment only draws them tighter.

That's why Jesus deals with you in a completely different way. He doesn't flatter you. Rather, he chastises you. He reacts to your ridiculous dual loyalty with holy irony. He makes every effort to appeal directly to your conscience with his uncompromising demands. He makes you ashamed of your own personal treasures so that you feel the prayer rising within you: "O my Lord Jesus, my Deliverer. Set me free also from this sin, from this heart's desire, from this shameful enslavement to material things."

In all of this, Jesus is heart and soul, so very human. That is to say, he understands completely what goes on in the human heart and how necessary it is for one born in sin to throw off attachment to sinful earthly treasures. But he also understands that for us to yearn for such treasures, to crave possessions, and to desire the glamor of wealth with all of our heart is innate. It belongs to the air that we humans breathe. That's the reason why the Lord in his love is sensitive to the struggle of our hearts. He doesn't simply say: "Stay poor! Live empty-handed. Stop yearning for earthly treasure." That's why he simply says: "Don't call gold everything that glitters. Don't let the pursuit of earthly goods become a heavenly quest! Have wallets, to be sure; but just let them be wallets that never wear out. Carry a treasure in them that cannot be stolen and that is not diminished in heaven." Make this wonderful saying of Ezekiel a proverb that you carry with you: " 'I am their possession,' says the Lord" (Ezek 44:28).

WORSE SINNERS THAN ALL OTHER GALILEANS

Jesus answered, "Do you think these Galileans were worse sinners than all other Galileans because they suffered like this?" Luke 13:2[1]

Success is not necessarily a blessing, nor prosperity evidence of God's favor. But that's what people often think, even Christians! For what's more common than hearing these two expressions among neighbors? "I was apparently doing what God wants, for my life has been blessed tremendously!" "Well, he obviously forsook the Lord's ways since God's hand has turned against him!"

Both of these opinions need to be rejected since they are extremely superficial and unspiritual.

Let's consider the subject of prosperity first. If a great deal of success in business, favorable outcomes to a person's best-laid plans, basking in fame and glory, and quaffing deep draughts of God's good fortune all qualify as indications of his favor, what are we to make of so many immoral theaters that bathe in luxury? What are we to think when they have it so good while the

---

1. The text is not printed in the republished Wormser edition of these meditations, although it was included in *De Heraut* when it was initially published.

local Christian school struggles to make ends meet? How do we explain the enormous profits made by bars and taprooms? How are we to understand the almost incalculable prosperity and sometimes baffling success of endeavors that proceed from the Devil rather than God and that people gloat over?

In the light of these considerations, therefore, shouldn't everyone admit not only that we may not talk glibly about blessings in connection with prosperity but that we cannot! Doesn't it follow from this that good fortune and prosperity in themselves can be a curse as well as a blessing? And doesn't it also follow that only the Holy Spirit can discern in individual hearts which of these two applies in any given situation?

This is just how it is in our day of wrath!

If someone meets trouble and affliction, if the course of their life is disrupted, if a cloud of thick darkness falls over them, and if all their best efforts come to nothing, then voices are raised everywhere. "They've been abandoned by God." "They're being tormented and oppressed by him." Job's friends appealed to him to admit his guilt and honor God. Those people in Jerusalem on whom the tower of Siloam fell were greater sinners than others! And woe to those Galileans whose blood Pilate had mixed with their sacrifices!

But such judgments just don't stand up!

The course of history indicates time and again that the best of people were whipped and assaulted more severely than all others. Precisely the faithful servants of God were hounded as though they were unfaithful and unworthy. That horrible and accursed wooden cross of Golgotha, scene of the most terrible suffering and the most bitter death imaginable, was reserved precisely for the One in whom God was "well pleased"! And experience still teaches that the godless here on earth prosper, while those who fear God suffer shame and persecution. And yet the powerful voice of the Spirit rises in the hearts of God's suffering servants to protest such cold, harsh treatment. Such treatment simply adds the bitter judgment of God-forsakenness to their priestly sufferings.

No, suffering is like prosperity in one respect. It can represent blessing or curse, favor or anger, grace or judgment. Whichever one it does, no one knows except the person favored or afflicted. And that insight comes not from that person, but by the light of the Holy Spirit.

What is relevant here is the directive "Judge not, that you be not judged."

Job's friends had to learn that belatedly, and only then did they understand that he was more righteous than they. His prayers had to reconcile their differences.

Asaph ultimately recognized that his perspective on the lot of others was wrong.

In Isaiah 53 the congregation recognizes that the one whom they had regarded as rejected because of his bitter sufferings is in fact the Son of God. Now with deep shame they flee to him as their Savior.

The coming of the Son of God himself refutes Israel's practice of judging unjustly. It demonstrates how the persecuted children of God, the poor, will certainly be saved. It opposes the verdict that the sufferings of the man born blind were due either to his own or to his parents' sins. It contests the angry suspicion that the Galileans that Pilate killed were worse sinners than others. It wants nothing to do with the accusation that the victims of Siloam were guiltier than others. And it culminates with the reward of pain and suffering imposed on his pure, sacred, innocent, and sinless head, bowed under the doom of the cross.

The lesson flowing from all this is clear. It has two dimensions, one with respect to others and the other with respect to you.

When we talk about what happens to others, look at it this way. If things go as they wish, this gives you no certainty that they are being blessed by the Lord. But if things go against them, you can be even less sure that they have forsaken God's ways and are being punished.

This may very well be the case. But whether it is or not is not for you to decide. God alone knows, and so does the person suffering if God wants to disclose that to them.

But before you suspend all judgment, or to put it another way, before you think that divine favor is being shown based on the nature of love or that angry judgment is possibly involved, think about this.

In your own case, is prosperity or suffering present that needs to be considered? You know your own past. You know about your walk with the Lord and his activity in your inner life. Be very careful, then, my brother and sister, that you not harden your conscience. You know that "the sun shines on both good and evil." Definitely examine yourself deeply before you conclude that the Lord is favoring you. And when you do, be very careful about concluding too quickly that the cross you bear is being carried because you're following him. He knows every step of your ways. So be very sure that you have thought through in his presence these questions: "Does the Lord have anything against me? Have I strayed at all from his paths?"

THE POOR AND NEEDY!

Blessed is he who eats this bread in the kingdom of God. Luke 14:15

Jesus is dealing here with the matter of our hunger.

He is the Bread of Life. Who hungers for him? Whose soul is quickened by the aroma of his life? Who opens their mouth when the Father of our souls and lives offers them this nourishing Strength?

Oh, that people's eyes would be open to the simple, clear message of the glorious gospel!

No, at Jesus' banquet and in Jesus' kingdom there is no room for wealthy neighbors, aristocratic appetites, or the spiritually satisfied.

People like that probably wouldn't come anyway. They are always preoccupied with buying more land, closely examining a new team of oxen, or keeping their women happy. They have no time left! But if in fact they would come, they wouldn't come to have Jesus do them some good. They wouldn't come to his table simply to be benefited, replenished, or satisfied. They would only come because it's not considered acceptable to stay away, or because they thought they were doing Jesus a favor and honoring or making him feel good by doing so. They would come entirely to see what Jesus was going to serve them. Then they would criticize what he set in front of them because they are finicky eaters, as the popular expression puts it, and afterwards simply go on their way again.

Could these be the people for whom the Son of God shed his precious blood?

Hardly! Listen well! We're dealing here with a completely different sort of person. We're dealing with a prodigal son, one who cries out—now, get this—"I am dying of hunger!"

What we see here is the Master's servant going out into the hedgerows and alleys to invite, even compel, the needy to come to the banquet in order that Jesus' house might be full. It's desperate, destitute, miserable people like this who jump at the chance to come when they hear about this fabulous banquet. They don't even get choosy when someone grabs them by the arm—in fact, they actually want to be forced to come! And when they enter, their eyes brighten at the sight of all the food. They attack it eagerly. They enjoy it as they never enjoyed anything before. It's all delicious and satisfying. And they can't understand how their wealthy host could have been so friendly as to let them in and be replenished with such abundance. And when leaving, all they can talk about is Jesus. They have nothing but praise and compliments for that evening's feast. Going home, they celebrate having such a merciful Savior.

That's why Jesus says as bluntly as possible that none of the spiritually self-satisfied and none of the rich neighbors will ever taste a thing at his banquet. That's why he praises, by contrast, "the blessed people who hunger." That's why he doesn't burden himself with the spiritually self-satisfied. That's why he takes care of "the poor, the blind, the lame, and the naked."

Jesus knows that for the rich nothing is ever good enough. They come critically, not hungry for bread. And that's precisely why they remain rigid in their pride rather than humbling themselves before the Lord.

No, his kingdom is for the poor! It's for the poor who feel that they'll die if they don't get any bread. It's for the poor who feel that everything is wonderful when they do get something to eat. How they feel is expressed well by what the writer of Proverbs says: "To the hungry, even what is bitter tastes sweet!" (Prov 27:7).

So, those of you reading this, put the state of your own soul to the test in this regard. Have you known that kind of hunger? Do you still experience it? Is a gnawing hunger driving you to Jesus over and over again? Not for the sake of having an abundance but simply in order to stay alive so you won't perish because of your sinful heart and the Holy One's condemnation?

Also think about these words of Jesus if you endeavor to approach others with this bread or when you invite others to Jesus' meal. Offering that bread casually and not genuinely is not evangelistic.

To offer bread where there is no hint or semblance of hunger, or where any sign of genuine hunger has disappeared, is totally lacking in mercy and is both irreverent and inappropriate. Then the only thing that you accomplish is to watch this precious bread crumble and fall between the fingers rather than be eaten. This merely nauseates the soul, and the Lord's saving benefits are despised.

But if you want to be truly merciful and at the same time respect what is sacred, do what Jesus himself said. Invite the poor, not your spiritually rich neighbors. Don't offer the Bread of Life to those who are overfed but to those who are hungry. Don't apply healing balm to the person who boasts about their good health but to the person groaning in pain because of their wounds.

The only thing that I ask is that you don't leave matters there, because the Word has to come to everyone, you as well as all others. This has to occur before you approach others with your bread, your painkillers, or your rescue effort. Then you'll bring what satisfies genuine hunger. Then you'll apply salve that soothes real wounds and shatters mere illusions.

14
VOLUME I

A CLOUD OF WITNESSES

Therefore, we have such a great cloud of
witnesses surrounding us. Hebrews 12:1

One of the most dreadful temptations experienced by God's children here on earth is to give in to a sense of being abandoned.

They are so insignificant. Their number is so pitifully small. One can count them easily, even in a large city. They are exceptions to the huge masses. They hardly count for anything compared with the vast majority. Each one of them stands in their own circles and surroundings as one against many. They feel all others are lined up against them alone!

The world, people generally, the public at large—or whatever other term you want to use for the great masses—don't search the depths of divine truth. They don't trouble themselves in the least about their break with Zion's daughter. On the contrary, they stand opposed to God and his Anointed One. They keep on making the same appeal they always have: "Let's cut our ties with them; let's sever any connections we have with them." They cheer once again whenever an attack on Christ's honor is successful. And when a word spoken by someone about Christ and his Word makes a momentary impression, they mumble a mocking response.

Truth be told, as soon as a person perceives what is going on around them, they come to the bitterly sad and deeply painful realization that the children of this generation as a rule do not embrace Christ. There are thousands and millions of them with whom we live in human society! They push away the glorious Son of God and merciful Savior rather than embrace him. And we, with our faith, our confession, and our love for him who is the One and Only, stand alone and abandoned. We are like a solitary individual lost and forgotten among the masses. That's when our evil heart easily whispers: "Can this kind of unique, old fashioned, unusual, rare person really be human? Are they actually for real?"

Seriously, almost no more frightening temptation exists than to feel so outnumbered.

Especially when, in clear contradiction with the words of Jesus, people keep on telling us that we have to become "a great multitude." It's a temptation to be afraid especially for so-called cultured and refined people. It's a temptation for an individual who has not yet died to the false sense of self-aggrandizement in their hunt for human recognition. It's definitely a temptation of the first order for men called by God to the study of his Word and to the educated pursuit of sacred theology, namely, to the Christ's teachings concerning doctrine and life. It's a temptation for those who still haven't learned to remain silent when hearing negative whispering because they still don't understand what the Lord's servant Paul said about "wisdom in the eyes of men" being "foolishness" in the eyes of God.

But our merciful God is mindful of this frightening battle of his redeemed people.

He also understands very well that our hearts need sympathetic handling. He knows that our confession needs supporting words. He recognizes that our faith in the Son of his love requires fellow believers. So, as the Fountain of all that is good, he will also provide for the needs of your heart!

For that very reason, he provided "such a great cloud of witnesses surrounding us" that, when we take one look at that immense host that no one can number, our eyes immediately brighten. Our courage is revived by that group of heroes that extends farther than the eye can see. The pulse of our faith quickens, fresh and strong, and our souls tremble with new vitality at the thought of this army of the living God packed side by side in spiritual battle lines century in and century out.

Think for a minute about the martyr in ancient times as a single, seemingly abandoned individual. When he entered the arena, he faced a roaring lion that wanted to tear him apart. The spectacle of thousands of mocking, laughing, yelling, and raging spectators made his heart stop.

But do you know what the Lord did then? He completely plugged that martyr's ears to all the shrieking. He pulled a curtain across that wild, seething mass of people so that our martyr did not even see them. And above that veil he caused the eye of faith to behold a glorious cloud of witnesses rising. It was a crowd of martyrs and prophets and men and women of God from all the ages. It was a huge mixture. And behind that cloud of witnesses, God caused a Milky Way of angels to rise up from their heavenly fortress and make it reverberate on his behalf with their beautiful, jubilant singing.

And why wouldn't the same thing be true for you in your own struggles as a follower of the Nazarene? God provides this in order to keep you solidly in your own precious, holy, universal Christian faith.

As long as you fix your attention on those who are great in this world, on those who are wise in worldly wisdom, and on those who make the most noise around you, you will be lost and abandoned. But close your physical eyes to that painful spectacle. With your spiritual eyes, contemplate the rising of that great cloud of witnesses. Consider those who "were persecuted on earth, mistrusted, and driven by life's storms." They beckon and appeal to you like this: "We struggled just like you, and now we are wearing crowns!" Consider those who wave you on and enthrall you with their holy gaze, saying: "Don't weaken. Don't give up. Don't give Satan the victory, because your downfall would be painful for us. Our honor is tied to your struggle!" And when you have been beaten down and are convulsing to the point of giving up, consider those who quietly whisper to you with irresistible seriousness: "You are more than conquerors through him who loved you!"

Paul writes to Timothy that he should fix his eyes on God's "elect angels" (1 Tim 5:21) when he wrestles alongside the struggles of God's people on earth. But even more powerful support than being involved with angels can ever produce comes from that great crowd of witnesses that includes human martyrs. These are people like us. They have been thrown into ovens, abandoned in pits, and forcibly held under water. They had sinful hearts just as we have. They struggled against the flesh just as we do. And just like us, they would have perished if they had not been saved by our exalted Leader's sacrifice on the cross.

This is why as soon as the voice of unbelief attacks you, echoed and repeated a thousand times over from the whole world, you should open your ears to that great cloud of witnesses. You should do it when your own weak response of faith sticks muffled in your throat. You should do it when in your sense of abandonment the sound of your testimony fades out. That's when you should listen to that countless crowd of believers from the Old and the New Testaments that surround you. They stand right beside you. They stand in front of you and behind you and all around you. They shout a hearty "Amen!" to the testimony you give by the power of God's Word and through his Spirit.

The Lord prepared that crowd of witnesses for you. You possess it! And you can't do without it!

Only One was ever able to say: "I alone have treaded the winepress." But even that One was strengthened for your sakes by witnessing the angels and their faith.

THOSE WHO
WERE GREEDY

The Pharisees, who were greedy, heard all these things. Luke 16:14

A subtle connection seems to exist between piety and greed.
The situation is like this. As soon as the ambition to be pious, to be seen as pious, and to associate with pious people occurs, this becomes the master of a person's heart! And this requires a great sacrifice on their part. It demands that from that time forward they will distance themself from all those worldly pleasures and attractions that the apostle so aptly calls "the vanities of this life."

We deny that we are pious and have desires at the same time. That's because to be seen at glamorous festivities, boisterous banquets, lighthearted gatherings, and immoral dramatic productions just isn't consistent with being pious. It's one or the other, not both at once. All who are attracted to the acclaim of piety have to turn their hearts away from such sensuous pleasures and relinquish what is inconsistent with their new status.

But is such a person now a saint? Is their heart thereby simply weaned from any desire for what is external or for possessions and recognition? Is a convert thereby delivered from their sinful nature?

Hardly! Those who are honest with themselves know better than that!

To be sure, an all-controlling change occurs in such a person—at least if it's a genuine work of God in them and not merely counterfeit. It's a change by which the entire contour of their life is affected. It's a change sustained moment by moment by ever-renewing grace and by the thoroughly new work of the Spirit, who makes "letting go of the things of this earth" and "thinking about the things that are above" a reality in their heart. The same sinful inclination toward glamor, greatness, and glory still exists in the heart, but life takes a new direction.

Piety forbids a person from spending money. It requires that they save it. The misguided heart regards the former as false piety and says: "We can't have that!" It can't be tolerated. It's worldly. People are expected to accumulate money. This produces the virtue of thriftiness. Piety consists of not squandering but in saving, of no longer being reckless but in being careful with what a person has.

That's the first stage of sinning.

If a person is not converted from this way of thinking, does not break with it and develop enmity toward it, this evil gradually becomes what Scripture calls "the love of money" or greed. That's when people become attached in their hearts to money as money. It becomes their god, and they practice idolatry. If this is not stifled by some higher intervention such as a terrible bankruptcy or a financial setback, this at first so seemingly innocent inclination of heart finally degenerates into an evil demon. And it even dares to deny God that sacred money when he asks for it. It dares to withhold it from people in need when they cry for help. Ultimately, every opportunity is evaluated in terms of whether their money will grow.

And when it comes to this, the wicked seed has sprouted in the soil. It shoots up. Then it bears its unholy fruit. All obligation and virtue are sacrificed to the god called Mammon. People become enslaved to him in a terrible kind of idolatry.

Thus, one can see how gradually and automatically greed can develop out of piety. Even more than the children of this world, the godly are vulnerable to being misled into greed. One can see what exceptional grace is required to break with the world and yet not be excessively tied to one's money. That's why Israel's prophets opposed almost no other sin as bluntly, unsparingly, and relentlessly as they did greed. That's why the Lord God, knowing very well what was going on in his people's hearts, developed no laws as fully as he did those about being merciful, sacrificial, and generous. They were all designed as a fatherly means of protecting Israel from the demon of money. That's why Jesus associated the Pharisees and not the Sadducees with greed. That's why greed is a terrible sin against which the apostles warned frequently. That's why

Jesus said that whoever bows to Mammon cannot kneel to God. That's why it is expressly identified as an obstacle to being invested with ecclesiastical office. And finally, that's why according to Scripture the love of money is the root of all evil and is numbered among those flagrant sins that shut a person out of the kingdom of God.

The experience of Jesus' church shows all too well how necessary this word of warning is.

Has there ever been a more lamentable and cutting complaint made about the church? Even in its best days? Especially by preachers of sin and repentance here in our country? It's the complaint about how impossible it is to distance ourselves from earthly goods. Is there anything that has been more deadening and stifling in godly circles than putting greater reliance on money in the bank than on God's blessing in highest heaven? Is there anything that more obviously impoverishes circles of those who confess the name of Jesus than that they are unable to separate themselves from their money? Oh, the bitter irony of God's divine judgment! In their hearts God's people crave and cling to what in their sacred songs they despise as filthy lucre!

Obviously, by saying this we are lumping two kinds of pious people together. There are devout people who really want to know that that's what they are. Then there are people whom God has actually made godly. Concerning the first, nothing more caustic can be said than what the apostle wrote when he stated that they are like dogs who return to their vomit. They are like a huge sow wallowing in her slime.

The others are the true children of the kingdom. But for their warning as well as for their comfort, I add that almost all of them feel the sensation of this sin pulsating through their veins. There is not one of them who by nature does not succumb to it. Not a few of them even yield for a time to it on the deeper level just noted. But with God a grace is at work that breaks that spell. Sometimes that grace works gloriously, even in our own day. And when a pious person who was once greedy is delivered from bondage to their money, the Lord God's mercy would be misunderstood if that person emphasized the mercy they now show rather than the mercy that was shown to them.

16

UNWORTHY SERVANTS

Even when you have done everything that you were told to do, you should say, "We are unworthy servants." Luke 17:10

What is left for that poor, highly sensitive man with all his false pretensions about whom Jesus is speaking here? Even if he is born again, not much. In fact, nothing at all!

Your Savior definitely comes to you with treasure far greater than the gifts that the wise men from the East brought to Bethlehem's crib. He will wash you whiter than snow. He will anoint you with precious nard. He will clothe you in the finest linen. He will cover you with jewels. He will honor you by putting a crown on your head. He will seat you on his throne. You will drink from his cup. He will make you shine like a star in the firmament. But he will do all this only on one firm, inviolable condition. You must first allow him to sear out of your soul by the red-hot iron of his holy Word the last remnants of your self-righteousness. The Lord knows very well what goes on in the human heart both during and after its conversion!

The first thing that needs to happen, verbally at least, is that you must deny yourself completely. You must be convicted of your sin. You must be overwhelmed by a sense of guilt and debt. You must confess, "Lord, you are everything; I am nothing," before you can be delivered and saved. If you are to receive grace, you must come to the foot of the cross as a lost, humbled person.

So far, so good! But when a person who has been delivered moves from being shattered to rejoicing, Satan knows just how to push the point of his dagger between the buckles of your armor. He does this ever so slyly. What results from that deadly attack is this at first seemingly strange attitude: "Now that I've been delivered, I'm a little bit better than others and much better than the masses." So, overflowing with goodness, you extend a helping hand to others. As a lovable, godly individual, far from being despised, you think of yourself as an asset to your little circle of pious associates. And that's exactly when you become poisonous!

But things get much worse should you now begin comparing "the very little" that those other pious folks do with the "relatively much more" that your spirituality undertakes. And sliding further down that slippery slope, you come to the conclusion that you are more authentic and truthful than they are. You now get used to characterizing them as inauthentic. Sad to say, you further entangle yourself by considering yourself so unblemished and filled with grace that you stand out as exceptional among the saints. That's when you hardly ever utter prayers for forgiveness any more. Then you take even more ungodly steps toward the fatal position of imagining that you "definitely have something to offer" God himself—your God! In all his holiness! Next, in your judgment, the blessings, successes, and good conditions you attracted from heaven mysteriously stop coming. The result is that in your hope for an eternal inheritance, you long ago lost the attitude of the penitent publican. But as a pious, virtuous, diligent child "who has certainly done well," you had expected that your God would give you a crown of glory.

How deep sin's corruption penetrates! It reaches bone and marrow and even infests the breath of our new life.

Then one avoids the remedy the merciful Savior has provided for searing out this cancer. It's the preaching of the Word according to Christ's teachings. Then one dares to resist that penetrating, heart-and-soul-enveloping preaching of the Word that applies to every fiber of our lives.

O you preachers of the sacred gospel, rise up! Have mercy! Tell those wandering around with their self-righteous delusions what Christ has told you. Have compassion on those suffering with a steadily rising fever of unruly, delirious spiritual attitudes.

Proclaim, "The Lord God is great! He is to be praised eternally above all else. Him alone! By everyone! Everlastingly! For you there is no greater glory than the sight of his radiance!"

You possess nothing that compares with him. Nothing above him! Nothing alongside him! You offer nothing from the time before your fall in Adam. You bring nothing from before your conversion. Nothing from after you came to him. And even now nothing from all your growth in Christ. And eternally nothing, should you participate in his glory!

A father derives nothing from his children, but along with God he gives them life. He provides them with food and drink, clothes them, cares for them when they are sick, and bears all their expenses. Look at your relationship to the Holy One in the same way, and even more profoundly.

You cost your Father in heaven a great deal. You cost him the best, the highest, the most precious thing that heaven possessed. You cost him what he carried in his heart. And you cost him even more. Every day that he allows his earth to feed you and clothe you and provide you with the air that allows you to live, you cost him. When he spreads his darkness that lets you sleep and causes the herbs to grow that relieve your pain, you cost him. Similarly, every day that he allows his preached Word to touch your soul and is willing to listen again to your prayers, you cost him. And when he has his angels serve you once more with his saving work, and when he again breathes strength into your will and a spark of life into your heart, you cost him. When he provides you with power from Christ to believe and with the power from his divine heart to go on living, you cost him. You cost him again when he sends you the Holy Spirit himself to keep you on his path and to comfort you when your soul is troubled.

So you cost him dearly. Even now! Every evening and every morning! You are indebted to him entirely. He has to take care of everything for you, and in so doing above all to uphold and support you. For if he ever withdrew his hand from you, you would perish in your own deadly turmoil and become just one more sad catastrophe! And for all of this, he gets nothing in return from you.

This is difficult for the flesh to comprehend this. It is hard to hear this. But there is no denying it. Nothing can change it. From you he receives not a single thing.

Not even if you pray and praise him and do good works?

Why not? You yourself would know this best!

But I say this much on the authority of the Word: "You have never prayed what in any sense might be called a prayer unless he had first awakened it in you! You have never exalted what amounted to really exalting in his praise, unless he qualified you to do so. You have never done any good work, unless he was the One who first moved you to do it, both to will and to work for his own good pleasure!"

So then, O man and O woman, what do you have that you have not first received?

And how can you argue with our blunt assessment: "You have received everything from him; he has received nothing from you"?

Listen to what Job already testified in ancient times: "Can a man benefit God? Or, what does it benefit the Almighty if you are righteous?" "If you are righteous, what do you give him or what does he receive from your hand?" (Job 22:2-3; 35:7). Listen to what the apostle impresses on your heart: "Who has first given anything to God, that he should repay him?" (Rom 11:35). Or better yet, listen to what your Savior whispers in your heart: "When you do everything that you were told to do, you should say, 'We are unworthy servants.'"

Listen to this, all you children of God who are not in total denial! Listen, and be wise!

17

VOLUME I

IMPOSSIBLE WITH MEN

Lord, then who can be saved? The things that are impossible
with men are possible with God. Luke 18:26b–27[1]

A man of God like Jeremiah needs to stand up among us once again. He needs to pour out the complaint raging in his heart and conscience: "They treat my people's wound lightly by saying 'Peace, peace!' when there is no peace."

Let's face it. We also go the deceitful route of playing effeminate[2] games with sacred matters. "People don't have to take it all that seriously!" "Jesus' yoke is easy!" "If people only emphasize Jesus in all his love, what more do they really need to believe?"

That's when people put feeling good religiously ahead of shaking their consciences awake. That's when passion rather than being shattered passes for faith. Then they think they're making headway and calculate the number of their converts.

Oh, who is there that will deliver our generation from the curse of such superficiality? It's a curse that now attempts to creep into that beautiful, miraculous, and completely amazing work of Almighty God, who in his inscrutable mercy brings dead souls back to life.

---

1. Kuyper cites only portions of both Luke 18:26 and Luke 18:27.
2. The word *onmanlijk* used here means "unmanly, effeminate, womanly."

Really now, is that work really that superficial? Does it happen so matter-of-factly? Does it depend merely on a stirring speech? Is that all it takes for you to turn a life around? Can you rip out by the roots the false values controlling someone's life and plant valid ones in their place, ones forever corruption free? Is this simply a matter of having the right approach? Of observing others? Or of imitating each other? And do you really shamelessly presume in the light of God's Word that that's the secret to your greater love, stronger faith, and fuller prayer life?

"This is impossible with men" is what you need to hear. This is a completely different tone set by your Savior, whose thoroughly serious approach to life you've never really measured. He says this so that you might once and for all unlearn those superficial notions that blow around like feathers in the wind.

"Impossible" because that great work has to take hold in the deepest recesses of the human heart. And you can't really fathom the heart at that depth. "Impossible" because you have nothing to go on except your own word. But the human heart lacks the capacity for comprehending even what you're saying as you're saying it. "Impossible" because even if the soul could comprehend what you're saying, it still can't create something from nothing. "Impossible" because the soul that you want to influence doesn't simply float freely in the air, but it is tied to this earth, bound to the world with powerful cords that Satan clutches between his fingers. "Impossible" once again because everything is consumed by sin's taint and poison. Sin has corrupted it all. It is a cancer on the whole person, body and soul. And that you ever, even if only for a moment, thought that it was possible, it's only because you have never understood the true condition of the soul that you tried to convert.

Oh, that you would just listen to Jesus!

In order to have everlasting life, a person needs to believe. And believing is not simply to say "yes" to something you present. Nor is it to have nothing against something that you affirm. Nor is it even to want to participate in the spiritual things that you are able to celebrate so enthusiastically. No, believing is this. It is what the Lord taught the father of all believers from the outset. Believing is to distance yourself from everything. It is to forsake everything. It is to relinquish everything. It is to hold back absolutely nothing for yourself, of yourself, or within yourself. It is to throw yourself with your accursed and depraved heart only on the complete possibility of God's mercy.

Believing, as Jesus made so clear to the rich young man in this passage, is not only to forgo all the pleasures and ambitions of this life, but all this world's treasures and possessions. "Sell all that you have" so that you have nothing left except God himself. Or to put it in the even more demanding sense in which Paul explained it: to have as though not having, to possess as though not possessing. To have something before you, around you, and within you; but then to be so fully detached from it that God is your only portion!

Pay attention! The Lord says that "to be blessed now and to have eternal life then" one first has to let go of goods and possessions, wife and children, friends and family in order then to possess them fully in him.

And don't say now, "That's good advice for those who are rich!" Because who, in their own way, is not "rich" in what they possess? This is even true of a child with her doll or a beggar with his crumbs. So this is true even for those who stood in Jesus' presence and didn't exclaim: "This is for the rich!" It applies to everyone. In response to the question put to Jesus—"Who then can be saved?"— he explains: "This is how it is. Being saved belongs to those things that are impossible with men! But be of good courage, for a greater possibility exists."

Yes. It is possible with God, who "speaks of things that are not as though they are." It is possible with God, who can raise someone from the dead. It is possible with God, in whose counsel nothing is so wondrous that it would be unthinkable. It is possible as a work of God accomplished in a thousand hearts that screamed for life and where thistles have been uprooted and replaced with myrtles. It is saving work that continues until it achieves its purpose despite people's hardheartedness.

Do you comprehend; do you understand how the Lord accomplishes this work? Have you traced the pathways of his Spirit? Have you walked in the ways of his Word? Have you ascended to that treasure store that can make you even whiter than freshly fallen snow?

My brothers and sisters, I understand very well that you worship and that when you do, you yourselves recede. Oh, that that reality would be true for you. Don't resist it; let it overwhelm you. For this is what it takes for you to do what the Word of the Lord commands: "Go forth. Proclaim my gospel to all creatures." Every one of you, proclaim it in your own circles. Let the mother do it in the home. Let the father do it in the workplace. Let the preacher do it in the congregation. Let each of you do it by word and by the works of your hands. Do it in conversation and by your actions. Don't proclaim just a slice of it; proclaim the whole Word, just as God revealed it. Don't do it just now and then. Do it with unspeakable earnestness, and for that very reason, in all of its inscrutable love.

And when you have done this, then as one of God's ministering servants do not quietly sit down the next day and write in your spiritual journal, "He was converted!" But in secret simply pray that it might please God "to do what is impossible."

And if you think that he has already done it, then you don't have to look back. Because then you have already forsaken yourself and given him all the glory!

18
VOLUME I

EVERYTHING
FULFILLED

*Everything will be fulfilled that is written by the
prophets about the Son of Man. Luke 18:31*

If only people would return to the simple message written in God's Word!
What's there is so clear. Jesus himself said emphatically that "everything
would be fulfilled that was written in the Old Testament" about him. Just a
moment before Jesus gave up his spirit on the cross, John reports, knowing
that everything said about him in the Old Testament had been fulfilled, that
Jesus cried out: "I thirst!" And all the way on the road to Emmaus, Jesus' conversation was one long reprimand of the disciples' spiritual dullness and misunderstanding about his program of suffering and death. They simply hadn't
discovered this in Moses and the Prophets, that is, in the entire Old Testament.

They didn't get a single part of it!

Don't make of this that the entire old covenant consists of one long lamentation over the suffering that a righteous person can expect, preeminently the
Messiah. And don't attempt to water down the whole old covenant to a single
dirge on Israel's suffering, or that the Messiah's extreme situation simply recap-
tures that of Israel. Even less, don't look for an explanation in the half-baked
interpretation that a suffering Messiah was prophesied to pay for our guilt

but that it doesn't delve deeply into the special sufferings he experienced in Gethsemane, in Gabbatha,[1] and on Golgotha.

By making such claims, the one as well as the other, you should know that you are contradicting no one less than Jesus himself!

For the Lord Jesus, prophecy thoroughly and uniquely presented his program of suffering. It was a program that with unwavering eye and absolute certainty he read, saw, and examined ahead of time. He grasped it all: the entire process of his suffering, shame, and death in all its vivid color and all its terrible contours. On those prophetic pages, he saw himself portrayed just as he would be—humiliated, oppressed, and broken.

From those prophecies, he showed his disciples not only that he would suffer but that he would suffer at the hands of the high priests. He did so after this was confirmed to him and after he had willingly accepted this outcome in his own heart. He also showed them that the priests would hand him over to pagans who would mock him, treat him shamefully, spit on him, and then scourge him. They would cause him to die and thereby prepare the way for his resurrection on the third day (Luke 18:31–33).

Each part of this majestic program of suffering that he endured with blood and tears as he struggled through it, he told them would happen so that prophecy would be fulfilled, just as had been foretold. His disciples later repeated that claim. When he finally took every step on the way to the cross, when he waded through the torrent of his continuous suffering, when all the details and parts of this divine tragedy were complete, he drank the last drops from his cup of suffering. It was a cup whose carefully measured portion he accepted in fear. He did this all with the clearheaded awareness that then everything had been fulfilled. Then he gave up his spirit.

This is how it happened. This is the way it was predicted. Is this also how you confess and believe it?

In the counsel and foreknowledge of God, everything had been predetermined. This was true not only of suffering in general, but down to the smallest details of what would happen.

"Predetermined," so that any appearance that as much as one moment, one derisive word, or one lash with whips in the life of the Son of Blessedness happened by the will of sinners simply doesn't hold up.

"Predetermined," so that you could never suppose that the powers of destruction overwhelmed what is sacred and holy on Golgotha, but so that you would

---

1. This is the Aramaic term for Pilate's judgment hall. See John 19:13.

understand that even the most terrible forces of destruction served to achieve God's purposes.

"Predetermined," so that instead of bewildering and confusing people, the cross of God's Son would seal the truth of God's Word to us.

"Predetermined," not least of all, so that Christ himself, in experiencing everything that he did, would in effect undergo a thousand deaths before he died. In doing so with a clear head, that is, with morally grounded willpower and submissiveness and not in some stupor that flooded over him, he grappled with sufferings that he discerned ahead of time with sober clarity.

Or couldn't that be possible? Is such a thing too amazing even for God?

But I ask you whether a mother whose son had been condemned to die by fire as a martyr wouldn't be able to experience what her child was about to suffer. She would see his struggles in her thoughts by day and in her dreams at night. Wouldn't she be able to anticipate what would happen to him? Wouldn't she be permitted to foresee his chains? His death procession! His funeral pyre! The flames! The stake! His executioners! His convulsions! And wouldn't Almighty God, when he gave his own beloved Son up to die, be completely involved with the details of those special events? Would he be unable to foresee them, comprehend them, and be completely accepting of the raw, overwhelming picture of the dark hour still coming?

And if that's the case, and if you are convinced that Golgotha was at the center of God's thinking already at the time of creation and covenant making, why do you still hold back? Why do you hold back when you know that this happened out of love and for the sake of your blessing? Why, when it couldn't be any other way than that God the Father was involved with his Son's suffering? Why, when all throughout his work of creating and giving life, he always had squarely in his sovereign vision the somber spectacle of the cross? Tell me, brothers and sisters, why do you still hesitate?

Or does the Lord, because of your insignificance, only pay attention to the important circumstances in your situation and not to the little ones? But I thought that every hair of your head was numbered! If that's so, why not the thorns that squeezed blood from that sacred head? Or maybe God the Father had all this suffering and sorrow in mind, saw it all ahead of time, but just couldn't bring himself to talk about it.

So if he, speaking to and through his prophets, as you confess, could not keep quiet about his Son and much less about "the Lamb before the slaughter," is it really so strange that that Son who became human opened the book of prophecy? Is it so strange that in it he found and read what his heavenly Father, in his eternal love, had predetermined for him? Is it so hard to understand that he disclosed his plans for him and talked about him? Don't you realize what large portions of tender love the Son drank before he entered his sufferings? Those divine insights, small and special, spoke tenderly to him and supported him in his suffering.

Consider those Old Testament prophesies of his sufferings. They are the pages from redemptive history in the Old Testament that deal with the Father's love for the Son in whom he is well pleased. This is not an indifferent matter. Now you understand why Jesus had to cling to that old covenant with his whole heart. You understand how he saw that what literally stands there accords entirely with God's will. He knew that "everything would be fulfilled" and that God's counsel would be carried out. He grasped in his soul that they were all one and the same.

And is this same for you?

THE HEM OF HIS ROBE

... and implored him to simply let them touch the hem of his robe, and as many as did were healed. Matthew 14:36

Quite a contrast, isn't it—between the dearly loved disciple who was allowed to rest his head on Jesus' chest at the Passover meal and the jostling crowds of sick people in the marketplace who could do no more in that surging crowd than reach out and touch the hem of his robe?

They weren't able to look him in the face. They had to squeeze in behind him. They weren't able to approach him as a group of suppliants but had to slip behind him unnoticed. They couldn't even shake his hand but had to settle for disturbing his robe ever so slightly, and then only its hem. They couldn't hold on to the hem but only brush it with a fingertip in their longing to be healed!

Tell me this: Shouldn't faith work more strongly and powerfully than simply reaching out to touch the hem of a robe in the hope of being healed?

And yet—and this is always the main point—it wasn't only the disciple allowed to lean on Jesus' chest who was healed, but also the sick who merely touched the hem of his robe.

No, there is really no comparison when it comes to the distribution of spiritual gifts, not even in the bonds of fellowship that unite us with Jesus. But simply let this better comparison encourage you and remove any anxiety you may have: everyone, regardless of whether they are a dearly loved John or one of the least in the kingdom, will be saved as long as they touch him!

As long as they touch him!

Look at it this way. Without touching him, there is no living fellowship with him. And without living fellowship, there is no transfer of sacred, healing power.

Your Lord Jesus has the power to heal. When the contagion on the skin or clothing of a diseased person creeps into your blood or lungs, it has a mysterious, penetrating ability. It makes you, who had been relatively healthy, sick as well. But in the case of Jesus, things are completely turned around. He is the only really healthy one, and he makes you who are sick healthy and whole again, just like he is. He heals you. It works the same way in both cases. An invisible, imperceptible, and mystifying transfer of something inexplicable and unnoticed occurs from one to the other. It is a transfer either from skin or the clothing, or from the hem of a robe.

Spiritually speaking, that's the rule!

Merely talking about Jesus, thinking about your Savior, even turning to him as a last resort doesn't matter! None of it can heal you.

There has to be contact—the contact of one's life, of one's ardent and animated living.

There needs to be a transfer of something from Jesus to you. A divine seed! A germ of higher life! A power, an action, a gift of the Holy Spirit! But whatever form it takes, it must always and unwaveringly be something spiritual that Jesus possesses and that you lack. It proceeds from him and overwhelms you. And the conduit through which it comes to you becomes, after your conversion, nothing less than the lifeline of your faith.

That kind of faith was expressed by the sick in the crowd who submitted to the point of bowing to the ground in their effort to touch the hem of his robe.

Pay attention to what the hem of the robe was like.

It consisted of an embroidered flower with a hyacinth-blue tassel stitched to it. Every Jew had to attach one to each corner of his clothing. He was to do this "so that he would remember the Lord's commandments and not allow his heart and eyes to lust after the things of this world!" (Num 15:39).

What a truly beautiful symbol! Life as a flower, displayed as a hyacinth-blue tassel that represents God's perfectly clear, azure heaven itself!

And now those sick people in the crowd reached out for the flower of life, for that blue tassel sliding along through the dust that was almost stepped on and torn loose. They stooped low and bowed down in their attempt to touch it. And in that stooping faith, those who were sick were healed from their miseries.

Oh, those craspedia[1] that the gospel writers recognize as the embroidered flowers whose tassels reflect the blueness of heaven, are even more beautiful than "the hem of his robe" itself. They are identified with a quiet faith that works by "stooping low."

That's always how it is. The need to bow deeply to the ground in order to touch him and have his power surge into you and heal you is constant. That was true in the day of your distress, and it's been true ever since. It will be true to the day you die. You need to reach out, as it were, with the hand of your soul, and touch Jesus in faith.

---

1. This is a daisy-like flowering plant indigenous to Australia and New Zealand.

ALL SHE HAD TO LIVE ON

But this woman in want, from all that she had to
live on, put in everything she had. Luke 21:4

What a widow, and what a gift!
She didn't only give out of her poverty. Not only what she could spare from her table. She gave everything that she had in the house. She gave everything she had in her purse. She gave all she had to live on.

She only had two small coins left. Taken together, they were worth hardly anything in our money. Calculated in terms of today's value, they were just enough to buy bread for one day. But she didn't take them to the bakery; she put them into the collection box in God's house. Then she went home empty-handed.

Has anyone ever given more? Has anyone ever given as much?

What, I ask you, could the hundreds and thousands of our well-off widows learn from this woman who had only two small pennies to live on?

"Sell everything you have and give it to the poor," Jesus proclaimed to the rich young man. And he still would have had wealthy friends who would have given him simple bread to stem his hunger. But what he didn't hunger for was what this amazing widow did! She had nothing to sell! But joyfully and calmly she gave God her last money.

Yes, you're right! Her act suggests despair. It's the despair of thinking: "With these two pennies I'm giving up. Maybe God in his mercy will send the ravens with some food. Maybe the meal in my jar won't run out." But what else is faith in the deepest sense, I ask you, other than despair with what we have in our hands and hoping for God's mercy?

The clink of those two coins hitting the bottom of the collection box rose as a song of resurrection hope.

She didn't merely give all that she had to live on, but she gave her whole life. Literally, that's what's here. And she dared to put it all into Jehovah's collection box. She consecrated all of it to the point of death on his altar of homage and adoration. Having done so and with nothing left in her hands, she anticipated receiving in return a richer and more glorious life from her God. With him all things are possible.

Who could doubt that in exchange for those two small coins that she gave away, she received thirtyfold or a hundredfold in return? Who questions whether in this case a courageous faith willing to suffer even death was not crowned with a life of fulfillment and glory? Oh, that this single story of Jesus would focus the attention of even one of his followers on this poor widow.

But she was most certainly helped, and very richly at that!

Oh, the marvelous insight of Jesus!

Isn't this an example of knowing everything? He knew that the two small coins that slipped from her stiff fingers and through the slot in the alms chest were all that she had.

And doesn't Jesus still know everything? Doesn't he still know what your fingers drop into his collection plate? Doesn't he know what still remains in your bank account, or what shortage you incur when you give? And doesn't he still possess, by the power given him from the Father, knowledge of who is lying when they make a contribution? Doesn't he know how to reward the person who respects his house's treasury? Doesn't he have the ability to make the poor widow's giving turn out to her benefit and to loosen the grip of the wealthy woman enslaved to her silver? Doesn't he still have the power, the glorious power, to grant the ability to give even today like the poor widow did—to give with a despairing faith, but as a quiet and regal act, all that she had to live on?

Sometimes we ask ourselves, my good readers, whether the Spirit still works magnificent things in human hearts. If Jesus had not noticed what the widow did, no one would have known. Likewise, you frequently are unaware of what glorious expressions of love happen all around you.

But Jesus sees them!

ON THE PEAK OF
THE TEMPLE

Then the Devil took him to the holy city and had him
stand on the peak of the temple. Matthew 4:5

This temptation of Jesus reflects a struggle of soul that each of God's children can also sometimes suffer bitterly, each in their own way.

God's holy temple can become a place of sinning for them too. Not in the same way that Hophni and Phinehas sinned when they took sacrificial meat behind sacred walls. No, that's not the biggest temptation. But it's when people are tempted to mix a cup of God's sacred blessings as a numbing drink that causes them to misuse the spiritual treasures of his house to glorify themselves.

But true worshipers don't frequent "the peak of the temple." You find them below, on the main floor, on the level where all God's saints bow and kneel. There they humble themselves, and in that act of abasing themselves they open themselves to receiving the flow of Christ's atoning blood.

But that's not where Satan operates.

He can't stand being down there in the temple. That's too far beneath him. That's where God's power prevails over people's consciences. That's where the Holy One is honored. That's where praise and celebration, weeping and praying happen.

No, he who by exalting himself to the level of a devil doesn't abandon the deadening work of stirring up self-exaltation in God's house. He simply climbs higher, to the top—all the way to the top—from one level to the next, until he reaches the highest point on the roof. And only then, when he has climbed to the highest point and stands safely behind the parapet of the "pinnacle of the temple," does he think that he has assumed his rightful position. That's when he's satisfied in his ungodly pursuit. Satisfied because, as Flavius Josephus tells us, then a person stands so far off the ground that they can no longer catch the smell of sacrifices burning on the altar or see the blood flowing from the sacrifices of atonement. That's when any sense of the holy God is lost in a pervasive haze.

So then, what else do we have here except a picture of spiritual arrogance?

This is a special sort of arrogance to which a worldly person is oblivious and that fails to fascinate both urban and rural people of high position. But it is a stumbling block and a scandalous pitfall that Satan sets for God's upright, tenderhearted children. The latter want nothing more than to live lives that are holy. They desire to be found in God's temple. "Just as the swallow finds a nest," their home is at God's altar. Their world is the temple of faith. It satisfies their souls. It is their all in all.

But in that temple what pleases them like nothing else can do is what is exalted, highly exalted, and beyond comprehension. So in that temple they always attempt to rise higher and higher, and if possible, still higher yet—even to the point of standing at "the pinnacle of the temple." To achieve that aspiration would be to satisfy the deepest spiritual desires of their hearts.

And isn't it lamentable when you see one of God's best children once again led up those ungodly stairs by Satan?

What is most sad about this is that they are hardly aware of what's happening to them. That's because, with this one exception in their spiritual lives, they are models of humility and modesty, of loving service, and of an unpretentious heart. They are models in such an effortless and natural sense that you hardly notice the pretense and fraud in their modesty.

But the pity is that beneath this external appearance, Satan is pursuing his murderous intent. On this precise point about spiritual life, he knows exactly how to get the soul so intoxicated with imagined bliss that people can't resist giving in to this danger. Thus, in spite of having the most exalted spiritual intentions, they are betrayed as spiritual persons. (But if they might be brought to their senses on the matter, it is God who is to be praised!)

In their deadly quest to be exalted spiritually far above everything else, even to the very peak of holiness at "the pinnacle of the temple," another threat slips in. It's indistinguishable from pride. It's an even worse delusion of the heart. It's that a religious person thinks they have climbed so high that they will occupy an especially favored place with God. And in that position, they feel that God will direct every situation and opportunity to serve their plans, their advantages, and their imagined glory. This, in turn, makes the proud person so presumptuous that they think that the ordinary limits and boundaries of God's ordinances are no longer binding for special people like them. And should they fall into evil ways, their sinful way of thinking leads them to believe this: "He will command his angels to catch me so that I do not strike my feet against a stone."

Among these people you will find those who flatter themselves as they stand on the pinnacle of the temple. They are so unconverted, hardhearted, and devoid of sensitivity that they dare to jump. Then they crash, smashing themselves on the cornerstone of God's holy temple. Among those callous hypocrites you can also probably find those who were regarded as spiritual leaders or prominent members. They amount to the blind who want to lead the blind masses. Totally disastrous, this is leadership by children of the night rather than of the day! The swallow suspends her well-crafted nest below, on God's altar. Only field mice build their nests high above, just below the peak of the temple!

And yet, just as I said at the outset, far and away the larger percentage of these members on the pinnacle of God's temple can be called God's finest and most noble children. Precisely because of the excellence of their spiritual gifts, they allow themselves to be enticed up to this high tower. But naturally, they don't stay there. They come back down. And once again they look to the blood of the altar. Once again they drench the floor of God's holy house with their tears of sorrow.

So, our brotherly obligation remains. We shouldn't allow anyone to grow spiritually numb in the bitter, cold air of such heights. Our voice should rise to the brothers and sisters who may be up there on the peak of the temple. Oh, that they might hear and come back down, clinging firmly in their hearts to nothing but what our Lord Jesus himself did as his source of support: to the unconditional, all-encompassing, self-denying affirmation "It is written"!

Written in the Word of our God!

22
VOLUME I

THEIR QUIET PRAYER

They uttered their quiet prayer when you
disciplined them. Isaiah 26:16

To have to pray quietly, and that's what the prophet is talking about here, always puts more pressure on those already under pressure.

Not daring to be too loud, not being able to pray together with others, not permitted to pray in public are all deficiencies in the lives of godly people. Oh, I know, there is also the silent prayer of a lonely child of God, barely whispered and heard by no one else. Stealthily, almost like a thief, it rises from your lips to highest heaven when your door is closed. But it is only sentimentalism, sick thinking, and completely contrary to Scripture to misunderstand the value of calling on God's name out loud due to a preference for that solitary, private prayer.

To experience the hour of prayer when one is winding his or her way up to Solomon's temple on Mount Zion is one of the richest and most magnificent religious experiences that one can have here on earth. The same is true of those special prayer days formerly held among our people. They were uplifting high points during turbulent times. In the same way, prayers offered in our houses of prayer or as morning prayers in our family circles add spiritual luster to people's lives today. The intercessory prayer in a congregation, however much it may have degenerated from its original intent, still has indescribable appeal for a person in need.

To be sure, kneeling and bowing the head still occur in solitude. But in addition and more important is "standing before the face of the Lord" and seeking him with the whole body of believers. This is the kind of seeking that does not depend on the words used or on comprehension. Close attention and praying along with what is being said are not the main things. But "praying together" is! Praying "before the face of the world" is! So is praying in "quiet reverence" while bowing before him who has created us! This is praying that may be designated as an act, as action. It is praying when the person leading the prayer only stammers the words.

But not infrequently the Lord denies us those more exalted experiences, just as he did in Isaiah's life. He does this in our own day when radiance dims and the luster fades from our open, public praying. Then we are left to enjoy only the supplication of "a quiet, solitary, secret prayer" while taking shelter in holes in the ground or in the clefts of the rocks.

That's when people can no longer enjoy the celebration associated with open prayer. That's when the racket of the world cuts off its possibility. Or when division among Christian brothers and sisters simply makes unity in prayer impossible! Or when the lightheartedness prevailing all around us leads to a complete absence of corporate prayer!

This is the all-too-sad picture of our own times!

Are you so certain, then, that with this muting and dying off of public prayer today an "outpouring of quiet praying" has begun?

Has everything that has been said about prayer fallen through the cracks? Has everything that has been believed about interceding been lost? Has everything expected from intercession disappeared? Is this what things have come to?

Is there still a yearning in this silence for "praying together"? And is that yearning marked by holy fervor?

Is the number of people who pray increasing? Not just those who pray about their own lot in life or their own hearth and home! But also those who have a heart for Zion! Those who weep when others suffer! Those who lament when what is sacred is desecrated, and who yearn for the kingdom to come quickly!

Does that kind of quiet praying still exist? Does it exist despite increased repression? Does it exist when prospects are dim? Does it exist when the Devil slips into our bedrooms and mockingly asks us whether all our kneeling and stammering do us any good?

Is it praying that the Spirit gradually injects with a spirit of prayerfulness that penetrates deeply? Is it becoming that? Is it more a continuous dribbling of empty words, or is it as Isaiah says, the pouring out of that hidden, subdued, "quiet prayer" to the Lord?

Above all, is the person praying someone who's not praying about or on behalf of a particular need? But are they praying because they themselves are in need and are oppressed by that need? Are they imploring God to be delivered from the bondage of that need? Note well, I don't mean someone who imagines that they are in need, or someone expressing empathy about another person's need. I mean someone who is sinking under the weight of their own guilt and sin. I mean someone praying that they will be delivered from their own guilt and their own sin because they have seen the spiritual damage they have done. I mean someone trying to climb out of the pit of a troubled, afflicted, and shattered conscience. I mean someone yearning for the blood that atones, like a person with a high fever thirsting for a drink of cool water.

If people were only led into paths of prayer like that! Then they would feel very small and insignificant in their own eyes, like they had sunk extremely low in their miserable condition. As a result, holding their breath, they would almost become so afraid of the sound of their own voices and so startled by their own words that they would prefer to sigh rather than whisper, to moan rather than implore. This spiritual condition is artfully sketched by the illustrious Isaiah in these beautiful words: "From your humbled position, you will speak softly from the dust; you will utter words while stretched on the ground, and your speech will be chirping from the dust!"

I am very aware that all of this, as a point of interest, can be mimicked hypocritically. Then it dishonors God terribly. It's terrible in a way that amounts to crude mockery and is hardly less provoking than outright lying.

But it can also be genuine, a dimension of worship in spirit and in truth. This difference is recognized by God, but not by humans. Then something very holy slips into the sighs of redeemed creatures. Then the appeals of God's children lying in the dust but saved by grace are precious beyond compare. You can't put a price on it. It comes from above, carried on the rustling footsteps of the One who brings peace.

Brothers and sisters, if that kind of "quiet prayer" is found in many bedrooms, many humble huts, and many clefts of the rock on Mount Horeb, lift up your heads once again! Cry out that your salvation has come! For behold, there's a bud on the fig tree, and a tender shoot is sprouting once more.

INSTEAD OF A THISTLE A MYRTLE

And instead of a thistle a myrtle tree will grow. Isaiah 55:13b

This verse is the beautiful conclusion of the prophecy that begins: "Come to the waters, all you who thirst." As you reflect on it, you naturally appreciate how exquisite, unusual, and glorious the myrtle really is. You consider its outstanding display among all God's plants with its always-green leaves, its luxuriant blossoms, its delicate and subtle aroma, and especially its exceptional double fruits of oil and wine!

To tell the truth, you can't imagine a more shining picture of what God's elect will one day be in glory: forever green and verdant, never barren or withered, expressing a united prayer and with one song of praise bursting out in the presence of the God we adore. Those exclamations are breathtaking and rich with a double fruit: the fruit of a broad, brilliant spiritual insight or knowledge of the Lord depicted in the image of excellent oil, and also the fruit of totally jubilant and celebrative joy captured in the image of wine.

And then to be able, to dare, and even to be compelled to believe that our own future and the futures of our dearest brothers and sisters are bound up in that prophecy! This is a future which we will share with all those souls who have been completely justified—an immense garden of myrtles! We will share in this, we who still sprout from the root of destruction! We who are still being pierced by the nettles on our own leaves! We who should be bundled up and tossed into the fire! Yes, it is definitely well for us to forget ourselves in our present condition and to be caught up in this glorious image of the myrtle's beauty. It is well to feel our souls overcome by the sense that "Yes, this is what true worship really is!"

But in your souls' bliss, brothers and sisters, as you're celebrating the amazing beauty of the myrtle, don't close your eyes to the thistle. For Isaiah also specifically mentions the thistle by name. You still also have to reckon with the thistle. How often doesn't that little voice in your conscience still say: "The thistle, that's you!"? "You are the thistle." No, not according to your faith. Naturally not! Even less according to your hope! And still less in terms of your life in Christ, since your name is hid with God in Christ! But, sad to say, this is definitely and all too frequently the case in terms of what your life is in the here and now. It's true in terms of your sad, earthly realities. It's true in terms of your ego and your self-serving flesh.

You understand that a thistle is recognized for what it is even by the blind, who know that anyone who touches it feels pain. Seen in that light, then, has the last prick already been removed for all time from your stem? Do the sharp nettles of the thistle, the pointed thorns, and the hot poisonous tips of its leaves never scrape your skin? Do their angry wounds leave you untouched? Have you never experienced the pain they cause? I'm not talking about the kind of pain that you cause in meeting your obligations, like a medical doctor does in his line of work. I'm talking about the other kind that applies to no one but you in your immediate surroundings simply by virtue of life's ordinary contacts. I'm talking about the kind that is caused by you and affects your neighbor.

No, you don't need to think right away about one of those huge thistles with monstrous thorns found in the wild. People definitely understand that those sorts of thistles are to be found in human society and need to be hacked out and burned. But then what remain, what spread, and what are incomparably threatening are those little plants with nettles. They are the hardly visible thistles. They are like hawthorns or like the little nettles hidden on the stem of a rose just beneath the most fragrant blossoms. They lure you deceptively with their fragrance wafting to your nose!

And do you dare to deny offhandedly and casually any connection with these, even now after your conversion?

My brothers and sisters, the work of calling forth new life proceeds so wondrously that the thistle becomes a myrtle. This happens just like the ugly chrysalis flies off as a beautiful butterfly! That the one becomes the other invites a comparison. The one shelters the other in such a way that the butterfly emerges at the last minute, and this is how it is between the thistle and the myrtle. The myrtle cannot swallow up the thistle before everything is accomplished and the last enemy, death, is swallowed up in victory.

So would it be good, then, to distinguish ourselves from those who are lacking in grace? Wouldn't it be better to at least consider that we are still thistles that have thorns on their branches and searing nettles on the tips of their foliage?

I think that if God's children would come to that self-knowledge instead of putting on blinders to it in their self-deception, they would cause a lot less pain and would suffer a lot less of it as well! O children of God, that's your exceptional glory and precious privilege. Become myrtles, then! You can do what others cannot. You can clip your thorns. You can make the tips of your needles supple. If you really want to! If in faith you want this, don't simply burn your nettles!

AND THE CHILDREN GATHER WOOD TOGETHER

*The children gather wood, the fathers light the fire, and
the mothers knead the dough and bake cakes for the Queen
of Heaven. And they cause me grief. Jeremiah 7:18*

Don't forget the beam and the splinter! And parents, be very careful about reprimanding others because they are blind to sin inherited through birth when you can't see your own actual sin infecting life's daily contacts.

The Lord had remorse especially about Jerusalem, the place that he himself had chosen, and about his own people who lived there. The godless practices going on in Babylon or the lewdness of Rome weren't an affront to his possessive love, but the scandals happening on the streets of Jerusalem were. Listen carefully! The Lord cries out: "Don't you see what they are doing in the cities of Judah and on the streets of Jerusalem?"

What was it that scandalized him and was so abominable in the city of his holy initiatives? To be sure, it was that incense rose to alien gods. It was definitely because the women "baked cakes for the Queen of Heaven."[1] What's worse, instead of acting like priests of the Almighty in their own homes, the fathers "stoked the fires" of godlessness. But the greatest of all these atrocities, the wickedness that the Lord emphasizes by mentioning it first, was that the fathers dragged their children into all this evil. They misled their little boys and girls before they even understood what was going on. Laughing and skipping, they sinned right along with their parents by "gathering and carrying the wood" that their fathers would light and over which people would offer their idolatrous gifts. That—especially that—was the most bitter of all bitterness for God in his tender love! And that's why the Holy One of Israel lamented: "They have caused me, their God, grief!"

But don't God's people in our own day reflect a sad similarity to ancient Israel in this regard?

Even in your best and most devout circles, isn't there a shocking lack of care for the children? They are the church of the future. They are the cherished darlings of our hearts. They are Christ's baptized little lambs.

Seriously and truthfully, then, aren't we giving practical expression to original, inherited sin when we don't attend to our children more persistently? Aren't we forcing them to absorb our own poisonous guilt and sin? Before they are even aware of doing so, aren't they drinking the numbing brew from our own infected cup? Aren't we consigning them to the sickness that cleaves to us and is then transmitted to their own tender, young hearts?

Please tell me where today you still find, even in Christian and ultra-Christian circles, the deliberate intent to make the law a tutor to Christ for the still unconverted hearts of children? Where do you find that kind of determined training? That kind of strenuous nurture? The kind of discipline that it takes to construct the fortifications needed to protect the precious safety of our children's hearts? For this is what it takes to prevent the ruin from outside from easily becoming the ruin inside. When sheltered there, it inflames and defiles.

Even now, perhaps more now than ever, you definitely find intentional pressure to resist the conversion of the young child and have them cling to the Savior. There's certainly a failure more now than ever to celebrate our small children achieving knowledge of Scripture. And we hasten to add that where

---

1. Kuyper uses the Hebrew term *Melecheth*, a reference likely to Ishtar or Astarte, Mesopotamian and Canaanite goddesses of fertility, respectively. Her worship by women in Jerusalem was popular in Jeremiah's day.

our children are concerned, there is scarcely any admonition, only minimal correction, and a lack of serious and faithful conversation.

And isn't all of this consistent with "the gathering of wood" for a father's altar and a mother's idolatry in Jerusalem?

Can you distance yourself very far from the idea that while you, your circle of friends, and even your own family saunter so piously through life with your children, in heaven there is complaining that you "have caused grief for your God"?

"Grief for your God" because you are so unloving as to involve your children in your own sinning! Whether you sin alone or sin together. Whether it's by arguing together as fathers and mothers. Whether it's misrepresenting the truth together, serving the world together, or determining together that your family will persist in the sinful practices that God has condemned and you should hate.

"Grief for your God" by yearning to abandon in your own time and way the basic requirements of restraint, integrity, and modesty that should mark your lives. Grief by promoting luxury, pleasure, and comfort in your own circles and your own lifestyle. These are things that worldly people, living without God, are worried about. But they are never appropriate for God's children.

You cause "grief for your God" above all when you wander down all these paths. You cause him grief when you sanction the demons of fame, greed, envy, and whatever else you want to call the Devil, for his name is Legion. You cause grief when you give them increasingly free rein and before you pull back on them yourself, but permit your children to see and hear such things. Then, even before they become adults, they themselves unconsciously become accustomed and enslaved to these things. Then, when your children rise above your level as participants in what is abominable to God, you involve them in playing out your inwardly unfaithful charade. Externally it all looks pious, but it really isn't. Now both you and they are caught up in the same unnerving, ruinous game.

I don't know! Maybe I've exaggerated! It might be that we've viewed life in Jerusalem too somberly. But I ask you, when time and again you hear about children who have succumbed to the same spiritual sins that have defiled their fathers and mothers and that were never blotted out with determination, what do you think? Can you avoid the terrible conclusion that the raging fire that ultimately consumed the children's souls was not kindled in the family circle?

A WHITE STONE

To the person who overcomes, I will give
a white stone. Revelation 2:17

People shouldn't misunderstand this inspiring, glistening, sparkling reference to a white stone.

This touchstone has nothing in common with the gem in a piece of jewelry worn on the chest. It also has nothing in common with the stone in a signet ring or the diamond in a crown. Jesus' expression deals with our acquittal from the sentence and curse of death, not with jewelry. This is talk about Judgment Day, about the hour when he will sit in judgment. It refers to the time when all the generations of the earth will appear before him. It is a reference to when the books of reckoning will be opened. It points to the time when every individual will receive from Jesus' lips either a death sentence or a gracious pardon.

In ancient times, people voted on a death sentence with small stones. They were either black or white. White stones were votes to set a person free. Black ones were irrevocable votes for the death sentence. And if there was more than one person being judged at the same time, the names of each of the accused were written on the stones, on black stones for those given a death sentence and on white ones for those acquitted.

Similarly, the elect of God stand as the accused until Judgment Day comes.

Oh, they have already been sealed inwardly. They have certainly celebrated the grace they have received. God's perfect love has driven all fear from their hearts. But—and you shouldn't take this lightly—as far as the public is concerned, whether in heaven above, in hell below, or here on earth, they have not yet been justified.

On the contrary. Their salvation is still a matter of faith. It hasn't yet been made obvious. This continues until everything is said and done, the outcome of their calling demonstrates otherwise, and God dismisses the case against them. Thus it seems as though they are perishing in their own unbelief, that all powers have turned against them, and often even that the Lord himself has abandoned them.

Our fathers understood such struggles very well. They expressed it beautifully in their confession when they said: "That great Judgment Day will be when the Son of God will acknowledge the case against them as his own and will publicly justify them against the tyrants who had tyrannized them."

That's why the child of God sighs and longs for that great day!

They long for the day when their oppressed, clouded, and perilous way of living will finally come to an end. Then in the presence of all creation, God Almighty will declare: "Yes, this beleaguered, wandering, lost soul was truly my child." That's why Scripture teaches that the elect as well as the hardened will appear before the throne of the eternal Judge on that day of days. There, in the hearing of every ear, they will publicly hear announced the lot decided for them. The righteous Judge, seated on his throne with the urn of black stones in front of him and the urn of white stones alongside it, will reach in and draw out those touchstones that designate either life or death.

This is what he testifies to the people of Pergamum. To each of the chosen, to every person "who has overcome," he hands a white stone of freedom and grace. He grants them eternal grace despite the fact that Satan, the world, and their own hearts would hand them a black stone.

Then Satan will cry out in protest: "Give him death!" And he will point out all the pain and shame we have caused. Then people with whom we have associated will scream, with Satan chiming in: "Sentence her to death!" They will point to all the transgressions and weaknesses they have witnessed in our lives. Even our own hearts, fearing death, will sadly acknowledge our unbelief and spiritual barrenness. But the tribunal will declare: "Who will bring any charge against God's elect? Who is there who dares condemn them?" Then, based somewhat on mercy but entirely on the blood of Christ, we will live. We will be pardoned and honored. We will live because we have been given the white stones that declare: "You have been set free." The names appearing on them are honored, and we are assigned an everlasting purpose.

Jesus strengthens you with his unseen manna until that day comes, however long that takes. On that day he will extend you the seal of your eternal pardon. This will be witnessed and celebrated by all God's creatures. He will hand this white touchstone to you personally, not to others on your behalf. He will give it to you as a token of his sacred friendship. Even more pointedly, he will not hand it out only to deliver you from death to life, but to usher you into a life of glory. On it, he inscribes the name of your everlasting identity. This is a profoundly intimate name that conveys his most sacred love for you—tenderly, delicately, intimately. It is so special that only you and your Savior fully understand it.

A PILLAR IN THE TEMPLE

He who overcomes I will make a pillar in the temple of my
God, and he will never leave it again. Revelation 3:12

The church in Philadelphia, with its profoundly prophetic name of "brotherly love," is standing on the ladder with seven rungs. In the book of Revelation, the Lord allows the congregation to climb and descend them as far as to the second and third rungs. Philadelphia undoubtedly rises above the others.

She has reached the highest one susceptible to receiving grace, for she has "very little strength." She has little social status and lives a humble existence. But she has also received the most glorious of promises. She will be counted worthy of bringing the most stubborn heretics and opponents to the feet of Jesus. By her Savior's love, she will be led safely through the most intense heat of persecution's oven. Then, finally, behind her she will hear David's key clicking shut the lock that will prevent anyone from ever diverting her from her salvation.

To seal the assurance that he gives her on the last matter, Jesus says: "You will be established as a pillar in the temple." By this Jesus understandably wants to disclose that she will blossom beautifully "in the perseverance of the saints."

The pillars of a temple are comparable to the trees of a forest, nature's temple, where the foliage is the roof and the birds are the singers in the choir. Visitors to the temple have this in common with these pillars. Like the forest's trees that evoke a sense of height, both the pillars and the visitors lift their arms and open their hands in giving praise and glory to their Maker. But the difference between the pillars of the temple and the visitors is this: visitors leave after a while, but pillars in the temple of our God always remain in place.

Intentionally staying with this image, the Lord gives this glorious benediction to the church in Philadelphia: "You will be like a pillar that remains in my house forever." To make perfectly clear that his promise is true and that it is to be understood with reference the perseverance of the saints, he immediately follows with these words: "and he will never leave it again." To strengthen this idea even further, he adds the picture of a serf who has inscribed on him both the name of his owner and the place where he lives. This assures that should he run away, he would be returned, either for good or for evil. In the same way, says Jesus, I will inscribe "the name of my God" and "the name of the city of my God" on them so that if they want to roam, my angels will recapture them and return them to their Lord.

Finally, that no other meaning should be attached to these wonderful descriptions is reinforced by the name of honor under which Jesus appears to the church of Philadelphia. He is "the one who holds the key of David so that what he opens no one can close, and what he closes no one can open."

These words are obviously an allusion to Jachin and Boaz, which were part of the temple in Jerusalem.[1] They definitely had left it and were carried off because of their aesthetic value. This reference is obvious from the expression "he will never again leave it." "Never again" means like the temple pillars in Jerusalem that had formerly been carried off.

Like everything in the sacred letters in this series that Jesus sent to the seven churches from the island of Patmos, this reference to "pillar" belongs to the sacred mysteries. It refers to the mystery of the perseverance of the saints. It is not intended to refer to a pillar that supports the temple. Nor is it intended to designate someone on whom others lean for support. Even less is it a reference to a place for posting sacred pronouncements to honor God. But simply see it for what it is, namely, an image for standing firm and not leaving. It represents standing firm in the sense of being supported. Supported at the base of one's

---

1. Kuyper is making an association here with the two bronze pillars that stood at the entrance of Solomon's temple. They were named Jachin ("He will establish") and Boaz ("In it is strength"). They were ornamental and symbolic, not structural in purpose. With the fall of Jerusalem and destruction of the temple, they were carried off (i.e., "left"—in Kuyper's imagery) to Babylon. See 1 Kgs 7:15–22; 2 Chr 3:15–17; Jer 52:17.

life on a solid foundation! Supported from above by the interconnected vaults and arches that achieve the holy purposes specified by God!

This is the glory experienced by God's saints. Not one of them can be lost. But while his grace sustains all of them, there are only a few congregations that are sufficiently humble and therefore sufficiently developed spiritually to really absorb the sweetness of this reality without having their maturation in Christ damaged.

Philadelphia would not be the only one that would persevere in holiness. But the advantage that she had was in being able to self-consciously confess the perseverance of the saints already now.

Blessed is the church here on earth that can confess that. Philadelphia could, and our Reformed church once could. Blessed is the church that can continue to grow and blossom spiritually in making that confession.

NOT FILLED WITH SWEET WINE

For these men are not filled with sweet
wine, as you suppose. Acts 2:15

S atan lives by conflict. With him nothing is original. There can't be, because he personifies the lie, denial, and only a spirit of lying.

So when God discloses himself to Israel, Satan posits his oracles in pagan lands. When God conceals his mysteries in Israel's holy of holies, Satan creates his in the Eleusinian mysteries. Just as soon as seers arise in Israel, magicians and fortune-tellers quickly appear alongside them. When Moses does the Lord's miracles in Egypt, their sorcerers perform the same feats. In opposition to Jehovah's true prophets, the Devil rouses his false prophets. Where God desires to establish his kingdom, this worldly overseer works to create worldly ones. And even when the Son of God takes on human flesh and speaks with a human voice, hordes of devils take up residence in the possessed, and Satan himself does so in wretched Judas—a kind of unholy incarnation, insofar as this is even imaginable! Even today, when the Holy Spirit dwells in a congregation, the forces of wickedness make every effort to force their way in as well.

We are locked in battle, says Paul so profoundly and experientially, not with flesh and blood, that is, not with wicked men, but with "the spiritual forces of the air."

What a somber shadow that frightening pronouncement casts over our Pentecost celebrations![1] And the shadow only lengthens with the passing of time.

Or doesn't the mocking accusation of being "filled with sweet wine" amount to some sort of prophecy? Could it be a prophecy of the form that this spiritual conflict will eventually take when the great apostasy occurs? That event will be like threshing machines moving across our poor, confused congregations.

For a very, very long time they have resisted, but now the dam has broken. Scandal has flooded the fields. Now the wild clamor and shouting we hear is not a fulfillment of Joel's prophecy; it is definitely an expression of "being soaked and filled with sweet wine"!

A spirit is roiling here, an evil spirit, Satan's spirit! In doing his clandestinely wicked work, Satan has dispersed this same terrible and malicious spirit to all parts of the earth simultaneously. Consequently, people everywhere are doped and enslaved by the deadly stupor they continually crave. That spirit rampages through all of Europe. It has been dispatched to America. It also corrupts impoverished China. Its devastating work is rumored to have reached Persia, India, and the Malay Archipelago.

Did you think that this was limited to those people? By some sort of agreement? That the sinners are the merchants and manufacturers who have been in some kind of collusion?

No, I tell you, that fire spewing out of the ground occurs everywhere, and the entire earth has to become a common hearth. The same wickedness is pouring out everywhere and in essentially the same form. Then it has to be obvious to everyone who is willing to see it for what it is, that there is a single force at work in it. All evil flows from a single source. One spirit is driving all of it.

But look, the Holy Spirit has now been poured out to illumine sinners inwardly. He makes them more human and also makes them participants in the divine nature. He makes them stalwart in their battle for what is more lovely. He causes them to trust in the love of God. But that other spirit that has invaded every bit of human terrain and resists the Holy Spirit is a demonic spirit. It has received the power to obscure rather than to illumine. It doesn't make people more human but more beastly. It makes them participants in Satan's wicked nature. It cripples all forward momentum toward what is honest. It throws its guilt-ridden sacrifices into the arms of despair and destruction, leaving them without faith.

Those two spirits continue to grapple with each other.

---

1. This meditation appeared in the Pentecost issue of *De Heraut*, no. 27 (June 9, 1878).

The Spirit of God has the goal of leading people down the path of glory to full glorification in the faith. The satanic spirit leads them down the path of shame that ends in nothing but doubt and desperation.

Look around you on this Pentecost. Which of these two spirits do you think human beings really prefer? Aren't those who prefer the Spirit of grace and who persist in prayer becoming fewer and fewer? And aren't those who follow the spirit that deadens and curses increasing in number? And those who are simply half-hearted, preferring neither the one or the other, and who are neither hot or cold but who are good for nothing but to be spit out on the ground, do you think that they are the ones who are going to rule the world for a very long time? Rather, haven't you noticed that they simply slink away as soon as they come under pressure?

And people say that we only fight over dogmas, quibble about incidentals, and split hairs!

Would that the church of Jesus Christ lived more fully into her dogmas! Into the dogma of the Holy Spirit as a person. Into the dogma of the personal existence of the spirit that lives in all that is evil!

Then the battle against the jibe that they "are filled with sweet wine" would become like a mighty, rolling stream. Then all ranks of society would be gripped in their hearts by the fear of the spiritual epidemic at hand. Then the civil authorities would realize that simply standing still and doing nothing in the face of this rampaging fire is worse than taking a wrong action.

But then the church of Jesus Christ would also understand that covenanting to fight the accusation that "they are filled with sweet wine" would come to nothing. Nor would shunning those who drink deeply of that sweet wine. Nor would diligence on the part of lawful civil authorities ... unless something else happened. None of it would amount to anything unless at the same time spiritual evil is opposed by spiritual means.

This will require opposition by the church. It will require resistance by those in the church who pray. Better yet, it will require opposition by him who alone has received all power to bind Satan, in response to the prayers of those who implore him to do so.

WISDOM MADE FOOLISH

*Has God not made foolish the wisdom of
this world? 1 Corinthians 1:20*

There are images that fascinate us: that of being persecuted, of mounting a scaffold for the sake of Christ, of feeling the sting of welts on our backs when whipped, or even of submitting our bodies to be burned. All of these invite an emotional response. But to acknowledge that man is a fool, hardly! Let's just admit that that image doesn't speak to our hearts.

One can admire suffering. Oppression can leave one speechless. Scorn often generates a sense of pleasure. But to glory in the fact that we are fools and don't even know that we are, that's too much! That's too painful to think about. The wisdom of our proud hearts can't accept that!

With the desire to be like God and to have the knowledge of good and evil, sin began its wicked rampage. That's why the ungodliness of intellectual pride persists endlessly.

The arrogance of the fallen angels is mimicked by sinners in the human fall. That's the way it still is, even for Christians!

Oh, your children can handle anything when they leave your home and enter the world. They've been raised to be religious. But don't let people ask them whether they're so narrow-minded as to simply accept all of that. Or whether they don't really know better! Or whether accepting it is really even thinkable for a civilized and intelligent person! Experience teaches us time and again that that's precisely when the arrow hits the target dead center and the urge to deny Christ rises in their hearts. Satan definitely knows the best trap to set for catching them!

It's always the trap of achieving or possessing something, whether that's money or knowledge. For Christ's saying applies as much to knowledge as to money: "It is easier for a camel to go through the eye of a needle than it is for a man rich in knowledge to enter the kingdom of heaven." Simply think about our professors, our doctors, our lawyers, our high school teachers, our authors, our police and military officers, and those who belong to our so-called civilized society. Cold of heart and barren of soul, with a few sterling exceptions, they live having veered far away from the living waters of eternal life. And why? Why else than because they think that they are wise. They feel the blood drain from their faces in anger if someone considers them to be foolish and ignorant. Or, if you will, they always think that the Tree of Knowledge is more valuable than the Tree of Life.

This is how Satan always causes division. I'm referring to the division between two sorts of people. On the one hand are the educated, the cultivated, the enlightened, the thinkers, and the knowledgeable. On the other hand are Christians, who are branded as narrow-minded, lightweight, gullible, and stupid. And people succumb to that division, because, look, people permit anything and accept everything, but their proud hearts won't tolerate being considered narrow-minded or taken lightly!

But sometimes it happens that even Christians introduce this division into Christian circles. (May God forgive those who do!) Then they talk about uneducated and narrow-minded Christians. And naturally an educated Christian is a term applied to oneself, one's friends, and other church members who think like they do. The narrow-minded, lightweight, and backward members are those who are foolish. They are those who hold tightly to what is passé and still believe it. They have no insight. The others make fun of them as narrow-minded, and they think of themselves as belonging to the educated circle of the very wise.

O sisters and brothers, how Paul would have been offended by that kind of pride among those "refined Christians." The man of Tarsus would have considered himself to be the narrowest of the narrow in order to show others that being refined is not what's really important. He would have shown that foolishness is what we should really be thinking about. He would have shown that in the sight of God it is the only thing that really matters as far God's glory and the salvation of our souls are concerned. What matters is whether we are willing to bow before God's Word and to the wisdom of the Lord. Our thinking should be concerned about exalting God and acknowledging how small we really are.

Do you want to win souls for Jesus? Then don't ever seek them by appealing to their wisdom, for that would be to mix poison with food. But challenge them first of all, relentlessly and directly, on the level of their understanding in an effort to make their arrogant thinking captive to him who "has made the wisdom of this world foolishness" before the cross of Jesus.

Furthermore, when you search the workings of your own soul, examine very closely whether the inner sacrifices that you have made to Jesus have included your own arrogant thinking. Has the Spirit's victory in you compelled you to acknowledge: "I am foolish; he alone is wise"?

BEDS AND CRIBS

They laid them on beds and mats so that when Peter passed that way, at least his shadow might fall on some among them. Acts 5:15

Nothing is as moving as the tender care Holy Scripture shows for the least among us.

During the time that Jesus was still on earth, people didn't need to be reminded of that. When he said "Let the children come to me," that was an invitation with magical charm. Or let me say it better like this: this wonderful saying has become a favorite in every Christian family with children. It is an expression full of warmth and luster that moves every Christian mother to pour out her love. It is an unfailing protector that makes it impossible for you to ever consciously cause moral harm to a child. It is an expression of love filled with magnetic power. When we remember it, it makes leaving our young children a very tender moment as we calmly and trustingly allow their hand to slip from ours.

What gets less attention but is no less lovely is presented to us in a pleasant scene from the life of the early church. It is the scene when Jesus' apostle had received power to heal the diseases of the sick by letting his shadow fall on them. Then all the citizens of Jerusalem carried their sick out of their rooms and laid them in rows outside their homes. They did so in the hope that their loved ones would benefit from this superhuman, miraculous, totally divine healing.

Then, as Holy Scripture tells us, this wondrous possibility for healing was not just extended to the aged or to mature adults, but also to little children. In order to guarantee for all time the bond between the church and little children, Holy Scripture also deliberately and emphatically tells us that those who were carried out were carried out on beds and cribs. The apostle's shadow fell on both with its divine, healing medicine.

Shouldn't you chisel that reference to "beds and cribs" into the cornerstone of every house of God? Shouldn't you engrave it on every residence where Almighty God has his people redeemed by the blood of the Lamb?

So much suffering also happens in those cribs. So much pain is expressed in the gentle tears of the crying children lying in them.

Don't forget that almost a third of all those to whom women give birth never make it any further than those little cribs. They are carried from their cribs to be laid in their graves.[1] Not just a few suffer in those cribs. A great many do!

What is even more heartrending is that there are so many of these sick little children who don't even have a crib to call their own. They have to sleep either on the corner of a big bed, on the floor, or in a feeding trough for livestock. Whichever way they must is so hard and uncomfortable that they cry their eyes out without being comforted. The little ones who will never recover are especially moving. Sometimes they languish slowly and for a bitterly long time on their cribs, which is even worse. Their pain is often suffered silently, not understood, and therefore especially heart-wrenching.

Shouldn't the loving shadow of Christ's church fall on such as these, lying on their tiny cribs? It might be the church in the form of a mother, a sister, or a nurse, should Christ move their hearts to watch, pray, and attempt to relieve suffering beside those cribs.

But there is something more they can do besides distracting such children from their situation. There is something more to do besides making them happy with a piece of candy. There is even something more to do besides lamenting their plight and spreading a soft blanket over them. It is to let the shadow of Jesus' love fall on them. This is far higher, much better, immeasurably holier, and definitely nobler. I certainly know that this is something that you can't put into words. But the deep mystery of that kind of love is felt in unbelievable depth by these children. They just drink it in!

But, sadly, so many of them go to their graves who have not had the shadow of that love fall on them, not even by their mothers.

---

1. The reference here is to the high child and infant mortality rates that still prevailed in the Netherlands of the late 1870s. Kuyper's title for this meditation is *Bedden en beddekens*, or "Beds and Small Beds." The meditation works because *beddekens* connotes children's cribs for him.

O church of Christ, what protests against your indifference rise to the God of mercy from a huge number of those touching beds of children! And they rise to him not just from the cribs of sick children but also from the little beds on which children who are still healthy lie slumbering. Those cribs can be found in many, many homes where night after night in children's bedrooms only God's holy angels are watching over the children with loving concern. But the shadow of their mother seldom falls on these children as they fall asleep!

It's sad that the number of cribs across which not as much as the shadow of a prayer falls is increasing greatly. Is it any wonder, then, that in time those parents will reap a handful of thorns from these cribs instead of a bouquet flowers?

I need to tell you in all seriousness that unless the shadow of your love falls across those cribs, Satan's terrible, dark shadow definitely will.

Then who will be able to calculate the poisonous weeds that sprouted already on those cribs from the seeds that Satan sowed there?

TAKE NOTE OF HIM

If anyone does not obey our words, take note of him. Do
not associate with him so that he will become ashamed.
Do not think of him as an enemy, but admonish
him as a brother. 2 Thessalonians 3:14–15

For some people, compassion can be harsh. But more often a lack of it passes for being loving!

They never dare to speak harshly. They lack the courage to address another person's conscience to the point that disturbs them. They think that it's being Christian in a higher sense of the word to dispense with all discipline.

Would that they would listen to these words of Christ's apostle!

Paul is not wishy-washy but always forthright. He is never sweetly soft-hearted and never just looks the other way. But he is always straight to the point and forceful.

He is conscious of the fact that there can be love even in anger. In fact, love shown in anger can often have more integrity and be more effective than quietly going along with what's happening. That's because Paul lives on a deeper level. He gets to the bottom of things. He does not deal with the here and now in a way that tries to guarantee the future.

Every sin and moral failure arouses his opposition. For him they are poison to be avoided. He battles them. They are inflaming, corrupting sources of the disease that impedes life. There's nothing else to do with them than to burn them out or to lance them like an abscess. This is the only way to save the person in whom they are found. For their own good, one should treat them as infected with the same contagion.

That's why Paul directs the church in Thessalonica to "take note of him." "Take note of him" who doesn't want what's good, who disturbs the good order, and who scandalizes Christ's good name. "Take note of him" and isolate him. Let him stand alone. Be on guard against untested appearances, lest you find nothing blameworthy in such immoral conduct.

"Take note of him" and "don't associate with him." Do so not because addressing him would inflame you, but so that your approach has a punitive and judgmental effect. This shouldn't be punishment that's high-handed or sanctimonious but that is an earnest reprimand given in love. It should come from the heart of a brother for the sake of saving, restoring, and sanctifying him. "Don't think of him as an enemy, but admonish him as a brother."

But what is still left of this apostolic requirement given in the Lord's name?

What is left of it in the church that no longer "takes note"? That has long ago lost the courage to "take note"? That no longer disciplines? That unlovingly and unmercifully tolerates in her own members everything that people call unholy and scandalous?

What is still left of it in the wider circles of those who confess Christ? Where people see no evil in what the Word clearly does and excuse it because "he is a brother"? Where the world worms its way into what is holy? What is left of it when the world quietly whispers, "No good can come of doing this"? What is left of it when dynamic love and merciful forthrightness are lacking so that the issue is avoided, peace is not disturbed, his anger is not aroused, and finally he is not punished by treating him like a pagan or a publican?

To this we simply add a word about what goes on in our own homes. There people act as though there is no difference between those who are right and those who are wrong. There we find a lack of seriousness, an absence of discipline, and no vigorous attack on evil until it's eradicated. There we peaceably tolerate their existence. But this only adds to the ungodly situation that we acknowledge could be better and where things should be different. So wickedness persists in the wife who is called "our dear mother," the husband who is considered to be "a good father," and the young man who is thought to be "a great son"!

It all comes down to this: people don't allow God's Word to have its way. They don't permit it to rule and control. They don't bow before the Word in either church or home. Stating that they live according to the Scriptures, they presume to delete what they please and to ignore what they think doesn't apply to them.

When this is so, the Word is obviously not a two-edged sword that penetrates to the separation of bone and marrow. Then all the blessing it is capable of bringing is forfeited because of your lamentable pride.

No, it's better to say that this is not pride as such, but more a weakness of soul. It's moral impotence! It's impotence dressed up with the deceptive, hypocritical slogans of "greater tenderness" and "deeper love" in an effort to maintain the pretense of being tenderhearted. But this only covers up a cancer that spreads and saps strength.

This is what happens when you define love on the basis of your feelings, what your heart tells you, and your own experience. Instead, a Christian injects that it must be based on the willingness to learn from your God in a quiet and childlike spirit.

CONTRARY TO SOUND DOCTRINE

*And if there is anything else contrary to
sound doctrine ... 1 Timothy 1:10*

A lot of logic chopping goes on with respect to sound doctrine. But who considers what God's Word says about sound doctrine anyway?

Almost always people depict doctrine as referring to a set of beautifully formulated propositions about the faith. Yet, doctrine is something quite different. To learn is to assimilate something into yourself. It is to allow yourself to be reshaped and transformed according to a set standard. It is to develop skillful capacities within yourself that you did not possess previously.

Similarly, there is a "doctrine" on how best to manage your household, a "doctrine" on how to pursue your calling in the best way possible, and a "doctrine" on socializing with others. In short, there's a "doctrine" for every one of life's endeavors.

All of life itself is really a school of learning. The workplace is that for an apprentice in one of the trades. The quiet family home is that for a daughter growing up at her mother's side. The rest bed is that for someone who suffers, and the sick ward is the same for someone who aspires to becoming a nurse.

In every one of these situations, "doctrine" points to the fact that we do not know how to go about things, how we will accomplish our objectives, or how things stand and will unfold. That's why we take the time to learn from others and have them instruct us. We allow others to shape us. Then, when the years of learning have run their course, we will have developed the same capacity and ability that they have.

Would a growing young man who knows a great deal about various kinds of leather, soles of shoes, and shoe making from reading books, but who has never benefitted from the learning experienced in a cobbler's shop, really be competent in that trade? And if he had already foolishly been approved for making shoes, I would ask you why that dry, abstract, theoretical learning in fact qualified him for that work.

Look, living from the heart is an art. Living with God is an art. And the greatest art of all is to live life here and now as life will be in the hereafter. A "doctrine" also exists for acquiring that art! You don't acquire that art automatically. You could never achieve it by yourself. No other way of developing it exists than by attending the proper school for it, or better said, to learn this doctrine from Christ himself.

Christ possesses this true doctrine. He instructs you in it by his Word. He applies it to you by his Spirit. He stimulates you by it throughout the course of your life. He accustoms you to what you first resisted. He develops your proficiency and capacity for living according to it. And like any good teacher, he shapes and qualifies you for this holy and totally glorious work of everlasting and completely blessed living.

So it's obvious that the Lord engages your awareness, thinking, and reasoning in this process. You are not a block of wood but a human being. In this process you do not sit on the sidelines like a spectator. He addresses you personally. He gives you insight. He opens your eyes. In his school of practical learning, he uses words. He employs clear, reasonable explanations of why things are as they are. He identifies components and explains how these parts work together. Regarding this higher plane of living, knowledge is not just about the fact that you are alive, but about why you are alive and how you should live.

So what do people do with this? They call this rational explanation "doctrine." They regard the map as the terrain itself. They take the catalog to be the treasures being put up for sale. They confuse the picture with the reality depicted.

And what, then, would it be to be healthy? We can talk about true and false doctrine, about lucid and obscure doctrine, but never about healthy or sick doctrine.

Your doctrine is "sound," therefore, when in all your work with the Word in your church, whether through discussions or presentations, you work in a way that shapes souls in the way prescribed by Christ. It is healthy when they receive the strength needed to resist Satan and when you can trust them to handle this by themselves. It is sound when they are growing and flourishing spiritually. It's healthy when they can smell what's false. It's sound when they yearn for what reflects the truth of God.

If your logical teaching is really pure, it's not the doctrine that makes you healthy.

To be healthy, people must first be alive. You know that even a skeleton can be positioned to appear like it's sitting beautifully. But it's not alive!

Similarly, your life isn't healthy simply because it exhibits moral strength that produces some ferment, activity, and higher aspiration. Even a fever shows strength, agitates the blood, and causes delirious activity.

No, to be sound, your doctrine must meet these three standards. First, it must agree with health as depicted by Christ and his apostles through their examples and in their normal teaching. Second, it must harmonize with the actual condition in which people find themselves; this applies to young and old, converted and unconverted alike, and it must demonstrate this with reliable spiritual clarity. Third, as your doctrine develops, it must be free from artificial or shocking devices; it needs to be solid and consistent with sacred realities; and in its development it needs the tact and sensitivity needed to purge itself of bizarre elements and to value what is genuine.

That kind of doctrine is consistent with what Christ taught. It is suited to people's actual spiritual needs. It is not static, but it continues to develop. And that development occurs rather naturally. Such doctrine is sound and healthy. Trust it readily. Dare to rely on it freely. Then it will become living doctrine. It will be living in the sense of teaching you the art of living a glorious, godly, and completely blessed life. The result will be a steadfast soul and integrity in God's eyes. Then already here on earth you will lead your life as a citizen of heaven, and above all, as a child of God.

32
VOLUME I

LOVELY THOUGHTS

The thoughts of a wicked man are an abomination to the Lord, but those of the pure in heart are lovely in his sight.[1] Proverbs 15:23

Thoughts proceed not from the head but from the heart.

Evil reflections come from people's hearts, not their heads. The head definitely shapes them. It clothes them. It determines the form they take. But their content, their essence, the urge and the force driving them, comes from somewhere deeper. That comes from within. It wells up from the very depths of our secret emotional life.

The head with its treasury of memories, imaginations, and associations performs the duties of a servant. But the heart plays the part of the master.

Living in the heart are the spirits of our emotional life. Those spirits are of two sorts and have two sources. There are spirits that are dull, somber, and black. They belong to our old nature. They spring from our old selves, from the flesh. They reflect the depths of sin, death, and the Devil. But dwelling in our hearts are also spirits that are pure, beautiful, holy, and loving in appearance. They come from above and fall on us from the Father of Light. They reside in us to enable us to talk about him. They stir in the depths of our souls as illuminating images.

---

1. Kuyper adds this footnote to his rendition of this verse: "This is a somewhat divergent translation in order better to capture the emphasis of the verse."

When the spirits of either sort want to expresses themselves externally, the path they have to take is through the head. That is to say, they have to engage our consciousness, reason, and thought processes. Then they take shape in the realm of our thoughts. That's where they receive recognizable form, a meaningful identity, and distinctive shape. That's when they enter the world of our imagination. That's where they are connected with other thoughts and considerations to ripen into full-blown possibilities. These are then proposed to the will that adopts them as its own and decides to act on them. By willpower in the context of opportunity, they become actions in our daily lives.

This is how evil considerations are produced. It is also how peaceable thoughts unfold in the presence of our God.

But what the world often calls lies, and what our hearts really don't want, and what our consciousness readily dismisses is in fact something different. We want them to be now and in the future secret, mysterious, inner voices, inaccessible to the God who is omnipresent, hears everything, and examines and fathoms all things.

Whether the heart's deliberation has already slipped through the door of our consciousness or is still hanging back behind it makes no difference. It also makes no difference whether it has already forced its way into the will or whether it is still suspended as a possibility. That possibility in and of itself, even in its first stages of disclosure and its earliest outlines, is an inner, hidden, but nonetheless undeniable reality. It is such just as soon as it has its first stirrings in our emotional life. Already at that stage, the heart is responsible for it. Because they are known to God, such ideas welling up within us, even in their earliest rustlings, always have the character of speaking to God.

Even within ourselves, we are never alone!

The thrice-holy God is always right there with us.

That presence is our conscience! And through it, God continues speaking. So he knows what we know. He hears what we are telling ourselves, and he is listening to what we are deliberating within the depths of our hearts.

This is why the writer of Proverbs says that when deliberations arise within our hearts, they first reach Jehovah. He is the first to know them. He is the One who evaluates them before anyone else can. And he is the One who detests or blesses them, based on whether they are in Satan's interest or come from on high.

Thus, your heart gives off a continual scent to God. If what rises to him has an offensive odor, he rejects it and pronounces a curse on it. Or, if what ascends to him from the altar of your soul has a pleasing fragrance, he is pleased and pronounces his blessing on it.

That's why Scripture says: "The thoughts of the wicked are an abomination to the Lord, but the deliberations of the pure in heart are lovely in his sight!"

Now, isn't that a glorious idea? Isn't it glorious to know that you never think or reflect on things alone, but that your God is right there listening to the solitary reflections of your soul?

And isn't it also a powerful incentive to have holy desires and pure thoughts, because you know that all your thinking is a form of speaking in God's presence? That what you think is discerned by him? That it is either detested as offensive or loved as lovely thoughts in the heart of the thrice-holy God?

And to think, then, that time and again even in the hearts of God's own children wicked thoughts arise, and that these trouble him and wound and dishonor his love!

Oh, doesn't this move you to pray, pray without ceasing, my brothers and sisters?

All of your reflections, all of your plans, all that flows from the fountain of your hearts, let it be one continuous stream of what is lovely to him. For he is more than the One who knows. He is also the One who searches the deepest recesses of your heart.

WALK IN THE LIGHT OF YOUR FIRE!

*Look, all of you who have set a fire and armed yourselves
with burning torches, walk in the light of your fire
and of the torches you have ignited. Isaiah 50:11*

The Lord has no patience with willfulness. Not even when one's pain is at its worst. Even if you should be overwhelmed by the waves and breakers, the Lord doesn't want you devising a way out all by yourself. He wants you to expect your deliverance in the way he provides for you.

This applies to your heart, to you as an individual, and also to all of God's people. Even his people escape from under his chastising hand in no other way than through the opening that he provides. All human agitating and conniving, all the inventiveness and cleverness that people are capable of showing in their attempt to escape by an act of sheer self-will, doesn't help us one bit. Those efforts only get us in deeper!

All glory must be the Lord's, even with respect to our foolishness and the path that we have willfully chosen.

When we sit in the ruins of our beautiful, sacred home and God gives us ashes for bread and tears to drink so that our souls flee in fear and a chilling desolation oppresses our hearts, then God provides us with a comforter. This is a Comforter who shows divine compassion and who is the only one among all comforters who is able to say: "I know just what to say and at just the right time to lift your spirits." And when that Messiah sees the people of his God humbled in sadness and fear, in darkness and gloom, he speaks words that grip our hearts: "Who is there among you that fears the Lord? Who is there that listens to the voice of his Servant? If such a person walks in darkness and has no light, let him truly trust in the name of the Lord and let him lean on no one but on his God!"

But that's not what the heart wants to do. It takes too long before light comes. So, taking control of our destiny out of the hands of the living God, we willfully reach for the flint and strike a spark. Holding the wick close so that it catches fire, we watch the torch burst into flame. Then we celebrate our own ingenuity, what we have accomplished, and the salvation we have achieved all by ourselves. That's when we call out to our neighbor: "Look, the darkness is gone; the fire's burning brightly. Everything around us glitters; it's bathed in a sea of light!"

No, don't be afraid that the Lord will blow out your fire. On the contrary, he will feed and fan it until it finally becomes too intense for you. At that point, you will become apprehensive about your own fire that to that point had been such a great delight to you. Now you'll begin to plead: "O Lord, help us! God of all power, please save us. Save us from this raging fire lest it consume us!"

However, at that point God will address us angrily. He from whose ways we have departed ... he from whose hands we have fallen ... he alone on whose name we should have depended for support ... he whose glorious light we scorned in favor of the choking smoke of our own torches. At that point the Holy One of Israel will say: "Behold, all of you who have kindled a fire on your own and have armed yourselves with torches, walk by the light of your own fire and of the torches you have lit. This is what you will receive from my hand; you will be humbled in your affliction."

And what an unquenchable fire that becomes!

It is the fire of bitterness and sorrow. It is the fire of an accusing conscience that singes and scorches and burns in our souls all the days that we have left here on earth. It first breaks out as a justly terrible fire. Then it grows into a flame that completely envelops us and whose suffocating smoke entraps us. This goes on until finally the windows are flung open, and the wonderfully fresh air of eternity wafts over us from the other side of the grave.

Even so, who is there who still waits for light from the Lord? Who is there who still anticipates the brightness that shines from the Lord's mountain? Who is there who still possesses a faith—a strong, deep, upright, childlike faith—who doesn't want to leave the darkness as long as the morning star of God's Word has not yet risen in his heart? Yes, what, what I ask, do you find even among God's people in many cases except that they go around with flints in their hands and wax dripping from the torches that they themselves have woven?

Thus, it seems as if darkness has fled. Then people devote themselves to celebrating instead of lamenting. No sense of God's wrath remains. They have no ear for God's voice of mercy. Then it seems as if the end of all suffering has arrived!

But what does this outcome produce except fresh disappointments? One after the other! One upheaval blends into the next. Unrest dominates. There is no more tranquility. The holiness of peace has become unattainable. All that is left is emptiness and dissatisfaction. Where people still think that they amount to something, they are consumed by the very fire that they have set. Always! They always have to come up with something new. They always need another incentive.

Over time, people lose any trace of being influenced by Holy Scripture and are left with nothing more than their own fantasies, resources, and delusions.

These amount to no more than random flames and sparks that dance and flit around our heads. That's when we want to smother the sparks and extinguish the fire.

But sadly, that won't happen. Every initiative just stokes the fire once more! Trying to blow out the sparks only makes them glow more intensely. If you try to escape the flames, they suck you in like a raging river. Because—now listen well—this is how the Holy One of Israel judges all willful conceit: "If you always want to walk by the light of your own fire," know that it will have disastrous results for you. This is what it will come to even for God's own people, should it apply to them as well.

May you learn once more to wait for the light that comes from your God!

34
VOLUME I

HOW THE GOLD HAS LOST ITS LUSTER!

How the gold has lost its luster! How the precious children
of Zion, once valued like fine gold, have now become
like the flesh of the earth. Lamentations 4:1[1]

"How the gold has lost its luster," Israel's complainer lamented when Jerusalem's glory had faded, the vessels of the temple had been looted, and the children of God were greatly troubled and severely oppressed by people speaking a strange language.

Once things in Jerusalem had glittered and glistened. That's when the poet stood in the courts of the temple and, filled with religious enthusiasm, exclaimed: "How everything in your house is radiant in its magnificence and splendor, my King and my God! How festive it all is!"

That's when servants from the lands of the Moors brought their gold from Ophir. That's when the queens of Sheba stared in amazement at Zion's glory and were overwhelmed by its splendor.

But now nothing more was left of that temple than a naked, bare wall standing here and there. The charred cedar wood had cooled. The gold overlay had

---

1. This is the only meditation in *Honey from the Rock* based on a text in Lamentations. It was published on August 4, 1878. In all, Kuyper wrote only eight meditations in *De Heraut* based on this book of the Bible.

been stripped off. Hiram's magnificent stonework had been toppled. Everything was one big pile of ruins!

That's when the seer wailed and lamented with a complaint that still penetrates to the marrow of your bones: "Streams of water fall from my eyes, they flow from my eyes and nothing can stop them. Nothing can stop them because there is no relief in sight. My eyes cause anguish in my soul because the daughter of Zion has been shattered."[2]

And shouldn't the Lord's people lament like that today?

For at one time here in our good land, the gold also glittered on the temple walls. There were days when people enjoyed a legacy of splendor and glory. The Lord's efforts on behalf of his servants were obvious. His church triumphed. Even opponents stood amazed at the brilliance and majesty with which the Lord our God had overwhelmed us.

That's when the gold shined!

But how sad that now, once again "the gold has lost its luster!" The glow of that golden sparkle has disappeared. Taunted and trampled, Zion now lies weak and humbled in its brokenness.

Sadly, that's the way it has to be!

Sub cruce! Beneath the cross! That's life's norm for Jesus' followers as long as they struggle here on this earth that bore his cross with him suspended on it.

Here he had no status or glory. If we beheld him, we would have seen nothing that compelled us to desire him. For him as the Son of God, glory would only come when he was exalted above this earth. So, church of that Man of Sorrows, what glory could you possibly expect to display, what gold expect to glisten, and what coals presume to glow as long as you still frequent the tabernacle here below and continue looking for the Jerusalem that is above, the mother of us all?

But consider this. For Jesus there was one moment of glory and exaltation here on earth. It occurred on Mount Tabor. Likewise for you here on earth there was a momentary legacy of honor and sheer majesty. It was when your appearance gleamed as in a bright light. Your face was radiant. Moses and Elijah seemed to descend into your own life. But as happened on Mount Tabor, it had to be temporary and passing also for you. It was an hour of totally abnormal brilliance granted to reassure you. It was given to refresh you when you remember it after having once again shouldered the cross you normally bear

---

2. Kuyper bases this quotation on excerpts from the Dutch translation of Lamentations 3:48–51.

and when you are disheartened like Isaiah was when he moaned that he was overwhelmed as by a flood.

So, O daughter of Zion, don't hide your face because you are no longer radiant. Rather, acknowledge that the glory you once knew can no longer return while you are still here. Don't let the question be whether "the gold has lost its luster." That is inevitable. But let it actually be whether what has lost its luster is still gold and still bears the authentic marks of true gold.

And by asking that question, there is no reason for a spiritual person considering spiritual matters or investigating the soul's inner working, like the angels in heaven do, to complain in any other way than Jeremiah did. There's no reason for One burdened by all your burdens to do anything else than to lament from the inner depths of life, from the hidden recesses of his temple, and from the work of praise adorning the lives of his redeemed. There's no reason for him to do so any less sadly than Jeremiah did, when he said: "How the gold has lost its luster!"

The gold of preaching has lost its luster in the tent of praise. The gold of prayer has lost its luster in the house of prayer.

The gold of godly scientific endeavor and of Christian doctrinal knowledge has lost its luster in the arena of the learned and in the halls of science.

The gold of discipline, order, and modesty has lost its luster in our homes and on our streets.

More sadly, the pure gold of faith, the glittering gold of hope, and the finest gold of love that once shined so gloriously have all lost their luster.

Then, even if we don't open our hearts, also the gold of salvation's inner mysteries will lose its luster. So will the gold of being introduced to the Exalted One who in a higher, tenderer grace clothes select souls with more than mere clothing, but adorns them with jewels that glisten: the emeralds of quiet humility and the sapphires of divinely consecrated hearts.

Even worse, my sisters and brothers, is that the times are so terribly perilous that even with the dimming of this life still worth living, Satan is at work. In this dimming he is not as interested in stealing gold as he is in replacing it with "earthly flesh," to use Jeremiah's words.

Then, should you still want to celebrate in your enthusiasm, let the kettle drums and symbols resound and drown out the quiet, lamenting song of the harp.

No, my friends, don't relieve your pain and sorrow with appeals for joy that have no basis.

Inner joy, oh yes, in the hidden depths. That's where there's true joy. In the holy of holies! Celebrate by always rejoicing in the presence of Jehovah your God!

But regarding what comes to external expression, regarding what you see of Zion with your eyes, reflect on the words of the preacher: "There is a time for laughing, but also a time for weeping." Judge for yourselves, then, whether the hour has not come for complaining to your God.

CRUMBS FROM THE TABLE!

*Even the dogs eat the crumbs that fall from
their master's table. Matthew 15:27*

Whether people should wish otherwise is not the issue. But this is simply a fact: the Lord has not ordained dispensing grace evenly in his kingdom.

Abraham was granted a richer portion than Isaac, David than Solomon, Isaiah than Amos, Peter than Thomas, John than Thaddeus. And what a gap existed between Martha of Bethany and Mary the mother of our Lord, even though both of them received gifts of grace.

What's true in the kingdom that God is establishing is true in his marvelous creation as well. Compare the little flower in a field with a beautiful rose, a water willow with an oak tree, and an emerald with a touchstone or even with the gravel you walk on with the souls of your feet. This is simply the way it is. Nowhere do we find monotony. Everywhere we see multiple colors and variation! But that variation sparkles only because of dissimilarity rather than sameness. That's the law and rule.

Every man possesses what is uniquely for him. Every soul baptized in the blood of the Lamb has what has been given specifically for her. An individual gift bearing each person's name and identity is directed at each one's heart. Beauty lies precisely in that wealth of the gifts of grace. There's no monochrome here but only a multicolored display!

So it's also true that in the kingdom the rich and poor come together because the Lord has made them both. This is true in the sense that in the realm of spiritual life the rich do not perish in their luxury, nor do the poor suffer shame in their meagerness. Each one receives as much as is good for him. Less would make him poor. Given more, he would squander it. Everyone's glass is different, and a different amount is poured into each of them from the fountain of life.

In the Lord's spiritual kingdom, no manufactured, one-size-fits-all model applies. Rather, every morning and evening a gift is sent from heaven to earth for each one of God's children here. It was prepared for them personally. It has their name on it. It is a gift of grace that testifies to the most tender and most personal of divine love. At the heart of its choice is that it is tailor-made for each person's unique character and calling in life.

These individualized gifts are not given to display the strength of our faith but God's great wisdom regarding the souls he has created, whether that is to make the wealthiest content or to bless the humblest.

There are those who live off the crumbs that fall from the table of those given a richer grace, and they are even prospered, inspired, and blessed by those crumbs. A small plate of gruel eaten in contentment is a better meal than the delicacies taken by those who always want more.

It's the same way spiritually. A life lived in simple grace, as long as one is satisfied with such a portion and not always self-centeredly reaching for more, is often lived closer to God than the ecstasy the most exalted vision produces when received arrogantly. Even the tiniest crumb is bread, and nourishing bread for the soul at that. That's because it falls from the table where nothing but the Bread of Life is served.

The question you have to answer, O my soul, is whether you have ever disdained the crumbs of other people's bread and whether you have ever denied them the crumbs of your own bread. For realize that in the kingdom of God things happen in amazing ways. Consistently! Repeatedly! At one time you may be the host seated at the table of knowledge, and your brother is the lesser person who longs for and lives off your crumbs. But soon after that, at another table where devotion and unselfishness are the dishes being served, the Lord designates that lesser brother to serve as host, and you have to crawl on the ground to catch his crumbs.

And the Lord does this to keep each of you humble by turns. He's concerned that you not exalt in your knowledge or he in his love. Both of you together should learn to give God the glory, to practice communion of the saints, and to share all things in common and in the service of the brothers and sisters.

36
VOLUME I

ANOINTED WITH NEW OIL

*You will exalt my horn like that of a unicorn: I have
been anointed with fresh oil. Psalm 92:10*[1]

Why do we avoid the dominant image of work in our era? The human heart is very much like a workplace filled with an amazingly ingenious and complicated set of machinery. It throbs and pounds with the movement of every gear and coiled spring. The powerful, driving vitality of that inner workshop goes on day and night, busily occupied with our dreams and aspirations.

Our hearts can handle this. They are suited for it. Our nerves need to relax, but not our hearts. Think about this: the well-being of our souls depends on this state of affairs. At least, it does as long as all this activity goes according to God's plan and established order. It does as long as godly thinking controls our hearts. This driving force comes to us from above. It descends to us from Jesus himself. One part engages another so quietly and smoothly that our hearts don't even notice it. They don't even think about it. They only consider what needs doing for Jesus' glory and are sensitive to suffering for his name's sake.

But we lack the kind of harmony just described. Sad to say, the parts of our hearts no longer work together that smoothly and harmoniously. Satan wants to be the driving power at work in them rather than Jesus. Our gears

---

1. This is verse 11 in Dutch versions.

move more at the direction of the world than that of Jesus. The result is that what was working smoothly becomes rough. What was polished becomes dull and speckled with rust spots. Our hearts cause us pain. The axle squeaks. The springs sag. The gears vibrate. We have the terrible impression that things aren't going very well for us at all. We sense that things aren't running the way God planned or wants. The result is that we weep. We cry tears of deep sadness in the hidden workshop of our souls. We yearn to walk in the ways of the Lord once again and according to his sacred plan.

If it comes to that, either in our prayers or without them, and always by sheer grace and never through any merit on our part, we are overwhelmed by the harmony that quietly and sacredly slips back into our hearts. It wipes away our bitterness. And in the depths of our hearts, we jubilantly cry out with the psalmist in his Sabbath rest: "Let God be praised. Strength has returned. I can function again. My horn is exalted like that of a unicorn; I have been anointed with fresh oil."

With fresh oil! It drips and flows between all the springs and gears in the soul's machinery. It makes smooth what was stiff and rapid what was sluggish. It causes the whole inner apparatus to work with its intended power and purpose once more. Now we feel that something good is going on again. We are being productive. He who is the inner Source of power in our hearts causes his Spirit and strength to pulsate through the cylinders and valves of our hearts. The result is that something good is designed, shaped, and produced for his kingdom.

Or, if you want to use another image, suppose that there was no opening to the inner parts of your heart. Suppose there was no way for you to gain entrance to the treasure store of resurrection life. But suppose also that your merciful Lord opened that door and brought those treasures into every corner of your heart. As long as there had been no such entrance, you existed only in a state of broken fellowship. It was definitely not in the fellowship that God intended. He really needed to return. But it was broken as far as you were concerned, broken with respect to your soul's enjoyment, broken in preventing your life from flourishing. Heaven's windows were closed to you; the door of your heart was closed to heaven. Suppose that you repeatedly tried to force open its jammed bolts and to wrench open its locks, but nothing worked. They wouldn't budge. That's how stiff and stubborn they had become because of this world's damp, cold atmosphere. That's what prevailed until a good dose of "fresh oil" was applied to what had refused to budge, and until the locks finally allowed themselves to be opened. Then the door was open to God, and he entered your heart again. All the while he had been a faithful watchman. He had kept on knocking. He had called out persistently. Then, when you couldn't create an opening, God himself did, and he now refreshes you in his abundant love.

Or better yet, brothers and sisters, consider the imagery of Scripture itself. It doesn't think in terms of a machine or the stubborn bolts on a door. It points to man himself. Wearied by the heat of the eastern sun, he frets and is discouraged by the stench of his own skin. He coldly, impersonally regards himself as disgusting because of the odor it gives off, while the sharp sand stirred up around him stings his parched skin like sharp needles.

Give that man a bottle of fresh oil! Even if it's not a bottle of alabaster or nard, you would see immediately the eagerness and pleasure with which he pours it out and smears it into his foul, parched, stiff skin. That's because the miserable fellow is refreshed and revived by the wonder-working power of that oil. The terrible stench of his own skin that revolted even him is replaced by a pleasing, refreshing aroma that strengthens his spirits. Instead of brittle and cracked skin from head to toe, he has skin and muscle that is soft and supple and tender to the touch. The stimulating and reviving effect of that fresh oil penetrating the pores of his skin reaches his limbs and joints. It's as though its power touches bone and marrow. That's the power that this divine oil has.

So yes, that's how it actually, truly goes with those who have become spiritually stiff and brittle. That's how it goes for those whose stench of death rising from their own hearts had become a loathsome hindrance. That's how it goes when God, through his merciful Son, is again pleased to create something glorious and to the praise of his grace from the misery suffered by sinners. That's how it goes when in his most tender compassion he pours the fresh oil of his indescribable good will over our dried out hearts. That's what happens when Immanuel, God with us, once more becomes real in our inner experience.

Then things become possible again. Then we can do battle again in the struggle shared with the psalmist. It's the battle of becoming conquerors in him who is already victorious so that we might participate in his victory. Then the anointing with fresh oil is a renewal of our anointed purpose, our calling, and our sacred destiny.

Simply by knowing this, we receive strength for the battle again. The battle takes on a higher purpose whose outcome is guaranteed by our only Surety. What a blessing! It makes God's children celebrate, stammering: "You, O Lord, are everything; I am nothing!" Those are the sounds of a reconciled, redeemed, and revived heart!

TAKE THE SHOES OFF YOUR FEET

Do not come closer. Take the shoes off your feet, because the
place where you are standing is holy ground. Exodus 3:5

There has to be a transition from being engaged on the lower levels of this world to lingering on the mountaintop of God's holiness. That's what the Lord expects of us!

To say that faith has to penetrate every part of our lives and on the basis of that principle to resist such profound awareness comes close to being overly spiritual in a way that undercuts all true adoration, praise, and worship of the Lord of Glory. That awareness is very obvious and real to others.

Whoever sets such a requirement wants already here and now what first of all is possible up above. They arrogantly imagine that they have attained it. This doesn't really lift us higher but drags us lower.

The nature of our lives, even as God's children, is such that they are still being lived in a world that is dead set against our Father. This is an opposition that exists outside us and all around us. But it is also an opposition that is definitely still found in our own flesh and the stirrings of our own souls. Such opposition demands that we clearly recognize the crass, concrete, and sharp distinction between the lower level of life in this world and the higher ground of Jesus' kingdom. It also requires that people reflect on the way the prophet

Ezekiel spoke about God. It requires that they always keep their eyes wide open to the real difference between the holy and the unholy.

Granted, we definitely have to pray without ceasing. The direction of our lives unquestionably has to be heavenward. Every thought flitting through our minds that doesn't come from God or turn us toward him, we have to stifle even as it's being born. But sadly, the reality of life now is simply that time and again we fail to pray without ceasing. We regularly veer off to the low level of ungodly thinking. We often indulge in sinful images before the battle against them has even begun in our hearts.

This is why Moses received the sacred command he did. It's why through that man of God every other human being does as well. Before we make the transition from unconsecrated to consecrated ground, we are commanded to "take the shoes off our feet."

More than anything, it's necessary for us to demonstrate and prove by what's on our feet that we no longer belong to the things of this earth and that they no longer belong to us.

Our feet are designed to walk in a Paradise where nothing hurts, bruises, or injures them. But they are ill-suited for terrain that produces thorns and thistles and where razor-sharp rocks jut from the ground.

That's the reason we take precautions for such terrain by putting on the footwear we do. That's why, like people in the Orient, we slip out of it when we walk onto the smooth surface and soft flooring of a well-appointed home.

It also explains why this footwear is associated with what was held in low esteem. It explains why a humble slave was assigned to untie and remove a person's shoes. It explains why an even lower-level slave was charged both then and even today to wash the dust and dirt off a person's bare feet.

This picture gives us both an image of as well as the basis for a correct understanding of our spiritual condition.

The person who is clean, says Jesus, has no need of having their feet washed, for they are completely clean.

Only feet that repeatedly come into contact with the fallen world make a person unclean. That's the reason why as brothers and sisters we are called to provide the service of foot washing for each other repeatedly and continuously. By that ministry, the dirt that sticks to us is removed and prevented from destroying us. It is removed by a higher spiritual strength that is expressed by us as brotherly love.

But this isn't enough.

In every sacred activity and with every act of worship, the Lord wants us to remember to loosen our shoe laces once again.

It's not enough simply to pray, to sit in church, to participate in the sacraments, or to listen to the reading of God's Word.

It's much more important to participate in each one of these highlights of sacred life in the awareness that we are walking on holy ground and that we have left the unholy ground behind us. It's more important that we first prepare our hearts by leaving the ordinary things of our lives behind and approach with a sincere and holy attitude. It's also more important that we come after having untied the shoelaces on the shoes with which we've been walking through the world and that protect us from it, because now they serve no useful purpose. Now we're standing on ground without thorns.

Well, "without thorns" is putting it too strongly. Thorns are still present in the burning bush. But the glory of the Lord exposes them. It even glows in them and shines through them so that we see them for what they are and pay careful attention to any power they have to hurt us, a power thereby diminished.

A lamp that guides our feet shines on that holy ground. It's a light that illumines our path every step of the way.

The Lord's will is that during this hour of prayer, praise, thanksgiving, and eternal celebration we experience freedom from the weight of the world and escape its filth.

What God puts in the hands of his children when they pray is not a spade for working the ground. It's not a trowel for building walls or a sword for waging battles. He gives them a golden harp for celebrating his praises.

That's how our shoelaces need to be untied and our feet scrubbed before we enter his tent to enjoy fellowship with the Almighty. Otherwise we'll be guilty of letting ourselves be diverted by the contaminating fellowship with the world.

Someday, when we have our last look at this world, we'll take off our shoes forever. Until then, every night as we lie down to sleep, we untie our shoelaces before we present our evening sacrifices of prayer to God. That's when spiritually—to extend the image, if we may, but using an image that definitely conveys the heart of reality—each of us once again needs to shake the dust off their feet as a prophecy of what's still coming. Then the expression "I am going up to God's altar" will convey what is truly in our hearts, whether we're in the house of prayer once again or not on holy ground.

UNCIRCUMCISED OF HEART

*Circumcision of the heart is spiritual circumcision, and
its praise belongs not to men but to God. Romans 2:29*

No, "to be circumcised of heart" is not to distance oneself from this or that sin. It is not to break with one unholy inclination or another. It is not to gradually prune the branches of the heart by cutting away what is evil, or cutting out life's cancers, or cutting off what's not holy, like a husbandman purges grape vines from sucker shoots.

Seen this way, it all remains your work—human work. It is also unfinished and frequently interrupted work in that case. It is completely useless for the purpose of getting at the eternal root of things.

Because, seen in terms of what Paul said to the Romans, it is just the other way around. Credit for the circumcision of the heart "belongs not to men, but to God."

You have to pay attention not to the act of cutting, but to the sacrament of circumcision if you are going to grasp the mystery of circumcision of the heart.

In Israel to be circumcised did not mean losing part of one's vitality or capability as small and insignificant as a snippet of skin. Nor did it represent loss of sensual desire. But it meant that a person was now marked, in those parts of the body kept hidden from human eyes among all peoples, by things that are mysterious. It meant that one no longer was part of the peoples of the earth as such, but that they were cut off from them and now belonged to the people of God.

People didn't do this to themselves, but it was something done to them. It was done as to a child who was only a week old. It was done so early that from the very beginning and throughout all of life, that person was an Israelite. It was an action, in short, that people only grasped later in their spiritual development. It was even an action whose all-embracing significance was in fact only understood by people of spiritual stature. This is because it was in fact a sacrament, thus a seal certifying that a person lived in covenant.

But what does it mean to say that a person is in covenant? This is first revealed in all its glory in the expression "circumcision of the heart."

The covenant of grace always conveys that our estranged and lonely hearts get a friend for eternity. This is a friend who locks us into a covenant that will never be broken. It's definitely a covenant that involves substitution. He takes on our obligation; we receive his glory. The exceptional beauty of the Christian faith lies precisely in this fact for us. It always has and always will—forever. This is the mystery of the work of salvation. This is what the soul treasures about the covenant. This is the goodness of salvation for the elect. This is the cup, the overflowing cup, of their peace and salvation.

Then you realize that being circumcised amounts to being rooted in the covenant.

No, it definitely does not amount to cutting something out of your heart. It amounts to cutting out your whole heart when it's a heart that just doesn't want to be in covenant. For then it wants to maintain its isolation. Then it's too proud to accept a substitute. It persists in wanting to handle everything on its own. Then what is grafted into that poor heart is the lie that imagines that all of this is what passes for circumcision!

That's why the whole heart has to go, not just a piece of it but all of it. And only then, when it's gone for good, is the circumcision of the heart complete in you. That's because now you have dared to relinquish your heart and to cast yourself entirely on Jesus. Now you no longer live without a substitute.

Now for the first time you feel, understand, enjoy, and experience what it is to live in covenant. This is a covenant with the One who will never forsake you and whose loyalty is unshakable. It is as solid as the mountain of the Lord. Now the truth of Paul's word to the Philippians is proven true: "We, we are the circumcised, we who worship God in spirit and glory in Christ Jesus" (Phil 3:3).

In that good, wholesome, and glorious sense, every bit of our lives needs to be sacramental. We shut the door on any inclinations in life that arise strictly from our own heart, and we unlock it for any that arise from our life in Christ and draw us closer to him. We are cut off from all the ways that proceed from our own sinful hearts, are intolerable to God, and are condemned by him. But we are opened to the royal highway on which Christ meets us, accompanies us, and overwhelms us with his grace. This is what circumcision of the heart is, nothing but this.

Oh, that two things would happen in you. First of all, that putting sin to death in your life would not amount to getting rid of the weeds, but to transforming the field in which those weeds spring up. That it would amount not to taking the axe to this or that branch, but to the root of the tree. Or, if you will, that it would not amount to taking aim at this or that sin, but at all sin at the same time. The second thing is that you would understand that neither the circumcision of your thinking nor the circumcision of your lifestyle ever does you any good unless you always confess your faith in the covenant meaningfully. May you always rely enthusiastically on your Substitute. May you always confess, "not I, but Jesus" with such devotion that in dealing with others they increase but you decrease.

But sadly, as long as the position of honor that you have so far reserved for yourself in your soul is not clothed with Jesus, you are still and will remain "uncircumcised of heart."

39
VOLUME I

GO OUT INTO THE MAIN ROADS

Go out into the main roads and invite to the wedding
as many as you find there. Matthew 22:9

How everything is being violated!

Right down to people's sacred, sensitive, inner character where the power of Jesus' kingdom is sheltered!

It is being misused by his enemies. It is being misused by his half-hearted friends. It is even being abused by those whom he has purchased, sad to say, in the times they lack spiritual passion and courage.

"Go out; face the day; reveal who you are," Jesus said. Unfurl your sacred banner. Let your rallying cry be heard. Don't hide in your corners and bedrooms. But get outside. Go into the marketplaces of life. Get into the middle of things. Show the great courage of displaying the emblems on your shields. Strip the veils off your faces. In short, "Go out into the main roads and shout it out!"

But what are people hearing now?

"No, no!" Jesus doesn't get it! He didn't intend those words for our day and age. To be dragged into the middle of the streets is totally inappropriate for something as glorious and beautiful as the Christian faith. It's much too sacred, tender, and intimate for that.

On the contrary! Just the opposite! Christianity has to be a religion strictly kept on a private, personal level. It has to be a religion that is sheltered, not displayed on the streets. There ought to be no trace of it in the centers of public life.

"God is a Spirit, and those that worship him must worship him in spirit and truth." The matter is obviously settled by that single religious saying, for what else could "in spirit and truth" mean except that it is to be practiced so quietly and secretly that no one notices.

That's how the power brokers of our time, Jesus' deadly enemies, attempt to mislead the world with that seemingly sensitive little refrain and to do away with the cross of Christ in public life.

Naturally, there should be freedom of conscience for everyone. Let those who believe, believe. But in the same way, let those renounce the faith, renounce it. Our whole, powerful society has nothing to do with whatever you choose! Neither does the government, or the civil authorities, or any king. You're completely free, at least as long as you keep your faith behind the closed doors of your house. Or as long as you confine the world-encompassing religion of Jesus to your private quarters! And preferably, even in your own home, as long as you take your faith along with you to your bedroom in the evening, when you've lived life for the day and there's nothing else that your weary bones need than a good night's sleep!

With that slogan, Christ is banished from our civil administration, dethroned in national life, and driven out of the public schools. With it the unbelieving Jews, the ancient enemies of Golgotha, continue to pursue their ungodly, destructive triumph in national affairs.

And who has paved the way for their triumph? Oh, don't ask! Don't talk about it, or you'll stir up a lot of pain all over again.

Or haven't you heard how the seducer has gone around among Jesus' followers to mislead many of them? He's seduced them so that they actually sang the same song as the prince of darkness and still sing it! Concerned about seeming overly pious, they show how affected they are when people tell them that they should only approach Jesus in the evening or should keep these things private out of consideration for the Jews.[1] This is how they demonstrate that they don't understand half the central, all-embracing call of Jesus' glorious gospel.

Oh, you know who they are, those friends who are against everything that causes a disturbance!

---

1. Kuyper's anti-Semitism in this paragraph is reprehensible. Rather than excusing it, we need to understand it in light of the emerging pluralism and the breakdown of Christian dominance in Dutch society and culture.

They are the ones who are at seeming peace with everything related to the church and the name of Jesus as long as they are permitted to pray silently, preach softly, and work energetically for missions behind the scenes. And, they are content as long as they are permitted to leave what is against what Jesus of Nazareth wants to the civil law and civil authorities, to the country and its citizens, to the people and their king.

Naturally, that kind of limp position would have no influence at all if the followers of the Nazarene had inherited even a little bit of courage from the Holy Spirit. But, regrettably, even that indignity would have to be concealed! No, no, those who confess otherwise just go along with all the others.

You realize that if they acted decisively, they would be mocked. If their Christian faith actually came out in the business world, their business opportunities would diminish. They would be scoffed at, taken advantage of, and persecuted. And even though they marvel at the martyrs, they themselves are completely predisposed to a calm and peaceable life.

Yet, however things develop, the everlasting gospel, the *evangelium aeternum*, is and always remains a calling and requirement that demands public expression. It definitely and truly expects that at its very core life is to be lived openly for King Jesus. The trunk is not for Satan, leaving only a few leaves for Jesus. But the entire trunk and all the leaves and branches belong to him who loved us even unto death.

So don't simply stand on the sidelines, brothers and sisters!

Don't be silent partners!

Don't make of what must be a world-embracing religion one that is concealed and withdrawn!

Christians stay in the streets, keep to the main roads, and are found in life's marketplaces. They may never allow themselves to be driven out, even at the price of their own blood.

LORD, TEACH US HOW TO PRAY

This, then, is how you should pray. Matthew 6:9

The deadening influence of modern life has no more disruptive and destructive impact than it does on prayer.

Then the human heart loses its innocence. It no longer yields to any impulse unless the all-controlling mind has first determined that that impulse is not self-deceptive or illusory. In that case, the tender plant of prayer is then stripped blossom by blossom and leaf by leaf until it finally just withers. It withers—and pay close attention to this!—for both ungodly and godly people, although that happens in a different way for each of them.

In the case of the ungodly, he is simply relieved of the obligation to pray. His heart was never in it; he never wanted to do it. He only prayed because others did. Out of custom! Because he was told to do so! But it always rubbed him the wrong way. It was always a relief to him if he could escape it. Now, now finally, the apostles of modernity have determined that praying is really nothing more than the soul talking to itself. Strong spirit, *esprit fort* that he is, he naturally no longer has any use for such childish activity.

Neither he, nor nine-tenths of all our "civilized" adults and young people do. It's terrible, but it's true. To the extent that refinement has gained ground, praying has died out.

What is even worse is that pious people are going along with this. Even those with more godly sensitivity are praying less. A modern lifestyle has not brought this about, but modern theology. Modern theology is continually calling for prayer that needs to be more worthy of God. It says that the human character of our praying needs to disappear and has to be replaced with a more divine dimension. It claims that it is merely ungodly muttering and not praying when most pious people only ask God for everything.

Oh, that sounds so enticing! It sounds even more enticing when so many hypocritical and churchgoing people fail to lament the thoughtless desecration of sacred things that not infrequently even happens in the chancel itself!

But it's not true that Almighty God, the living God himself, needs to be approached in a godlike manner in our prayers for them to be a blessing and delight or for them to glorify his majestic being.

To strive for praying in a godlike way is an appeal being made by modern theology in virtually every pious context today. Consequently, people increasingly avoid in their praying whatever involves the needs of daily life. Offering petitions on behalf of those who are suffering by actually naming them is avoided at all costs. Even praying for the king is largely falling into disuse. All petitions and requests to be given something are being lost. More and more, prayer is merely becoming an unbosoming of the soul, like a paragraph from a speech cast in the form of a prayer. In the end, so little of actual prayer remains that the need for it disappears from one's heart, and people seriously ask themselves what good it does to keep on praying that way any longer. For the great governing forces of all things are going to go their own way whether we keep on praying or we go dumb. The appeals of a mere creature can't divert that powerful enterprise one whit from its determined course. And how often doesn't it happen that one person prays precisely for something that another person pleads against? In summary, is there still room for prayer in the life of someone who fears God at a deeper level of faith?

The outcome for him is the same as for one who lacks piety: prayer becomes flatter, more sluggish, and more lifeless until finally prayer only crosses a person's lips in moments of fear and desperation.

No wonder! For what is being proposed is simply and thoroughly false. No, God wants us to pray in an exactly more human way, not in a more divine way.

Praying in a more divine manner is, in short, absurd because God, since he is the God who is all-sufficient, does not need to pray and cannot pray without first becoming the Son of Man. Then he prayed out of the depths of his human heart. Then he lived into our human needs, prayed in human language, and assumed human posture. In short, he prayed in a thoroughly human way and learned through his experiences what prayer is and what it should be.

On the topic of prayer, all this rationalizing about God's sovereign control, about the consequences that our prayer might have, and about who knows what else, is simply foolishness.

Praying is the breathing of our souls. We do it automatically, without asking how it works. Furthermore, our own souls are the first to recognize true prayer. All philosophy is a deadly poison for your prayer life. It annihilates prayer. Very few ever return to a revived prayer life from it.

If you want to pray like a human being, with complete openness and freedom and expressing the needs of your human heart as well as your human hopes and desires, the issue for you won't be about prayer itself!

The disciples asked this of Jesus: "Lord, teach us how to pray!" And look what the Lord did. He laid petitions on their lips. All petitions! Like a child would bring to his father. Requests that never ended, included everything, and were as intimately human as any prayer could possibly be. That's what he taught them, he who was One with the Father, who was from God and who was with God.

Our souls must trust in him where prayer is concerned and not in the arid reasoning of our minds.

My good brother and sister, the unfathomable mercy of the eternal God is seen in this: he bore our humanity, was willing to become as a little child, and took pleasure in becoming simple. Yes, the glory of his matchless compassion is that he created the breath of prayer in your human heart, and that he wants you to listen to that quiet call that comes to you from his throne of glory.

41
VOLUME I

THE FRUIT OF LIPS

Let us then always through him offer to God a sacrifice of praise,
that is, the fruit of lips that confess his name. Hebrews 13:15

It's not the food that crosses our lips and goes into our mouths that matters. It's the grace-filled thanks and praise to Almighty God that crosses our lips as it comes out of us that do. They are the fruit of our lips that he intends and wants them to produce.

This explains why the apostle says what he does in the ninth verse: "It is good that the heart is strengthened by grace, not by foods." In verse 15 he points to what, according to divine arrangement, the fruit of Christians' lips needs to be. It needs to be "a sacrifice of praise" and a confession of the Lord's name.

The lips are the most sensitive of our human organs. On them the ways of flesh and spirit intersect. Body and soul find their strongest connection in what comes off the lips.

"The fruit of the lips" for the body is the food and drink supplied to it by way of the lips. This is the subordinate, lower, and entirely material purpose that our lips serve. Beside and above it is the higher and entirely different, spiritual calling that they have been assigned. This is the purpose of expressing what's in a person's heart and spirit, what rises from the depths of their soul, and what the state of their inner emotions happens to be. These things need to be expressed.

That God has created all things for his own purposes, including the lips, is certain and true for every good and upright heart. If that's so, then it is obvious that the fruit of the lips best ripens, that is to say, achieves the intended purpose for human lips, when those lips serve as instruments for praising the Lord and confessing the name of Jesus.

A passive, silent godliness is the kind of fruit that is contrary to Scripture. God would have you love with all your heart and all your soul, but also with your entire mind and all your strength. This is still the first and great commandment. And what surpasses the strength of the word, brothers and sisters, when it is expressed in speech and song? The word is the vehicle of the mind and has far-reaching possibilities and influence, particularly as the fruit of the lips.

Paul definitely wants us also to offer our bodies as reasonable, pleasing sacrifices to God. But the kind of godly fruitfulness that wants to devote the soul and its inner life to God, but withholds our bodies and our public lives from him, is unprincipled half-heartedness. It is spiritually false, without courage, and lacks spiritual fervor. That's what the entire cloud of witnesses and martyrs condemns and resists.

You owe God the complete integrity of soul, spirit, and body. Remaining silent is not confessing. It is denial, and it is a denial that is worse than unbelief. It is being unfaithful to the Lord!

Use your capacity to speak and to sing. Let your power of word and song be expressed in the presence of ungodly people and the devils so that the grace of a higher way of living is a real force in your lives. Let it shine as the glory of your souls before godly people and the angels. This is an amazing, worshipful, and incomparably rich capacity entrusted to you by your Creator. To be able to express anger and opposition with the lips, to be able to chastise and denounce scorpions from the Word, and at the same time to be able to pray and praise, to be able to give thanks and bear witness with those same lips in order to magnify the great acts of our God is our crowning glory as human beings. Even Darwin could never crown his gorillas that way. "If they could talk, they would be human," said a deeply reflective philosopher about that unusual, highly developed animal. Yes, definitely; everything is tied to this! "The fruit of lips" for an animal is only that it can feed itself and make sounds, whether shrill or beautiful, but always only noises. Only human beings are capable of speaking. Only what is born of a woman is able to praise with songs that makes sense. Only a human being reborn in Jesus Christ can confess with a power that overthrows kingdoms and makes tyrants quiver on their thrones.

A prophet in Israel is actually known as "a man who cries out." He is someone who is unable to hold back. He is someone who puts his open lips to good use as a fountain of eternal life. He is someone who under the impulse and urging of the Holy Spirit dares to break silence and proclaim, praise, and profess.

Even on Pentecost, the first fruit of the Spirit was "the fruit of lips." Then the apostles and disciples "proclaimed the mighty acts of God, each in a different language." On every scaffold and every martyr's pyre there was speaking, celebrating, and testifying, sometimes through and in spite of the billows of smoke. It was the dying glory of God's elect children.

No trying or shocking time ever fell on the church of Christ that was not accompanied by singing. Time and again singing, whether that was a psalm of David or one of the Sea Beggars' melodies,[1] was its most effective and glorious weapon in her battle against tyranny. Look, the Devil's preference is to render dumb those who are persecuted. But the One who came to shatter the Devil's work takes pure delight in loosening people's tongues so they produce "the fruit of lips" to the Father's honor.

So, if all this is true, do you still dare to deny that you are misusing and profaning your lips when you avoid their intended purpose? When that glorious instrument of speech by which the soul is heard and grace is made intelligible is either dumb or used for what is empty, vain, useless, or merely passing? When a steady stream of inspiration never crosses them—inspiration that expresses jubilance before the face of the Lord, even in the depths of the soul's lamentation because a huge measure of his boundless compassion is evident?

Shouldn't there be more silence regarding what is talked about these days? Isn't there a whole lot of empty chatter going on? Isn't a great deal of human interchange amazingly comparable to the buzzing around a beehive? Isn't it more degrading than uplifting?

On the other hand, shouldn't a lot more be said that now remains coldly stifled behind the lips in cowardice? Aren't our own Christian people well down the road of stealing all sacrifices of praise from God's altar? Of holding back on professing his name? Therefore of robbing the fruit of the lips from the Holy One? God will definitely pass judgment on such things. That's precisely why the Lord wants everyone to judge themselves. Brothers and sisters, do you have the courage to do that regarding your speech, the fruit of your lips? Have you done so?

---

1. The Sea Beggars were the valiant underdogs and heroes of the Dutch struggle for independence against the imperial forces of Roman Catholic Spain. They were persecuted for their Protestant, substantially Reformed faith.

Now I understand that there are those who will respond by saying: "I sing all the time! I'm brimming with enthusiasm. I'm never silent." Then I would simply want to ask them: "Isn't there some fruit of lips that is still impure? What if the seraph flew down right now with a fiery coal from the altar in order to purify your lips? Or briefer yet, what have you brought to that altar from your lips? Was it on your lips by the Spirit of God or by your own spirit? In other words, what fruit has been harvested for God from your lips? Was it fresh fruit or spoiled fruit?"

UNIFY MY HEART

Unify my heart in the fear of your name, O Lord my God, and
then I will praise you with my whole heart. Psalm 86:11–12

Whoever prays, "O God, unify my heart!" recognizes that his heart is not unified but divided. He confesses to God, who fathoms the depths of our souls, that in a manner of speaking his heart is shattered into bits and pieces. He is no longer ashamed to admit that he is powerless to put them back together. He can't reunite them or weld them back into a coherent unit. Now, recognizing that he is unable to achieve this in his own strength, he approaches the Almighty, who has power over all things. He entreats God: "Please, Lord, work deep within me. Truly, O my God, unify my heart again; unify it so that I might fear your name."

Unity of heart. That's what this is about. That's what it comes down to.

Is there anyone who has achieved the incalculable strength needed to put such a smoothly operating heart to work? Wouldn't this require putting all the counsels and devotion of our souls into play? And even if that were possible, is there as much as one human heart that has the strength, capacity, and determination to work with the required purpose and intensity to achieve this? There isn't!

But that's the secret to understanding Satan!

Satan's heart is definitely unified. There is no division or disunity in him. There's not a trace of contradiction in the depths of his unfathomably evil heart. There's not a hint of any struggle in it. His heart is totally unified, and it's also thoroughly wicked. It's not only capable of hating God with his entire mind and all his strength; it's also filled with a passionate desire to do so.

That's also the secret that explains the influence that radically godless people have in church, state, and society today.

As long as we were dealing with a generation of people who were half-heartedly godless and only half-heartedly religious, the flood of godlessness was not overwhelming. It couldn't be while they were in control. They were too double-minded, too compromised, and too weak for that to happen. Their hearts were divided three or four ways.

But that's not the way things are now with the present pace-setting generation. Now a kind of person has appeared on the scene who has a unified heart. He wants to banish the fear of the Lord's name with all of his heart and with all of his soul. Just take a look at how things are going. Look at how people want to turn everything upside down and sweep away whatever gets in their way. A demonic, almost superhuman power has broken loose.

But yet, don't despair, my brothers and sisters. Simply pray that you will get what these evildoers have, namely, a unified, fused, and undivided heart. Do it because it's perfectly obvious that with a compromised and double-minded heart you won't be able to accomplish a single thing against those doing battle with you from the amazing strength of their own undivided hearts. As things now stand, half-hearted and divided efforts are completely useless, powerless, and ineffectual.

You can see how these swarming deviants daily gain more influence and how the half-hearted are simply sidelined. There's nothing at all to be gained by half-hearted piety, compromised orthodoxy, or half-baked theology. Now that the heat of the day has come, its light has burned off all these mists like shadows. The only thing that won't wither is what is deeply rooted in good ground. Only it can resist and remain standing.

This is how good comes from evil and God's people are aroused to jealousy by the unified hearts of godless folks. But this will happen only if they are provoked by the disgusting condition of half-heartedness and restored to wholeness. It will happen only if God Almighty hears their petition, "Unify my heart," and their hearts become one again. It will happen only if he hears that prayer and it convinces him that they "love him with all of their heart" and that they "wholeheartedly belong to him," the God of mercy.

Wouldn't that be worth celebrating?

So let's give thanks! Let's give thanks with lips that are resolutely serious about experiencing the beautiful days of renewed commitment once more. Evil has broken out, to be sure. But so has the richest, most glorious expression of heavenly power possible!

Let people focus only on this one thing. Let every individual first of all examine how things are in their own heart, in the heart they carry around in their own chest. Let them examine whether it is unified, whether it speaks with one voice, and whether it is whole.

And if it is not, then pray, pray without letup, pray at all times, pray to the Spirit who is within you and who prays with you, that the sacred peace of "a unified heart" may be given also to you.

I know very well that here on earth this is a petition that is never fully granted. But I also know that whatever is lacking in this respect is covered and fully completed through the unified, fully divine and fully human heart of the Mediator. It was never shattered. But through all the days of his life and all the times of his suffering, even unto death, it remained unified in the fear of his Father's name.

43

VOLUME I

LIGHT IS SOWN FOR THE RIGHTEOUS

*Light is sown for the righteous and joy for
the upright of heart. Psalm 97:11*[1]

Light is sown for the righteous! It is carried outside and buried in the ground. While for a time it is invisible, it is in fact germinating and swelling in the womb of the earth. Shortly the day of harvest dawns and overwhelms him with a wealth of light and brilliance.

Admit it! As an image this picture is choice and unbelievably beautiful.

The person who chose for God and in doing so broke with the world in his heart and with all that glitters here on earth sees that everything around him is gradually becoming darker. One light goes out in front of him, another behind him. Candelabras with their ungodly glow once burned wherever he partied, but now he has blown out their candles. Other little lights that could have kept on burning the world begrudged him. It blew them out just to torment him. Then there were also many other lights that the Angel of Light extinguished so that his soul might be purified. And now, step by step, he walks the path of his pilgrimage in almost total darkness. He becomes as exuberant as a child when now and then by God's mercy a lovely ray of light still falls across that path.

---

1. The Hebrew original and most English translations, like the Dutch, use the mixed metaphor here of "sowing light." Kuyper develops this meditation around that mixed metaphor.

Pay close attention! We're not playing word games here or exaggerating. We can still talk about light, luster, and sparkle. The otherwise quiet joy and family happiness is still known to a fairly large extent by God's children. Who doesn't experience this and give praise and thanks to God for it? But what they lack and are compelled to do without is the worldly limelight, the glow of recognition, and the glitter of earthly glory. They aren't permitted to have it here on earth or it would cost them their faith and the soundness of their spiritual lives.

Yet such light is a big part of life today. We long for it. We've been promised that we can have it and not be limited to just a little subdued joy and sedate happiness. Our hearts are drawn to raucous shouts of laughter, the glamor of victory, and the glory of crowning recognition. But here on earth, we have to leave all that to those who are opposed to God. Those who kneel at the foot of the cross are not permitted to enjoy these things in their worldly, ungodly forms.

Daily experience makes this clear to you in repeatedly new ways. In our world here below, in the great drama of human life, slaves to their own egos bask in the light of recognition, just as Mammon in general and Satan do. Meanwhile, God's saints and devout children are pushed into the drab background, where they are lost in a haze of darkness and obscurity.

The Holy Spirit knows all this. As the searcher of our human hearts, he also knows what this costs us, how this saddens us, and how this frequently threatens our faith. Remember, that's why he comes to us now as the Comforter and reassures us in this amazing song of suffering. He whispers in our souls: "The light of glory seems to have disappeared for you. But it isn't gone. It has simply been sown, that is, it is hidden in the womb of the earth so that when the world's day has run its course and your day has come, you will overflow in abundance—thirtyfold, sixtyfold, and a hundredfold."

So does the sower grieve when his barn is empty and his pouch drained because he carried his seed to the field and scattered it across the plowed ground? No, just the opposite! Now he finally feels completely satisfied. The seed is gone from the storehouse, and the field now shelters all of it beneath its cover. He knows that his seed grain is at work for him. He knows that God is causing it to flourish. He knows that by being hidden away, his precious seed promises to yield him a far richer harvest of wheat.

Should you be sad then, O my soul, because when Christ entered your life his angels followed him to carry out of your house the light of great honor and glory? That they dressed you in the clothing of obscurity? That people forgot about you and the world laughed at you? That the sons of Belial dragged you through the mud? That you were deprived of esteem in the eyes of men?

Understand that your light is a better light, a far more brilliant light. It definitely is and it always will be. It exists, although you may not see it during the long days and years given you. It doesn't shine far and wide, but it's hidden there, right at your feet, just in front of you, beneath the surface of your daily living. It's sheltered there for a purpose. It isn't inactive. But it's being protected by your God. There its luster is being steadily increased by his majesty, multiplied instead of diminished. It's gaining purity, clarity, power, and luster until it will eventually burst out. Then it will engulf you and wash over you like a flowing stream, O righteous person. It will flood over you and many others who are righteous along with you. It will make you shine with the splendor of your Lord, like a star in the firmament!

The psalmist sings that life for the ungodly is like a dense black thundercloud. Lightning flashes from it and lights up everything, but with a brilliance that consumes, destroys, and discredits (vv. 1–7).

But for you who follow in the footsteps of the Man of Sorrows where you live, love, and struggle, life may also be dark, to be sure. But that darkness is like that of the gray field holding the kernels of seed in its womb. They are sheltered there from the light while you ripen and swell until the time when everything that surrounds you is light, splendor, and glory (vv. 7–11). So "rejoice in the Lord, you righteous, and praise him in honoring his holiness!" (v. 12).

The one who said "I am the Light of the world" needs to be heard in terms of this light when he expresses the sobering prophecy: "If it is not sown into the ground and dies, it will always remain just one seed; but if it dies, it will produce fruit a hundredfold."

And he's that One whom we keep on following!

YOU WHO CARRY THE LORD'S VESSELS

*Leave their midst and purify yourselves, you
who carry the Lord's vessels. Isaiah 52:11[1]*

This appeal to Israel appears here in a prophecy of redemption. This is a prophecy of deliverance from Babylon's painful, humiliating, and shameful captivity of God's people.

It comes from a time when the seer saw an end coming to a sentence to humiliation and shame. By the Spirit's illumination, he saw those sons who had once been carried off into the house of bondage clothed in sackcloth returning with shouts of triumph. How the command "Leave, leave!" must have resounded like a song of life in the ears of people sick with grief as they languished in exile. It was a heavenly melody. This is the setting when the guardian of Israel's honor gave the precious command to "leave their midst and purify yourselves, you who carry the Lord's vessels!"

It naturally made the first and fullest impression on the choirs of Levites, the retinue of priests, and people of Aaronic descent. These were the ones chosen by lot and bloodline who were regarded as worthy of ministering to God's saints. Now the sacred utensils designated for this work could be carried

---

1. As originally published in *De Heraut* on October 13, 1878, as well as later republished in book form, the text is erroneously given as Isaiah 2:11.

back through the desert to Zion with overwhelming joy and submissive hearts. At one time they had been dragged out of the temple by coarse, savage, thieving, plundering warriors and hauled off to Babylon.

Those designated to carry the Lord's vessels had to lead the way on the return trip to Jerusalem, ahead of the others. They were to set the mood for breaking with Babylon, entering the barren wilderness, and crossing the uncharted sea of sand in search of the holy mountain. Jehovah had selected them in their yearning for Jerusalem. This is why the prophecy puts it the way it does: "Leave here. Lead the way, you who have been chosen to carry the Lord's vessels. And purify yourselves before you pick up your sacred loads."

So they purified themselves, those who had been selected by the Lord. And they did lead the way, ahead of all the others, with their important, precious, sacred loads. They proceeded through the valley of the shadows and into the wilderness for no other reason than for the sake of the Lord's utensils they carried. They had eyes only for those holy vessels. All their effort was devoted to them. They raised no objections when their feet hurt, their faces were pelted in a sandstorm, or their clothing got dirty. If only the vessels of the Lord could make it intact through the desert, across the Jordan, up the mountains, through Jerusalem's side streets, and be carried into the temple of the Lord again!

Doesn't the picture of that Levite procession moving through an immense desert represent for you the pilgrimage of God's saints traveling through the valley of this dreary life on their way to the city of the living God? Aren't you carrying a vessel of the Lord as well? Have you been chosen as well for this task in his boundless grace?

Let me ask you this. What is the heart that you carry around in your breast if it isn't a precious vessel? Jehovah wants to equip it as a utensil for his glory. He does this by sprinkling it with sacrificial blood and anointing it with the Holy Spirit, thus consecrating it to himself.

Doesn't your soul belong to him if you are children of the kingdom? If you are regenerate and thus alive through your life with Christ? Doesn't it belong to him so that you have no other right or obligation than to keep your soul pure? Than from now on to direct your life toward the New Jerusalem that is above, where your soul will be presented to the God who takes care of you as an ornament and trophy of his grace? That's where it will be added to that vast, beautifully crafted display of God's immeasurable mercy.

Won't carrying that vessel of the Lord overwhelm you with the same difficulties on the way? The same heat of the day? The same dangers of the trip? The same fears about what you might encounter as those in the Levite procession expected on their journey through the desert and in crossing the rivers of their captivity on their way to "the river of God that makes Jerusalem rejoice"? Shouldn't this command resonate with you as well: "Leave there; and purify yourselves"?

This is a timely word that tells you to break with the world around you. Isn't this command to "go out" the incentive you need to stop forever saying "I should go," without ever actually doing so? And isn't the directive to "purify yourself" meant for you too, so that you don't just drag the world along in your heart when you physically leave it? And should the order to "untie the shoelaces on your feet" be ignored with respect to the sacred things of God?

Hundreds upon hundreds are still sitting beside the rivers of Babylon with "the vessels of the Lord" that have been entrusted to them. They certainly look toward Jerusalem with enthusiasm. But they dare not exchange the comforts of luxurious Babylon for the arid desert. There are also whole groups of others that definitely do leave, but they are so weighed down with the alluring things of that sinful city that they have hardly any strength in their bodies or room left in their arms for carrying a vessel of the Lord.

And yet your own vessel of the Lord, your soul redeemed by Jesus' blood, is so precious that you will devote everything to bring it to the Lord in his holy temple.

Not immediately! That you cannot do.

But for now you and those like you carry their vessels as pilgrims on life's pathways. You do this until you too reach the shores of the eternal Jordan. There you will shake the desert's dust off your feet. Then you will pass through the valley of the shadow of death and enter the glorious, marvelous Jerusalem, where a place has been reserved for every "vessel of the Lord." Even better, an uninterrupted use in the worship of God has been foreordained there for every one of the Lord's vessels. There, in the heaven of heavens, they will be retained in endless, completely blessed service.

CHILDREN OF THE RESURRECTION

They are God's children, children of the resurrection. Luke 20:36[1]

What are children of the resurrection?

Jesus is an enemy of sentimentality. He lives and works, he struggles and dies for what is sacred to God. But he dismisses weak, emotional excuses with the directive "Let the dead bury their dead!" For him, it's all about God and God alone. No creature is exalted by God, and consequently even the holiest of all creatures must serve the holiness of his great majesty. "He who loves father or mother more than he loves me is not worthy of me." Put even more strongly: "He who does not hate husband or wife or child for the sake of the gospel of the kingdom" falls from his place in that kingdom.

This also applies to life in heaven. In yearning for heaven and thinking about what it will be like, we should focus only on God. All speculation about what is coming and all imagining about what the blessed state of our dearly departed loved ones is like in heaven is condemned by God because it pushes him into the shadows.

This sort of thing drags the relationships of this world and of this life into what belongs on the other side of the grave. It should be just the other way

---

1. As originally published in *De Heraut* on October 20, 1878, as well as later republished in book form, the text is erroneously given as Luke 20:86.

around. What belongs to the age to come should already control what belongs to this world. What will then come to be should be carried into our present daily affairs by the instruments of our reborn hearts.

That's why when they approached Jesus with questions regarding what the relationship of husband and wife here on earth would be after they died, Jesus quickly brushed off that whole approach with a sweeping gesture. One could even say he did it mercilessly! There is no place for it in the human heart. He did this with his beautiful revelation about the future life, whose marvelous conclusion goes like this: "There we will live only for him!"

There they will no longer live for each other, but for him. He is the one and only center to whom all life of the soul returns. He is their completely satisfying portion. He is the strength of their lives, their purpose for living. He is their only good.

Oh, we will definitely recognize and see each other there. But that will be incidental, subordinate to giving glory to God. When she awakens in that totally blessed life, the wife will first walk right past her husband because her love for the Holy One will consume her. Later she will find her husband back, but in Jesus.

We certainly realize that this is considered insensitive because it doesn't take human longings into consideration. It does not stir up the emotions. But it is consistent with Scripture. It is straightforward, manly, and required by the sacred material. It's also completely true!

In that age people will no longer die, nor be born, says Jesus. Nor will they marry or be given in marriage, whose purpose was to make "being born" a reality. That purpose simply falls away in the higher life to come. No rationale exists for it any longer. It shouldn't be allowed to continue. Heartfelt relationships will definitely be present there, but they will not be defined by earthly standards. They will be holier, different.

And this also applies, Jesus continues, to the relationships between parents and children. These above all will fall away. Well, to say it better, they don't fall away, but they are transformed into an enduringly more exalted relationship. People will no longer be known as "children of this or that earthly father or mother" but exclusively as "children of God."

This will be the case not merely because that's what they'll be called but because in that fully glorious day that's what they'll in fact be! In that glorious age, the Savior says, they will not be your children or their mother's children, but "God's children" because they are "children of the resurrection."

Once, prior to this new age, they were your children. You brought them into being for this life by the efforts of your quickly fading strength and from your motherly womb. You gave them their existence. You bore them.

But then, in that age, when they will shine in the fullness of light, it will not be you but God who has brought them to life. They were initially born here, from the womb of sinful life. Then they will be finally and fully born into that blessed future. This will happen by means of an all-encompassing strength and out of the womb of the grave. It will happen when death is overtaken and annihilated. Then they will have been raised to eternal life.

With that resurrection, the glorious work of rebirth that is rooted in God's eternal election will finally have accomplished its purpose.

Then they will be God's children fully. Nothing that is from God will be withheld from them. They will be children of God in a far richer and more glorious sense than they first were here on earth. For then their entire personhood, body and soul, in totality, will have been born of God. This is why they will be known as "children of the resurrection." The resurrection will be the final labor pains preceding their birth.

Or you could say that it will be the final contraction of the eternal God in making you fully his child.

HE PASSED AWAY TO NO ONE'S REGRET

And he passed away to no one's regret, and they buried him in the city of David, but not in the graves of the kings. 2 Chronicles 21:20

Jehoram was a miserable fellow.

And yet, his father was one of Judah's most pious kings. But he was a father with a weak spot for his son. This is seen in giving his consent to the marriage of one of David's seed to an unbelieving princess.

Jehoram had gone traveling and found Ahab's worldly court compellingly attractive. There he became acquainted with the thoroughly wicked Athaliah, and this wanton woman caught him in her snares. The devout Jehoshaphat had finally agreed that Jehoram, his oldest son and the youngster who would one day wear his crown, might marry this cunning, foxy, lewd, and unbelieving princess. So Jehoram took her as his bride into David's palace.

What followed was predictable.

Jehoshaphat had barely closed his eyelids and Jehoram been made king before Athaliah took the reins into her own hands. She dragged Jehoram into all sorts of abominable and scandalous activities. This began with the murder of all Jehoram's brothers and the elimination of the heads of Judah's nobility. It continued with the construction of temples for idols and by erecting high places for their worship. Finally, as written, he literally compelled his helpless people to "go whoring after other gods."

That's when the Lord stepped in and showed mercy to his destitute people. Pestilence, plagues, and the disaffection of tribute-paying vassals followed. The Philistines invaded. All this was designed to sensitize the people's consciences. But the miserable Jehoram no longer felt this prodding. Finally, the reverses touched him personally, and he was seized by "an illness of the bowels that was incurable." Eventually, "his bowels came out and he died a painful death!"

What lay there was the deformed corpse of the fallen king. It occasioned no tributes whatsoever in his memory.

We read that the people withheld paying him any kind of royal homage and "lit no fires in his honor." They accorded him no place in the crypt of the kings. Finally, the saying was passed around on Jerusalem's streets: "Jehoram passed away to no one's regret!"

The paths that Jehoram followed and how he fell out of God's favor are not the same sinful ways in which we cause God sorrow. That's obvious because we live under different circumstances. The temptations we face have different dimensions and forms from those that he did.

But in the end, what difference does the form of our sins make when light is also snuffed out in our eyes? When we are laid out? When we are carried off? When the opinion people have of us in their hearts finally comes out?

If it comes down to that and if people's opinion of us becomes a prophecy of God's coming judgment, isn't the expression "and he passed away to no one's regret" also widely recognizable in our own circles? Answer me, those of you who dare to be honest.

Don't be misled by the temporary clamor of grief when we pass away. When we cease to exist, the sorrow won't last. Death is always threatening. Shuttered windows are always sobering. A funeral procession evokes emotional responses that pass quickly.

No, no, this is not what lasts; what lasts is what comes later. When heartfelt tears have been dried away and the shutters opened again, and when the symbols of grief have been put away, there is really not a deep desire to have back among us those who have been lost. That desire is not all-consuming. And is it what we really want in our heart of hearts?

If we're honest with ourselves, we have to admit that seven times out of ten, a year or so later almost all memory of those who have passed away has rather automatically disappeared. Isn't that true, my good readers?

When someone else speaks about such a person, when something occurs that causes us to remember the deceased—perhaps their birthday or the date of their death, or when we visit their gravesite—then fleeting memories recur.

I know that. But sad to say, even most of these pass quickly. Or they cause such bitter sadness that in our hearts we really don't miss them. We feel no genuine sorrow, no emptiness, and no wounds in our hearts.

There are certainly still many who are living among the silent and largely forgotten people of the land who are not unaffected by death's disruption. In their small and limited social circles and through their genuine love and self-sacrificial demeanor, people become deeply rooted in the hearts and lives of others. When they pass away, an indescribable and heartfelt sorrow is often felt concerning them. They are mourned and missed. People do suffer in their souls over their loss.

Nevertheless, brothers and sisters, numbers don't lie! Instances of genuine mourning are very rare and remarkably occasional. In our restless age, the impact of one heart on another has become superficial. The bonds knitting one soul to another today are very loose.

This contributes to our superficiality! It causes our total annoyance that permits no quiet devotion or self-sacrifice. This, in turn, reflects a terrible shortage of love and deeply grounded faith.

This shortage is so blatantly awful that even genuine mourners almost always express a sorrow marred by bland sentimentality and unchristian superficiality.

How distressing this situation can be. It is so distressing that it literally severs the bond between one generation and the next. People no longer feel that there needs to be a connection between those who have gone to their rest and those still living among us.

Because monuments are no longer erected in people's hearts, they put them somewhere on a street corner or chisel into the granite of a gravestone what ought to be inscribed on their hearts.

It's all external! In stone! So cold! So frigid! So heartless!

Maybe this is how people will carry you out! Brothers and sisters, does it have to be the case that the children of God "pass away to no one's regret"?

AND SETS ON FIRE THE WHEEL OF OUR BIRTH

The tongue is also a fire. It is a world of evil. It is placed among the members of our bodies as the one that corrupts the entire body and sets on fire the wheel of our birth, while it itself is set on fire by hell. James 3:6[1]

Everyone understands the phenomenon of a wheel that's turning too fast and, because of the heat generated on the axle, catches on fire, as people put it.

That happens with the axles of windmills, with poorly maintained cart wheels, and with cogwheels that are turning too rapidly. It always happens for the same reason, for example, when the blades of a windmill are turning too fast because of a strong wind, or when a wheel is rolling along with too much speed because of a high-spirited horse, or when a wheel is being driven too hard because the pressure of steam on a cylinder is too intense.

---

1. "The wheel of our birth" (*het rad onzer geboorte* in the Dutch) is often translated into English as "the course of our life." The idea here is that the tongue inflames, corrupts, and compromises the entire direction and purpose of our lives. Kuyper allows his imagination to run with the term "wheel" in developing this meditation.

This is the image James introduces in connecting the tongue with our inner lives. He compares the inner life to a machine that is being driven forward and kept in motion by a wheel. Our inner lives have two dimensions. The first has to do with living out of our rebirth, that is, out of our new humanity. The second is living out of our first birth, that is, out of our old humanity. If one were to introduce the image of a machine at this point, the first needs to be called "the wheel of our rebirth." And it's obvious that living out of our old humanity would be called "the wheel of our first birth," or shorter yet, "the wheel of our birth."

These two wheels are each driven by opposing power sources. The wheel of our rebirth is set and kept in motion by power that comes down from heaven. By contrast, the wheel of our natural birth runs by power that rises up from hell. Like the sources of their power, the results of their respective movement totally diverge. When the wheel of our rebirth is turning properly, we praise God our Father. In contrast, when the wheel of our first birth is turning freely, it produces what is accursed in people who are created in the image of God.

Nevertheless, both of these wheels that generate life's movement involve the same heart, that is, the same person. They have to turn on the same axle. And that axle, says James, is the tongue. The result is that the tongue is very uncontrollable, and it governs the complete machinery, if we may express it like that, of our person (our body). The entire, mighty individual person is controlled by her tongue, just as a large and powerful horse is by a bridle, or an ocean liner of enormous size is by a small rudder, or a heavy set of gears is by a thin axle. What is more impossible than gripping and stopping a rapidly spinning shaft? Just as impossible, says James, is to stifle the tongue, the axle on which the wheels of our lives turn. Once set in motion, it is virtually uncontrollable!

It is uncontrollable when the wheel of rebirth, that is, the new life driven by God's Spirit, is set in motion to the praise and exaltation of God. But it is equally uncontrollable when the wheel of our first birth starts revolving on its axle, that is, when the passions of unsanctified living are set in motion within us by the spirit of hell. Slander and cursing are the result. Then all restraint disappears. The axle of our tongue is set on fire by the heat of our restless passions that originate in hell itself (v. 6c). And when that axle is red hot, the tongue itself is set on fire (v. 6a), and nothing can prevent the wheel of our natural birth from being set on fire. Thus, the wheel of our birth is ignited by the fires of hell.

Naturally, at that point a person is no longer the master, and wicked words slip out that were better not expressed. We find ourselves standing, quite literally, in the flames of our passions. Worse yet, we cause fire to spread to everything involved with our hearts. It all goes up in flames.

And people still say that of all things in life, words don't really matter. What we do matters more than what we profess. The power that works unnoticed matters more than the words that we consciously, heatedly express. "No, no, no," says James three times over. The tongue is definitely more powerful, certainly more dangerous, and even more damaging than the hand. The heart bursts into flame by coveting, envying, slandering, and cursing until finally an entire part of the world is ablaze.

No, no, a spoken word—even your word—is not just noise that dies out. It is a driving force on the axle of your life, the rotating of the wheel of your natural birth, a spark of fire that can either destroy or inspire. Words, also the ones that you speak in your conversing, whispering, or murmuring are like an onrushing stream that always leaves a residue behind at the foundation of your life. It may be unnoticed, but it's permanent.

Speaking is not just saying something to someone else. It is at the very time we speak an expression of who we are as persons. It displays whether our speech is driven from above or from the depths. It expresses whether our tongues are in the service of "the wisdom that is from above" (v. 17) or of "the wisdom that is earthly, natural, and devilish" (v. 15).

Tongues are the organs that show whether they are working toward your inner sanctification or toward your spiritual destruction.

THOSE WHO WALK UPRIGHTLY

He will enter into peace. Then they will lie down on their beds to die, every one of them who has walked uprightly. Isaiah 57:2

Properly understood, the only thing that the Lord requires of us is that we walk uprightly. To those who do, he promises the most glorious reward imaginable. They "will enter in peace." They "will be spared from evil." They will rest quietly on their beds.

It all comes down to being truthful; to banishing all falsehood, especially all falsehood with respect to our piety; to being truthful before him who searches the heart; to truthfulness before God in our inmost beings.

Note well that truthfulness in the inmost being according to God's Word certainly does not mean what worldly people mean by "being candid." And it doesn't mean what Christians often mean by adding to that "and still be truthful."

The candor of the world is not truthfulness but ungodly brutality. This is evident when worldly people have shaken all respect for God Almighty out of what they say. When there is no fear of the Lord left in their hearts, they are fully capable of opening their unholy mouths and, without so much as flinching or blushing, break out with the most terrible language that they dare to use against the living God.

What people mean by "not being truthful," particularly in recent years, does not come close to the root meaning of righteousness according to God's

Word. The cherished expression of "being truthful" usually only means that the mouth runs ahead of the heart. And that's a habit very worth breaking! Admittedly, it also has a justifiable side and only becomes a sin when excessive. For an individual who is not fanatic but lives out of the Word, confession precedes spiritual experience, as the opening verses of Romans 5 make plain. This is a chapter to which many erring brothers would do well to take to heart. Whoever begins with experience and even hesitates to confess his faith prior to having a confirming religious experience opposes the salvation order.

No, according to Holy Scripture, "to walk in his righteousness" means that you do the truth. And since for you it is all about doing the truth, it means that you look for that truth in him who is the only one who can provide it for you, namely, God himself. "All men are liars, God alone is truthful." This is the reality on which all you desire and are willing to risk needs to be based.

And understand this clearly. Taking a risk is not something isolated to which you can make all sorts of exceptions or to which you attach all kinds of contingencies. But it is expressing clearly, plainly, and transparently what is true and real.

"Only God is true!" If you are really serious about doing the truth, then you will simply go directly to God's Word and ask what he has said there about those things on which it pleased him to express himself. Then, if you are certain and sure, convinced that things are like God says they are, you will do the truth. You will not first put your finger in the wind. You will not first wait until your religious emotions tell you it's true. But without any additional testing and even when those feelings are missing, you will joyfully and ardently profess it as the absolute, solid, irrefutable truth.

But now you have to take one further step if you want to be sure that you meant what you said and that the truth is really in you. You have to examine yourself pointedly in wanting to know who you really are by consulting yourself, other people, and in fact God himself.

It's not true that it's only you who has the greatest interest in this effort.

If you go to God with all your other questions, but consult other oracles on the most important one of all, namely, the one about who you are and how matters stand with you, all your parading around with God's Word is nothing more than a meaningless game.

So go to God's Word in examining yourself closely in order to know who you are and how things stand in your life. Only it has the answers.

Given that, my good readers, who is "upright of heart"? Who qualifies if God shows them from his Word how spiritually distorted and corrupt, how deeply sinful and accursed they are? Who can escape knowing that they are alienated, lost, and completely broken?

Oh, a prediction of their ruin seems inevitable!

But who takes that position? Who lives out of that reality? Who offers no other explanation than that in themselves they are no more than the deeply depraved sinners that God's Word talks about so often? Is this the rule in God's church today?

But that's the all-determining reality. That's what it comes down to. And without that recognition, all your praise of the Word only amounts to a very wicked posturing of a fear of the Lord that just isn't in you.

"Uprightness," properly understood, is the only thing that matters.

For the person who knows that they are lost is the person who is upheld! "Whoever knows that they have to lose their life will in fact gain their life!"

So you should always stay focused on that dimension of salvation known as "uprightness." You should never let your lying fellow human beings or the deceitful inner emotions of your own heart answer the important question for you of whether you are included in the little group of those living truly. Sadly, thousands upon thousands are doing just that. Rather, take that question only to God, the only one who knows the answer to it. Learn from his Word how a transformed soul upon examining itself can learn that answer. Second, examine yourself to see whether your own soul is inclined to do what the Word says it should.

That is how to read Scripture. That's how to examine God's Word. That's what it means to walk spiritually before the face of Almighty God "in uprightness of heart."

ALL THE INTENTS OF HIS HEART ARE ONLY EVIL

And the Lord saw that the wickedness of man was great
on the earth and that all the intents of the thoughts in
his heart were only evil all his days. Genesis 6:5

In his Word, God judges the heart of man in a totally different way than the man himself judges his daily interactions, his conversation, and even himself.

We also know that ugly things can be said about the human heart. That's especially true when we become appropriately angry with our fellow human beings. When we hear reports about horrible atrocities! Or when we become pessimistic about their terrible outbursts!

Never forget that that's when we always make a distinction between evil and good people, and usually we quietly put ourselves in the latter category.

Then we're no longer dealing with the evil of people as people. Not with the evil that applies to all people without exception. Not with our nature and the race to which we belong. Then we are dealing with a few inhuman people, as they are characteristically known and more specifically with people in their inhuman moments.

What remains firmly entrenched in our hearts is that a person as such is not an evil being but a good one, not hateful but amicable. We often go to great lengths to find more loving words for what is more lovable in people. This is especially true of entertainers in their songs, eulogists in their tributes, and graveside speakers in their blessings. Then a child of dust actually seems more like an angel. No, I say, it seems more like they have become a demigod.

Yet, this is the highest kind of deception. It is delusional and a flat-out lie.

It's a lie for the simple reason that God's Word often says just the opposite. It turns things precisely around. God tells you in his Word: "You know, O man, that the intents of your heart are evil. All the intents of your heart are only evil. Yes, all the intents of your heart are only evil all the days of your life!"

That was the case before the great flood.

But also after the flood of waters and under the covenant with Noah, we read: "The intent of man's heart is evil from the time of his youth" (Gen 8:21). "Look how he puts no trust in his holy ones (his angels), and how the heavens are not holy in his eyes. How much more, then, is the one who is offensive and stinks before him, the one who drinks wickedness like water" (Job 15:16). "Perversions are in his heart; he is evil all the time" (Prov 6:14). "The heart is deceitful, sick unto death" (Jer 17:9). In order to silence what is spoken from people's hearts, Jesus identified "evil thoughts, murder, adultery, sexual impurity, stealing, bearing false witness, and slander."

In his Word, God leaves no trace of doubt! These quotations are so bold and vivid that nothing is spared.

There is nothing whole about you, from the crown of your head to the soles of your feet! But you might say: "That just doesn't compute. It's in conflict with the facts. It contradicts everyday experience." And isn't there a wealth of goodness, devotion, overwhelming love, and compassion that make life livable on a daily basis and work like a healing balm on your heart?

Completely true! But don't forget four things, I beg of you.

First, never forget that there are the converted here on earth for whom the ax has been laid at the root of the poisonous tree and who no longer live for themselves but for Christ who lives in them. They certainly don't simply write poetry because of the evil in their hearts. But the Holy Spirit often sings there because their hearts are in Christ.

Second, remember that there is a preserving grace that is also at work in unconverted hearts. That grace has nothing at all to do with saving grace (see Heb 6). But it is nevertheless a priceless treasure that tames the wild animal in people's hearts and operates as a restraint between them. This is how a civil social order is made possible. Its presence creates room for the existence of the church of Christ. Our forebears called the fruits of this grace "the virtues of those without grace."

In the third place, keep an eye out for the fact that in many things that appear to be brave and courageous, the evil intents of a wicked heart often predominate in what's going on. A kiss is an expression of love, but it can also be the kiss of a Judas. Don't many expressions of seemingly good conduct, therefore, actually intend to blind us to what's really going on? Here we're talking about intent, that is, about the inner motivations to achieve something, to make something happen, to realize an objective that God says springs from evil intent. This is about a person creating something for his own ends rather than allowing his God to create what's in his heart. This can never lead to anything but a bad end. But even if the end is bad, we are not dealing by a long way with all the factors at play.

Consider in the fourth place that our generation has been weakened and is rapidly becoming too weak to curb the wicked content of its heart, to put it bluntly. Just allow fermentation to continue to ferment. Let the lion come out of its cave and for once be the hunted. Let restraint and discipline and order disappear. Then who would there be who wouldn't cover their face because of the shame and atrocities committed by the sort of beings that people had become?

If you want to know whether slime and mud lie on the bottom, you mustn't look into a stream when the waters are gently gliding along. You need to come when they are being churned up by big waves. Then you'll see what lay beneath the surface when it was flat as a mirror. The scent of a flower can be so beautiful and fragrant. But let it lie for a while and come back in ten days. Then judge what kind of smell that fragrant flower with its beautiful petals emits.

Isn't this how things are with human beings?

THEY DON'T KNOW
WHAT THEY DO

*And Jesus said, "Father, forgive them, for they
don't know what they do." Luke 23:34*

One of the most profound but least understood mysteries about the work of salvation is that sin is intoxicating.

The person who is once committed to sin no longer understands fully what they are doing.

The Devil certainly does. For that reason he is beyond forgiving. That's not true of people, who are conceived and born in sin and have always lived under its deadening influence.

To be sure, in that stupor a turning point can occur when the Lord whacks them so hard that they either have to yield or harden their hearts. And if they risk taking the option of hardening, as Pharaoh did, they succumb to the judgment of becoming confirmed sinners.

But that's not the rule.

Usually sin just keeps on working its numbing power year after year.

It's not as though we are not aware of doing something bad when we sin. But it is the case that we don't grasp the long-range consequences that our offenses have.

That's how it was with the Jews who mocked Jesus while he was on the cross!

They knew that mockery is always bad, especially that mocking a dying man is always evil. But they were completely ignorant of the fact that the person they were mocking was the Son of God.

Peter himself said: "And now, brothers and sisters, I know that you acted in ignorance, just as your civil rulers did." Paul repeats this idea in his letter to the Corinthians when he writes: "For if they had known him, they would not have crucified the Lord of Glory."

But why do we need their testimony when we have that of Jesus himself? His is preferable. He prayed: "Father, forgive them for they don't know what they do."

So it is really the case that something inherent in sin causes the sinner almost never to know what they are doing. It's precisely that not knowing what they are doing that constitutes a hook for grace. It is not a basis for grace. It is not the cause of grace. But it establishes a point of contact for grace. To put it another way and perhaps a little more pointedly, it's that not knowing what they are doing that constitutes the lasting human condition in which the forgiveness of sin is still possible.

Jesus says explicitly: "Forgive them, my Father, because they do not know what they do." And in the well-known parable he says: "The man who does not know the will of his master and does things worthy of punishment will be beaten with few blows."

Consequently, no one says, "I didn't know any better, therefore I am innocent!" That is the mindless mumbling of a godless individual who is not paying attention to the ways of the Lord. No, those who live by the Bible know better. Sin is always sin. And sin incurs guilt even when a person doesn't know what they are doing.

Jesus certainly didn't say: "Father, they really aren't guilty because they didn't know what they were doing." He said just the opposite. He understood that they were definitely guilty and that's the reason he invoked God's forgiving grace for them. This also demonstrated that a way remained open for them to have their sin and guilt forgiven.

Similarly, Jesus did not say in the parable just mentioned: "The man who does not know the will of his master may not be beaten." On the contrary, he indicated that the severity of his punishment would be less, for although he also would be beaten, the number of blows he would receive would be fewer.

This is a standard that clearly indicates how entirely differently God sees the level of guilt in one sinner as opposed to that in another. God does not measure with human standards. To the degree that one knows better, to that degree one's guilt is greater. Diminished guilt requires that a person's path through life has been walked in relatively greater darkness.

That's why the guilt of those of you who know God's Word is the greatest of all. With the light of fuller exposure, guilt becomes greater. And the worst of all guilt falls on a child of the Lord!

Sad to say, judgment always begins in God's household!

Think that through! Note well what light exposed the atrocity of Adam's sin. Surely no one since then has sinned with the sobriety, full consciousness, and determined willfulness that he showed.

Everyone who came after him sinned with a fairly high degree of the fogginess he lacked. With him when he fell, there was almost none. It was as good as unnoticeable.

If the proportion of guilt is diminished to the extent that its numbing effect becomes more appalling, it also increases to the extent that that numbing effect is diminished. Therefore it was greatest with the first sinner, who gave in to sin before sin had worked its intoxicating effect on him.

Only he was totally accountable for his transgression, and through that one transgression guilt spread over all humanity.

The doctrine that all people who come after him share in Adam's guilt cuts so deep and is seen as so grim, that it might better be regarded as the necessary flip side of atoning grace. That is the picture that the Man of Sorrows paints in his petition: "Forgive them. Forgive them, O Father, for they don't know what they are doing!"

UNTIE THE KNOTS OF WICKEDNESS

Isn't this the fasting that I choose, that you untie
the knots of ungodliness? Isaiah 58:6

"Let out a full-throated cry. Don't hold back!" is what the Spirit testifies through Isaiah.

But what should a person call out? What shouldn't be held back? What does God forbid you from smothering on your tongue?

The answer from Jehovah goes like this: "This is what my people should do, the ones who call on my name and still look to me when they approach me daily. They should untie the knots of ungodliness in their lives!"

Too little of this is being done for God's people here in our country! The leaders hunt down worldly folks. They cast their baited fishing lines in the direction of the unconverted. They don't let up on those who live for sensual pleasure, and they appeal to them to leave their ungodly ways. But what do they do for God's people? What do they do for those who confess their faith with conviction, but who exactly for that reason are in double jeopardy of being severely attacked by Satan? What do they do for the friends of biblical Israel who are at constant risk of being tied up in the knots of hypocrisy? What do they do for those who are truly converted but not yet living in the heavenly city and who often in the depths of their beings yearn for what the child of God that lives in them detests, shuns, flees, and abhors? And really, what do you shepherds actually do in this regard for the sheep in your flock?

Oh, that people would completely reject this approach and want nothing to do with it. Would that they reviled and disparaged it. That wouldn't be the least bit damaging! But they knew that much beforehand.

But what did those of you who chose their ways as your own do? What did those of you who have been participants in the same faith they have and who find strength in their confidence actually do? What did you do for those who call on the Lord's name but are often still deathly sick?

Have you comforted them? Have you encouraged them? That may be fine, but could this also be so soothing and flattering and evasive that it doesn't shake them awake or grip them with compassionate correction? Have you stopped short of confronting them about the wrath of the Holy One toward sins against his Zion? Have you wanted to say something but sealed your lips, kept it quiet, held it in?

Well, then, listen to what the Lord lays on our hearts: "You mustn't let this die on your tongue! You may not keep quiet about it. You may not hold it in. You have to make a full-throated appeal and confront them compassionately. You have to talk to them with such overwhelming love that they cling to the hem of your clothing as the consoler and liberator of their souls."

Let no one close their eyes to the fact that a great many ties to ungodliness still bind the hearts of God's children. They are frequently cinched even tighter by pious activity rather than loosened by it. These are ties to ungodliness, thank God, that only infrequently come to external expression, but that are much more terrible and frightening in the eyes of the living God in the way they ruin, invalidate, and corrupt the inner life. Truly, these are fetters in the fullest sense of the word. They are knots that are so tightly tangled that as soon as a person's fingers attempt to untie them their fingernails break off. Then a person simply gives up and lulls them self to sleep thinking: "O God, you are the One who's going to have to do this!"

Now I realize that a child of the world sees no danger in this black side of the soul's hidden life. But for the children of God it's a chilling reality. That's because they always feel that through it they cause their dear Father considerable distress and offend him. By the Spirit's light, they also clearly understand that this desecrates the blood of the Son of God. They sense that in it they offend God's holy angels. It makes them detest themselves. It robs them of blessing. It arouses God's wrath against them. By it they suffer, as with a cancer whose relentless advance corrupts and destroys everything.

And yet, people simply acquiesce to it.

Preaching that calls people to repentance seems fine for those who are superficial. But for the purpose of penetrating and gripping the hearts and souls of God's children, it seems excessive. People don't go that far! That would be to act as though the children of God are indistinguishable from children of the lie. Thankfully you can dispense with cutting that deep into matters of the flesh or drilling down that far into the conscience. As children of the covenant, when admonished you're greeted by the better side of what's in your hearts.

Look, if Christians here in our country would take an Arminian approach to achieving salvation, we would say: "Back off. Stop being contentious. It's hopeless anyway, and of no use." To be truthful, evil has broken out so powerfully and holiness has withered in God's house to such an extent that the strength to fight it just isn't there anymore. Well, yes, there is still some strength remaining among superficial people who take things lightly and just don't want to hear about a sharpened conscience. But it's not there if you're paying attention to those who pray more deeply. These people have felt its pain more bitterly in their own hearts. Certainly, lonely recluses exist without a shepherd for whom God provides special guidance when they are simply lost in a general population that God doesn't recognize or are banished to isolated places. But as a rule—really a set rule in God's arrangements—these people of his definitely will be pastured and their shepherds will understand and generously help them in their struggles. It is merciless, reckless, and derelict when such help does not come to them from their shepherds, or when such shepherds are lacking because they have not been sent to them from their brothers in Christ.

For the knots of ungodliness must not be allowed to remain. Although the Lord God could definitely cut through them, that's not what he wants to do. He wants you to untie them. You by yourself! He wants them untied not so you'll be free, but so that he will no longer be offended and his Holy Spirit no longer grieved. He wants you to untie them out of your love for your Lord.

And when you set about doing this, straining your crooked fingers and challenging your soul, and it doesn't seem like it's going to work and you are ready to give up, do you know what helps? Then, my brother and sister, a timely word of warning helps wonderfully. It hits home like an arrow finding the bull's-eye. That's when a reprimand makes us tremble inside. That's when the admonition of a loving brother humbles us to the ground and makes us feel small in God's eyes. That's when a man of God who knows exactly where to sink the knife does so and it penetrates deep into the flesh and wounds our soul. That's when God uses all those words, like so many tugs on the knot of ungodliness, to achieve the same result. The God of all that's holy knows that that kind of brotherly concern and fidelity breaks through the heart's darkness like light coming at daybreak.

That's when the heart truly cries out:

> Lord, my God, I have gone astray,
>> Restore me once again.
> This depends completely on your goodness, Lord!
>> For my heart has deserted me
>> Farther than I can measure!
> Oh, draw me that I may return to you.
>
> So that I might sing your praise forever
>> May I be compelled
> By Jehovah's strong right hand
>> That has found my wayward heart
>> And bound it to him alone
> With bonds that cannot be broken.
>
> That my Sun and Shield and Strength
>> Might do their work within me,
> May you who in but a moment,
>> Can make all darkness disappear
>> Come and shine within me.
> Jesus, please come quickly![1]

---

1. Kuyper's note: "A mournful cry of the soul, to be sung in the style of Psalm 61 as it appears in *De verloren zondaar gezocht en gezaligt*, sixth printing (Amsterdam: G. de Groot, 1717)." This was a hymnal whose versifications were made by Nicolaas Simon van Leeuwaarden (1648–1730), a popular poet of good standing in the Dutch Reformed Church whose devotional poems were frequently reprinted. This hymnal was also reprinted by Höveker in the nineteenth century. This Amsterdam publisher specialized in devotional material read avidly by followers of the 1834 *Afscheiding* or Separation. The rhymed Dutch reads:

> *Heer, mijn God, ik ben aan 't dwalen*
> *'t wederhalen*
> *hangt al aan uw goedheid, Heer!*
> *Want mijn hart heeft mij verlaten,*
> *boven maten!*
> *ai, trek mij, dat ik wederkeer!*
> *Opdat ik voor eeuwig zingen*
> *mag, het dwingen*
> *van Jehovahs rechterhand,*
> *die mijn dwalend hart gevonden*
> *en gebonden*
> *heeft met onverbreekbren band.*
> *Dat mijn Zon, mijn Schild, mijn Sterkte,*

Then let all glory be to the One who does all things well! But he is also the One who is pleased to use these efforts to chasten you with double-pronged words of repentance and warning.

---

mij bewerkte,
Gij, die in een oogenblik
al het duistre doet verdwijnen,
kom verschijnen,
Jezus, kom toch haastiglijk!

WE FUMBLE ALONG IN THE MIDDLE OF THE DAY

We feel along the wall like blind men, groping like those who have no eyes. We fumble along in the middle of the day. Isaiah 59:10[1]

People here and in surrounding countries who are still seeking God want to make spiritual progress. But they are unable to do so because they often lose their bearings. They go straight ahead when the road curves, and they turn off where it simply continues. They swerve to avoid an obstacle that isn't really there, but they unexpectedly hit their heads against the branch of a tree that hangs over the road. They get out of the way of someone who isn't approaching, but bump against the brother walking beside them. They come to the point of not knowing where they should be going, repeatedly make the wrong decision, fumble along, and finally they get the feeling that they have simply lost the way. Then, discouraged, they just stand still and lean against a nearby wall. This is a situation like the one the Lord describes here in the words of Isaiah. It's the picture of a people that coos like a dove and waits for a deliverance that never

---

1. While the original appearance of this meditation in *De Heraut*, no. 52 (December 8, 1878), gave the biblical reference correctly, its reprint in 1896 mistakenly cited the text as Isaiah 59:16.

comes. They are like a blind person feeling along a wall, not on a pitch-black night but in the light of high noon and the clarity of full daylight.

You can be sure of this: the hand of the Lord is not shortened, and his light has not run for cover.

If we only had the eyes to walk in his light, God's people would complete their journey rejoicing and singing glad songs. They would walk and not grow weary. They would stride ahead without stumbling. They would make progress without being diverted. Then the fruit of their souls' effort would bring praise and honor to our Mediator and our Surety, our King and our Covenant Head.

God's Word is still with us. His Spirit is still at work. And where Word and Spirit shine, light shines in all its fullness. This is light that is more glorious than any other that we will ever receive here on earth. This is light sufficient for all our needs. By it we will find our way in every situation, be able to spot every obstacle, and detect every enemy who lies in wait against us.

But this is what our people forget. That light only shines in the homes of Israel's children in the fertile land of Goshen. In the houses of the Egyptians, there is only darkness, the thickest possible darkness. What carries over from Isaiah's imagery and what it intends to convey is that we can only see by the light of God's Word and Spirit when our souls are not always looking at and hankering after the ways of the world. We see only when we embrace absolutely the separation between God's people and the people of the world. Then we'll have nothing to do with their song and dance, either in our hearts, our heads, or our homes.

That's how our fathers felt. That's why they became staunch Puritans, that is, people who had the courage to break with the ungodly world that the Lord so accurately describes as people "who hatch lizards' eggs and weave spiders' webs."

Our spiritual fathers yearned not to be conformed to this world. That's why they thought differently, sang differently, lived differently, ate differently, clothed themselves differently, and raised their children differently. They didn't allow the world to dictate their standards, but they reverently bowed their heads to God's law. When the world called out: "Come along with me!" their ready, stalwart, and bold response was: "We can't!" And they didn't either, but held to their own path and thus reached their destination.

And that's also how we should proceed, brothers and sisters, guided by the same rule. We shouldn't introduce a Mennonite kind of avoidance, nor play the part of "Precisionists," nor expect repayment from God for satisfying him with the self-righteous work of chastising ourselves. All of this is deadening, under his curse, and yields nothing at all.

No, but remaining in this world, as often as the demands of this world's words come into conflict with the Word of God, we need to stand relentlessly and immovably on God's Word. We need to cling to it tenaciously. We simply need to proceed on the basis of that Word with deadly seriousness in opposition to all earthly powers, friends, kinsmen, and human talk and gossip.

We must never conceal that Word in the folds and creases of worldly clothing.

That's what often happens today. It does with respect to raising children. It does in socializing with relatives and neighbors. It does in choosing enjoyment and entertainment. It does in selecting clothing and a lifestyle. It does in the conversations that people have and in the literature they read. All of this makes the Lord angry. Then, in his anger, God allows all this worldly smoke to swirl around us and blind us so that we can't see our hands in front of our faces any longer. Then, although we want to make progress, we can't, and we simply fumble along.

This is when evil advances toward worldliness dressed in the garb of our flesh. From the flesh it creeps into our thoughts and reflections. And if one still believes in Christianity, better yet in God himself, and still values Christianity, Christianity becomes nothing more than embroidery on the threads of worldly fabric.

Naturally, the truth finally then just stumbles down the street. What's right no longer makes an impression. People get so far off course that even God's anger no longer has any impact on them. When in his zeal God directs his anger against our sins, we always think this applies to someone else.

YOUR INIQUITIES CAUSE DIVISION!

Behold, the hand of the Lord is not shortened. But your iniquities cause division between you and your God. And your sins have hidden his face from you, so that he no longer hears you. Isaiah 59:1–2[1]

This is what the Lord says, not to the people of Tyre and Sidon, not to those who offer sacrifices to Moloch or worship the sun, and not to the uncircumcised Philistines, but to the children of his own people. This is what he says to the ones he has chosen and carries on his wings, like an eagle does her young. This is what he says to those designated to receive an inheritance and be made rich by his saving work.

This people once had the truth. They had an understanding of truth like no others. So, when seen in the light of their profession, the lofty knowledge of the Greeks must be considered empty and the wisdom of the Egyptians idle chatter. In fact, it can be said with certainty concerning them and only them that the truth as they professed it has overcome the world. And it still constitutes the realm of power and thought that possesses all the resources needed to banish sin and falsehood.

---

1. While the reference in the original is only to Isaiah 59:1, Kuyper actually quotes select portions of verses 1–2.

Nevertheless, that people still lay terribly entangled in sin and iniquity. They refused to walk in the light. So the Lord disciplined them with a rod of iron and smote them in his anger. He did so not because they did not possess the truth, but because they did not do what they professed.

And that's when that people prayed and ran back to God like a rapidly flowing river: "O Lord, help us!" But the Lord did not help them. He smote them all the more severely. His anger burned even more intensely, so that you would think that that people would finally rend their hearts and fall down before the Holy One.

But no, people can live so appallingly far removed from what is on their lips that they become incensed and have the courage to complain against God rather than about themselves. They dared to talk about "the arm of the Lord that was is too short"! They thought they could find an explanation other than that of their own sins to the question of why, when they prayed, God wouldn't listen. Or you could put it this way: why, when they cooed like doves for salvation and deliverance, did God leave them lying in their misery? And in opposing that pervasive, shameful assault on God's sacred majesty, the Holy Spirit angrily responds to that unfaithful and wicked people: "No, the hand of the Lord is not shortened. But your iniquities cause a division between you and your God."

Doesn't this also apply to us today? Doesn't it also hit the people of God where it hurts in our day and age? Doesn't truth still dwell with them? Doesn't it often surprise you how, despite the fact that they slog and slave to follow the truth, they veer further from it? Aren't the well-educated class here in our country also tainted and tarnished, despite the fact that they seem to grasp truth so fully and completely? And shouldn't individual theologians return to Scripture in order to get their feet solidly beneath them again?

Doesn't it strike you that, when you once again take hold of what you profess, you are overwhelmed with the wonderful sensation of being able to breathe again? Don't you feel that you've gotten rid of that nauseous sense of empty-headedness? Don't you know once again where you're headed? What direction your life is taking and where your destination lies?

Don't the people of the Lord still bear the true light, however mocked and dismissed they might be by this world? And yet, yet, these people who still bear the truth, don't they wrestle and struggle without results? And doesn't Jehovah's contention with them just keep going on? And don't they pray and cry out to him then? Despite this, doesn't the Lord's opposition to you continue and never come to an end? Isn't it true that sometimes the oppression is interrupted, but then for just a moment when you are granted grace from on high?

Now I ask you, what else except our own unrighteousness could the reason for this be? What else could cause this than ignoring the truth in our hearts and lives? And what else could turn the saving arm of the Lord toward us than that we untie those knots of unrighteousness and once again make a broad highway for our God into our hearts, our heads, and our homes?

For far too long God's people have been spared and dealt with leniently.

Because in its unrighteousness the world wanted to mislead them, falsely alleging that their truth was not the real truth, God's people became withdrawn and inward. An attitude of resentment arose in their hearts. They forgot to exercise their brotherly service or to meet their mutual obligations of confronting Israel about her sins day and night and of calling Judah to repentance.

The mistaken position "that whoever does not live the truth does not possess the truth" has been unknowingly taken over by us in evil days. But since we now know that we possess the truth, we imagine that we also therefore live the truth. Oh, what a deceitful, thoroughly false, and terribly wicked conclusion! As though truth did not originate with God but came to us from some outside source! As though it were something conveyed to our souls by flesh and blood!

In truth, brothers, such false impressions corrupt us. They bring death to a people. They're the reason that warnings and discipline are unknown. They are also why repentance and conversion don't occur. They explain why essentials of Reformed identity are simply missing in those who profess the Reformed faith.

Reject that false notion. Prove that you don't hesitate for a moment to recognize that what this people profess is God's truth. That it is the only truth. That it is the truth by which you want to live and die. Then you'll see immediately how your heart will bond with the hearts of people like you. And if you then approach them and talk to them about their sins, pressing them intensely about them, they will listen. They will pay attention if you apply the Lord's discipline firmly, and if you implore them to break with their old selves until nothing of it is left in them. It will be like they have been backed against a steel wall by your appeals for their conversion of heart and life. It's then that we become a refuge for one another! Then those people will not turn their heads away from you, but they will kiss the hand with which you struck them!

Know this with certainty: they will be deeply moved because you offer them spiritual counsel. They will understand that they needed to hear strong words, even exceptionally strong words!

But you need to do one more thing. You must never challenge their sacred profession, because that doesn't come from them. It's truth that comes from God!

A JEWELED CROWN INSTEAD OF ASHES

The Spirit of the Lord of Lords is upon me for the Lord
has anointed me ... to give those who lament in Zion
a jeweled crown instead of ashes. Isaiah 61:1, 3

This is what's stirring once again from the clouds, in our churches, through our homes, and off our lips. It's the lovely name of Jesus and the cherished gospel sung to us by the angels: "Glory to God, and on earth peace among people with whom he is well pleased!"

This is a glorious shout and song. It is celebration by someone with whom the Spirit of the Lord is a continuing presence, by someone ordained and anointed by God. This person comes with glad tidings for the tenderhearted. He wants to bind up the brokenhearted. He brings those who are bound in chains the prophecy that for them the prison's doors swing open!

"Comfort, comfort my people!" the Holy Spirit had implored through the seer of old. And that Spirit had prophesied that this is what would come to pass: "O Jerusalem, you are the proclaimer of good news. Climb up a high mountain and let it be heard in every city and marketplace. Your Savior has arrived. To you a King is born. Let every oppressed and broken heart celebrate with sacred delight. For behold, he has come. Look, here is your God!"[1]

---

1. Here Kuyper is quoting rather freely and loosely Isaiah 40:1 and 9.

And that prophesy has been fulfilled. The Messiah, the King of Glory, the Savior of our souls, was born. He has been seen. He is worshiped as God in the flesh.

We remember once again the glory of Bethlehem. We remember the mystery of the enormous devotion shown there. We remember the coming of this Son in our flesh, as our brother, for the sake of our eternal happiness.[2]

But how, how, I ask you, should we think about all of this? For whom can these memories of Immanuel be real, genuinely spiritual, and intimately true? Just listen to this:

He brings a joyous message for those who are genuinely tenderhearted.

He comes to bind up those who are completely brokenhearted.

He comes to proclaim liberty for those who really do sit in prison.

He throws open the prison doors for those who are actually chained.

He comes with salvation for those in Zion who are oppressed.

He brings the oil of gladness to those humbled in their sorrow.

He will dress in garments of praise the one whose heart is filled with anxiety, even though this is not apparent and he doesn't want it known that it is.

If you want to put it more bluntly, more directly, or more powerfully yet, know that Immanuel comes to bestow a jeweled crown! But only on those who carry ashes on their heads as a sign of their sorrow and heavyheartedness. And who is it who carries ashes on their heads more than one whose heart is like a pile of ashes in their breast?

Ashes! That's all that's left of our appearances when they are thrown into the furnace: our reputation, our honors, our strength, our wisdom, our love and generosity, even our piety and spiritual fruit. That's all that's left when all this has been destroyed in that oven and nothing remains at all.

Ashes! That's what's left when strength has been drained and when even the little that remains has all but disappeared, and its glow and warmth have gone cold.

Ashes! What are they except the residue of everything that's been consumed, gone up in flames, and has no standing whatsoever before him who sees right through our souls?

Ashes! Totally burned out, stone cold, and dead!

Now that's how the souls have to be on whom Jesus will confer a spiritual crown. A bejeweled crown, with pearls and rubies ... but, in exchange for ashes! Conferred, therefore, not for what still remains unconsumed on the altar. Also

---

2. This was an advent meditation first published on December 22, 1878.

not in exchange for what is only half burned. Not even for what still flickers, smolders, and is still capable of throwing off a few sparks. But only for ashes and for what are nothing but ashes!

To profess to God that we are insignificant and worthless doesn't make a difference. To profess that we are dust doesn't do it either. But to cry out with Abraham, "I am only dust and ashes," and to reject ourselves completely, is what it takes.

Now a person should understand us very well, brothers and sisters. We are not saying without further elaboration that grace is not already at work. We are not saying that there cannot already be a covering over of our nakedness. But what the Holy Spirit is testifying to us through the prophet is just this: "A spiritual crown is given to someone in exchange for nothing else than ashes."

These saving gifts, these tender mercies, these heavenly treasures, and these precious jewels from the trove of God's divine gems he distributes only to those here on earth who have discarded all of their own jewels. He confers them on no others. He gives them only to those who are covered with ashes.

O church of our God, in this Christmas celebration would you like the glory of your Lord Jesus to be highly exalted? Then be humble and lowly. Consider yourselves of little account, not by the face you put on, but by what your soul tells you about yourself. Not from your lips, but from the depths of your heart.

Then be humbled in your own ashes, and you will be given a sacred, jeweled crown by him!

LIKE A FLOWER
OF THE FIELD

All flesh is grass and all the good things it does are like the
flowers of the field. The grass withers and the flower fades ...
but the Word of the Lord endures forever. Isaiah 40:6–8

Every year that passes is like a messenger of God traveling through the desert who asks, "What shall I announce?" He always gets the same soul-stirring and heart-rending answer: "Announce to the children of men not only that all flesh is like grass, but also that all the good things they have done are like the flowers of the field."

All flesh, including you! Just grass! But certainly not grass in the sense of grass in a Dutch pasture that is luscious and fresh and has large blades. Not grass that grows year round and stays green even when the sun singes it! Not grass that keeps growing even under the snow!

Goodness knows that among us you can use grass as an image of toughness and vitality.

No, by "grass" is meant grass in the Middle East, grass in waterless places, and grass at the edge of an arid desert. This is the sort of grass that is stunted and grows sparsely. It has little root or substance. It lacks juice and rigidity. And when it breaks ground, as soon as the sun gets hot and the south wind starts to blow, it quickly yellows, goes limp, and shrivels. It is ripped out of the ground, coated with sand and filth, and blown around in the air.

The Holy Spirit compares you with that kind of worthless grass. He compares your dearest child with it. Your beloved wife. Your cherished mother. He compares with worthless grass the entire circle of those dear and friendly people whose loyalty invigorates you, whose devotion sustains you when you suffer, and whose love adorns your home like precious jewels.

Look, don't say it! Don't say that in his Word the Lord doesn't have any heart or appreciation for the kind of loving, cordial, sustaining attention these people provide!

Listen! He doesn't only talk about grass. He also talks about a flower. A flower is something beautiful, elegant, and eye catching that is designed to unfold above that stunted grass. The Lord knows very well that this stunted grass is bedding for the fragrant flower of the field and that this field flower is both beautiful and appealing. But what you want to forget, the Holy Spirit does not! That beautiful flower of the field wilts. Like the grass, it withers. Its petals fall to the ground, and its splendor is gone. Nothing of it remains. It leaves nothing behind. It once existed, but it no longer does.

Now, that applies to all the mercies that humans enjoy and to everything that is kind, valued, and appealing about your life. Oh, there are certainly flowers strewn on your life's pathway, even beautiful ones. But, but … , and this is what's disturbing, if it were only about flowers of the field and nothing more than acts of goodness that we enjoy, then everything that is so appealing is merely snapped off at the stem when death occurs. It just fades and withers and disappears. It really existed. It really did, just as certainly as the flower did. It was just as real as the loyalty of your dog who will grieve on your grave. But just as certainly as that dog's loyalty soon disappears without a trace, things that are so appealing also sink into oblivion. Look, that said, this is how the Lord is talking here.

But that's not how the world talks. That's not how you usually do, either. "All flesh is grass!"—but you imagine that it's not your turn! The south wind will spare those close to you. Like grass, but the season for withering hasn't arrived for you yet. That's how young people talk. Even older folks still do.

How we still fool ourselves!

For what other reason does God's Word come to you than to say: "You are flesh. And your flesh, that is, your entire existence, is as brittle as withered grass"? This is what it asks of you personally—you yourself and not someone else—directly, emphatically. So pay attention to how you live. Put the house of your soul in order. Pay attention to how the breath of God's Holy Spirit sweeps over you and how you will wither and wilt and fall to the ground for eternity—either with or without God. The Holy Spirit takes this so incredibly seriously that he first totally exposes you, strips you of all your clothing, removes all jewelry, then makes you see yourself as you really are.

What do you have that would sustain you from that kind of withering?

Your physical strength? But that will fail you when the time comes. Your great reputation? But that will die along with you. Your money and material possessions? But they simply turn to ashes for your heirs. The honors heaped on you by others? But that's not enough, for they are too busy chasing their own honors to crown you with yours once you are dead. No, the only thing still left for you to suppose might still satisfy you and that you might be able to take along with you is your own goodness. By that I mean the winsome qualities of your heart, the praiseworthiness of your inner life, your integrity as a person. For isn't it true that about such things you would at least dare to think and hope: "These things will last. They are eternal. They will stay with me."

No, just listen now. Even these last reeds bend over. These final sources of any support fail you. For, exactly because you get it so completely wrong, Holy Scripture speaks to your heart with this soul-piercing insight: "O mortal man, never build on that; don't in any way build on your kind heart. For I, your God, tell you that even all your mercifulness is just as vain and perishing as you yourself are. Just as you perish like grass, the flowers of the field in your own life will wilt forever!"

And should you ask anxiously and in your restless soul whether absolutely everything will perish and nothing at all will remain, hear this. My good reader, listen to what the Holy Spirit answers so gloriously and comfortingly in the solemn hour of your departure: "Yes, there is definitely one thing that will last forever and will never disappear. It is the Word of your God, and therefore also all the good things that have been worked in you and in your life on earth by the power of that Word!"

PEACE ON EARTH!

Do not think that I have come to bring peace on earth. No, I tell you, but a sword. Matthew 10:34

How hollow and empty the interpretation of God's Word can be. That's true of what people make of the "peace on earth" in the angels' song at Christmastime.

How vague, shallow, and shockingly superficial all those allusions are to Afghanistan, Aceh, and whatever other corners of the world are then judged worthy of mention.[1] It's as though the expression "peace on earth" refers to nothing richer, more exalted and uplifting than putting an end to fighting and conflict!

Preachers, authors, and commentators who come down on such a shared interpretation really understand bitterly little of the real battle going on. This one is not fought at the expense of blood but of souls. It doesn't occur in one isolated spot but to the ends of the entire earth every day and at all hours. It happens wherever people live, and it is endlessly fought against the living God.

Isn't Satan stronger and more powerful than the mightiest emir? Aren't his attacks and battle plans incomparably more dangerous to the heart and core

---

1. In the mid-1870s, Dutch colonial forces fought a sustained, cruel war in an attempt to subdue the powerful, wealthy Muslim ruler of Aceh on the northern tip of Sumatra. One strategy and initiative after another failed and almost bankrupted the kingdom of the Netherlands. Kuyper's reference is to this heatedly debated involvement at the time he wrote this meditation.

of our human existence and to our way of life? Isn't the soul more important than the body?

Is peace with God for you, all our brothers and sisters, and all our fellow citizens something attained in just one day? Like conquering Aceh?

Aren't the horrors of the battlefield like child's play compared with the ones that those defeated by the Lord will experience in the depths of their destruction?

And don't you realize that already in the fearful conflict going on here and now the person who feels trapped can become so overwhelmed and puny that they would rather take their own life than resist any longer?

And yet, what is the suffocating pressure and terror experienced here compared to that which is coming in eternity? Or if you prefer, compared to the inhuman suffering that the Son of God knew when sweat rolled off his face "like great drops of blood"?

Oh, in wars and little skirmishes, soldiers devastate a small piece of ground for a year or so. But the conflict that God's Spirit wages against all that is unholy about us and against the Evil One at work within us is the source of all suffering! It is the source of all anguish. It is the cause of all regrets and every unnamed misery poured out daily to the ends of the earth on people bearing our flesh and blood. It is the very cause of the wars and skirmishes just mentioned. But above everything else, it is the source of all that is lodged in the hidden recesses of the heart, all that is eventually brought to light, and all that contends with anyone who cannot come to peace with God.

But people simply shut their eyes to that ocean of human misery. They only deal with the dribbles of unhappiness that betray the emptiness of their thinking. And those, my good people, are your struggles!

I would tell you to turn away from these blind battles. Turn to those loving angels that definitely did not wave palm branches of peace over the battlefields of our soldiers when they appeared above Ephrata's fields. They actually unfurled them above our spiritual battlegrounds. When they sang about "peace on earth," they definitely had in mind the unfathomably deep, immeasurable misery that already for sixty frightening centuries now has incurred anger and wrath because of our enmity with our holy God.

Peace, then, when we have fought the good fight to the end!

Peace, on the soil of our heart when faith receives the good seed that falls on it.

Peace, in him who is our peace, not as the world gives peace but as he does. That is what the angels celebrated about you. That is what God's children bear witness to out of their soul-felt experiences.

But what, I ask of you, does this sacred peace have to do with that more lowly hushing of enmity, damping down of the hearts' desires, or setting aside of human differences? Aren't these examples of yearning for peace in exactly the same way that the world does when people see in Bethlehem's crib a satyr at war with the unconverted masses? Or when one witnesses an outburst of differences between believers over a question of faith, and an individual is eager either to offer counsel in order to put the matter to rest or to find a reason for preferably keeping quiet on the subject?

I always thought that if that's the rule by which we're guided, then it would be better if the crib of Bethlehem had never happened. For, if there has ever been a cause for a great deal of warfare and bloodshed, and similarly, if there has ever been a source for a lot of bickering and division here on earth, it has definitely been the gospel about the Man of Sorrows who once lay in Bethlehem's crib as a little child. And what is even more telling is that the same Man of Sorrows expressed himself so clearly that he removes any misunderstanding!

He certainly knew that they would see also him as one of those false comforters who wants to bandage wounds with the words "peace, peace!" instead of actually healing them. That's why he warned his disciples so strongly when he addressed them by saying: "Don't misunderstand me! Don't regard me as someone I'm not. I have not come to bring peace on earth but a sword and to divide people into two groups!" Yes, definitely two groups, two that both confess him but without agreeing with each other in their hearts. They need to be needled by the Holy Spirit for as long as it takes for them to have the courage to put him and his name above some false, weak, and deceitful stranger.

And you ask me about the basis for such distortion?

What other reason for it is there than that people passionately think of themselves and their neighbors too highly, think far too superficially about sin, and fail to see it as the aggressive cancer that it is. For, in truth, whoever comes to see clearly by the light of God's Word what a jumble of mocking, ungodly forces are mixed together in humanity, the world, and one's own heart understands one thing all too well. They understand that people who are as white as the driven snow cannot fall into that kind of slimy morass and come out clean! Or, if you want it straight and without the imagery, they realize all too bitterly that Christ cannot descend into a world that is as contentious as ours is without engaging all the conflict already present there and without adding to it. He enters into conflict with that kind of world, that kind of human heart, and that kind of half-heartedness for the honor of his holy name.

REFINING SILVER

And he will sit refining and purifying silver. Malachi 3:3

Among all those bearing witness to Advent, Malachi is everyone's cherished prophet. How could it be otherwise? Just note his final words that appear immediately prior to Matthew's birth narratives: "The Lord for whom you are looking will come suddenly into his temple. He is the angel of the covenant whom you desire. Behold, he is coming, says the Lord of Hosts!"[1] And shouldn't people celebrate this joyfully in Christian circles and depict it even more vividly on the cards they circulate during the weeks of Advent? They want to show that these words are fulfilled in the coming of the Christ child to Bethlehem's crib.

But might you not forget the seriousness of the event in all this beautiful religious language?

Don't forget what follows this prophecy with such sobering force: the Messiah comes to sit in judgment! There it stands! It belongs with the preceding! "And he will sit refining and purifying silver."

Have you forgotten that this beautiful religious language about "coming suddenly" also applies to the cradle, and even more pointedly that that "refining the silver" is not limited to the judgment day? The process of refining the silver is already underway. It's happening now. And mustn't this also apply, therefore, to those said to belong to Jesus (it will eventually be recognized that

---

1. Kuyper is quoting Malachi 3:1 here. The meditation was first published just after Christmas, on January 12, 1879.

this is true!). For the silver refers to all the redeemed, and the gold to all the elect in the estimation of the Protector of Souls.

He does not see them as throwaway trinkets but as jewels. They are no longer *Lo-ammi*. They have become *Ruhamah*.[2] For what he achieved by this process, what he created through it, and the priceless things he fashioned are like precious metals in his eyes.

But if the silver still exists in the form of silver ore and not yet as pure silver, it still needs to be placed in a crucible and smelted in the flames. The silver must be separated from its impurities before the refined ore can glisten and shine to the glory of God.

I definitely know that the total and complete separation of refuse from the ore mixed in the clump of earth being refined only happens with the death of everything that is sinful. What is sinful has to be discarded, root and branch!

That will only happen at the exact hour in your soul, mine, and every other person's, when the intense level of heat is reached that is needed to separate all the refuse that clings to them. That's when the smelted silver in all its brilliance is poured into the mold shaped by God.

Is the labor involved in the refining that is already happening something to be taken lightly?

Could you be a child of God and be at peace with the impurities still clinging to you unless you knew that the work of refining and discarding the dross was going on continuously? Would you be able to have fellowship with the Lamb of God for as much as one instant if you didn't know that the wickedness still sticking to you was being skimmed off at the same time? Could you, unless you experienced that he was busy separating them from you and smelting them out of your life?

Is this even thinkable for a reflective person who has been converted but not yet unfettered, freed but not yet an indwelt child of the Lord, unless Jesus is present doing his purifying and refining work on their behalf?

Note well, not just carrying it on once in a while! Not just now and then! But regularly, continuously!

And if you don't understand this experientially, go to the refiners' furnaces here on earth where they are busy working with gold and silver. Observe them. Notice how the operators prepare the furnace. How they assure a fuel supply. How they light a fire. How they process the ore. How they make the fire hotter.

---

2. The two names are from Hosea 1:8–9. *Lo-Ammi* means "Not-Loved"; *Ruhamah*, a reversal of the name Gomer gave the first child (*Lo-Ruhamah*), means "My-People."

All of these steps are part of the same, entire process. One step cannot be separated from the others.

Now apply this to what Scripture is indicating here. Apply it to the continuous, unified, and unstoppable work that Jesus devotes to you.

He's refining you continuously, even when you don't know it's going on because you haven't seen the glow of the fire around you yet. Its heat still hasn't penetrated. He has just begun preparing the furnace, providing the fuel, and igniting it for the first time.

Although that may not be the way it goes with someone else, isn't that the way it does with you? You experienced so little chastising that at first it almost seemed as though you must be a bastard. And when there was no mention of fruit to peel, you thought that you could peel off the skin of your personal habits by yourself, like a snake sheds its skin. Then, feeling increasingly holy and celebrating that fact, you began to think: "I've arrived!"

Still later, when the hour struck that you stood before the face of God, all of that seemed to be an illusion, self-deception, and false hope. And when the Lord Jesus finally got through to you with his refining fire, you were overcome with the horrible feeling that you had always been and still definitely were that unappealing, old, unrefined ore. Then you also felt that the actual refining would get under way for the first time. You felt that from then on it would begin working. You felt it would give you a lot of pain, a piercing pain in the tenderest part of your heart and on the skin of your soul!

Pain, definitely! But your neighbor thinks, "My neighbor has really got it good!" Your children never suspect the depths of your suffering. Truly, there's no one on earth and only One in the heavens who feels oppressed by all the oppressiveness you feel. He's the only one who can console you.

When we finally get to that point, the pilgrim in us emerges, and all that is around us that once had so much appeal begins to fade and disappear. Then we either bow our head in shame or we possibly see something of the coming glory or the crown that awaits us.

Or if you'll allow me, let me say that the person who gets to that point then understands Calvary's cross and the Man of Sorrows for the first time. They understand that the cross does not need repeating but that the work of that cross has been completed.

THIS IS WHY I GAVE THEM MY SABBATHS

*For this reason I gave them my Sabbaths, that they
might be a sign between me and them so that they might
know that it is I who sanctifies them. Ezekiel 20:12*[1]

Three elements are present in Christian Sabbath observance.

On Sinai, God Almighty said: "Remember the Sabbath day to keep it holy, for in six days the Lord created heaven and earth, the sea and all that is in them, and he rested on the seventh day. Therefore the Lord blessed the Sabbath day and made it holy."

Notice the reference back to the work of creation. The life of a human being who is created in the image of God is a reflection of God's creating activity. This refers particularly to your natural, physical, and creative activity as a human being. It indicates that individual people, families, and nations have been appointed to be creative. They have also been assigned and created to rest for one day in the seven-day cycle. You could also say that this is a requirement for life here on earth and in human society. They are to conform to God's ways of doing things. This is a fixed rule for temporal matters that conforms to his governing providence. This is a stipulation that echoes the rhythm of God's

---

1. Either Kuyper or the typesetter erroneously gave the reference as Exodus 20:12.

own divine life. The day laborer rests from his work and toil, and the human spirit is revived by reflecting on the Lord his God.

But the matter is stated a little differently in the book of Deuteronomy. There Moses, as the mediator of the old covenant, folds the law originally given at Sinai back into the admonition he gives Israel in his departing speech. Guided by the intentional inspiration of the Holy Spirit, the reason he gives for the Sabbath when he comes to the fourth commandment jumps from the work of creation to the work of redemption. This is what he binds on Israel's heart: "Observe the Sabbath and keep it holy, for in doing so you will remember that you were slaves in Egypt and that the Lord your God led you from there with his strong hand and outstretched arm. This is why the Lord your God has commanded that you observe the Sabbath."

Here the Sabbath is exactly the same Sabbath as before; it is God's Sabbath. But here the reason for it is not based on or explained in terms of the creation of humanity, but in terms of the deliverance of God's people. This is a deeper meaning with higher significance. It lifts the Sabbath above the ordinary, natural order to the extraordinary and amazing spiritual order. There is also talk of rest here, but this is rest as a symbol of the soul's glorious rest when it was first set free and led out of Egypt, the house of bondage. Then it escaped from stooping in front of brick ovens and feeling whiplashes on the back.

The explanation is something else again when the Lord explains the Sabbath for the third time. This occurs in the book of the prophets. Here he looks back to the tabernacle, and in the words of Ezekiel he appeals to Israel and also to us: "For this reason I gave them my Sabbaths, that they might be a sign between me and them so that they might know that it is I who sanctifies them." Once again he takes a leap, just as he did from creation to redemption. This time it's from the work of redemption to the work of sanctification.

No more beautiful, inspiring, or pleasing idea can be repeated on this subject than the one that Ursinus expressed in the Heidelberg Catechism: "That all the days of my life I turn from my wicked ways, allow the Lord God to work in me by his Spirit, and thus begin the eternal Sabbath already in this life."

Accordingly, the Sabbath is based (1) on the work of God the Father and our creation, (2) on the work of God the Son and our salvation, and (3) on the work of God the Holy Spirit and our sanctification. Its fullness is captured in this threefold summary. For life here on earth, the shadow of the three-in-one, Trinitarian God falls across the Sabbath.

Consequently, it needs to offer you rest from the pressures of this world. That's first. In the name of God you need to be properly able to stop the workday activity of this world every seventh day. With all other creatures you need to set aside your regular expenditure of energy. You need to restore the strength you have lost. And you need to receive from God once again the resources you need for your daily work and efforts. With them you'll be able to face the six new days awaiting you at the end of the Sabbath.

Then it also needs to offer you rest from the attacks of the Devil. That's second. In the name of God you need to be equipped to escape bondage to the works of the Devil. That's when you enter the Year of Jubilee, your year of liberation by the atoning work of your Surety and Redeemer.

And also, it needs to offer you rest from the powerful urges of your own heart as well. That's in the third place. In the name of God you need to be equipped to give up bondage to your own evil heart. You need to abandon the empty way of living that serves no useful purpose. You need to pull back from drinking from springs that never provide pure water. You need to enter that blessed, completely glorious rest that consists of letting go of self so that God's work may be completed in you through his Holy Spirit.

This in the full sense of the word is the Sabbath of the Father, Son, and Holy Spirit.

This is what he who stood calling meant by Sabbath when he said: "Come to me, all you who are weary and heavily burdened, and I will give you rest."

Oh, may you never forget that it is not you who create this kind of Sabbath in order to glorify God, but it is a gift of God to you in his grace that you may share in his riches.

That kind of Sabbath comes only as the fruit of grace and prayer!

59
VOLUME I

CHANGING DIRECTION AT HIS COMMAND

They change direction according to his wise counsel
and accomplish on the face of the ground throughout
the whole earth whatever he commands. Job 37:12

This verse is a message from the clouds of heaven, not from the children of men. Nevertheless, it is a communication from the clouds of heaven that immediately reminded Job of people because it so clearly mirrors human life. It both has and must have direct application to each one of us personally, to our lives and our very persons!

How beautiful clouds are! They are, aren't they? How majestically they move across the firmament! One time they are bright with the sun's brilliance, strewn with gold, and etched with silver at the edges. The next time they are dark, threatening, and overwhelmed with blackness as they hang over you.

And have you ever seen how fast, almost beyond following with the naked eye, clouds can sometimes move when driven by a high wind? They push and shove, and even seem to be shoved aside themselves by the wind's breath. Where are they going so fast? What's their destination, these clouds that are now in flight directly over your head and at other times are being nudged aside?

Sometimes they're covered by other clouds. Over there one spins like a whirlwind and then moves backwards. Another time it lacks any sense of direction and just stands still. Doesn't it appear as though all this is devoid of any order and that everything is merely jumbled together in some sort of dance or game?

Yes, that's how the clouds twist and move, says Elihu on the pages of Scripture: "That's how they change direction at his command" from one corner of the sky to the other. They flutter like the shadows cast by the moonlight on the surface of the earth. They dance like the waves and billows that also turn and change direction on the ocean's surface.

And doesn't that turning and changing of direction capture with frightening accuracy what you call "my life"? Isn't there constant unsteadiness in your own personal life? It is never the same. It's always in motion, aflutter, twisting, and changing direction. It's just like what Elihu describes for you about God's clouds.

You want to make progress and advance, but what have you gained? Aren't you just like the clouds played with by the wind? Yanked in this direction, then in that? Turned around? In flight? And tomorrow don't you find yourself in the same spot where you started the day before yesterday?

Are you capable of keeping an eye on your own life? Are you able to see where your life is actually headed? What you really want out of life? Where that constant change of direction will eventually land you? Why have you made hardly any progress in the steps taken in one direction? Why can you suddenly be driven sideways, then go around in circles and even move backwards? Why is your life consistently like that of the clouds, lifeless, or at least a life without purpose and direction? Why does it seem like you are continually "changing directions"? Why does it remind you of living in a maze rather than with steady, determined purpose? With respect both to what you love and cling to and to what you discard or lose, you are driven without any control or purpose. You are moved in turn by the rustling of cool evening breezes, the driving force of some storm's winds, or the deathly frightening rage of a hurricane.

What about all this?

Does it actually amount to any more than being slung this way and that way without purpose? Doesn't it make you retreat into yourself one time and to be confidently expansive the next? To shine brilliantly now, but then to be overwhelmed in darkness, just as the clouds of heaven are?

Is God only playing with you in your changes of direction, just as he enjoys playing with the clouds in his spacious heavens?

Playing? What picture do you get here? How do you think of yourself other than like this? What do you imagine? That the turbulence among the clouds could only be a game? That all that turmoil and pressure in the light of the moon is just accidental and that it has no plan or purpose? That there is no order in all that turning, no plan for all those changes in direction, no guidance involved for what is driven and swerving?

Well, then listen to what the Holy Spirit says through the mouth of Elihu. If you think those clouds of the heavens are simply involved in their own whimsical game, know that their changing direction never happens except "by his wise determination."

"You don't know," declares the seer, "how God has determined their order or how he makes the lightening flash in the clouds" (v. 15). Even so, there is order involved. Every gathering of the clouds, he declares, is in "balanced position" (v. 16) and is in fact stable, however much the clouds swerve and turn. In all their churning they only "do what he has determined" (v. 12) for them to do in the heavens above and over the earth's surface. This is how the prophet is stirring you and all other creatures to praise the wonders of the One who "knows all things."

Consider, then, the clouds in how they are driven. They don't know from where they have come so speedily; and they don't have any sense of where they are going. Nevertheless, the Spirit tells you that even the contours of your best-laid plans never swerve very far from their divine determination. He who sits on the throne steers the changing directions of the clouds in their innumerable host.

So why should you be concerned about the restless changes of direction in your life, O you of little faith? Isn't your life of more value than the clouds? Isn't your soul more precious than they in their entire host, O you who have been called by him? And if God directs in their changing direction the clouds of heaven, that are here today and tomorrow are poured out in the rain, won't he guide the changes in your life? Won't he be much more involved in leading you, O you who have been delivered by the blood of his Son?

In all of the driven activity, the pressure, and the fast pace of your life as it affects your soul and spirit, isn't there woven also into it an orderly course, a set plan, a secret counsel, and a divine knowledge? Isn't everything that seems to move here and there without purpose in your life like the pumping up and down of a piston in the cylinder of a steam engine? It changes direction, but all the up and down motion produces the power that yields forward motion. Likewise all the movement in your life has a predetermined order.

And if your clouds sometimes simply hang heavy and motionless rather than moving you forward, what do you need? Or if at other times they seem to pile up, smother and depress you, and if almost no ray of God's consoling face seems to penetrate your soul, what do you need, my sister and brother? Even when we no longer have God's light to comfort us for so much as one moment, his counsel abides as the unshakeable foundation for peace in our hearts.

May this be our watchword: "While directions may change, they do so by his wise command."

I WILL PAY THEM BACK IN THEIR BOSOM

Behold, it was written in my presence. I will not keep quiet, but I
will pay them back. I will pay them back in their bosom. Isaiah 65:6

Obedience is the noblest characteristic in which the beauty of human nature comes to expression after God has restored it. If people obey and submit to God's authority once again, their humanity is elevated. That's the case if they do it gladly, not grudgingly, if they do it not because they're overpowered and forced to do so but from an inner motivation. That's when they show that they want to obey and that they are capable of obeying again, my sisters and brothers.

That's when God will give you a medal and pin it to your chest. That's when something beautiful happens in your soul.

Dominating, commanding, asserting, and making a show of strength—that's not where things are! All of this is still an expression of the flesh. Those are all old ways of trying to get what you can't accomplish. It's an attempt to hold on to a crown that you had stolen and robbed from God, and that you'll have to remove in his presence.

But you need to bow down until you buckle over, you tiny, meek, and lowly creature. You need to follow the Lamb wherever he goes. With whatever he gives you. In however he wants you to serve. Then you need to willingly acknowledge, making continual progress in doing so, that whatever is noble or outstanding or holy about you is nothing unusual or special, but it is simple obedience. This is what raises the value of the new wine pressed from a bunch of grapes and why men don't throw it out, noting "This is pretty good stuff!"

Obedience is definitely not just doing what you are told to do. It is to cooperate with those in whose service you stand. It is to do so completely and wholeheartedly.

A warrior obeys on the battlefield from a sense of honor and not only from a desire to do precisely what he has been ordered to do. It's not just about promptly accomplishing his assignment, but it's about devoting all his energy to what his captain wants to achieve and accomplishing it as his only mission. In erecting the walls of a building, construction workers obey not by simply following the blueprints, but they play their part in creating what the architect had in mind by poring over those prints and making sense of how their work harmonizes with his plans. In the same way, you don't obey merely by keeping God's commandments one by one, but basically by developing an appreciation for what the Lord is doing and becoming deeply involved in that work yourself.

The Lord himself said as much in Isaiah 65, where he pits his faithful servants against those who work against him. The Holy Spirit says that those who work against the Lord are people "who have chosen things in which the Lord has no delight" (v. 12). Over against them are the faithful servants to whom the Lord appeals: "My people, rejoice forever in what I am creating" (v. 18).[1]

"As the eye of a maid is on the hand of her mistress, so my eye looks to you, O Lord!" And serving always involves thinking about nothing else and wanting to do nothing else than this one thing: pleasing him whom we serve, working hand in hand with him, and if possible appearing in his presence even before he calls for us. It is to have such desire, joy, and satisfaction in the walls of the Jerusalem that he is building that we yearn to participate in that work. We long to obey him in this because we know how pleasing it is to him. We develop the spiritual instinct to follow God's plan. Grasping the style in which God is building, each one of us does their part in achieving the higher level of obedience

---

1. The original meditation and its republication give the reference erroneously as verse 15.

that doesn't exist under the covenant of works but is the crowing jewel of the covenant of grace.

Actually, our obedience needs to be like that which only the Son of God could achieve. He said: "Behold, I have come to do your will." In saying this, he meant: "I'm the only one who can do this, who can obey you like this. After I had understood in the depths of my soul that 'I love the Lord and his house,' you held my complete attention and prepared my body to do your work." Christ is the only One who truly obeys. He is the only One who has ever reached the level of honor and glory of such heart-stirring obedience. He lived it. He dedicated himself to it. It penetrated the depths of his being. He also perfected and accomplished it!

Our only boast is to share in that indescribably beautiful and glorious obedience of Jesus. It is a work of art! Our only glory is to be covered by it completely. To have it work in and through us until it transforms us and renews us in his image!

Then we will be wondrously blessed.

Then we will be embraced. Then we will no longer live aimlessly. Then we will know where we are headed. Then all of our effort will be worthwhile and all of our pathways level. Then we will discover how wonderfully glorious it is to live into and to live out that plan that is eternally well pleasing to God. Then we will find the peace that comes through nothing but obedience to our God.

Sadly, this is not the case with most people. What causes this other than that they contend against God? They "kick against the pricks." They flagrantly want to oppose God. They always work against and never according to God's purposes. Why take more time trying to describe why? The answer is simply captured in what verse 12 says so sharply and pointedly: "Because they have chosen that in which the Lord has no delight, and they have no delight in what the Lord chooses"!

But this doesn't only apply to worldly people. It also applies to many good and honest people, even to many Christians. Among them, you even find many who are sterling examples of self-denial and loving service.

Examples of loving service, but that still doesn't matter!

Examples of a solid confession, but peace still escapes them!

Examples of precise and attentive living, but even that still doesn't melt their hearts!

Naturally, because you can be the epitome of loving service itself and still insist on having it your own way. You can be as dedicated as Phinehas and then realize that people give you no recognition. You can be the embodiment of conscientiousness but still be serving your own purposes.

Thus without obedience! Without working along with the Lord, but still always working against God's purposes! So how could you possibly find peace?

Isn't this when the Lord says: "In their bosom, yes in their bosom I will pay them back"?

If the invisible God causes you who are disobedient to become unsettled in your bosom, deep inside yourself, in your bowels, in the depths of your soul, how could you possibly be at peace in your heart? If he afflicts you, and in his righteousness lets you become a source of murmuring and resentment, how could you possibly ever know the joy of such sacred peace?

HE HIMSELF DOES NOT KNOW HOW

*He is like a man who sows seed on the ground, goes to sleep
at night, and gets up in the morning. The seed sprouts
and grows, but he does not know how. Mark 4:26–27*

It's usually the case that people pay far too much attention to what they do themselves and far too little attention to what God does. We're talking about him who is the Creator of spiritual life, or you could say more precisely, about the Holy Spirit.

Jesus tells this parable about the field in order to reprimand us about this. He wants us to see how foolish it is to think this way and to make us stop doing it. He wants us to reflect on the fact that it is the same way with spiritual soil as with soil in a field.

Everyone knows that a farmer contributes nothing to the actual growing process. He can neither hasten it nor slow it down. What he can and should do is prepare the ground, see that he acquires good seed, cover it well with soil, and weed it when needed or keep the weeds under control some other way. Beyond this all he has to do is keep an eye on things and bide his time until the ripened grain begins to sway in the breeze of its own accord. But the effort of growing and the forces behind that are not his doing. That's the work of another. He can't make the seed. He must accept that as it comes. Someone else, not he, has hidden the germ of life in the grain concealed beneath the husk and chaff.

He is even less capable of making the kernel germinate. If he starts interfering with that process, he will only ruin things and assure that it never does. No, the germinating is also caused by another. And that someone does this work mysteriously, in secret. No one notices it or is able to trace it. Through the forces in the ground, by the warmth of the sun's rays, with the effect of the falling rain, the seed sprouts. First it swells. Then it sends out a shoot. That becomes a blade. It produces a bud that in turn becomes the ripened grain. And the farmer definitely sees all of this happening! That's because this part of the process is all visible. But he is totally incapable of contributing anything here as well. Apart from having the understanding that something is happening, "he himself does not know how!"

And that's exactly how a person has to deal with what's happening on spiritual terrain, says our Savior.

He has to prepare the ground, either by turning it over or plowing it. Yes, he has to do that properly. Then he has to have a very sharp eye in choosing the seed he sows on that ground; it must not be bad seed. Good seed and bad seed often resemble each other very closely, but making a seemingly small mistake in selecting the seed grain could cost him the entire harvest. More than this he cannot do. And as far as spiritual work is concerned, he's as helpless as a small child standing in front of a locked door. The growing, flourishing, ripening, and producing of fruit is not his doing. Someone else has to do this; he cannot. Just as his inventive powers, best efforts, concentration, and spirituality are in no position to create so much as one kernel of seed, so he can contribute no more to the actual sowing than to scatter diligently that which has been entrusted to him. He has to do this as instructed and on the field pointed out to him. As to what happens to that kernel of seed beyond this, he is unable to add anything at all. That happens by itself, that is to say, that occurs by a mysterious hand and a secret power. It humbles and shames him to realize that the germinating, growing, and ripening in fact do happen, but that "he himself does not know how!"

If he is unwilling to accept this fact and resists simply waiting quietly, if he becomes restless and impatient in wanting to see some progress, and if he keeps turning the ground over, the only result he'll get is that he'll just snap off the newly emerging little shoots. He'll impede the maturing process, if not destroy the sprout completely!

People see parents doing that kind of thing with their children. They see teachers doing it with their students. Worse yet, they see pastors doing it with their congregations. Such people never give the seed time to germinate, sprout, or flourish. They're always too intense. They always think that they have to get the results. Oh, they don't put their faith in their own efforts, for they're all too aware of what that accomplishes! But they don't see God at work in people's hearts, God's hidden work. And that kind of spirituality really amounts to unbelief! It arouses the Holy Spirit's zeal against them and only hinders their own spiritual growth.

Look here! Properly understood, they can hardly add anything to the beginning or growth of this life. Everything really comes from the Lord. He makes the living seed available to them. Beneath the heart's surface, the Holy Spirit peels back that seed, unwraps it, and makes it grow. He nurtures it with the Son of Righteousness, moistens it with the dew of his love, and sends the gentle spiritual rains that cause it to swell and flourish. But people angrily turn this entire process upside down. They suppose that they are actually contributing everything and that the Lord God is doing very little on which you can really rely! They become unsettled, pressured, and erratic enough to always be disturbing that poor kernel. They're disrupting the process. They want to take control of it.

Isn't that the complete opposite of giving God the glory? Doesn't it militate against the nature and spirit of his work? Isn't it highly irreverent?

Nothing! Nothing! I can't say it strongly enough! A person can bring nothing to this endeavor other than that they prepare the ground in quiet obedience, pay attention to the quality of the seed, and beyond that do the required weeding. All the rest needs to come from above. And it does. The Lord God is at work in all of it. He never slumbers or closes his eyes. His power is always at work in the hidden depths of one's inner being in order to realize his purposes and bring about the praise of his name.

So, you who fear the Lord in all righteousness, give him the glory due his name.

Curtail your estimation of your own contributions; cut them down to their actual, trivial size. Peek behind the curtain of external appearance; look at the miraculous, comprehensive, and majestic work of the Holy Spirit in your heart. Consider the work of the Son of Righteousness in your heart. It is grace that causes the beginning, germinating, and ripening of that work in you. It is to his glory.

That's when you'll find peace—peace, because now you'll be honoring God!

That's when you'll be better able to let go of what has been entrusted to you than you've been able to do up until now. That's when you'll be able to focus much more on what only God can do. That's when you'll immediately put far less of a premium on your own work, realizing that when you turned the ground over, you only pushed the spade in halfway. You'll realize that you sowed bad seed in your child's heart and did a far from perfect job at weeding. You'll find peace when you're converted, perfected, and gripped by God's power in this way.

Furthermore, you'll also discover that you've been delivered from your fears. It will no longer be the case that when you sow today, you'll moan and groan tomorrow because you don't see a stem or blade. Calm and content, you'll know that the Holy Spirit is busy at work. You'll know that because he is, things will flourish in an orderly way: "first the bud, then the flower, and then the full head of grain."

That's because God's doing the work. He's the real worker! The blessed, saving work of God belongs to him alone—in its beginning, its progress, and its completion. This is what you first failed to see in your unfaithfulness, but what you now confess to your comfort.

62

VOLUME I

THE PERSON
WHO TREMBLES
AT MY WORD

*This is the one I regard, the person who is poor and contrite
of spirit and who trembles at my Word. Isaiah 66:2*

I need to tremble at God's Word. The Lord himself says so because it is the
Holy Spirit who testifies through Isaiah: "This is the one I regard, the person
who trembles at my Word." It's beyond dispute that the expression "This is the
one I regard" means nothing less than "This is the one to whom I will show
my grace." The result is that the Lord is in effect saying that he will withhold
and withdraw his grace from any individual who doesn't exhibit "trembling at
his Word." According to this, any individual who longs for salvation, searches
for the secret to being saved, and wants to live in the eternal courts of the
tabernacle knows that "trembling at the Word of our God" has to be found in
them as well.

So what does it actually mean "to tremble at God's Word"?

Naturally, it doesn't consist of the extraordinary experience the prophet had
when the Lord revealed his burden to his soul and sounded it in his ear. That
can't be, because the text says: "This is the one I regard, the person who is poor

and contrite of spirit and who trembles at my Word." This obviously applies to all God's children and not only to one who holds a special office.

Also, it does not mean to say that we need to be filled with fright or fear upon hearing God's Word and thus flee from his presence. For the first words that always cross the lips of angels are "Don't be afraid!" The Word of God comes expressly to bless and comfort.

Even less does it convey that we always need to hear judgment echoed in God's Word, for the heart and core of God's Word is the gospel. That didn't begin only when Bethlehem's manger held Mary's child. It began already in Paradise.

No, that you should "tremble at God's Word" means something entirely different.

It means first of all that you mustn't approach that Word with your most profound observations and reflections. It means that you should in all humility show God the honor that every father expects from his child. It also means that you should think of the God who addresses you in this Word as the only gyroscope of all wisdom, knowledge, and science. Accordingly, he is the source of all progress and deepening insight in life. His eye sweeps across the ages. He fathoms the depths of all things and their causes. His thoughts are higher than your imaginings by as much as the heavens are higher than the earth. For that reason and on that basis, bowing in awe before that Word, you should immediately submit your own humble spirit in obedience to the divine Spirit in his majesty. You should quietly, thoughtfully listen to what God is saying to you.

But "trembling at God's Word" means even more.

When we tremble at some sound or voice that reaches us, we react strongly when the sound only reverberates off our eardrum. But we get weak-kneed if that sound goes through us like an electric shock. Then the eardrum sends a message through our nervous system that ripples through our whole body. Our whole being is visibly shaken, and we are driven to our knees. Well then, that's like the effect the Word of God should have on us. It shouldn't merely bounce off our eardrum or glide smoothly through our soul's networks. But it should directly, immediately, intensely, and totally penetrate our whole being. It should grip us in our entirety as spiritual beings. Its message should touch every spot in our soul. It should make us quiver in our total being. Not externally like the Quakers' experience, as though our lips and hands should tremble. But internally, so that our hearts quiver in our chests. It should also mean that our spirits tremble "because the Word of God is living and active and sharper than any double-edged sword that cuts to the cleaving of soul and spirit, joints and marrow, and is the judge of all thoughts."

But even this does not yet exhaust the meaning of trembling before God's Word.

That's because a lofty and inexpressible Majesty is involved here. God's Word is so powerful that it always expresses might. It always creates something and accomplishes something.

It's like the wind playing with a shriveled leaf. The wind doesn't say to the leaf, "Pick yourself up and go lie down over there," as though the leaf calmly listens to this command and immediately picks itself up by its own strength and floats over to the spot where directed. No, the wind itself picks up the leaf and relentlessly pushes it ahead, farther and farther, until it deposits it on the other spot.

That's exactly how God's Word has to work with us.

Just as the leaf trembles at the wind's breath, our souls should tremble at the breath coming from the Spirit's mouth.

So it's not the case that we just listen calmly to the Word and then decide whether we will do what it says. At some time that suits us better! By our own strength! By our own wisdom! And at our personal convenience!

No, but this is how it happens. When the Word of God impacts our soul, our entire soul is immediately set in motion. It is caught up by the Word itself and is brought, not by its own strength, to the place where it has to be.

If this is what's happening with us, we are living in the "fear of the Lord."

That's when we are "poor" in the sense of being driven like that leaf and are "contrite in spirit" like a leaf that is shriveled. Then we tremble and quake and are pressed forward farther and farther as soon as the Lord's breath leaves his mouth. And that's when we also experience this glorious comfort: "This is the one I regard, the person who is poor and contrite of spirit and who trembles at my Word." Then it's not we who accomplish what needs to happen, but the Word. And the glory of that Word is that in it God himself is with us and receives all honor.

MY FOOD IS TO COMPLETE HIS WORK

He said to them, "I have food to eat that you do not know about." Then the disciples said, "Has someone else brought him food?" And Jesus responded, "My food is to do the will of my Father who sent me and to complete his work." John 4:32–34

The nature of spiritual life often stands in stark contrast with physical life. The flesh strives against the spirit the minute a person's spirit is inspired by God.

Flesh and spirit do not see eye to eye. Very often they make competing demands. They don't work in harmony, but they oppose each other.

If the spirit wants to go right, the flesh takes a left. When the spirit wants to move forward, the flesh goes in reverse. As soon as the spirit flourishes, the body complains. The body reaches for what's below, and the spirit stretches for what's above. Now, this sharp opposition needs to continue as long as it does because our spirits have not yet been liberated, crowned, and delivered. This will only come when the physical is put off, carried to the grave, and through some chemical process disintegrates.

Look! This is what Jesus is indicating when he uses the expression "to eat food" in a context explaining how spirit and flesh are poised against each other. Understand it this way: by working the body develops its need for food, while by working the spirit diminishes its need for food. After it has worked hard, the body becomes exhausted. But precisely by doing its work, the spirit overcomes its exhaustion. Or one might say that the flesh never experiences less hunger than when it has done no work for several days, but hunger arises in the soul precisely after days of drought and inactivity. The body never experiences more intense hunger than after expending enormous energy, while the spirit is never more wonderfully satisfied than when it has expended great effort in all that it does. In short and put most pointedly, the body eats in order to work, but the spirit works in order to be fed. As Jesus says, "My food is ... my work."

The entire discussion with the Samaritan woman turns on the contrasting needs between spiritual and physical life. We would quickly add that it can only be understood from that perspective. That's why John 4 first presents the contrast between physical and spiritual drinking and then between physical and spiritual eating.

The person who drinks physically, says Jesus, always has to come back for more in order to be satisfied. They need to draw water again. Following more strenuous exertion, a person experiences more intense thirst and swallows even bigger amounts.

By contrast, the person who drinks spiritually comes but once. They don't need to draw again, for they receive. The water of eternal life flows and splashes in their soul. And the more fully their soul is aroused, the more wonderful they feel as they drink deeply and as that water flows fully.

Then, after Jesus had communicated this beautiful thought to the Samaritan woman with the image of drinking, he repeated the same idea with the image of eating food. It's the same wonderful, basic thought applied to the same contrast between flesh and spirit.

But the disciples continued to be preoccupied exclusively with physical food. They were concerned only with the fact that Jesus might be hungry. They worried that their trip and now his discussion with the woman had exhausted him. But instead of finding him completely exhausted, they find him completely reenergized. And they have no other explanation for his condition than that "someone else must have brought him food."

All along they keep telling him: "Rabbi, because you have worked so hard, you have to eat!" (v. 31).

And what does Jesus do?

He immediately changes the subject to spiritual life and says: "Eat because and after I have worked? My dear disciples, you still don't get the point. To work for me is my food. Working is precisely the means by which I am satisfied. My food is that I am able to do so. This is what fed me and renewed my strength so that I can now complete my work!"

All of this is to say that for a believing child of God there may be a desire and passion for working and striving merely to get ahead, as though that can ever satisfy their soul. For think about it. Jesus had not pressed to make good time on his trip. Rather, he took the time quietly and calmly to have a serious discussion with a person that he had met on his journey. Does it really need to be added, then, that the work about which Jesus is speaking is not something extraordinary but that it's very ordinary work? It's what occupies us every day. Faith always has to permeate and enliven what we do. Jesus added so beautifully that by itself doing work is not what satisfies, but it's only doing God's will that does. By itself work irritates and wearies us. That's when the only thing it can do is make us hungry. But if our work amounts to being occupied with what God has assigned us, then our work satisfies us.

It comes down to activity that is not arbitrary or selfish or unfinished, but to totally setting aside self-will and personal preference in addressing and completing the work that God assigns. This holds for everyone in their own calling and in their own home. It holds for everyone in their own heart and in the hidden recesses of their own conscience. It holds for whatever they have been charged to accomplish for that day.

This approach tolerates no deadness, no dryness, and no diversion! These only produce weakness and deterioration. But working at cultivating something more in our work is what is satisfying. Doing so as long as and with as much determination as is required to produce results is fulfilling. This is what quenches thirst and removes hunger. That's because whoever works this way keeps busy moment by moment only with what has been received from the hand of God. That person never makes things up but listens carefully and responds to what God says. That person never concocts something on their own but thoroughly enjoys what they see that God has already provided. They live with the provision that he has made. That person does not operate under their own power, but they employ as much strength as is necessary from what God provides. In the end, they find that they have baskets full of leftovers. With that person it's about always praying about everything. It's about imploring God and then waiting patiently. It's about then being thankful for what is received. That's when praying and giving thanks amount to always hungering, but at the same time being so completely satisfied that experiencing hunger is thoroughly enjoyable.

And now what about that portion given you for your life's work? What about the strengthening graces you need for that? What about receiving them in overflowing abundance? Is there anyone else in whom these are guaranteed to you other than Jesus Christ?

Isn't the endless and measureless reservoir of living water needed by every thirsty soul found in his divine heart? Similarly, isn't the basket of bread capable of feeding all hungry people, if we may put it that way, also found in his merciful heart?

Well then, what Jesus says about his own food in John 4 is exactly the same idea that he expressed in Capernaum, as recorded in John 6: "I am the Bread of Life. The person who comes to me will never be hungry and the person who believes in me will never be thirsty!"

Do you believe that?

ONE SOWS AND ANOTHER REAPS

But the saying is true: "One sows, and another reaps." John 4:37

What's our way of doing things? Oh, we sow and think that before we came nothing had been done to the field. We also think that after we have sowed, we have to wait a long time before something is produced that can be cut with the scythe.

We think that our mowing always has to be the mowing of our own sowing!

In imagining that everything happens by our hand and that no one else is at work except us, we are always mistaken. We are wrong in thinking that everything comes down to what we do and is to be credited to our account. We err in supposing that every field continues to lie fallow until we drive the plow's blade through it and unless we scatter the seed on it by our own hand.

It's just like Jesus said about his disciples. They thought this way. And we do too.

Jesus put it like this: "You say, 'we have just finished the sowing, and now we have to wait another four months before the harvest comes.'" Their sowing! Their mowing! Doing it all themselves!

So obviously, when things don't move along on schedule, we become impatient. Then we talk about our disappointment. Then we say our work was in vain. We talk about working in vain with our children, working in vain in the Lord's vineyard, and working in vain as a people and nation. It's vanity all around us!

Naturally enough, sowing isn't that enjoyable. It amounts to throwing something away and burying it in the cold ground, where it sinks out of sight. The person who sows leaves with plenty but returns home empty-handed. It's like the poet who versified the Psalms put it so aptly:

> The one who carries the seed he sows
> goes out weeping and sows it all.

No, what gives pleasure is not the sowing but the reaping:

> For without dreading a catastrophe, before long
> he will return a happy man,
> rejoicing in that fortunate hour
> carrying home the sheaves he stores.[1]

The one who mows always goes out empty-handed, but he comes back with his arms full! The one who sows becomes poorer. But the one who mows becomes wealthier with every swish of the scythe.

The glory and enjoyment lies in the stroke of the sickle and not in the fruitfulness of the bare ground. For sowing is entrusted to the earth, therefore to dying and burying. But mowing has to do with resurrection and living. Its focus is the wealth of the harvest.

Aware of this, the One who comforts our souls calls us first of all to be involved in mowing, not sowing. In his tender love, he has assigned us the lot of rejoicing with the mower, not that of weeping with the sower who goes out to scatter.

Pay close attention to this. Jesus says: "You imagine that you still have to wait for many months before the harvest is yours, but this is due to your pride and spiritual blindness. They are caused because you trust in nothing but your own effort, your own sowing. You are preoccupied with nothing other than the bleak, dark earth. But I tell you now, get rid of that pride. Lift up your eyes and consider the fields, for they are already white unto harvest."

Where is your sickle, O you of little faith? How you hold back, mumbling and complaining to yourself! Oh, you definitely also have to sow, but you first have

---

1. This hymn is obviously based on Psalm 126: 5-6. Untranslated in rhymed form, it reads:
Wie 't zaad draagt dat hij zaaien zal,
Gaat weenend voort en zaait het al!
Want hij zal, zonder ramp te schromen,
Eerlang met blijdschap wederkomen,
En met gejuich te goeder uur
Zijn schoven dragen in de schuur!

to mow! You have to mow before anything else. You have to mow and gather into full sheaves all that I have worked for when I plowed and sowed and moistened and watered and caused to ripen. I did this all before you or anyone else realized what was happening. I did it in my mysterious and wondrous grace.

"O that you would simply mow. For mowing is so glorious," says the Lord! "Even now he who mows receives his wages and gathers a crop unto eternal life, so that the sower and reaper may rejoice together" (v. 36).

Your spiritual mistake is concealed above all in the fact that you always think that you can't mow unless you have first done the sowing yourself. But I tell you: "One sows, and another mows" (v. 37). And "I have sent you out not first of all to sow, but to reap what you have not sown and to gather in the fruit of their efforts" (v. 38).

What a beautiful, glorious way of putting it by my Savior!

My own effort is not self-standing and isolated, therefore. It is connected with the efforts of others.

It is related to all the effort expended during those long centuries that lie behind me. It is connected to what was achieved by grace during those times and prepared for our times. It is also connected with all the effort that those alongside and around me expend in the broader and wider fields that constitute the lush pastures of the Good Shepherd.

Yes, and it is connected above all with what is being accomplished so amazingly by my Savior in the background of all of life generally—quietly, mysteriously, and by the soft and cool rustling of his work everywhere. He is busy in every human heart. He is achieving something every day and in every soul. He is aware of everything. He knows everyone by name and appeals to them "on the basis of his great power and because he is able to do great things."

And look! Now I'm connected to the complete body of that divine work that has been accomplished through the centuries by all the efforts of God's children. I'm connected not for the purpose of contributing anything major but something modest to it. The main reason why the Lord sends us out is not that we might contribute so much to that work, but that our souls might be inspired and our hearts quickened by the glorious sight of his miraculous work. It is the sight of fields white with a bountiful harvest!

But by our pride we would like to destroy all of that and turn things completely around!

We would like to see it as a bad thing that the sowing was not our doing. Our darkened eyes would like to see the whitened fields as bleak, bare ground.

Our self-serving natures have too little of the childlike abandon that would let us play happily in those fields with our sickles.

How ungrateful we still are!

Oh, how miserable we would be if God only put us to work on human hearts where nothing had been done as yet! In human hearts that kick up nothing but the dust of sin and anger and are raw and untamed!

But in his mercy God doesn't do that. He protects so much of the harvest in the lives of our children and congregations. He sometimes even causes it to ripen by his saving grace, when in our evil hearts we would rather complain than rejoice and weep rather than celebrate.

Then we feel like martyrs.

Then we complain about our having become complainers.

Then we plow on rocks.

Then people become discouraged and simply give up.

Then, when we've spoiled everything in our self-serving pride, we think that we've been misunderstood and haven't been appreciated!

Shame on our souls!

But know this! This is exactly how you blow out the candlesticks that have to blaze with the light of Jesus' glory.

What then should weigh heavily on your heart is that this is how you corrupt your child instead of nurturing and building them up properly. This is how you destroy a congregation instead of strengthening and building it. This is how you poison the atmosphere rather than purifying it. Then your face falls. Your eyes become downcast. Everything looks black in your soul and in the depths of your being.

Oh, then lift your eyes again, you elders and pastors and members of Christ's flock. Look at the fields. Look how white they are. It is time for the harvest!

ALL JUDGMENT GIVEN TO THE SON

The Father judges no one, but he has given all judgment
to the Son. ... He has given him the authority to judge
because he is the Son of Man. John 5:22, 27

The honor of God depends on the fact that all creatures, saved or condemned, will eternally acknowledge and must acknowledge that "God is righteous."

In the scene revealed to us in the book of Revelation, the Patmos apostle hears what seems like the roar of a great, heavenly host shouting: "Hallelujah! Salvation, and glory, and honor, and power belong to the Lord our God! For his judgments are true and righteous." And just as the saved extol God's righteousness in that scene when they see judgment being exercised on the ungodly, the people who fear the Lord celebrate throughout all of Scripture the fact that "God is righteous." Sometimes they do it even more loudly and forcefully when God's chastisements humble them and when they are pressed down, body and soul, in God's winepress.

"Rivers of tears flow from my eyes," laments the psalmist. "But you, O Lord, are righteous and each of your judgments is right."[1] When Jerusalem lay in ruins and "Zion stretched out her hands but there was no one to comfort her,"

---

1. Here Kuyper quotes Psalm 119:136–37, bridging two distinct sections of the psalm in so doing.

the people still acknowledged God's honor and exclaimed: "The Lord is righteous, for I have stubbornly resisted the words of his mouth."[2] And when Jerusalem had been rebuilt and the breaches in her walls had been healed, sin broke out yet again. This was once more followed by judgment. Then the aged Ezra threw himself on the ground and, weeping bitterly, testified in the presence of God and all creation: "O Lord, the God of Israel, you are righteous and we lie here before your face in our guilt."[3]

But even this is inadequate. The complete, strict, not-to-be-shortchanged requirement of God's sacred honor will only be satisfied when the most ungodly among all the ungodly recognize and confess in the depths of their damnation what Paul expressed: "Their damnation is righteous."[4] This cannot and must not be otherwise.

Even the suspicion of his unrighteousness would make this inextinguishable fire an insult to God's majesty. Morally speaking, God must be the victor with every one of his creatures, whether that is in restoring them forever or in bringing them down everlastingly.

This is exactly the reason why judgment must not remain with the Father but is transferred to the Son. It is also why in his judging the Son must secure God's righteousness by becoming one with us and by conducting judgment not as the Son of the Father but as the Son of Man. "Who is it that condemns?" Paul asks. His answer goes like this: "Christ is the One who has died for us!" And Jesus himself clearly explains that for this reason the Father "has given all judgment to the Son because he is the Son of Man."

There are two reasons for this.

First, a mere creature must never be able to say that they were blinded, shattered, and totally devastated by God's exalted character, his indescribable majesty, or his boundless power. That we ultimately lack every excuse for doing so is essential. But the lack of any objection must always be grounded in the conviction that the sinner is guilty. It may never be based on the excuse that they lacked the courage to speak so much as one word against such an exalted God. Not being able to understand this is what makes Job's objection to Eliphaz unintelligible to so many. That Job in his desperation also spoke against God sprang from a love for God's honor. Wanting to spare God from such talk,

---

2. He splices together Lamentations 1:17a and 18a here.

3. See Ezra 9:15.

4. Romans 3:8. While modern English translations such as the NIV and NASB soften this verse, Kuyper and the *Statenvertaling* do not.

however, is nothing more than laughable arrogance in the human heart. This doesn't exalt God's honor but diminishes it.

A creature must dare to say any and everything against his judge, as long as it is based on justice. This must be done respectfully, to be sure, but it may be done nonetheless. They mustn't hold back anything, so that after the judgment has been rendered they can never say: "If I had only spoken out on this or that, my sentence would have been quickly dismissed."

So this is why God has provided us with the kind of judge who himself was "the most despised among men." He was one to whom the most despised among the children of men can tell everything and one to whom they dare to say anything. He is a friend of publicans and sinners. He is one who washes feet. He is one among you. He serves you.

But there is more! In the second place, it needs to be emphasized in the most powerful way possible that the condemned person must never be able to say: "My judge was biased!"

All sin is always a violation of God's exalted, sovereign majesty. It is an affront to God in person and an offense to the Father himself. So if the Father would be the one sitting in judgment, he would be the judge in his own case. He would be judge and plaintiff at the same time. Then the sinner attempting to justify himself could get the impression that his judge was biased. That's how they would see it. That's another reason, therefore, why the Father turned over the judging to another, to one who stood between him and the creature and who was evenhanded toward both. This other took on our humanity and was related to us flesh and blood. He became our brother and a human being in the full sense of the word.

Thus, if a person wants to protest the judgment of his Judge by complaining to the Father: "That judge was also your Son!" the Father can respond to his creature by saying: "But he was also your brother!"

THE FIRSTFRUIT OF HIS HARVEST

Israel was holy to the Lord, the firstfruit of his harvest. Jeremiah 2:3

If there can ever be talk of God longing for something, desiring something, or hungering for something, there can certainly be talk of him wanting the love of his elect creature.

Naturally, our holy God is totally blessed in his own being without having the enjoyment of that love. He is, because he is God. He is all-sufficient unto himself. He is also self-sufficient in his own love.

This reality is concealed in the mystery of the Holy Trinity. The mutual exchange of love finds its fulfillment within the Divine Being itself. By it he loves without end, and he is loved with unending love. Along with the Holy Spirit, this everlasting and personal love is both in God and is God.

But with the decree to create, this changes.

Now it is simply God's will and intention to no longer restrict his love to himself, but to extend it to his creature. This same decision of God also entails that the elect creature shall love their God in return and that they also have a need to be loved in return. The yearning to be loved in return is just as inseparable from the Divine Being as is the immutable decree that the response of loving in return can only be powerfully activated in the creature by the Holy Spirit.

The Scripture beautifully calls this responding love "a harvest that the Lord receives from us." To capture it literally in the words of Jeremiah: "his harvest."

This is a harvest that consists of the firstfruits, the full harvest, and the gleanings afterwards. This is the harvest that will be completely carried into God's holy temple when the entire host of the redeemed will love God eternally before his throne, just as they are loved! It will be with an unfailing, fervent love!

This is the reason why the Lord our God is so jubilant and displays such perfect joy over "the firstfruits of his harvest." That's also why he complains so bitterly when this first love is rejected.

That jubilation was heard alongside the Sea of Crystal above. It arose from the millions upon millions of Israel's redeemed who stood around the throne of their Savior, who sheltered them there. Their eyes were radiant with happiness and glistening with gratitude as they were caught up in tender love in that firmament above. That's when the Lord drank in their responding love. That's when he received a gathering of the firstfruits of his harvest.

But the full harvest itself, sad to report, still had not been gathered in.

> Oh, his people will not
>> Listen to his voice
> Israel has forsaken God
>> And his covenant.
> It has sought another,
>> Led by its own pleasure.[1]

The tone of thanksgiving died, and the love cooled. A once-holy people grieved the Holy Spirit yet again. They brought sorrow to the Lord. With guilty hands they tossed aside the crown of his glory in their in sin and idleness.

But that's precisely when that "firstfruits of the harvest" began with the God of unfathomable mercy. Then God approached Israel through his prophet, not to remind them of his love for Israel but to make them aware of their own love with which they once loved him. "Go and proclaim in Jerusalem's hearing" is how it begins when Jeremiah says: "Thus says the Lord, 'I remember the devotion of your youth, your love when we were betrothed, when you followed me in the wilderness and in a land not sown with seed.'" Then Israel was holy to the Lord, the firstfruit of his harvest. And with all the sadness of

---

1. The rhymed Dutch original of this hymn reads:
   Och, zijn volk wou niet
   Naar zijn stemme hooren,
   Israël verliet
   God en zijn geboon;
   't Heeft zich andre goôn
   Naar zijn lust verkoren.

a wounded lover, the Lord now asks them whether he had shortchanged them. Had he stopped talking to them? Was there something wrong with the love he, their God, had shown them? "Listen to the Word of the Lord," God continues in his speech, "you families in the house of Israel. What unrighteousness did your fathers find in me, that they strayed so far from me and pursued idolatry, becoming even emptier than the idolatry they pursued?"

What gave him the greatest grief in all the heartache that the Lord felt was that the children of Israel didn't even miss him now that he their God had to leave them. He missed their love bitterly. But his people no longer felt any sense of loss over losing his love. They raised no complaint. They didn't say: "Where is the Lord? Where is the Lord who carried us out of Egypt? Who led us into the desert, into a wilderness of traps and snares, into a parched land, into the shadow of death, into a land through which no one passed and in which no one lived?"

Oh, this lament cut deep, deep into his soul, deep into his Fatherly heart. But if there is still anything strong enough to make the shriveled love in the hearts of God's people set a bud again, wouldn't it be that weeping divine love?

Or is it different now? Better today than in was then? Better for God with your heart or mine?

Maybe this still applies: "I have this against you, that you have forsaken your first love." Whoever of us reads this cannot do so without blushing deeply with shame. They think back with bitter self-incrimination on the indescribable blessedness of their first love. They also recall the shameful forgetfulness of God's boundless mercy, into which they repeatedly sank.

But because God's Word is still sharper than any double-edged sword, this short quotation about "the firstfruits of his harvest" makes a sacred impact on us, my good reader. It is bound on our hearts. It might even wake us up and stir our souls to respond. For they can find no other peace than in penitence and self-critique: "O my soul, I will stand up and return to my dear Father and say to him, 'Father, I have sinned against your love and made your heart sad!' "

BECAUSE YOU ATE SOME OF THIS BREAD

You seek me not because you have seen signs, but
because you ate some of this bread. John 6:26

The miracle of the loaves is directly connected to the sentence that was pronounced on humanity in Paradise.

It is definitely not only a display of Jesus' power, nor even exclusively a revelation of his love. But in a narrower and very special way it is the first step in lifting the heavy burden of work from people's shoulders. This burden was imposed because of human sin.

In order to understand both Jesus' words and his works, one must always keep Paradise in mind. Leaving Paradise, he carried the seed of glory in his heart. The Messiah's ultimate purpose was to restore that Paradise in an even more beautiful form than it once had in Eden. And when he bestowed grace on the murderer on the cross, this didn't only prophesy the man's salvation. It also predicted his own pleasure when he cried out: "Today you will be with me in Paradise." In effect he was saying: "I'll be with you there as well." He wasn't thinking here about Paradise from the perspective of God, to whom all glory is given eternally. But he was talking about it from a human perspective and as the

Son of Man, as one daring to think about his own glory. For outside Paradise, a person is not truly human. Paradise belongs to being human. It involves a person's second body. It is the context in which their life flourishes unencumbered. Only in Paradise, in the absence of a cross or crown of thorns, will a person be able to worship for the first time without falsehood in their heart.

As things presently stand here on earth and outside Paradise, what are needed for deep, wholehearted worship are the pressure of the cross and the burden of work. We are incapable in this world of the kind of continuous spiritual engagement that is directed to God and is nourished by him. This is the reason why external labor has been imposed on us here. It is a punishment— obviously! But it is punishment in the same sense that all God's chastisements bear, namely, as a simultaneous protection against evil. For to be able to eat bread earned by the sweat of our brows is one of the greatest means God has provided for offering resistance to Satan and our own flesh. And where labor becomes slack and diminishes with those who are not converted, we find little else than loss of self-esteem and sense of purpose. Even when they do keep busy and their hearts are in what they do, they are proud and inflated with what is empty and ordinary. Sadly, even with God's born-again children this kind of weak spiritual activity persists. It's only the direct, inner work of the Holy Spirit that produces brief moments of sacred, heavenly spiritual engagement in their hearts.

But even this does not diminish the fact that the work of our hands is always at the same time a symbol of our shame. Whether in Paradise or before God's throne, working with the hands will be unworthy of human beings. Like the birds of the air that neither sow nor reap nor gather into barns, it should really be improper for human beings as the rulers of creation to be preoccupied with material struggles and labor. They shouldn't be overwhelmed and constantly thinking about what they need to survive.

This is how it was in Paradise, where every tree offered the man and woman its fruit and where the pangs of hunger and thirst were unknown. It was the same way in the desert, where manna simply fell from heaven without the children of Israel having to plow the sands or stomp a spade into the rocky ground. And this is how it will be in an even more glorious sense above, when we will eat of the Tree of Life and drink from silver streams. Then we will eat even more wonderful manna and drink undiluted wine at the lavish meal that the Lord will prepare for all peoples after he has wiped the sweat off their brows.

Recognize from this what was lost in Paradise, what was demonstrated once again in the desert, and what we so expectantly long for in the glory to come. Jesus gives us a sign, a sample, and an assurance of these things. He does so first at the wedding in Cana and later in his miracle of feeding the crowds.

When the thousands upon thousands received bread without working for it and were satisfied, the peace and glory of Paradise reappeared for a moment. It glistened there on the shores of the Sea of Galilee without sweat so much as beading on their foreheads. It was as if Jesus wanted to provide solid proof by multiplying that bread for which the people hadn't worked, that his talk about the coming glory was not so many empty words. He handed the people solid evidence of it. He carried in his own person living confirmation of that glory. He wanted to show that he was the mighty hero who possessed the power to distribute that glory to whomever he wished.

If people only ate for the sake of eating and did not taste the coming glory in that miraculous bread, they would have completely misunderstood his miracle. They would have missed seeing it as a sign of his messianic power displayed so that we might obtain that glory. This explains the strong scolding that Jesus gave the excited crowd the next morning once they had cooled down: "You look for me not because you have seen a sign of something greater in me, but only because you ate some bread and nothing more."

And if some individual gets more out of it than that, Jesus blesses that person!

For we are repeatedly overwhelmed by an abundance of joy, a lavish sense of well-being, and rich blessing. When we are highly favored, it is not simply due to the fact that we exist. It is not based on something in our being. But it is simply God's freely given favor flowing our way. This can be a source of blessing to us when it is a sign of something we see in our Savior. When it is proof of the riches we have in him. When it is a foretaste of what will come in eternity. When it makes us give thanks. When it exalts our hearts. But if we are guilty of the sin committed by the people of Capernaum and simply enjoy bread for the sake of enjoying it, and if our hearts simply get used to that kind of enjoyment as though we had a right to it, then we eat the manna to our judgment and are cursed in drinking from the cup.

That's when our souls get confused. Then we are merely self-satisfied. Then we receive the little gifts, to be sure, but we completely miss contact with the generous Giver.

DISTRESSED!

In all of their distress, he was distressed, and the angel
standing in his presence saved them. Isaiah 63:9

To be in distress is not being able to see the light. It's to gasp for breath. It's
when everything seems to be in turmoil and closing in on a person. It's
when they just can't go on. It's when they feel beads of anxious sweat on their
forehead because nothing changes.

But worse than feeling tightening in the chest and throat is the oppressiveness felt in a person's soul. Then their spirit is choked, their heart is squeezed,
and their soul cramps up. They feel walled off from everything and feel like
there's no way out. They're on lockdown, and the "grim tormentor" walks all
over them (Isa 51:23).[1] They are tied up in knots, imprisoned, and dying a thousand deaths. All the waves of the Almighty are crashing over them.

Oh, we can suddenly become that inexpressibly distressed at heart! This
can be a distress against which we feel completely powerless. Then it seems
like we've been thrown into the deepest possible pit where lions snap at us
from every side, where no light is shining, and where we don't have as much
as a drop of water to cool the tip of our tongue.

When a person is still young, they don't believe such things happen. They
maintain that feelings like that are only imaginary or fanatic. So they aren't
drawn to the Word that offers comfort in such distress and speaks to oppressed

---

1. The Dutch text erroneously gives the reference as Isaiah 51:73.

hearts. In fact, you can even find gray-haired men and women in menopause who mock such complaints about the soul's distress. Sometimes this short-sightedness goes so far, in fact, that even sincere Christians regard these experiences of heartfelt depression as no more than sour, dark exaggeration. They attribute them to a person's temperament. To an overly serious disposition. To a much too bleak outlook on things.

That kind of ridicule and smirking only continues until someone appears from nowhere. When he talks, he's deadly serious, and there's the look of terror in his eyes. He's a frightened soul that dares to tell such folks: "You know what? I'm a man who's known that kind of distress!"

This happens often in any number of circles.

You won't read about it in the papers, but it happens nevertheless. God makes a note on it in his book up above. The angels pay attention to it. And "the Savior of those in distress" (Jer 14:8) looks down on what's going on with the look of mercy written all over his reassuring face.

Whether the world wants to admit it or not and whether superficial Christians want to believe it or not, the cry of those in distress touches the hearts of others. It has an incredible impact on those who hear it. Exactly the kind of distress experienced by someone "who has fallen into such a pit" is more powerful than anything else in cutting through the superficial complacency of indifferent hearts.

Anguish is enormously disturbing in the effect it has on us!

There's weeping in an anguished soul like that of a woman in labor. But that's precisely why something is born out of that terror. It produces strength. Fear bears fruit.

To be distressed in the soul is to be involved in the work of the kingdom of heaven. It is to be in pain for a higher life. It is to die a thousand deaths in a single moment so that out of such death new life might sprout and grow. This is all true unless—and this is the most terrible thing imaginable—unless such anxiety is born in hell and leads back to hell because it arises from your own evil nature and pressures you to take an even more ungodly stand against your God.

But that is simply the exception. So pay close attention only to the distress that the Lord God uses to oppress us until we acknowledge that there is in fact an entirely divine involvement in it. For then God's hand squeezing your soul is just like you squeezing a leather pouch until it is completely empty and all the air has been pressed out of it. Then, as soon as you stop squeezing, the wine is automatically sucked back in until the pouch is filled. So all that unbearable distress is nothing else than God squeezing all the impure, ungodly air that you had sucked in from here below entirely out of your soul's lungs. His intent is, once you have been emptied, to create the pressure that sucks into you the fresh, blessed air of heaven. He wants you to drink it in deeply.

Your soul is truly like your lungs! They are designed to inhale air, and it is designed to inhale and suck or drink in life from God!

As long as the space in your soul is filled with other gases and air that are not from God, the life of God can't enter. For that to happen the Lord God first has to squeeze you and press you flat until all that is not holy is forced out, and room is made in you for the breath of God. This is what really belongs in the lungs of your soul.

Whether your distresses come from outside or inside pressures makes no difference. They might pounce on you at your place of business or in your home. They might be due to your children. They might come with respect to your best-laid plans or be tied to what you produce. They might emerge even in your musing and reflecting. On the other hand, they might creep into your soul from within due to a blood disorder and make themselves at home in your body. There they could attack through pain and disease. They could be directly spiritual distresses based on a sense of God's justice and your own sense of damnation and impotence. What is still more distressing is that they might arise from attacks by the Evil One. But all of these differences are only matters of degree. Being in distress is being distressed! Closely examined, all feelings of being overwhelmed are terrible. They are God clamping down on the souls of his children. To whatever degree they occur, they are his means of putting your old self to death in order that your Savior might rise to life within you.

And that's exactly where things stand!

A woman in labor would simply give up if she didn't know that "all of this misery is about having my baby!" Similarly, your struggling soul would simply give up and die if it didn't know that all the distress was about getting new breath!

But now that it knows this, it celebrates. And what does it know? The distressed soul knows that shortly it will put on "the garment of praise." It knows that the hour of darkness will pass and that it will enter "a spacious place" once again. It knows that, being tightly squeezed for the moment, it will then be glorified. "O Lord! You alone are to be praised, praised because your ways are just. It is pleasant to give you praise!" Now the soul rejoices with Habakkuk:

"I will wait patiently in the day of my distress."[2] It prays with Jonah from the belly of the sea monster: "When my soul is overwhelmed within me, I will still call upon the Lord!"

But this gracious and merciful God does even more. He is that kind of compassionate and empathetic God. He will never put you into some deep pit unless he will descend into it with you and sustain you there. He will never bolt you behind some door but that you will feel his everlasting arms of mercy beneath you and holding you up. He does this in a way that calmly says to you in his holiness: "Through all of your distress, I am your God and I am in distress along with you." So tell me, my good reader, can God in his boundless mercy do any more for us? Then isn't our complaining in our anxiety nothing short of a scandalous lack of love?

We once again find ourselves in the season of Lent.[3]

Are you living close to the cross?

Are you living into what Jesus suffered in his tortured soul? Are you living on that even deeper level?

When he was hard-pressed in the winepress and alone, and when there was no one there with him to sustain him?

When he was in distress to the point of death itself?

When he was so afraid that sweat dripped from his forehead like drops of blood?

Oh, that you would thank your Savior for all this when fear overwhelms you. Oh, that you would stay close to Jesus, be less frightened, and find peace in his presence.

What is most gratifying for a mother is when she sees that her child is less frightened because they see that she is with them. And do you think that Jesus would do less for you than a mother does for her child?

So never forget Jesus when you feel overwhelmed. And think about Jesus when you see one of your brothers or sisters in distress. Because, once again, to be distressed is horrible. But to comfort others in their distress is a blessed thing to do. It is almost godlike! It is also the suffering of your Lord bearing fruit in your own soul.

---

2. Kuyper is quoting the first half of Habakkuk 3:16. The second half reads: "to be visited on the nation that invades us." Kuyper must have assumed that his readers would understand the entire context of the passage.

3. This meditation was first published on March 30, 1879.

WASH AWAY THE OLD YEAST

Wash away the old yeast so that you may become
a new batch of dough without yeast, since you
are in fact unleavened. 1 Corinthians 5:7

The feast of unleavened bread belongs to the Passover.

This is not an incidental point that we quickly read over. But it's an important matter that was described in great detail for Israel on two occasions. In fact, it was detailed as a sort of illustrated prophecy because Jesus' apostle applies the Passover to the Son of God and his church: "For our Passover has been sacrificed for us. So wash away the old yeast and let us celebrate the feast with the unleavened bread of sincerity and truth."

What's the meaning of being a lump of dough that's in fact "unleavened"?

Yeast agitates the dough; it lifts it higher; it makes it rise. Thus, it makes it appear to be more than it really is. Yeast is still essential for bread in our day and age. The Bible itself calls unleavened bread "the bread of misery" (Deut 16:3). The absence of yeast is what makes for unleavened bread. Its presence in the dough gives bread its lightness and makes it easier on our digestive system.

Bread is the basic part of the diet that sustains human life, and for that reason it is the symbol of human life itself.

But our human life is actually a "life of misery." Simply left to itself, it is a pathetic, dreary existence in your own heart and all around you.

This explains the persistent interest in what's stimulating. We're always looking for something that can lift us above the ordinariness of everyday life. We want to rise above it. People create all sorts of ways to make life more livable for human beings. (I hardly dare put it that way!) This is true especially in our larger cities. There stimulation depends on creating excitement, exerting ourselves, and stirring each other up excessively. What's still worse is that all spiritual life is preoccupied with everything except what has to do with salvation! Yet it makes every effort of displaying the sheen and beauty of genuine virtue and loveliness. But this pretext of piety is nothing more than a leavened, puffed-up way of living! That is to say, it's a way of living that's unnatural and is the result of adding the ingredients of ambition and pride to the human heart. It's a consequence of adding more than the recipe calls for, of agitating spiritual stimulants, and of increasing the pressure and turning up the heat!

If people didn't include any such yeast in the mix, human life among us would be like it is among the Kaffirs and Zulus: very flat, disheartening, and tasteless!

There are two routes open to avoiding that frightening and bad prospect. The first is God's way. The other is man's way.

Concerning the latter, man's way, people will simply tell you that the lump of dough is what it is and left to itself it won't change. God created the dough that way. To get something more satisfying out of it, the only thing to do is for you to add something to it. They let it rise and turn into a beautiful, airy loaf of bread.

But when it comes to God's way, people say: "No, don't look for salvation from leavened bread. Leavened bread is only beautiful in appearance. You only have to wait ten days or so and the freshness is gone, mold appears, and it loses all its good aroma and taste."

So what you need to do, my good woman, is not to mix some ingredient in the old dough that makes it rise. What you need is different soil, a soil that produces a different grain that yields different flour and produces better dough. You need dough that rises by itself, that works by itself, that produces its unique aroma and flavor. This produces bread that never crumbles or becomes moldy but is always fresh and smells fine, even when it travels with you to the other side of the grave.

For Israel to learn all this, it first had to get rid of all its yeast. Then it had to eat the unleavened bread of its suffering for many a long day. Finally, it had to accept the manna that needed no yeast but that descended from heaven fully prepared.

And God also directed that his people, including every one of his children among them, had to begin to wash away every bit of their yeast with all of its stimulus, excitement, excessive agitation, and sense of amounting to something. Then by God's design, emptied, deflated, and humbled, they would have to eat the bread of their own misery for a very long time. After that, he would bring the Bread of Life to their lips. This is bread from heaven that needs no added, unholy, or artificial ingredient.

Now do you understand what the apostle means when he says: "Our Passover has been sacrificed for us, so wash away the old yeast and celebrate the feast with the unleavened bread of sincerity and truth"?

Do you understand this? Will you act accordingly?

For the Lord our God will not allow his holy Christian faith to be abused by a kind of yeast that is really good for nothing but continues to work and ferment in the dough when it only gives the appearance of being good. God regards Christ as too sacred for anything like that! No, in you that dough needs to be better dough that rises on its own, without outside agitation, and produces bread that can truly feed you.

That's how it has to be in your life. Every morning and evening your soul has to have a healthy slice of the Bread of Life, properly prepared and without any deceptive ingredients. What you pick up with your hands and what crosses your lips has to be prepared and made with complete integrity and absolute truth. It has to be bread like it's supposed to be!

But this can't happen with and for you as long as your soul only wants to go halfway. Not if one time you have a piece of Christ's bread of life, baked with healthy wheat, and the next time you take a slice of leavened bread baked according to your own recipe.

It's all about him as the Bread of Life. Nothing else!

The soul that it's intended to nourish can never tolerate as much as a single grain of such yeast mixed in with what it eats. Only such bread can feed you. Otherwise all of its nourishing power will be of no benefit to you.

For the Bread of Life to nourish your soul, the last bit of bad yeast has to be washed out of it.

70

VOLUME I

THOSE WHO CANNOT KEEP THEIR SOULS ALIVE

*All those that bow to the dust will kneel in his presence, even
those who cannot keep their souls alive. Psalm 22:29*[1]

Who clings tightly to the resurrected Lord? The One who rose again and had the ability to walk out of his grave? The One who snatched his life from the jaws of death? Who is there that runs to him for help? Who is the person who never lets go of him again, come what may?[2]

Who do you find at springs of water? It's always those who are thirsty. Who attacks their food heartily? It's those who are hungry. Who looks for shade? Those who are overwhelmed by the heat. And who, I ask you to tell me, are those who should run to Jesus, who rose from the dead, and cling to him? Who should never let go of this Jesus who endured all that he did? The people that the psalmist describes in Psalm 22 are definitely good candidates! They are the ones "who can't keep their souls alive"!

---

1. The original gives the reference as Psalm 22:3, when in fact the text is Psalm 22:30 in the Dutch and 22:29 in English versions.

2. Knowing that this meditation was published during Holy Week, on April 13, 1879, helps to understand it.

Believe me when I tell you that those who have first tried everything else and tried it everywhere else are the ones who make his most devoted disciples when they finally come to Jesus!

Being alive is what we're concerned about!

People stake everything on living and on maintaining life. They measure everything in those terms. Everything that draws breath struggles and works hard to keep on living. All our struggles and exertion are aimed at living fuller and richer lives. Heart and head are determined to do just that. And by living, we struggle all the time with what it means to be really living.

When life doesn't go like it should and death in some form intrudes on it, we become disheartened. We become discouraged and tense. Finally, no matter how long we may have struggled and pushed the issue, we get to the point of throwing ourselves to the ground and lying in the dust. This whole process represents what's deeply tragic about life robbed of delightful satisfaction.

This explains why we fight dying.

Fools who think that life consists of what's physical do this very superficially by acquiring material things. But those who are wise understand that the soul is the essence and core of human existence. They profess: "I need to concentrate on my soul. The soul needs to sustain my life." So they naturally focus on the spiritual vitamins and medicines that strengthen the soul.

Oh, the ability, the wonderful ability to change a stone-cold soul depends on finding a way of first bringing it to life and then of sustaining it in that life. It's finding a way to do this without rupturing its connection with our bodily existence more than just temporarily.

Then it's all about a footrace.

One person expects to find it in an exceptionally pious, unnatural, and fastidious spirituality. Another does in being honest, virtuous, and conscientious, while a third person determinedly torments their self with charitable giving, thinking this will work some kind of magic for them. But however much any of them frets and struggles in their attempt to act with integrity, it's all useless in bringing them one step closer to what they're chasing. All three eventually get to that point. The man who is superpious does! The one who is totally honest does! And so does the woman who torments herself! For matters don't turn on a good crease in your clothing, or on a good reputation with others, or on resolute self-control. They turn on living and on the life of the soul! It depends on the kind of living that can deal with anything and that never gives up. But sadly, all those spiritual vitamins don't get you a hair's breadth closer to it. For you are simply too weak to achieve what you want and desire, namely, the one thing that determines everything else. You are totally incapable "of keeping your own soul alive."

You have to get to the point of recognizing that fact. You have to express this in words that are not merely mumbled. They have to be completely frank and come from deep in your soul. Your heart has to be in them! In the presence of God and others you have to say:

"No!" "O my God, no!" "O my brother, no!" "I can't keep my soul alive!"

"I wanted to do it. I tried to do it. I worked at it so hard that my soul sweated!"

"I would have done it by myself. I should have done it by myself. I would have finally succeeded if I had just yearned for it passionately enough, wanted it badly enough, and persisted at it long enough."

" 'My God,' I said in my soul, 'surely in your mercy you will not disregard my intense struggling. Surely you will bless it in the end.' "

"But no. The Lord didn't respond like I hoped he would. He, the Holy One, did just the opposite. He demolished all my efforts. His billows overwhelmed me. His strong winds sucked my lungs empty."

"For now I know that he loved me more dearly than I loved myself. That's why he saw to it that all these efforts came to a dead end. That's why all the paths I took were cut off. They all ended in failure, frustration, and disappointment. In the end, all my vain pride died. My willful determination disappeared to my shame. And the result was that I finally admitted what I had not been willing to acknowledge to the entire world: 'I can't do it! I can't keep my soul alive. I'm powerless, despite what I do or attempt to do. Everything that I attempted only succeeded in deadening my soul further. It sapped my strength. It virtually killed me!' "

And if such a person finally exclaims: "To keep my soul alive—that I simply cannot do," they are already celebrating a true Passover. I tell you that if such a person hears once again about a Jesus who arose, a Jesus who was resurrected from the dead, a Jesus who brought his life through all that he experienced and who thereby demonstrated that he could "keep his own soul alive," I tell you plainly, my good reader, that you certainly don't need to tell such a person anymore: "Just go to Jesus!"

"Just go to Jesus?" That person is there already! They already cling to Jesus. His life is their life!

You know, that's precisely the mystery of true faith. In order to see with your own eyes during your Passover celebration that Jesus lives, you first have to see with your own eyes that in yourself you are dead! Oh, life doesn't lie in the excitement and festivity of a celebration.

The Ruler of Life doesn't appear to any other people than to those who lie in the dust and in the shadow of death!

WE HAVE BEEN RAISED WITH HIM

And he has raised us with him and seated us in
heaven with Christ Jesus. Ephesians 2:6

What a miracle this is! You and I, my brother and sister, "have been raised with Christ"!

What is this mystery? What will it be? That we are buried with him in his death, are raised with him, and are seated with him in heaven? It's that we have become one vine with him, equalized with him in his death and therefore also in his resurrection.

The text does not say: "He will raise you with him," but that he already has raised you with him.

It doesn't say: "He first raised Christ and afterwards, at another point in time, he raised you as well." But it says Christ and you were raised at the same time and in the same moment. Your resurrection is tied and bound to the single act of Christ's resurrection.

There is no talk here of your resurrection after your death. Nor is there any mention of the act of you being made alive in your conversion. And no, there's not a word here about something that will occur only over a period of years or of something that happened just recently. But the text is about an act of God in your soul that happened more than eighteen centuries ago!

But doesn't this just make your head spin? Isn't it the essence of absurdity? Doesn't it completely contradict all sense and reason? Were you really resurrected centuries before you were actually born? Even before your parents were born? Were you resurrected then, there, in Joseph's garden in that sepulcher in which no one had ever been laid before? And did that huge, mighty act of grace that set all the angels and serifs to singing happen to you then and there?

Oh, we're definitely dealing here with a miracle, an unfathomable mystery, and an insoluble riddle of divine omnipotence.

So then, may I ask you a question?

Do you believe that there was a universal flood caused by sin? Do you actually believe that in that flood all flesh died? All lambs, for example, so that after the waters receded, no other lambs ever grazed in the world's pastures than those that came out of the ark with Noah? Well now, if you really believe that, let me ask you one further question, if I may. Weren't all lambs that have lived on earth since that time also saved at the same time that Noah's lambs were saved? Isn't it true, then, that if those lambs had not been preserved from the death brought by the flood, all subsequent generations of lambs would have perished with them? Weren't all lambs born subsequently tied and bound in essence and identity to those few?

Isn't it more than mere imagery, therefore, and in fact completely clear reality if I said that the lambs that are living now were preserved with those in Noah's ark? Wouldn't this be a useful way for you to think about the matter?

But why do I need to be talking about lambs? Doesn't the same thing apply to Noah's sons? Is it only imagery, or is it reality when I say this about the people in the ark? If they had not been preserved, the entire human race would have perished. As a result, as far as natural life is concerned, all who are considered human were saved, rescued, and preserved along with Noah in God's ark.

And if you understand and concur that what we've said about the ark applies to life in the flesh, wouldn't the same clear application apply just as much to Jesus and his saving work from another flood? Would it apply any less to him preserving people from the depths of death and destruction? Look, the ark that preserved the lambs was simply a symbol and prototype of the refuge that elect people have in their Savior.

This isn't just something that those who allegorize say, but it's what Scripture itself says. Baptism in Jesus' blood is literally "symbolized" by the salvation of Noah's eight people from the flood (1 Pet 3:20–21).

And how is Jesus symbolized here by what happened then?

Most definitely in this totally transparent way. He assumed the office of Messiah. By becoming the Son of Man, Jesus was not simply assuming human nature. He became the head of a new humanity and thereby included all those who would become children of God. He embraced them in his high-priestly heart. In an act of eternal love, he incorporated us into himself, after the Father gave us to him.

From that moment on, we live in him. In his heart! In his high-priestly person! From that moment, we were in him. We were still impure and unholy in all our sins; but he carried them all away as the Lamb of God.

So he stood there, then, with all God's children bound up in him. There were those who lived before, those who lived then, those who are living now, and those who will come afterwards. The entire race of the elect was bound up in the Son of Man. Because of this, Christ sank down under the flood of unrighteousness belonging to God's children that poured over his heart. These are the sins that oppressed him with "the enormous burden of God's anger."

This is how he met death, descended to hell, and was buried under a curse. But naturally, not he alone but also we with him, since we were in him. Where he descended, we descended as well. We were buried with him in his death. When he died, we died. When he lay in the grave, we lay in that grave, bound in his heart. In him, in a shared lot with him!

And when he rose again, broke the bonds of death, and triumphed over hell and the grave, the Messiah did not dismiss us from his heart. He didn't simply leave us lying in the grave, my brother and sister, to triumph only by himself. No, he took us along with him in his resurrection. Along with him out of the grave! When he stepped back into life, we stepped over the threshold with him, out of ruin and raised to new life. When forty days later he ascended to heaven, he did not leave us behind here on earth. But he held us close, bound in his heart. And he took us above with him so that we have now been seated with him in heaven. And because he is praying for us in his heart, we may be at peace in that heart of his.

So now do you understand?

Are things clearer for you?

And if you're still asking: "But how can these things be true? How could I be in Jesus already centuries before I was born?" I have only this to say: "My dear man, don't you know anything about the 'new man' that has to be born in you and has replaced the 'old man'?" And doesn't that new man possess the seed, the root, and the kernel of true existence that "has been foreknown by God from all ages?" Where else would these be yours as a child of God than in Christ Jesus?

So now I tell you straightforwardly that a mystery is hidden in all of this. If you have eyes to see it, it is the same mystery that repeats itself every spring in every flower seed and every little bird's nest. If you do, you'll never say: "These things in nature are clear to me, but I don't understand anything at all about me being in Christ."

Being in Christ is truly about only one terrifying question: "Do you have assurance about your calling; have you made your election firm and sure?" Answering it is all about dying with Christ in his death, being raised with him, being seated with him in heaven, and always being found in the Messiah's heart.

"Child of God" is definitely a title of honor that belongs to you.

Is that who you really are in the eternal depths of divine truth? Not because you've misappropriated it! But because it is yours by right, on the basis of pure grace!

72
VOLUME I

STAYING AND BELONGING

We are always of good courage, therefore, knowing that we are
present in the body and absent from the Lord. 2 Corinthians 5:8

What is the difference between simply staying somewhere and belonging somewhere?

Search your soul to see whether it doesn't come down to these three points:

1. that you place less emphasis on the inconveniences of the place where you are only staying temporarily;

2. that your status and position are based more on the family to which you really belong;

3. that all your arrangements of a permanent nature are made with a view to the home where you really belong?

At least this is the practical way we look at matters in daily life.

Live with someone for a while, or as we usually express it, take up lodging with them. Then notice how quickly you make light of little inconveniences. At home everything bothers you. You're able to tolerate very little. When things don't go your way, it weighs on you heavily. But if you're lodging somewhere else, what does it really matter to you if things are a little more difficult, less to your liking, or don't exactly meet your needs? It matters so little that you put on your friendliest face, and without saying a word about it you roll with the punches. And if someone talks to you about the problem and offers to help out, admit it, you quickly respond: "Oh, it's nothing!"

So I would say that since here on earth you really only occupy your body, think of it as taking up temporary lodging, as we put it. Why, then, wouldn't you apply the same easygoing spirit and roll with the punches concerning inconveniences that hamper you in this life? Take inconveniences caused by your body not doing what you want it to do, for example! Don't take things too seriously. Just think like this: "I'm only staying here for a little while." Take the approach of saying about the situation: "Oh, it's nothing!" That's to have a healthy attitude.

It's nothing if there are a few bumps in the road, if my bed isn't as comfortable as I'd like, or if things don't develop the way I think they should. This isn't my house anyway, and I don't make the rules. It's not my place to insist that my demands are met. I'm only staying here temporarily.

Yes, "nothing!" It's nothing if your sick and ailing body just won't do what you want it to do. It can't walk as spritely as your spirit moves. You regularly have problems with it, and it's the source of aches and pains. So you should be able to say about it too: "It's nothing! It's just my body. I can't blame myself for what's wrong, and I certainly can't do anything about it." When things are difficult, people simply often have to bite their tongue. But you can still do things and accomplish things as long as you never forget that you're at most only occupying your body in its present condition on a short-term basis. You don't actually live there; it's not your real home.

Having said this, we easily get to the next, more advanced, and higher consideration: your status and position are based more on the family to which you really belong. For isn't it true even in society at large that your position does not depend on the house where you are only lodging. But it definitely does depend on the home of your father and mother. That's your own home. So doesn't this apply to what we are dealing with here? A king can spend the night in a shack, but he's still a king. Similarly, you will always remain "princes in the kingdom of heaven" if you have Jesus as your brother and you stand to inherit your Father's house. Wouldn't it be mocking him, therefore, if you fussed around with trying to get a higher position here on earth and risked your glorious standing in the everlasting kingdom? Doesn't it truly give you a greater inner appreciation of the honor and sacred value that you have? Doesn't it mean something to you in your heart of hearts to know this to be solidly true, and that only by grace? Will this glorious understanding of your status and position above have consequences? Will it give you peace and contentment with your assigned position and cause you to accept it here with appreciation? At the same time, will you make every attempt to express the nobler, more exquisite, and more exalted dimensions of your glorious status in all that you do? In all of your conduct? All of your interaction with others?

If you would only make your real home with Jesus!

If you would only remember that your bedroom above is being kept open for you!

If you would only remain convinced that up above there is already an intense longing for you to come back home!

Persuaded of this, if you would only express from the depths of your soul the abiding love that you have for those above who you call your own!

What follows immediately and almost automatically is the third point: that all your arrangements of a permanent nature are made with a view to where you feel most at home.

On this there is virtually no difference of opinion in ordinary life.

Everyone without exception never considers the opinions of those with whom they are merely lodging temporarily when it comes to the important decisions they must make. But there are very few who don't seriously consider the convictions of those in their family circle, where they feel completely at home. Small, passing matters that occur daily are easily settled. Those aren't relevant here. But ones that are of lasting significance and will have enduring influence are definitely not left to mere chance. A person reflects long and hard on them. They think about them in terms of their personal opportunities and circumstances. And when it comes to judging and evaluating these, they're not so foolish as to follow the advice to those where they're only staying for the time being. But everyone without exception actually pays strict attention to the consequences in the place they call home.

On this subject, I simply ask you, my soul, whether there isn't something here that applies to you. You say you are absent from your Savior but that you are living here in your body only temporarily. Isn't there an obligation we have here? In all weighty matters, serious considerations, and decisive decisions in life, should we be so unspeakably foolish as to measure things as superficially as we do temporal matters? The only honorable and permissible thing for a Christian to do is to apply the standards of the home that is above, with the Lord, when it comes to taking such steps.

Exaggeration can cause damage in this regard.

We can't inject these incredibly exalted and sacred guidelines into each and every inconsequential decision. That would demand exertion that we simply couldn't sustain. It would be unnatural. It would miss the point being made here. In secondary matters, we are permitted to consider the opportunities of this life. We have to proceed on that basis.

But when it comes to major decisions in life, determinations that affect people where they actually live, and choices that impact the lives of your children, that's different. That's even the case when it's less obvious what the results will be, or whether they will have a lasting impact, or what bearing they might have on your own future. In such cases, my sisters and brothers, I would only tell you that we should be practical and follow the course that everyone does. But we should always make our decisions not in terms of the house where we're only lodging temporarily but in terms of the place where we are truly at home.

Really now, if the spirit of that higher order isn't found in us, what do you think? Do we really prefer being at home with the Lord?

BY ONE MAN

Just as sin entered the world through one man, and
through sin, death ... Romans 5:12

Moved by the Holy Spirit, Paul used two expressions that are almost the same, yet different. They are about the origin of death.

In Romans 5:12 we read: "Just as sin entered the world through one man, and through sin, death ... " And in 1 Corinthians 15:21 almost the same is said, but it's different: "For, since death came through a man, so also the resurrection of the dead comes through a man."

The difference between them lies in this. Romans 5:12 expressly says "death through a single man," while 1 Corinthians 15:21 simply says "death through a man"! This is a difference that in translation is less striking but that in the Greek is obvious. While in Romans 5:12 the numeral "one" is intentionally added in the original text, 1 Corinthians 15:21 merely says that "death is through a man."

Is there a contradiction here?

Not in the least.

At least not if one considers that the Holy Spirit wants to reveal something entirely different in Romans 5 from in 1 Corinthians 15.

In Romans 5 the entire, determinative comparison is being made between the covenant head Adam and the covenant head Christ. That's why the emphasis falls on the fact that as far as God is concerned we are dealing with more than our own individual sin since Adam's guilt is added to our account. By way of further clarification, the point is that there are not as many origins of sin as there are individual people. All guilt has one common origin in the one man Adam.

In 1 Corinthians 15, by contrast, the Holy Spirit intends to disclose that death does not have its basis in nature, but that it entered nature through a man. Consistent with that thought, he is also saying that the resurrection to glory is not achieved by the power of nature, but is only achieved by the same route by which death entered, namely, through a man. In our way of putting it, we might say that death is not a completely natural event, but that it also has a spiritual dimension. In the same way, also the resurrection cannot be a merely natural phenomenon, but it necessarily carries inherently spiritual force. And whereas that spiritual element does not reside in nature but uniquely in humanity among all creatures on earth, so both death and resurrection cannot be achieved merely through human instrumentality. The first is an expression of God's wrath, the second of his grace.

And yet, one would be hugely mistaken if one thought on the basis of this explanation that Romans 5:12 and 1 Corinthians 15:21 are contradictory.

To the contrary, even what the Holy Spirit reveals in 1 Corinthians 15, while the emphasis does not fall on the point, is very intentionally designed and intended to convey that both death and resurrection came into the world through one individual person.

Two contrasting positions are possible here. One might certainly ask: "Are death and resurrection attributable to nature, which lacks a soul, or to humanity, which possesses a soul?" To this question, 1 Corinthians responds: "Not to nature, but to humanity." But one might also ask: "How? Is it the case that they originate anew in every individual person, or are they transmitted from one person as head to all others?" And to that question Romans 5:12 and 1 Corinthians 15:21 both respond: "Not anew in every individual person, but they originate for all people with one individual person who is the first person to exist and who is their covenant head."

Accordingly, 1 Corinthians 15:22 immediately continues with the following: "For just as all died in Adam, so all will also be made alive in Christ." That's a definite explanation made obvious by the causal use of the little word "for" that begins the sentence. It shows beyond any doubt that the thought rests on the previous verse, and it also definitely requires that the reference to man in verse 21 not be understood as every person head for head, but as the first man, the father of all humanity, who is our covenant head. Something by way of still fuller explanation appears in verse 23. There we read: "Every person, in their determined sequence, will be raised, Christ the firstfruit and then, when he returns, those that are in Christ." Here two ideas are expressed. The first is that humanity is not regarded head for head as a loose collection of individuals but as belonging to a determined succession that is organically connected. Second, in this organic union, Christ is the firstfruit or progenitor and original person, while others appear only secondarily as those that are in Christ. This refers to those who proceed from him spiritually.

Take the expression "For, since death came through a man, so also the resurrection of the dead comes through a man." In light of the indisputable demonstration of the foregoing union, it should not be taken as though it simply means that death has its genesis in something man does and not in the law of nature. Rather, it is properly understood in the sense that "man" in this expression means progenitor, original person, and covenant head. Accordingly, in both references we are dealing with the notion of one. Whereas each and every tree has one progenitor, so each and every covenant can have only one head.

Indeed, every other explanation of this important expression needs to be rejected—not only because of what follows it, but also because of what precedes it.

Yet, it was said that Christ has not only been raised from the dead, but that in his resurrection he has become the firstfruit, that is, the progenitor, the covenant head, and the root of all those who have died but who will one day be raised in him. And now, given that line of reasoning, says the Holy Spirit in effect: "That this is the case is obvious from the fact that death came into the world through a man, and that definitely happened through a man who was the progenitor of everyone. Also the resurrection can come into the world in no other way than through a man. And that, once again, is through a man who is the progenitor, the firstfruit or covenant head of all children of the resurrection."

The agreement of this passage with Romans 5:12 should not rise or fall with the accent marks placed on the numeral "one" in the phrase "through one man."[1] That's definitely not where to look. That ignores the entire contextual train of thought. Rather, find it in the fact that the word "man" in 1 Corinthians 15:21, both in terms of what precedes and what follows the verse, neither can or may be understood in any other way than as referring to the sort of man who is simultaneously the firstborn, the progenitor, the source, and the covenant head of all those who are saved!

---

1. Kuyper's point about emphasis here is with reference to the two accent marks placed above the numeral one in the Dutch language: één.

DOING GOD'S WORK

This is the work of God: that you believe in
him whom he has sent. John 6:29

Are working and believing contradictory? Is not working something to be celebrated by Christians? Is doing nothing honorable for them? Will idleness be their crown of glory?

If not, what does it mean to be working? Isn't it simply an expression of life? Doesn't it indicate that they are alive? That they are living, breathing people?

Someone who's dead doesn't work. People don't work during the night. Someone who is stretched out unconscious isn't working. But the voice of the Great Shepherd calls to whomever has any life in them at all. He appeals to all for whom the light shines, to every individual who knows that they exist, who is living, and who is standing before the face of God. He says: "Work while it is still day, for the night is coming in which no one can work!"

No, it's not working that we need to avoid, but working for selfish reasons. We're not like ants that gather in order to enjoy what they've gathered. We're even less like spiders that store up in order to produce a toxin. But we work like the honeybee that produces honey in the hive not for itself but for the beekeeper who sells it.

Well then, the church of Jesus Christ needs to be like a beehive. There everyone strives to contribute their very best. They use their gifts without letup in order to pour out the purest honey from the honeycomb. They do this not to consume that precious, virgin honey themselves, but to offer it in honor of him to whom the entire church belongs. And if someone asks whether Jesus hasn't expressly said: "God's work is all about believing in Jesus!" then we give the following answer. "Definitely, as long as you're convinced of that and do so in the way he has prescribed!"

Believing ... when it comes to knowing the truth. This means that I regard myself as a complete fool in order to honor Jesus as "the wisdom of God."

Believing ... with respect to atonement. This means that I cannot bring or offer as much as a grain of sand in payment of my debt, but that Jesus is the Alpha and Omega where the work of atonement is concerned.

Believing ... in finding my way forward. This means that I don't dare to put one foot in front of the other based on my own insight, but that I follow Jesus my faithful Shepherd closely, step by step.

Believing ... when the seas are raging and the waves are crashing over my lifeboat. It means knowing with absolute certainty that I'm going to die and sink into oblivion if I have to depend on my own rowing and navigating. It also means depending only on Jesus, who calmly clamps his divine hand on the tiller.

Believing ... where life's struggles are involved. Then it means being convinced that I will fall and be totally defeated before I even know it if the outcome depends on me. It also means being absolutely persuaded that no arrow will pierce me and no spear strike me as long as my Defender leads me and his shield covers me.

So believing always has a different sense depending on the matter at hand, on what you happen to be facing, on what the issue is, and on what the discussion is all about.

Every situation in life poses the same question: "What now?" To it there is always one and the same answer: "Believe in Jesus!" Always believe! Never do anything else than believe!

That's also true when it comes to your work. Even then it comes down to believing. And yet, it involves the kind of believing that applies specifically to working.

Suppose that a palace is being built. In the morning the carpenters, masons, and foremen all arrive. They have to begin working. But how should they go about working? Should each of them follow their own sense of how to proceed and take their own approach? Definitely not! Rather, they should do so trusting the architect! They should believe that nothing is going to turn out well unless they follow his plan, listen to his orders, and consult his blueprint. They should also believe that everything is going to turn out well and fall into place if they unquestioningly follow his directives. They should believe in him unconditionally. They should believe in him knowing that he anticipates things before they do. This should give them confidence and inspire them. They should believe that he is the invisible tie that binds them together. They should believe in him knowing that he provides all the materials on the construction site required to raise the walls.

Shouldn't this be the way it is with Jesus' construction project?

Or isn't Jesus building a temple of praise in which the glory of God will shine? And isn't his entire church busy constructing that temple? And if the project is going to turn out well, shouldn't your entire life, all your strength, your money, your possessions, and your love be devoted to building that temple?

But how should you be involved in working on it? Certainly not with materials that you have brought and prepared, but definitely with those that Jesus has provided. Isn't that true? Certainly not by following your own ideas, inclinations, or good intentions, but by believing in the Architect. By believing that he alone knows everything and understands it completely. By seeing things through his eyes. By being inspired by his inspiration, flooded with confidence in the words he has spoken and whispered in your soul. Yes, by believing that he must be the One and All in whom you find fulfillment in order to avoid plunging into your own bungling failures.

So think about this. When a section of the wall has been finished, and you step back to examine it from a distance and you like what you see, your soul feels an inner need to say something. Then you don't say to some passerby: "Look at that! I laid those bricks!" No, you feel the need to exclaim: "Look at that beautiful sight. It's just what Jesus ordered. He deserves all the glory!" That's when you'll find peace in the depths of your heart, my good reader. That's because then you'll have done your work in the only satisfying way possible: by believing in your Lord!

ASCENDING TO WHERE HE WAS BEFORE

*Does this offend you? Then what about seeing the Son of
Man ascending to where he was before? John 6:61b–62[1]*

With respect to the ascension of our King, because of our interest in the
heaven to which he returned, we may never lose sight of the ascending
itself, the reality of rising up, or the fact of being elevated.

Our thinking should not be focused only on Jesus being in heaven. But
it should concentrate in the first place on what it is called today and on how
it has been remembered through the ages. It should be a commemoration of
Jesus' ascending.

Then we will be remembering the ascension appreciatively and in the way
that the Lord himself indicated, namely, in contrast with his earlier descending from heaven. The being taken up again into the sphere of glory where he
was before is in direct contrast with this.

---

1. The passage reference in the original Kuyper text is only to John 6:62.

Otherwise, my good reader, how can you understand the striking saying of Jesus spoken to the people of Capernaum that they found so difficult to comprehend: "I am the Bread of Life that has descended from heaven"?

That's also when the Lord said to them: "Does this offend you? Then what would it be like if you saw the Son of Man ascending to where he was before?"

The heart of the matter to which we need to pay attention is the contrast between first descending from heaven and then ascending into heaven again. Only when seen against the background of "first descending" is the "ascending again" understood in its true light.

Are you asking what's involved here, what's being said, what deeper thought is buried in all this?

Look, many a man has jumped into a stream to save someone who is drowning only to go under himself and never come up again. Along with the object of his compassion, he died and sank to the bottom, sacrificing himself.

But with our Mediator it was a completely different matter when he jumped into the stream of our unrighteousness and misery in order to grasp us and hold on to us tightly. The ability he had to pull us out of that flood of misery and bring us up to the surface was something else again. Clutching the lost in his arms! Bearing his bride in his heart! Holding tightly those he had purchased! His descending was a demonstration of his overflowing love. But the ascending to the surface was a demonstration of his overwhelming strength.

Mercy and compassion are needed in descending from the throne of glory. To step down! To enter a woman's womb and become a poor man in this poor world! To suffer as the most despised and rejected of all men in that world! Under that burden to endure the most bitter of all deaths! That's what makes the rescue effort shine so brilliantly. That's what it means to love the sinner. That represents self-denial. That reflects the triumph of divine determination and perfect grace.

But ascending is totally different.

To jump into a stream after a drowning child is something anyone would do who has any love, compassion, self-denial, and mercy at all. That includes a young boy, a crippled man, and the child's mother. But who could pull the child to safety? Only a person who has the ability to pull himself out as well!

That kind of rising up again doesn't depend on love or mercy, but only on strength and power and the ability needed to do so. It depends on the stalwart, extended arms that powerfully rule rivers and winds and floods.

But where do you ever find both of these together, overflowing love and overwhelming strength?

Here on earth, don't they almost always stand opposed to each other? Doesn't someone who is extremely strong almost always suffer from a lack of love and tenderness? And doesn't it seem as though others almost always take advantage of someone who is unusually loving? That all strength fails him? That going under is his pathetic destiny? Doesn't that beautiful and eloquent name "God's Suffering Servant" suit every servant of Jehovah who succumbs in the battle here on earth between love and power? And in that struggle, aren't those weakest who yearn to fight by using the resources of this world?

To gain a crown from God, definitely; but then by succumbing in the conflict!

Look! All of this might seem lovely, or tragic, or even emotionally stirring to eyes that are fogged over. But you say that it doesn't appeal to you!

The Lord God doesn't play around with tragedies.

With God, death is never a game.

And even a demonstration of the most remarkable moral greatness, as long as it remains just an exhibition, is far below the dignity of God's divine majesty.

No, the Lord God saves! Actually saves! He saves both body and soul.

And what's truly beautiful is not the apparent defeat of saving love, as tragically moving as that may be. No, the only thing that is truly beautiful, moving, and holy is the saving love that also triumphs. It not only descends into the stream but is also capable of rising out of the stream. He not only succeeds in rising from the stream, but he carries the drowning person out of that stream of misery with him and sets him on the throne where he himself had been before.

This is the reason why the ascension of Jesus is so beautiful, my good readers. It's why it's so majestic and so completely glorious. For here we see overwhelming power. Here is complete victory. Here we have ascending once again out of a majestic and beautiful struggle. Here we witness climbing higher, being lifted up until he is again finally "where he was before"!

He's there despite everything that opposed him. The laws of nature opposed him. The elements opposed him. The human flesh that he assumed opposed him. Even the love found in the hearts of his disciples opposed him. It all pulled him down. It all held him down. It all resisted his ascending.

But even so, nothing withstood him.

He vanquished it all.

He ascended.

And oh, the miracle of divine omnipotence! In ascending he carried the entire church of the redeemed along with him on high. Those who dwell above! Those living now! And those who have yet to live! All God's children!

Look! Look at him standing there in heaven with his treasure, the souls of the redeemed in his arms.

All the angels are adoring him.

All the martyrs and prophets are kneeling before him.

The Father is crowning him!

A GOD WHO HIDES HIMSELF

You are a God who hides himself. Isaiah 45:15

But doesn't God reveal himself, then? Do we have to hunt him down until we find him? Do we have to hold on to him tightly so that he doesn't shut us out? Must we hang on until he shows us his great glory?

In our hearts, we thought things were so different!

We supposed that by our sinning we had caused a thick haze to arise that made the Holy One invisible to us. We thought that with our own hands we had stretched out a veil that prevented us from seeing the everlasting God. And about the Lord God we imagined that he is precisely a God who reveals himself and who works hard in all of his merciful power and through the blood of his own Son to break through the haze and rip down that veil. We imagined that he would eventually find us and, breaking through to our souls, whisper to his people in ravishingly blessed words: "Look. Here I am, O Jerusalem. Look, here is your God."

But this doesn't seem possible because Isaiah says quite emphatically: "Truly, you are a God who hides himself!" He doesn't merely say: "for the time being you are still hidden" or "are hidden in spite of yourself." No, but he says: "You are a God whose divine nature requires by an act of your own will that you stay hidden!"

What sense does this make? What does the prophet intend to say here?

If a person reads Isaiah in context, there can be no dispute about the immediate and contextual meaning of this saying. Isaiah is speaking in the middle of Israel's deepest humiliation. He is talking with a view to the even deeper suffering that Israel would experience in Babylon. And now he is prophesying that this apparent abandonment of his people will at bottom really be nothing other than God's well planned, chosen, desired, and implemented means of glorifying Israel.

"You are a God who hides himself" is intended in Isaiah 45:15 simply to say straightforwardly: "You keep your plans and decisions hidden; you don't allow people to know immediately the intent of what you're doing."

Israel had thought that something completely different was going on. It had imagined that God had withdrawn his love for his people. It had been afraid that Jehovah's faithfulness had been shattered forever because of its sins. It had characterized God as unloving in his seething anger. But in retrospect, it becomes obvious that nothing but loving impulses were involved in all of this and that God is totally different from what people thought he was based on what he was doing. That's why this is not a lament but should be understood as a joyful celebration: "O God, you totally surprised us! You are completely different from what we had imagined. How we misunderstood you. You truly are a God who hides himself!"

But this deeper insight is not totally satisfying.

That's because, while this saying is consistent with ones we read elsewhere, in another sense it is completely different. Elsewhere we read things like this: "My thoughts are not your thoughts"; "the secret things belong to the Lord our God"; "his judgments are beyond finding out"; and also what Paul exclaimed: "How untraceable are all your ways!" But what's expressed here is completely different because it touches a feature of God's being. It expresses an act of his will. It represents something that God intentionally does because he is God. "You are truly a God who hides himself."

Apparently beneath this further explanation lies a still deeper principle that captivates the soul, like something deeper shining through a shimmering reflection mirrored on the water's surface. A person scrutinizes it and wants to comprehend it. But is that deeper principle really so difficult to grasp? Or is it just the unique nature of things that are noble, pure, and tender to stay hidden?

Everybody calls an adulteress a "public woman," but the pure, chaste young woman stays discreetly hidden. Our body is visible and can be seen in public, but our soul is hidden from view. With respect to the body, the less attractive parts such as the hand and foot can be seen, but the more essential parts such as the lungs, heart, and blood are hidden. The last ones, of course, are momentarily visible when a person's face blushes in shame or from joyful excitement.

This principle is universally true. A cobblestone is publicly visible as it lies in the road, but a nugget of gold remains hidden deep in the mine. Snail shells can be picked up on any beach, but you have to dive to the hidden depths to find a pearl-bearing oyster shell. The stars begin shinning in the night's dim light, but they retreat and hide in full sunlight. So shouldn't God stay hidden? He is the source and pivot of all that is pure, of good report, lovely, and noble in heaven and on earth.

Could he still be God if he exposed himself completely to his creatures and scattered pearls from the depths of his divine heart to be rummaged by dogs?

Wouldn't a God who is transparent to any and everyone be a God of very little depth? Wouldn't he be a God lacking a private, inner life? Wouldn't he be a God who lacks precisely the deepest, most inner being that makes him God?

Isn't learning to know God—learning to know him with ever increasing intimacy, depth, and accuracy—nothing less than the single most blessed effort that is permitted for his children here on earth and throughout eternity? And what would it be like if you could actually say: "Now I've completed my knowledge of God"; "Now I understand him completely"; "Now there's nothing left for me to learn about God"? Wouldn't your sense of blessedness disappear at the same time? Wouldn't the fascination of everlasting life in heaven be gone?

And if that full knowledge persisted, would any kind of everlastingly hidden depth be left to discover?

And if it did and you could ever find the boundaries of God's being, wouldn't God at that point stop being limitless and in fact cease being God?

If God ever stopped being hidden, could your God ever again be completely glorious and fully blessed?

My brother and sister, if God stopped being hidden, wouldn't you even stop worshiping him?

Is all of this to acknowledge that there is no knowledge of God possible for your soul?

If a person never dived for the pearl, wouldn't it stay hidden in the depths of the water? If there is no mining for gold, doesn't gold remain buried in the bowels of the earth? If you don't gradually get to know your wife's soul, doesn't it remain hidden behind the veil of her flesh?

Is it any different where God is concerned?

Or is he asking too much when he requires that people dive into the depths in order to approach and find him? Probe the depths of his being? That they test and search in their struggles in order to cling to him? Isn't God permitted to require that all knowledge of his glorious being shall be gained by the sweat of the soul? That it be a reward for spiritual hard work? Won with strength and won from him? Gained with a will that he stiffened? But nevertheless achieved with real exertion?

Is any other kind of knowledge of God possible or even thinkable?

What does it take to know God? Your thought processes? Your memory? Your mind? Your conceptualizing? Your feelings? No! You! You yourself! And how will you know, unless such knowledge delves deeply? And how will it be able to penetrate in depth, deep into your being, unless you are engaged in this in the depths of your being? And does that ever happen, my sister and brother, without tremendous exertion in your soul?

And that's the reason why even when it seems to our souls like the Almighty is covered in thick, black darkness, that's precisely when his hiddenness is the reason we should to flee to him.

We should when we face the most difficult circumstances of our lives. We should when our souls feel spiritually abandoned and our hearts are virtually lifeless. We should even when we die a thousand deaths for fear that we are about to lose touch with God and our souls will die within us.

That's exactly how it is with our own children! They walk closest with us when we know something that we are not sharing with them or won't allow them to see. That's when they refuse to let go of our hands!

DEFINITELY BLESSED

*That man is blessed who does not walk in
the counsel of the wicked. Psalm 1:1*

Isn't it wonderfully profound that our Psalm collection dares to begin with a sinful, lost, no-account man who is struggling in misery, dying in his distress, and mouthing one complaint after the other, but who is still blessed? No, blissful! Even praised as definitely blessed!

Not only definitely blessed in the hereafter, but already now. Not that that man will be definitely blessed, but that that man is already definitely blessed.

Everyone knows very well that we yearn for happiness in our hearts. All human striving and endeavor is directed to that end. They are attempts to remove the hindrances that impede the way to our happiness. We don't and we can't rest until we are able to say that we are blessed.

"To be a blessing to the poor" is the approach taken, the promise made, and the prophecy announced by every form of idolatry. It's the same with every reformer, crusader, philosopher, and world conqueror. And the afflicted masses turn away from such people after they see that the promised blessedness hasn't arrived. Then the sting of discontent produces even stronger unrest in their hearts.

But now consider your Bible, God's Word. It also makes an approach, offers a promise, and announces a prophecy of blessing to you. But it is much stronger and more powerful in tone than the longing created by the crusader's approach. This Word doesn't only promise less suffering and to ease pain but offers an infusion of real blessedness. And that happiness is so complete that it can even be called "definite blessedness." You can drink that kind of blessedness in such deep drafts that even the term "definite blessedness" is inadequate. That language can't begin to capture the full richness of the peace and joy involved here.

But how and in what way does the Bible promise that kind of definite blessedness?

To understand that, simply open the book of Psalms and notice how in many places the man who doesn't want to walk in the counsels of the wicked is wasting away.

You would think that God would deliver him from all his illnesses. But notice how he complains in his chains, calls out from the deadly dangers he faces, and simply moans in the bottom of some pit where there is no water.

You would think that his cup is brimming over with prosperity and wealth, but instead you see that he is hunted down like a doe in the mountains and that all the waves and breakers of the Almighty are crashing over him.

You would expect that he would be surrounded by a circle of faithful companions. But notice that all his acquaintances have abandoned him, and that the man who ate his bread has repaid him with affliction.

If then all these earthly blessings continue to be threatened, you would at least imagine that this most blessed of men would walk in quiet peace before the face of the Lord and enjoy uninterrupted holiness and devotion. But you find just the opposite, for over and over again his lips complain about his sin, and he prays for forgiveness. What rumbles from the bottom of his heart are the struggles that leave him a broken man and a contemptible sinner in his own eyes.

You might ask how it is possible that Scripture still calls such a person "definitely blessed." My good reader, here is the key to that wonderful secret.

That man is the most miserable of all people in every other respect. No one has said it better than Paul did: "O miserable man that I am. Who shall deliver me?" But in one respect the page is completely turned, and that's precisely where salvation emerges. That man knows that it's not he who possesses God, but God possesses him! He lives by and with that faith. That's all he needs. He doesn't desire more. Now the pit without water becomes God's pit. God put him there. God is working in him there. God wants to lift him out of it, and he will.

So do you understand now?

Definitely blessed because God possesses him, God upholds him, and God wraps his soul in the bonds of his divine will. Those bonds tie him securely to Christ, the Son of his love. God is present in his Son and present in himself.

This is truly a miracle. All those other proposals, plans, and strategies for making people happy have long ago been discarded, mocked, and then forgotten, and the multitudes in their inflamed bitterness have stopped following those who made them false promises. Then the plan in the book of Psalms for finding definite blessedness emerges once more. It's three thousand years old now. But in every land and among every people you still find living examples of which the Holy Spirit describes: "Look over there! There's the kind of definitely blessed person I'm talking about!" And if you were to take the entire world together, there would be a whole multitude that would be celebrating and saying in unison: "Yes, I'm one of those who have experienced that glorious grace!" You'd be able to hear over and over again how those people who are hunted and hounded are still singing. Sometimes they are lying in a deep pit. Sometimes the lions are growling around them. That's when they sing their way through their fears and even rejoice in their pain and oppression: "As far as my situation goes, it's good for me to be near to God."

Is that how it is with your soul, my sister and my brother? Are you being definitely blessed like this?

THE SINS OF MY YOUTH

Do not remember the sins of my youth. Psalm 25:7

We all learned this beautiful verse by singing it from our psalm books as children:

> Never again remember the sins
>> That I have committed in my youth.
> Remember me in your kindness
>> That I may always benefit from your goodness.[1]

But in our youth did we ever think or even suspect how the verse from the Psalms on which this stanza is based would bother our consciences in old age? How it would cast our souls entirely on the grace of God?

Every individual among God's people feels sad and burdened about "the sins of our youth." That's because those sins are simply there. They lurk behind you

---

1. The rhymed versification of Psalm 25:7 as sung in Dutch Reformed worship services for over a hundred years before Kuyper included it here reads as follows in the Dutch language:
Sla de zonden nimmer ga,
Die mijn jonkheid heeft bedreven.
Denk aan mij toch in genà
Om uw goedheid eer te geven.

in your memories. You can't get rid of them. They still haunt you. And what is worst of all is that they get bigger every day.

You ask how that's possible. How can the sins of his youth become larger with every passing day for a person well along in years? Look, the answer is obvious and is really very simple. It's by the holy light of God's Spirit that time and again something from your youth is exposed as sinful. When you did it, you didn't see it as sinful at all. But now you are definitely conscious of the fact that it went against God, that it grieved the Spirit present at your baptism, and that you are accountable for it.

Permit me to add this as well: the further along you get in life, it won't get any better. For, if I could put it this way, suppose that in your past there's a part that is white and another that is completely black. And suppose that these are blotches that lie beside each other. Then you have to reckon with the fact that the black one will expand and the white one will only contract until the question finally occurs to you of whether there was anything wholesome there at all.

The sins of youth are doubly disastrous. They amount to the appearance of an angry abscess in what appears to be sound and healthy tissue, or to the steady dripping of poison into what is still developing. Except that for the entire remainder of something's development it wreaks damage and destruction.

The sins of youth! Oh, how they control the formation of a person's entire character, the whole tone of their life, and the total shape of their future.

They eat so deeply into us because youthful character is doubly soft and impressionable. They put at Satan's disposal the boundless youthful energy and passionate spirit that thrives in the hearts of young people.

Oh, who can ever measure the terrible evil involved in those "sins of our youth," including the "secret sins" buried there? For, and understand this clearly, they are not readily detected. People think better things of you. Your youth itself is like a shield that protects you. It causes anyone admonishing you to focus on better things about you. And that's a license for you to persist without interruption or impediment in doing what's evil.

Still worse is that after you commit them, they continue working for as long as you live. Even when you have been reconciled and saved by God's inexpressible mercy, that old enemy is still lying in wait inside you and evil constantly roils up, "as though from a polluted spring," to use the words of our confession.[2]

Oh, where could we hide if we didn't have a Savior who covered the sins of our youth with the burial shroud of his divine mercy? Think what it would be

---

2. Kuyper is referencing article 15 of the Belgic Confession here.

like if you could never get rid of those persistent memories. How frightening that would be for you.

But also think about how inexpressibly gracious it is on the part of God's Son that he stands between you and your youth. And he says to you: "Forget what is behind you. Stretch out toward what is ahead of you." Already from his cradle, he quietly whispers a word of blessed reconciliation to you!

Oh, if our young smart alecks, our children, and our youngsters would only know what those "sins of our youth" will be for a still-unreconciled heart! How they should flee to God. How they should flee from the world's contamination. How they should find their shelter close to him who said: "Let the little children come to me!" That's where his protective grace is at work even for unconverted youth.

Don't underestimate "the sins of your youth," you children! Pray them away before they happen! Fight against them with your whole heart. This much I know: there is no youth without sin. So why don't you turn, heart and soul, to that which is lovely and of good report?

Church of the living God, help your baptized children come to that point. Parents, you especially should do this! So much can be avoided. So much can be resisted. The pores of a child's soul are so receptive. You penetrate them so easily and so undetected through your own sinful surroundings. But the Lord also wants to use you in unnoticed ways to inoculate your children with good medicine.

Once again, "the sins of our youth" represent such a sad and deeply depressing chapter in the history of human sin. At the same time, so much can be done from the Word of God for, with, and in our young people to restrain and limit them as well as remove incentives to commit them.

So guard yourselves, my readers both young and old. Stay faithful!

YOU SET ME BEFORE YOUR FACE FOREVER

But as for me, you uphold me in my uprightness and
you set me before your face forever. Psalm 41:12[1]

Many apparently insignificant expressions over which a person reads quickly exist particularly in the book of Psalms. Yet, when a person plumbs their depths, they yield rich comfort and are a source of grace. That's true of the words from Psalm 41 that stand above this little meditation. Think into it for a minute and let it register on your soul. What wonderful grace is tucked away in those brief words!

I should have died, says the child of God, but I didn't! I will triumph over my enemy and over the man who torments my soul. But this certainly won't happen because I'm able to withstand him or because I'm stronger than he is. It will only be because I am a child of my God. It doesn't depend on me his child, but only on God! It's because the honor of my God and Father is involved. That's why, and for that reason alone, God's child ultimately perseveres, no matter how much unhappiness may be involved.

Ultimately getting through categorically doesn't happen without righteousness. Otherwise all the devils would raise objections and scream to high heaven

---

1. Psalm 41:13 in Dutch versions, including in Kuyper's meditation here.

from the depths of hell: "God is unrighteous!" And if things unfolded like that, the devils themselves would also find themselves in heaven!

No, God's child holds out with righteousness and without the least bit of unrighteousness. And the mystery of how that can happen the psalmist solves from his own spiritual experience. Again and again he resists clinging to his own righteousness, but he finds that God establishes that in him and for him. "Lord, as for me, you uphold me in my uprightness!" Uprightness! That's even more than righteousness, for in effect that amounts to saying: "I am made righteous by you, and I would never claim that I have gotten to that point by myself!" Uprightness confesses in and from the heart: "The Lord himself accomplished this, and he alone!"

And how does this work of his unfold?

Very simply said, my good brother and sister, it is accomplished because God in his love does one very simple thing: he "sets you before his face forever."

He did that in eternity and before laying the foundations of the world. In that act of setting someone before his face forever, both your election and the root of your salvation in that election are bound together.

"Setting you before his face" also included your regeneration by infusing your soul with the capacity to believe when you were brought to life from death.[2] Recognize that all of your worldly living and abiding in death amounted to standing outside of his light and happened because you were estranged from him, your God. Your awakening to new life through faith was precisely your coming to stand before God's face and immediately seeing by the light of his presence both your eternal death and the unfathomable depth of his grace. And this much you know for certain, that you did not go and stand before God's face! He was the one who placed you there!

Oh, the divine moment of your eternal rebirth, when the All-Compassionate God looked down on you. Then it became impossible for you ever to leave him, for now you were positioned in his presence, standing before his awesome and yet so reassuring face.

And is that the way it's always going to be?

For you and I remained so ungodly that after his miraculous work of mercy and after briefly enjoying our presence before him, we suddenly decided that a person is not capable of looking upon God continually. Our souls told us that we had had enough of God and that there was not a lot of life in such a monotonous

---

2. This is an explicit statement of Kuyper's controversial and hotly contested doctrine of "presumptive regeneration."

existence. We wanted to get back to what was really visible. Naturally, we did this with the idea that later we could return to God. But for the moment, at least, we were going to enjoy something good away from him. But in turning away from him, we really wanted to do so while still singing: "Yet it's really good, it's a source of blessing to me, to be near to my God!"

Truly, how perplexing our human hearts actually are! We really scare ourselves sometimes, don't we?

But the fact is, a child of God can't have or do what they want. They may want to run away from God in order to be free, but God doesn't let them do this. All the running away happens only in a dream. They imagine that they're out of God's presence. They picture themselves as now being free. They dream that later they'll go back to God. But in reality, all of this is nothing more than a mirage.

They simply can't! For God has "set them before his face forever"! At best, they can only touch their lips to the cup of sin before a terrifying light shines all around them and a fire burns inside them. So what is this heaviness of conscience? This sadness pouring over their souls? That terrible weakness in their legs? What else is it but the face of God, in whose presence you are standing forever? That's the reason why a child of God can't sin without the sinning being followed by terrible turmoil in the soul and soul-wrenching remorse.

But remorse is followed by praise. For God always succeeds. If you humble yourself and cry out with a submissive heart: "O God, just give up on me. I don't deserve to lift my eyes and look you in the face!" then God always does the same thing. He sets you before his face once again. But now it's before his comforting face, and the love of Christ begins flowing quietly into your heart.

And so, God be praised, that's how it will be forever. "You set me before your face forever." That's why, whatever may come and whatever may threaten us, we are never overcome by it, and it always turns out well. For God is God. And when we are once above, all desire to be away from God will be gone, because that's how our own wills will forever want it. Then God will place all his children before his face to enjoy his everlasting presence. Jehovah exalted in his saints!

Oh, may his mercy grant this glory also in you and me!

YOU DO NOT SUPPORT THE ROOT, BUT THE ROOT SUPPORTS YOU

*So do not exalt about the branches; but if you do exalt
about them, remember that you do not support the
root, but the root supports you. Romans 11:18[1]*

W hat a perceptive and illuminating statement this is when considered
just after Pentecost. It reawakens what went through our hearts during
that important religious holiday: "You don't support the root, but the root supports you!"

When it was Pentecost, we considered the body of Christ that was conceived
in Paradise, showed the signs of life in Abram's call, and was finally born from
mother Israel's womb. That event marks the incredible moment when the Holy

---

1. This meditation was first published in *De Heraut*, no. 129 (May 30, 1880), where the reference was given correctly. When republished in book form, the reference was erroneously cited
as Romans 11:28.

Spirit, given to our Head by the Father up above, was poured into the church of the living God by that Head through all the veins in its spiritual tissue.

This is a powerful reality that is very reassuring for the souls of God's children, at least as long as they remember that the Holy Spirit will never abandon the church. Or that the divine breath of life will never be sucked out of the church's lungs. Or even that, when it seems like a member of that church (perhaps a hand, perhaps a foot) seems ice-cold, frozen solid, and stone-cold dead, the Holy Spirit himself will revive such a member and maintain them in life. He will do this as Comforter, Giver of Life, and Regenerating Agent.

So what is Paul, Jesus' wonderful apostle, teaching us in this statement about you not supporting the root but the root supporting you?

In his mind's eye, he sees the church of the living God standing before him like an olive tree. It's something living, therefore. It's pulsating with inner life. And it is so constituted that all its branches and twigs draw sap through the pith and up the stem from the roots. A tree simply has life within it, and if it doesn't, it's no longer a tree. A tree whose roots are devoid of life and whose life-giving sap has dried up is just dead wood. It ceases being a tree. Every naturally grown or grafted branch and twig, and every blossom and piece of fruit that ever flourished on it and might still hang there, now no longer has as much as a single drop of life-giving fluid left in it. Otherwise, they would have drawn it from the earth, through the roots, and up the stem.

And applying this to the church, the apostle teaches us that something similar is going on with the church of the living God. For the church has not been created by men cutting living branches off some other tree and immediately grafting them onto a second one in order to assure that they have roots under them that sustain the new branches. No, no, not at all! That would be to reject the outpouring of the Holy Spirit, the living union of the church with its Head, as well as the fact that all spiritual realities are rooted in divine election. No! And it would also be to deny that the church of the living God was first present in the Word of God, like a future oak tree is already present in an acorn. Nor does it recognize that God first laid it in the soil of this world, that it began to grow there as a small sprout, that in time it shot up and was tended by God in the garden of the nation of Israel. But in that first garden plot, it grew too wildly, although it definitely did bear some fruit in the elect (v. 7). But as a tree, a trunk, and an olive producer, things went awry. So the Lord God lopped off the entire crown of the tree. He temporarily rejected Israel. Then he grafted shoots from the wild olives of heathen nations onto the trunk of his elect, where they were nourished by the sap of his church, drawn from the living roots of his Son's glorious organism.

The height of folly would be to think that these added branches that are now the only ones showing green on the once-naked trunk have nothing to do with what preceded them. It would be to forget that all their present beauty depends, both now and going forward, on Isaiah's root out of dry ground that is now blooming again.

But that's in fact how they want to think. In their foolishness, they yield to that notion. Then they think they are free of Israel. That's when they think that they have accomplished what's happening. And that's exactly why Paul admonishes them so sternly: "You do not support the root, but the root supports you." For—and if all my brothers would only listen to this word—being cut off from the root does not yet amount to being cut off from Israel. This least of all! But it does mean being separated from the Son of the living God, from your Mediator and from the Stronghold of your life. For Israel is nothing and Abram is nothing, but when they are planted in him, the living sap of your Lord rises!

Impress that on your heart and never let go of it until all your brothers grasp it.

The frantic searching and pressing by the many enthusiasts among those who are orthodox, also in our day, cannot and will not last very long unless the children of our time once again reflect on the tree where they are only branches. Let them reflect on the trunk crowned by the branches, on the sap that flows up that trunk as the source of life, and finally on the roots on which the trunk rests.

When you once grasp that, you will naturally be connected again to the doctrine, vitality, and spirit of our fathers of old. Remember that it wasn't the case that Calvin amounted to something, or that Gomarus accomplished so much, or that the fathers of Dort caused a great deal to happen. Simply tell it like it is. Learn it well. Calvin was a mere creature. Gomarus was a guilty sinner. The entire circle of Dort fathers in and of themselves was of no account with God. Then you and your children will really feel tied to the lives of those men, to the monuments memorializing them, and especially to the Scriptures on which those monuments rest. That's because in doing so, you'll be confessing: "That was also the body of Christ in their day, and it was also Christ who was working in that body then." Or you could put it this way: "It was Christ who was already at work in those days through the roots, the trunk, and the rising sap by which my soul is alive today."

I AM AGAINST YOU

Prophesy and say: "This is what the Lord God
says, 'I am against you.'" Ezekiel 35:2–3

There are two ways of doing things that the Lord God has in his dealings with people and nations.

On the one hand, he shows divine patience and long-suffering. On the other hand, in a given situation he definitely and noticeably breaks with a long-suffering approach. Then in his wrath he attacks the rebellious and obstinate sons of men, humbles them in his anger, and terrifies them with the over-whelming force of his judgment.

What is the reason for either? The deepest reason is that he does so only for the sake of his name and its honor.

Remember that the Lord God does not only have to deal with sinners, but also with the Devil. The book of Job makes this very clear. Why do you think all the waves and breakers of the Almighty pounded on pious Job's tired, hurting head? It certainly wasn't because of his exceptional sinfulness. It wasn't to sanctify him further through suffering, either. It wasn't even actually to test his faith. It was only because the Devil taunted God about his servant Job, and with a laugh from hell on his lips he charged that God's work in Job was not genuine but only seemed so because of Job's wealth and privilege. That's why Job had to suffer. Not because God doubted Job, but precisely because God did not doubt Job. So now, for the sake of his name's honor, he wanted to demonstrate to the Devil just how authentic Job's faith was and how a child of God could withstand such affliction without falling away.

And the Devil was also after something else in badgering God about his people and about his elect children when things were going their way and they, like Job, were free from scandalous sin. Do you really think that Satan would take little notice if God's people would rebuke him?

So, child of the resurrection, what do you think? Do you really think that there can ever be one single sinner who becomes a child of God who is not a thorn in Satan's eye? Do you really think that Satan isn't watching God's children carefully in order to catch them backsliding? And if they do backslide, don't you think that Satan would rub his hands in glee and laugh in God's face because his pious, beloved, and elect children still seem to be such terrible sinners? Satan would taunt God because they were such hypocrites.

And when Satan points his finger at God's children like this, how does the Lord God react to Satan?

Wouldn't it be the reaction of an embarrassed father? A father who has to acknowledge the truth of the matter? One who could offer no rebuttal? And wouldn't he also feel keenly that in Satan's eyes the shame of such a terrible sin doesn't fall only on the sinner, but also directly on the God who had made that kind of sinner his very own child?

Consider the sins in your own life from that perspective for a moment. Then tell me whether you don't get an entirely different feeling about the inexhaustible capacity needed for divine patience. In spite of Satan's devilish laughter, God forbears with you in his indescribable long-suffering. Instead of immediately rejecting you, he causes you to scarcely notice the pain that you have caused him. In his fatherly compassion, knowing what kind of creature you are, he admonishes you and moves you to do better by the power of his Word. He sends his angels to rein you in. Then you pray by the power of the Holy Spirit that you will not grieve the love of your Father.

As far as God himself is concerned, note well that as the All-Merciful One he will definitely continue to be unceasingly long-suffering. But if the Lord God in his opposition to Satan risked depending on your love for your Father, and that didn't help, and Satan noticed that it didn't and laughed at God's expense, wouldn't it be different? What if in that case Satan said to God, in his demonic tone of voice: "Look there, Lord! You said they are your children and they don't lie; but look again, what do you think about your children now?" Tell me, my good reader, wouldn't there finally have to come a time when the Lord God, for the sake the honor of his name, might stop being patient and long-suffering? A time when he could wait no longer?

What if you just persisted in your insensitivity and continued in your wicked ways while Satan was busy taunting God? What if you weren't concerned about God at all and remained undisturbed about it? Wouldn't your Father have to take strong action?

Well, that's just what he does in such situations!

He did in fact once say: "My children will not lie!" But he was talking there about children about whom it becomes obvious that they are true children. You can read about them in Isaiah 63:8. In fact, it must and will become obvious already in this life that such children can be found.

But now in your case it seems impossible that you will see the light by means of divine patience, so God has to finally resort to the means of his divine anger.

"Behold, I am against you," says the Lord of Hosts, or rather the deeply aggrieved and indignant Father to his offending child.

THE HANDS OF ZALMUNNA

The officials of Succoth said to him, "Are the hands of Zalmunna already in your hands that we should give you bread here?" Judges 8:6

Gideon is a hero of faith.

He's not an overconfident hero. He doesn't charge ahead recklessly. And he doesn't brag about the strength of his faith.

No, not at all. Gideon is like a weasel that creeps close to the ground and takes no chances. He's not very daring and just lacks confidence. And now his God serves him notice in an extraordinary disclosure that he should pay strict attention to the various signs he has provided for fortifying his faith and lifting him above his lack of confidence.

But how then did the One who works out all things awaken faith in Gideon's heart? How is it that he no longer hesitates but grabs the hilt of his sword and pursues the Midianites? He along with twenty-two thousand troops! Think about what a host that must have been!

But naturally that only weakened his faith once again. A leader who has twenty-two thousand men with him depends a lot less on God than he who stands by himself. And because the Lord God wants to demonstrate to us that Gideon was a hero of faith, he has to get rid of the army. But it has to be reduced not by an act of God. This has to be done through an assignment that God gives

Gideon. Gideon himself has the terrible responsibility of sending that army on its way.

The Holy Spirit works in him in such a way that enables him to do this. So he does it. He says: "Whoever is afraid and fainthearted may leave!" With that offer, more than half slink away, and only ten thousand remain with him.

But even that isn't enough. "No, Gideon! With ten thousand men you're still operating with faith at only one-fourth strength." So now Gideon has to sift out still more chaff. Only those who lap water from their cupped hands without kneeling at the brook may join the pursuit, but none of the others! And Gideon now certainly must have thought that at least half the men would get down on their knees to drink. But no, only a very small group did—a handful, a tiny little band that amounts to nothing. And at this point, Gideon faces this question: "Do you have enough faith to tackle the job now that almost everyone has walked away? Enough to know what has to be done? Enough to do it?"

Remarkably, Gideon is given that faith by the Holy Spirit. So he follows in hot pursuit. He attacks. And he slays the Midianites who fled before him, fled in terror and fled in confusion.

Faith dared and faith triumphed!

This is Gideon the hero of faith! But consider the contrast between this shining example and the shadow cast by the faithless leaders of Succoth.

The people of Succoth trifled with faith.

To be sure, they are also on the side of the Lord and his sacred kingdom! Definitely, they will also participate! Of course they will do their part with the people of the Lord ... except that they first want to see "the hands of Zalmunna."[1]

Zalmunna was the mighty king of Midian. He was a plague on the Israelites' houses. He was a feared tyrant. He was the scourge of Israel. He was someone who would exact bitter revenge if Succoth dared to rise up against him.

That's why they are afraid and shrink back. Oh, they surely want to be rid of Zalmunna. Hail to the hero who will deliver them from that tyrant! But before they can be openly identified with the campaign, they have to be sure that they will suffer no bad consequences from doing so.

If it is first successful, if they can see that it has worked, if the victory has been won, yes, then they will get behind it. They operate with Gamaliel's wrongheaded theory: "If it succeeds, then it is from the hand of God!" Only

---

1. At this stage in biblical history, body parts of defeated enemies were brought back as trophies and confirmations of victory.

then could they fly the flag of the Lord of Hosts. When the attack is no longer needed, then you'll find them prepared to join the charge.

And this is what passes for believing! This is what they call an act of faith, the fruit of prudent faith. And should it be that remaining safely at home back-fires, then such people say: "You see there how well we did by not participating, by not immediately going along with that plan! It's quite obvious now that this was not God's cause!"

Naturally, a person has to protest unconditionally against those who haughtily want to condemn those lovers of "the hands of Zalmunna," thinking: "I definitely have a much more vibrant faith than they do." Please understand that the Gideons of this life already know from experience all the pious singing of Succoth's sons. But although they pursue the Midianites courageously, in their heart of hearts they tremble like reeds in the wind before God. And like faithless children, they implore him for a sign, then for still another in their quest for certainty. They yearn to be reassured by the Holy Spirit.

There's not a whole lot of difference. The Gideonites are in essence people of Succoth, and in silence they yearn just as intensely to see the hands of Zalmunna.

But here's the difference.

The Gideonites see this in themselves and condemn it. So they turn again and again to the Spirit. But in the end, when they undertake their pursuit it's not the hands of Zalmunna that they desire but symbols of God's faithfulness. So they proceed in faith, and in that faith they perform miracles! But the lovers of the hands of Zalmunna stay comfortably at home. They are at peace with their faithless state of heart and mind. What they want most is to project a Pharisaic appearance: either that they have been very discerning in knowing that the whole endeavor would fail, or that they were stouthearted heroes who shared in the victory celebrations when they came.

The latter alternative will not stand the test of eternity because it is not of God and is actually against him.

This is what is to be learned from the people of Succoth.

Gideon triumphs. He ultimately brings back "the hands of Zalmunna." That's when Succoth wants to give bread and nourishment to the Gideonites and sing them a song of triumph.

But Gideon despises them. He stays as far away from these ostentatious fools and their unbefitting homage as possible. In celebrating, he takes thorns and briars of the desert and uses them "to teach the men of Succoth a lesson."

This is how it is with heroes of faith in God's Word. And this is how, by God's will, all who come from Succoth perish because they put more emphasis on seeing the hands of Zalmunna than on the hand of the Lord that is never shortened!

TWO OR THREE SEEN AT THE TOP OF THE HIGHEST BRANCH

*But gleanings will still be left behind, as in the shaking
of an olive tree when two or three olives are still seen
at the top of the highest branch. Isaiah 17:6*

Because of Golgotha, the cross was once and for all impressed on God's children as a symbol and seal of life in this world. As such, that cross can appear in one of two invariable ways. First, if there is peace with the world so that it doesn't persecute, vilify, or kill us, we then mostly languish internally. In the second way, it can point to the fact that the world obviously persecutes Christians and cannot tolerate them. That's when God's children are blessed the most spiritually. Then they are inspired and filled with faith and the Holy Spirit.

The second is by far not the saddest thing that could happen. For if the world banishes and expels you, mocks and taunts you, and finally lays hands on you to persecute you, the first thing that happens is that you get rid of the hypocrites. They become very careful not to identify with you any longer! The second thing that happens is that the hypocrite within you receives a solid body blow of divine grace. You don't have to worry about making a good impression any longer, only about inner resoluteness and conviction. Most of all, then the

Lord gives you a double portion of his grace. He anoints his own people with holy oil day by day. All the strength of his own power gloriously floods the hearts of his redeemed and is expressed by their lips.

That's why a much, much heavier cross, if you're seeing things straight, is laid on Jesus' church in relatively peaceful times. In days such as ours, there is no shortage of opposition, subversion, and reviling. But people still quietly and decently allow you to be who you are and tolerate you doing your own thing, as long as you don't become too intensely zealous about it. Of necessity they still greet you respectfully.

You have to realize that in such times you never really know who you can count on. Partial and wholehearted friends are all scrambled together. In your own life, you always find yourself on side streets and you frequently don't seem to have the energy to travel on the royal highway. The Christian life is dull and uninspiring. It's as though it hasn't pleased the Lord God to raise up people of strength. The entire Christian legacy is receding into the shadows. If not a spirit of deep sleep, then one of sleeping lightly or merely snoozing seems to pervade those who confess Jesus. Wrangling goes on everywhere. You almost never find loyalty that lasts until the end of life. Clinging to fundamental principles doesn't exist anymore. People sullenly recognize that everything is being torn loose. And a frightening question assails your own soul. You ask how you can reach any certainty, any stability, and any insight on how to find the good, tried-and-true path in life. The circle of sisters and brothers lulling around you prefer to offer you the counsel of despair rather than show you the sure road that leads to God and peace in him.

And if you sink under the weight of all this and it finally does you in, what difference does it make? For you know that the world in which the church of Jesus finds itself and out of which it came is impure, sinful, and powerless. It will not tolerate the snow that falls on it white as wool to lie glittering on it in its unstained whiteness more than momentarily. God's truth is certainly fast, sure, and pure. But our own lives, hearts, and consciences are too tattered, fragmented, and flaky for that truth to be anything other than broken and wobbly in our spiritual existence.

What Rome teaches and promises would definitely be wonderful, if it were only true, namely, that the church can provide absolute certainty about anything. But, in fact, it cannot because sin is so terrible, and because it is not permitted for sinners to do anything except to cling to the eternal certainties in the life of faith. And what is the life of faith? What else than to experience those rare, totally blessed moments when the riches of faith are at full strength and it pleases the Lord God to shine with full clarity in our darkened hearts.

That's the situation now, and that's how it will remain until the end. We can't escape such struggle. And until the day we die, we will fall from belief into unbelief in order to once again be raised to faith from unbelief. Meanwhile, the church will stand exposed. And conflicts among the brothers will tear at your heart. Should you long for unity, it won't come. Should you thirst for complete purity in confessing the truth, you will discover spots and blemishes. Your soul will become weary when you see how others aren't bothered by the burden of such struggles. Many will exchange the truths of God for man-made formulations that are an attempt to "be relevant," as the saying goes. The number of those who hold fast to the truth of God's holy Word will shrink. Time and again you are disappointed with the defenses you should have been building. You realize that you fall short daily. And you finally and sadly ask yourself: "Is there no one any longer who fears God? Has all knowledge of him been lost? Are the waters of Pharpar[1] all that's left, and have the little brooks flowing into the Jordan dried up entirely?"

That feeling of abandonment is the most oppressive one imaginable. That's when the cross presses even more heavily. That's how lonely it can become! Then we doubt whether there's anyone left with us! Then we sometimes cry out: "O my God, O my Father, are all these people really that ungodly; do I still dare to take a stand for you?"

That kind of spiritual fear may not be squelched. Its bitter dregs must be swallowed. For "all people who have breath left in their nostrils simply give up." They fall into complete despair in their spiritual abandonment about ultimately finding in God everything that they need. The dearest people here on earth slip the quickest and furthest in their souls.

But if you dare to keep going, that's the moment when you'll find the way out. That's when the Lord God comes to you in his Word and comforts you again. He fills your emptiness and banishes your loneliness. That's when he tells you that this is how it's been throughout the ages and that he, your God, has nevertheless helped his church through it. He also says that others will be reassured by you and by your witness. They will be solidly grounded in the faith through you. He promises that you are not alone, and although you may not know who these people are, God does. He assures you that they are in your immediate

---

1. See 2 Kings 5:12.

surroundings, that they are praying for you, and that in unseen ways they are living right alongside you.

Then our situation is the same as it was with Israel in Isaiah's day. Everything seems to have been harvested and picked bare. It even looks like it has been gleaned. You might almost say: "The olive tree is completely bare." And that's not only true of the part closest to the ground, but also way up on top, where God, looking down on a thin little branch that human eyes had missed, sees a few little olives hanging. There they are, above the heavy branches that have been picked clean. They're swollen with oil and nourishment.

Isaiah says it so beautifully: "Two or three olives are still seen at the top of the highest branch." God's precious sun is shining on them, and his holy eyes didn't miss them!

Yes, let the Lord be praised! That's how it was then. That's how it still is in our own days!

Our amazing Lord is beyond finding out in his saving work.

DISLOYAL TO THE GENERATIONS OF YOUR CHILDREN

If I had said, "I will say it like this," I would have been
disloyal to the generations of your children. Psalm 73:15

Nothing makes as powerful an impression on a person who is isolated, abandoned, and living in loneliness as knowing that they belong to a people and generation for whom nothing can ever get any better.

If you only focused on yourself, you would simply give up. What kind of struggle is that when one weak person faces the whole world with all its smart, powerful, and influential people entirely on their own? They just laugh you off because of your beliefs, right? They just shrug their shoulders at your simple-mindedness. Meanwhile, they fully enjoy the world. They are honored. They get ahead. And it's very obvious that they don't do with less because Immanuel is nowhere to be found in their lives.

But when you were first converted, that wasn't all so bad. Isn't it true that then you thought to yourself and a little voice inside you said: "Why do I need them? Let them have what the world has to offer. I have my God and his Christ, and I'm totally enjoying the love of Christ. Am I not even richer than they are?"

However, things didn't stay that way! While it's true that when your faith life was first kindled, its glow was indescribably beautiful. You were swept off your feet. It was like the warmth you felt from the hearth when, frozen stiff, you first came in from the cold. The inner sensation you had when first converted was even more glorious than that! That was the turning point. That's when you first drank from the Fountain of Everlasting Water. That was your coming through the Red Sea and seeing Pharaoh drowned; that was your celebration, deep in your heart, on the far shore.

But then you had to go through the desert. God's Word put it well for you: "The sufferings of the present time cannot be compared with the glory that will then be revealed." And the Lord's ambassador said it well when he exclaimed: "We walk by faith and not by sight." "In hope, we are blessed, and in nothing else!" But those positive words didn't register with you, and you thought that things would get better. Already now, in this life!

This happened because originally you did not understand the essence of faith. You still didn't grasp that believing is having nothing in your hands. And that was the complete opposite of what you were experiencing to be true. You hadn't yet seen that the certainty of God's blessing doesn't depend on what you experience, but on what God holds before you in his Word. Your response is not surprising. Faith is not something you learn from some little book. Not by going to a catechism class. Not in a sermon. Nor from what someone tells you. Only God teaches you what faith is when he causes you to believe and leads you spiritually into the faith. That's how he taught Abram to believe! And David! And Paul! He did it not by explaining it to them ahead of time, but by leading them into it. And that's how the Lord also does it now, today, with all his children.

It couldn't be otherwise. It had to be like this. That first overwhelmingly blessed experience had to eventually wear off in order to make room for fear, dimness of soul, empty-handedness, being at a loss for words, and branches without fruit. And that's when you first really got serious. The situation now became like this: those worldly folk really did have it good. They were at peace. They really did mock you. Now with respect to those people you in fact came to think that the world did have a lot to offer. But inside you felt so deprived, naked, and miserable that you would have been ashamed if they had been able to see inside you.

That's when faith actually broke through!

Having nothing, but still rejoicing! Rejoicing not based on your experience, but rejoicing because God's Word says you should! Believing based more on what God tells you to your face than on what your soul whispers to you. You got out of the way. God became everything—everything even in the inner working of your soul and in your becoming more holy. Believing, knowing, and being convinced that you were becoming holier in no other way than by, in, and from him. That was the change! He was accomplishing all this in you. He simply couldn't abandon this effort because it had been determined in his eternal counsel that all who are elect are chosen to become holy and blameless before him.

Whoever dares to acknowledge this comes to that point. Better said, they are there already!

But that happens only through fear, apprehension, and dying a thousand deaths. Then you will experience what Asaph did when his feet almost took him out the door, that is to say, when the thankless Asaph was ready to give up on his good and faithful God. He was at the point of allowing the most terrible curse to break loose in his soul. Then he thought it would be better to abandon God and to take up with the Evil One. But what restrained Asaph from such a curse at that moment? Or you can ask what likewise restrains every child of God dealing with a similar situation. God's grace does, you say, and you are correct! God accomplishes this. What I mean is this: How does that occur in the deliberating that such a troubled child of God does on those occasions? How do they work that out in the depths of their soul? Do they think about God? About Jesus? About his atoning blood? Oh, all of that only comes later! Their first response is completely different. It's totally understandable and completely human! They simply think that there's more of the same coming, that it's always been like this for the children of God.

If I were to say anything different, "I would be disloyal to the generations of your children!"

Whether he saddened his God didn't matter to Asaph very much at that moment. What did matter was that he was recognized as one who kept faith with his brothers. He thought: This huge crowd of witnesses has endured things like this for all these centuries. Now I'm one of them. I'm giving up and I'm going to find out what they loathed and identify with them in their drudgery.

Faithless? Not at all, for God has preserved me for this!

I'll never be a traitor!

That's when the loneliness disappears. That's when the spirits of all the completely justified surround us and when the martyrs wave their palm branches of victory over our heads. That's when we hear the angelic hosts rejoicing.

Praise God! I'm there!

The battle is over. Let the world enjoy itself and even mock me. And if in so doing they even scoff at God, I remain filled with holy confidence. I testify to them that I may definitely be despised, and naked, and have but few possessions, but in order to become a king ... by faith!

8 5
VOLUME I

EMPTY, SWEPT CLEAN, AND NICELY DECORATED

Then the unclean spirit says, "I will return to my house
from which I came"; and returning, he finds it empty,
swept clean, and nicely decorated. Matthew 12:44

When we hear Jesus talking, then the battle going on between Satan and our souls about our salvation takes on unbelievably serious proportions. This begins when wicked, unclean spirits nestle into the folds of our heart, like night owls and field mice nest in a hollow tree or the crevice of a rock. We're not talking here about the Devil, the prince of darkness, or about the terrible Satan in our own inner person. No, we're speaking about the spirits that he supports there, that he inspires in his wickedness, and that he uses as his instruments for robbing souls from God. These impure spirits force their way into us gradually and postage free. Then they become bolder. While in the beginning they get comfortable in some hidden corner, ultimately they play the part of boss of our entire heart. They act like they're lord and master and finally claim: "This person's heart is 'my house'" (Matt 12:44).

That's when resistance on the part of our soul begins. The ungodly side of us still wants to accommodate these impure spirits. It tolerates them as live-ins by way of exception. But when that impure spirit takes off its mask, instead of serving us it starts giving us orders in our own home, our hearts. Then our pride causes us to resist, and we do our level best to give that impure spirit no peace, to make life unbearable for him, and thus force him to start looking for a change in residence.

Most of the time that works.

That's what Jesus means in this parable when he talks about an unclean spirit leaving a man, not because it was thrown out by Jesus, but leaving of its own accord because it was "seeking rest." This is definitely a sign that the person into whose heart the impure spirit had penetrated had made things uncomfortable for it.

We're not talking here about a converted person, but on the contrary about an unconverted person whom Beelzebub the overseer of devils in his craftiness caused to motivate and compel the unclean spirit to take flight.

Just look at what happens next!

When the impure spirit was gone and moving around through waterless places, that good man went to work on the home that was his heart. His plan worked. The last occupant had taken to his heels. Things were falling into place nicely. Now he was boss in his own heart once again. He was a free man once more. He could do what he thought best just as before. But he also wanted to get some recognition for what he'd achieved. So the first thing that occurred to him was to clean his house from top to bottom immediately and thoroughly. For the unclean spirit had been sitting everywhere, and everything with which he had come into contact was filthy and stained. Thus, the man literally swept the house of his heart clean, bottom to top, until there was not a single spot or speck of dust left by the unclean spirit that could be detected anywhere. This done, he could truly say that now everything was neat and lovely once more.

But he didn't even stop at that! He also wanted to decorate his house, that is, he didn't only want to get rid of what was bad, but he wanted to redecorate the place with virtues. Yes, it seemed to his neighbors as though the man living next door had not only broken with all his sins, but that above all he had become the epitome of quiet goodness and virtue.

The only thing was, his heart remained empty! Besides himself, no one else was living there. The impure spirit had fled in order to find peace and quiet. But no one heard about anyone else coming in to take his place.

That's the way things stayed for a little while, and it went well. But that didn't last long. For the impure spirit had left looking for rest. But it wasn't obvious that he was finding it anywhere! What if he, instead of finding peace and rest out there, was discovering that things were only worse? And he did. So he immediately decided that he would rather live in continual conflict with the owner of that heart than to continue running around so restlessly. What if that impure spirit would return?

Yes, the owner of the heart had considered that possibility. But he wasn't perturbed about it. He had taken his own measures against that happening. He had chosen for the good. But above all, even if the unclean spirit were to force his way back in, he was now stronger morally and in a position to throw the intruder out by force, if necessary. No, no! Just have a look at his beautiful heart now swept clean and nicely decorated. What would anyone with a heart like that have to fear about evil? A clear conscience is a reliable charm for warding off the Devil!

That's how the man thought.

But he miscalculated badly. For something happened that he had not considered at all. The unclean spirit returned, but he didn't come alone. He was crafty as well. He knew that he was at considerable risk in trying to carry it off alone. That's why he was so careful that he took accomplices with him. Eight of them came. This is how the Lord continued telling the story: "Then he goes out and takes seven other spirits with him, more wicked than himself."

Oh my! Who would have suspected such a terrible state of affairs? How could the man put up any resistance?

What kind of drivel is this about you "keeping them out of your house"? Before you can even think about it, you're thrown completely off balance. You find yourself flung to the ground. And the eight frightening spirits have set up their devilish style of housekeeping in the house that you have swept clean and decorated so nicely.

You fail. You fail miserably. And the neighbors of your heart just shake their heads about life there now; it's a curse on the man who yesterday was living so serenely.

And they won't leave again, those unclean spirits. Now "they live there." And "the last state of that man becomes worse than the first." What troubling words! "Worse than the first"! And hadn't he had good intentions? Hadn't he broken confidently with his sinning? Didn't the neighbors talk together about his exemplary good-heartedness? It all seemed possible, but in the end things got worse instead of better, and now in a very real sense he had become a football for the players on Satan's team.

When that unclean spirit returned with seven other evil spirits, what was really involved? Isn't it that in the beginning his sinning was expressed mainly as one specific sin, but later all the major sins gripped his soul equally? The outcome was that his entire way of life was now in the service of the Devil.

Are you asking how that happened? Jesus himself tells us how. Arriving, that unclean spirit found the house "swept clean and nicely decorated," but "empty." The unclean spirit had left, to be sure, but the Holy Spirit had not come in. Satan had definitely been thrown out, but Jesus had not been brought in. The result was that the heart was empty. No one was living there.

No one, that is, except the pathetic little "I." Simply because Jesus had not been brought in, it was an "I" that revealed that it was deeply enmeshed in hypocrisy and imagined that it could save itself. This gave every appearance of conversion, but it was not genuine conversion. It was nothing less than wanting to do by oneself what only the God of mercy could do.

Sin in fact remained in that house that had apparently been cleansed of sin. For being "empty" on the inside is also sinful. It is in fact the ultimate sin, because it's as though a person is saying to Jesus: "I can make it apart from you. I can be saved even in my own emptiness." And that goes directly contrary to all God's ordinances.

You are intended to be inhabited, O man, O woman. You are intended to be a temple. You are intended to be led by a spirit holding the reins and who is mightier than you. That could be Satan; it might be Jesus!

The person who says: "No, I'll just inhabit my own heart" has let go of Jesus and becomes Satan's prize.

"This is how it will be for this evil generation," says Jesus.

O Lord, have mercy, have mercy on us!

YOU ARE LIKE GILEAD TO ME, AND LIKE THE HEIGHTS OF LEBANON

This is what the Lord says to the king of the house of Judah: "You are like Gilead to me, and like the heights of Lebanon. But will I not make of you a desert and uninhabited cities?" Jeremiah 22:6

W hen the Lord our God looks down on our little world from his throne of grace, then it strikes him very differently than it would us.

If we on some occasion were to look down from a high tower or a mountaintop, what would we see? We would see fields and forests, cities and hamlets, brooks and rivers. It would all stretch out as a glorious panorama at our feet. But we would hardly notice the people, who looked so small that they were the size of frogs or grasshoppers. Our eyes would almost exclusively drink in the grandeur of nature and appreciate the lay of the woods and streams.

But it's very different for the Lord our God. For him the trees and valleys scarcely matter, but the world of people is what he finds beautiful, wonderful, and exciting. In Proverbs 8:31, the Messiah said—or better said, sang—through the Holy Spirit: "My delights are in the children of mankind."

The sacred Scriptures frequently present all living souls as objects of the Almighty's faithfulness. In the broader circle of human beings, God does what we do with natural panoramas. We distinguish between deserts and arid places on the one hand, and areas of ordinary beauty and a few spots that are especially striking on the other hand. Similarly, Holy Scripture identifies the people of God as the Lord's garden, a "court of his delights," and "the vineyard that he has planted." The Holy Spirit goes so far as to say about the noblest of God's elect: "House of the kings of Judah, you are like Gilead to me, like the heights of Lebanon, and like a forest of cedars to my eyes."

Wonderful, isn't it, to hear that whispered to us from the Word of God?

And to think that God, who is so invisible and holy, looks down on this intricate world that he has so ingeniously created and scarcely notices the valleys of Gilead and cedars of Lebanon. When we insensitive humans do, on the other hand, we can hardly contain ourselves and feel compelled to cry out: "Isn't nature amazingly beautiful!" God fixes his gaze almost exclusively to those puny little sinful creatures that we call human beings. When he does, he exclaims: "My delights are in human beings." Those are my forests! They, for me, your God, are the most beautiful part of all creation. All of my desires involve the world of humans!

You would say that this is almost unbelievable.

The world of human beings frequently knocks the wind out of you. You consistently avoid it and favor finding your delight in God's creation. Even those in your closest circles irritate, grieve, and sadden you. That holds for those who are Godfearing as well as those who aren't. Sometimes the former vex you the most. Then to hear from God: "My delight is in human beings"! Or to listen to your God saying: "You are like Gilead to me, and like the heights of Lebanon!"

Incredible! Are we mistaken on this point? Aren't people really as terribly impure, wicked, godless, and scandalous as we had imagined?

Well, let God's Word give you the answer to those questions. Then you'll discover that you're still thinking much too highly about human beings. They have sunk much lower than you imagined. Take your own soul and your own person, for example. Where you're concerned, things are much worse than people think or than you will admit. You can see this clearly in the Bible verse that stands at the beginning of this meditation. Those monarchs and princes about whom it is being said: "You are like Gilead to me, and like the heights of

Lebanon" were scandalously ungodly people. In the eyes of the Lord God they had become thoroughly bloodthirsty.

If you want to understand the mystery involved here, O my child, recognize that this glorious and holy God never takes his delight in what the creature does, but only in his own work. God's work can be seen in every tree and in each flower. His work is obvious in every bird singing in the forest. But infinitely higher is the work that God does in his human children. We see it already in how they are able to think and speak and pray. But highest and best of all is his work of saving grace. From beings whose breath is in their nostrils and who are made from the dust to which they will return, he makes sparkling stars in his firmament, children of his own life, and eternal beings to celebrate before his throne forever. That surpasses all the other ingenious work of the Supreme Builder.

If God displayed the power of his majesty to his angels, then like Solomon did for the queen of Sheba, wouldn't the All-Merciful God pass in review on his holy mountain the entire gathering of those who are fully justified in heaven? When he does, wouldn't he exclaim: "All these were at one time ungodly; but look at what I in my grace have made of them"?

This is how a person comes to understand how the Lord God has greater satisfaction in this work precisely because humanity had sunk so deeply. He wanted to enhance the reputation of his mercy through what he had accomplished with the mass of ungodly humanity. This is where we grasp the riddle of his delight in the dry, dead branches made alive again through his grace.

Every human heart where grace is at work is a workshop that exhibits the creativity of amazing, divine grace. Every human being who was dead and who crossed from death to life is a gorgeous garden of the heavenly Gardener. And all those souls collectively, in whom the life-giving sap of God's Word is flowing and working and producing spiritual maturity, constitute God's Gilead. They are his cedars of Lebanon. About them, Psalm 92 says: "The righteous people will grow as though in Lebanon, nourished by the sun, the palm, and the cedar together. You who have been planted in the house of the Lord, in his courts, will mature and increase by the hand of the Lord."[2]

So where does the Lord in his holy omniscience see the dividing line when he looks down on the children of men? Where is the dividing line between the desert places, where everything is shriveled, and the plains of Gilead, where

---

2. Kuyper is taking exceptional liberty here, perhaps citing from memory parts of Psalm 92:12–13 and other places.

everything is blooming? Just before this, in verse 3, the Holy Spirit answers this through the prophet: "Do what is just and right." Mercy attends them. Let mercy dwell in your soul. "Deliver the person who has been robbed by the hand of the oppressor. Do not oppress the stranger or the widow and orphan." And if you show mercy like this, I will be your God. "Otherwise, will I not make you desolate? Yes, I will sanctify your oppressors, each of them prepared to chop down your spreading cedars!"

Don't simply slide over these soul-searching words, brothers and sisters! Give them an "Amen" in your hearts.

It can't be any different than this. It has to happen this way. The godless will have no peace, says our God. And this is when you cry out in the depths of your poor soul: "Then what about me, for how can I act righteously?"

Now then, if you do lament that uprightly, consider the cedars of the forest and how they grow. They do not labor. They do not weave their own leaves, and yet Solomon in all his splendor was never more glorious than one of these.

Just pull that tree from the ground by its roots. Bury it in your cellar, without the fertile earth from which to draw its sap, without the life-giving light from which it draws strength, without the sun shining down on it and giving it warmth, then watch what happens. The tree dies; it withers and rots. But when the tree is deeply rooted in good earth, it doesn't declare: "I think I'll start to grow!" That happens naturally. It grows just by living. It exhales the air again that it first breathed in. Its leaves shine.

And that's how you should proceed.

Apart from Christ, beyond the influence of his Holy Spirit, resistant to the warmth of highest heaven, you're going to shrivel and die in ungodliness and shame. You'll languish, and your complete disappearance will be close behind. You'll loathe yourself. You'll be a hindrance to God's angels. You'll offend the love of God's Son.

If you want to grow and blossom, don't be a fool who spreads his roots in the air and buries her branches in the earth. But live your life rooted in Christ. Allow all your leaves to drink in the air of the Spirit. Cherish the Son of Righteousness in your heart.

Being rooted, drinking in, and cherishing—what is all of this if it isn't believing? You, nothing! He, everything! And whatever there ever will be in you, let it be only what he has first imparted to you. Oh, you know it well. It is the centuries-old but ever-fresh living testimony of that great cloud of witnesses: "A righteous person lives, but only by faith!"

That's how it is in the courts of the Lord!

87
VOLUME I

HAVING FALLEN ASLEEP

In the same way even these men, having fallen asleep, pollute
the flesh, reject authority, and slander heavenly beings. Jude 8

Along with the profound and wonderful comfort found in the notion of
the soul falling asleep is the even more frightening thought of deadly
danger and spiritual death.

Everyone understands the comfort involved.

For when a child of God wanders off on ungodly paths, that's when the
sacred Word of God comes to them in their doubting faith and talks to them
about their spirit sleeping. It happens when their faith leaves them. When
there's no longer any sign of the Spirit's presence. When their heart is so cold
it's like the chill of death. When their heart is even cold toward God, Jesus,
and about their own salvation. When despair envelops their heart so totally
that they already hear hell claiming their soul. It's as though it whispers to
them: "Don't despair. Simply believe. Your soul isn't dead yet. Praise God that
what you're experiencing is only your spirit in a deep sleep, one that Satan has
thrown over it like a blanket."

Then the soul revives. "So I'm not really dead! I haven't committed the sin
against the Holy Spirit! There is still mercy and forgiveness for me from above!
I wasn't dead after all, just sleeping! Wake me up, since I've only fallen asleep.
Raise me from among those who are without facial expression and appear to

be dead. Wake up! Stay awake! Get up! Then, O Lord Jesus, shine in my soul once more just like you did earlier in your most tender love."

That comfort is certainly wonderful for the guilty child of God. Who can count all those who have almost expired but who are precisely at the point of hearing the verdict "not yet dead but only sleeping" and of being snatched from ruin and the grip of the Devil?

But, and this is a big "but," is this all that needs to be said? Isn't there a great deal more packed into these frequent scriptural references to our souls being asleep? Isn't there a voice making an urgent appeal here?

Look, when the child of God is in real despair, is genuinely afraid, and their heart is so barren that they think they're already sliding toward hell, they really aren't sleeping anymore. Then they're already awake. They've already been shaken awake. Then a ray of light from the everlasting morning has already touched their soul. A child of God stays asleep only as long as they don't notice being on that slippery slope descending toward hell. They can still pray during that kind of sleep. They can still dream about God's counsel and his decrees involving salvation. They can think hard and long about such profound mysteries. But all of this is only the imaginary activity. There's no reality in it. Their prayer isn't really praying. God's counsel doesn't lift their spirits any more. The mysteries no longer have a holy beauty for them or make any impact on them. They no longer comfort the soul no longer yearning for comfort.

And that's how the poor children of God sometimes sleep stacked like piles of cordwood, sometimes as an entire congregation. That's when things are at their worst, for there's no one to warn them. There's no one to shout: "The Philistines are upon you, Samson!" On one, that is, except the One who never slumbers. The Shepherd of Israel. Your Father, O child of God.

Where does that cold sleep originate?

It overcomes you by the inscrutable determination of him who called you into life, as no one denies. Apart from his will, not a hair will fall from your head. How then will he not cause a deadly sleep to fall on your soul? And God is righteous, always compassionate. Then if you have to experience that kind of sleep, there's a definite reason for it. There's some reason within you why that light needs to be withdrawn from you for a time. There's some reason why you seriously forfeited the glory of staying awake.

But who was the instrument of putting you in a deep sleep? Who drugged you? Who administered the sleeping potion? Who sang into your listening ear the lullaby that put you to sleep?

Don't be concerned about the fact that what we have here is a book that's only one chapter long, my good reader. Jude, a servant of Jesus Christ, writes something very remarkable in this single chapter. He conveys that already in Christ's early church terrible sinning had broken out. Men of Sodom had slipped in among the brothers. The church and its overseers had taken such a weak position on this that these people were even admitted to the church's love feasts, where men and women sat together in the name of the Lord.

Do you want to know how that was possible? Do you want to know how already in the early church such terrible impurity of the flesh, such blasphemy against holy ordinances, and such rejection of divine authority could occur? Then read what this servant of Jesus Christ says in verse 8. He writes that they "fell asleep." This is obviously to say no more and no less than that they succumbed to such blatant evil and became oblivious to it when they were lulled to sleep by the Devil.

Putting people to sleep, drugging them, rendering them unconscious, causing them not to notice things, rendering them senseless, turning them into putty in others' hands, and making them deaf to the Word of God, all of this is definitely the personal work of the Devil.

That's what a thief does when he wants to steal from you! That's what he does when he wants to rob you of the wealth, security, and treasures that you have from God.

Now do you understand why the disciples were sleeping in Gethsemane? Do you understand why time and again Jesus stirred their souls in both parables and sayings to "watch, watch, therefore"? And do you also understand now why the apostles, once awakened for all time, so persistently appealed to the church exactly because of Gethsemane? They warned the church to be vigilant against such sleeping. And when it was already half asleep, do you see why they had to quickly wake it up again?

"Wake up to righteousness and stop sinning, for some of you have no knowledge of God. I say this to your shame."[1] "Wake up, you who are sleeping. Arise from the dead and let Christ shine on you." "We know the timely opportunity we have; the hour is here for us to awake from sleep." "The night has passed and the day has come. Let us put off the works of darkness and put on the weapons of light." "You are all children of light and children of the day. ... So then let us

---

1. 1 Corinthians 15:34. Kuyper's Dutch version, like the KJV and unlike most modern translations, uses the command to stay awake here.

not sleep, as others do, but let us stay awake and be sober."[2] "We who belong to the day, let us put on the breastplate of faith and love!" This is the tone of intense seriousness that runs through the entire Scripture. It's the tone in which God addresses us in Scripture because he knows his own children are at the point of slumbering. And he also knows all about the frightening feelings that sleep of the soul can produce.

Oh, it's a battle to stay awake against the power of such numbing sleep, as I well know. When the eyelids get heavy! When fogginess crawls over our spirits and every attempt to stay clear-headed fails! When we still want to cry out, but our voice sticks in our throat, and our lips quiver but shape no words! When we grasp at the chance to see heaven, but a veil falls across God, his throne, and his angelic hosts! When we no longer pay attention to what we should! When everything around us becomes dull and gray and lifeless! When we still want to pray but are disgusted with our empty muttering and we simply quit without speaking an "Amen" over what isn't worth one!

Yes, it's really awful when even then we see the image of our Savior through the veil of such mists. We see him moving around from a great distance and we still want to shout: "Come, Lord Jesus. Come quickly." But the problem is that Satan is standing right next to us. We want to struggle and get loose, but we just can't. Things have gone too far. We quit struggling. Our eyelids sag. The mists engulf us completely. That's how terrible it gets! There's nothing left to do about it, except that your God still has the power over you even in that sleep! With his thundering voice he calls out to your soul. Satan has to leave. And you wake up again. In your self-criticism over the sleep into which you had fallen, you soberly realize that all of it has been left at the foot of the cross.

That point is never lost on God's children. Once they are awake again, they never say: "O God, Satan did this to me!" Rather, they blame themselves. They confess that it happened because of their sinning, and now contrite and converted, they approach their Father and say: "Father, I have sinned against heaven and against you. I am not worthy of being called your child. Treat me as one of your hired servants."

That's not some dream; it's real! For understand this clearly, my sister and brother. Whoever does not want to succumb to the numbing effects of sleep jumps up as soon as Satan tries to close the windows. And they say: "Stop, you dirty Devil! Leave the windows open. I want the fresh air coming in off God's holy mountain to keep me awake!" Or, if you want to use a different illustration,

---

2. 1 Thessalonians 5:5–6. Kuyper omits part of verse 5.

you won't stretch out on your bed when Satan wants to sing you a lullaby. You'll stay on your feet, pacing back and forth. You'll plug your ears and sing a psalm of praise in a loud voice instead.

So, watch out, those of you relaxing on a soft pillow. You're going to slip off if that's how you're lying down! Lift your head off that pillow. As one of Jesus' warriors, you have to stay on your feet, fresh and alert. Let the light shine in your heart, because Satan lurks in the darkness. And where the light from above is shining, Satan flees; he can't withstand it. So if you keep the candle burning beside you and don't blow it out, he'll never be able to sing you his deadly lullabies.

EVEN THE REBELLIOUS LIVE IN YOUR PRESENCE

Yes, even the rebellious live in your presence,
O Lord my God. Psalm 68:18¹

No position is more seriously disappointing and more sadly disavowed in its outcome than the opinion that people can be divided into the unconverted, who rise up against God in rebellion, and the converted, who walk behind their Shepherd as obediently and submissively as sheep.

That was never the case! It's never been like that! And it never will be!

Just ask yourself who is more persistent in asking for the forgiveness of sins. Who does so from the depths of their soul and in spirit and truth? Who consistently feels deeply sorry? Who continually lies in dust and ashes before their God, brokenhearted and with psalms of penitence on their lips?

Do you think this is happening with the unconverted? Do you suppose it's the unconverted that resonate with an expression such as "How everyone laments, complaining about their sins?" If you do, you'd be sadly mistaken!

---

1. Psalm 68:19 in Dutch versions.

No, we do not question the fact that even the most defiant people now and then experience twinges of conscience and are unsettled. They have some impression of God's terrible anger. We know that even outside Golgotha's cross people can be shocked by their own wickedness. There can even be a tearful search for relief from sorrow without a tormented soul ever finding such a place.

The actual, steady, and increasing thirst for the forgiveness of sins you don't find with the children of the world. Nor do you find pleas for mercy there. Rather, these you find precisely with those that you would think rise far above the need for them. You find them only with the children of God. And you find them there not only at the time of their conversion or shortly afterwards but until the day that they die.

They were rebellious. But because they are bound to the horns of the altar with cords of everlasting mercy despite themselves, they are always convinced in their heart of hearts that they are capable of fleeing that altar should their High Priest whom they confess ever cut those cords. But they are definitely no longer what they once were! On the contrary! They have become changed people! Earlier they would have found it horrible if they had thought that Jesus could capture their rebellious heart. But now, by way of contrast, they would find it horrible to think that Jesus would ever let go of their rebellious soul. Despite that being so, they remain rebellious people who are tied to Jesus with strength far stronger than their own.

To be sure, the stronger force with which they are bound to Jesus is no external force. It's not like the rope that a Levite used to force a bull or ram to lower its head before the altar. No, Jesus uses inner bonds. You can't see them. This is spiritual work. He binds you, and you don't understand how. He holds you securely, and you don't notice what he's using. Jesus even gets to the point of using that stronger force to keep your will in check, so far, in fact, that your will finally desires what at first it did not want.

But whatever is used to achieve that inner submission, the child of God here on earth retains the feeling until the day they die that something else keeps tugging at their soul. A power is working on it! The sense remains that if that power ever stopped working, they would snap loose like the stave of a barrel or like a rubber band released and that they would regress, far away from Jesus.

In actuality, things are going far better than that child perceives. But inwardly they feel deeper forces at work within that pull them away from Jesus. They want to follow along when Jesus leads with his tether. But even in that desire to go with him, a resistance is tugging and pulling in a different direction. It's as though the doorposts and window frames of a person's soul are sagging and crooked! The depths of their heart are exposed. And the pool bubbling up within is frightening. With brighter light, all the filthy splattering it produces can be seen. In the end, the self-conscious child of God sinks into deeper dejection that doesn't weaken but becomes stronger as time passes. They complain: "O Lord, how could my miserable heart be so terribly ungodly?"

That's what gives rise to the appeal "Cleanse me with hyssop!" And to the complaint "Lord, Lord, hear my prayer!" And when they hear from others who claim that they can no longer pray the fifth petition of the Lord's Prayer, they don't understand them. But they don't condemn them either; they simply say that they live by a different gospel than he does. They admit that they would be lying to God if they suggested otherwise.

Yes, God's children are rebellious until the day they die. But when they first recognize that Jesus is tugging at them, they know by that tugging that they are rebellious people who must live in God's presence. Living with God! Above! In the Father's house! Willingly! In one of the many rooms that Jesus will have already prepared!

But for now they are still living in that hidden Zion, in the house of God that constitutes the church. In sweet communion! Enfolded in that secret fellowship of the redeemed! No longer living along with the world, but dwelling with God!

Yet, how?

In such a way that the Lord of the house could freely throw open all the doors, could dismiss the watchmen, and could loosen all ties to it! But look, if the Lord God did that, as terrible as it is to admit this, then all God's children who had not yet walked through the gates of death would scamper their way out of God's holy dwelling and fall into ruin. They know they would!

And just because they know that, and because they find it so horrifying should they lose touch with their God, they don't say: "O my Lord, I love you so much and am so confident of my situation that I know that you are capable of overlooking everything and that I will still dwell in your presence!" No, they say just the opposite: "O my God and Father continue to uphold me. Let your watchmen stay alert so that I do not slip away. Don't loosen the bands of your everlasting love, for things are good only in your presence. Only with you are things wonderful! Glorious! But my own heart would mislead me and my fleshly appetites would kill me. Like a sheep, I have so often wandered off and looked around instead of staying with you as your child. Show me your favor. In your grace, favor me by living in my heart.

The Savior hears that prayer!

And when he sees that we are rebellious and would like to flee from God but still want to live in fellowship with him, he comes with his reassuring comfort in the words of this unwavering promise:

> I have determined for the people's comfort
> that even my conflicted children
> will always live near to God.[2]

Then he accomplishes it. He does what he promises. The outcome is that your rebellious soul is still living and keeps on living in the presence of your God.

---

2. Untranslated, this portion of the rhymed hymn Kuyper quotes here reads:
Ik heb gaven tot der menschen troost,
Opdat zelfs het wederhoorig kroost
Altijd bij God zou wonen.

LIKE A LOST SHEEP

I have gone astray like a lost sheep. Look for your servant, for
I have not forgotten your commandments. Psalm 119:176

The lost sheep of Psalm 119 is not someone who is foolhardy and estranged from God. They are not a child of the world whose prayers are frivolous. They are not unconverted. But they are a child of God and servant of Jehovah. They are someone who keeps God's law and is penitent and converted. But they are the kind of person who, after believing, once again strays from the way of salvation. In the realities of daily living, that happens to such a "sheep" through mere negligence and lighthearted inattention.

By nature, a sheep doesn't act that way! It seems like the sheep of any given flock cling together so tightly that they can't live without each other. That's why they crowd together the way they do. It's as though they mimic God's cherubim living together. You can literally say about sheep and their flock: "Where one goes, they all go; where one stops and stands, they all stop and stand still as well."

A sheep is the most defenseless, helpless, and dependent animal imaginable. It is so constituted that it doesn't act, but it reacts like the others do. It doesn't lead, but it follows. It doesn't take initiative, isn't assertive, and isn't curious. This just isn't in its nature! Someone else has to find the pasture. Someone else has to lead them to a meadow and show them where to eat. Then a sheep eats. Then it lives. Then it is wondrously carefree.

But now consider what a separated sheep is like! The psalmist expresses it so graphically in a single word. A separated sheep is "lost." It's not only the case that such a wayward animal feels tremendously unsettled, but it looks for the other sheep of its flock. But they're not around. So it bleats for its shepherd. He doesn't answer. It longs for the meadow, but all around it are sand and rocks. What's even worse is that a separated sheep is totally helpless. Accustomed only to following, it hasn't a clue how to find the way back. It sees no path. It wouldn't know a path if it saw one. If it did, it would take it the wrong way. It just walks in circles there in the wilderness, without any idea where to go. Finally, it just collapses, tired of walking, totally fatigued, and lying against a rock, it begins bleating, and crying, and simply shrieking. What would it ever be able to do in such a situation if it weren't for the nipping of the shepherd's dog? The shepherd, the shepherd! He's the only one who can bring it back. Otherwise it would die. It would languish and expire.

Bless me with life, O my shepherd. Search for your separated, lost sheep!

So you can clearly see that by the lost sheep the psalmist is referring to a child of God and absolutely not to someone who is unconverted. What also strikes you is that he is talking about himself and not about someone else. "I, I myself am that lost sheep," he is in effect saying. "It is I who love God's law. It is I who find my satisfaction in keeping God's commandments. It is I who has been singing: 'Your loving care has never disappointed me.' But I have disdained your flock. I have lost sight of my shepherd. So now here I lie, gone astray and dead tired, humbled and lost. I'm left with only one defense against fighting off complete destruction. I can still simply cry out: 'Pour life back into my soul!' I can still confess: 'I have gone astray like a sheep that has unwittingly lost sight of its shepherd.' But, contending with the Devil, hell, and the reproach of my own heart, I still glory in the language of faith that professes: 'I am steadfast in wanting to hear your call once more!' "

The psalmist did not get to the point of acknowledging his shame all on his own. The Holy Spirit forced it out of him. This is first of all and naturally because he was the one who was searched for, found, and rescued. He was the one who was returned to the pasture of God's hidden joys, to the flock that God loves, and to the watchful eye of the Good Shepherd. But all of this occurred for a higher purpose.

The apostle says that all that was written earlier was written for your benefit. It was written so that you might find hope in the patience and reassurance expressed in Scripture. This is why the Holy Spirit compelled the psalmist to describe the state of his soul like that of a lost sheep. It's why he moved him to put it in song and to sing it. It wasn't only for the psalmist's benefit but for that of all God's estranged children. It was to shed light on the separated and lost condition that can overcome your heart. It was so you might discover yourself in these closing words of the psalmist's song. It was so you could grasp the clear, helpful, pure truth about yourself once all the empty, imaginary interpretation of these verses has been wiped away. It was so that you could be brought to the point of exclaiming: "Yes, that really lays out my situation with God truthfully. That's how it is with my soul! O God, be gracious to me, a poor sinner!"

This creates patience. This brings comfort from Scripture. And by way of patience and comfort comes hope. Hope, yes; but definitely not the hope that we will be able to stumble across some little stream or find a small patch of green pasture grass by ourselves. That's not hope at all. It's false hope. For if our souls react like that, it's as though the sand is more parched, the rocks are all the hotter, and everything around us is mocking our separated souls' sense of being self-sufficient.

Nor is it the hope that by trying once again, we will finally find the correct path back. That's because if we take to heart what the psalmist spoke from his heart, we are blind to that path. We can't see it anymore. We wouldn't recognize it if we could. And we wouldn't be able say whether it headed east or south.

No, that hope consists only and entirely in the fact that we're able to believe again. We're able to believe that we have the kind of gracious Shepherd who would leave his other ninety-nine sheep behind in the wilderness in order to start looking for the one that was lost. We're able to believe in a Shepherd who is incapable of thinking: "Well, that sheep is gone anyway. It's his own fault. Just let it stay lost!" Rather, he says to himself: "That one sheep is also one that I received from the Father!" So out of respect for his Father's will, he sets out and searches for that sheep until he finds it. He doesn't quit until he does.

That kind of hope comes because we believe again. It comes because we believe that we have such a mighty Shepherd that he has the ability to find the exact spot where we're lying down. He's so strong that no matter what the distance is between us, he's able to hear our souls moaning for him. Whether it's over cliffs or through treacherous terrain, nothing is too painful or too difficult for finding "the lost child" and returning them to their God and ours.

Let me ask who is so lost that they cannot be found?

Not someone who says: "Lord, I'm going to come looking for you!" But one who cries with all the energy left in their faith: "Lord, search for me, your servant!"

Not one who appeals: "Save me so that I may yet live!" But one who implores: "Favor me with life so that I may still praise you!" One who dares to testify, even when they lie near death: "I am steadfast in listening to our voice!"

Yes, truly, God comes quickly for such as these. He finds them again. They shall yet praise him!

If this is how things are with you, my brother and my sister, then lift your eyes to the mountains, from where your only help can possibly come. That's where he beckons. He beckons from afar. Your good and faithful and divine Shepherd beckons to you!

To see him again is to live again! Isn't that true?

The person that sees him again can praise him once more.

Therefore, praise him, all his people! For all his people have gone astray, but they have all come through that experience.

We were all lost sheep, each in our own time and in our own way.

90
VOLUME I

FORGIVENESS AND THE FEAR OF THE LORD

With you is forgiveness, therefore you are feared. Psalm 130:4

The twelve articles of the Apostles' Creed don't only include "I believe in God the Father, the Almighty"; or, "I believe in Jesus Christ, his only begotten Son"; or, "I believe in the Holy Spirit." They also include that more puzzling and more incomprehensible "I believe in the forgiveness of sins." Does this affirmation really speak truthfully to your heart so that you can add a hearty "Amen" to it?

To believe that an actual, living being called God exists; to believe that that God has revealed himself in the flesh; and to believe that this God really lives in people's hearts—all of this is already so indescribably immense and so unspeakably glorious that no human heart could have ever actually come up with these ideas by itself!

But if you once get to the point of confessing these things because God gave you the gift of faith, can you go further? Can you add the confession that this invisible God, this thrice-holy Being, forgives all your misdeeds? That he does not hold you accountable for your sins? That he has covered all your transgressions? Admit it, my sisters and brothers, doesn't this require a uniquely special grace? Doesn't it rise astonishingly far above anything that can possibly come from the depths of the human heart?

"I believe in the forgiveness of sins!" To say that and to mean it, and to really cling to it as completely true is something else. To do so when you have been shattered by wrestling with the depths of your sin is to understand something quite amazing! Or to do so when you have felt Satan's traps snap shut on your soul! Or when you have discovered how your enemies the Devil, the world, and your own flesh are capable of attacking you from three sides all at the same time! Or when you have experienced the indescribable anger of the Trinity against you as a stage in your salvation! Or when in the frightful oppressiveness in your soul you come to know that in the final analysis your sin is the most terrible sin possible! Or when the prayer "O God, be merciful to me, a poor sinner" is transformed from a prayer for conversion to the despairing cry of one already converted! So now you tell me, in the light of all this, when your soul has been shaken in its depths and you have been deeply shocked by your own shameful sin, whether even then you can calmly, with complete certainty, and in a spirit of quiet thanksgiving confess: "I believe in the forgiveness also of my own sins." Isn't doing so a much deeper mystery than confessing to believe in the three persons of the Trinity?

Oh, I know that people play games with the forgiveness of sins. They play with that tender reality like we play with other holy things of the Lord. We sing thoughtlessly. We pray when our heart isn't in it. And we all also talk about the forgiveness of sins without any feeling. (Lord, how is any of this possible?) It is considered unimportant, even less than unimportant, that people admit that they don't have a clue how the sacred Lamb of God could possibly be a substitute for us.

Worse yet is that we have not only played games with the forgiveness of sins, but that each of us has sinned in this connection in our own way. "God is so good and God is so loving. Even to ask for forgiveness is really unnecessary. God forgives automatically. How could he stay angry, this loving Father in heaven?" That's not only the way modernists talk. It's also the way the modern sinner living in our own heart speaks, or better said, the old sinner in our own heart. Just think about this for a minute. Satan knows how to manipulate everything. He even sees an opportunity in the forgiveness of sins to cause new sins to grow in our evil hearts. Listen up; it's all really very simple. He does nothing more than push aside preoccupation with sin itself and replace it with a focus on the forgiveness of sin. When he does that at the point where we are about to sin, our minds focus on the grace of God. We say to ourselves as we are about to fall into sin that we will be forgiven immediately! That's when the last connection we have with God's covenant of grace is cut. And we fall. We fall deeply. We do what God sees as sin. Oh, the unfathomable mystery of evil! Then our impure lips pray the prayer asking God to forgive us even for that sin.

Children of the kingdom, you have to realize this. Nathan's word applies here. It applies to your soul and not to someone else's: "You are the man!" But that point has not yet sunk in. The promptings of your own heart don't get it! Seen another way and equally true, there is a type of faith in the forgiveness of sins that is not from God but from the Evil One. This is a faith that dares to say, "With you, O God, is forgiveness, therefore all fear of your holiness is gone from left my heart."

But that is not the confession of the church of Jesus Christ.

What sets the tone of her life is exactly the opposite. It is expressed in the ancient song of ascent: "With you is forgiveness, therefore you are feared!"

"Feared" not with a fear that causes us to flee from God! But fear as a holy emotion and a profound awe that, approaching God in his exalted majesty, causes us to stop in our tracks with reverential silence. It purges us of unholy thought. It compels us to uncover our heads, to open our ears, and to listen respectfully to what the Lord says.

And what he says is this: "My child, don't commit that sin any longer." When God's child hears their Father say that, they find that they cannot, even when in their wickedness they are still inclined to do so. For then the voice of God is like a restraint operating in their souls and holding them back. This is the God who has forgiven all my sins. This is the God who caused the precious blood of his dear Son to flow. And this is the God that continuously appeals to my heart, "My child, don't commit that sin!" That's when the untrustworthy and afflicted soul shows fear, and that's when it neither wants nor dares to go against the voice of God. For he who calls out to them like this in his soul-piercing voice is the same God who has forgiven all their sins.

This is how evil is disarmed. This is how sin is stifled at birth. This is when a sneering Satan retreats. In this God is praised.

And this is how the fear of the Lord comes through being forgiven.

At this point the church of all ages exclaims, "Yes! Amen! With you is forgiveness, therefore God is feared!"

So tell me, with what choir are you singing?

Where, when your soul dares to confess, "I believe in the forgiveness of sins!"?

Does it sing that song superficially and without feeling to the tune of the thoughtless? "Forgiven ... so, not really so concerned about sin!"

Or for you has it become an overwhelming power of God in your chest? "I am no longer able to commit sin, because God forgives!"

Reader, be discerning in answering that question. For once don't trust your own notions, or your personal feelings, or your own understanding with respect to this confession. But examine the actual way your own soul works.

Does your faith that God forgives sins render your conscience more sensitive or more indifferent?

How terrible if you have to admit "more indifferent."

But, then, it is better that you are startled now than that you enter eternity with a devilishly misled faith in your heart, only to stand quivering and shaking before God when you do.

That particular sin, the sin of your misled and unrealistic and false believing, is especially abominable. It is an abomination in the presence of our Holy God.

But there is still hope.

That's because there is even a way back to the thrice-holy God for the soul that is suffocating with that particular sin. It is to come with the language of the psalmist on one's lips:

"Lord, with you is forgiveness, forgiveness even for this sin, therefore you are feared!"

91

VOLUME I

LIVING BY FAITH

For the righteous shall live by faith. Galatians 3:11

The promise with which God enriches his people is that they will live by faith.

This is not simply a promise that the Lord will help us get through some situation. Nor that he will jump to our help when some danger threatens! Nor that he will listen to our prayers! Nor that he will crown us with honors! Nor that he will clothe our naked bodies!

The Lord God certainly knows that if there's nothing more than all this packed into his promise, a person may leave with all these valuables, but they will be just as poor as when they entered. That's because they'll have to keep on crying out: "O God, my God, the honor is priceless. The clothing shows how much you care about me. Your listening ear reassures me. But if I only had life! What do these other things matter as long as my tired, embattled heart is still always yearning for life? I keep on grappling with questions about my existence, about being able to breathe, about eternity, about my inner being. What does honor mean to someone who's dead? What do beautiful clothes mean to someone who yearns for the life that's still missing?"

The Lord understands!

He knew this was true of Israel in the wilderness. That's why he didn't only command Israel to conqueror Canaan but began by giving it life. He gave it life first of all by paralyzing Pharaoh's hand that quite literally had it by the throat! Next he did by giving it life in the hollow of the sea, whose floor is usually just a graveyard for people. But he transformed it into a pathway of life, and that's how it came to be known by his people. Then he did by giving it life in the desert itself, where the barren landscape was covered with manna and the rock was split open so that water gushed from it for the people of God.

And the Lord God still knows that his people today, just like his people of old, are first and foremost concerned about life. That's because what goes on here on earth is open and exposed to his holy sight. Those called out from among the children of men are truly, definitely regarded by him as a flock of sheep that has gone astray. It can't make any progress because it has. It has fallen down. It doesn't have any breath left in it. It can't help itself. It can't do anything about its situation unless its Savior first begins to explain how these winded people can begin to live again!

The eternal God of Love reveals himself to those that this describes. The measure of how lost these poor creatures needing salvation are is the measure of the mercy by which they'll be saved. And before he promises them anything else, that's exactly how the Lord enters their crushed hearts. He comes with the most comprehensive, profound, and gracious of all his promises: "I give you life. You'll definitely live, as long as you live by faith."

But what does it mean, then, to "live by faith"?

Does this mean to say, as so many imagine, "If you'll only start by firmly believing a few dry, abstract truths, then when you die I'll give you life as a reward for your quiet submissiveness"?

Or if it doesn't mean that, might it mean, "If you simply believe that things are as I say they are, then somewhere in heaven I'll assign you to a life that is far above and beyond anything you can now imagine"?

Well, my brother and sister, if it doesn't mean anything more precious, heartwarming, or wonderful than either of these, do you seriously think that anyone would ever be revitalized by these words? Would anyone ever lift a song of praise in response to them? Would the language of holy rapture ever be heard from human lips about them?

Not at all! Listen to me carefully! Much richer grace than any of this floods your lives from the promise about "living by faith." "To live" means several things. It means that strength is restored to what was totally stripped of strength. It means that what was choked and stifled breathes again. It means that what lay as collapsed and motionless as a corpse in a grave rises and starts moving again.

Look at being restored to life from Ezekiel's perspective of those dry bones that began stirring. Bleached white skeletons yielded to the hues of living skin and tissue. Bones disassembled were reattached. Finally, ultimately, the spirit began stirring and returned from the four winds of the earth until what lay motionless became erect and stood straight up. It didn't only give the appearance of existing, but it knew that it was alive.

These glorious things are what the Lord is promising you in his blessing. You will live, but only if you live by faith! Such life doesn't come through your own struggles! Not by your own effort! Not by what you do! Entirely to the contrary! In fact, to the extent that you tire yourself out in the attempt, by that much you're diverted from faith and restrained from really living. And the kind of life involved here doesn't come through what others contribute. Nor by what they lay out for you! Nor by what flits through your imagination! That's merely a mirage in the desert that yields no water. It only makes you thirstier. No soul can live on that!

No, such life comes only by faith, not by sight. You can't see it, and it can't be put on display for you. It may not be entrusted to you for protection. No, it has to stay with him to whom God entrusted it, namely, Jesus Christ. You have to drink in that holy, strengthening, and revitalizing power from him drop by drop, breath by breath, and bit by bit. There's a veil hanging in front of this Fountain of Life. This deeply mysterious source of life recedes, and woe to you if you reach out to pull that veil aside. At that very moment, it disappears entirely, and you won't be able to find it back. Faith has to stay faith!

Don't believe only with your head or only with your heart. Believe with both your head and your heart, with both the will and the emotions. Believe with your entire person and with everything within you. For everything about you is equally miserable, naked, unsettled, vulnerable, and powerless.

In fact, believing is nothing more than feeling like you've been snake bitten! It's recognizing and saying: "The snake venom is spreading through my bloodstream. It's over! I'm going to die!" Believing in that kind of desperation, with death advancing through your system, is to look up at the brazen serpent and with a deep sigh of faith to profess: "There! There's my life!" Don't ask how; don't ask in what way. Look up! Look away from yourself. I don't think about the bite or the venom anymore. I think only about him, in faith. And, O my God, how blessed it is! Life starts stirring, then bubbling, and finally flowing! O my God, how is this even possible? By believing, I'm living again! And it's eternal life, life from Jesus himself.

Just as I can deaden my finger by pressing intensely on a blood vessel, I can temporarily deaden my soul by allowing Satan to apply intense pressure on the veins through which life flows to me from Jesus.

But why should I be afraid? The veins are still there. Jesus is still there. And in him the pressure to bring me life persists as well.

I can't lose my faith completely either, for I am not its source. He created it within me and for my benefit. But faith can be temporarily inactive. And if it depended on me, then faith once inactive would always remain inactive. For if truth be told, we have sunk so far that we would put this to the test. We'd do this either out of sheer willful determination, haughtiness of heart, or I don't know what other devilish desire. But we would do it, and I don't know how long we'd hold out apart from Christ.

But he whose love we have grieved and saddened by doing so doesn't permit this to happen. He keeps a watchful eye on us. And when he notices that the force of Satan's hand on the veins of our soul has continued too long and become too deadly, he in his boundless mercy wrenches Satan's grip loose. Then life flows through them once more. Then we return to living by faith. Then we praise him again with all that is in us. He is our Comforter, full of unending mercy, and in his divine love the Savior of our soul.

VERY SLIPPERY PLACES IN THE DARK

Therefore their ways will be like very slippery places in the dark; they will be driven away and will fall. Jeremiah 23:12

Every one of us needs to make progress and get ahead. But to get ahead, there has to be a clearly marked road to follow. And it's all about that road! The person is triply blessed who can say: "I've found that road!"

That road is not only found in our initial separation from the world. That road is not only found in a person's first turning to Jesus! No, but that road is where the soul finds real life. It's the well-traveled road! That road is taken by the saints of God! That road is where our souls can never travel without noticing that the Lord God is also walking that road, and so are all his elect children and his angels with him!

Having no road at all is really terrible. But that's not the worst by far. The most frightening prospect is when we deliberately cut ourselves off from taking the road of life, thinking: "I'd rather stay where I am!" It's frightening because then the Lord God comes and shocks us by saying: "I'll never allow that! If you don't want to walk my road, then you'll simply slide down the slippery slope toward hell. But there's no peace in that. Either walk toward me, or walk away from me. Choose either the path of the saints that leads to what's above, or trudge toward what's below at the expense of your soul. But if you simply want to stand still, I'll personally see to it that you're moving somewhere. You have to move until you fall and disappear."

Hear what the Lord is also saying through Jeremiah the seer to the people of our day: "Repent! If you don't, I'll make the road you're walking like very slippery places in the dark. And if this makes you shudder so that you're afraid to put one foot in front of the other, I'll force you to move. I'll hound you and drive you until you stumble and your feet slip from under you and you fall."

God's complaints against his people in this chapter are just that frightening!

"Look," says the Holy One, "I bore you as my child. I girded you with strength. I lavished my love on you. And now these are the indignities you heap on my Holy Spirit! Then I sent you a priest to testify to my name, to pray for my people, and to hold you to my law. But the priest himself left the road and turned out to be a hypocrite. So then I sent you a prophet to shake both my people and the faithless priest awake. But even the prophet chose to oppose me. Everything human cursed my holiness in unison!"

This is how the Lord God deals not first and foremost with deviant priests and prophets like those who served in Bethel of the Levites in biblical times. Nor is it how he deals first and foremost with their modern counterparts who are inspired by some idol or pet idea of their own, but then who still call on the name of Jehovah!

This is still only simply absurdity, says the Lord (v. 13).

What is much worse and what upsets our holy God much more pointedly is what the ultraorthodox prophets of Judah do. They present themselves as very pious. They pray at length. They sing God's praises lustily. They act like they're keeping God's Word to the letter. But behind their pious façade is a festering unrighteousness. "I have seen the offenses of Samaria's prophets. But in the prophets of Jerusalem I see abominations!"

When you think about such prophets, don't think only or mainly about orthodox preachers who are hypocrites. For they'll bear the most severe condemnation, to be sure. Woe, woe to the shepherds! For in the age of the new covenant, all God's people belong to the priesthood. That's where the prophet's prayer is answered: "Oh, that all God's people were prophets!" This word from the Lord is aimed at every one of us!

The abomination is on us. It's in our homes. It's in our hearts. It's in the entire way in which we present ourselves and in how we behave.

That's what's so terrible!

To be godly is the highest ideal, but it's also the most dangerous to practice.

For either you really are and are blessed, or you actually aren't and the false pretense produces a spiritual lie within you. The lie poisons you, and Satan comes along to inflame your thoughts and desires. That's how what's abominable, deeply abominable, occurs in people who present themselves as pious and as really wanting to be godly but who have only dry bones in their souls.

Oh, don't look for hypocrites only among the educated, deliberate fakers. Scripture almost never concerns itself with opposing these spiritual children of the Devil. They don't listen anyway. No, the spiritually ill with whom God's Word labors are the naïve, spiritually compromised children of God who cling to the appearance of piety. They do so not primarily to please others, but because they know that "life comes only by living piously." Yet, knowing and confessing this, they don't let God into their heart of hearts. Golgotha remains very far away, even though they can always be found busy with Jerusalem's activities.

These are terrible situations. They are often the source of bitter suffering and struggle, and sometimes of even more bitter crying. But people simply can't wiggle out of them, any more that a fly can struggle free from a spider's web.

In such situations, then, it's a gift of grace when the Father of all mercy causes darkness to fall over us and places our feet on slippery surfaces.

Grace, yes, really! Divine grace when God makes it impossible for us to put one foot in front of the other in such situations.

It's grace when God doesn't listen to our calling and shrieking but makes things so slippery, dark, and fearful all around us that we can't stand it any longer. We simply slip and stumble and fall down.

And when we're lying there, it's all over!

Then a person no longer pleads from the heart: "O God, just show me some light so that I can make some headway!" They can only sigh and moan: "O my dear God and Father, I can't handle this any longer. For Jesus' sake, carry me!"

When a person gets to that point, they begin living again. Their prayer actually amounts to praying once more. The soul revives. The aroma of nard wafts from their heart. The hypocrite is amazed at what's happening. They can actually pray now, offer praise again, and talk meaningfully about their Lord. There's something authentic about them again, something truthful buried deep inside, and their conscience no longer condemns them.

If it comes to this, people definitely notice! Authentic talk about the King is never uncertain.

Look, the spiritual glad-handers in Israel talked about spiritual feelings that they themselves had never experienced. They reported about an inner working of God that was nothing more than a proud figment of their imagination.

And that sort of thing made the Holy Spirit powerfully angry. "Behold, I will rise up against those who prophesy false hopes, who spread them around, and who mislead my people with their lies," says the Lord.

No, where God is involved, it's very easy to discern whether the Almighty is working in the soul. If a fire crept up on you and began singeing you, wouldn't you notice that? Similarly, observes the Lord, "Isn't my Word like a fire?" To put it even more plainly, "If my Word penetrates a person's heart, isn't that like me hitting them with a hammer capable of splitting rocks?" Does a quiet traveler who suddenly hears a lion growling behind them ever doubt what's going on? "So," says the Lord, "my Word is the growling of a lion that first strikes terror in your heart! Only after that does the wonderful sense of being spared overwhelm you."

My dear sisters and brothers, is this how the Lord has come into your hearts too? Not only once, but many times? Are you still capable of hearing the roar of this Lion in the tribe of Judah? If not, then don't go any further! If so, see to it that you don't withhold any of the honors due him. If you long to give him these, then yearn to do so even more powerfully!

There is living water to be had from your God!

THE FRUIT OF THE SPIRIT

But the fruit of the Spirit is love, joy, peace, patience, kindness, goodness, faithfulness, gentleness, and self-control. Against such there is no law. Galatians 5:22–23

It's important, in fact it's more important than anything else, that the Lord who is our great God and Savior be glorified. To glorify him is the ultimate purpose of all creatures, but especially of human beings. In the most special sense of all, this is true of Christians.

The glory of God on earth does not consist of mere appearance or of external worship. Rather, it consists of something going on daily within the souls of Christians. This is something that everyone experiences and acknowledges as not arising from within the person them self. Its source is higher, for it has the power of God in it.

There needs to be fruit. Beautiful fruit! Lovely fruit! Fruit that others find appealing! Fruit that clearly, indelibly bears the trademark of God himself!

And it's not enough that the fruits of sin are diminishing in your life. That definitely has to happen as well. Anyone who lives with the conviction that they are a child of God and whose daily life still bears the watermark of sin is living dangerously. They have to take stock of what the characteristics of being a child of God are. A temporary falling back into sin by someone who has been saved is certainly thinkable. But continually living in those old, former sins certainly is not.

Even if a person gets to the point of exclaiming: "Praise God! This and that sin are diminishing in my life," they understand perfectly well that those sins haven't disappeared entirely. They can still be at work in your life. But an indication of a genuine work of God in you that causes your specific sins to lose their grip is obvious only when all "the works of the flesh" are simultaneously becoming weaker.

Wanting to do away with sin on a one-by-one basis is counsel from the Tempter. Abandoning the very fountain of all sinning that boils up within you is the sacred work of God.

Be sure to catch this difference, brothers and sisters. Your strength depends on it. So does your sense of well-being. Peace in your heart does as well.

But suppose things got to that point with you. In yourself, by yourself, and for yourself you're still the same old, scandalous, ungodly sinner sold out to the sins of the flesh. But in Christ you are pure and holy and blessed! That happens only by believing. It happens in no other way than through faith. You have the conflicted experience of detecting more and more sin in your life, but at the same time you find that the power of all sin is weakening in you. If your soul is operating on that level and with those results, good for you!

Even so, would the Lord God thereby be receiving the honor due to him? When that which is offensive in God's holy eyes is being tempered in you, is he actually being honored? Suppose once more that the fruit of all sinning ceased entirely in your life and in the lives of all other people, what does that amount to before God in his holy courts?

Nothing, really!

Not a single bud! Not one blossom! And not one piece of fruit!

It's only when the fruit is presented that the glory shines. It radiates with honor to God.

Pay close attention to the fact that I'm not talking here about fruits of the Spirit, but about the fruit of the Spirit. For, as was true with the diminishing power of sin, so is the case with the budding of the sacred vine. When the Spirit is at work, all sins diminish together; and all virtues are stimulated simultaneously by his work as well. There are not fruits of the Spirit. Rather, there is only one fruit of the Spirit. Notice that this is stated in the singular in both Galatians 5:22 and Ephesians 5:9. But everything is involved in that one fruit: one love, one joy, one peace, one patience, one kindness, one goodness, one faithfulness, one gentleness, and one self-control.

This isn't the way humans calculate, for then the virtues would be tallied one by one. But when the Spirit is behind what's happening, when God is at work, there is one fruit.

Are you seeing a lot of evidence of that fruit?

Sad to say, we appear to be living in spiritually adverse times when God's own people are guilty of bearing very little of it.

Oh, I would quickly add, let there be times of bitter persecution once again! Let the Lord use dagger and sword once more to cut us off from conforming to this world! Let him scorch and singe the pharisaical wool off our souls on a martyr's pyre. For as far as God is concerned, the devastating effects of sin appear to be so deep that the saving power of the gospel doesn't have a tenth of the strength that it did for the churches under the cross.[1] This is true of even the most submissive and devout believers of our day.

"You shall have no other gods before you." "You shall not steal." "You shall not commit adultery." People understand these commands. But would that they had power so that behind and under them the power of God's own being were felt! Would that you had a passion for God alone. Would that you had a passion for giving and for showing mercy. Would that you had a passion for devotion and for serving and for self-denial and for living humbly. Not because you were forced to show passion! But because you expressed it as exuberantly as a child who leaves the house and runs out to pick flowers and weaves them into a wreath to braid into her hair. That kind of passion is missing in more than one person!

And the God who knows that this kind of passion has passed us by has carved the diamond-pointed directive into his Word that we must express the fruit of the Spirit.

That Word is restated for you in these lines once again.

And should it happen that today or tomorrow the result is that you display more of the fruit of the Spirit, this short meditation didn't accomplish that. And you certainly didn't! But his Word served as an instrument in God's hand for promoting the penetrating and compelling work of the Holy Spirit within you. So, understand very clearly that what you display is in essence the fruit of the Spirit, and it always will be. He is its source. It is a work of the Holy Spirit, and therefore not of your doing or of any other person's doing.

---

1. *Kruisgemeenten*, or churches under the cross, is a reference to the Protestant churches of the Low Countries that endured persecution under the Spanish Inquisition prior to the time the northern provinces of the present-day Netherlands gained independence in the 1570s.

To carry the Holy Spirit within us is amazingly magnificent! So is knowing that our bodies are his temple. And when we are alone, or wandering around and feeling lonely, or are busy with our work, may we reflect on this thought: "Right now the Holy Spirit is working in me, a poor sinner; he who with the Father and the Son is the true and everlasting God!" What a magnificent thought.

To play games with something that magnificent seems to be fearfully ungodly!

But that's precisely why the anointing of the Holy Spirit penetrates the membranes of your soul like fine perfume does your clothing. Anyone who is granted a fresh supply is doubly energized!

The result will be, must be, that the fruit of the Spirit will be expressed in you. You will find that you are richly blessed in bearing this fruit. You will have an inner peace and will display this fruit externally as well. In this he will be exalted. And he alone is to be exalted; in comparison with him all creatures are to be counted as less than nothing. He is the breath in our nostrils!

TWO BASKETS OF FIGS

The Lord showed me two baskets of figs. ... In one basket were very good figs, but in the other basket were very bad figs that could not be eaten because they were so rotten. Jeremiah 24:1–2[1]

A re there two or are there three kinds of people?

The Lord God showed Jeremiah only two baskets. What lay in the one was "very good," and what lay in the other was "very bad."

Good or bad refers to how they looked to the Lord.

But if we go by what we human beings see on close observation, shouldn't a third basket be included? You tell me! Shouldn't there be a third basket placed between the other two? Shouldn't it be a basket that contained some fruit that was not entirely good and not entirely bad? One between the other two! Half and half! Not completely dead yet! But not entirely alive either! Hanging like that halfway between heaven and earth!

But that's not how Scripture sees things. It simply doesn't acknowledge a third basket containing what's in between. "Very good" or "very bad," and there's no other choice! But pay close attention to the fact that good or bad

---

1. The reference as originally published in *De Heraut* and as republished in book form was erroneously given as Jeremiah 24:24. The text as cited is a portion of verse 1 and all of verse 2.

depends on the extent to which people are already converted. It is determined entirely by how they have been tagged according to God's promise.

Notice what follows in verse 7.

Those who lie in the basket on the right and of whom verse 2 says that they are "very good" still don't have the seed of life in them. They're not yet converted. They still don't know God. What clearly stands in verse 7 is this: "I will give them a new heart so they might know me, for I am the Lord. They will turn to me with their whole heart." If it's written like this and states that God will give them a new heart, then they obviously still have their old heart. If it states that they will turn to him, then they obviously are not yet converted! Nonetheless, there they lay, in the basket of good figs. And the Spirit testifies that they are "very good."

It's the same way with Jacob and Esau. Before either of them had done anything good or bad, things were decided according to their election. And that would stand fast.

Shouldn't we give all the careful attention to this that our souls can seriously muster?

What do we look for in making our distinction between the two types? At what we see? At what we believe to be true? At what evidence of the new life each day happens to bring? When we notice it, or at least think we do, we label people as "converted."

We label them as "anxious" or "concerned" if we see a little of it stirring in them, but not much. And when we see no evidence at all of life in the branches, we identify them as "still worldly."

But when you operate that way, don't you think that you're including as "worldly" a whole lot of people who by God's eternal determination are lying in the "good basket"? Ones that he judges to be "very good"? Even though that's not evident to you?"

And then don't you also think that a lot of what's lying there in the good basket probably doesn't belong there at all. It's only expressing temporary faith! Don't you think that you might be wrong in approving what you approve of being there?

Worst of all, you don't have a clue in operating like that how the most sensitive souls, those who are "anxious," as you call them, simply perish in their deep concern. You don't understand how they are being tossed here and there and in their own minds are lying on the ground, outside either basket and entirely missing faith's joys and blessings.

This is what happens when people build on seeing rather than on believing!

Then infant baptism gets thrown out.

Then the certainty of salvation walks out the church door.

Human effort supplants God's work.

And ultimately, you lose all sense of justification by faith.

My, oh my! That third basket!

Get rid of it! From your heart! Throw it out of your home and out of your congregation!

You're not the one to divide the figs between the baskets! God has already done that. And his division holds for time and for eternity.

Just believe in what God is doing. Doing for you! Doing with you! Doing to you! Stand amazed that that eternal order is being worked out so gloriously. Whatever militates against it does not build up the church. It only breaks it down.

Then those poor, anxious souls crumple in fear and never enter spiritually spacious places.

Then the church in its religious pride postures itself against the world instead of serving it in love.

Then those who play God in their pious existence forfeit the riches of grace in their self-preoccupation and introversion.

Make no mistake. There is no ambivalence here. No uncertainty! The bad figs are such that "they cannot be eaten." And all the others are good, even "very good" as green, lush figs that have just ripened. They are good not because they are so in and of themselves, but because that's how God sees them in and through the Son of his love.

This is when the Holy Spirit comes and helps us to see ourselves not as the wretches we think we are, but as the people God says we are in Jesus.

This amounts to believing! It's the kind of believing that blesses us.

Then comes the fruit. Not before you get to that point, but once you're there.

BROKENHEARTED

A broken and contrite heart you, O God, will
not despise. Psalm 51:17[1]

To be "brokenhearted," if you really think about it, is really the most difficult demand that can be laid on a sinful human being.

To be curbed a little isn't objectionable to our big egos. You hardly ever come across someone who won't acknowledge that they don't fail sometime and at some things. Everyone acknowledges that they could do better than they sometimes do. As long as there's talk about nothing worse than curbing a person's lavish excesses, you're not going to get an actual objection from most of them.

That kind of curtailed person walks around by the thousands on the biblical broad road, strutting their restraint and modesty. Hemmed in by the fences of their own self-righteousness, they live and work in their own kind of hell.

But that doesn't matter to God. It doesn't matter to him in his mysterious judgment as long as his light penetrates and exposes what's going on.

But as far as the Searcher of every heart is concerned, you don't make a lick of progress by punishing, curbing, subduing, and if necessary even cracking and breaking your bodily members. Every child of God knows the failed track record here.

But things can't stay like this. The sails of sinful living have to be trimmed. It has to be reined in. The body has to be forcibly subdued. But people don't

---

1. Psalm 51:19 In the Dutch versions.

want to do this any longer. And this will destroy them. It will kill them. Sins, to be specific, need to be rendered ineffective. Things that appealed to people before no longer do. Change is noticeable. Progress is being made. And this amounts to more than merely curbing. It consists of circumcising the old, wild nature.

And yet this does not get you to where you should be. It can't. For however much you mutilate your way of living, this is not yet taking a stand against it. Then you're simply replacing the natural leg you amputated with a wooden one, or if necessary, with a crutch, and you keep on stumbling along in your old ways with artificial support! Oh, even mutilated spiritual strugglers are under the constraints of hell.

No, our physical members behave like unchecked growth. They are untamed sucker shoots in daily living. When it comes to dealing with God, you have to deal with life itself. The divine medical doctor doesn't just examine your foot or your hand. He examines everything. Even what's beneath your clothing! Right down to your heart! And he doesn't hesitate or doubt for a second. He talks straight from the shoulder! Man-to-man! "This heart has to change!"

Listen closely! Objections arise immediately to that diagnosis by the Lord our God: "My heart can't handle that! I'd die if I tried. I live by what's in my heart. Test me! Take everything else, O divine physician, but don't let the scalpel of your Word cut into my heart. Take this hand; here, I offer it to you! Take that leg; I can do without it! Just let me keep on creeping along and stumbling forward. I'm willing to do anything to be saved. I'm ready for anything. No pain frightens me, no matter how intense it might be. But whoever heard of a person having to give up their heart? That they had to cut it out? That they had to crush it to a pulp? How could anyone endure that kind of procedure and remain alive?"

With talk like that, the willful, self-righteous heart bent on protecting itself reappears!

But no, O Lord my God, I will not withhold even my heart from you. Even my heart needs to be changed! It is too arrogant. It needs to be humbled. My heart and my will truly do want to bow before you!

But God in his holiness remains adamant.

But no, emphatically not! A yielded heart is still not enough! The promise of salvation is held out only to a broken heart. A yielded heart doesn't matter, because in the first place it just doesn't go far enough. It's still too inflexible. Even if it might bend over and bow down today, tomorrow it will snap right back up. And that amounts to only playing games with the Almighty. That's dealing in appearances, not inner truth.

That's why not a jot or tittle of God's Word can be changed! Broken! Really broken! Shattered to pieces in the full sense of the word! That's what has to happen to your arrogant and resistant heart.

"But ... then it's all over for me. Then I'd stop existing. That amounts to dying!"

That's definitely the case, my good readers. That's what it's all about. And that's exactly why it has to be as stated. Your heart has to be broken. You have to die. You have to stop living for what's in your old heart. Because if you really do get to that point, then you won't die, but you'll start living again!

There's room for everything else in hell. Just not for a broken human heart!

When living for self disappears in brokenheartedness, that's the precise moment when living in Jesus begins. In the instant that you lance a vein and drain the bad blood of living for self, the life-giving blood of Jesus flows into your soul.

This is why the text uses the word "broken." "A broken heart!" A heart shattered to pieces! A brokenness that endures until the heart lies in smithereens!

This doesn't happen all at once. For some people the hammer of his Word pounds on the rock pile of their heart for years.

First he trims a little. Then he cuts more deeply. Then he applies more pressure on you. He sends judgments that frighten you, and he compels you to take swallow after swallow from the chalice of his fury. His intent is to oppress your soul.

Your joy flees. Your favorite plaything is gone. Your circle of friends melts away. Every night you long for the morning. Every aspiration is dashed.

That's when every crushed person weeps and laments, complaining: "The world doesn't offer me a thing anymore." They feel like adding: "This last blow has simply broken my heart!"

Then God answers: "No, no, no! What broke in you is only what you imagined to be the love and hope of your heart! Your heart itself is intact!" And now the real spiritual work begins. Blow after blow was the tugging of a higher hand within you. Blow after blow was the prodding of your soul. Blow after blow was the pounding of God's hammer, his Word, on different parts of your heart.

That's what happens to the idol Dagon. An arm comes off. A foot falls off. Finally the whole idol is cut in half, its proud bearing devastated. And God keeps hammering on it until its will, its emotions, its honor, its self-worth, its virtue, and its piety, even its praying and charitable giving, all lie in the dust, pulverized at God's feet.

When that happens, a miracle occurs. When Dagon has been toppled, the godless ego is rendered impotent. Everything that was our pride and strength lies there as pulverized dust. But lo and behold, in the same heart where Dagon lies dashed to pieces, Someone else, Someone better has forced his way in!

Don't you know him?

He's your Savior. "Comforter" is his name!

NOW THESE THREE REMAIN

And now there remain faith, hope, and love, these three.
But the greatest of these is love. 1 Corinthians 13:13

"And now there remain these three, faith and hope and love. Of them, love is the greatest."

They remain? Now? But for how long? Does the apostle mean that they remain until we die? Or does he mean that they will remain with us after we die and accompany us into eternity?

The latter alternative is being increasingly preached in our churches today, just as it was preached by itinerant messengers in former times. But the church of God, which is the pillar and ground of the truth (or better yet the Holy Spirit in the church), has held firmly and still does that the words "now these three remain" do not mean continuous existence throughout eternity.

That can't be! That interpretation is as unthinkable as it is impossible.

Faith is setting aside what is visible and holding onto what is invisible. Faith is clinging with spiritual strength to what you do not now see. The very essence of faith itself is tied to not seeing and not tasting. "Blessed are those that will not see and yet will believe!" How, I ask you, can people possibly imagine that faith like that of Thomas is the standard for the exalted life to be lived in heaven?

And a child can tell you what hope is. Hope is having the illusion of already possessing what has not yet been received. It's to enjoy what's still coming! It's reveling in what has been delayed but will eventually definitely be given to us. In Holy Scripture, therefore, hope or Christian hope is certain and unshakable. It is the prospect that God's children have of the glory that will be revealed to them when Christ returns on the clouds of heaven.

It's certainly true that there are those who say: "But even life in heaven has its ranks. People start on one level of favor and meanwhile hope to rise to a higher level after a time." But that doesn't make sense. That's using an earthly yardstick to measure things in heaven. We may not do that. Up above things are everlasting, and what is everlasting doesn't exist on one level today and on another level tomorrow. From the outset we possess in full. In heaven there is no such thing as a succession of time.

When Jesus' apostle says: "These three remain, faith, hope, and love," he can't mean anything else than in this life. At the same time, you shouldn't understand them as remaining only until your death. Rather, understand that these three forces in life that belong to his people, his fellowship, and the church of God remain until the return of our Lord Jesus Christ.

In this respect, these gifts are to be sharply distinguished from those other spiritual gifts that Paul talks about in 1 Corinthians 12; 13; and 14. That's because the gift of speaking in tongues will pass away. The gift of performing miracles will cease. The gift of prophesying will stop. These extraordinary and unusual gifts are given to only a few people. And then only for a brief time! But here he masterfully poses the other three against all of them. He does so for the comfort of God's people. These are gifts given to every child of God. They belong to the everyday living of God's children. They are not dependent on place or special talent. For that reason, they will endure as long as the church of Jesus Christ remains on earth.

Remember that the Holy Spirit moved the apostle in his writing and that the Holy Spirit then already knew that the church of God still had to pass through many centuries. And remember that it would be adorned with these exceptional, miraculous gifts for only a small portion of that time. Remember that afterwards those special gifts would cease entirely. And also remember that then as its only and all-sufficient comfort the church would rely on nothing else than its faith in, its hope on, and its love for Jesus Christ our Lord.

People are well advised never to be mistaken about these matters.

Among those extraordinary gifts there is also one that both Jesus and his apostles called "faith." Take a look at verse 9 in the previous chapter, where it reads that one person is given the gift of healing and another "the gift of faith." Naturally, that cannot refer to saving faith. For that kind is not given to only a few Christians but to each and every child of God. By the faith in 1 Corinthians 12:9 is meant, therefore, a special and unique faith, that as the writer says, is "the faith to work miracles." This is the same kind of extraordinary gift of faith that Jesus talked about when he said: "If you have faith the size of a grain of mustard seed and say to this mountain, 'Be thrown into the sea ... !' " And pay attention to the beginning of 1 Corinthians 13, where Paul deals with this gift of extraordinary faith and says that it is not faith unto salvation. He writes: "And if I have all faith so as to say to this mountain, 'Be taken up and thrown into the sea,' but have not love, I am nothing."

Similarly, just as the apostle speaks there about a separate, nonsaving faith, he also talks there about a separate nonsaving gift of exceptionally strong hope when he says: "Even if I give my body to be burned (in the hope of glory, wouldn't you think?), and I have not love, what good does it do me?"

And after having expressed himself on the extraordinary but nonsaving gift of faith to work miracles, and on the extraordinary but nonsaving gift of martyr-like hope, he adds a word about the special gift of exceptional love that also is weak and useless when it comes to salvation. For he says: "If I divide all my earthly possessions to support the poor, and have this unusual gift for showing love, but it is not a deep and saving love, of what eternal benefit is it to me?"

With respect to and by way of contrast with these extraordinary gifts of faith, hope, and love treated at the beginning of the chapter, he turns to something else at the end of the chapter. There he definitely deals with the saving, nonextraordinary, and generally shared inner working of the Spirit that yields true faith, unshakable hope, and divine love. In the name of the Lord, he explains that the extraordinary manifestations of these gifts disappear in time. He says that centuries ago there were people from whom martyrs' blood flowed, but that these were followed by centuries when in their nations it no longer did. But now these three have remained through all ages and among all peoples for the common good of those in fellowship with Jesus: faith and hope and love. He says that they will remain until he comes again, when we will see him face-to-face.

Verse 12, therefore, does not depict life in heaven. It only expresses what our response will be when we see Jesus returning on the clouds. Now we see as in a mirror, but then it will be face-to-face. Now we see from afar. Then we will know with the force of full contemplation.

Then follows: "But now—that is to say, in expectation of the Lord's coming—there remain these three pledges of salvation for the church: faith, hope, and love!" And among these, love is the greatest, just as in your estimation (as far as sheer enjoyment is concerned), the cluster of grapes is greater than the branch from which it was picked and the root that caused the vine to bloom.

NEEDFUL THAT STUMBLING COMES

*Woe to the world because of the stumbling it causes. It
is needful that stumbling comes, but woe to the
person by whom it comes. Matthew 18:7*

The terrible battle for God's children is how to navigate between the two reefs of despising the world on one side, and of getting completely tangled up in it on the other side.

The Lord's people are not permitted to leave the world. They have to live in it. Their calling is to be the salt that prevents rotting. A light in the darkness! A city set on a hill! But ... , and herein lies the difficulty, to be able to prevent the rotting, the salt has to be in close contact with what's spoiling. And that's precisely what nips and clips our faith!

We're talking about faith that has to walk the walk full of courage, thinking: "I will not falter!"

But two steps down the road it encounters an unexpected stumbling block, and a person trips and falls. A little farther along, a ditch has been dug; the person didn't anticipate it and falls into it. Still farther, a spiritual bandit sneaks up unnoticed and assaults them. They fall to the ground, knocked down by his heavy blows. So the soul becomes worn out and almost gives up as a result. It develops misgivings about trusting its faith. It sinks into despair and finally asks itself: "What good is my faith to me, anyway? It doesn't get me where I need to be!"

If only that battle were waged confidently in a believer's soul, they would ultimately get where we need to be. But, moving forward, a person actually seems to be moving backward without even noticing it. That's when the Lord God steps in and brings us there. To him be all the glory!

Meanwhile, the soul lives in fear, especially because in addition to all these dangers and obstacles a person also meets stumbling blocks. Stumbling blocks are all those words, circumstances, and other things that are met by a child of God and that tempt them into sin. That's because they give evil a beautiful and pious appearance. Or it's because a person plays around mentally with some indwelling sin. Our lives are full of these kinds of stumbling blocks.

It can't be otherwise. In the depths of its being, the world hates Christ. It feels that the Christ of God is its death. It succeeded in putting Christ to death on the cross. But that didn't help. He rose again. He ascended into heaven. And now from heaven he's a threat to the world once again. He lingers. He bides his time. He waits. But the world knows very well that his lingering, tarrying, and waiting are strictly for the purpose of gathering in his elect. When they are finally gathered into his kingdom, nothing will then restrain him. It knows that then its hour will have struck and all its glory will be finished. Then it will taste death at the hands of the Son of God.

This is why the world is motivated to oppose God's Son in its deep malice and bitterness. It's also why it's afraid of him and tries to drive him off, lest he destroy it with his outstretched arm. The world is like a snake being trampled by the Lion. So it hisses and spits poison and curls up to strike him. It's compelled to do this. But it won't pull it off.

This describes its hellish struggle against Christ. And however often it has attempted to bring its battle with Christ to a successful conclusion, it hasn't worked and hasn't helped the world's cause. Christ gives it no peace. New streams of its bitter, old enmity keep on welling up and flowing from the depths of its wickedness.

And God's children are caught between the snake and the Lion. That's where the snake promises them that it won't bite them as long as they don't acknowledge the Lion.

This, then, is the deep offense that is the cause of all stumbling blocks.

Christ says that the world is ungodly. And if the stumbling blocks looked ungodly, they wouldn't divert you from your course. But pay attention; they don't look ungodly, at least not when they present themselves to you. In your home! When they seek your approval at the gateway of your heart. Then they even look religious, sensitive, and vibrantly pious.

But from the other side, Christ sounds a warning: "My redeemed are pure!" But then the world approaches. It creeps into your heart. It mocks you and whispers so devilishly deep within you: "What a pretty, pure heart!" Having said that, it hauls up one by one all the miserable content of your inner life and causes that filthy pool of unrighteousness to bubble over from the depths.

And that's discouraging, for then our poor soul concludes that "the world is so much better and we are so much worse than we ever thought." Then we're offended. In a very real sense, we're offended in our heart! Offended by ourselves! Offended by the people of God! But above all, offended by the words of Christ that always turn out differently than he promised us! At times like that, our heart does a double take. We become despondent. Watching, Satan sees this and in all sorts of ways sends some ungodly message in our weaker moments that trips us up.

For anyone who has lived on a deeper level and experienced more frightening struggles, those times are a living hell. They're times when you wouldn't make it but for the words: "I tell you that the angels in heaven continually see the face of my Father who is in heaven." That's the reason why the words of this text come to you at such times. They prophesy that times of stumbling will come. They prophesy that they must come. Finally, they prophesy a "woe to you," but not about God's children. It's about what will be experienced by the world! The one who causes the stumbling will experience it most deeply.

That's comforting!

It's comforting because I simply know that it has to be that way. It's comforting that Jesus knew that this is what will happen. So then, what I experience is nothing strange. Nothing against which Jesus has not made provision! In the hour of fear, therefore, I lean undismayed on the Lion of the tribe of Judah, who is powerful and will protect my poor soul from the striking snake.

The greatest danger for God's children is not that they will suffer offense. The greatest danger is that you will let Satan use you as a stumbling block to your brother. May the Lord protect you from that in your going out and your coming in.

This is why the Lord adds the serious warning: "Woe to the person who causes them to stumble."

Now look around you in the world. Look at those who profess their faith in religious circles and ask yourself whether it's not often true that they cause "these little ones" to stumble.

No, I tell you, look into your own heart rather than at the circles of others around you. Study what's in your own heart. What do you think? Is there as much as one Christian who has not at one time, perhaps many times over, caused their brother or sister to stumble?

THEY THOUGHT THEY WOULD RECEIVE MORE

And when the first ones hired came, they thought they would receive more; but they also each received one denarius. Matthew 20:10

A difference, in fact a very big difference, exists between people's spiritual lots in life. Every child of God walks their own road. Each redeemed person has a unique situation. A name is engraved on a touchstone that applies to no other person than the one to whom it belongs. Every pilgrim bears their own cross and dies on it in a way uniquely their own.

This knowledge should make you very careful about judging another person's state of grace or spiritual journey. Admittedly, you would prefer seeing that things go with others the way they went for you. That your own conversion experience became the standard for all God's children! But that's not how it is. The eternal power of the Lord of Lords is too majestic not to be expressed one way for one individual and another way for someone else. It is ultimately displayed in whatever ways please God!

But there's more here. There's also the idea involved of putting a wayward soul immediately back on track.

Note that among those who confess Jesus as Lord are those who have it pretty easy in life. This even includes people who have enjoyed the world deep into their old age and have lived sinful lives. Then after at most only a few years of spiritual struggle, they have entered a state of grace and died peacefully in the Lord. On the other hand, there are others who were converted in their youth. For half a century or more they endured the heat of the day, went through intense inner struggles spiritually, and had the weight of the world on their shoulders.

Note that some people have lived in very loving family circles. They have witnessed nothing but the sweet fellowship of salvation all around them, and they themselves have possessed a tranquil spirit. After a life of uninterrupted peace, they have gone to sleep and then awakened to the eternal morning. By contrast, others have lived a very lonely existence amid mockers and blasphemers. They had a volatile temperament and daily endured pain and conflict. Consistently they were on the verge of forsaking the faith. But then, in their fear of dying they looked on high and with faltering voice asked: "Lord God! Do you still have room for me?"

Once again note that some folks can honestly say that they have never known the troubles of this life. They have never felt heavy blows imposed by their lot in life waling on their own heart. They have prospered in virtually everything they've done. They've had a smooth ride, walked among the roses, been accustomed to loving laughter, and hardly noticed the streams of tears softly flowing from human eyes. Alternately and just the opposite, others drink only draughts of bitterness, they are cut by one grief after the other, and every plague held in God's angry hands is visited on them by turns—or worse yet, on their loved ones.

Why is it that those who make their way "through very quiet waters" look down so calmly and reproachfully on those whose eyes are red from crying and whose souls are bloodied by struggle? Their looks from on high are so offensive, detached, and pitiless.

Doesn't this amount to sinning that stings?

It definitely does! As far as God is concerned, sinning stings when it comes in the form of a haughtiness that exudes peace. That's because this amounts to a peace devoid of love and mercy.

But let's turn things around! Doesn't the person who struggles in God's kingdom all too often disdain the pilgrim who goes quietly on their way? A person suffers. They battle. They wait. Their heart churns. Night after night they pour out their overwhelmed soul. And they look at those others, the ones who have it so easy! What about their faith, if it really is faith? Aren't they really deceiving themselves? Don't they just imagine that they believe? Don't talk about faith to me, you who are so spiritually superficial. If you only had to walk in my shoes for a while, then you could talk to me about faith. Who really thinks that that plastered on, varnished, and deadening quiet life is an example of our Lord having wrested a person's soul out of Satan's grip?

That's how this person in turn expresses a lack of love. That's how they also become judgmental, rather than leaving judgment in God's hands. That's how they can become so proud that they glory so much in their cross and personal difficulties that they stray from the pathway of grace.

Our Lord prophesied correctly! The workers who were hired early and had to endure the heat of the day were in little danger of not being offended because those hired later also received a whole denarius. Their anger flares up because Jesus is generous. The thought occurs to them almost automatically that as much suffering of soul and as much extensive struggling as they had endured entitles them to a little more, to special consideration!

There's no doubt about the fact that in eternity those who endured more will receive a greater crown. At least that's true as long as by enduring more a greater grace is also glorified and the soul doesn't exalt in itself! Otherwise it loses its reward! And that's exactly what's so lamentable: that so many frightened sufferers allow themselves to be misled by Satan's whispers and glory in their suffering. Then all fruit is forfeited.

If only people would see everything in our spiritual life in terms of God!

What do people work on longer and more persistently than on a piece of ordinary crystal or a very precious diamond?

When the Lord God polishes your soul with his sharp tools and once again files on your heart as long as he does someone else's, is that really so bad? Is it so bad if he expends double the effort on you and polishes you personally with three times as much divine intensity? Does the diamond have a reason to complain if it's worked on longer and harder than the ruby? Or the ruby because it's held tighter and ground down farther than polished crystal? And if it pleases the Lord God to grip your soul so much tighter and to work so much longer and to pay the price of expending his divine majesty on you, is that reason for you to complain? If he applies much more pressure in polishing you in order to bring out more sheen, tell me, why lament so glumly? And if you endure and suffer all this effort, should that ever be a reason for claiming glory? May the diamond ever claim glory because it let itself be chiseled and cut and polished with the sharpest of instruments?

Now apply all of this to the soul of a person who wrestles with their lot in life. Take that hard diamond that was polished so intensely. Who thinks about what happened during the polishing? Who doesn't simply admire the outcome? Who doesn't simply appreciate the pure light produced by that polishing? And if the work is to be praised, who would praise anyone other than the one who did the polishing?

Would you have it be any different?

If your soul is that kind of hard, precious stone, and if the Lord God can't have it produce gleaming light in any other way than by using intense pressure to chisel, cut, and polish it, to whom else should the glory and honor be given? Shouldn't it be given to the One who lovingly worked on you without letup until you radiated pure light?

All of this tremendous effort is not something that you expended, so that God is now indebted to you. Rather, it reflects the intense love that he has for your soul. For that fact you owe the faithful and merciful God all the more thanks, quiet devotion, and intense love. What follows from this is that you not calculate what God owes humans, but what humans owe God. This is what Scripture requires and what our forefathers emphasized. If you calculate in terms of what God owes you, your suffering becomes a real trial. It's a struggle to be overcome. Then you distort your suffering and proudly exalt in it. But that blunts how you receive grace.

But if you start with God and view yourself as he sees you, all of your afflictions and chastisements from God are the price paid for greater grace. The result is that you should live quietly and submissively under the crafting of his saving love. Give him thanks instead of giving glory to yourself. Such thanksgiving is enriched with grace upon grace.

A HOUSE OF PRAYER

My house will be called a house of prayer, but you
have made it a pit of murderers. Matthew 21:13[1]

The temple standing on Mount Zion represented the heart of Israel. Not the heart of a single, pious Israelite, but it stood for the heart of the entire national community. It symbolized the hearts of the people in whom God had chosen to dwell as his resting place. This is a house not of wood and stone, but one represented in wood and stone, namely, the hearts of God's people.

When Jesus appeared, the hour of destruction had arrived for that temple of stone. For what was he as Messiah other than the heart of the nation, the itinerating temple of God, the resting place of our God and King?

That stone temple had merely served the purpose of pointing toward the Messiah. Now that the Messiah himself had appeared, he could rightly say about the temple of his own body: "You will break down this temple and in three days I will rebuild it!" When Jesus died on Golgotha, the veil in that stone temple was torn completely in two.

When after his resurrection, Christ was elevated to his throne of glory, a temple of God remained here on earth in the form of his church. It is a temple that he as the Lamb of God had purchased at the high price of his own blood and

---

1. While English translations and the Greek original talk about a "den" or "cave of robbers" here, Kuyper and his Dutch version say "a pit of murderers." That metaphor comes into play later in this meditation, so we leave it as Kuyper wrote it.

into which the Holy Spirit had descended. According to plan and purpose, the human heart is the real temple of God. It's a temple that he enters and where he makes his home. It's a dwelling place where sacrifices are made to him. It's a house of prayer. And that's the glorious, the unspeakably majestic, and the enormously sacred nature of the human heart.

Its nature doesn't reside in the fact that it has strings of emotion extending to every part of life that, when softly strummed, make music. Nor does it lie in the fact that it possesses a virtually inextinguishable zest for life and an almost unrestrained passion to preserve it. Still less that it is an organ endowed with the capacity to love. All of these are only means and instruments serving a greater purpose. The actual purpose and reason for the existence of the human heart is to provide a place into which the Holy Spirit can descend and wants to live and from which he can speak. That's the heart's royal purpose!

When the Holy Spirit speaks and prays with groaning that can't be put into words, he does so in the heart of a human being. This is his temple. This is the place where God has chosen to live. This is his haven of rest. And the glory of God will only fully shine in his temple when the unimpeded Holy Spirit is admitted into every human heart and into the hearts of all people together.

That a house of stone had to be built in Zion was only because God's temple in human hearts had become uninhabitable. That God created that kind of royal dwelling in the human heart of the Messiah was only because the human heart had distorted his royal existence.

When Jesus entered the temple of stone on Mount Zion, therefore, wove together a whip of cords, and drove out the evildoers, overturning their tables, he angrily said that this is what had been written: "My house will be called a house of prayer, but you have made it a pit of murderers." That's when Jesus actually directed that intense act of holy anger toward us! He aims that penetrating reproach at our hearts. He lays the angry lashes of his whip on our hearts. He wants to drive out the evil transactions going on in our hearts. Pay sharp attention to this: Zion's temple is no more than a large mirror reflecting what's in your heart and your bosom. It's a mirror of what's going on in your own heart.

Jesus is painting a picture here designed to promote self-examination. It's intended to foster a teachable moment. There has to be a house of prayer in your life. Pay attention to your own sinful activity going on in your house of prayer.

"A house of prayer" is designed to convey that in your heart your ego regularly drives you to your knees with twinges of your deadly guilt and total unworthiness. There you quietly pray to him who is the source of all that's holy, the fountainhead of all goodness, and the origin of all glory. From him, one blessing after another flows to a person who truly prays. They come like waves rolling in on each other.

So what is there left to say? What is left to discover? I tell you, nothing at all as long as you're putting your best foot forward! But once you conduct that examination of the way you've been walking, unobserved by others and all by yourself, you discover for yourself what's there!

Examine the heart in your bosom, therefore.

"But I'm not a murderer," you exclaim defensively. "My heart certainly hasn't become a pit of murderers!"

Praise God for that! Not in the usual bloody sense of the term! At least, not yet! But don't be too sure! Let the person standing be careful lest they fall!

But I contend that you are, even in a criminal sense! For what would Jesus' own apostle understand by these words? This holy preacher of repentance who comes in the name of Jesus puts it like this: "Everyone who hates his brother, even only hates him, is already a murderer!"

Who hasn't hated. Doesn't the plant of resentment grow in your garden too? Is the weed of envy a stranger there? Does wishing them away—far, far away—prevent them from taking root? So don't talk too confidently in God's presence! He knows all about these things. The most inner and hidden secrets are open and exposed to his holy eyes.

If you place your heart in front of the mirror of God's searing law, do you really have much reason to boast or congratulate yourself. Tell me, my sister and brother, do you? When you let light, bright light, the light of God, shine on the secret ways of your heart, do you ever call other people to come and have a look? Don't you prefer to just keep that between God and yourself? And what does limiting it to something between God and your own soul tell you? Doesn't it tell you that things are so unspeakably scandalous that you are ashamed and can't even lift your eyes?

Oh, so much more than murder is going on in that pit of murderers! You find stealing going on there. And lying! Cruelty! Sensuality! Also brazen pride! It's no mystery that in that cave of bandits there's even a perverse shadow of piety, for you might even find a crucifix on the wall! You can find thieves falling to their knees when God in defending his honor causes his thunder to roll through the forest.

What's especially coldhearted is when you hold all this at arm's length and say: "At least I'm not involved in any of that!" But wait a minute! Think about

Zion's temple when Jesus drove out the sellers. What were those merchants doing? They came to bring their sacrifices. They came to donate their money to the treasury. They came to worship. They did what the Jews of former days had done, and against whom Jeremiah spoke out in the words that Jesus is quoting here. In their deceptive sighing they said: "The temple of the Lord! The temple of the Lord! This is the Lord's temple" (Jer 7:4). Against them, the prophet countered: "Will you steal and commit adultery and offer sacrifices to Baal? Then will you come and stand in my presence here in this house and call on my name? Will you actually say: 'We have been delivered,' when you commit all these abominations" (Jer 7:9–10)?

It was too much trouble for them to take a small dove along with them from home or to buy one in the city market. No, they had to defile themselves. Look, they could buy a dove right there in the temple, out of a basket, close to the altar, and lackadaisically hand it to a priest. That's what the veneer of piety had come to in Jerusalem. That's what Jesus' anger was directed toward. So he hit them right between the eyes, those hypocritical, self-satisfied, contemptible folks.

What about us? What about our piety?

What about the piety of our hearts? Those hearts that are intended to be a house of prayer? Isn't it frightening that in our perplexing hearts the shadow of true piety is so often married to the spirit prevailing in the murderers' pit?

"Have mercy! Have mercy on us, O Lord" is what the blind man whom Jesus had just healed called out. Shouldn't that be echoed by those who recognize the blindness in their own hearts? And shouldn't they add: "Do even more; do even more, O my Savior. Come with your whip and drive out the evil remaining in me!"

STAY AWAKE

What I say to you, I tell everyone: Stay awake! Mark 13:37

In God's Word, sinning is compared to sleeping. "Wake up, you who are asleep. Rise up from the dead, and Christ will shine on you," says the holy apostle Paul in Ephesians 5:14. "Wake up to righteousness and do not sin," the same apostle says in 1 Corinthians 15:34. In Romans 13:12, he compares the state of sinning to a "spiritual night" when he says: "The night is almost gone, the day is at hand. Let us therefore set aside the works of darkness and put on the armor of light. Let us live honestly, as in the day." Expressing himself in even stronger terms in 1 Thessalonians 5:6–7, he warns Jesus' church: "So, let us not sleep like others do. For those who sleep, sleep at night. But we are not children of the night, but we are children of the day and of the light."

If I were to say to someone, "Stay awake!" that would not mean in this context: "Watch over this house; keep watch on that ship!" That's when someone designates a person to stay awake in the sense of being alert to what's going on around them. Nor does it mean: "Stay awake with this patient in case she needs something in the middle of the night and there's no one around to help her." But "Stay awake!" here pointedly means "See to it that you're not overcome by sleep again," or "Don't let the situation be repeated when you're sleeping rather than staying awake!"

It's not the same with the soul as it is with the body. The body needs sleep at set times, after which it wakes up once more. Then it goes about its work, after which it slumbers again. It does each in turn, sleeps and stays awake. It does this throughout all of its life. But the soul must never sleep! Sleeping for the soul is just as bad, just as sinful, just as damaging as a healthy night's sleep can be a welcome blessing for a weary head or a worn-out body. Sleeping of the soul applies to the soul what applies to physical life. It doesn't belong there! Sleeping is deadly for the soul. It destroys it.

Our soul has to be fresh, clear, alert, effective. When it is, it can stay that way without interruption, needing not as much as a trace of rest. The body is exhausted by work; but the soul goes from strength to strength and from grace to grace through spiritual work.

Staying awake for the soul means lifting its head above the world's over-whelming clouds of smoke and seeing things as they really are. It means recog-nizing the Devil for the Devil he is. It means seeing Jesus seated on his throne. It means noticing how the dew of God's grace falls on his children for Jesus' sake like a shower of refreshing rain.

Staying awake is being able to explain how when they dream people often do crazy things. How they sin! How they are frequently seduced by gold, or fame, or leisure, or lusts of the flesh! But also how, when they wake back up from that shameful life of dreaming, they see how unsightly, disgusting, and offensive it all is. It's seeing that genuine rubies dazzle only in the heavenly Jerusalem and that the standards prevailing here on earth are only poor imitations.

So, we all need to take a stand, every one of us at their own post. How glo-rious and glorifying life would be then, if we all stayed awake, with our eyes open and on fire for the Lord!

But then one comes along who numbs us, dims the lights, drugs us, and gently rocks us so that we are literally overcome with sleep again. We and our entire family! With such a deep sleep that our darling little children are already born with dozing, slumbering souls! The result is that when they grow up, they require lighter doses of this sleeping medicine. Sometimes we find these boys and girls in a spiritual sleep that is so unruly and obstinate that they don't wake up even when we call or shake them! Oh, we have to admit it. That's just how it once was with us when we were sleeping deeply in the sleep of sin!

This is not to say that the sleep of sin always has to result in those kinds of outbursts of sin. No, it's not just about the outbursts; the sleep itself is already sinful. Even if no frightening dreams torment you, aren't you still sinning by simply lying there unconscious? Why wouldn't the quiet little girl who walks around the house with her sleeping soul be just as sinful in God's sight as the dreaming boy who runs out into the world?

Oh, it's definitely true that those vivid dreams can make sinning so much worse. But in principle it's the same thing. Such sleeping in and of itself is just as deadly, terrible, and sinful in God's eyes. It's that terrible because no individual by himself or herself can free themselves from that kind of sleep. However much you may want to, Satan is always standing right there with his bottle of chloroform. And the minute he detects any movement at all, he reaches over and applies more of his numbing poison.

Only the One who grabs Satan by the arm can save you. He's the only one who can bring you out of that sleep and keep you awake. He intervenes at that moment and makes sure that the chloroform never gets to you. He calls your name. He lifts you from your cot. He applies his eye drops to your eyes. Then he leads you out into the refreshing, invigorating air of God's glorious grace. That's when you've been awakened. You woke up! You're awake! Your will has been renewed. You've reached a higher level of consciousness. You're now aware of God as well as of yourself. Now you're really awake.

But now a worse danger intrudes.

How can you stay awake? How can you prevent Jesus from losing sight of you so that you won't fall back into bed and slip back into the same old sleep of sin? How can you prevent undressing and taking off your Christian armor? How can you prevent falling back into the arms of self-forgetfulness and imbibing a soul-deadening overdose?

Well, Jesus anticipated that danger! He foresaw it with his disciples. And he foresees it with each one of us. That's why, before he died, he told his disciples so emphatically: "What I say to you, I tell everyone: Stay awake!"

It's as though the Lord wants to tell you that you've just woken up, but that your eyes are still listless. You're inclined to go back to sleep. Your eyelids are still heavy. He wants to make you aware that the one who drugs and numbs the soul is watching you closely and that he'll take advantage of you every chance he gets. There are people who are willing to help him. They're ready to mix up a sleeping potion for you to drink and to sing you a lullaby. And if they ever notice that you're sitting down again and shortly after that stretch out and lay your head on sin's pillow, they'll become even quieter. They'll softly hum you a deadly tune. And when you're completely quiet, they'll tiptoe out of the room. Then, with a devilish grin on their lips, they'll whisper to each other: "We won! He's sleeping again! She's not thinking about God anymore!"

So, "stay awake!"

Stay awake not because that's what makes sense, or because you think it's to your advantage. Not because someone else tells you to, but because the Word of God tells you to.

"Stay awake" is what's written here. And the expression "It is written" is the only foolproof spell against slumbering again. It's the only antidote against the sleep medicine. It's the only thing that will close your ears to the lullaby. It's the only thing that keeps you from lying down again, but keeps you on your feet.

Jesus appeals: "Stay awake!" Whoever pays attention to these words from Jesus' mouth and really hears them discovers that his promise is fulfilled: "Even if you were to drink poison, it will not harm you." To their ears Satan's lullaby is hoarse screeching that only keeps them from sleeping rather than puts them to sleep. For them there are only sharp, pointed objects on the bed where they used to snooze; they prevent them from ever being able to lie down again.

"Stay awake!" says Jesus, and that command has wonder-working power! The soul can't sleep any longer. It has to stay awake, because Jesus keeps on repeating this to it. And isn't it true that as long as Jesus keeps on talking to you, your soul finds it impossible to slip back into the arms of sin. It doesn't, because it loves him!

VOLUME II

1

VOLUME II

KEEPING WATCH OVER THEIR FLOCK AT NIGHT

And there were shepherds in the fields nearby keeping
watch over their flock at night. Luke 2:8

If we should ever be envious, shouldn't we envy the shepherds out in Bethlehem's fields? Those men singled out for their exceptionally glorious privilege! The ones awestruck on that holy night by the flood of heavenly glory that no one else had ever seen! Those who saw God's heavenly hosts swooping and glistening above the fields! The men whose ears were ringing with the resounding angelic anthem "Glory be to God in the highest!" The shepherds who then made their way to Bethlehem and saw for themselves "the little baby wrapped in swaddling clothes and lying in a manger," basking in Mary's motherly gaze! Shouldn't we envy them?

That's the way our imaginations work about those shepherds! From the time we were young, that's the way that little band has struck us as they huddled down or half reclined on the sloping hillside with their white-wool sheep and their even whiter lambs still grazing or bedded down around them.

And when we think of how the silver moonlight bathed the whole scene just before it was completely overwhelmed by the glory of the Lord, there's hardly anything more beautiful or inspiring than the thought of those shepherds keeping watch at night over the flock entrusted to them there outside Bethlehem's gate.

But is that where we should leave matters? That they inspire us so that we envy them? Is that it? Don't they speak a word to our souls? A serious word? A word of warning?

Think about this: there are many others who are also shepherds, even though they may not tend actual sheep on the green grass of an actual field. The person tending real sheep is not the greatest shepherd. The Shepherd of all shepherds is the Lord, the great Shepherd of our souls. That's the first thing to say about this full, rich, prophecy-fulfilling notion of shepherds. He, our own Lord Jesus, is the Greatest Shepherd—he alone.

And because he is the Shepherd, the shepherd metaphor works so well here on earth. It does so for two reasons. It does so partly because actual people guide herds of cattle or flocks of sheep into green pastures. But in a much higher sense, it also works because the Lord God so arranges things that a given person is assigned to be the shepherd of a "flock" of people.

Who qualifies as a shepherd over a flock of people?

Aren't the king and governing authorities shepherds of the people? Aren't ministers of the Word also shepherds of the church? Aren't fathers and mothers shepherds of their children and their entire family? Look, aren't all those who are vested with authority over other people shepherds? This includes leaders over hundreds, managers of organizations, people with responsibility for the needy, teachers in all schools, and even those who lead the huge flock of human society by their influence, example, or directives.

To all of these it can be said: "You are the shepherd of those entrusted to you; they are your flock!" And there, in Bethlehem's night, the all-knowing God comes to all of us asking whether it can really be said of us: "And they were watching over their flock at night!"

The shepherd keeps watch at night out of concern for his profit margin. If he didn't, some wolf would snatch his lambs. So he better do so. He needs to keep bread on the table. His sheep live on grass, but he lives off his sheep.

That's basic.

The little band in Bethlehem's fields is picturesque and inspiring. But in itself that image conveys no great moral truth.

A shepherd only becomes great, prosperous, and praiseworthy when their shepherding is all about people's souls. That happens when the shepherding of their flock is not about what they can get out of it but about what they put into it. It happens when they are totally dedicated to that kind of shepherding. It occurs when shepherds dedicate their lives to their work.

Don't think now about the kings, who will have to give account to God. Don't think about the ministers of the Word, who are answerable to the One who sends them. Think only about yourself. Think about your shepherding. Think about the flock entrusted to you. Think about your own responsibility to keep watch over that flock at night. What does your conscience say to you about that? The year is coming to a close. Days are flying by. Give an account of yourself, reckoning with your own soul. Brothers and sisters, I ask, what have you done with your flock? What have you done with those about whom the Lord said to you: "I entrust these to you!"

So, tell me then, how do things stand with you on that matter? Are you keeping watch at night?

"Keeping watch at night," as you well know, does not mean that you sit along-side the little bed of a darling child when they are sick. You could do that night after night and the wolf could still drag your little lamb off. No, the real night is life lived without light. The circle of people who live in the light of God's grace and on whom his face shines live in the daylight. By contrast, night is the darkness of sin, the bleakness of the world devoid of holiness. That's the world your children have to live in. That's where they stand naked, confront-ing a double danger. That's where this world's darkness poses a double threat to their tender souls. The day watch over your children is the light shining around you in your home, where they are safe. But the night watch over your children is that heavyhearted responsibility you have when dangers encroach and bleakness descends and they could suddenly be gone.

That's why I said that sometimes there have been mothers who sat up all night a week at a time beside the bed of a dearly loved, sick child who never "kept watch at night." They simply lost sight of their little treasures when the blackness of sin descended on them and a soul-snatching wolf roamed around seeking to carry them off.

But the real kind of "keeping watch over your flock at night" requires dedication.

A good shepherd, Jesus tells us, dedicates his life for his sheep. Most people understand this to mean only rushing in to fend off the wolf the moment it attacks the sheep. But they forget that this requires that at the moment of attack you have to be there with the sheep. Always! You have to organize your life around your flock. You have to dedicate your life to your flock.

Sitting up with your child for two or three nights is asking a lot. But it passes, and that night watch is over. But the night watch over your children that we're talking about here is ongoing because your children always go about their lives in the night of sin. That's why they are always in danger. And that's also exactly why "keeping watch in the night" of sin is so exhausting.

How terrible—truly terrible—when parents are guilty of neglecting their care in this regard. Time and again a person encounters flocks in the night of sin that are left without a shepherd and have to find their own way. Their shepherd is relaxing in the daylight, thinking: "God will certainly take care of my youngsters!" Who can count the lambs that have been snatched and dragged off because a mother's eyes were shut and a father was indifferent to "the night of sin"? That night of sin is present out there in the world, but it also settles down over the school, over circles of little boys and girls, and over the parental home right down to the blankets on children's' beds.

But then there are also parents who "keep watch at night" even over some flock beyond their own door. These are the ones who have it really busy! That's why they sometimes leave their flock in the hands of another caregiver. That's turning God's ordinances on their head! They're keeping watch at night, all right, but not over their own flock!

Can there be peace in such an arrangement?

Will the heavens be able to open for us then?

Think about this. If the shepherds in Ephrath's fields had not been faithfully involved in keeping watch over their flock, they would have seen nothing of that night's brilliance, witnessed nothing of the Lord's glory shining around them, heard no angel song, and would never have paid homage to God's Holy Child.

Doesn't the same apply to you? The heavens still sometimes open. The holy light still sometimes shines down on the earth. God's ministering angels still sometimes bring blessed peace. And God's Holy Child is still paid homage.

In the name of the Lord, may these things be true for you, brothers and sisters—for the sake of your children and for the sake of your own souls. But you will never experience these blessed events, and the heavens will never open for you, unless the Holy Spirit testifies about you as well: "Also these shepherds kept watch over their flock at night!"

YOU COMPLETELY TRANSFORM HIS ILLNESS

The Lord will support him on his sickbed. In his illness, you will completely transform the bed on which he lies. Psalm 41:3[2]

Our sick and afflicted!

What an overwhelming amount of quietly endured pain and hidden suffering lies hidden behind that expression "our sick and afflicted"! Other people don't much notice, but there's often a lot of fear behind that curtain. How many illusions are exploded in the rooms of the sick! How many flickering hopes extinguished! How many little flowers snapped off their stems! Add the actual pain that goes along with this. Pain that is very intense! Constant pain! Pain that never ends! Pain that burns so deep that it penetrates our bones! It's all covered up so well. The majority of people hardly take any notice of it at all. But for our sick it's a different matter. Theirs is a different kind of world, and you can safely say that it's a terrible world, at least as long as people endure their suffering without God.

---

2. Psalm 41:4 in the Dutch text.

Do you pay much attention to those who are sick? Are they a living part of your prayers? Aren't they confined pretty much to the formal prayers of the congregation, although with pity and compassion, when it meets on Sunday?

They are "our sick," and you have a sense of what that involves. They belong to us. They are part of our circles. They are part of our congregation. They have left our homes and gone to their sick rooms. They are our flesh and blood. Our sick are lying there in order to send us a message. They're there to appeal to us in our casual superficiality by in effect telling us: "It won't be long before you'll be where I am." Our sick became sick so that we may shower our love on them. So that our faith might be evident to them! So that we might comfort them by what we say to them! Our sick that are lying in front of us dressed in their white gowns are like priests and priestesses who whisper: "This is all because of our sinfulness, and that involves you too!" Yes, why should we be writing only about "our sick"? They are salt to us in our corrupt and corrupting lives. If sicknesses had not come into their lives, how many others would never have found God? How much devotion and self-denial would never have seen the light of day? How much more unrestrained would those who light-heartedly pursue worldly pleasures have been? Illnesses serve as a restraining grace in our circle of the living. And that's the glory associated with those who lie ill among us. They suppose that they are doing nothing, but they are actually blessing us! They imagine that all their suffering is useless, when in fact it strengthens the bonds holding the Lord's household together.

Amazing, isn't it? To prevent all supports from collapsing under the weight of material pursuits and superficial diversions, the Lord God sends an attacking angel. From its bowl of wrath, it sprinkles some drops on a dearly loved, rosy-cheeked child who becomes pale and wastes away. Next a few more fall on a pious child of God who is zealous for the Lord of Hosts but is suddenly blocked in the prime of life.

If there has to be sickness at all, you say to yourself, why doesn't God afflict the godless or the aged who are going to die anyway?

Naturally, as long as you think about being sick as a useless waste of time, it won't make any sense. But if you see it as a time when the power of the kingdom can be displayed, then it's something else again. For through sickness, God can bind the Devil's work in the social order and open up opportunities for the greatest tenderness. Then you understand how a sick person sometimes is far more useful and accomplishes more for the Lord than a person in full health. Then you can also see why God often allows so many of his dearest children to become ill. It's because they are the ones through whom he can do his best work. God's dear children always have other children of God who love them dearly. So the situation turns out beautifully. God's dear children are Satan's favorite target. For that reason, they carry a heavier obligation to guard their soul than other people do. It's also true that when they're sick in bed, things often turn out better for them than for children of the world. Rivet and Witsius were both highly learned professors. But they may well have contributed more to building the inner kingdom of God during the few days that they were sick in bed than they did through all their scholarly writing! We can't calculate that, of course, but the spiritual power of a God-glorifying sickbed stretches incredibly far! It's a spark that starts a fire and that in turn starts others generation after generation. It's a seed buried in the ground that always produces even more grain at the tip of the stalk when it ripens.

So now ask whether God is acting unjustly! Ask whether he is being unfair by causing his dearest children to suffer!

Well, remember Golgotha! "He laid on him the iniquity of us all! By his stripes we are healed!" Now you'd like to drop your question, wouldn't you?

But not so quickly! Show a little of Job's courage and like him tell your would-be comforter: "God's ways are not always easy! I will accuse the Almighty and make my case before him!" For there's a definite solution. And it's presented in the words of the psalmist at the beginning of these reflections.

No, the Lord God doesn't act unjustly when he lays suffering on his dearest children. For, in the words of David, the Spirit says: "In his illness, you will completely transform the bed on which he lies."

The God who possesses such mysterious powers deals freely with his dearest children. And what is the mystery involved in this "complete transformation"?

Isn't it the mystery of Marah? Early in its pilgrimage, Israel came to a well in the desert, but it could not drink the water because it was too bitter. Then Israel's shepherd called on the Lord, and the Lord showed him something. He threw it into the water, and what happened? The bitter water became sweet. Then Israel continued on its journey in the wilderness until it reached twelve springs of water and seventy palm trees. And it camped by those waters.

And precisely that is the sacred mystery involving God's dearest children when they make their way through the wilderness of life's illnesses. He completely changes everything for them.

Not always! Sometimes he goes away and leaves people alone. That could be because they don't love him or because he wants to test their love. That's when things get very bad and seethe in the depths of their soul. That's when dark clouds roil, and when sometimes just a brief flash of faith's lightening still pierces the gloom.

But that's not where things stay. After a shorter or longer time, the Lord returns. Then a miracle happens. Even if the condition remains unchanged or the illness perhaps becomes even worse and the oppressiveness more frightening, it no longer involves what it did before. "God has completely transformed the bed of illness on which the person lies!"

The bitterness remained, but yet it became sweet.

That's because the Lord came. He embraced the soul. He breathed strength into it. He brought the comfort of his most tender reassurances.

Then a journey of faith commences. Everything takes on a new appearance. The branches of the palms sway softly in the distance as they stand among the refreshing springs of water. That's where God's children make camp. The onlookers think: "How terrible! How bitterly painful!" But God's children take no notice. "They find that what has crossed their lips is sweet rather than bitter!"

What makes all the difference is whether a sickbed is endured with God or without him!

ASK ABOUT THE ANCIENT WAYS

*Ask about the ancient ways where the good paths lie and walk
in them. Then you will find rest for your soul. Jeremiah 16:6*

Ancient ways!

Those are the paths on which people like us walked in ancient times. They had the same needs in their human hearts as we do in ours. They committed the same kinds of sin we do. They carried the same kinds of crosses in their lives. And they found rest for their souls where we do.

Today everything is in turmoil spiritually in the church of Christ, and therefore also with the spirit of our times as well. The yearnings of human hearts are in turmoil too. The cords of salvation that people hang on to are all tangled up.

This explains why the children of God in our day and age lack courage, are so worried, frightened, and weak. Everyone stumbles around on their own. They don't see a clear path ahead of them, one on which they can plant their feet and where they have an unobstructed line of vision. There is no clearly marked path. Looking for somewhere to rest, they find nothing. They go off in this direction or that and wander around until they finally collapse, unable to go any farther.

God in his mercy sees what's happening. He also sees that beyond where we are wandering around aimlessly, there's a wonderful, broad highway stretched out that leads where his people used to go. They had walked it calmly and with stamina. They had made progress confidently and found peace in their hearts on it.

So from heaven, our faithful Father calls to us in his compassion, pity, and tender mercy: "Ask about the ancient ways, where the good paths lie, and walk in them. Then you will find rest for your soul."

Who is listening to that appeal? Who is responding to it?

Praise God, there are those who do! Tired of their roving and wandering, they're looking once again for the peace to be found on that road!

"Ask about those ancient paths," admonishes the Word of God.

Not about each and every path that men wanted to walk in ancient times, but about those paths that were walked with such wonderful results by our forefathers. These are the paths that produced strength and courage, sacred joy and peace. They are the ones leading to the cross and to the Jerusalem that is above, the mother of us all! Divine strength comes to those who walk them. An inner working that is from above! An infusion of the power of the coming age into fragile creatures! It fills them with it!

In ourselves, we are nothing. As creatures we are mere vanity. In and of ourselves, we are incapable of any good and inclined to all evil. That's what's so unsettling. That's what wearies our souls. It exhausts us to the point of collapse.

But the ancient paths, that is to say, the ones that our fathers walked, were ones on which they made progress. On them they experienced that God is gracious. That's where they discovered that he wants to work in his creatures, reassures their souls, and is glorious in the lives of his saints.

This is the same thing to which God is calling us!

He doesn't summon us to an atlas or map where these paths have been drawn. No, he calls us to the paths themselves. He calls us to the paths where you know you're walking when you experience what our forefathers did. The same creaturely sense of full-blown misery! The same display of divine strength at work in us.

Oh, these are the paths where Satan is standing on the shoulder, looking to devour the souls of those who are walking there. But while he can glare at them in anger, he can never snatch them. They continue walking in safety, protected by the hand of the Lord!

But for that to happen, these paths actually have to be walked!

"Ask about the ancient paths and walk in them" is Jeremiah's divine directive.

Simply longing to take a look at the old paths isn't enough. Nor is being curious about what it would be like to actually set foot on them! Nor is having a slow, sluggish spirit that is so apathetic that it has to be coaxed to flee down them.

Not in the least! With the Lord our God everything has to be vibrant. And when his strength falls on one of his creatures, that liveliness needs to be expressed.

A path is meant to be taken. A road is designed to be walked on. And when you're scarcely on the right path, you hear the divine imperative: "Hurry up! Make progress!" For the old paths that people brag about and celebrate simply because they have discovered them but on which they fail to walk provide no blessing in your heart, but only destruction.

What's old and dormant doesn't provide rest for the soul. It only makes it musty!

How people merely jabber in response and only gape at shapes and sounds.

Yes, they're still serious about taking God's holy Word seriously so that they can trifle with that old toy of "then finding rest for your soul."

But no, rest for the soul by way of the old paths is not the rest of sitting still or lying down. But rest for the soul means that you've gotten rid of the fearful unsettledness of having to create your own road if you want to be on the right road. That's what causes real fear and tension!

Look! Formerly, everything demanded so much wearisome effort. But now your soul is like a horse that gloriously scampers down a mountain, as Isaiah puts it, and makes its way to streams of water.

But let me simply add this.

Following God's directive to "ask about the ancient paths," Jeremiah registers a harsh conclusion about his contemporaries. He adds: "But they refused to walk in them!"

They saw with their own eyes that the heathen around them offered no path.

They understood very well from historical sources that their fathers traveled the ancient paths.

They certainly heard the appeal: "Turn toward the ancient paths again!" But they didn't want to. They refused because they had proud hearts. They resisted because they understood perfectly well that to return to the ancient paths was to recognize that the path they had chosen was the wrong one. And they couldn't bring themselves to do that. That would have been a negative judgment on their own egos and their own insights.

No, better that they just put up with their unsettled hearts! They had once said that these ancient paths were antiquated and impassible. And they stood by that!

My good reader, are you going to fall for their conclusions? There's no salvation in them!

4

VOLUME II

FROM THE SEEDS TO THE SKIN

All his days as a Nazirite he shall not eat anything produced
from a grapevine, from the seeds to the skin. Numbers 6:4

The Lord our God is an amazing King, and his majesty knows no bounds! He will always be God. He conducts himself as God. He wants to be acknowledged as God. And as God, he exercises the power of his divine rule over all things, right down to the core of every one of them. As far as he's concerned, halfway measures don't apply. They simply don't exist! For him to be involved in something halfway would be to deny the attributes of his divine existence.

To halve something is to divide it! To divide something between God and another would be to accord it rights alongside and equal to God's. And this is precisely what God opposes with every fiber in his divine being. That's impossible. It's unthinkable. To name the "eternal name that is above every name" and in the same breath to mention it half-heartedly just makes no sense.

That's why God's Word always demands an unqualified "All or nothing!" God entirely, or you have no part of him! In various forms and ways in Scripture, the Holy Spirit literally and consistently rejects as intolerable any half-heartedness on our part with respect to God Almighty. He expresses this in ever-stronger terms and more compelling language.

Look, it's not just about loving God. But it's about loving God with all of your soul, with all your mind, with all your heart, and with all your strength. This basically expresses the glorious presence of God's unfathomable mercy in the inner being of a child of God. That's a mercy that continues despite their sense of continuing weakness.

As far as Scripture is concerned, therefore, it's not enough to say that God looks at the heart. It must be added that as our almighty and glorious God he sees what's beneath and behind our hearts. He sees to the hidden depths of our inner being. He searches us by the light of his holiness. And what he discovers by way of sin in our heart and inner being, he not only cuts off as branches, but he also pulls out by the roots.

To what does Scripture call us? What does the God who tests the heart and inner being and who fights sin root and branch require of us? What does he ask of us who confess his name? It requires that we distance our entire unrighteous existence from sin. Not merely from the sweetness of its sap! But as is so grippingly, pointedly, and soul-searchingly expressed here: "from the seeds to the skin!"

"From the seeds to the skin!" applies to the freely taken vow of the Nazirite. It is an example of one of those many means and instruments for promoting godliness in Israel. Nazirites were provided to serve the people of God in their battle against the Devil, sin, and the world.

A Nazirite took a vow not to drink any wine for a time. But the Nazirite's heart could be crafty, just like ours sometimes are. He could play games with the Lord and with his own soul. Like a Jesuit, he could look for exceptions to the rule. He could devise escape clauses and thus give the appearance of denying himself the enjoyment of the vine while behind the back and in ways covered by extenuating circumstances, he could take a few enjoyable sips! But he nevertheless maintained that he was really keeping his vow to God.

It's those extenuating circumstances that the Holy Spirit relentlessly forbids in this passage. There need to be unshakable, unfailing consequences tied to making vows to God. To make this transparently clear to the Nazirite in words than can never be taken ambiguously or have a double meaning, the Holy Spirit says what he does. His explanation emphasizes that he has to separate himself so completely from wine that he has nothing at all to do with a grapevine, with what could be called a grapevine, or with what is produced by a grapevine. He must not hang around wine like a gnat flits around a candle. He must forsake it no matter what form it takes or by what name it's known! He must do so for all the days covered by the vow! He must never so much as touch a bunch of grapes! But he must shun and flee the grapes hanging so temptingly in front of him! Absolutely and completely! From within and without, or from the seeds or pits within to the skins and peels without!

These words show divine passion, don't they? They come with divine determination. They penetrate to bone and marrow. Or to use another biblical expression that is just as powerful, he is "to hate even the smell that rises from the flesh!"

Who can measure up to those words? Who dares to claim they can? Who is willing to raise their hand and say: "Lord, neither the pits nor the skin cross my lips"?

Oh, every one of us from the best to the least is humiliated by the divine thoroughness reflected in these words. They expose the vanity of our half-heartedness and the unworthiness of our pretentious, haggling, and calculating behavior. We can each ask why we have not been called out on this score and why our trifling with the holy things of the Lord is not exposed.

What is even worse is when people defend such half-hearted living. When it becomes a pattern in their lives that passes for evenhandedness! For the rejection of extremism! As a restraint on one-sidedness, exaggeration, and fanaticism! Oh, what does it mean to act like Roman Catholics, either inside our churches or outside them, other than to embody that kind of pretense? Never to get to the heart of the matter! To have an aversion to being thorough! To always find excuses!

Sisters and brothers, what else is the battle in which God's children are engaged other than resisting tooth and nail that kind of endless dissembling? What else, fundamentally, is the struggle for God and his truth in which this generation of his people find themselves, if it isn't this? It's the struggle against dividing the honor of salvation between ourselves and God. It's the struggle against dividing our hearts between what is above and what is in this world. It's the struggle against dividing our awareness between what we believe and what we think. In short, it's the struggle against dividing into two parts all that is essentially one. By doing that we lose the energizing power of Reformed living and slip back into the laxness, pride, and ungodliness of a false faith that doesn't serve God but merely plays games with him.

So if you really want to prepare yourself for that battle, you'll be welcomed by the living Lord of Hosts. Even though that battle may exhaust you, God will give you the spiritual strength for it. He will exalt you in it, and he will fill your soul with a kingly power.

Just never forget one thing: whoever engraves this inscription on their shield, "Against All Half-heartedness!" but in their heart of hearts is really only playing games with God is not qualified for the battle! Nor have they been called to the honor of bearing royal power.

OUR DAILY BREAD

Give us this day our daily bread. Matthew 6:11

Who still prays for their daily bread?

That people still give thanks for it, praise God, is understandable. So is the fact that they still pray for a blessing on their daily bread. But that every morning people would still call on the Lord to provide their ordinary food, their daily bread—let me repeat the question—where is that still practiced?

Oh, our faithful Father in heaven is much too rich in mercy to expect that!

He has almost completely delivered his people living in Christian countries from famine. That someone living in a baptized nation would die of hunger is a terribly sad exception. Anxiety about how a person will be able to maintain life in the face of severe shortages is almost exclusively found only in very large cities. By far the majority of people are born, live, and die without ever having experienced actual hunger in their lives.

God is so good! He provides bread, the staff of life, so quietly, generously, and abundantly that our attitude seems to be that our daily bread simply falls into our laps every morning by itself.

I certainly am not forgetting the thousands upon thousands who have to work long and hard by the sweat of their brow day in and day out merely to earn "a few crusts of bread" for their wife and children. But a person would be completely mistaken if they expected that in those circles people implored God every morning for their daily bread.

Where there is little of no money, people still pray for work. A person can't provide for themselves without a job. But where there is employment, people think that the money will come and with it their daily bread. Most folks in such circles think that employment actually is provided by "good people" and that this is what allows a father to bring home the bread over which he asks no more than God's blessing.

That this is a very unbelieving approach is obvious immediately! As though you with all your money have the power to grow as much grain as goes into the flour contained in a lump of bread dough! As though you have the wisdom and knowledge needed to figure out how to turn that loaf of bread into nourishing food suited for human beings! As though you control why it doesn't make people sick but is always appetizing and, as Scripture says, is the staff of life on which our human existence depends and flourishes! As though you can ever achieve all of this by all your slaving and toiling! And especially as though the divine favor and determination of God's providence is unnecessary for providing exactly as much freshly baked bread as is needed! In every city and village! Every morning! From the oven and into the pantry! In every house! Then from the pantry to every single person in all those houses! Just as much as is needed every single morning! Every noon! And every evening! For feeding the millions upon millions of people living in a Christian country!

So it's not simply all about having a job and earning money, not by a long shot!

Even if you earn money hand over fist, even if you are never denied the pleasure of a hearty meal, even if you are bathed in wealth and abundance, then—especially then—you and your family need to implore God for your allotted portion. It behooves you as a small and insignificant creature to do this every morning, for he is the amazing God who has not only conceived and created our bread. He is the very One who provides and distributes it.

Even so, still more needs to be said.

Look, the prayer "Give us this day our daily bread" is actually a prayer that people can only pray when they believe and when they live by faith. People say so offhandedly: "Anyone can pray that prayer." They imagine that the spiritual gift of faith is necessary only when it comes to praying. But people are sadly mistaken in saying that. No, as long as faith has not renewed our hearts, that prayer for a bite of bread may sometimes cross our lips but never come from our heart. For apart from faith, it makes no sense at all to pray for bread that is already standing on the table in front of you. In that case it would make sense to pray that you would have bread tomorrow, but certainly not for today!

And if you should ask what difference it makes, then, whether people believe, here's the answer.

Without faith, a rich person thinks: "My money is my money, and as long as I have money, I'll have enough to eat!" That's why the idea of first asking God for something to eat just doesn't occur to them. Similarly, the day laborer thinks: "I have to work in order to earn my bread, but as long as I'm employed I don't have anything to worry about!"

But it's something else entirely when faith is involved and doing its work. Then the rich man says: "My money is money from God that I have to devote to his service; then, because I'm serving him, God ministers to me by feeding me and taking care of me." Then the day laborer says: "The work I do, I do by the will of God. I do it not for the purpose of earning a living, but in order to be faithful in my calling. If I take care to serve God, I have no needs because God sees to it that I have my bread!" Without faith it's about working for pay; but in faith it's about being children in the Father's house.

For isn't it the case that a child doesn't do what their father says in order to earn their bread, but they obey their father and the father gives the child their allotted portion?

6

VOLUME II

YOUR CHILDREN HAVE FORSAKEN ME

How could I forgive you for this? Your children
have forsaken me. Jeremiah 5:7

No one can comprehend how long-suffering the Lord God actually is.
For if you could grasp that, you'd have to be like God himself! You'd have to be able to see everything just as accurately and sharply as God does. You'd have to be able to listen to people's sorrows like God does. Even more importantly, you'd have to be able to feel in your own heart just as much abhorrence as God does for sin and everything that is called sin. Only then you would actually be able to understand what God suffers because of us. Then you'd be capable despite all this of knowing how tremendously far God's long-suffering has to extend in still reaching out to us and in being patient and gracious toward us.

Oh, do you really know what this long-suffering God once had to announce to Jerusalem?

Jerusalem had to be destroyed! The enemy was already pulling down her walls. Soon, very soon, the temple would collapse. And that's exactly when the Lord God made this extremely gracious offer through his prophet Jeremiah: "If among all your inhabitants there is still one single person, whether man or woman, whether young or old, who seeks what is true, then I will spare them and be gracious toward your city!" (Jer 5:1).

And that's also when Jeremiah started looking. That's when he began searching for that one person on whose account Jerusalem would be saved.

He went around in the marketplace. He searched the alleys and hedges where ordinary folk went about their daily activities. He looked where the day laborers were doing their jobs and where the beggars were begging. But, sad to say, he found no one. They were all distracted. Deeply distressed, he had to complain to God: "O Lord, if you are looking for one who is true, I have to admit that even those who are worried and suffering have hardened their hearts against you; their faces are hard as stone" (v. 3).

But Jeremiah didn't give up. These were only the poor, simple, uneducated people who didn't know the law. So now he would go to the more refined class of people, to the important and powerful people who lived in the palaces on the canals (v. 5).[1]

Yet, he met the same disappointment there and he had to register the same complaint to God about them: "They're all in this together, the rich along with the poor, for they have broken your yoke and ripped off their holy, divine ties to you" (v. 5).

But even then Jeremiah did not give up in his compassionate quest. This thought occurred to him: "What would happen if this generation died off and passed from the scene, and if the Lord would build a new congregation with their children?" Then standing their ground would be assured. Then they would be spared from what was coming. Then, with new tongues, these people's descendants would give God the shining glory due him in Jerusalem! And the outcome would be their salvation!

And even this was a possibility!

Sometimes it pleases the Lord to allow his grace to skip a generation or two and to have the children give him the glory once again that their parents denied him. But that's exceptional. Most often that's not how it goes. As a rule, the children diverge even further than their parents have. And that's how it was in Jerusalem as well.

This is what produced Jeremiah's plea: "Lord, forgive them for the sake of their children!" But the terrible, heart-wrenching answer came: "How could I forgive them for this? For their children have also forsaken me and stray even further from God's ways in their pursuit of other things."

So it was all over for Jerusalem!

---

1. This is Kuyper's none-too-subtle attempt to apply the prophecy to the Dutch scene. Jerusalem had no canals!

But what do you think about our own situation?

Are we any better? Do we have room to celebrate? Is there definitely a large crowd of people seeking the truth among us? Also among our children?

Look around you!

Does it amount to seeking truth when you see people sitting down and enjoying the reading of some orthodox book? Or reaching for devotional material? Or happily listening to pure, error-free Reformed preaching? If this is what it means, then "Yes, there are people by the thousands who are still seeking the truth."

Or does seeking the truth amount to being opposed to lying? Not cheating a lot? Being who they say they are when they talk a great deal about "being truthful"? Once more, if that's what it's all about, then "definitely!" You find those who seek the truth in huge numbers among people who don't follow the Word of God.

But if seeking the truth is not either one of these, but if it's basically rather about finding someone who tells the truth about what they think of us, then doesn't almost everyone fall outside what's involved? For telling the truth means saying what God's Word says about us! Isn't seeking the truth all about finding out what God thinks of us?

Isn't it about not becoming too angry and hotheaded when a person tells us the truth about ourselves? About not simply dismissing someone like that out of hand? About suppressing our excuses and sometimes just being willing to listen to such a person? And when we finally have no excuses left and are convinced somewhat unwillingly, isn't it about admitting that they are right? That's when you're definitely seeking the truth, even though you may only do it occasionally.

But who has any desire to listen to someone who tells us the truth? Man-to-man? On a personal level? Who humbles us in the sight of God until we are empty-handed? Who has any desire to go looking for him ourselves? Much less to reach out for the hem of his garment? To pray that he conceal nothing from us? And when he wounds us, who has any desire to reach out for the hand that struck us and to bless him who pushed us off the pinnacles of our pride? Just tell me, who is up for this? Who does it? Who wants to?

Or haven't you noticed or encountered the smooth talkers who bait people. Haven't you noticed how people seek out flatterers? Haven't you discerned all the falsification of God's truth that permits people to freely go their own way? Haven't you seen all the games being played with our conscience? The half-truths told? The way matters are relativized and excused? If not, then you have to be told that all these enemies of the Word are for all the world nothing more than wicked attempts to evade its moral judgments.

And simply let me add this yet: Have you ever realized that the person to whom the Word truly speaks cannot fail?

But maybe there's more hope for our children! For the second generation. For those who succeed us.

In Jerusalem, the parents were still doctrinally orthodox, or you might say that they still believed in the Trinity (v. 2). But because in fact there was no truth in them, the children strayed still further and ended up denying that God was even God. Accordingly, they walked in even more wicked ways.

And what about now?

Those who are older still hold somewhat to "the heritage of the fathers" while the children let it slide. They acknowledge that they have to be upright, but that to be upright they also have to be progressive. The result is that they believe nothing! The situation is terrible. This cancer rages in our offspring! Our sins live in worse forms in our children.

And now you want to meet that terrible evil with a few warnings, by singing some simple songs, and by offering a new generation Sunday school lessons in an attempt to shape them to fear the Lord!

What a horrible delusion!

For sure! Double your warnings. Sing beautifully to your children about Jesus. Spread your Sunday schools to every corner of the earth. That's obligatory. That's excellent! And as long as you do all this according to the demands of the Word, these are godly efforts! But by themselves these efforts won't change the situation. And it won't save your children.

It's only the truth that has power in the face of such destruction. You have to be willing to hear the truth that people speak to you. And this has to cause you and your children to enter the truth. Only then will the bewitching power of the lie be weakened.

Only then, my good reader, will an unshakable foundation on which they can build solidly be laid in the hearts of your children.

LIVING WITH HOSTILITY TOWARD THE LORD

If for this reason you do not listen to me, but would rather behave
with hostility toward me, then I will also act with hostility
toward you in my own intense anger. Leviticus 26:26–27

Hostility is something entirely different from adversity. By "adversity" we understand that things don't go as we wish. They don't meet our expectations or aren't successful.

But when Scripture talks about "hostility," it intends to convey something much deeper. Then it has in mind God being against us. It conveys that the Almighty is contending against us. It indicates that the Lord confronts us with wrath and anger in our lives.

"Hostility" does not simply mean "disastrous events" in our lives, therefore. But it refers to attacks by Almighty God on our hearts, our very existence, and our lifestyle. They are designed to shatter our pride and arrogance. But God's hostilities toward us are always preceded by other hostilities, namely, those that we show toward God.

Listen to me carefully in my attempt to clarify for you what the Lord says to Israel through his servant Moses in this beautiful twenty-sixth chapter of Leviticus. This is laid on our hearts already in verse 21 with mounting seriousness and considerable force: "And if you act with hostility toward me and do not listen to me, I will afflict you sevenfold because of your sins."

He puts it even more sharply in verse 23: "But if you are not self-disciplined in these matters, but act with hostility toward me, I will afflict you sevenfold according to your sins."

And finally and most forcefully, he says in verse 27: "If for this reason you do not listen to me, but would rather behave with hostility toward me, then I will also act with hostility toward you in my own intense anger and will discipline you sevenfold according to your sins!"

Pay close attention, my brothers and sisters, to this struggle that God has with his creatures. It's not comparable to the Almighty's contention with Pharaoh in his pride. No, here it's not a struggle with God's enemies, the ungodly, or children destined for destruction. This struggle is against his own people, the children of the kingdom, his covenant partners. It is "covenantal vengeance with which I will take revenge," says the Holy One of Israel.

That's why we're dealing here with a wrath of God that no Pharaoh could arouse in him or that no Belshazzar could provoke in him. Rather, it's anger that cries out for satisfaction on the part of our commiserating God when his love is denied, his mercy is scoffed, and his compassion is trampled underfoot. It's an anger, then, that is even more terrible than the wrath visited on Pharaoh, but at the same time it's to be distinguished completely from the destructive anger seen there. The purpose of this hostility of God toward his people is always to be seen in the context of his covenant. Its purpose is always to render his chastised people tenderhearted and to have them celebrate once again their experience of God's love.

Any Christian would be completely wrong who imagined that all of God's chastisements are only designed to test our faith. Or that they amounted to suffering with Christ for the purpose of our being cleansed in him. Or that all conflict that God might have with us can be explained entirely by our narrow-mindedness or less-than-Christian ways of thinking.

No, the conflict that God has with his people arises when it becomes obvious that our intentions are to oppose the flow of his holy benefits toward us. Then such conflict with his church, his servants, and the children he loves is not only thinkable but actual. It happens when we oppose his laws and ordinances. It occurs when we persist in our desire to resist his will. It results when we act in hostility to the Lord our God with mind and will. For the Lord never, ever tolerates that kind of thing.

He doesn't tolerate it because it would result in our complete apostasy.

He doesn't tolerate it because such erroneous direction in our living would completely disrupt the proper functioning of his covenant.

But he also doesn't tolerate it because the honor of his name is at stake.

This is why the moment that your unbelief, faithlessness, infidelity, and absence of tender affection toward him assume the proportions of hostility to God, he confronts you head-on! He does so even though your opposition to him has only a tenth of full-blown hostility toward him. He does so because it reflects determined opposition toward him. Then as sure as his Word is "yea and amen," he will oppose you, discipline you, and chastise you as long as it takes until you yield to your God, fall to your knees confessing your guilt, and in tears of humble remorse admit: "Lord, you are just!"

But now you're still perplexed about one thing.

Considered superficially, it makes almost no difference whether the Lord God deals with someone in hostility or whether he is chastising that person in tender compassion in order to test their faith. A person can almost never discern the difference with the naked eye. They usually see the horrible discipline in hostility and the chastisement in love as two virtually indistinguishable drops of water.

Remember Job. His high-minded friends stoutly maintained that his afflictions were "Jehovah's hostility toward his servant" when that wasn't the case at all. Job's suffering was terrible. But it was definitely not "an expression of the Lord's hostility."

Just as Eliphaz, Bildad, and Zophar were mistaken, it's also possible for you to be mistaken when you witness one of your brothers suffering terribly and think to yourself: "That's because of his sinning. He never did do what I told or advised him!"

Be very careful, here, my brothers and sisters! That's never appropriate for us who cannot judge the heart. But you may definitely assert that about God's people taken as a whole.

When you experience bitter suffering yourself, you definitely ought to examine yourself and ask: "Am I resisting the flow of God's sacred benefits in my life?" But where you're not involved, and this is happening to someone else whose hidden motives and ordained outcome have not been disclosed to you, don't be quick to express an opinion. Let your lips be sealed.

Whether the bitter suffering of someone else's soul is actually an expression of God's angry hostility or of his purifying love is known only to that person in the depths of their own heart. Don't forget it!

It's also known to God, who truly knows their heart. But you don't!

IF YOU ABIDE
IN MY WORD

If you abide in my Word, you are truly my disciples. John 8:31

What is the Word of Jesus in which we are to abide?

This is certainly not to be taken as his demands, requirements, or commands! For then the "blood of the new covenant" would no longer be a means of reconciliation in the covenant of grace. Then we'd be right back at the foot of Mount Sinai! "Do this and you will live!" Then we poor Christians would be worse off than the Jews in ancient times, and in our natural powerlessness we'd be the most miserable of all people.

So then what is his Word?

In an effort to enlighten you on this, let me take you into the bedroom of your little children.

You certainly know what sometimes makes your little ones difficult in the evening. Sometimes they are terribly afraid. What makes them so afraid is their unsettledness due to being overly stimulated or overly excited. Or it may be due to a troubled conscience. It might be caused by an insensitive nanny or a brother who teased them.

But whatever it is that makes them fearful, that fear is something terrible for a small child.

Then they actually see grotesque figures in every corner of the room and ghastly creatures behind every bed and dresser. They glare monstrously from every nook and doorway. Children see them so vividly and definitely that they can't be dissuaded of this for all the money in the world. So they cling to you in their deadly fear. With trembling voices, they plead with you to stay with them, not to leave them, and above all to leave the lights on because in the darkness … "they" will come out!

Nothing helps! Not threats! Not punishment! None of this matters to a frightened child.

Well, no—one thing does! There is still one thing that can calm this kind of frightened child. It's a word from their mother!

When their mother is a tender and loving woman to whom her children cling, then it sometimes helps if she quietly, calmly, and patiently sits at the foot of the bed for the entire evening, maybe even for a whole night. It helps when she bends down over the child and pulls them tightly against her breast. It helps when those wild eyes find shelter in the recesses of her heart. What ultimately calms the child and restores their confidence is when their mother very quietly assures her little darling that there is no bogeyman in the corner and that there are no wolves leering at them from behind the doors. And what really helps is when she simply walks over and shines light there, then quietly suggests to her already-calmer child that there are probably angels filling the room instead. Then the fears are hushed. Then the mother's words often set the child free and their anxiety is diminished. Then the little head lies down peacefully and begins falling asleep.

As long as the child believes the mother's word, they remain calm, and fear no longer grips their heart. As long as they believe that what they thought they saw in the corners and behind the doors are not there, they're fine. But if they forget their mother's word and return to their unfounded imaginations and suspicions, then their eyes start rolling around in fear all over again. But if the child "focuses on the words" of their mother, then look what happens. They remain calm; calm brings rest; rest turns to slumber; and very shortly their slumber produces sleep. The child is happy!

Shouldn't that small child provide us with an example of what it means for us children of this world "to abide in the Word" of our Lord Jesus? Don't we find ourselves in virtually the same position as that child?

Don't we also see almost everything other than it really is? Our own heart? Our own personhood? Our ability? Our happiness? Our surroundings? Our fellow human beings? Our personal sin? Our death and what awaits us after our death? Heaven? Our God? Don't we have impressions of all these that are entirely wrong and aren't consistent with reality?

Is there as much as one person who ever sees what's behind things without being mistaken? Is there as much as one of us who peers through the cracks and crevices of human reality and discerns what's really going on? In fact, is there as much as one of us who fixes their gaze on the corners and behind the veils of their own heart who calmly, truthfully, and with resignation perceives what's really going on there? Do they discern how matters actually are?

Don't we wander around as though in a haze?

Aren't we living in one continuous state of self-delusion? And isn't that enormous self-delusion precisely the source of all our weakness and trouble? And doesn't being converted from that realm of illusion, mirages, and self-deception finally and ultimately require nothing short of daring to look ourselves in the face and seeing ourselves clearly and honestly in the mirror for what we really are?

How do we get to that point?

And what is that mirror?

I ask you to tell me what it is if it's not precisely this "Word of Jesus!"

The Word of Jesus is something fundamentally different from him saying to you: "You've got it all wrong! Things are not what you think they are!" It's when he says: "Look, this is how it is!"

This is how it is. So listen when Jesus starts speaking. Now his Word is coming. Now that Word describes reality as it is. Now it describes what's going on in your own heart, in your thinking, in your deliberating, in your gut. It's a description also of what's going on in the hearts of others, and in the world, and under the world in Satan's realm! But on the other hand, it's also a description of what death is and of what follows death. It's a description of life with God, of his sacred dealings, and of life in the tents of his mercies!

So that's his Word. It's a world of ideas. Or to put it more accurately, it's a world of true thought about this world and the world to come.

Now the question occurs to you: "What now?" The way you visualized and imagined the way things were in, around, and above you with your distorted vision was thus and so. But according to the Word of Jesus and the way he represents them, the things within, around, and above you are turned totally upside down! So what do you now hold to be true? Do you say: "I see things exactly as they are; Jesus gets it wrong"? Or do you acknowledge: "My vision is distorted; Jesus' Word is certain and sure"?

If it's the latter, from that moment on you no longer live with your perception of things, but you abide in Jesus' Word.

Yet, as far as your Savior is concerned, that's still not enough.

Sometimes, when a mother slips out of the bedroom, the little one who has just fallen off is startled awake because they have forgotten their mother's reassurances and now see the wolves again.

Jesus knows that the same thing all too often happens with us. He doesn't want that to happen. It would mock him if it did.

So he whispers quietly in our soul: "It's not enough that you enter into my Word. No, if you're really my disciple, you have to abide in my Word!"

9

VOLUME II

HEARTLESS!

*You foolish and heartless people who have eyes but do not see and
ears but do not hear, will you not fear me? Jeremiah 5:21–22*[1]

The world apart from God says that in order to gain knowledge, achieve scientific understanding, and become wise, you have to develop, use, and sharpen your mind. In our era, the worth of a person is based on the knowledge that they possess in their head. The first and most important recommendation that our generation makes about someone is that they are smart. People put all the emphasis on a person's brains in assessing proper development.

To be stupid, particularly to be clueless and devoid of any understanding, makes a person a fool and a lunatic. This seems to be the most horrible, terrible, and dreadful condition that could befall anyone born of a woman.

Oh, our century lives by what's in the human head. It looks to human thought for its strength. In doing so, this rational age slips into an imaginary world. Imagining that it hungers for what is real, it pursues nothing more than the fleeting shadows of its own thought processes.

How totally different this is from what the Lord God teaches us. In his Word, God says: "The gateway to knowledge is not found in your head, but in your heart." It's not the case that your head is the means by which you accumulate knowledge and that your heart only serves to express your feelings. No, not in the least! Rather, in order to develop understanding, accumulate knowledge,

---

1. Kuyper cites only a portion of these two verses.

and even share in wisdom, the driving force within you is not your brain, but it's found in the recesses of your heart.

Consider for a moment how often a very plain woman is so much further advanced in a practical understanding of life than her very educated husband. She has a deeper insight into things, a fuller awareness of what's going on around her, a better understanding of people, and a greater wisdom in dealing with matters than he does.

Or notice once with what sensitivity and clarity the simple folks of the countryside taste and smell that this or that preacher deviates from the truth despite appearances to the contrary. While at the same time, the town's mayor, doctor, notary, and all those with some education in the community proceed confidently and give no evidence whatever of having detected anything wrong.

And even observe how sometimes a mere child can immediately discern in its heart the crafty character of someone it has just met. You stand amazed at the resoluteness with which it resists such a person and how in just a few critical moments it knows how to respond.

All of this is natural, isn't it?

Just ask yourself what it takes for a steamship to slice its way safely through the waves of the ocean. That only happens when there is vigilant attention in the engine room, a sharp eye on the bridge, immediate obedience of orders with respect to the mast and rigging, and a complete comprehension of external conditions like currents, tides, winds, the clouds above and the waters below, and whatever else is around, above, or behind that ship. But just imagine what would happen if the man at the helm were asleep! If those responsible for the mast were inattentive! If no one thought about currents, tides, or winds! And if all reliance were pinned only on the solid, quick, and fine work in the engine room! You'd be dealing with a ship of fools!

But isn't that what's going on in our day and age? In the wheelhouse of the heart? With respect to the rigging of emotional life? Concerning the spiritual tides and currents of the day? Relative to the dealings of the Lord our God above, behind, and around us? People aren't inquiring about these matters. They're not concerned about them.

They're only paying attention to the engine room of the brain! Everything is sacrificed for it. That's where everything has to be responsive, well maintained, and glistening. So the ship plows ahead and steams through the waves without anyone ever asking the question: "Where is our age headed? What direction are we taking with all our knowledge?"

God's Word identifies as "foolish" the person who is heartless. Or one who is dull-hearted. Or someone who neither looks within nor looks up with the eyes of their heart! It calls "foolish" anyone whose ear no longer catches the whisper telling it to look up or within.

Just read Jeremiah. We cite him chapter and verse above.

Isn't it even more than foolish when you find people who confess Jesus but who reduce the knowledge of God to a matter of memory or an exercise of the brain?

Isn't it even worse than foolish when you find heart and head pitted against each other in Christian circles in a way that asserts: "Knowledge is less important; the heart is what it's all about"? This would be to act as though God's Word advocates that the heart is not the instrument for acquiring true knowledge of God and of divine matters. But get this very straight: the heart is not merely the source of emotions. It is the place within you where God works. From there he also works on your head and on your brain.

Isn't it more foolish than foolish when you see parents of baptized children allowing those children's hearts to become dull by emphasizing sharp thinking and getting smart by focusing so heavily only on what they think is genuine science?

Isn't it the height of folly when you see born-again Christians, children of God, who have closed the eyes of their hearts and never learned to listen with the ears of their heart? They simply muddle along with an impoverished knowledge of God until the day they die!

And isn't it the pinnacle of all foolishness when you even find ministers of the Word who are heartless, that is, who are devoid of any knowledge of the essence of things? They simply stand in front of an equally "heartless" congregation, a church with a stunted sense of the truth, and attempt to make things better by appealing to the heart only on an emotional level and consigning all knowledge only to the head.

Isn't all this foolishness obvious among you, the Israel of our day?

10

VOLUME II

A MURDERER FROM THE BEGINNING

You are from your father, the Devil, and you want to do what
he wants. He was a murderer from the beginning. John 8:44

Recently people have mockingly dismissed Christianity in Germany by saying that its distinguishing feature is not that people there believe in God but that they believe in the Devil. And there's an element of truth in that apparent paradox.

Someone who doesn't go any deeper than the superficial, casual affirmation "I believe that there is a God" is really operating on a considerably lower level from someone who confesses with dismay: "I definitely believe in the existence of a personal Devil." To believe that there is a God is so customary that by saying so a person suffers neither scorn nor ridicule because most people still do. With that vague testimony on their lips, people can simply go on living as though there really is no God. They can fashion a God of their own imagination who has very little likeness to the living God of the Word and thus in fact really doesn't exist at all.

But it's a completely different matter if you believe in the existence of a personal Devil. That brings you into immediate conflict with respectable, refined folks. Then you can expect to be mocked and scorned. People will scoff at you as a narrow-minded religious fanatic. Yes, that's a confession that takes moral courage to maintain without wavering. The fact that nine-tenths of the people still attach significance to the existence of a God, while at most only a tenth still do on the existence of the Devil, demonstrates that a lot more is at stake with respect to the latter than the former.

But that's just obvious.

To believe that God exists can simply mean repeating what you've learned from others. It doesn't really register or make a difference internally. But when you've really battled, doubted, or been in denial and then finally prevailed, you come to recognize and understand that the Devil really does exist. You admit it, and behind that profession is a wide battlefield of moral conflict witnessed by God's angels. You've had to engage sin in all its power. You've discovered something of the depth of the abyss. Sin ultimately emerged as so horribly frightening to you that you exclaimed: "That should never take root in a person's life. It has a much deeper source. It arises from the pit of ruin. It comes from the Devil himself!"

Precisely because you then understood that such horror could not be rooted in humanity but had to originate with the Devil, you were also able to believe in the possibility of rescue, atonement, and the restoration of what has strayed off course. You saw that humanity is still salvageable, while the Devil can never be rescued and reconciled. He is forever consigned to drag the chains of the abyss around behind him.

Believing that there is a personal Devil is to believe in the depths of misery and in the possibility of deliverance. Even more profoundly, it is to believe that rescue can come in no other way than through a personal Savior. As long as I see sinning as only a bad habit, it's perfectly understandable that I'll keep trying to replace it with good habits. But once I recognize that it's not merely about a bad habit but above all about a powerful person who enslaves me, my heart begins feeling the need for another, more powerful person who is capable of destroying the work of the Devil and becoming my Deliverer.

We really don't need to haggle over the fact, therefore, that the belief that the Devil is a personal being provides a greater guarantee for moral courage, genuine spiritual experience, and orthodox teaching than the superficial acknowledgment that there is a God.

Even more, it's worth emphasizing that belief in the existence of the Devil can't happen without believing at the same time not just that there is a God, but also without believing in that God!

If that were not the case, even momentarily, the Devil would then be the stronger of the two beings for such a person. This would in effect make the Devil their God. What nonsense that would be!

We don't want to lose sight of this apparent paradox in the thought of the mockers. Rather, we emphasize it with some urgency in order to urge the church of Christ to develop its thinking about the Devil much more deeply than it has in the past.

Jesus himself set the example for us in this respect. He always kept the Devil in mind. His whole battle and all of his struggles, in fact the whole purpose of his life, were to tear down what the Devil had built up. His intent was to rebuild what Satan had destroyed. All the suffering he endured originated with Satan, the ruler of this world.

All prayer should be supplication to be delivered from the Evil One. All sin that occurs is, as far as Jesus is concerned, nothing else than doing what Satan wants. In an attempt to characterize how terrible this enterprise in all its horror really is, Jesus does not shy away from the hard-nosed judgment that fundamentally all sinning is to commit murder of the will and conscience.

He calls it murder from the beginning! But not murder in the beginning! It's not just murder in Eden, but it's always murder! It's not just murder in the case of Adam, but in the case of every newborn infant, in the case of every person who has ever lived, in the case of each and every one of your loved ones for whom you pray!

To be a murderer means to attack human beings with intense effort. It means being preoccupied with digging their graves, handing them poison, and sucking out their lifeblood. It means doing all this in an effort to render them defenseless, senseless, and so weakened that they are eternally estranged from God, their Source of Life. This is what murder means here.

So now I ask you in all seriousness where and with whom in our ordinary, daily lives do you find even as much as a feeble sense of the urgency with which such a belief in Satan should grip and constrain us?

Who lives with it?

Who prays against it?

Who strives for their own and their children's salvation from the danger it poses?

"A murderer!" No, that conviction still constrains almost no one!

If you would return to the circles where you live your daily lives, my brothers and sisters, with that frightening word from Jesus squarely before you, I would think that you and I would hardly need preachers anymore! We wouldn't need them to strengthen our faith concerning the Devil. What we would need are ones who warn us much more than they do, who impress that awareness more deeply in our consciousness, and who give it sharper definition for us.

IN THE SPIRIT ON THE LORD'S DAY

I was in the Spirit on the Lord's Day, and I heard behind me
a voice as loud as the sound of a trumpet. Revelation 1:10

The first chapter of the book of Revelation is preeminently a Sabbath chapter.

First comes the regal greeting of peace with which Jesus' apostle blesses the congregation: "Grace to you and peace from him who is and who was and who is to come, and from the seven spirits that are before his throne, and from Jesus Christ, who is the faithful witness, the firstborn of the dead, and the ruler of the kings of the earth." This is a greeting of peace that is so glorious because it immediately transports the congregation from the immediate, limited present to the eternal. There that which "is, and was, and is to come" all converge. And that's where all the powers of this world lift their eye of faith to the Prince of All Life, who extends his control over all the rulers of this earth.

Like a refrain, the homage of the congregation to the one and only ruler follows immediately: "He who loved us and washed us from our sins by his blood has made us kings and priests in the service of God his Father; to him be power and glory through all eternity!" This is worship of the congregation that reflects the same sense of eternity and the same acknowledgment of Jesus' exalted royalty.

But understandably, matters don't end there.

The Christian Sabbath is not when someone else speaks to a person on behalf of Jesus. It's not when they then respond by expressing a word of homage for the Mediator to that other person. For Jesus as the Son of God, the Sabbath is basically when he himself discloses himself to them and when he himself testifies to them with a soul-piercing effect. It's when Jesus himself speaks to them and when they listen to his voice in the depths of their soul.

That's why this chapter immediately points us above, to him who will return on the clouds of heaven. It focuses on the living Christ, not one who is dead. It directs us to the Christ who speaks from his throne in glory and who declares: "I am the Alpha and the Omega, the beginning and the end." The Lord adds: "I am the One who is, who was, and who will come again; I am the Almighty!"

But who actually hears that voice? Everyone?

Oh no! But only John! And why John?

Look! Here's the answer: it's because the other inhabitants or visitors on Patmos were involved with their own spirits or caught up on the spirit of this world. He, on the other hand, "was caught up in the Spirit," that is, in the Holy Spirit, the Spirit of God.

What this intends to say is very clear. As soon as and to the extent that any thought, idea, suggestion, or event reflecting the spirit of this age enters, fills, and controls you, you stand outside and beyond yourself. Then you no longer set the tone in your soul for your thinking and living. But you concede them to the spirit of the world, if not to the spirit of the Evil One himself. Similarly, a person is "in the Spirit," that is, in the Spirit of God, whenever the Holy Spirit enters, fills, and controls them. Then they no longer set the tone in the hidden depths of their own being. Then what they think, imagine, and intend is the result of the work of God's Spirit and is devoted to his purposes.

Then a person is overcome in another sense with what sometimes recurs in their dreams when they are sleeping. In dreaming, our consciousness, thinking, and planning retreat from the world of our daily living, and we are opened up to a completely different world. There "the spirit within us" receives guidance and direction in some obscure way from a hidden power that controls us in our dreams. And that's how it is "to be caught up in the Spirit" and to be drawn out of our daily routine and our ordinary working world. Then quietly and peacefully our emotions are enveloped by the sacred realm of the Sabbath. There all is different; other rules are obeyed; other interests prevail. When we find ourselves in that other, better, sacred realm, the Holy Spirit is allowed to work and dictate and freely have his way.

That explains how John was "caught up in the Spirit" on the Lord's Day.

Naturally, that happened in a way consistent with his position and calling as an apostle.

He was influenced for the purpose of revealing things that needed to be disclosed to the entire church and brought to it through the Word. That's why it was shown to him as an apostle with completely unique clarity, in direct communication, and through an intentional appearance.

This was completely different from what is experienced by an "ordinary" child of the resurrection, even though they are a companion in suffering, in the kingdom, and in persecution. But however starkly we pose the contrast between us and the apostle John and emphasize this difference, the main idea is the same for both of us. Like him, we must be caught up in the Spirit on the Lord's Day.

Overexertion makes no difference. It needs to be recognized that it is impossible for a child of God here on earth to be completely "caught up in the Spirit." That makes life itself impossible for them.

With the exertion of all their strength in their divine calling, but at the same time being diligent in their calling in this world while simultaneously being "in the Spirit," are two things that are mutually exclusive. The most we can ordinarily achieve is that in the context of our daily work and all our troubles is that the Spirit of God supports and guards us, maintains and warns us, stimulates and inspires us, and protects us from destruction.

But to realize something greater and higher as our basic condition all day long, and not just during the moments we pray, so that everything working together serves that purpose, we need the Sabbath, the Lord's Day. This means that we need a day when the Lord works in a special way and when we are still. To that end, two things are true simultaneously. First, the Sabbath serves to bring us into the Spirit. Next, being in the Spirit is the only thing that makes the Sabbath a reality for the Christian.

When those converge and complement one another, the Sabbath encircles us with a quiet freedom, and we find ourselves in the Spirit. That's when we hear behind us that voice that sounds like a loud trumpet. It is clear and penetrating. Then our soul experiences a blessed fellowship as he lays his right hand on us and tenderly says: "Don't be afraid, for behold, I was also once dead but am now alive. Yes, I live eternally, and no one else but I holds the keys of death and hell."

This is when there is Sabbath in us and around us!

This is to receive the eternal Sabbath already in this life.

The prayer rising from the hearts of God's children is that that Sabbath might increase in their lives.

12
VOLUME II

LIKE A DEAF VIPER

They are like a deaf viper that has clogged its ears. Psalm 58:4[1]

Holy Scripture everywhere displays great courage with respect to God's holiness. God himself dares to speak out against proud and important people in an effort to humble or break them so they fall on their faces. He neither spares them nor is intimidated by their position in life.

Thus, also here in Psalm 58, God addresses the sinner and says: "Actually, seen for what you are, you are no more than a deaf viper."

A viper!

It's a nasty, repulsive animal that automatically causes revulsion. People avoid it. They warn their children about it, telling them: "Don't touch it!" "A brood of vipers" is the harsh, sharp, cutting expression that Jesus used in striking back at the Pharisees and unmasking them. "The human heart is cunning and deadly; who can know it?" exclaims the prophet.

And here in this context the psalmist says that the ungodly person is "a viper" that spews out their poison. Behind their fangs is a venom that wounds and kills when they strike. Note well that this viper is not limited to an intentional deceiver, a thoroughly evil person, or a perverse corruptor of other souls. Not at all! It is saying that every person, every sinner, whether they do so willingly or unwillingly, can do nothing except corrupt the hearts of others. They incite those around them. They become a source of moral and spiritual death to them.

---

1. Psalm 58:5 in the Dutch versions.

To do so, you don't only have to talk about or do wicked things. But your mere presence, your personality, and your unwitting way of living have a polluting effect. They have an evil effect and nurture evil in others.

Just as a viper can poison you regardless of whether it does so intentionally in order to protect itself or whether it does so merely instinctively, the result is the same. It doesn't think about whether the poison it spews lands on the grass and ground or is injected into your hand or arm. The same is true of what emanates from the sinner, whether it's their breath, their language, the fire in their eyes, their example, or their influence. So much of what comes from the poisonous glands of their own hearts never has a cleansing effect but has damaging results. When it goes to work, it produces death.

Now, it's the case that God has medicine, an antidote, for that poison that you spew on other people. It's comparable to the pharmaceutical measures that our medical doctors have at their disposal. They take poisonous materials, including snake venom, and have the knowledge of how to use these with certain diseases and under specific circumstances to counteract illness with a healing rather than destructive effect. Naturally, this doesn't change in the least the deadly nature of the venom itself. Nor does this detract at all from the evil nature of what is generated spiritually by you.

For you the concern is not what God may do with the poison you generate. Rather, it should be what effect you have on others. Is it a healthy or destructive influence?

The Holy Spirit confronts that very question here through the mouth of David. He applies it to the ungodly person who is unregenerate. But he applies it as well to the regenerate individual to the extent that they often fall out of fellowship with their Savior and then generate from the cells and glands of their soul only what is impure, sensuous, and poisonous.

It's very obvious that the evil is worse and that they are more accountable for it when people express it by choice, like the viper does in striking intentionally either by defending itself or by attacking. Then people exhibit a lust for evil. They behave with such premeditated counsel that evil bursts out of their souls' glands and splatters over others, infecting their lifeblood.

Now we're dealing with full-blown wickedness! Now an unholy force has power over our souls! Now we are not merely unwitting instruments but fully aware servants of unrighteousness. And that's much worse!

Even then, the fullest measure of corruption has not yet been reached. The worst is what is unique to us as sinners, and this goes far beyond what is found in an angry viper. Isaiah says emphatically that a person is not only like a viper, but that "your work is still worse than that of the viper" (41:24).[2] And the most revolting thing about what is worst is stated here in what the psalmist says in the verse I have quoted, namely, that people are not just vipers but especially that they are often like "deaf vipers!"

The animal that we identify as a viper can be charmed. There is a power in the human voice that, well developed for that purpose, has power over wild, poisonous animals. Particularly in the Orient in former times, the human voice was well developed, and people mastered the art of mesmerizing, so-called charming, and controlling snakes and other poisonous creatures.

Applying this to people, a person could say that a certain power exists in God's voice that has the capability of subduing the viper in our soul. It can render it so powerless that it becomes incapable of spewing out poison. It is disarmed, and its capacity to inflict damage disappears. God's Word can be seen as a charm that casts a spell over the inner threats of the human soul.

While a viper or a snake is never deaf and is incapable of clogging its ears and is always definitely rendered powerless when it hears the soothing voice of its charmer, that's not true of people. Sinners, you and I and everyone else born by and in sin, frequently know how to play the part of a deaf viper. We know how to close our ears to the Word of God! And in speaking to our souls here, this is precisely what the Holy Spirit addresses and reproves in the remarkable image of the deaf viper. He's not just addressing a viper who is capable of spewing poisonous venom but especially one that is deaf to its divine charmer! He desires to disarm the viper within us by his amazingly miraculous Word.

That's why we can do no better than to understand how to expunge the poisonous fluids from our corrupt hearts. Nothing helps do this better in this regard than our full, totally enthusiastic confession of faith in Christ. And things will not be as they should be with us until we willingly draw every drop of life-giving fluid that nourishes us and those around us from him who is the Spring and Fountain of Living Waters.

---

2. While English translations do not reference a "viper," the Dutch translation used by Kuyper says *ulieder werk is erger dan eene adder*.

13
VOLUME II

THAT GRACE
MIGHT INCREASE

*What shall we say then? Should we continue in
sin that grace might increase? Romans 6:1*

Frequently, in fact very frequently, the same old question raised by Paul resurfaces in pious circles. "Isn't sinning really the way by which grace comes to fuller expression?"

What a terrible, horrible, frightening question! And yet it sometimes strikes too close, very close to the hearts of God's children, while superficial Christians are never even tempted to raise it. But for God's children at certain times in their life of faith, raising that question is definitely a temptation. So it didn't seem strange to me at all when recently in a certain pious circle in our capital city the tempter of souls moved someone to raise it.

Think about this!

If sin had never entered the world, wouldn't eternal compassion and God's rich mercy always have remained partially hidden? If we had not been conceived and born in sin, our souls would never have experienced the sweetness of being shattered or the blessed glory of being shown grace. If Jesus had never found sinners, Christ the counselor would have remained in the shadows forever. While he would be radiant in his regal glory, no one's tears of sorrow would ever fall on the Savior's feet to be dried by their own hair.

What says even more is when we compare the children of God with self-righteous folks. Who can deny that precisely the sliding off into the pathways of sin before falling completely has often been the painful spur to return to the Father and say: "Father, please take me back as one of your hired servants"?

Who hasn't often noticed how even among God's children those who have at one time fallen deeply are now the most zealous, motivated, and warmhearted, while others always seem somewhat cool and more measured in their faith? And what's worst of all is that the depth of your sense of guilt, even after your conversion, doesn't comport with your tepid response to grace. Isn't it the case that our sense of guilt never shocks our souls more deeply, stirs our hearts more profoundly, or compels us to make supplication than in the moment we again fall into the sin that we cherish most in our hearts?

Seriously then, is it even possible for a serious person who is intent on being truthful and who understands through experience what it is to live with integrity to deny what I've been saying? Is it so amazing, strange, or unthinkable, then, that Satan, who also understands all of this perfectly well, repeatedly tries to tempt God's children just to keep on sinning "so that grace might increase"?

I know that self-righteous Christians don't understand any of this!

But I do ask this: "Is there as much as one Christian who lives by grace whose poor soul hasn't been seared by the flames of this very temptation?" For that reason, it's so patently wrong when thoughtless preachers who have no sense or patience for any of this haughtily dismiss as "scandalously antinomian" people who struggle with it in their souls.

No, the love of Christ takes a completely different approach. It engages those who are sick of soul. It points them back to the correct way of salvation. It encourages them. And it delivers them from their soul-suffering wounds. It does so first of all by taking a different approach that investigates that condition. Then it tries to expose how the soul became entangled in it. It acknowledges that the heart, even the born-again heart, is nakedly exposed to such temptation. And it assists us in overcoming it only by the Word of God that cannot be broken. Someone who has never been in the wilderness can't understand this temptation. For one who has, no other weapon against it exists than definitely and resolutely affirming "But it is written!"

With your mind you have to affirm that it's true: in sinning, grace is increased. So then, if your soul longs for greater grace, wouldn't sinning be the way to receive it? With God, not at all! "Get behind me, Satan, for it is written: 'That can never be! For those of us who have died to sin, how can we still live in it?' " The approach to take with Satan in meeting this temptation is not to reason with him. It is to attack and repel him with the power of the double-edged sword of God's Word.

Sin is always under the curse. Sin and all that goes by that name is forever under the condemnation of destruction. God's Word wants nothing to do with it, never tolerates it, doesn't wink at it or look at it between the fingers! But it rejects it relentlessly and always with this refrain: "Holy, holy is the Lord. No sin can exist in his sacred presence!"

Your own conscience, the memory of your earlier struggles, and especially the witness of the Holy Spirit within you if you've always been a child of God, all unconditionally and emphatically tell you in the most definite way possible that what Satan whispers in your ear can never be true. What he says is totally devoid of God's grace and is an abominable assault on God's holiness. You immediately shudder when you hear it. You resist it with your whole soul.

And yet, my sisters and brothers, all of this is to no avail. It's shaky. It's subjective. It's slippery in your very soul. It shifts around before your very eyes. And Satan knows just how to manipulate and entangle you so that you finally have the overwhelming impression that your own conscience and even the Holy Spirit at work within you no longer object.

That's why you mustn't rely on reasoning, be guided only by your own conscience, or even depend only on what the Holy Spirit says internally to you. All of that can wobble!

No, there is only one shield that can deflect the poisoned, fiery, venomous arrows of Satan. It is and always will be the affirmation "But it is written!" It is the Word that can never be broken. When Romans 6 says, "That can never be!" it pronounces eternal judgment against this horrible temptation.

"God's foundations stand fast. They have this seal: The Lord knows his own, and everyone who calls on the name of Christ stands opposed to all unrighteousness!"

14
VOLUME II

AND SCRIPTURE CAN
NEVER BE BROKEN

If [the law] called them gods to whom the Word of God
came, and Scripture cannot be broken. John 10:35

What Jesus says here is worded very strongly.

Not because Scripture is unshakable. Not because it takes firm positions. Not because it cannot be ignored or pushed aside or manipulated. But because what Jesus says here references and applies to a single very strange and obviously loaded word that appears in Scripture.

What comes to the mind of a reflective person here is all the new, modern monkeying around that rejects the full authority of Scripture. But for the individual who still confesses: "When Jesus speaks, that's the end of the matter," things are settled once and for all.

Consider for a moment the usual way that orthodox theologians in our day understand the authority of Scripture. They acknowledge and confess, don't they, that Scripture contains the Word of God? Upon investigation of what they mean by the Word of God, a person finds that they distinguish basically between the spiritual content of Scripture and the framework within which that content is embedded. And then when it comes to sorting out what that spiritual content actually is, they take this very generally. They hold that it's not something that should be applied too literally, precisely, or in trivial detail. Those who do so they identify as "literalists."

They think that their subjective feelings, impressions, and conscience as illumined by the Holy Spirit are a reliable enough guide for distinguishing between what is universal, important, wonderful, and spiritual, and what is insignificant, incidental, and circumstantial.

This approach is spiritually seductive! People by nature want to be free from submission to absolute authority. So if you can make it possible for them to appear to be submissive to God's authority and at the same time allow them to actually determine for themselves what is or is not authoritative in Scripture, you do two things. You satisfy their need to believe and you caress their love of self-determination.

Eating from the Tree of the Knowledge of Good and Evil is still going on!

Such an individual does want to yield to Jesus. But to submit to Jesus in such a way that their understanding, their critical reflection, their thought processes, and their whole realm of ideas would be captivated by the text of Scripture as written rubs them the wrong way.

Because we know that many people in the church are beginning to yield to freedom's allure, and because they find such a position more spiritual, loftier, and more attractive, we direct them to the argument in this context to which everyone must bow: the words of Jesus.

The way Jesus thought about Holy Scripture is the way you should.

What Jesus confessed concerning Scripture, you should.

What Jesus accepted as the sacred charter of truth, you should as well.

If you don't agree, we can't talk any further.

If someone dares to assert: "Jesus was simply wrong in how he thought about Scripture. He attached a value to it that it simply does not have!"—we don't need to deal with such a person any longer. They reject the crucial fact of Jesus' inner veracity. If he who was the Word of God made flesh could be mistaken about the written Word of God, he is diminished in both his divinity and in his authentic humanity at the same time. Such a person has unknowingly adopted a view of the Lord that the Christian church has emphatically opposed, fought, and discarded.

Much less, either by rationalizing in terms of Oriental thought patterns or some notion of the progressive development of Jesus' human nature, may we yield to the excuse "That's certainly what Jesus said, it's what he thought and intended, but that doesn't mean that's the way it was!" That's a position often either thought or stated.

And let's not dress the matter up in pretty bows by alleging that this or that half-truth is being circulated today only by many contemporary orthodox biblical scholars. If Jesus did not know exactly, precisely, and completely what we need to hold and believe and confess from Holy Scripture, say so straight out! But then honestly recognize that you won't get behind what he stated, not even with all your dazzling intellectual ability.

Then just give up in the conflict over the authority of Scripture.

All the particulars involved are only so much dust swirling around you and being scattered by the wind. They'll never produce the stability or certainty on which a person, a household, a school, a nation or its government can really build. All your qualifications and exceptions will never inspire you spiritually.

Are you willing to concede that, my sisters and brothers?

Don't you feel it? Don't you sense that it's beyond dispute? With the acceptance or the rejection of Jesus' absolute authority on this matter, Scripture and scriptural authority rises or falls.

So then, I pray of you, I implore you, to think through clearly and calmly what Jesus said to the Jewish leaders in John 10:35. That's when he uttered of his own volition and in a forceful voice the completely unsolicited words "The Scripture cannot be broken."

And by not "breaking" or maintaining Scripture in its entirety, he did not mean a number of things. He wasn't referring to maintaining it as revealed truth. Or to accepting the mysteries of salvation in it. Or to meddling with any commandment in it, or anything like that. He wasn't talking about accepting the truth of a miracle or mighty event contained in it. Finally, he wasn't referring to not recognizing as inspired a prophecy, psalm, or divine utterance in Scripture.

No, by not breaking the Scripture, the Son of God meant maintaining and accepting to the letter the truth of every single word that Moses wove into his writing of the ordinary civil laws for Israel. Jesus meant accepting it without changing its sense in any way, even though Moses could have substituted another word for it.

He meant keeping the word "gods" in the sense that it had when it first appeared in Exodus 21:6 and that was maintained when it was repeated in Psalm 82:6: "You shall bring such a slave who wants to remain a slave to the authorities of the people, or bring him to the 'gods.'" The sense is completely the same. That's more apparent because there's no hint here of administering justice by the authorities but entirely of the official recognition of a freely taken decision. The slave wanted to stay a slave, and now that had to be registered on a civil level, we could say.

Obviously the use of the word "gods" in Exodus 21:6 is entirely incidental. Despite what we are taught from an ethical or some other angle, this word "gods" is simply a figure of speech that Moses chose and for which he might just as well have selected another term.

But what does Jesus say and teach in contrast? That term, Jesus is saying, was definitely not chosen by Moses, but it originated with God. What Psalm 82:6 teaches is that in Exodus 21:6 God is speaking, and that it was God who in that context assigned the honorable title of "gods" to the people's authorities. This is no figure of speech, Jesus is saying, but the calm, sober truth.

It's true that the same Holy Spirit who had inspired Exodus 21:6 can say in Psalm 82:6: "I was the one who said, 'You are gods,' not Moses!" And whereas that word, that term, that title of "gods" is one selected by God and as such appears in Scripture, it's obvious that precisely for that reason the title of "gods" expresses an actual, enduring, sacred truth that can never, ever be broken.

So now investigate, brothers and sisters, the extent to which most preaching of the gospel diverges from this belief in Scripture reflected by our Lord Jesus. Investigate how much of the confession taught by Jesus concerning Scripture still remains in the church. Above all, examine your own heart to determine how deeply Jesus' reverence for the Word has penetrated your own soul.

And should you find a frightful shortcoming in these matters, don't be too severe, but tenderly warn those who have strayed in this regard and call them back. At the same time, never leave off the hook those who have strayed on this matter. You have to stand rock solid in the conviction that "What Jesus says is completely true!"

AND HE WAS TROUBLED

*When Jesus saw Mary weeping and the Jews that
came with her also weeping, he was therefore deeply
moved in spirit and troubled. John 11:33*

The true fruit of godliness is sharply tilted away from extreme emotionalism. It's not as though we should blunt our feelings. Nor should our soul and senses always remain impassive. Nor should we aspire to a proud, stoical glory by always staying dry-eyed. On the contrary, in this world of sin and disappointment it's unthinkable that we wouldn't be strongly moved emotionally from time to time. That's simply the expression of tender piety in our hearts.

But what a godly way of living fights and seeks to overcome is the passionate emotionalism seen when a flood of feelings overflows its banks.

We become emotional, of course, about anything that stirs our feelings in an unusual, striking manner. The suffering going on around us rattles our nerves. It arouses an empathetic emotional response in us. It creates the impression that our inner feelings are like a turbulent brook whose waters tumble this way, then that.

We can't do anything about that kind of response. It's normal.

Not to acknowledge such impressions and emotions and not to be shaken by suffering, you would have to harden yourself to a degree to your natural human feelings. You'd have to be insensitive and heartless.

But here the question is whether, when you have that kind of emotional experience, do you give in to it? Do you let it continue unchecked? Are you content to let it sweep you along, as though your will has no role to play here? Or do you offer some resistance? As a child of God, do you make some attempt to control it?

Jesus did the latter.

His was an extremely sensitive, very compassionate emotional life. The painful things of this life therefore made a powerful impression also on him. Our Lord Jesus was frequently shocked by what happened around him. So, at the grave of Lazarus, when "he saw Mary weeping and the Jews who came with her weeping as well," that immediately affected him. It affected his nervous system, and his nerves generated an emotional response: "Jesus was deeply moved in spirit." But in that instance, Jesus' will also came into play. He had to decide whether he was going to allow his emotions to overwhelm him or whether he would check and resist them, whether he would repress them.

At Lazarus' grave, although he initially wanted to give in to his emotions, it was not his emotions that "troubled" him. But it was that they continued to stir within him to the extent that they did that troubled him.

Look, this is what's true here. It's what our guideline will be that's highest and noblest in such cases.

If you become overwhelmed with passion, then you allow your emotions to become your master. Then your emotional responses become too intense and too strong. Then you give in to them and they become oppressive. And when your feelings completely control you, ultimately you can't do anything about it!

People sometimes see this with young children who are unsettled by the smallest things. If something happens to them, they can burst out in tears and scream so hard you think they're going to choke.

It's the same later in life, when all too often their emotions exhibit an irrational control over women.

And sometimes you find people who are unable to control their crying and sobbing at wakes or funerals. That's particularly true of otherworldly folks. Then, when they want to say something, they choke on their own words. They fall on each other's shoulders. They shriek. They collapse. And when they become overwrought, their emotional display of crying can sometimes only be ended by bringing out the smelling salts and cold water!

Matters must never be allowed to go that far. It demonstrates weakness. It shatters the harmony of one's inner being. It is contrary to God's will.

A person needs to learn how to take a measured response to life's pain. They need to learn self-control and restraint. Even with respect to the most intense emotions, they should always remember that "the spirit of the prophets must be subject to the prophets."[1]

About Jesus we do not only read that he was personally troubled, but as our writer so beautifully and sensitively puts it in his account, that he also "shed tears."

Mary "cried" and the Jews "cried." Concerning both, the Greek word used is *klaiein*, which means to cry really hard. But what appears here concerning Jesus is that "he allowed a drop of moisture to slip out and shed a tear." This is the same word used to describe honey dripping from the comb or gum oozing from the bark of a tree. Even Jesus' tears were subject to the control of his will. In that sense, Jesus' weeping was a very personal act.

So how, we ask, does anyone in the church of Jesus dare to allow the provoking of the kind of emotional response characteristic of an easily swayed public? I'm talking about one where weak people lack self-control and are overcome with passion characterized by crying and sobbing. I'm talking about one where the preacher, when he's finished, descends from the pulpit in the sweet awareness that he succeeded in deeply moving his audience.

Our spiritual fathers strongly opposed such false tendencies in our worship services.

Naturally, the emotions definitely have an assigned role to play in the work of God in our hearts. They need to be sensitive, tender, deeply moved. That's both permitted and required. Being moved must not be resisted, but embraced. That's part of being human. That's why God gave us hearts!

But what is not permitted is that we find a kind of enjoyment in our painful emotional responses. We may not intentionally arouse responses as we imagine they should occur. Nor may we celebrate the kind of piety based on them. And when they arise unintentionally, we are not to give them full rein and allow them to gain control over us.

A Christian learns from Jesus how to remain calm in their pain, quiet under God's judgments, and submissive to their Lord in all things, including when they are troubled in spirit.

So be strong, sisters and brothers. Definitely don't become insensitive or close your hearts. But be Christ's people by embracing every emotional response you have in a way that's superior to the world. In your Savior you are stronger

---

1. Kuyper is citing 1 Corinthians 14:32 here, a verse governing prophetic utterances in the context or worship.

than the world. Every emotion that would overpower you, you are to control in your hearts in such a way that they serve to glorify Jesus.

HE LIVES TO MAKE INTERCESSION FOR THEM

This is why he is able to save completely those that call on God through him, since he always lives to make intercession for them. Hebrews 7:25

As a rule, Christians say wonderful things about their own praying. But who ever talks about Jesus' praying?

People make a kind of idolatry of a sinful creature's praying. And telling someone else that you have been praying for them can border on being insensitive and immodest, as though doing this is something so special. But who among us is overwhelmed by the glorious thought that Jesus is praying for us?

I'm not saying that there might be someone among us who denies, disparages, or discounts Jesus' praying. Oh, I'm totally convinced that any person who holds to the Christian faith definitely includes Christ's intercession among those ministries that Jesus the High Priest performs in the holy of holies before the throne of God.

But what I do contend is that Jesus praying for her is not a living reality for his church. Nor is the fact that he lives for the very purpose of always making supplication for her a living reality for her. Consequently, she's deprived of the comfort that flows from Christ's intercession.

Sadly, people have thought too highly of the praying that people do. They've thought too highly of public as well as of private prayer. We don't point this out in order to discourage praying. Rather, we wish to God that the spirit of grace and of praying would be poured out so mightily and powerfully on us that our praying would be doubled.

But what we object to is excessively valuing the worth of our own praying. That can be damaging. It's as though ten of our deadening prayers are worth more than one of our living ones! It's as though the great length of our praying eclipses the value of its depth and intensity. It's as if our prayers could really be praying without them being aroused and awakened by the Holy Spirit or without him infusing them with a worshipful spirit. In short, it's as if in praying we never continue wrestling emotionally with the evil spirit of thoughtlessness, lack of spirituality, superficiality, formality and mere habit. It's as if there's not already cause for thanksgiving, rejoicing, or giving glory. In contrast, true praying is praying in the Spirit, praying in the name of Jesus, praying with the saints of all ages, praying in the certainty of being heard. Sometimes, by way of exception, that kind of praying can slip out of our hearts and across our lips!

No, the answer does not lie in our own praying. According to the word of the apostle, as far as our being really blessed is concerned, this depends on Jesus praying for us and not on our own praying. Being blessed does not depend on anything that we do.

It's not that there is first a decree, then the coming of our Surety according to that decree, and now the automatic, unspiritual, and mechanical bestowing of salvation by that Surety on the children of God.

No, but the whole process is dynamic. The decree is one that is borne, maintained, and enlivened every moment by the merciful power of God. That Surety provides no guarantee that is not permeated and strengthened from moment to moment by his glorious divinity, manifested in Golgotha's saving power. Similarly, the salvation provided by that Surety would have no enduring resonance in the souls of the redeemed, if the Mediator did not pray for them moment by moment.

Rome talks about providing an enduring efficacy of Jesus' sacrifice in the mass.

We reject that. And why do we?

In order to preserve nothing more than a cold, bleak emptiness and hollowness?

No, a thousand times over, no! It's because only the intercession of Christ maintains the efficacy of that sacrifice! It also provides the unceasing effort and all-enabling strength that sustains the souls of the redeemed day and night. It blesses them!

So don't ever think that the praying that Jesus does happens now and then based on your petition, your request, or you imploring him for his prayer. It's not like your Savior has to be asked to pray on your behalf before the throne of grace. Look, Jesus doesn't just pray for you some of the time or only once! He does so ceaselessly. Praying for you is his preoccupation; it's his purpose for living! He lives for it. His life revolves around praying for you.

Do you ask how that can be the case? I don't really know. But I do know that the apostle himself lays the demand on us to "Pray without ceasing!" So it goes without saying that a demand he lays on us he wouldn't consider unthinkable for our Intercessor.

And this is what he actually does: he prays continuously, without letup. He lives for uttering his supplications on our behalf before his Father's throne. Such praying is his very breath. It amounts to pouring out his soul on behalf of his people. Such praying reflects the sacred effort of our redeeming Hero on behalf of those still struggling here on earth.

That's why Jesus' praying is the lifeline tied to your soul that prevents it from sinking.

Jesus is praying for you even while you're sleeping.

He's praying for you even when in the busyness of your daily life you are no longer thinking about him.

As your Savior, he's praying for you even when you cause him sorrow and distress.

Christ imploring God on your behalf is your constantly flowing stream of life. It's the wind that fills your sails and moves you forward, even when you lie down exhausted in your little boat and give up struggling.

Yes, even when you approach death and hover between heaven and hell, it will be the praying of Jesus that upholds you, offers you support, and ultimately saves you.

And if these thoughts in and of themselves are already so unspeakably comforting, so effective in deflecting sin and restraining you from unrighteousness, they are also of priceless value for your own prayer life. Just test the evidence for this.

Before you begin praying, simply first lift your soul to your Savior, who is already busy praying for you. Make an effort, force yourself, and try to hear with the ears of your soul what Jesus is imploring from the throne of grace on your behalf. Yes, if you take the praying of Jesus seriously, it will become perfectly clear to you how your own praying, with all that it lacks, stands by comparison with the praying of Jesus. It will become evident that your own praying is simply repeating what Jesus has already been beseeching on your behalf. Discounting all value that your own prayer has, your soul will come to rest completely on Jesus. Then the peace of God will flood into your inner being, because God's own Son draws your soul into his own heart and takes your name on his own lips. Then, always living with Jesus, you find that no sin can ultimately affect you any longer, not even death or the Devil.

17

VOLUME II

DRAW THEM ALL TO ME

*And when I will be lifted up from the earth, I
will draw them all to me. John 12:32*

God's ways consistently involve the most unusual contrasts, paradoxes, and disparities. And the Lord definitely wants us to pay close attention to those differences. This is obvious from what Jesus says here about his being lifted up.

Sinners would lift him up by hanging him on a cross. The Father would lift him up by seating him on his throne in glory. And he himself would lift up those who believe in him by drawing them to himself, that is, above and beyond this world.

Jesus and this world that lies under a curse don't really belong together.

So it's one or the other. Either this world is too good for Jesus, or Jesus is too good for this world. The first option is the one that sinners take. That's why they shout: "Rid the world of this Jesus!" The other choice is God's determination that his Son would shortly be lifted up in glory. But both sinners and God in his holiness recognize that it is impossible for this Jesus to remain in this world. And with that same image of being lifted up, Jesus captures the outcome of this contrasted judgment.

"Hoist him above the ground!" This world can't stand him any longer! He's not worthy to place the soles of his feet on the ground. Hoist him on the timbers like a reject, a criminal, a curse. The law of Moses already said: "Cursed is everyone who hangs on a cross!" The entire wicked world shouts the same thing.

But "Exalt him above the earth!" is also God's command to his holy angels. Lift him above the oppressiveness, the intolerable conditions, and the decadence of this fallen world. Give him honor and worship, and let him ascend his throne!

And if that's the way it goes for Jesus, can it be any different for those he has delivered, namely, his servants and his holy disciples?

"Jesus and this world don't belong together!" Doesn't this mean that those who belong to Jesus may not get involved with the world? Or that they may not be at peace with the world? Or that they have to be lifted up above this world?

Isn't a child of God a living embodiment of "the condemnation of the world and all its ambitions"?

Isn't a child of God someone whom this world could not and cannot produce on its own? Isn't theirs a spirit not poured into the sons and daughters of men, but one that is imprinted on their nature and that awakens in them the impulse to react to the world by rejecting what the world thinks and says and does?

For what does it mean to be "a child of God" other than to be implanted with the seed of a higher, different, and holier life? That life is like a drop of oil that floats on the waters of this earthly life without becoming one with them, dissolved in them, or indistinguishable from them.

Doesn't saying "I belong to Jesus" inherently involve regarding the world as too unimportant, too inferior, too ignoble, or too downright ordinary that a person should no longer be concerned with it? And doesn't it involve spiritually regarding it as too unholy, too sinful, and too depraved so that a person's soul should no longer be troubled about with it?

And naturally this is definitely not to say that a person has to take a condescending attitude toward the people of the world. That's because, in the first place, I don't really know who God's children are. It could very well be that fine elect people exist under the cover of those who right now look like the most flagrant sinners around. But even more than that, the world and I are not two totally separable entities. For the world can be found in me too, in my own flesh and blood and in my own heart. And every condemnation of the world needs to begin precisely with the sharpest condemnation of the world in my own heart. Otherwise, I will forfeit all moral strength, be rooted in hypocrisy, and never stand in God's presence as justified.

No, the Spirit at work within us needs to be the spirit that condemns the world so that we break with it, put it behind us, and rise above it.

This is what Scripture wants. And this is also what the intensely earnest Puritan quest for the devout life is all about.[1]

We're talking here about the serious and devout life that Christians exemplify in our own era of so much superficiality. Think about it. People find it so hard to say no to things today. They're not able to deny themselves very much at all. In thousands of ways, they find the means for going along with the world in this, that, or the next thing.

Can it be otherwise?

But look, it's obvious that God's children don't really belong to the world and need to rise above it.

However, people can be lifted up above the world in one of two ways.

Either I can put up my own ladder and, standing in front of it, try to climb it by myself, rung by rung. Or I can be lifted up by Jesus.

Pay careful attention to the fact, sisters and brothers, that Jesus' work of lifting us up does not depend merely on our own striving or your blessed entrance.

"Lifting up" is Jesus' work. It's the work of the Jesus who is already exalted in heaven. It's his work, heart and soul.

"So when I am lifted up, I will draw them all to me" means "as soon as I am exalted above the earth." It doesn't refer to the hour of death that comes for everyone. But it means throughout our lives. It means being lifted up beginning with the outset of the new life in you and me. It means the being lifted up that accompanies and promotes all the growth in that new life. And more gloriously yet, it even means the "being lifted up" to heaven that is still coming. It also means that the Lord is drawing the redeemed to himself ever more closely, quickly, and intimately.

The secret of disengaging from the world, therefore, does not consist of you and me systematically erecting a barrier between ourselves and the world. What it does mean is allowing the barrier to fall that exists between us and the Jesus living within us.

Go to him more often! Live with him more consciously! Attach yourself more intimately! Then the ties that bind us to the world will fall away!

Then avoiding the things of this life will no longer consist of keeping "rule upon rule, precept upon precept, law upon law, standard upon standard." It won't consist of not touching and not tasting and not getting upset. But it will consist only, exclusively, and definitely of living your faith.

---

1. This is an obvious appeal to readers who appreciated Puritan and Dutch Further Reformation devotional material.

For if you truly believe, your believing will consist of truly and essentially "being drawn to Christ himself." It will consist of believing in such a way that faith is the driving force in your life, a force that enlivens you, warms your heart, and brings you where you need to be.

It involves being drawn by his love.

It includes being drawn by his power.

And means being drawn to him for as long as it takes for you to be with him fully.

18
VOLUME II

LET THE DEAD
BURY THEIR DEAD

"Lord, let me first go and bury my father." Then Jesus said to
him, "Let the dead bury their own dead." Matthew 8:21–22

Jesus could be severely cutting. Like here!

Isn't it true that nothing is more natural than that this young man would first want to go home and pay his father his final respects either yet that evening or the following morning? He'd want to do that as long as his father's body was still above ground!

Imagine that some Christian in our own day would miss his father's funeral because he was too busy evangelizing or had to preach somewhere. Wouldn't there be a huge public outcry in the media over such a degenerate son?

But Jesus demands nothing less than this!

That young man might not go home. He had to suppress the tender feelings welling up inside him. He had to leave to others the work of carrying his father's corpse in the funeral procession. While his entire family and the entire public in his hometown would be scandalized because he dared to stay away, this sad young man had to quash the sorrow in his heart and begin going around from village to village while heralding: "Your Messiah, your Messiah has come, O Israel."

No, don't dress this up in ribbons and bows. Don't soft-pedal or sweeten it! Recognize it for the unbelievably harsh demand that it is. It clashes with our natural human instincts. And if Jesus had been a human being like us, he would never have been able to make a demand like this. He would not have dared to do so!

What lies behind this requirement?

Here once again Scripture is best explained in terms of Scripture.

What do we read in Leviticus about how to handle Israel's dead?

Just this: that with respect to burying the corpses of precious loved ones, there are three types of regulation. First, there are those concerning an ordinary citizen who is required to be involved in the funeral procession and the grieving process of all his family members and next of kin. Second, there are those that apply to a priest, who may only participate in the burial of his closest blood relatives. And third, there are those that apply only to the high priest, who is never permitted to be involved in a burial, not even in the funeral procession of his father or mother.

In Leviticus 21:1 and following, the requirements involving priests are given clearly: "A priest is not to defile himself through involvement with a dead body, except in the case of his closest blood relatives such as his mother or his father, his son or his daughter, and his brother or his unmarried sister."

Those involving the high priest are even more explicit: "He who is a high priest among his brothers, whose head has been anointed with holy oil, shall not come into contact with a dead body. This even applies to his father and his mother; he shall not defile himself through contact with them. Out of respect for his sacred status, he shall not participate in the funeral procession of his father or his mother, so that he does not defile that which is holy unto the Lord. For the crown of his God's anointing oil is upon him. I am Jehovah!"

There cannot be the least doubt, therefore, that within Israel there existed, as specified in the law, precisely what Jesus expressed when he said: "Let the dead bury their dead!" This applied to all priests. And at the highest level, it applied to the high priest, who was ordered word for word not to attend to the care of the corpses of either his father or his mother. He had to let others attend to this.

In saying what he did, Jesus was understandably and obviously appealing to Leviticus 21. In explaining this puzzling and harsh demand, people could avoid a great deal of astonishment if they had paid more attention to what was in Israel's law.

In the light of Leviticus, Jesus' severely cutting words meant nothing other than this: "I am anointing all of you as priests, and what in Israel applied only to the high priest now applies to all of you, head for head."

Those who wrote the marginal notes for our Bible got it right. Concerning Leviticus 21:12 they expressly stated: "He was not to abandon what is sacred" meant that the high priest might not leave the tabernacle to "walk behind the corpse," even it was that of his own father.

So what is the meaning of what Leviticus ordered and Jesus affirmed?

Understand that there are two kinds of family, two types of blood relatives, and two sorts of bonds between successive generations. For both converted and unconverted people there is first of all their family according to the flesh with its relationships in the flesh. This constitutes the bonds with which we are born as well as the ones into which we marry.

But for a converted person an entirely different connection is added to this one. This is the sacred connection to the heavenly family, the relationship with the saints who are above. This is the living bond that connects them with God and all his elect. So the child of God has two sorts of family: their family according to the flesh here on earth and their spiritual or heavenly family. Accordingly, they have two kinds of kinship: a kinship based on the flesh and a kinship based on spiritual rebirth.

The result is that they have a double connection in life. They experience a temporary connection with their relatives here on earth. But they have an enduring, everlasting tie to those with whom they share the one life in Jesus' kingdom. This second family relationship, kinship tie, and living connection ranks far above the former in importance.

Because a person's calling in the kingdom is so much higher, they must exercise the willpower never to value that first family connection above the second. They must never allow it to impede or damage the second one.

This requirement was already partially imposed on the priests in Leviticus. It is completely required of all God's priests today.

You see it in the life of Jesus: "Woman, what have I to do with you? My hour is not yet come. Do you not know that I have to be about my Father's business?" These are expressions that demonstrate that Jesus was following the same principle.

Jesus spoke even more strongly when he said: "Behold, those who do the will of my Father who is in heaven are my true family; they are my mother, my brothers, and my sisters!"

And remember this one: "He who loves father or mother more than me is not worthy of me."

Have you, my good reader, already been born into that sacred family? If so, what is the relationship between that family relationship and your family tie according to the flesh?

19

VOLUME II

THE HEART HUMBLED BY HARD LABOR

Wherefore he humbled their hearts through hard labor. Psalm 107:12

Is it really above human nature to put someone down who thinks more highly of themself than they should and to keep them there?

And doesn't a Christian always struggle with thinking more highly of themself in their heart than they should? They know that they should be modest and humble and unpretentious because they live by grace, and that grace comes only to those who are lowly of heart. Still more, they have learned through experience that when they were proud, they became vulnerable to all kinds of bad things. Yes, they have learned that pride inflicts spiritual pain on their life and robs them of the sacred peace that God provides. But really now, what does that knowledge, or that conviction, or that experience really matter? Their arrogant heart won't obey them. It remains haughty no matter how much they beg and cajole it to be more modest once again. They have no control over it. Their heart controls them!

This is an extremely painful situation.

For a proud heart is not always expressed as craving greatness, fame, or honor in this world. Understand this clearly! It can just as often be an unholy desire not to be inconvenienced by anything, to not go out of their way for anyone else, and to always be headed in a selfish direction. It can be expressed ultimately in the most sinful pride of all, namely, in pitting one's own will against God's!

Don't be too quick to say: "That doesn't apply to me at all! Such thoughts never occur to me!"

Because, properly seen and measured, what else is every transgression of any of God's commands except elevating our hearts above the living God? He says: "This is the way it will be." But we protest, replying: "No, but this is how we'll do it!" In making that decision, we elevate our hearts above God. Ultimately, what the Lord commands, we oppose. It helps us as unholy mortals achieve what he forbids.

This is how transgressing God's commands always expresses an evil heart that exalts itself above God on high. This is the case with ungodly people as well as with those who have been born again. The only difference is that the ungodly do this without even thinking about it, but the born again are conflicted over it.

A child of God loses sleep over this. They are not at peace with it. They neither can nor will ever be satisfied with it. That's not because they are any better than the ungodly. Rather, considered in and by themselves, apart from Christ, they live in constant death. But the Holy Spirit is at work in the heart of a born-again child of God. A new person is emerging. And this new person "experiences a heartfelt joy in God through Christ. They possess a desire and love for living according to God's commandments." And so, when they feel like they're being attracted to sin and sucked into it, they sense an unaccountable oppressiveness slipping into them. This is being worked in the hidden recesses of their soul by the Holy Spirit, and it stirs them to want to circumcise the foreskin of their heart. They would rather die than upset and offend God any longer with their proud heart. They see with their own eyes what a contemptible creature they really are.

This is part of the suffering that God's children experience here on earth. This is the most painful and agonizing wound they feel.

Then they scrutinize everything, test everything, and evaluate everything in an attempt to rein in their proud heart. They pull back on those reins, manipulate them, and grip them so firmly that they think they have won the battle and can now sleep soundly. They think: "Things can't get out of hand now!" But sadly, all that effort only yields disappointment. The reins are ripped from their hands, and the first chance it gets, that proud heart suddenly swells again and rises up against God's commands. This happens even though they know and feel at that very moment that this must flout God, grieve their Mediator, and sadden the Holy Spirit.

But they can never afflict the Holy Spirit to such an extent that he does not return and comfort these "struggling children." They can never grieve this Mediator so much that he stops praying that they will return from their wandering ways. And they can never flout God but that he extends his hands and comes to their aid. And he does this by sending them "hard labor," since an arrogant heart is never humbled except by being burdened. Except by being pressured by the weight of divine anger! Then it is ultimately brought low and humbled by his strength and power.

At first the child of God doesn't realize this. Their first instinct is to push back against these afflictions when they come, to not want them, and to resist them in their heart. But that's only a momentary reaction. For then the gracious purpose God has in sending these burdens is made clear. This happens externally from the Word and internally by the Spirit. This heavy-handedness is not intended to shatter them but to help them in their continuous battle against their pride of heart. They realize that it isn't anger but mercy that is motivating God because he recognizes their frightful struggle to become humble without being very successful at it.

It's for this reason that he, your Father in heaven, the Always-Faithful One, and the All-Compassionate, has summoned these heavy burdens to descend on your heart. He desires the proud heart to bow down, to be brought low, so that in that humbled position the full stream of sacred, glorious, saving grace might appear and flow into your life again.

Then God's children rejoice!

They do so not because they realize that God is not vindictive. They do so not only because they are able to say: "This, too, has a saving purpose for me!" They do so much more because this is what they experience more profoundly and gloriously: "My proud heart has been genuinely humbled. Praise God! Grace has come!"

That's when they find themselves in the song of deliverance sung for them by the Holy Spirit in Psalm 107.

Because they had rebelled against God's commands and had rejected the counsel of the Most High in their unfaithfulness, he humbled their hearts through hard labor until they stumbled and realized that there was no one to help them.

But when they called on the Lord in their distress, he delivered them from their fears.

He guided them out of darkness and the shadow of death, and he broke their bonds.

Let them praise God for his tender mercies and for the wonders he has worked among the children of mankind.

20

VOLUME II

YOUR JUST DUE!

Who would not fear you, O King of the nations?
For this is your just due. Jeremiah 10:7

People usually put a great deal of stock in knowledge, science, and wisdom! If a person lives quietly in their community, is piously guided by their conscience, and walks uprightly, it doesn't produce awe in the hearts of others. It doesn't compel respect. People don't go out of their way to comment on it. But if someone appears who has observed much, has read widely, and knows a great deal, it's another matter. If they are seen by their associates as being wise, or if their community regards them as highly educated, they will bow willingly to their knowledge and ability. They will burn incense to them if they are regarded as excelling others in knowledge and science, cautious judgment, and good discernment.

"Knowledge is Power" is the motto glittering in gold letters that the world displays. All effort in our day and age is expended on the goal of becoming smarter, gaining knowledge, and being more discerning. This is the most highly praised and most sought-after fruit growing on the Tree of Knowledge in our Dutch garden. Preoccupation with being smart and gaining a lot of knowledge and wisdom has gone so far, in fact, that the great majority of those "accomplished" in this regard have intentionally and with great delight sold out their salvation as well as God and heaven to attain it. With their proud hearts, they want full and unimpeded access to the Tree of Knowledge.

This is how knowledge comes to be pitted powerfully against piety, science against the fear of the Lord, and an able, wise, and highly educated person against his God.

In our day a minister of the Word even stood up in one of our Christian churches and with his own lips propounded the following radical, idolatrous conviction: "From now on we should emphasize our efforts instead of the faith, our scientific endeavors instead of sacred theology, and humanity instead of God!"

Many, upon hearing this, imagined that this was something new.

But that's not the case.

Even this sin is as old as Paradise!

Knowledge has always wanted to oppose God. Science throughout the ages has built its own kingdom in opposition to God's. In every nation and in each generation, wisdom has fervently struggled against the living God at the city gates and in the streets. If this wisdom were to be hallowed by God's special grace, things would be different. But flourishing independently and simply left to its own devises, knowledge has never done anything other than set up a pedestal on which humanity exalted and worshiped itself. This applies to the development of human understanding and the power of human thought as well. Together they have tried, unsuccessfully, to see higher than our always more highly exalted God!

You should understand that it's not only highly educated people who are guilty of this. It clings to every heart. Even yours! Every moment that you, like a weaned child, are not protected by the Lord your God, your trivial knowledge renders your praying empty. And by thinking that you know better than God how things should go, your soul is alienated from him.

But when you are drenched with the dew of heaven and soaked with rain of the Spirit, and when you long to be anointed with his anointing, then "yes!" Then the light of wisdom and knowledge can shine gloriously. But just as soon as they are pursued in a way that is neither baptized, reconciled, nor conse-crated, a person's ability to understand and think and exercise incisive judg-ment is deadened. Then they carry a person away from the Holy One. Then all awe, reverence, and godly fear before the Creator's majesty and for God's overwhelming power are severed and rejected in the human spirit.

That's exactly how it was already in Jeremiah's day.

And what did the prophet do about it? How did he fight it?

Did he warn against research? Did he resist knowledge? Did he disparage science?

No, not at all!

But taking the presumptuous man at his own word, he thundered this penetrating, shattering question to him: "Do you really want to bow to knowledge and wisdom more deeply than to anything else? Well then, to whom could you bow more deeply and before whom could you better bend to the dust than to the living God?" And after posing those admonishing questions, he testifies, as it were, to the Holy One: "Who would not fear you, O King of the nations? For this is your just due; among all the wise men of all the nations there is none like you."

Jeremiah reaches for the same plumb line that sways pedantically and primly in the world's hands! He doesn't do this to go hide timidly in a corner. No, but he does so in order to needle all such presumptuous folks on the very basis of wisdom, knowledge, and insight so that they might rethink the notion that they are actually wiser than God. Or, if they're not capable of this, he does so in order that they might simply bow reverently to that God whom they have in fact been opposing.

So you want to revere wisdom above holiness, you say? Then listen! Let me tell you about the wisdom of God. And when I do, admit this, if you really want to be honest with yourself: "O God, measured by this standard, there can be a crown for no else by you; this is your just due, yours alone!"

How is it with Jehovah's servants today? What's going on with those humble folks who still revere his name? The good souls who have not been completely alienated from him?

They continue to speak out against measuring things by the standard of knowledge. They want to keep their distance from it. They protect their children from it. To be sure, they preach about the love of God. They talk about his majesty. They praise his grace. But the wisdom of God—what about it?

People still hear about it from catechism books. They read of it in the Belgic Confession. What they remember best is that God's Word in both the Old and New Testaments often speaks of it.

Everything compels you to still acknowledge this glorious attribute of the living God, namely, that he is omniscient.

But still, the value of that attribute, that power, and that wonderful quality of God has dropped out of sight for believers. People don't think about it any longer. They don't extol it any more. They don't even talk about it in their houses of prayer.

How cunning Satan's tactics are!

Precisely in this century when the appeal for wisdom is stronger than ever and when knowledge seduces the soul, he puts blinders on the eyes of Christ's church. It is no longer capable of seeing the wisdom of the Lord our God, which exceeds all knowledge and is the only truly praiseworthy wisdom.

"Collect all the trivial clutter in the land and throw it out," cried Jeremiah in his day. Shouldn't we take those words on our lips today, church of Christ, when we see what those who have gone before dared to unwittingly parade as wisdom?

Oh, that all wisdom, especially your own, would fall to the ground so that only the wisdom of the Omniscient One would remain standing to be praised and honored among us. For this is his "just due!"

REMEMBER THE SABBATH DAY

Remember the Sabbath Day so that you keep it holy. Six days you shall do all your work, but the seventh day is a Sabbath to the Lord your God, and on it you shall not do any work. Exodus 20:8–10

Old and antiquated questions asked a long time ago always have a way of popping up again among those without any historical awareness.

So now we are hearing about Saturday Sabbath day observance.

When people don't regard the scriptural text as a gold mine that produces ore that must first be crushed and then refined, but as a jewelry store displaying each artfully crafted piece that has been completely finished and appealingly laid out under glass, they ask the wrong question. They ask: "Can you show me a text that demands Sunday observance?" The questioner knows very well, of course, that such a text doesn't exist, so they immediately take the obvious next step and announce this conclusion: "If that's not the case, then either we should return to Saturday observance, as Exodus 20:8 explicitly states, or we shouldn't have to observe a day of rest as at all obligatory!"

Some people have very tender consciences in raising that kind of question. And there are more people with even tenderer consciences who are upset when they do! This calls for a brief response.

We need to say immediately that those who want to tie God's will to a date on the calendar will never be able to do so. That's because, first of all, with the introduction of the Gregorian calendar an uneven number of days was simply ignored. Second, it's because the Jewish year in Moses' day was not as long as a year is in our time. Third, it's also because the beginning and the end of the day were determined differently at the base of Mount Sinai than they are by us now. So even such folks have to concede a more general determination with respect to the last day of the week as that day and week were determined in any given time and place.

Furthermore, a person needs remember that no one who lives outside Canaan can take the law as contained in the Ten Commandments literally because the promise attached to the fifth commandment is obviously not applicable to them. Also, the naming of the ox and the ass as the only draft animals or beasts of burden used in that country at that time may not be understood by anyone to mean that the horse, which is used in those capacities today in our own country, shouldn't be included as well in that reference.

That's why our forefathers repeatedly made the distinction transparently clear between the moral and the ceremonial or temporary applicability of the law. The former has fixed and enduring applicability, whereas the second has an application that can change with different times, places, and circumstances.

In the case of the fourth commandment, the moral sense consists of observing one day in seven as holy. It is ceremonial within the context of the Old Testament dispensation, when rest was prescribed only after a person had first expended themselves in their daily work.

Therefore, it's not the case that observing Sunday or observing the Sabbath is simply a matter of convenience, or that it is no longer a compelling obligation in God's law.

We are not free to decide whether or not to keep a day a week holy, depending on whether it suits us or we want to or not.

No, where the observance of keeping a day of rest holy is involved, our consciences are very definitely bound by God's will. This discloses that the basis for such observance is grounded in an act of God, namely, the act of creation, and that as such it holds true for the entire world as long as it exists. This is evident from the way in which a Paradise tradition is found among all non-Christian people groups. It is also observable from the fact that the human constitution cannot flourish without a day of rest.

The fourth commandment given at Mount Sinai restores and applies to Israel, therefore, what already existed as a general ordinance binding on all creatures.

It is an ordinance that serves the purpose of openly telling us that creation is not an endless process. This is the notion from which the abominations of pantheism and materialism arise. Rather, it is an ordinance that considers creation to be a work of God that has a beginning, a specific duration, and then a definite conclusion. Furthermore, it is a work that stamped every creature with limitations and with the need to have its strength replenished.

The intent of this ordinance was to honor the all-determinative truth that God freely willed his creation into existence and that at a definite point in time this work ended. It had been completed. The intent is not just to pay this ordinance lip service but to observe it by our actions. It is to be kept by human beings throughout the entirety of their lives. Keeping it is in fact a confession that God is the only Eternal One and that we are finite and fragile.

That's why when this holy ordinance was lost over time, God in his grace restored it for his own chosen people Israel in this specific form. It is a form suited to their time and place. In Israel's case it was intended to apply after they had worked and were exhausted. It was intended, therefore, to refresh them with blessed rest at the end of the week. But to assure that it would function as a blessing for his specially chosen people under the new covenant, people who would be called out and gathered from all nations, it was intended to bestow the blessing of rest in a way applicable to their situation. Now it applies after Christ's appearance, after he has come out of the shadows, after he brought the first expression of everlasting rest. Now his people work in the strength of that anticipated eternal rest celebrated on the first day of the week. This change occurred under the oversight of Jesus' apostles, who inaugurated a new dispensation for the church.

If in former times salvation was about deliverance from Egypt and of the created order, now it is about deliverance from sin and about a new, spiritual creation in Christ. The form that the day of celebration now takes reflects this significant change. Celebrating the day in Christ Jesus is not only about earthly rest, but from now on it is about exalting him more highly in the life of the assembly of the elect. At the same time, it is about remembering the miracle of his resurrection in its implications for both creation and re-creation.

The Holy Spirit has sealed this change for the Christian church of all times and stamps it with a twofold seal. The first is that of a peaceful conscience where opposition to the change is concerned, for such opposition cannot last and soon disappears. The second seal is the blessing that rests on the change. Remember our own recent past as well as England and America now.[1]

---

1. While it's not terribly clear what Kuyper has in mind here, the reference may be to Sabbath observance that prevailed earlier in all three places.

In accepting that we may not overlook the change from promise to fulfill-ment, the church of Jesus Christ is being subject to the spirit of Scripture. Then she proceeds with the feast of creation and re-creation, enjoying the rest that was obtained through celebrating the Sabbath day historically but that is now tied to the resurrection of Jesus Christ from the dead.

But the moral content of the Sabbath law remains in force today. So cele-brating that day also involves interrupting our earthly work. We do so not out of obligation or compulsion but out of respect for God's ways. Then we break with the rhythm of daily work. We quietly take distance from it. And we focus internally on ourselves.

The point is not about doing nothing, then, but about not doing what would impede that change in rhythm.

But we can't leave it at that. Interrupting the flow of our daily work is not sufficient. Another sort of labor begins at that point. We're talking about the work of God's kingdom insofar as that is imaginable only on a day of universal rest. This is work that also continues alongside our daily work on other days but that is only pursued to a greater degree on that day.

And there is still more. The rest we are talking about does not mean that we stop living. It's not about collapsing in laziness or idleness. Completely to the contrary; it must be resting in God, entering into his tent, finding shelter under his wings, raising him above the flow of whatever is passing and enslav-ing—rest as exalting in his royal majesty.

This is the kind of resting in his majesty that renders the Devil powerless at his feet because the wings of Christ's total power completely overshadow a person! In the deepest sense, therefore, this is to rest from one's evil work and therefore to receive already in this life something of God's "eternal rest." It is a rest that will be unsurpassed above and of which we have a foretaste already here below, at least to the extent that we deny ourselves and emphasize Christ's work for us and in us.

THE LORD IS YOUR KEEPER!

*Behold, the Keeper of Israel will neither slumber
nor sleep. The Lord is your Keeper; the Lord is your
shade on your right hand. Psalm 121:4–5*

Isn't it in conflict to say on the one hand that "God only gives grace to the humble of heart" but to say on the other hand that "one to whom grace has been given knows that they have been elect from before the foundation of the world"? Or doesn't the sense of being elect make a person arrogant? If so, isn't this the direct opposite of being humble? And doesn't that render a person unsuited for receiving grace?

And turning things around, if my soul lives in a state of being genuinely humble, don't I find myself so far down in the dumps that it becomes impossible to believe that such a miserable person as I can be one of God's elect?

And here's the proof! Don't you consistently find callous, proud people without an ounce of humility who offend and repulse you when you consider that they might be elect ahead of you? And don't you often encounter genuinely spiritual, tenderhearted souls who exude the fragrance of the Holy Spirit and who, with their low self-esteem, hardly dare to hope that they are chosen? They wonder whether there is as much as a twig or sprout inscribed with their name among the living branches grafted onto the True Vine!

So tell me, can you ever avoid the impression that those who say they are elect are often far from it, and those who don't dare to think they are really belong there?

And how do you see yourself on this?

Or doesn't the tension of this contradiction burrow its way deep into your soul? Don't you experience the following struggle? On the one hand, you sometimes believe that you are elect, it's true, but then you immediately feel trapped by your pride. But on the other hand, you subsequently become dispirited and stand before God in fear and trembling that you dare hope to share the joy of God's children.

Is this normal? Does being bounced between the poles of pride and fright have to endure to the end? Or according to God's Word, might not the Holy Spirit seem powerful enough to work both effects in you simultaneously? Isn't he capable of keeping you humble before God and at the same time joyful in the complete certainty that you are one of his beloved children?

Should you ask where the key to reconciling that apparent contradiction might be found, just read what the Holy Spirit says in Psalm 121 about keeping your heart. For what do we find there?

Just this: it says that "the Lord is your Keeper"—definitely that! But it also says that he is your Keeper because he is "the Keeper of Israel, of his church, of his Son's body"—and right here is the key to the secret.

Think about a pocket watch, one for example that you carry with you wherever you go. It contains any number of rotating little wheels and spindles, tiny screws and springs, minute nuts and shafts. And you protect that entire device encased in gold or silver with the greatest possible care, so that not even a speck of dust gets into it. You protect the entire thing, and in its entirety every small, insignificant, and trivial stem and screw that's part of it. You do this not because that little steel shaft is so valuable in and of itself but because it's part of the whole.

Removed from the watch, such a little pin would not be worth a tenth of a cent as a piece of steel. Thus it has very infinitesimal economic value. And yet you encase that infinitesimal little pin in silver or gold and attend to it with the greatest of care. You do so not simply for the sake of that small stem but because the entire intricate device that constitutes that watch simply cannot do without it. Taken by itself, it is scarcely worth the trouble of even throwing away. But as a part of the whole, it is just as essential as the little wheel spinning on it. In fact, so much of the entire device depends on that small shaft that the manufacturer has selected it with the greatest care. He did so not because of the value it has in and of itself. But by choosing it and inserting it into the entire device, he made it valuable.

This is exactly how things are between you and the God of Israel.

The Israel of God, the church of Christ, the body of the Son, is an intricate and well-crafted watch, if I may put it like that. Divine mercy is transmitted through its rhythmic functioning and daily ticking. In that watch there are likewise a countless number of little parts. We call them believers. Brought together in the whole body, they have their place like the rotating little wheels and springs, the spindles and tiny shafts, of a watch.

You, too, when considered in isolation and by yourself in that marvelous device called the church of God, are a completely worthless little shaft, maybe the most infinitesimal and insignificant one of all. You couldn't think of yourself as small and insignificant enough, therefore. Literally, hardly worth throwing away, like a tiny shaft or screw in the watch! But when God incorporates you into that device, and when he devises a place for you somewhere in that watch so that you are clothed with a purpose in it, the picture changes completely.

The Lord God has made and shaped and elected you for a place in it with unending skill and care. He's done so with even more skill than the watch maker in Geneva chose his little nuts and spindles. The holy God of Israel bestows, confers, and assigns a value on you that does not inhere in your own insignificance. Not for a moment! But it is yours only when you fulfill the service assigned to you in that role of a lowly little part in that beautifully crafted whole.

Then God protects you. He does this not because you are so insignificant. He does so because you are part of the whole, an intricate part of the entire and beautifully crafted timepiece. This is the church, the Israel that is the product of his desire. And now he encases you in silver and gold. He shields you from damage. He even sees to it that no speck of dust finds its way in. This is when the Lord is your Keeper, but only because he is the Keeper of Israel.

So now can your own soul tell to me whether there is really any so-called conflict between being "lowly of heart" and yet "chosen of God"?

BEARING THE WEAKNESS OF THE WEAK!

We who are strong are obligated to bear the weaknesses of
the weak, and not just to please ourselves. Romans 15:1

Does the Holy Spirit guide all God's children to equal depth on this matter?
Both Scripture and our experience compel us to answer this question in the negative.

It's not only that there are some newborn children of God who are still only
drinking milk and others who are mature and already enjoying solid food. It's
not about still others of whom the apostle writes: "As many of us as have been
made perfect, let us live by that standard." But it's that even among those who
have been perfected or are mature there is a great difference in the gifts of grace,
as well as in the leading of the Spirit. Some of those who are called are strong,
while others will remain weak and frail until the day they die.

By those who have been made perfect or who are mature, the Scriptures
naturally do not mean people who have achieved complete holiness. It means
exactly what we mean by "mature" in ordinary human language. With respect
to every individual, mature means someone who has reached their full stature and in that sense will grow no taller. But we add that because that person

is now physically mature, they are just beginning to develop or ripen with respect to spiritual maturity.

Likewise, the Lord has determined the definite measure or height or girth that every Christian will attain spiritually and that they will never exceed. Because they are limited like this, the initial working of the Holy Spirit in them is intended to develop their spiritual limbs and organs to the designated level. Having reached that level, they have achieved their spiritual measure or height or proportions. They have in that sense then reached maturity. They have been perfected or completed.

However, this is not said to leave the impression that people have already achieved that level. No, it's intended to indicate that the powerful work of the Holy Spirit in producing this development, this spiritual nourishment and nurture, this ripening of maturity in Christ, is just beginning.

For the moment we leave aside small children and youth. We are thinking only about those Christians who are regarded as adults. And among them, Scripture tells us, are found all sorts of gifts, strengths, and abilities. No two are completely alike. Each has their assigned position and portion. This is different for each of them. For the Holy Spirit assigns each what he chooses. This may be ten talents, or five, or three, or sometimes only one!

The result is that in any given congregation a distinction has to continually be made among adults between the strong and the weak. Furthermore, the weak must not be looked for only among the unconverted or the recently converted. They can be found among those who have been converted for a very long time already and who have already reached the full level of their spiritual growth. Also among them an unevenness of strength and ability exists, just as is the case with the parts of our own bodies. The pinky finger is not the lower back. The shoulder can withstand a blow that the shin cannot.

By God's design, will, and determination there are some in the congregation who are spiritual giants. Others must get along as dwarfs. There are some who have been given the spirit, insight, and faith that is strong enough to withstand the worst things possible and to accept the greatest challenges. Others crumple and retreat from the worst and succumb to a burden ten times lighter.

That's just a fact!

You may not dismiss it. In fact, you cannot. But you do have to ask yourself how the Lord wants you, if you are one of the stronger members, to bear the weaknesses of the weak. And when you do, I'm afraid to say that you'll find that there's all too much sinning against God's sacred command.

Nevertheless, God's command is that the stronger will bear the weakness of those who are weak, and that they will not do so in order to please them-selves. But in actual practice, we find just the opposite. We see that those who are stronger demonstrate that they take a great deal of satisfaction in being stronger than those who are weak. They repress those who are weaker and in the great majority rather than supporting and uplifting them. And in their arrogance, they often reproach those who are weaker for not being as strong as they are.

Naturally, this is not what the Lord wants! That's not why he blessed you with more. That kind of attitude angers him. By showing it, you waste in wicked ways the sacred strength that he has given you. What is even worse is that it leaves the weak to perish in their weakness.

Consider the example of a stronger husband and a weaker wife living together. The weaker wife stimulates her husband's tenderness, and the strong husband fortifies his wife. This is how it should be in the church of Christ.

Whoever lives more deeply into this reality experiences it more fully and receives more from it. That's where they need to discover both their desire to humbly serve the less blessed and their love for doing so. Likewise, the spiri-tually less experienced and mature need to open their hearts and senses to live from the abundance of others.

But this is not what people do. They do something quite different. And even when by God's unusual mercy someone might have something of that deeper, rock-solid faith grounded on God's eternal decree and that expresses the high ideals of Reformed living, it's not unusual to witness something different. One sees how people are filled with conceit and regard themselves as higher than others who haven't reached their level and just don't get what it's all about. Then it's not unusual for them to take a great deal of pleasure in laying out for these others in a bewildering avalanche of words the heights that they will never be able to achieve. They are also pleased when they see these others leaving empty-handed because they carry with them the impression from us that we rank so far above them.

Brothers and sisters, this must never be the way thing are among us!

Those who behave like this are not building up the Reformed church. They are destroying it. For such people are definitely doing what God strenuously rejects when he tells them not to act in order "to please themselves." They hav-en't shown the love that has learned to uphold their brothers and sisters. They alienate rather than attract them. And that distorts the spiritual balance that God has ordained for his church.

This is not the standard of Christ and his cross, but the wicked practices of an evil world applied to a sacred inheritance. If we could ever once rid ourselves of this, how the church would blossom and how truth would triumph!

If only people found satisfaction in upholding, supporting, and guiding one another instead of despising, condemning, and trampling them. Doing so is by no stretch of the imagination an expression of weakness or of abandoning as much as one jot or tittle of God's truth.

The Lord preserves us for this!

How could anyone who has received greater light ever hide it under a bushel?

No, but this is what's required: that you let that greater light illumine the path of those walking in darker places, and that you always consider their weaker eyesight.

24
VOLUME II

THE GOLD IS MINE!

The silver is mine and the gold is mine, says
the Lord of Hosts. Haggai 2:8[1]

O nly God can create gold. All that human beings are capable of producing is baked bricks! Not gold! Not silver! Not even copper or iron or even a piece of wood! A human being can't bring any of them into existence. All they can do is make bricks from clay, and then only with the clay that God has first created and with the heat that God has called into existence.

There are crude, rough, worthless things on earth. And there are other things that are exquisite, noble, and very valuable.

Typical of the nobler things is the precious metal that Scripture often extols as gold. Scripture frequently reminds us that this fine, pure gold is a beautiful feature of God's creation. He was pleased to bestow a number of excellent qualities on it. That people slave so hard sluicing for gold is certainly not just because it's so scarce, hard to find, and unusual. It's also because in and of itself gold is so gloriously beautiful and exquisite.

Concerning gold, the Lord God says here: "This is mine. I made it. You can't possibly produce anything like it, you sons of men. All that I allow you to do is to work with the gold that I've given you. You might be able to give it some sort of artistic expression or to refine it so skillfully that its beauty is enhanced. You might give it a place among my temple's treasures. You might utilize it for

---

1. Kuyper and the Dutch translation give the reference as Haggai 2:9.

the even higher purpose of expressing love artistically and thereby working miracles of tenderheartedness."

But is God's creature willing to live with this?

Go ask the Middle Ages, when the brightest minds poured their energies into alchemy and the art of men making gold. They endeavored to have men do what God had reserved for himself. That's an apt picture of the Roman Catholic Middle Ages, when all the meanderings of Christ's church were devoted to the effort of reproducing the gold of his atonement.

That's the reason why God shamed and scandalized all those attempts to create gold by means of alchemy. They couldn't succeed because of what is written in Haggai 2:8: "The silver is mine and the gold is mine, says the Lord of Hosts." And just as soon as the mere creature once again tries to see what they can do, God points them back to the account of the tower of Babel in his Word. There people baked bricks from clay and used them for stone in building a tower whose top would rise to the clouds. But God knocked it down and destroyed it with a single blow. Or you can recall the brick kilns of Egypt, where God's people had to expend all their best efforts in shaping and baking building blocks from clay.

And if you want to feel intensely and fundamentally how futile man's baking of bricks really is, think about this: They will soon be reduced to rubble. Now compare that with the granite of God's enduring stone mountains. Ask yourself, also, what endures of that stone when God exclaims, "Here are my stones, O man," and strews out his emeralds, sapphires, rubies, and diamonds that sparkle and glitter before your eyes.

Isn't there a lesson in all this? And doesn't this lesson apply to every aspect of life? In all of one's genius, creativity, thought process, willpower, character, and striving for virtue and godliness, isn't there both gold and dross, just as there is in the goldsmith's crucible?

And doesn't God teach you time and again that he, the Lord of Hosts, reserves exclusively for himself the making of gold in all of these matters?

Does the best military organization ever create even one grain of talent in some general? Does the most ably crafted body of laws ever produce a wise king for a nation? Can a society itself ever create one poetic genius? Are you able to give your children a good set of brains? If it's not innate, can you make geniuses of them?

Oh, to shape something, to help something along, to modify something one way or another—all of this you can do. You can modify the appearance of something because you're clever, have learned something about it, or because of what you've experienced. But can you modify its character? Above all, is it within your power to create the gold of living with God in another person's heart?

Or mustn't you simply confess this in quiet humility about the gold of a person's talents, virtue, or spiritual life: "You, O powerful Creator, you alone are capable of creating these! This gold is yours and yours alone!"

And if you in your heart can say "Amen" to this, don't all the sins of our era, of false teachers, and of our own upbringing amount to spiritual alchemy? Isn't this what all the attempts to create by ourselves the gold of our own characters amount to? The gold of our own genius? The gold in our own hearts? Even the gold of our own justification and sanctification? They are all irrational and senseless attempts! Instead, we should be praying to God to provide them for us!

And how did the spirit of such foolishness come to pervade our generation? Surely not just by itself! Didn't it come as the judgment on our sin from the One to whom all gold belongs? Didn't it come as his judgment on the sin of human presumption in using God's gold against him rather than to his glory?

For when the Lord says: "The silver is mine and the gold is mine," he first of all means: "I'm the only one who can create it!" At the same time, what directly and properly follows from this is this: "Thus it must be used to my glory."

But consider for a moment what people did with the gold they had received from God.

First of all, consider what they did with the gold ore taken from the gold mine and that should have been for the purpose of showing mercy. It was misused for luxuries. And if it wasn't used in actual sin, it rusted in the miser's treasure chest, if it actually could have rusted.

Then also ask yourself what people have done with all that gold given them by the grace of God in the form of genius, talent, and knowledge. Consider how instead of being sanctified in the service of God these became a source of pride that first mocked God, then scorned him, and finally denied him altogether.

Or consider the gold that has been conferred on the will, conscience, character, nature, and disposition of the humble people in our own country.

And above all, inquire about the gold of spiritual rebirth! Oh, all you children of the Almighty, won't even we be judged if we allow that most precious of all gold to lie unused in the form of mere ore, or worse yet, if in our selfishness we rob God of his honor by how we use it?

25

VOLUME II

YOUR HEALING WILL HAPPEN QUICKLY

*Then your light will break forth like the dawn and
your healing will happen quickly. Isaiah 58:8*

The entire congregation now knows that it's sick. All the people lament in their inner chambers. They complain mournfully in their assemblies and houses of prayer. God's true children in any case no longer think about healing the rupture.

That's why among the children of the kingdom all attention is focused on the future. They want to escape the present and experience better conditions. Understood more profoundly, they long for the everlasting condition that will arrive with the Lord's return.

For whoever is sick is looking to be restored. They try to heal their wounds. They look for healing day and night. And that healing will certainly come. Eventually a trace of improvement is evident, but the healing of our souls and the healing of God's people comes so very slowly.

All sorts of remedies are tried. First they are looked for from the east, and then they are thought to come from the west. One hero after another comes along who would sink a well-placed stone in Goliath's forehead. But it is as though the torrent of impotence, futility, and inadequacy resumes its course after having been stemmed momentarily.

People definitely know the road they have to take. God's Word speaks clearly and distinctly. People genuinely want to walk the only true road. Their lives bear witness that they "daily seek the Lord and have a deep desire to know his ways as people who live in righteousness." But when all is said and done, they make no progress. They gather stones, but no wall is built.

And yet, things don't have to stay like this. Better said, this situation may not be permitted to continue!

As far as God is concerned, our illness always dishonors his name. Our failure is a source of grief to the Holy Spirit. Our weakness bitterly disappoints the Son, in whom all power resides. Most importantly, the Lord's promise pointedly testifies: "Your healing will happen quickly." The All-Merciful One, who is faithful, says: "Your light will break forth like the dawn!"

So if things don't happen quickly, it's obviously proof that while we might be on the right road, we are not walking according to its requirements. We are more corrupt and worse than we had imagined.

And should you really want to walk as you should and if you cry out with your whole heart: "O God, let your Word show me the better way and lead me sure-footedly," it will do so powerfully. But then you have to make that appeal to God with a sense of humility, smallness of soul, and genuine misery.

For what does the Lord say through Isaiah about when your healing will come quickly?

When you seek him daily? No, I tell you. For the Lord himself bears witness to Israel that his temple is crowded every day!

When you live more seriously and submissively? Even less so, for Israel tormented its soul and piled one fast day on top of the other.

When you search for a deeper knowledge of the Lord? Even this doesn't determine the outcome, since the Lord tells Israel: "You do have a deep desire to know the Lord!"

No, the basic idea on which this admonition of the Word rests is this: godliness must soak your whole being like oil soaks clothing.

God saw that his children were filled with lying.

They ran to him like a flowing stream and thought that they were serious. But they didn't mean it.

They went through the motions. They said what they should have. But their words did not rise from the depths of their lives. They did not flow from them like Aaron's oil flowed down onto his clothing. Their profession, their prayer, and their songs of praise were too far above them. They couldn't really aspire to them. Their words were above their heads. The result was that they were actually living a double life. The one was very pious, very enthusiastic, and full of sacred fervor. But beneath and behind this one was another. And it was pathetic, powerless, and base.

But the Lord our God cannot and will not tolerate this kind of double-mindedness. He wants diamonds. Nothing but diamonds whose sparkle and shine glisten from their deepest depths—from their hearts!

However, the situation is this. Our hearts, our deeply corrupt and miserable hearts, can be compared either to the blackest coal or to the most brilliant diamond. But just as in the natural order coal and diamonds differ according to the degree of heat that formed them, in Christ's kingdom there is a power to transform coal-blackened hearts into gemstones for God. That happens every time the Spirit shines through our hearts as they live in union with Christ.

In order to deliver you from this state of disgrace and chronic illness, the Holy Spirit shows you a more excellent way through the prophet Isaiah. It is this: "That you loosen the knots of injustice; that you discard the yoke of bondage; that you free the oppressed and smash all their yokes; that you share your bread with the hungry and welcome the dispossessed into our home; that you clothe the naked that you encounter; and that you do not turn away from your own flesh and blood."

Does this indicate a realistic way of living?

Show a little more respect with your question, my brother! These are the Lord your God's very own words being held in front of you! You can simply read them in Isaiah 58.

Yes, the Lord definitely stirs you to one great act without delay. It might be the most difficult one of all. It is that you dare to give away your wealth!

The love of money is the root of all evil, which is why the One who nurtures your soul begins by chopping at that root with his axe. Pity, empathy, compassion, and mercy need to be cultivated in your heart and nurtured in the hearts of your children. Surely this is what must happen in the presence of the Lord. This is how you should act and teach those entrusted to you to act. Without this, you will find no peace. For then you are a miser; you'll always be one; and you'll never inherit the kingdom of heaven.

But once you have gotten beyond that, you face all the devils in your heart whose name is "Legion." And we know that they'll continue assaulting us until the day we die. Oh, the knots of injustice, the bondage of that yoke! A thousand times you've wanted to break them, but they continue to tie your wrists. And now would you merely live in peace?

No, I tell you in the name of the Lord, to the degree that you want to be genuinely Reformed in lip and heart and life but don't have peace is the degree to which the One who breaks all bonds responds. He hears the anguished cries of your soul and breaks your chains.

> In response to all their prayers
> He sets his Israel free
> From all their terrible snares,
> And he'll do the same for me![1]

---

1. The rhymed Dutch versification of the hymn stanza reads:
Hij maakt op hun gebeden
Gansch Israël vrij
Van ongerechtigheden,
Zoo doe Hij ook aan mij!

26
VOLUME II

DON'T PRAY FOR THESE PEOPLE!

*Then the Lord said to me: "Don't pray for the welfare of this
people ... " Therefore, we will wait for you. Jeremiah 14:11, 22*

In their spiritual struggles, how terribly anxious a child of God can be because
they've not only been devastated by the Lord, but they have the sense that
he's holding them down there.

Take for example the dedicated Jeremiah, one of God's heroes!

Jerusalem taunted him on their streets. The kids booed him. Upstanding
members of society simply smiled at his "foolish prattle." Ungodly folks gnashed
their teeth at this doomsday preacher that nobody respected. And he could do
nothing at all about it. He simply had to put up with it.

But then hard times fell on foolhardy Jerusalem. A terrible plague afflicted
the people. The wells dried up. The cisterns were emptied. There was no more
water. People were overcome with thirst.

And what does Jeremiah say now? "Lord, I thank you that you have vindicated me"?

Not at all! That solid, tenderhearted man fell to his knees and began praying
and pleading for God's mercy toward the Jerusalem that had been jeering at him.

You might say that that's too much to ask of any human heart! But that kind
of pleading and imploring didn't rise from his own heart; it arose from the Holy
Spirit working in his soul.

You would think that his praying would be crowned with triumph and that the heavens would be opened and it would begin raining again. But they didn't. That wasn't in God's plans. To the contrary, God's insulted love and offended holiness turned against that sinful city all the more terribly. The response that Jeremiah got was this almost-unbearable answer: "Don't pray for the welfare of these people, but banish them from my presence!"

Had Jeremiah been praying too presumptuously? Isn't it sometimes overlooked that confessing our guilt and having our souls shattered in everyone's hearing needs to precede our praying?

But no, just listen! This is how he had been praying: "Lord, although our iniquities testify against us, respond for your own name's sake. We have often departed from your ways. We have sinned against you!"

That's as tenderhearted as it could be! He didn't pray that "those Jerusalemites" have sinned but that "we" have sinned. He included himself as part of the sinful city. He lumped himself with the transgressors.

And then still to be refused, still to be turned down, almost as though he were being punished for praying like that! My good reader, you'd understand, wouldn't you, if Jeremiah, after having received that kind of answer from God, prayed: "Let Jerusalem die, then! The Lord has vindicated me!"? It would be as though he had caught his second wind and could breathe again!

And that's exactly how Jeremiah would have prayed if he had been master of his own lips! But now you can see why we confess a Trinitarian God. Not just the Father and the Son! But also the Holy Spirit!

Oh, I know that the uninitiated call this a fruitless dogma! But, O my Lord, it has always been the most blessed truth about your own being, a totally wonderful revelation, and a source of comfort to my soul!

We see that here once again!

Israel had offended its covenant God. God's only response could have been to show his anger. But in the context of Jehovah's anger, the Holy Spirit entered Jeremiah's heart. He stirred up a prayer that never otherwise would have risen in Jeremiah's heart. It's only source could have been that Spirit who is God himself. And the Spirit set him free in his struggles of faith to resist the urge not to pray. He moved Jeremiah to keep on praying: "And yet, O Lord, we will wait for you, for your hand is in all these matters!"

So do you sense what it is to confess that the Holy Spirit is also God and is sent by God? And wasn't the conclusion of the matter glorious, when with his own lips the Lord said: "Thus, it will not go well with your remnant!"

Just as he did with Jeremiah, God often deals this way with his children.

They believe. They even have a profusion of faith. And in that abundance they appeal to God in exalted language, or so it seems. But this is actually offensive to the Lord.

Then the Lord does with them what a person does with a beginner in a swimming pool. They push their head underwater so they can't breathe. They can only think that they are going to choke and die. This goes on until the person with him finally pulls the beginner by the hair and lifts their head out of the water. Then, with lungs bursting, they can breathe again, wonderfully and freely!

Faith is the breath of the soul. The Lord dunks his overly confident child under so that all the waves and breakers of the Almighty overwhelm them. That's when his submerged child frantically appeals to him, but it doesn't help. God seems cruel; he doesn't respond but pushes his child farther down. What cruelty! How terrible God is! In its deathly fright, faith thinks it's choking. But then, when they've been under long enough, with his other hand the Lord lifts his child up. Above water, their soul feels like it can breathe again. They see the reassuring face of their God once more. That person then whispers to themself: "How completely I misunderstood my dear God and Father!"

WHEREVER THE SPIRIT WENT, THEY WENT

Wherever the Spirit went, they went. Ezekiel 1:20

The privilege that Israel's prophets had was enormous. They had to endure much because of the Lord's name. But they also drank deeply of the sweet delicacies in that name things that would never cross our lips. Just think, for example, about Ezekiel's ravishing vision of God's cherubim.

One gets the impression from all of this seer's prophecies that the wonderful spectacle of these angels always stayed with him. It often reinvigorated him. The memory of it enlivened him.

The world of angels is something that sweeps us off our feet!

It is a swarming, swelling, seething life of holy and blessed spirits surrounding the throne of incomparable glory. Everything that God's Word discloses about it is spectacular. It is one glittering spectacle of radiance and glory, something to behold! And among the angels, there is continuous celebrating and rejoicing and praising in the presence of the everlasting God. In their faces one sees tenderness, loveliness, and great beauty. And by covering their faces with their wings in the presence of God, they display the profound depth of their adoration.

How much more spiritually cordial life would be for God's children if they were more attentive to the sacred truth that these friendly beings surround them at all times. How much better it would be if they were always aware of these ministering, celebrating angels and of what the Lord God is striving to do and accomplish through them as they polish our discouraged, unfinished hearts.

To pay attention to these angels and their work is not heretical in the least! Just because the erring Church of Rome misuses the ministry of angels, we should not neglect the life of angels. In his holy Word, God tells us that he provided them as a treasure and a rich resource for our souls.

Didn't our Savior himself make use of angels to minister to him in the desert? Didn't they support him in Gethsemane? Moreover, didn't the Prince of the Heavenly Hosts, when he taught us how to pray, include the petition "Your will be done on earth as it is in heaven"? And doesn't that very pointedly refer to the angels' total dedication to the Lord's service?

So then, how could you as a child of the kingdom ever pray: "May I serve as your angels do," unless you reckoned with the life of angels? Those words would never cross your lips naturally if you didn't think their existence is true. They wouldn't unless you think longingly about how they attend to your personal needs every day and every night. About how they surround God! About how they are resplendent in holiness in God's eternal sight!

The latter is above all what exhilarated Ezekiel about those blessed cherubim when he so appropriately said: "Wherever the Spirit went, they went!"

Now, that's what I call real following!

When you truly follow someone, you follow them blindly. You turn when they do. You wheel around when they do. You stand stock still when they do. You pick up the pace when their footsteps quicken. And it may definitely be asserted that Ezekiel was saying the same thing about God's angels when he said: "Wherever the Spirit went, they went!" They understand much better and more deeply than we do what it means to follow Christ. They are much more keenly sensitive about imitating Christ and about doing what Jesus does than the taskmasters who are always prodding us to "imitate Jesus" and "do what Jesus would do!" Our souls keep on responding: "But, who is equal to that task?"

No, then we're really better off observing this ordinance given the cherubim, given to the vast armies of heavenly hosts: "Where the Spirit goes, we will go!"

For living gloriously is first of all precisely that! It's for you never to hesitate. Never to waver! To always know that what you're doing is good! It's seeing to it that that you keep your eye on the Spirit!

Yes, living blessedly is when you never spiritually resist the breath of the Spirit, but when the Holy Spirit is always visibly ahead of us and when we are always moved forward by him, come winds and high tides.

And it's a royal blessing when we never need to strain at rowing or dragging our little boat ahead.

When we never have to put the pressure of a steam engine on ourselves to do so! But when we're always pulled forward by the Spirit! "Wherever the Spirit goes, we go!"

What spiritual rule about living explains this?

But you hesitate and waveringly ask: "Should I do this, or should I forget about it?" "Should I go that direction or simply go along with the crowd?" "Should I wait or forge ahead?" In all of these instances, you have to decide in your heart whether the fresh air of the Holy Spirit is to be found on that path, by making that decision, or in having no direction at all.

This is definitely what characterizes a child of God. The spiritual person discerns all things spiritually.

The world does not. It neither sees nor knows him. But those of you born of the Father definitely do, for "you know him and he lives in you."

Just be aware that it's very well possible that left to yourself you sometimes hesitate. And sometimes when the Spirit is definitely present, you still don't dare to take a definite position. Well then, simply be patient, bide your time, hold back. But it would be impossible for you ever to say: "Look! That's where the Holy Spirit is leading us," and having received that sacred clarity, then to pursue a sinful path.

It is a glorious, invigorating thought to see in your imagination the Spirit of God moving forward slowly and calmly as the standard bearer and a long train of God's children following behind him. Following behind, yes, but with a few who momentarily linger because they think they know better than the Spirit, but who then quickly fall in step behind him too. And also, to see others who run ahead but then fall back and wait until the Spirit has moved ahead of them again. It's glorious to witness this procession until finally, on the edge of eternity, all those redeemed by the blood of the Lamb find themselves moving forward in that sacred army, each according to their rank and assigned position.

My brothers and sisters, are you in step with this?

Do you see the Spirit leading you? If so, then praise your ever-holy God with all that is in you! But if you don't, hurry to walk in God's strength by being brokenhearted and fall in step behind the Spirit!

28

HOW YOU DESPISE
YOUR BROTHER

I wish that all people were as I am. But each one has their own gift
from God, the one this and the other that one. 1 Corinthians 7:7

Despising your brother is a frequent, full-blown evil, especially in our day!
The Holy Spirit warned against this intensely when he appealed to the
Romans through the apostle Paul: "Why do you judge your brother; and why
do you despise your brother? For we will all be placed before God's judgment
seat" (Rom 14:10). But in defiance of this warning, this terrible evil continues to
creep forward little by little. Sadly, showing contempt for your brother persists,
especially contempt for those who are more common, less distinguished, and
less gifted among them. This is getting worse instead of better.

Whoever has amassed a great deal of knowledge and possesses keen judgment usually looks down from their presumptuous height on others who barely
get by with their limited knowledge and are often mistaken. Those who have
achieved positions of honor in church or society are accustomed to being condescending toward those who are not as keen as they are. Nimble, clever people
sometimes conduct themselves scandalously toward the slow, sluggish ways
of others. Even so, we all too frequently encounter accomplished people who
have received from God a great deal of insight into sacred matters, yet who
disparage those who are spiritually dull and simpleminded, with whom you

just can't hold a meaningful conversation, who will never amount to anything, and at best can only be regarded as the least in God's kingdom.

This sin does a lot of damage. It's a knife that slices into two souls at the same time. It wounds two hearts with one thrust. It always inflicts arrogance and overconfidence on the person who strikes the blow. And it discourages and diminishes the one attacked. In combating this sin, people simply have to confront it with the truth of God's Word, the pure truth as it shined in our spiritual fathers' hearts in their powerful ways of stifling it.

If the Pelagians, the Arminians, and those who advocate free will are correct, despising your brother is, of course, completely defensible. For look, then it's your unusual excellence that explains your high rank. By contrast, it's the other person's sluggishness and tragic failure that explains why they haven't reached the same level you have but have remained so insignificant that they scarcely matter. If Pelagius is right, you have to praise a smart child to high heaven because they're so exceptional, and you have to come down hard on one who behaves stupidly and even despise them! In such cases, there's no objection to the very gifted person thinking: "Look how superior I am to that individual and how insignificant and unimportant they are." This attitude thinks that such people only need to show some ambition and self-confidence. Otherwise, the only thing to do with them is to shove them into a corner. It's thought that the more richly endowed person has earned what they have achieved, while the shameful deficiency with which the other walks around is their own fault. To the extent that the entire Roman Catholic Church, almost all modernists, and most proponents of the newer orthodoxy either openly or covertly espouse free will in our day, it's no wonder at all that despising your brother is on the increase! By nature we're all inclined to it. And when preaching spurs on human ability rather than reins in this sin, it's not hard to understand how it flourishes as wildly as weeds after the rain!

But contrast this with the simple, clear, unmistakable truth of God's holy Word. It teaches all people that "no one possesses anything that they have not been given!" This truth completely changes the way that you look at yourself as well as at your brothers.

Imagine that you yourself are a very gifted as well as a deeply spiritual person. Imagine that you have been given one talent after the other and that you excel your brothers in many respects. If so, remember that then you are nothing more than an empty glass into which your owner has poured an exquisite, fragrant wine that they intend to drink later. Or remember that you yourself are no more than an empty porcelain cabinet into which your owner has assembled a collection of porcelain for which he paid a small fortune so that its admirers would praise the owner, not the display case. Or again, remember that you are an empty ship that your owner fills with a valuable cargo that he intends to unload at some other port.

In such examples, there's nothing about the content that you have earned. It's all simply been entrusted to you. This imposes a heavy obligation on you. It also exposes you to enormous dangers. It also obliges you to serve in a much deeper sense than it does your brothers. You are the person designated to be the standard bearer in the army of the less fortunate. You have to understand that this means people will take aim particularly at you and will attack you hardest of all. While others in the column have been assigned to carry either a table or a chair, you have been charged with transporting its sacks of money. This means that any robbers are going to attack you first. You feel no greater pressure than being tempted in your heart. Greater demands are placed on your strength. You need to be more disciplined in your living. And you are favored with no greater or purer pleasure than the honor of having carried and endured more for your Lord than others have!

This is how the doctrine of free grace trims back boasting, arrogance, self-centeredness, and pride.

The "earthen vessel," the expression that Jacob Cats[1] uses to describe you, serves no other purpose than to help you withstand the heat of the fire and serve up a fine meal.

At the same time, the corollary of this doctrine is that you reject the poison of despising your brother. For, in fact, there's nothing left to despise!

Or didn't God have the freedom to create sixty or a hundred people who are really quite ordinary, thirty on a second level, and only ten whom he festooned in special ways? And when that little man who is less accomplished and not as highly gifted has been entrusted with only one talent, isn't that one talent also a God-given talent? And doesn't the person who disparages and merely dismisses that one talent really offend God?

Tell me what you have to say about the spiritually dull and simpleminded! "Everyone has received their gift from God," says the apostle. It would be just as foolish for someone who weighs 170 pounds to think less of someone who weighs only 150 pounds, as it would be to disparage someone on crutches with a broken leg. It's irrational, senseless, and just plain wrong to look down on spiritually simple and ordinary people who haven't developed more fully, to

---

1. Cats was an esteemed seventeenth-century poet of the Dutch "golden age."

whom the Lord God hasn't accorded a full grasp of things, and who can't stay in step with your own quicker pace!

This is how people come to realize that God needs to be afforded his due honor if we are to be set free from our sinning in this regard.

Admit it! Confess it! Worship the Lord God because of it! He is the completely free and sole dispenser of all intellectual, physical, and spiritual gifts. Because they flow from him alone, forsake all pride and self-centeredness once and for all. Likewise, develop a deep aversion to despising your brother. Rather, value the smallest gift that you detect in him. This worshipful attitude will at the same time cause the less gifted brother not to be envious any longer nor to complain that he has been given so much less than you have received.

What will happen, in short, is that because there is reverence for God, there will also be reverence among people for each other. The only sin remaining to be resisted is that of the person who has three talents but who thinks and acts like they have five! Also to be resisted is the sin of the discontented person to whom God has given only one talent but who thinks and acts like they have received none!

Both sins always need to be resisted. That's because both of them are lies. Both of them are lies that misrepresent what God has done.

29

AND I ALSO AM
AT WORK

My Father is at work until now, and I also am at work. John 5:17

Laboring and working to our way of thinking and in our language are as good as the same thing. Both suggest "slaving away by the sweat of your brow" or "grinding it out" and "working your fingers to the bone." People automatically think of working physically with one's hands and muscles when the term "labor" is used. And if someone is busy but never needs to use their hands, a great many people say that that person is not exerting themself.

While such misunderstanding may seem innocent enough, it in fact is not. In no small measure, it is in fact the source of considerable damage to our spiritual lives. For just think about it! If the false impression that all work has to be visible, outward, physical exertion gains traction, then it's obvious that Sabbath rest here on earth, the eternal Sabbath above, and even the rest of the everlasting God himself all convey a totally wrong idea!

Sabbath rest then amounts to doing nothing! Heaven presents a picture of us sitting alongside each other century after century and singing God's praises. The concept that we create of the Lord God is in the fullest sense one of a God who is virtually asleep and almost dead! People think of our Surety and Mediator in terms of someone sitting at the right hand of the Father, doing nothing, reclining, praying a little, and just waiting for the day when he will return on the clouds of heaven.

This all amounts to denouncing and condemning the Lord's riveting exclamation: "My Father is at work until now, and I also am at work." It also demonstrates unmistakably that we only understand God's divine rest, therefore also the rest of the redeemed and Sabbath rest, when we perceive and grasp how this holy rest in fact imposes a heightened form of work on us human beings. It depicts the real work to which we who have been created in God's image have been called by virtue of our divine origin and our true nature.

The valid understanding of this wonderful affirmation completely turns our usual understanding upside down!

Or don't people already grasp this from our earthly life? Don't they already understand that to the extent that a person holds a higher position, they are called to expend a more demanding level of effort? Don't they see that although a person's external effort may be less, it's because their work is more comprehensive and strenuous?

Consider for a moment what goes on in a colossal factory where people are filling all kinds of orders that come in telegraphically. Look at how many people sweat and slave and toil and slog and walk and run in response to the orders that one single person sitting in an administrative office passes along! He commands his assistant to distribute them minute by minute. Or think about a general perched on a hilltop far above the turmoil and din of the battlefield below. He calmly issues orders through his adjuncts. Or notice how a ship's captain leisurely strolls back and forth on the bridge while everything is hissing and clanging in the engine room below and men are wrestling with the fishing nets on deck. And if you now ask who is working harder, the factory manager or his workers, the general or his soldiers, or the captain or his crew, then everyone senses immediately that it's the first three. They are doing so even though they are sitting down, only standing, or strolling casually. They are doing nothing more than watching what's going on and speaking a few words. Yet I tell you that those three are the real workers! It's their spirited work that's driving that of all the others. That of all the others merely flows directly from their own. Theirs is work on a higher level than that of the workers, the soldiers, or the sailors, even though they had all been frantically and intensely active. So when the factory produces a beautiful art object, or the army wins a battle, or the ship returns safely, no one will say: "That's what the workers, the soldiers, or the crew accomplished!" Everyone will testify: "That's what the manager accomplished." "The general won the battle." "That engineer produced such beautiful results!"

So already here on earth people can sit very quietly, not lift a limb of their body, be completely at rest, and nevertheless be intensively engaged in exerting themselves and be undeniably at work. The philosopher, the thinker, the poet, the statesman, and whoever else is engaged in the finer, nobler expressions of life can be working while almost totally motionless physically. They are working when they only move their lips, use a few fingers to push a pen, or sometimes just turn a page.

So think about applying the same kind of explanation just a little bit further. Suppose that the same lips, fingers, and senses were free of any external exertion and remained at complete rest in order to allow the inner spirit to work. Tell me, then, haven't you just captured the picture of complete rest that at the same time involves the highest form of work?

And if you move from there to the spiritual activity of God's children, penetrate to the work of the soul, and from there rise to the level of being engaged with Sabbath rest, is it still so puzzling how there can be Sabbath rest in heaven above? Is it puzzling how Jesus can say: "My Father is at work until now, and I also am at work"? Is it surprising that he is at work and also the redeemed with him?

No, labor in the ordinary sense of the term doesn't ennoble a person. It does ennoble a sinner. For a fallen sinner, work is a wonderful instrument for preventing Satan from gaining influence over their flesh, senses, and heart. Banished from Paradise, the sinner had to live by the sweat of their brow as a punishment. But this is a punishment that at the same time is a blessing.

But that kind of labor is not "noble" for us. Rather, what is noble for God's children is that after they have been at work, they return to their real glory found in Sabbath rest. Then already here on earth they receive the eternal Sabbath that constitutes their hope and longing.

That's when they find rest. And in that rest they receive a blessed expansion of strength. And in that quiet increase of strength in the Lord's house they discover the secret of how the cedar and the palm tree grow.

The stranger to all this wryly observes: "The cedar's not doing a thing!" But God says: "The cedar is definitely doing something. It is accomplishing a lot! It achieves the greatest thing imaginable. It grows. It increases. Its blossoms ripen!" And to grow in the Lord, to increase in Christ, and to flower in the Holy Spirit—what do you think, sisters and brothers? Isn't that enough work for the here and now as well as for the blessedness of heaven above?

BECAUSE I WILL SHOW YOU NO GRACE

There you will serve other gods day and night, and
I will show you no grace. Jeremiah 16:13

What's terrible is to fall into the hands of the living God. It's truly terrible!
It's terrible not because he punishes us so harshly, chastises us so
severely, reproves us so sharply, and tests us so intensely. Even a storm and
bad weather can be lovely as long as God is present in them. Even though the
Lord rains powerful blows on you, this is a sign of God's merciful favor more
than of wanting to oppress you and make you miserable.

No, Abraham on Mount Moriah or Job sitting on a pile of ashes were not
rebels for whom it was terrible to fall into the hands of the living God. That
was true for his opponents such as the Pharaohs, the Nebuchadnezzars, the
Ahithophels, and the Judases.

You ask why?

Because in fact there's only one thing that's really terrible, and that's to be
consigned to hell! And even that's definitely not terrible because the physical
suffering there will be so terrible. It's first of all and primarily because in hell
every person is condemned to follow their own ungodly heart without any

restraint whatever. They are completely turned over to their own evil nature. Nothing reins it in! Nothing, nothing at all holds them back anymore from drinking the full dregs of their own filth and unrighteousness.

You poor soul! You presently, desperately need every diversion and distraction possible when you remember the evil or wickedness that drives you and that you can't shake. But in hell, a person's disastrous existence can never escape it. You simply have to live forever with the fullness of your unrestrained evil and sin.

Why does that happen? Only because in hell there is no longer any divine grace. The absence of grace is what defines hell!

Here on earth, hell is already present in, on, and around you every moment that it pleases God to withdraw his grace from you. For when God withdraws his grace from you, at that very moment nothing remains any longer to restrain your sinning. You pursue it totally, recklessly.

Note carefully that we are not talking here about saving, regenerating grace. We're dealing much more with that restraining, curbing, and restricting grace that God applies to human life in general. If people were turned loose without it, they would attack each other like tigers and other wild animals. But because they are held back and restrained by it, human society is still made possible for them. Because of it their lives are also sometimes adorned with civic virtues.

This is a grace shown to you in your unconverted state. As such, it is a divine power that protects you from the force of your own sinning that would otherwise sweep you away and suck you into complete ruin. It assures that you remain a good citizen, however much the world, the Devil, and your own heart attempt to make you throw that all overboard by giving in to sin and injustice. And although on the inside you stand guilty before God, you are not overwhelmed by the destructive, hellish power of sin over you.

But sometimes—and this is what's truly horrible!—the Lord God ultimately withdraws this restraining, curbing, and restricting grace from a group of people or from an individual.

To some extent the Lord did this in his just judgment on the heathens "that he gave over to their depraved mind to do what should not be done." He allowed them "to walk in their own ways" so that "they were consigned to impurity" and "dishonest living" according to "the desires of their own hearts."

It's the same terrible reason why in his glory he sent his prophet with the command: "Make the hearts of these people fat. Make their ears heavy and shut their eyes so they cannot see." Something comparable is said in the book of Job: "If your children have sinned, he has delivered them into the hands of their transgressions." The Holy Spirit conveys entirely the same message through the psalmist: "I have given these people over to the intentions of their hearts." He puts it still more strongly in the letter to the Thessalonians: "For this reason, their God will send them the power of delusion so that they might believe the lie." And this is what the Lord threatens to do to his own people when he has Jeremiah say in this passage: "If you would do this and then that ... then you will ultimately bow down to other gods, and I will withdraw my grace from you."

Don't awful words like these cause us to get very serious?

Brothers, my brothers, think very hard about this. God is still helping you to refrain from sinning. And when you sneak away through the back door in order to sin again, God still comes immediately with his grace to hamper you in a way that won't let you sin. But the Lord God will not be patient with you and put up with this indefinitely. He won't if you persist in your yearning to sin. He won't if you're drawn to it. He won't if you find it burdensome that God is still so gracious toward you that you actually refrain and are prevented from sinning.

But then, when God's long-suffering has run its course, things will change. Then it will occur to you that the Lord was also talking about you when he said: "This soul will just not quit sinning. They will pursue it with all the strength left in them. They find my restraining grace oppressive. Well then, just let them sin! I'll simply withdraw my grace from them. Then they'll slide into the depths of their sin and totally lose any control over it. The pace at which they'll sink into it will quicken. Nothing can stop them then!"

Just ask yourself, "Wouldn't that be terrible?"

Terrible if you couldn't do anything about it?

Terrible if you simply had to sin?

How terrible if you became the prey, the completely powerless prey, of the one who murders souls!

What do you think? Wouldn't that literally be hell on earth?

So "remember his voice today!" Remember what brings you peace.

Our holy God can tolerate a great deal. But not the mocking of his mercy and his grace!

WITH AN IRON POINT!

*Judah's sin is recorded with an iron pen, with the point
of a diamond. It is inscribed on the tablets of their
hearts and on the horns of the altars. Jeremiah 17:1*

Judah's sin is not the sin of the unbelieving world. It is the sin of God's peculiar people, who have been named after his own name. It is the people who bear the sign of the covenant and are adorned with the knowledge of his holiness. We're talking about believers here! We're talking about those who have been instructed by his Word.

And here the Holy Spirit through Jeremiah is talking about that sin that the Lord God inscribed not on a slate from which it can be wiped off or on a sheet of paper that can be ripped up. But God himself etched it with "an iron pen and the point of a diamond." This indicates that the Lord engraved it on something very hard, on something from which it cannot ever be washed off, in a sealed record book from which it will never be expunged. In fact, it stands there as though it had been chiseled in granite in the presence of God himself. This is the One of whom it is said in verse 10: "I the Lord search the heart and examine all thought in order to repay everyone according to their works."

But that's not all. The Lord God very specifically engraved the sin of his people "on the tablets of their heart." This means on their consciences! Deep in their inner awareness! Imprinted on the walls of the inner person! At the base of their minds! That's where a record is kept of every way that you abuse the love of God and the Savior's mercy and of every time that you grieve the Holy Spirit. It's all there—in plain words, in clear and legible handwriting engraved with God's own finger. And if it appalls you that recalling your sin gives you no peace, you should know that this is only because your God has inscribed it with such detailed precision and unspeakable clarity on your conscience.

To be absolutely clear that the Lord regards his people's sins as murdering his love, he keeps record of them in blood! He addresses them in flaming letters written in those secret places and hidden recesses to which you have banished your sin in an effort to conceal it. That's why it's added here that the Lord also inscribed Judah's sin "on the horns of their altars." Those altars stood on the high places and under every green tree. These were the spots far from the presence of their God where Judah committed its abominable, idolatrous adulteries!

Why does the Lord deal this way with his people?

Is it from any other motive than an inner compulsion to be merciful? Why should it be anything else than because he loves his people? For this is what you should understand and experience: knowing that your sin remains on your conscience like an indelible bloodstain and that it keeps on reproving you—"from the beams and walls," as Hosea puts it—is the most trustworthy beacon on the sea for God's children. It can guide us safely through the storms of life and prevent our shipwreck on its reefs.

But more comes to mind in this regard.

Consider this fact. By going into your sin in such great detail that he records it with his iron pen, God sends a very disturbing signal of how he is grieved by the sins of his people. That grief permeates everything. The sinning troubles him so terribly much that he can't get rid of it. It keeps on staring him in his holy face. He can't forget it. Actually you are the one who, by sinning against God's love, inscribes by your own hand an account of your sins on God's consciousness! You do so with an iron pen! And after you've written up your sin on God's consciousness as a source of grief to him, God comes to you. He in turn inscribes the same sin on your own conscience so that you will know in your own heart exactly what God knows about you! This is him addressing your conscience with love, not in a spirit of opposition, rejection, or condemnation. He does it with love so that you will lament his sacred disappointment with your sin in the depths of your emotions. He does it to register his anger, not with the frightening display seen at Mount Horeb, but with the look that Jesus gave Peter after he had denied his Lord three times.

The din of that loud, sharp, powerful memory talking to you about your sin against God's mercy keeps your conscience troubled as a child of God. This is a blessing. It is a shaming grace that proves to you that your Father has not forsaken you.

But notice that verse 9 says: "The heart is deceitful above all things; who can understand it?" Among God's people there are false healers who attempt to quiet the unsettled conscience with sleeping medicine. You're strongly attracted to what they offer. And when that begins working on your heart, God has to write that much more deeply on it with his iron pen. At least that's the case to the extent that you've been reborn into the truth. So remember this well: nothing militates against the state of grace in the lives of God's people more than the numbing of the conscience.

The situation comes down to this. When your conscience accuses you of sinning against your God, you should immediately recognize that you're dealing with the living God himself. He's registering that sin in your conscience out of his grieving heart. A conscience unattended by the living God is nothing more than a ledger of your guilt that you simply toss into a corner and forget about. No, to have a conscience requires that you hear every thought that comes to mind about wrongdoing as the voice of the living God talking to you. The conscience only does its work effectively when in communion with God's majesty. Then it doesn't torment you but helps you move forward.

Remember, brothers and sisters, because God inscribes their sins on the hearts of his people with an iron pen, it's God the Holy Spirit coming to you when your conscience is troubled. He doesn't come in his wrath. He doesn't come to cut you off eternally. But he comes softly and with the intent of saving you. He comes exactly at the right time to admonish you and to give you exactly you what you need. This is provided by him whose blood has such unlimited power that even what has been inscribed with an iron pen and the tip of a diamond is eternally washed away. It is blotted out in the power of his love. It disappears forever because of his sacred, atoning blood.

32
VOLUME II

TAKING UP
ONE'S CROSS

Anyone who would come after me must deny himself,
take up his cross, and follow me. Matthew 16:24

To have to walk around as punishment for days, weeks, months, or even years while carrying a cross on your shoulders was and is unthinkable. If the purpose were to oppress a guilty person for their entire life by letting them struggle under a heavy load, then there's no reason at all why it would have to be a cross. A heavy timber or iron pipe or sack of rocks would do just as well.

Every application of Jesus' words about "taking up one's cross" to some specific burden that we struggle under for a long time must be rejected as illogical. Taking up one's cross applies only to someone condemned to death who must then drag their cross all by themself to the spot where they're going to be crucified.

This is a splendid saying given by our Savior: "Anyone who would come after me must deny himself, take up his cross, and follow me." But it's almost always misunderstood. It's misunderstood by people who would apply it to all sorts of affliction. These are the ones who produce secret pain and constant sorrow, the kind they wake up with every morning and take to bed with them every evening. As a result, God's people think of themselves as a great host of pilgrims struggling down the long road to the heavenly gates with their crosses on their backs.

But the meaning of Jesus' words is much deeper.

Jesus doesn't just require that every Christian willingly bear the same suffering laid on them that is also laid on worldly people. But he is saying above all that as followers of God's Son they have to shoulder a unique cross, one unknown to a child of the world. And this involves nothing less, my brothers and sisters, than Jesus demanding that you accept a death sentence. He expects that you will willingly make your way to the place of shame where that sentence will be fully carried out! He also expects you to pick up that cross and to carry it to that place of disgrace, where you will be stretched out and left to die.

This is the only explanation that does justice to those perceptive words of Jesus.

If anyone would come after him, that person needs to (1) deny themselves, (2) pick up their cross, and (3) follow him.

To deny yourself is definitely not what you do when you sacrifice something for the sake of a brother. It's not to dedicate yourself to something. It's not to go out of your way for another person. No, to deny yourself is in stark contrast with denying your Savior. Protecting yourself at all costs is to give up on Jesus. So is asserting that you're always right or justified. So is continually looking out for yourself. If you live like this, you're sending Jesus on his way! Then denying Christ completely dominates your soul. But, by contrast, if you just allow Jesus to be Jesus, that is to say, if you accept him as your Savior, truly embrace him as your king, and stop obstructing even the smallest recognition of his honor and majesty, then you have to dedicate yourself to these matters. You stop putting yourself first. You totally discount yourself in his presence. You are no longer preoccupied with how things are going for you. It doesn't matter what happens to you anymore. You don't calculate what's in it for you any longer. This is what it means in the full sense of the term to literally deny yourself.

So that's the first step: to deny yourself. But how, pray tell, could an even greater demand follow than the one not to complain about your pain and sorrow? This is no more than is required even of those who haven't been born again!

The second, higher step is completely different. It's nothing less than being willing to suffer death. Self-denial has to lead to accepting a death penalty in order to demonstrate that it's genuine. Even so, accepting a death penalty isn't self-denial in the complete sense of the term. For in any case, Jesus wants to delay carrying out that death penalty. Or he at least wants to substitute another kind of death for it, one that suits him better. In the case of a genuinely self-denying person, Jesus intends to say, resistance to the sentence itself has disappeared. As long as Jesus is in control of a person, he's satisfied. He manages things according to this regulation: from now on the person's life has to be a constant, daily dying. This is the kind of dying accompanied by pain and humiliation. It's dying on a cross. But now the question is whether people will have to drag this person to their cross by force. Or will a glorious heroism be awakened in them so that they resolutely grip their cross, take it up, and carry it to their personal Golgotha?

The cross on which they have to die quite literally involves their entire lives. It involves the evil desires of the flesh that have to be killed and buried. It involves the desire for honor and glory and for happiness and peace in this world that they are obligated to crucify. It also involves crucifying the world around them. That cross includes gradually breaking, wounding, and putting to death everything in them that causes pain and shame. It includes putting an end to everything they desired in their own hearts, within their own circles of family and friends, and even about their own salvation. They literally have to rise above everything about them that was a source of pain and suffering. And they have to quit once and for all their repeated efforts to resist diminishing their own egos!

If all of this is what a child of God really wants … , if they have confessed their Lord and denied self … , and if in doing so they have not resisted or resented its rough wood but desired it and placed it against their neck … , then Jesus says that the third thing follows. It is to follow Christ in dying.

This immediately puts everyone to the test. The conclusion can only mean "follow me to Golgotha in dying."

The cross that we lift up and now willingly struggle to carry must not be borne simply to make a good impression! We don't do it to make a point or show off. We must not do so in order to demonstrate how strong we are. We mustn't do it to please ourselves. No, but we need to bear that cross to our own Golgotha without hesitation so that it can be lifted off our shoulders, raised up as a sign of disgrace, and our ego can be nailed to it. Then the full force of the cross's pain and suffering will fall on us.

In the age of the martyrs, it would have been said that we would have to lay our heads on the block. In less intensive times, it can mean that people will take your bread away from you. Or it might signify that people declare you to be morally dead or that they murder you socially. Even if it doesn't come to those kinds of storms and turbulence, the outcome is substantially the same. A child of God needs to die. Their life must be a constant death. Time and again a part of their ego must die. Living branches need to be cut off and left to die. You understand that "any person who would keep his life must first lose it." But once you've experienced that death, brothers and sisters, gladly listen to what Paul celebrates: "It is no longer I who live, but Christ is living in me."

33
VOLUME II

TO SIFT YOU
LIKE WHEAT

*Simon, Simon, know that Satan has fervently desired
to sift you like wheat. But I have prayed for you
that your faith will not fail. Luke 22:31–32*

Those who confess our Lord Jesus Christ find themselves in an extremely dangerous situation these days. They readily and dependably go about things as "believers." They are known as "the faithful" and deserve high praise in distinction from "those who fall away." In their circles, they are very often leaders and pace setters. That's how they live, responding to the demands of orthodoxy and without being put down very much by others or being persecuted. All too often they live this way without giving it much thought.

Little sensitivity or brotherly courage exists today for admonishing and spiritually challenging those under our care. That's especially true because the human ego has become so overly sensitive that a person hardly dares to say anything critical to someone else. A church that is vigilant and attempts to stay pure through the exercise of discipline is a thing of the past. The whole situation in which believers find themselves is so unprincipled, so influenced by various sects, and so twisted out of joint by self-interest, that people simply no longer become righteously indignant or exercise diligence in confronting a sinful brother or sister about their offense. Meanwhile, the leaders of all kinds of sects are ready to welcome them with open arms, whispering quietly: "My dear brother, if people claiming to be your friends make it too difficult for you, we'd love to have you join us. We're not that judgmental by a long shot. Everyone is accepted here!"

And all this would amount to nothing if Satan were unemployed. But, sadly, he is not! Moreover, the Lord God has judged it necessary for us that this enemy of our souls continue attacking us relentlessly with respect to the world and the sin in our own hearts. So Satan keeps on aiming his arrows directly at our hearts. You know, of course, that he's as sly as a fox, a liar, and the murderer of human hearts.

The Devil is the all-time Old Sifter.

He knows full well that Christ Jesus is preordained to someday test and judge every human heart. He also knows that's why Christ is holding a winnowing basket in his hands. This is a winnowing basket or sieve with which he will sift souls in order to clean up his threshing floor and to gather into his eternal granary clean wheat minus the chaff.

But as we also know, Satan is always intent on mimicking Christ. That's why he wants to single out people and test them too. He has his own winnowing basket. Like Jesus indicated to his beloved disciples on the night of his betrayal, no sinner can follow Jesus without Satan also trying to sift them like wheat. That's how devilish he is at heart! To put it even more strongly, Satan even asked God for permission to single out believers, especially those who are very precise in their Christian practice,[1] and the spiritual fathers in the Christian community. He wanted to test them to determine whether they were in fact pure gold. He proposed doing this in order to expose hypocrites and unmask their pretention.

And to that, my brothers and sisters, God gave his assent. Never forget it!

God would not, God could not, deny Satan this request. If he had done so, what would Satan have been able to say? "Look at that! He doesn't dare to allow that kind of test! We obviously can't be dealing with pure gold here!" And God's honor can't tolerate that kind of response. When the Lord God once declares: "This is my child," that has to be solidly, actually, and truly the case. In fact, even though we might be dragged through the very depths of hell ten times over, we will in the end be purified and saved and will enter the everlasting brilliance of God's presence.

---

1. Kuyper uses the term *fijnen* here. It is shorthand for an identifiable group of Dutch Reformed Christians who lived so carefully, so intentionally distanced from wider cultural patterns, and so distinct in dress, speech, and mores that they were also known as "precisionists," "legalists," and "hyperspiritualists."

Now, being sifted by the Devil is certainly terrible. If we genuinely love integrity and are honest about it, on the inside we are still very bad. There's nothing whole about us. Our best of intentions crumble. When Satan's approach is crafty enough, we have the cold, deeply damnable experience of really hankering after what Satan proposes. And our deviating hearts give us the greatest difficulty in ultimately holding on to the Lord.

I certainly know that those of us who are in Christ Jesus will not fall away. I know that however much Satan may sift God's true children, their faith can and will never fail. This is true however much he manipulates them and tests, afflicts, jolts, or twists them around. But ... but ... doesn't their election also have to be unequivocally confirmed? Don't we look to our works for repeated assurances of our election? And doesn't this frightening question often cross our minds in times of spiritual drought: "Am I a hypocrite too? Am I only a Christian outwardly? Am I a hyperorthodox person who is repulsed by Jesus rather than attracted to him?"

Then, by grace, we have to admit freely and calmly, just as the intensely sifted Job did: "I know that my Redeemer lives!" Persisting, I then have to ask: "Is maturing in Christ something that doesn't matter then? Aren't we being coldhearted when Satan becomes more dominant in our lives than the Lord our God? Can we tolerate Satan celebrating in the depths of his soul, as he often does, when he brags: "We got that and that believing woman to fall into sin once again"? Can we accept that in such cases the Holy Spirit is grieving in heaven above over our impurity and lack of holiness?

By focusing our attention on the Savior's cross, the Lord urgently warns us about Satan's sifting. He does so in the name of the blood of the Spotless Lamb. It has all the power needed to wash away our sinful spots. He also does so by the prayers on the lips of our great High Priest. It's his suffering that keeps our faith from yielding to temptation. Oh, in the name of all that's holy to the hearts of God's initiated children, how intensely is this urgent question being pressed home on your heart: "How are you holding up under the Devil's sifting?"

Look, Satan doesn't warn you before he sifts you. He begins sifting before you realize it. You find yourself in his winnowing basket before you even know where you are. When he approaches, do you see Satan or an angel of light? But that apparent angel is really Satan.

But how is it possible for your heart go along with this?

You keep on confessing! That's natural, for Satan saves that fact for his final attack. At first he leaves your orthodoxy in full play. He leaves it unchallenged.

Otherwise he could never turn you into a hypocrite. Precisely this strategy is the only chance he has.

He makes his next move by appealing to the evil side of your nature. He relies on stealthy, gradually advancing sins. He's not very open in his approach. It's best that no one notices it. And if something comes of it, he very craftily creates the illusion that something good will happen to you—something different for you than for someone else. It will succeed for you. It will be good for you. In fact, it's exactly tailored for your benefit.

And if it should happen that sometimes your conscience is aroused, Satan whispers: "That's because you are much more sensitive than all the others. They won't admit it. If you knew everything about them, you would agree that in your case this definitely isn't so bad."

If you're still uneasy, he misleads you by promising that next week you'll stop. If even that fails, he whispers that whatever is involved will put you in an even better position for going to heaven. That's when you're thrown back on work righteousness and removed from your only Surety.

Through all these devices the lie slips into your soul. You become unfaithful. You cling to sin, the world, and the Devil instead of to your Savior. The outcome is that your growth in Christ disappears. You become estranged from your own heart. Your prayers are hollowed out and become empty shells. Spiritual warmth cools until finally you make the only sacrifice that pleases God: you become disgusted with yourself. With a defeated heart and a shattered soul, you fall on your face before our God. Then he takes pity on you and helps you. He does so despite the fact that you have terribly and miserably disappointed him.

Oh, the ways of the heart are so mysterious!

And all these ways, in a word, are laid bare.

Some of you feel compelled to wander. Stop in your tracks; turn around now, today!

The path of sin can never be your way of life as a child of God.

"Be holy, for I am holy," cries Jehovah Sabaoth!

34
VOLUME II

IN THE JUDGMENT HALL

They led Jesus into the judgment hall. John 18:28

Our Savior allowed himself to be led into the judgment hall.

What's this all about?

Isn't the judgment hall the house of his Father? Isn't all justice from God? Isn't God the one who preserves justice? When a nation develops to the point that it opens a hall of justice, isn't that also a blessing to them?

You know that in days of turmoil and anarchy, when violence reigns and the blind passions of the heart have a free hand, the judgment hall is on lockdown. The judge isn't sitting on the bench. That's when the fires of hell rise to the surface. Remember Paris in 1870.[1] The devils were turned loose!

But as soon as the uproar had subsided, the power of mutiny broken, and brute force clipped, the doors of the courthouse were opened again. The judge resumed his place of honor on the bench, and the scales of justice tipped in his hands once more.

And when light and life had been restored in the courtroom, the better citizens could breathe again, and the criminal element trembled at the prospect of retribution.

---

1. The reference is to the radical turmoil that followed the collapse of the Third French Republic in September 1870 and to the revolutionary socialist turmoil that ensued for some months.

A judgment hall in human society is certainly a godly thing! It's a divine institution that reflects something of God's presence and honor. "Gods" are seated in a court of justice, says Scripture, and God is in their midst.

With God, it's all about justice.

It's not just about making us pure and holy and blessed. It's not only about treating us medically and healing us. It's not even about dealing with us on the ethical level and fostering a new and holier life in us. No, more than all of this, the issue of justice is at the heart of the living God's dealing with his creatures.

It's about establishing justice.

This is because the Lord God is a God who is aware. He knows what he wants. For this reason he has established his will and expressed his life in ordinances, commandments, and directives. He drew boundaries through the entire creation. He determined every limit and restriction. For each of his creatures, he has determined the way in which they are to serve him and exist in his presence.

If the Lord God were a being who is simply unaware of things and has no will or issues no commands about them, it would be enough for us merely to receive new life from him or to be healed of our wounds by him.

But God possesses a self-conscious will about all things. This will governs his ordinances. So there are laws and regulations that determine what God expects of his creatures. And they will be realized just as surely and definitely as a star follows the course that God has defined for it.

As far as God is concerned, those laws cannot be annulled. His lordship through those laws extends so far that he even has control over Satan, the fallen angels, and those who will ultimately be lost. While he is capable of winning strictly through the exercise of sheer power because he is God, he chooses not to do so. He chooses to win only by means of his laws. And in this reality we have the only real key for explaining the suffering of Jesus.

The world into which Jesus entered is governed by laws, as distorted and falsified as they may be. Yet these are laws that always have their place and always have their advocates. The deeply fallen world always has a stake in upholding them. Its honor is involved in doing so. And now Jesus definitely wants to capture that world as his prize and to win back those entrusted to him by the Father. But according to the ordinances governing this earth, that had to be done lawfully.

God had determined that one standard exists for all people. He had also determined that there was nevertheless one nation where law had achieved a greater, purer development. That nation was not that of the Jews but that of the Romans.

The right of condemning to death had not been granted to Jewish law, therefore.

Israel was in possession of a God-given law as well as of a humanly developed system of justice based on it.

This divine law was sacred, and according to it the Man of Sorrows was Israel's Lord and King.

But according to its humanly developed system of justice, Jesus could definitely be apprehended, but not justly condemned. This is why God had arranged it that the masters of law, that is, the Romans, were in control in Jerusalem precisely at that time. That's why he also determined that they alone had the authority and competence to impose the death penalty.

So in Jerusalem there was not only one judgment hall but also the best courthouse on earth available at that time. It was a court with a Roman as presiding judge. This is why we profess in the Apostles' Creed "suffered under Pontius Pilate." Pilate was that Roman in the judgment hall. "Suffered under Pontius Pilate" expresses faith in God's divine leading and guidance.

So the One who bore our sins entered that judgment hall in the full awareness that the sentence of death awaited him there.

Dead or alive, Jesus wanted justice.

Justice in the hall where the man sat who held power because the Father had given it to him! Jesus loves the Father everlastingly. Because God is just, because he lives by justice, because he acts justly, and because he administers justice, Jesus could not escape justice even though that justice would condemn him to death.

He did this so that he might lead you into the eternal judgment hall, namely, into his Father's house.

He did this in order to establish a judgment hall in your own heart, your dwelling place, and to seat the Judge of Every Thought back on the judgment seat there, which is his place of honor.

Yes, he did this to create a refuge for justice in his church here on earth.

So let me know, my good reader. Is your heart that kind of judgment hall? Is your home? Is the congregation to which you belong?

Do you love justice? With a deep, pervasive drive to do God's will, even when it doesn't go your way?

3 5

VOLUME II

LIKE A GREEN OLIVE TREE IN GOD'S HOUSE

I am like a green olive tree in God's house. I rely on
God's mercy now and for eternity. Psalm 52:8[1]

Christ is living! And the life of our Lord Jesus Christ is a continuous source of the power of life flowing, pouring from it. This power pervades everything. It is not limited by distance, but it springs from the heart of Jesus and is here on earth in a split second. It is present in your daily activities, your home, the privacy of your own bedroom, and at the doorway of your heart. It is a power that searches for you and does not give up until it finds you. It always ends either with you crushing and discarding it or by getting through to you. The latter is absolutely wonderful! For then it permeates you, inspires you, exalts you, sustains you, and roots you in the life of God himself.

All the glory of his church, all the preeminence his people may possess, and all the strength of his elect are rooted in the living Christ.

His church receives nothing at all from a dead Christ, or even an unemployed Christ who is now seated somewhere high above us in heaven and is

---

1. Psalm 52:10 in Kuyper's Dutch version.

so far away from us that we have to shout to him and hardly get back as much as a faintly whispered answer. That's when the church is like a lamp without oil, a streambed without water, a parched skeleton without marrow or nerves.

When seen without the steady outpouring and infusion of Jesus' life-giving power, his church, every one of his elect people, and even your own heart are all no more than dead, shriveled carcasses. They are devoid of life's glow and inner appeal. They are worthless, good for nothing, and like a diamond in pitch-black darkness.

But that's not the case, praise God! The Son of God, our glorious Head, is never absent from us in his majesty or with his grace and his Spirit. The diamond is never without bright light shining on it. The root is filled with sap. The streambed is always brimming with flowing water. This is the case even when the church thinks it has no energy and vitality left at all. It's the case when an elect child of the Lord feels worthless and gives up. But that's when the living Christ comes to them, inspires them, and upholds them. That's when he speaks sacred, splendid words to them: "I'll be with you all the days of your life, even until the end of the world!"

This is not what the soul senses, however. It rarely has experiences like that. It's only been able to examine them a few times. If we had to rely on religious experience, we'd have to complain: "The Lord is absent from me three hundred days of the year! And it's already saying too much if I said that on the rest of them I only detect him from a long way off!"

If a gospel had to be fashioned on the basis of the religious experience of God's children, it would go like this: "Those who are superficial glory in their impression that Jesus is always with them. But those who reflect more deeply know that he has visited them on only a few occasions, and then only to spend the night!"

This is precisely the reason why God the Holy Spirit hasn't left the writing of the gospel up to us. That's why he did it himself. Thanks to that divine decision, what we have in his Word is not what we think about Jesus. We have him there as he really is. This is the Jesus presented to God's children there. He is the Jesus who has received all power in heaven and on earth. He is the divine Immanuel. And yet, he is also our brother. He is the Jesus who is ever living, always working, and continuously causing his power to flow from him. He is the Jesus who is always close to his church. He is always enlivening the souls of his elect, even when they take no notice of it.

On that basis, a child of God dares to exalt even during times when they feel abandoned. They exalt as David did when everything seemed lost, all hope was gone, he was walled off from everything, and the Holy Spirit enabled him not to complain even then: "I won't go down that road, but I will exalt and rejoice. 'I will be like a green olive tree in God's house, always and forever.' "

To speak such heroic words at such times is not based on mere religious experience but on a deep faith. It's a faith that relies on a God who is with us even when he doesn't seem to be. It's a faith that calls out to him as though he is present.

An olive tree! I'm an olive tree! That is, I'm such a precious plant that I never shrivel but always stay green. I'm a tree on which people see no fruit from a distance, but when they shake me, the little olives rain down on them on all sides. I'm a tree beautiful in every way, and even my shape is enchantingly beautiful. I'm a tree whose chopped wood—although that's a very displeasing thought— even has a soft, lovely appearance.

That's the kind of olive tree, says David, that I'll be in the house of the Lord. It won't be standing alone on some naked rock like a one-eyed king. It won't be in the desert, where some brushwood passes for a tree. No, it will stand in the most splendid, beautiful courtyard of God's dwelling. It will be in that garden where the cedars and palm trees are on display and where the martyrs' descendants are nourished by their blood. It will be in that magnificent spiritual court where the selection of all the specimens has been coordinated. That's where I'll be, always green, green forever, the shoot of an olive! That's what David dared to exalt in at the very moment that everything seemed lost, when men were hunting him like the gazelle, and when Satan was attacking his sinful heart with thoughts of Nabal and Bathsheba.

So tell me. Do you understand now what the inspiration of sacred Scripture is all about?

It comes down to this. David himself did not really, truly know who he was. But the Holy Spirit did. And here the Holy Spirit is speaking for David. David repeats what he said. David believed what he said. And by means of that faith, David knew that he was God's child. That's how he moved beyond his sin and the shriveling of his soul. That's how he knew he was actually an olive tree, green on the inside. That's how he knew that such green growth didn't come from within himself but that it came from the ever-living Immanuel, who fashioned a greening olive tree from a parched David.

But what about you?

Are things any different for you?

Do you think you can really build anything on the basis of your religious experience?

Do you understand how matters stand with you? Do you know your own situation?

My dear sisters and brothers, consider those who are sick. So many who are sick actually feel very healthy. Their doctor just shakes his head knowingly. Feelings can really fool you!

On the other hand, there are a great many sick people who think they're not going to make it through the night. They are that deathly afraid. But their doctor tells them: "Don't worry. You're going to be fine!" It's only their imagination that threatens them.

And this is exactly how things are in that enormous hospital for souls. Only the Holy Spirit, the Great Physician, actually knows our condition. Our own feelings are misleading.

For that reason, the person who feels good shouldn't celebrate all that much. The person who doesn't shouldn't complain all that much, either.

But even when things are dark and bleak in your soul, believe him when the Holy Spirit comes to you and says: "The battle's over!" Simply respond: "O Holy Spirit, I really do believe you." Stammer the way David did, and confess that you are like "an olive tree in God's house, green now and green forever!"

36
VOLUME II

UPRIGHT IN HEART

Rejoice in the Lord and be exalted, you righteous. Sing
for joy, you upright in heart. Psalm 32:11

T he most intense struggle that a child of the kingdom can experience is
with unrighteousness.

I'm not talking about the everyday, external wickedness that consists of
lying to or deceiving a neighbor. For those temptations as well as the inclination
to all other sins are lodged in his wicked heart. But, schooled by the Word and
Spirit to understand that lying and deception are works of the Devil, a person
is able in the Lord's strength to abstain from such wanton service to the Devil.
The Word commands this: "Let every man speak the truth to his neighbor." By
the power of the Word, he does just that.

No, the insincerity with which a child of God struggles until the day they
die goes much deeper. It's lodged inside and touches their spiritual standing
before our All-Knowing God. That's why Almighty God, the Father of believers, says consistently: "Let me see that you walk before me sincerely." Psalm 25
says: "Let uprightness and godliness protect me." Christ was amazed to find that
Nathaniel was a genuine person "without deceit. Truly, no deceit was found
in him." And the great, glorious promise found in the New Testament is "that
true worshipers will worship the Father in spirit and in truth."

The deeply insightful Psalm 32 provides light on the question of what the
Lord God means by the uprightness of his children. The struggling person
who by the Spirit's leading pours out their soul in this psalm is a child of God.

But they're a child of God who deviates, struggles, and falls into sin. And now, after having fallen into sin, they find themself standing in God's presence as insincere. After they fell into sin, their heavenly Father sought them out. God scrutinized them with that holy, godly, penetrating look of his. By that look he intended to wound them as well as to connect with them.

But the fallen child of God didn't want to see that disturbing look on God's face. They didn't dare to return it. They didn't look up at their God looking down on them. And when they very clearly felt and understood that God wanted them to say something, they didn't say a word. They remained silent. This is how David put it: "When I stayed silent … , your hand was heavy on me all day and all night. My strength was sapped, as in the heat of summer." But that silence was wrong on David's part, for in the immediately preceding verse he confesses that "my spirit was deceitful."

But then he comes clean and says very frankly that this was foolish on his part. He should have spoken immediately when God confronted him. He should have confessed his guilt. He acknowledges that he had been "like a horse or a mule, like an animal that has no understanding."

Of what benefit to him was it that he had been so insincere in God's presence? Did it help him at all? Did it remove his sin? Did it prevent God from knowing his sin? Was his soul uplifted a little by this silence of his, by his proud and arrogant silence?

Not at all! In fact, his heart languished. His soul was torn apart. He felt oppressed inwardly by it. It made him very tense to avoid looking his holy God in the eye! In fact, it made him miserable.

Just listen to his jubilation, however, when his soul finally broke through his silence: "Oh, how blessed when God forgives someone for their transgressions and covers their sins. How unspeakably blessed I am now that the Lord no longer counts my iniquities and that my heart is free of deceit." He had moved from death to life, from despair to joy.

But initially he had not wanted to have anything to do with that blessedness or with that amazing grace. He had spent the whole day, every day, making a lot of noise; but through all that clamor, his soul had remained totally silent. He had simply left God standing there, tested him, and held out on him. "But when I was silent," he confesses now, "my bones wasted away."

That's because opposing God and holding out on him causes us pain. It gnaws at the marrow of our bones.

Finally, he could hold out no longer. The large dike of his own pride was breached. The waters of God's grace flooded into the fields once again. "Then I made known my sins. I no longer concealed my unrighteousness. I said: 'I will speak; I will confess my transgressions to the Lord!' Oh, blessed experience! As soon as my confession crossed my lips, my faith was restored 'and you forgave my sin and unrighteousness.' "

Now set free, he is jubilant and he professes: "Therefore, all who are holy will worship you in the day they are found. And even a flood of great waters will not touch them!" Then he adds: "Rejoice in the Lord, O you righteous! Sing for joy, you upright in heart!"

Scripture itself teaches us what it means for God's children to be "upright in heart." It intends to say that they should not merely think: "God certainly knows what I've done wrong!" But they should remember that they are obligated and accountable to make known to God themselves what their sins are. They're required to spell them out for him. They're obligated to confess them, not keep quiet about them. They're expected to do so continuously and to admit to suffering the deepest humiliation that a child of God can possibly endure with respect to the eternally merciful love of God.

And don't just say that all of this doesn't matter all that much, or that it will happen rather automatically. Don't think that pretty much everyone responds this way. The experience of the soul tells us just the opposite! It demonstrates that sin produces something quite different. It weakens and reduces the ability to pray. It sees to it that people really do want to drop to their knees, but that they seldom get around to it. It makes sure that when people pray, they pray in generalities. It guarantees that their praying lacks the moral power to force them beyond the outer court and into the holy of holies.

The destruction that sin produces is quite awful. Compare a bud on a stem that you think is going to open and blossom. Then sin comes along, and like a worm it chews on that stem. Before you know it, the bud that should have opened just withers away.

Ahhhhh! But there's still an enduring power of life remaining in the root! Sin no longer brings death to the plant cultivated by God, even though sometimes there's fear that it might. Grace, nothing but grace, is what finally turns the heart in a new direction. Heated passions die down in the heart. Calmness is restored. This is the sensibility brought by the soothing strokes of a higher hand. The soul that so recently was still angry and untrue shuts down to unrighteousness, and it no longer yearns for what it shouldn't. Then it opens and unfolds and emits a wonderful fragrance. From the depths it is now able to profess: "Father, I have sinned against heaven and against you. I am not worthy of being called your child." That's when it realizes once again that what it thought was gone was really present all along, namely, "the everlasting arms of mercy!"

Sisters and brothers, when your soul genuinely confesses your guilt, you are enabled to pour out your hearts to the Lord. But then never exalt in yourself. That you are able to do this, that you now feel that you're being completely truthful, and that this comes very easily for you is due only and completely to God's merciful grace!

This still needs to be added, however.

A child of God doesn't experience this struggle only in unusual spiritual circumstances. It doesn't happen only when they're dealing with a blatant sin that goes against their better judgment and is persistent and brutalizing. The intense battle against wickedness needs to be waged constantly.

To suppose that there is as much as a single moment in their life while a child of God is here on earth when sin doesn't grate their soul is an abhorrent self-delusion. Sin oppresses them. It restricts their spiritual maturation. It puts them in tension with the image of the Son of God being renewed within them.

The person who judges casually imagines otherwise. But the person who uses a more exacting measurement knows better.

Look, sin produces inner discord. When we examine ourselves closely, very closely, we feel we're good for nothing. Everything about us falls away. We've nothing left to offer. And then the tempter whispers: "Is this really a child of the God who reigns on high?" And when the world comes along and regards us as being so much holier than we really are, or when Christian brothers and sisters see a holiness in us that really isn't there, then our hearts are split down the middle. Then there's a chasm between what's in our hearts and what crosses our lips! That distance is what's false, insincere, deceitful, and even self-deceitful, about us. It shouldn't exist. It has to be closed. "Lord, let my tongue and my mouth and the deepest desires of my heart be well-pleasing to you!"

To realize this, you need faith! You need faith to understand how miserable you are, how glorious Jesus is, and how richly merciful God is. With such faith, you will be able to see and understand and experience this truth: "The All-Merciful God has addressed my miserable condition from the riches that are in Christ Jesus."

Such faith is the ax wielded against the root of wickedness.

MY ABUNDANCE

My people will be satisfied with my abundance, says the Lord.
They will flock to the Lord's abundance. Jeremiah 31:14, 12

To whom does all abundance belong?

This is a question that covers every form of bounty your soul holds dear. Every single thing that might be considered good! Every possession that makes you wealthy! Each thing, whatever it might be called, that enhances your life as a human being! Makes it more beautiful! Adds luster to it! It's a question of bounty, therefore, not only in the sense of spiritual abundance but also in the sense of earthly possessions. It involves the family you love, your friends, the influence you have, your colleagues at work, and all your talents.

So don't overly spiritualize the question. When the Lord God announces through his prophet: "My people will be satisfied with my abundance," don't interpret this to mean that we really have no interest in the things of this world. Don't think it means that believers will be enriched with "an abundance of heavenly manna!" For then someone who knows the Scriptures well will ask you with deadly seriousness to take a good look at what precedes in the twelfth verse. There Jehovah says: "They will flock to the Lord's abundance." They will point out that the verse goes on to refer to grain, new wine, oil, and newborn sheep and cattle. It says that the people's lives will be like "a well-watered garden." Even more pointedly, a spiritually mature person will be incensed and ask whether you still haven't learned from God's sacred Word to stop making a false distinction between the internal and external realities of your life. They'll want to know whether experience hasn't taught you what a hypocrite and traitor you've become because you like the smell of money so much, as well as the trivialities of this life. They'll note that after muttering this distinction, you'll just close the Good Book and become completely absorbed again in all the vain things "here below."

No, the Lord God definitely doesn't command you to act like a monk in the course of your daily living. He doesn't even expect you to outdo a monk who stays in his cell. He doesn't demand that you despise all material things as though you don't care a whit about them. Stronger yet, he doesn't want this! He doesn't permit it! He rejects it!

How could it be any different? How can you possibly imagine that God wants us to be unfeeling, indifferent, and even dead to all things visible? Especially when he compels us to be busy with them on a daily basis for our entire lives! Even when he imposes the calling on the vast majority of people to spend their lives in the coarser, visible activities of the kitchen and shop, of the field and stalls in the barn? This is a God who created us with bodies afflicted with constant weariness day and night because of our earthly activities, especially the more menial ones.

Those who do imagine such possibilities become confused. They live with an inner contradiction. They nurture a fragile little plant of academic, bogus piety best suited for a religious practitioner or teacher who doesn't have anything better to do. But it's the sort of piety that's totally impractical for a housewife, a laboring man, or for an ordinary citizen in their daily calling.

And when you've once and for all shaken off that overly spiritualized sense of the faith imported from monastic life, something good happens. It does when the notion that all things visible belong to the life ordained for us by God penetrates our souls fully, powerfully, and deeply. It does when it bores into our consciousness until we understand that it applies to the more menial as well as the more refined sides of life. This includes hacking out chunks of coal deep in some dark mine shaft. Yes, in fact everything is designed to be a channel, a funnel, a vehicle, and a kind of electrical cord for conveying our obligations to God and giving him glory and honor. When you get to that point, you've purged the false spiritual leaven out of your system, and your practical world-and-life view has become Reformed!

That's when the emphasis disappears that always imposes on you the impossible dilemma between meeting your obligations to God and meeting the pressing realities of daily life. That's when the confusion is gone over wishing that you didn't have to deal with life in this world so that you could give yourself to the cause of the gospel. That's when you embrace human life instead of kicking it away as something contemptible. That's when you hold it to your heart and love it for what it is with the quiet prayer: "If only all of this beautiful life would glorify you, O my God!"

What the Lord's people should totally exalt in, therefore, is not in rejecting ordinary abundance, but in embracing that abundance in an extraordinary way!

"My people," says the Lord, "will be satisfied with my bounty!"

"With my abundance!" That's where you should place all the emphasis. Really apply that in your lives. Walk around in your house with that conviction, for it is really a house of the Lord. He created every beam and board, every brick and molding. It stands on his lot. He holds the title to it, and it belongs to him. He accepts you as his guest and as the occupant. Or look at your money similarly. "It's your bounty," O Lord. Your precious metal! It's so good, so wonderful, and so impressive. Because of the power inherent in that precious metal, you can exchange it at your discretion for all sorts of material things. That's for you to decide. All sorts of household necessities! All the things filling your cupboards and chests! All your clothing and garments! They're all God's abundance. So is that piece of ground; it's his field! The cows in it are his. That magnificent horse! Those chickens in the courtyard! Yes, even that valuable collection of books! Especially that large, particularly beautiful one, your old family Bible, just as it lies there; it's his bounty. It's part of his abundance; I'm permitted to live with it and to depend on it. So admit it. Aren't our lives a thousand times richer? And when ungodly folks sometimes talk about abundance but don't really have a clue about what the child of God knows, feels, and lives into, isn't it literally true that being a child of God makes you incredibly richer than they are? Even when the furniture itself doesn't change a bit? That's because the Lord God has inscribed on every single piece of furniture or clothing or jewelry the simple words "My bounty!"

Continue in that line of thinking and apply it to the living people who are close to you: your children, your husband, your wife, your beloved parents, your maids, and your close friends. They all belong to God. They are human beings that he created. He brought them into association with you. He instilled in them a feeling of love for you and a devotion to you. So tell me, brothers and sisters, when you stop to consider this divine initiative, isn't it as though God has freshly baptized your entire household? Anointed every soul in it? Allowed all of you to live in a whole wing of his palace?

If the Holy Spirit leads you in such a way that upon hearing this you don't merely give it a "yea and amen" but really own it, then what? Then your whole soul is illumined so that you see everything around you in the light of this vision. Then you see everything, everything at all, as belonging to God: your time, your brainpower, your imagination, your emotions, your will, your talents, your influence, and your control over other people. You see that for all these long years you have really been stealing all of this from God. And once you've discovered that you've really been a thief, you find that it is not all taken away from you, but you see that God has entrusted all of it to you as his gifts. O pilgrim on your way to the city above, your cup is full to overflowing! How inexpressibly wealthy God has truly made you! You're always worried about asking for more! I would have thought that you would get to the point of giving thanks! You're of the opinion that you possess a field filled with nothing but thorns and thistles. But now that you've started digging, look what a treasure is buried there! Now you see that all of it is the Lord's bounty and that you are so unbelievably wealthy!

From that vantage point, the child of God finally becomes aware of possessing an even more immeasurable spiritual wealth. They find in this prophecy of Jeremiah a glorious promise of an inner wealth of the soul. Then the earthly treasures are but a small and minor beginning. They are a prelude to the beautiful song that follows. They are the threshold that a child of God must cross upon entering the actual house of the Lord.

Then there is no eye adequate for the soul to see, no ear able to let it hear, no heart equal to have it enjoy all that sparkles like jewels and is on display in the Lord's sacred dwelling.

Then it's as though leaving some poor hut we enter Solomon's palace and exclaim with the queen of Sheba: "The half has not been told me!"

Then all the treasures we have in Christ stream to us, flow over us, press in upon us. Grace for grace!

Glory after glory! One unending banquet of the Lord, laden with bounty and the sweetest wine! A wealth of blessed forgiveness! The most tender of tender love! The depth of everlasting light!

None of these remain outside us, but the Holy Spirit makes them real within us.

And this is what amounts to wonderful enjoyment.

This is when the people of the Lord are completely satisfied with "the abundance of the Lord."

38
VOLUME II

UNTIL I VISIT HIM!

"And he will remain there until I visit him," says the Lord. Jeremiah 32:5

"Until I visit him!" What a wonderfully comforting expression this is for those who are dying.

This is said of Zedekiah the king during the captivity. He was taken to Babylon in chains. He was kept in prison there. But he was nevertheless honored in Babylon, where he died. There he lay in state and was carried to a royal grave, having been paid homage by both the people and the king of Babylon.

Under the inspiration of the Spirit, Jeremiah prophesied concerning Zedekiah, a son of David, a man standing in the royal line, and a person who was one of the types of Christ in the Old Testament, that he would remain there in Babylon " 'until I will visit him,' says the Lord." What this means is "until he dies."

The question remains as to whether Zedekiah was a recipient of grace or whether he perished under judgment without receiving it. Those are questions we don't have to decide. They're questions that we are incapable of deciding! Who knows, and who is able to say what the Lord God has done and brought about in a person's soul without us having noticed? It all comes down to the work of God in their heart, definitely not to what that person reveals or says about themself. So I don't know. But I do think that on that day of days, that great and celebrated day of the Lord, there will be many big surprises. Many who are *Lo ammi* ("not my people") will then be called "my people." And who knows how many who are now known as "my people" will in the final outcome actually be *Lo ammi*?

So we make no judgment on Zedekiah's state of grace. We can only conclude that the Lord of Hosts says that when Zedekiah would come to his end, the Lord God would visit him and that that visitation by God would be his actual death.

With that in view, it can be asked whether that final visit produces the glorious light of God fellowshiping with his creature, or whether by contrast that intrusion by God doesn't primarily explain dying in the deepest sense of the word.

But don't be too quick to separate what actually belongs together!

Your life is a single entity. All parts of it belong together. The moments that separate one from one another are merely fictitious. They represent time that actually doesn't exist. They fall away in the eternal depths of all things that stand in the presence of God. For him, a thousand years are as one day; and your entire life, even if you should reach the age of ninety, is at most as but one day. This means that it passes as one single burst of life.

Your life exists in the context of your death. Your death is nothing more than the end of your life. They belong together. All those distinctions of years and days definitely exist in your own personal awareness. They don't for God. In his eyes it all converges, and the convergence is the reality. In actuality things don't exist as you see them, but as they are seen by God.

This faithful God and Father comes to visit his creatures constantly and continuously throughout the length of their entire lives. He's done this with you and he continues to do so. So once again, I'm not asking whether you are always aware of this or whether you never are. That doesn't make any difference. The Shepherd of Israel is a searching God. He stands and knocks daily. He rushes to you at every serious moment of your life. He's present with you when you feel oppressed. He stands at your right hand when you're struggling. He extends his hands of blessing over you when the wolf in sheep's clothing threatens to snatch you.

This God who is always searching visits us far more often than we think. He never tires of coming. He never quits.

Suppose once that you are a person who had discovered that you are a recipient of irresistible, faith-implanting grace. Then you belong to the very few who have noticed that they were visited by this holy and exalted God. One of the few who has knowledge of this! Who is pleased by it! Who has sometimes felt so glorious and enraptured by it that they can testify how blessed they were by this encounter! Who sometimes even had such intimate fellowship with the All-Compassionate that they knew the adoration of love and the love of adoration! Who have been visited by the Holy One so that the afterglow left behind in their souls sustained them for days afterward!

Consider this. To all these wonderful results, Jeremiah's words add something new and enriching. For here the Holy Spirit teaches you, if you'll just listen to it, that these visits of God have another purpose than to bring you home by means of passing grace. Their purpose is to accompany you and to bring you home to be with him.

With every visit of God in our souls, if it goes as it should, he takes a piece of our heart along with him to heaven above. Time and again he loosens something of our personhood to live and dwell directly in heaven.

The Lord comes, and he finds the little ship of our soul tightly moored by ten anchors and held fast by chains and cables. And now every time the King of the Jerusalem that is above comes to visit us, he loosens one of those bonds. He does this to increasingly free us and to give the little vessel a more definite direction. He does this until finally he makes the last and real visit, the visit that accomplishes his ultimate purpose. After cutting loose the last anchor, the little ship begins moving, either driven by or against the winds that determine the course of the soul as it moves toward the eternal shore.

In the light of all this, think about the departed and the departure of your loved ones. A "visit" by your Lord! Think about the coming of the Lord, who already had come so often, and who finally came to take them along with him. He, the Lord, doesn't really belong here. His home, his palace, his heavenly dwelling is above. It's in that other, more perfect world. It's in that everlasting, inexhaustible, and tranquil blessedness surrounding the throne. That's why his Spirit returns to that Exalted, Eternal, and Divine Being after every visit he makes. And those visits of God are put to rest and fulfill their ultimate purpose when you finally accompany him to that home above. There all the visits of your God fall away and you live with him, dwelling there forever. He no longer comes to you merely to spend the night, but he puts you up to live with him always.

This occurs in his magnificent palace. Or you could find yourself in his wretched hell! For God also has a hell. He does because he is God, because he is holy, because he takes everything so very seriously. He means what he says. He carries out any threats he makes. This is the place of which the ever-loving Jesus spoke when he talked about "that outer darkness where there will be weeping and the gnashing of teeth."

With that in mind, my good reader, I implore you to let every deathbed say this to you: "The Lord God has been here!" Let every struggle with death make this appeal: "God's holy activity can be seen here!" Let every grave that is dug once again proclaim: "We don't belong here. We belong where the Lord God dwells. Our true existence is in eternity—there and there alone. That's our purpose for living. That's why we were delivered from our mother's womb, after the Almighty had brought us into existence in such secret places."

"Until I visit him!" That's what it all comes to for you. Your time is coming. Every visit from God is a foretaste of it.

And when it finally does come for you, may it be a visitation from God that results in sacred peace.

May it be a departure for you not into "outer darkness" but into everlasting light!

THE NECK AND
NOT THE FACE

*They turned their neck away from me and not their
face, even though I taught them.*[1] *Jeremiah 32:33*

T he nature of an animal is to turn its neck. An animal certainly has eyes, a
mouth, and a nose. But it doesn't have a face. To have a face is the sacred
privilege of humans. The face is what a person takes when they go outside. It
reflects their soul. It reveals to their neighbors who they are.

The Lord God created humans in his image, not like the animals, but as
something different from them. He created them to give him praise and honor,
things that no animal ever could. What is distinctively human, higher, richer,
purer, holier, more exalted, and what the Lord God wants from a human being
is not found in their hands. It does not reside in the feet with which they walk.
It is found even less in some other part of the body, but it is located exclusively
in their face. It is found in this mirror of their being, in this engraving that
reflects their entire personality, in this indescribable and inexpressible something that a person takes out in public. It is seen in the depths of their eyes.
It's apparent in their facial features, the pursing of their lips, and even in the
blood beneath their skin that makes them blush.

---

1. English translations uniformly use "back" where Kuyper's Dutch translation uses the word
"neck."

The Lord God wants to look you in the face so that he can see right through you to the bottom of your being and understand what it expresses. He wants you to turn your face toward him so that he can read in your eyes what's going on in the hidden recesses of your soul. He wants you to lift up your face toward him. If it's in guilt, then he can see the shamed redness of your embarrassment. If it's in your brokenness, then he can see your tears of sorrow and remorse. But it's always your face that he wants to see so that he knows that you're not straying from him in ungodliness. He doesn't want you trying to hide your face from him.

Although this is what God wants, what do people want?

"God gets my neck," people exclaim in their angry, rebellious hearts. They whisper it to themselves, even while songs of praise boom from their lips. We know this not first of all by experience, although experience does confirm it. No, not by experience, soul searching, or examining heart and conscience, as some prefer to do! For if you had to depend on searching your own soul, your self-satisfied heart would always water down the truth. Your heart would say something like this to you: "Others may be stiff-necked where God is concerned, but not I! I love him. I willingly bow to his teaching." This is how you would think, just like those who stand outside the Word! This is what you'd imagine!

So no, not at all! It's not the false, unreliable word of your own heart that teaches you this, but the only true Word, the one that comes from God. This is what he says through his seer: "They turned their neck away from me and not their face. Their princes did, and so did their priests, upstanding citizens, seers, and the inhabitants of all their cities." And once you learned this from his Word, then hesitantly and not willingly but in the end emphatically you had to acknowledge: "That's true; that's how it is. The Lord in his Word confirms what I've experienced in my own heart."

"God gets my neck," which is to say, I refuse to bow or stoop or humble myself. I will do so to some extent and if necessary in many things. But God asks for everything, and I won't give him everything. I'll hold back something for myself, even if it's only just one small idol. I have to keep something for myself, however little, that lets me feel and know: "Look, I'm not yielding here. I'm not giving in to God on this one. It remains mine!"

With most people it gets worse yet. With most of them, their whole heart is rebellious and mutinous against the Lord, the King of kings. But for you to avoid being compared with everyone else, person for person, it's required that you yield in everything, on every last item. Otherwise that one single thing will assure that you're counted among the worst of the stiff-necked and rebellious.

Like a beast of burden that refuses to yield, the heart of every person is disposed to resist the sovereign Lord.

To turn your neck away from God means not letting God look you in the face. It means keeping him in the dark about your life and activities. It means not making eye contact with his all-searching eyes. It means behaving as though you needn't be disturbed by him, as though you don't notice him. It means just letting God be who he is and then going your own way.

So what will it take to change this?

Will it be by finally realizing and telling yourself: "This can't continue, O my God; look at my face!"?

The prophet Jeremiah teaches something different.

No. Israel remains stiff-necked. So God then casts her off. He consigns Israel to death. He buries her in the Babylonian grave. By then, when Israel is at the end of her rope, imprisoned in the cells of an alien ruler and bound by his chains, the Lord comes to her. He says: "Realize this, my people. I myself will cause your hearts to fear me so that you no longer turn away from me" (v. 40).

That's when it happens. For the Lord God accomplishes it. His Word is unbreakable and trustworthy. But it doesn't happen because the Lord God implants a new heart in our chest so that we are enabled to fear God in the strength of that new heart. As though through it we can turn our neck and show him our face by ourselves.

O my sisters and brothers, it's much rather like it is with bread. Your body gets hungry. Here's bread, says God. And now that you have bread, can you simply feed yourself with that bread? No, a thousand times no, says Deuteronomy 8. It is still the Lord God who has to give you the strength through that bread to be capable of change. And as someone who knows this very well, you first pray: "Lord, bless to me this otherwise dead bread that can only nourish me at your command."

The same thing is true spiritually.

It's definitely true that the person in whom God has implanted a new heart has everything; but yet they have nothing. That's because everything that's in that new heart can only bring salvation if the Lord God now accomplishes what that new heart believes. And what does it believe? It believes that God can and will bring salvation; so that he's not only the one doing the work, but the one to whom all honor is due as well.

That's why, when a sinner has been converted, the vertebrae are loosened so that the head can be turned; then God turns the face instead of the neck toward him. That was impossible before. Then the vertebrae were stiff and inflexible. But now the person is converted. Now it's possible. But just because it's possible doesn't mean they can do it. Their own ego is still disposed to hide their face from God. But now the Holy Spirit begins working internally. And the Holy Spirit causes the ego to relinquish all opposition so that it now both wills to turn and actually does turn. It does so with an inexpressible sense of both shame and blessedness. Even so, the person is now truly seen by God.

So realize this. People do not dare to lift up their faces, but with the encouragement of the Holy Spirit they actually do so.

We respond this way while shrinking back as the Holy One peers into the core of our entire sinful and detestable existence with inestimable judgment. But he does this in a way that exalts us and confirms our blessedness through the unimaginable love of his reassuring face.

"O wretched person that I am! He saves even me!"

O God, can anything be too wonderful for love like this?

Hallelujah!

I SHALL NOT WANT

The Lord is my Shepherd; I shall not want. Psalm 23:1

"I shall not want!" Whoever believes this has arrived! They have peace. They know contentment. They have turned to the Lord with body and soul, spouse and child, in life and in death. They trust the All-Powerful Being, the Complete Provider, the only Totally Satisfying One, and our most highly exalted and absolutely holy Source of All Good.

Such a person understands, reflects on, and knows this in their heart: "I exist because of the exalted God who has created me. When he did, he already knew that there was a place for me in his world. He determined that I have a calling to fulfill in it. And I believe that he is powerful and determined enough to provide me with everything that I need to fulfill my calling. He does so at precisely the right moment."

Whether that calling is prominent or ordinary makes no difference. Perhaps I have to be careful as a boy when I walk under a ladder on which someone else has climbed high to make a repair or to paint the peak. Perhaps I have to stand for my entire life alongside a busy street with a sign inviting people to turn in and buy what I'm advertising. Perhaps a young woman's job of putting up displays in a store window may not seem very important, but she's indispensable. Never make comparisons! Pay attention to your own work, never that of someone else. And definitely never let yourself think or say: "God certainly could have given me something more important to do!" Because if you do, with that single thought you attack God's absolute sovereignty. And the

Lord has no patience for that kind of talk. He knows how things should go. He asks for no one else's advice. And when you complain against God without knowing his intentions, you are attacking him and murmuring against how he arranges things.

This is what's primarily involved in the statement "I shall not want!"

The manager of an enterprise gives every employee as much orientation, material, and other resources as they need to do their own job. In the building trades, for example, a contractor gives the rough carpenter basic instruction, the finish carpenter more advanced preparation, and the sculptor the most precise training. But to the lad who assists them, he gives almost no direction at all. But even he lacks nothing he needs. And if he simply accepts his role, he is happy, whistling his tune while he works, and he feels good about what he's doing. He doesn't need another thing.

Be absolutely sure of this. You will lack nothing for the work the Lord has assigned to you in his circle of servants. But when you step outside that role and want to do something for which God has not called you, then this promise definitely doesn't apply to you. Then you will "want" or lack a great deal. The Lord God provides you with nothing in that case. And you won't be able to buy it and you can't generate it yourself.

But if you accept the position where God has placed you, you will definitely experience that you live without apprehension and a load of concerns. Fear and misgivings under those circumstances definitely indicate a lack of faith. This amounts to a lack of faith that you are in your real calling. They reflect a lack of faith that God the Lord rules over all things. A lack of faith that God is all-knowing and really does know what you need! A lack of faith that God has a purpose for which he has considered and calculated all the details! A lack of faith, in a word, that God is really God! That kind of doubt at work in you is really nothing more than God-forsaken despair in your heart. It's the sin of Paradise. It's Eve's horrible wickedness that is now rekindled in your own heart and renewed in your life.

"I shall not want!" This definitely is not to say that you have here a promise that you will bathe in luxury. My dear brother or sister, it might well be that you have to stand in the fiery furnace like Shadrach did. But it is a promise that even in that kind of oven you "will not want." It is even possible that your life is one long succession of disappointments, of suffering poverty, of bitter pain in your heart. It is possible that God has destined you to demonstrate to Satan that however much poverty, suffering, or humiliation you endure, he knows how to nurture your faith and maintain your joy as his child. The Lord God is mysterious in his ways. He causes some to be blind, others to be deaf, and still others to be emotionally ill. But all of these serve his inscrutable purposes. And the only thing of which people can be sure is that in their suffering or in their rejoicing they will lack nothing in dealing with their situation.

How does a person become a martyr? How can someone in living life submit to fire and sword and still sing psalms? I don't know how! And you don't know how, either, because neither of us has ever been given what was assigned to a martyr. They were given what belongs to their situation, but not to ours.

"I shall not want!" may never be construed as a fortress to which we can flee to avoid suffering. The affirmation should only be taken as a sure promise that we will be able to endure it. I would never say that we can endure it to assure us that we will enjoy a happy old age. No, we are enabled to endure it so that we might enter an eternal day following the dawn of our eternal morning.

"I shall not want!" ultimately means simply this: God will never fail us. In God we have the highest, holiest source of all that's good. So what do we really have to complain about?

This applies to both body and soul.

That's why for your body you will lack nothing that is necessary for your soul. Similarly, you will lack nothing for your soul that is needed by your body. The text does not say: "I will lack nothing needed for my body." It says, "I shall not want!" The focus is on the whole person, on you and me as we are.

If we need oil in our lamps, God provides oil. If the garden is parched, the rains come. If you thirst after the living God, God himself arrives. His messengers climb the highest mountains and shout: "Look, your God is here!"

If you stand too tall, God cuts you down to size. If you sink too deep, the everlasting arms mercifully appear to lift you up.

All of your grappling, all of your soul's contortions must come down to this one thing, that you believe. And what do you believe? Simply this: that you have total access to what already exists in God's storehouse, ready and waiting! And that storehouse is Christ himself. Faith is the movement of the soul by which the Holy Spirit dispenses from Christ's storehouse everything that you need.

Do you need good works? Behold, God "has prepared them for you so that you might walk in them." Receive them and give thanks.

Do you need to be more submissive? God the Holy Spirit will control you like a difficult horse with the bit and bridle, and you will grow compliant and grateful. He will humble your resistant heart with faith in the Word.

Do you need faith itself so that you come crawling on your knees but still can't pray? Do you feel like a thick cloud is hanging between you and God?

Then your only deliverance comes not by torturing or tormenting or forcing yourself, because such responses only create more intense sin that pushes you even further away from God. It comes by reading God's Word, where it says: "The Lord is my Shepherd; I shall not want." It comes with the promise in hand and stammering with a quiet voice and a proper attitude: "Lord, teach me how to pray!" Even being able to pray is a gift given by our Lord God when in his all-sufficient grace he mercifully turns toward us.

May God the Lord grant that from now on you never go to bed without having that prayer answered. I realize that perhaps days will go by before true prayer flows freely from your heart. But what does that indicate?

It always says that whatever you might be experiencing at that moment, the most important thing is not the prayer but what you need to learn in your situation. It involves learning to depend much less on your own mutterings so that after a while you learn what godly prayer really is. Then you will come to realize that even the disappearance of a deep prayer life was a gift from the Good Shepherd, one as necessary as daily bread. Then you will see that it was given without your even knowing it is a gift.

Oh, the Faithful Shepherd, who had much preferred to listen to the voice of your suffering in faith, first carved out in you a riverbed along which your prayers would eventually flow. He did this so that you then might lack nothing that you really needed.

41

VOLUME II

COME, BUY AND EAT!

All you who thirst come to the waters. You who have no money, come and buy without money, buy wine and milk at no price. Isaiah 55:1

Things are wonderful in God's sacred, glorious kingdom!

In every other kingdom, people would say: "Buying without money is not buying at all!" Buying without money on the spur of the moment and agreeing to pay later, sure, people understand that in the kingdom of this world. But that's not what's involved here. Not by a long shot! "Come, buy wine and milk without money and without price" means to carry something away as your own without paying for it. It means that you didn't give anything for it and that you will never have to.

Now, people could say: "That may be the case. But then it's not purchased. Then it's merely handed to you, donated, given to you as a gift."

And naturally, who among all God's children would have anything against this? Grace behind us, grace all around us, and nothing but everlasting grace in front of us! We know nothing else. We recognize nothing different.

Don't you understand when you think like this and live into the notion of completely free grace more deeply that you can't possibly meet your eternal debt of gratitude? Look, brothers and sisters, the Trinitarian God simply gives you that indescribable, unfathomable, matchless salvation as a gift! And when he offers it to you, doesn't that put you under an eternal moral obligation to be thankful for it? Doesn't your conscience tell you this? And until you meet it, will you ever find peace?

Even if you toil and slave to pay off that debt of gratitude to the Lord your God, you'll never get there! Never! Never! Not by half! And your soul will always be oppressed by the nagging reproach that you haven't gotten there.

As we might sometimes say to a good friend who all too often overwhelms us with their good deeds: "My dear friend, you're discouraging me!" Likewise, the enormous magnitude of God's love could have the effect of oppressing us instead of uplifting us. How could you ever get from under it?

That's why, aware of this, God through the Holy Spirit calls out: "Come and buy without money!" That's intended to say that you don't ever have to pay a penny. Not for all eternity! Yet you'll possess it free and clear as though you had purchased it. And the Ever-Merciful God will never, ever, come to you and ask: "What are you going to repay me for all the goodness I've shown you?"

No, child of God, you bought it. Salvation is yours. It's yours by right. Against all right, it has become yours. And your totally glorious God bestowed on you not a single but a double grace. The first is, namely, the grace shown in your salvation; the second is that you now possess that salvation as purchased. This is a purchase very definitely followed by gratitude, and that's gratitude on a much higher level. It's a heavenly gratitude, not a worldly one. It's not a gratitude that thinks it must or can wipe away a debt. Rather, it's gratitude that blooms in quiet love. This love is expressed as fellowship, fellowship with the Holy Spirit in thought, words, and actions.

All calculations, measurements, and weights with respect to determining gratitude for grace need to be discarded, therefore.

"Come and buy!" calls the Holy One of Israel. And that which is not sold obligates a person to greater, deeper, and more profuse thanks rather than to less. This is thanks rooted in another principle. It is thanks that liberates rather than oppresses and thanks not to be dismissed but deepened. It is thanks always obligated to be increased and repeated. It is thanks committed to dwell with the Fountain of All Goodness, the Source of All Blessedness, and the Living Spring of Our Salvation.

That's why what follows tells us to "eat."

Nothing is worse for the Lord God than to see those who are hungry and thirsty flowing toward him like a mighty stream, walking into the storehouse of his favors, purchasing more than wine and milk, buying without paying a price, and then calling out to others while holding up the Bread of Life: "Rejoice with me, brothers. Look what I bought!" Nothing is worse for God, I say, to see all this, and then to see that these people still don't eat!

To purchase the Bread of Life but not eat it, what is that all about?

Have people just pretended to be hungry? Or didn't they trust the Bread of Life? Were they afraid that it would not nourish but perhaps harm them, that the bread would not bring them life but death?

This is what it is to despise God.

This is what it is to despise his unspeakable gift. To despise the Son, who is God's unspeakable gift to us! This is to despise him who said: "I am the Bread of Life!"

Will the Lord God leave this unpunished? Won't he take revenge on those who despise the Son of his most tender love? Won't he seek revenge on you by starving your soul?

That's why, my sisters and brothers who have purchased food, if you would not abandon thankfulness, you must first of all also eat. Eat the Bread of Life. Eat and your soul will be delighted with plenty. Eat and you will flourish in your fruitfulness and be glorious in appearance.

"A tree planted by the stream will bear fruit in its season, and its leaf will not wither!"

Blessed is the person for whom this happens.

IF WE SAY!

If we say that we have fellowship with him and we walk
in darkness, we lie and do not do the truth. 1 John 1:6

"If we say ... " Oh, the false tongue! Always talking, bragging, having big spiritual discussions! "Saying" that we belong to the Lord; "saying" that we are God's children; "saying" that we take refuge in him! "Saying" that there's fellowship and that communion exists between your heart and the living God in his glory and holiness!

"Saying" so that someone else hears it! Also "saying" in order to be granted stature, higher value, and more importance in the eyes of others! Putting the tongue to work in order to create a higher estimation and better image of yourself, to guarantee that people think of you as devout! Oh, that shocking misuse of both the tongue and the grace in your soul while always supposing that you're telling the truth!

Your tongue is a precious organ. It's a thoroughly divine and amazingly creative instrument. God has given it to you in order to express what lives inside you, what roils and presses to be expressed to others. And when it reveals to them what's there, they are internally affected as well. Your tongue and their ears! Those are the amazing organs by which what's deep inside you can be conveyed to the depths of the other person. Without tongues and ears, human beings would stand alongside each other like trees in a forest. They'd brush against one another externally. But they'd never reach out to each other internally and never have personal fellowship with each other.

So your ability to speak, to say something, and to express yourself is a completely amazing gift of God. But obviously, that wonderful gift from the Lord God was not given to you as a toy. Much less was it given to you to spread evil. It was entrusted for a lofty and holy purpose. It was given so that you could glorify him along with other people as well as to make you a blessing to them.

Now we can understand why speaking, putting something into words, and expressing ourselves can be misused. Sharing what's deep within us can be abused by putting on a show and rallying others behind us. Then we in effect say something like this: "Come over here! Let me tell you a little bit about the beautiful things deep in my heart. Let me share with you what an important and blessed person lives down there. Here's what God Almighty especially esteems about the person living in me."

When the tongue stoops to that level, would it be too cruel to cut it out? Wouldn't it deserve that?

You have to decrease. You have to deny yourself, your own ego. Nothing of self should remain. Your God must be magnified. But now you've gone out and abused that precious gift of speech. You've done it to put yourself first and to glorify yourself in the eyes of others. You've done it to focus all the attention on you. You've done it so they'll see what a great person you are!

But perhaps you'd excuse yourself by saying: "My dear friend, that's the way I used to be when I was bloated with a sense of my own virtue. But not now! You've heard me. My only glory is to glory in what God has done in my heart!" That's when the Word of the Lord stings your arrogant, inflated heart just as sharply and intensely as before. It causes you to realize deeply that such interference with what's sacred actually leaves you much worse off rather than better off!

For it's definitely the case that the great tempter produces that kind of craftiness in your heart. You can take enormous satisfaction in such things while giving the appearance of great humility. Nothing is more suited or susceptible to flouting sacred matters than to talk about them incessantly.

Say that you're forthright and people compliment you on it to the point that you boast about it. Say that you think of yourself as personable, but people regard you as conceited. No, you can't chalk up any glory for any of this. But if you say that you're one of God's saints, they don't contradict you concerning this greatest of all pretentions. Then they defer to you and think to themselves: "What an unusual fellow he has to be if he dares to talk about himself this way."

That happens so easily!

Well, not at first. The first step is difficult. The words almost don't come out. Shame is the faithful guardian that the Lord God has established to warn us about opening our mouths; it won't let us.

But once we get beyond the initial hesitation, we simply start speaking our minds. What we say flows freely. Oh, then pay close attention to people who are particularly glib and for whom speaking is habitual. The words gush over their lips, and virtually all holy restraint disappears from impure lips.

Note that when the prophet was called to speak on behalf of God, who is holy, he lamented from deep in his soul: "Lord, I'm unable to talk about your holy matters with these unclean lips." Then a seraph flew from the altar and purified his tongue and lips with a burning coal. What does this tell us? Does it mean to say that Isaiah would not have been able to intelligibly explain sacred matters in words unless his lips were seared clean through this painful ordeal? Naturally not! By themselves, his words were no more than the ones used in everyday life. But this is what's being said: Isaiah was afraid that with his impure lips he would contaminate sacred matters. He sensed that his talking about them would only amount to being just so much jabbering and blabbering. He feared that talking about them would only exalt him, as is so often the case with us.

If a champion of God such as Isaiah felt a deep need to restrain his lips out of fear that he might misuse either them or the sacred things of the Lord for selfish ends, what does that say to us who are exposed to even greater dangers in that respect?

So pay attention to what's going on around you. Then ask yourself whether you still find much of Isaiah's humility today. Rather, doesn't everyone seem to be living with the delusion that their lips are good and pure enough to allow words about sacred matters to pour over them like a river?

"If we say … " Oh, Jesus' apostle knew well enough what a temptation, danger, and delusion lies buried in that expression! That's why he warns us so passionately to put a stop to all this "saying." That's why he admonishes us to discipline ourselves to speak seriously and in truth. It's preferable, in his judgment, not to say a thing on ten occasions when we could have spoken than to speak even once, yes, even once, in a way that offends God's holiness.

Christ's teaching is so compellingly serious!

Listen to how every mouth among all peoples to the ends of the entire earth brags and buzzes and raves on endlessly. It's exhausting to hear it all! All the laughing, howling, and crazy talk! The tiny tongue always wagging! The lips always moving up and down! But then the teaching of our Lord Jesus comes with its commentary on all this human verbal brawling: "You people will have to give an account for every idle word that you've ever spoken!"

Yet here John's teaching goes even deeper. Here this apostle who was the most quiet of them all, who said very little when he laid his head on Jesus' breast, speaks to us and to the entire church of Christ when he says: "If we say ... " He definitely doesn't have in mind here all the idle prattle, small talk, and chattering that goes on. He has his eye on a much more serious abuse of our speaking, namely, that we reduce sacred subjects to meaningless drivel. That can happen when we talk about God's matchless truths or about what we are dealing with personally.

That first danger exists especially for those who hold office as ministers of the Word. Oh, preachers are entrusted with a very desirable office. They are allowed to be God's messengers to sinners, and they are permitted to pray as though God himself is praying through them: "Be reconciled to God!" That's a magnificent, captivatingly beautiful calling! But never forget that it has a shadow side. Preachers face a thousand dangers of abusing what is sacred. They risk making their office a throne for themselves. It's possible for them to imagine that the people exist for the purpose of listening to them, not that they exist for the purpose of encouraging God's people. They might think that the church gathers around them rather than around the Word of the living God. Above all, they can say many sacred things over and over again when their heart is not in it and when it's not the truth that's on their lips. Incredible dangers! It really is easier for a camel to pass through the eye of a needle than for a man—and couldn't we add here, for someone who bears the office of minister of the Word?—to enter into the kingdom of heaven!

Congregation, pray for your preachers! They face dangers on a daily basis, but particularly on the Lord's Day.

Pray for them, but pray for yourselves as well. For you are just as exposed. You are exposed to the other danger involved in the expression "If we say ... that we have fellowship with him!"

Every redeemed person believes this.

But to say this, and how and when to say it, is the issue!

For this much is certain. If this is genuinely the case, may there not be times to keep quiet? On the other hand, may there not also be times to untie the tongue and to testify about what God has done in our hearts as an absolute obligation? There's a big difference between the two!

At times God the Holy Spirit frees the tongue! Who, then, can hold back? If the lion roars, who shouldn't listen? That's when you have to speak!

But there are also times when your tongue should be tied but when you just keep on talking about sacred subjects for your own benefit and not God's. And that's what John opposes when he says: "If we say!"

That's when your "saying" is a curse.

43

THAT WE HAVE FELLOWSHIP WITH HIM!

If we say that we have fellowship with him and we walk in darkness, we lie and do not do the truth. 1 John 1:6

"Fellowship with him?" With whom?

Fellowship with the exalted, holy, and glorious God! O my soul, do you experience what a wealth of blessing is involved in that one idea of fellowship with this completely glorious and blessed Being? Do you fathom and grasp it?

No, fellowship with him is not just saying that you sometimes think about your God. Nor is it that now and then you imagine that you've been transported to heaven! Nor that in his presence you work hard not to offend him or to stop doing so!

All of that is so superficial. Fleeting! Artificial! It's all a kind of contrived fellowship that doesn't have solid footing. There's no truth to it.

So then, if the Lord our God is Absolute Perfection, could fellowship with him be anything else than complete union with him? Could it be anything else than something he causes for his own satisfaction, rather than something we bring about by our own praying, singing, or exalting?

But, your soul asks apprehensively, "How complete does that fellowship have to be so that it doesn't mislead or dupe us? Ah, then all my hoping has been futile and the foundation of my trust crumbles."

Well, I'm not going to shrink back even from that disheartening question, sisters and brothers. I'm just going to let your own conscience talk to you about this concern. If it's your praying, reflecting, striving, and loving that you think establishes your fellowship with the eternal, holy, completely blessed being we call God, you're being completely misled. And that's the truth! You contribute nothing whatsoever to establishing fellowship between God and your own soul. Only God can do that. All of your praying and loving and praising do not create that fellowship. That's not what constitutes that fellowship! And where that fellowship does not exist, least of all can these make it happen. At most they are the flowering, the fruit, and the consequence of that fellowship.

In fact, we have to go so far that we dare to say: "Look, see to it that your prayers, love, and piety don't get in the way of your fellowship with God!"

The question comes down to what the condition is of the faith planted in your heart and of the righteousness in your soul. Is the faith deeply rooted? Is the crown of righteousness lifted high? Or, as is unfortunately true of so many people, has the crown toppled to the ground, and are the shriveled roots poking up into the air? Is this an image you understand?

The crown is your praying and loving and striving and sacrificing. The roots are what God is doing to you and for you. Now it's simply the case that this activity of God is the root on which your life, your condition, and the expression of your faith all depend. Many people turn this completely around. They make their praying and their devotion the root. They think that these are the basis of their fellowship with the everlasting God. Those poor misled people! It's almost as though they can't grant him this because they won't bow to the horrible idea that God really is God!

Yes, he's the One who's the source of your fellowship!

But how? What is it? Of what does it consist?

Think of it like this. One is weak. Three off by themselves are as well. But three together are strong. They are because they are connected, because they are in fellowship. This is why sin, death, the Devil, and the world are in fellowship. Because God is so strong, if the enemies of God were going to have any hope at all they couldn't go it alone but had to join forces, unite, and have fellowship with each other. That's why in all their striving, forcing, and pressing for all that's sinful they had to work together. Like the gears in the same huge, frightening, hellish machine, they had to support, incite, and help one another. Think about how one sin leads to another in this world. One attaches to the other and completes it. Everything that is unrighteous and ungodly is connected. It all forms one complete, cohesive whole. It is all one in fellowship!

And how did Satan come up with such an idea? Where did the hellish hands of sin ever acquire the amazing capacity of working together so harmoniously in all their endeavors? Did Satan think this up? As though he could ever do anything except imitate God! Mimic God in his devilishly false ways!

So we're led to conclude that Satan did not conceive of the idea of fellowship. God did. The prospect of everything that he had created and everything that he recreated working together pleased him. It pleased him so much that he conceived of one glorious fellowship. As a result, all things belong together as one body, one kingdom, one organism, and one majestic whole. It's not a fellowship that people would foster in order to be together but a fellowship that reflects God's eternal being. It flows from him. It lives out of him. It is enlivened by him. It is designed for the revelation of his everlasting glory. And it settles on every personal fellowship with the Lord of Lords.

What in all of creation definitely belongs to this fellowship and what does not is determined by God's eternal good pleasure. That applies to every single piece, member, part, wheel, axle, or spring of his created apparatus. And when once established that that entity is part of it, it is part of it forever. It can never be outside that fellowship. It cannot escape it. But whatever is far off and separated by a great distance is always being drawn ever closer and more intimately into the depths of everlasting Light.

If you have fellowship with the All-Glorious One, this does not mean that you always experience that fellowship. This doesn't mean that you won't have the impression, sometimes for hours at a time, that it's gone. Even less does it mean that you're going to enjoy the blessing of its most tender love minute by minute. No, it only means that you'll know that you've been delivered from fellowship with Satan and have entered into fellowship with him who is holy. It means that you'll know that you've been transposed from the kingdom of darkness into the kingdom of the Son of his love.

To have fellowship with the everlasting God means being a little wheel or spring in his huge machine, or to change the metaphor, a little vessel or cell in the body known as the church of his Son, Jesus.

That fellowship is therefore totally complete. Once you stood outside it, but now you are included in it. Once you were unconnected with it, now you are bound to it. Fellowship with God was available but beyond you, while now you have been taken into it and become a small part of it. This happened through nothing but the miraculous work of your God.

Why, then, is this called "fellowship with God"?

Understand that things can intrude on that fellowship that really don't belong there, like a sliver that you sometimes get in your finger. It has to be dug out. So it's not enough to know that you're in that fellowship. It's important to know that you're actually having fellowship with God, for that's the true mark of being in that fellowship and that you belong there. All who are in it and cling to God belong there. Every person who is included in that fellowship but who does not cling to him rejects it now or for eternity.

Who is the person who will stand up and say: "I have genuine fellowship with this God," but then shows no evidence of knowing what it's all about? Who is the person who even has to be pressured and forced into it, but then in their heavyheartedness breaks out jubilantly, saying: "Yes, God be praised! I have that blessed fellowship!"

Who?

No one other than the person in whom God has brought it about! No one other than the one in whom the Lord God through his Holy Spirit has instilled the freedom to freely confess they have received it as a second gift of grace!

The person who says that they have such fellowship when they actually do not is blowing soap bubbles. It will result in their destruction. The person who has it and talks about it with less than the Spirit's freedom is spiritually rigid. Their life lacks spiritual vitality.

But the person does of whom two things are true: both that he is in true fellowship and that the Spirit testifies to him, "Speak!" That person will testify before God and others: "Yes, by the grace of God I am alive, and I am standing in that fellowship and I am having that fellowship with God."

When such a person says that, their words are like a flash of lightning that suddenly illumines the darkness in the hearts of others and reveals what's in their own. They speak in a tone that reverberates with power. It shakes others awake. It strikes like claps of thunder in the stillness of many nights. It impacts many others who are languishing in their graves.

And this is glorious!

But if this is just so much empty talk that sprouts like weeds in a pond, if it's only trumped-up testimony devoid of any glory or inspiration, people are only going to be disgusted by it. It will only leave anxious and quietly weeping folks in their bad predicament.

O God our Lord, guard us against such distortions of spiritual fervor. Fellowship with you is the holiest, highest, and most glorious thing that word can express. Grant it to those we love. Give it to many others. In your mercy, bestow it on us. Most of all, breathe it into affected, imagined, and pretended fellowship, for you test our souls and know our hearts.

AND WALK IN DARKNESS!

If we say that we have fellowship with him and we walk
in darkness, we lie and do not do the truth. 1 John 1:6

Two things have to stand like solid walls for Christians.

First of all, they have to be able to say this clearly and plainly about themselves: "We are not walking in darkness, but in the light." But they must also recognize and just as definitely and emphatically confess: "We have sinned. And because there are things of which we're not aware, we also need to appeal for the forgiveness of our unknown sins. God knows our hearts better than we do. What we don't know, he does. In his holiness, God watches us with his all-seeing eye."

Abandon either of these convictions, and you immediately find yourself outside the Christian faith. You've become a liar. Simply listen to what the apostle says: "If we say that we have fellowship with him but nevertheless walk in darkness, we lie." Just as emphatically, verse 8 says: "If we say that we have no sin, the truth is not in us."

The holy apostle simply allows the apparent contradiction to stand just as it's written. By doing so, he cuts off at their roots both the loose living of antinomianism and the smug self-satisfaction of perfectionism.

Both realities have to be found in you simultaneously: "walking in the light" and "the continual confessing of your sins." This is a riddle. It's a moral mystery.

But that's the way it is! At least it is if you live according to the Word and don't stray from it either to the right or to the left!

How does that work, then?

Zanchius, one of our old and respected spiritual fathers, said this: "Dear brothers, it's certainly the case that I can be walking down a well-lit street and still fall flat on my face. But if I'm walking down a street when it's pitch-black, even though things go pretty well for a while, I'm eventually going to have a fatal accident."

"Walking in the darkness" is impossible to reconcile with the Christian faith. The person who does but still affirms that they are a Christian is nothing more than a Pharisee in the fullest sense of the word. They are a hypocrite and a pretender. They destroy their own soul and are a threat to others.

That sort of spiritual vampire has always existed in the history of the Christian church. They are spiritually horrible people even though they may be staunch confessors of the faith. They are people who give a very good impression of their Christian character but who compromise that faith in many ways, although probably not in everything. In doing so, they weaken the Christian conscience of others all around them. And they leave the impression with Christian young people that they don't have to measure up to the standards of Christian circles as highly as they once thought.

That's why it's important to expose these whitewashed sepulchers. Respect for them should not be tolerated. Their "dry bones" need to be exposed by others. Who they really are needs to come out!

This is the important intent of the Word when it speaks out against the thorns and thistles in the spiritual courts of the Lord, as it so frequently does. It also imposes on all preachers of the Word and on all instruments of Christian witness the unavoidable obligation of unmasking these immoral monsters. It's their duty to say: "Stop making such a sacred testimony with your sullied lips. Stop parading around with the cross of Christ in your filthy, dirty hands!"

Understand this clearly, my good readers. "Walking in the darkness" really means longing for the darkness. This is in contrast with someone else who really cherishes walking in the sunshine because the warmth does them so much good, makes them feel so good, and inspires them. The person walking in darkness and hiding there does so very intentionally because that softens the sting of their wounds. It conceals their inner turmoil and makes us more sympathetic to the nature of darkness.

To walk in the darkness is to avoid God and to make every attempt to stay out of his sight. It's a deplorable condition of our souls that is like that of the birds of the night. They still have eyes and can see in the dark, but they can't tolerate the light. This means that with their unconverted and unrepentant hearts, people brood in secret and enjoy dark places.

Then there can certainly still be talk about spiritual things and even praying and involvement with religious activities. But these are either no more than the reflexes of religious custom or emotional games being played in the heart. Worse yet, they may be pure hypocrisy that's intended to influence others and gain their confidence for evil purposes. Or a person might simply think: "Because I appear to be pious, perhaps God will still be gracious to me when I draw my dying breath."

The children of God never walk in the darkness understood in any of these ways. They must never be tempted by the misguided urge to conclude from Scripture that someone can walk both ways: by the light in the morning and in darkness during the evening. As though a person can plant one foot on a well-lit path while at the same time setting the other down in darkness!

Nothing doing! It's not possible. You're either dead or alive! You walk either to the right or to the left, but not both ways.

And now don't people say: "But what about those who are spiritually anxious?" Dear readers, think about this! Isn't it a thousand times better that you are unsettled and that the Scripture reassures you of belonging to the Lord than that you simply come and go with those who "are at peace in Zion" and your great Judge eventually scares you to death with his eternal verdict?

And please never rely simply on religious experience, but only on the Word of God. For then there can be no doubt that every child of God walks in the light every day of their new life and that they can never go back to the way things were. That's true even though they may now and then temporarily walk on the paths of darkness.

But this can definitely happen. You can know that you're walking in the light even when your soul is shrouded in darkness.

Then something happens. You're compelled to decide: "What's really going on here? Am I dealing with walking on the paths of eternal splendor while experiencing temporary darkness? Or am I still walking on the gloomy paths of everlasting darkness?"

God be praised, the difference can be determined easily!

How?

So simply in actual practice!

Just examine what you know to be true.

Are you at all inclined to think: "Hey, this darkness is really pretty nice"? Do you pull back into that darkness? And when people confront you fairly directly about it, do you excuse your darkness as really being the light? Or, on the other hand, are you afraid for the salvation of your soul and for your heart? Do you curse what you see happening? Do you immediately cry out for mercy and for forgiving grace?

If it's the former, you're a miserable hypocrite! If it's the latter, then you're a prodigal son, a sheep that has gone astray, and a very troubled child of the Father who is still genuinely bound to Christ as your Surety and Mediator.

This is what he who is merciful and holy says to the hypocrite: "Turn from your evil ways. If you repent, there is forgiving grace for you! If you don't, know that it's going to be terrible for you when you fall into the hands of the living God!"

To his own child who has lost their way and gone astray, the Comforter says, even though they may not hear it all that clearly: "Your sins have been thrown into the depths of the sea; return to me, my child, and sin no more!"

In that connection, how does walking in the light proceed?

Rather naturally!

"Are we not his workmanship, created in Christ Jesus for good works that he has prepared for us to do?"

You need to do nothing more than believe.

Believe also that the Holy Spirit is at work in you.

Then you will experience this about yourself and in your pathetic self-centeredness: no good work can possibly exist in you. But the Holy Spirit will produce good works in the person who is continuously struggling and saying with a humble heart: "No, this really can't be happening! But yes, it really is! It is in and through the help that exists solely in the name of the Lord our God!"

WE LIE AND DO NOT DO THE TRUTH!

If we say that we have fellowship with him and we walk
in darkness, we lie and do not do the truth. 1 John 1:6

To listen to the way people talk, today everything is about "being true." You scarcely hear them talking anymore about "speaking falsely" or "doing what's false." The chief evil against which they do battle at present is "being false." The expression of "being false" seems to possess such a powerful fascination that it has made its way from the writings of philosophers to the works of theologians and from there into sermons and poems. And now it's living on the lips of evangelists, religious speakers, and refined church members.

Is this a good thing?

According to God's holy Word, no! That Word emphasizes that we are unable to make a judgment about someone else's inner being. That's God's department, not ours as human beings. We have to be satisfied with the more modest role of discerning the truth of what crosses someone else's lips and of what they do and how they live. So it comes down to what someone says and does, not what they are. It's good that we understand these things. God will judge what they are. All such cherished prattle about others "being false" is fundamentally presumptuous because it invades God's territory.

An even stronger reason for warning against always weighing in on "being false" is this. It leads, almost without notice, to paying less strict attention to "speaking the truth." And attention to "doing the truth" also recedes step by step.

The two are tied together.

If I could ever penetrate the surface and reach the hidden depths of someone else's inner being and be able to judge if they are really true, then what? Then that major issue would be followed by the comparatively secondary one of whether that person is speaking the truth or telling it like it is. That would become a subordinate matter. I'd be a lot less interested in it. Moreover, since that deeper penetration in and of itself attaches less value to what's on the surface, the force of words is weakened. One becomes accustomed to understanding everything about everything!

To probe this matter a little more deeply, to ascribe "being truthful" to a human being is actually something that they don't deserve. Every person is "prone to lying." This is true of those who have not been born again without them even realizing or acknowledging this fact. The eyes of those who have been born again have been opened to this reality. And it's when the child of God wrestles against their inner self that they come to a proper insight of the untrue, false, and lying nature of their own being. Every effort to put a stop to that condition here on earth is fruitless. The contradiction between their being and their believing persists. And unless they have drunk deeply from the numbing chalice of perfectionism and fallen into the stupor of their imagined bliss, the gulf between who they are and what they believe persists until the day they die.

"Being true" also doesn't simply amount to being Dutch! Concerning a person who is actively employed, it should never be said that they "are true." Rather, it should be said that they "are truthful" in the sense of our Bible translators, who everywhere that the original uses the expression "is true" consistently translate it as "is truthful."[1]

So the matter of "being truthful" applies only to God and not to us. Wanting to apply it to ourselves is presumptuous arrogance. It can't be attributed to us. What we are able to do from our untruthful disposition is to lift our arms imploringly to him who is the Truth. To him who is the only one who is "completely truthful" and who can help and sustain us! It applies to him who as Jehovah "is who he will be." Therefore he is the only one, among all others, who in his own being is the absolute "guarantee of all truth!"

---

1. Here Kuyper adds this footnote: "In 2 Cor. 6:8 the expression 'are true' is used of the apostles, but this is done from the perspective of inspiration."

Through Isaiah the Holy Spirit laments about those who "confuse darkness with the light and light with the darkness" (5:20). This means that a bat could pose the question to an owl of whether the daytime isn't really dark and the nighttime really light because that's when he can see well. And that's exactly how we deal with the Lord God. Because we avert our eyes from the light and stare so intently at what's sinful, we get things exactly backwards. Then in our pride, we say: "Now I can really see things; the lighting is very good!" That's when the Lord comes in his majesty, trips you up with the things of this world, and thunders in your heart: "No, the light in you is actually darkness. I, your God, and I alone, determine what is light, what truth is, what the reality of things is, and how they need to be identified!"

Then no longer being able to determine the how and why of things, we grope along the wall and plead for a touchstone or standard that will help us to be discerning. And then Jesus comes to us and says: "I am the Truth." Confessing that he is the Truth, I change directions and recognize that within myself "I am untrue, a liar, a fraud, not real, conflicted, and a contradiction." I also recognize that "the truth is in him and in him alone. He is the only One who is completely truthful and in whom pure and complete harmony exists."

That's why, brothers and sisters, you should see to it that you do not allow yourself to be misled by talking about "being true."

Whoever thinks that they are competent to make the judgment that others are "not true" in effect has concluded that they themselves certainly are! But that's how the tongue misleads the soul! This is sheer arrogance! All the drivel about "being true" only leads a person further away from him who is the Truth!

No, what's appropriate for us poor creatures is to show quiet humility in coming to the deepening conviction that he who is the Truth is up above! The only One who is really truthful is in heaven. All people are deceitful, ourselves first of all.

If it's the case that we have been converted by grace, that is, that we grasp all of this and that the Holy Spirit dwells within us, then we will long for the Truth that is above. Then we will also confess our faith in that Truth and desire that that Truth will rule in us and everyone around us. We will bear his yoke, my brothers and sisters, and we will not attempt to plumb those depths that we can never measure. Rather, we will listen to the Scriptures, to what is practical, and to the teachings of our spiritual fathers. We will place a sentry at the door of our lips so that you and I become responsible for what we say. We will assign a guard to our comings and goings to assure that we are actually walking on the paths assigned to us.

But if none of this is true for you, you sentence, judge, and condemn your-self. You are really telling yourself: "I'm lying!" "I'm not doing the truth, either."

When the verdict of the Word is effective, your pride is shattered. Then you stretch out your hands again toward him who is the Truth. Then God's Word in judging you delivers you from the lie and brings you into the Truth.

YOU ARE SMELTING MY INNER BEING!

You lift me on the wind. You cause me to ride it. You
are smelting my inner being.[1] *Job 30:22*

Don't complain too bitterly, even when your harp only plays dirges and your organ becomes the voice of weeping! In order not to be overwhelmed in your bitter complaints, learn from Job what the lofty purposes of the Lord are in shattering his sacred offspring here on earth.

Take a look. Here's this Job. He's a wonderfully holy child of the Lord. He's not holy in the sense of being above sin. Not at all! Job is one of us. He's like you and me. And so that he might live with integrity, he is directed and upheld by the Spirit at work within him. Job is holy because God has been discerning about Job's life. The result is that even when Job's heart is parched, God causes things to sprout and grow. He's holy because, falling or standing, he's been set apart as God's vessel. He's been made an instrument. He's been designated as one of the rods or gears in the glorious mechanism of divine grace.

So what has overwhelmed Job in this setting?

---

1. While some modern English translations employ dynamic equivalence to render the last sentence of this verse in a way that continues the imagery of the wind (NIV and RSV: "toss about"; Berkley: "blow away"), the KJV, ASV, and RASV all use the etymologically more precise word "dissolve." The *Statenvertaling* used by Kuyper was close to this notion, employing the idea of "melt or smelt" (*versmelten*).

Exactly this! Satan is baiting God. Satan is badgering God with respect to his pious children. Satan keeps on whispering that it's not genuine work going on in elect children, even though it is the work of the Holy Spirit.

So in order to silence this taunting, one of these dear children of God has to be designated for the refiner's furnace. In order to show Satan up, God has to do this with one of his elect people. He has to wound him more deeply and test him more intensely than anyone has ever been wounded or tested before. The Lord God will withdraw all comfort from this completely trampled individual. Nothing but the vinegar of many other painful afflictions will be poured into his wounds. Instead of reassuring and reviving him, the Holy Spirit will go into hiding, and he will have no sense of the Spirit's presence in his heart at all. Then, when things get to the point for this pathetic figure that Satan finds that he cannot entrap him, he will tire of trying and will have poured out all his anger. This pitiful man will finally be dragged out of the slime and mud. Then God will ask Satan to examine Job's heart for himself. He will ask him to judge whether the gift of grace in and through all of this suffering hasn't preserved Job by keeping him just as glorious, solid, and pure as he had been before.

This is when Satan leaves in shame. God is glorified. The inexhaustible quality of grace radiates just as gloriously here as it does the genuineness of the grace-filled life. It was Job's great honor to have been given the assignment of displaying and upholding God's glory. He had been an instrument in God's service.

But don't ever forget that Job only realized this later. While he was consigned to the refiner's furnace, he was unaware of it. Otherwise he would have been a martyr. But here he has just been another sufferer under the old covenant.

If he had understood what was happening beforehand, that awareness would have been oil on his wounds. He would have sung psalms as he sat on his heap of ashes. But now that he didn't understand any of this, he simply thought: "I'm dying, and for no good reason!" He had nothing to support him. And precisely that made his suffering all the more unbearable and so indescribably heavy.

Nothing, nothing at all, could be permitted that Satan could possibly have used as an excuse! He could not be allowed to say: "Yes, but Job had the hope of gaining a martyr's crown!" Even Job's faith had to be overwhelmed so that all honor and glory could be ascribed to God who worked it in him and not to Job himself. Even though Job cursed the day of his birth, Satan could not wrench him out of God's hands.

And this was the source of Satan's defeat. It was also the Lord our God's triumph. It was likewise the reason for Job's suffering that was beyond description. It explains the roaring of a soul that couldn't take any more and that screamed and moaned and shrieked as the heart was being shred to pieces.

The shrillest note sounded from the parched lips of a sufferer in the middle of their groaning is heard when they cry out to the Lord: "Lord, you are smelting me in the core of my being!"[2] Within every person there is a core, a center, or something about which they say: "There, that's my inner being." Everything else is window dressing. All sorts of things are found there and are part of their existence. But they do not constitute a person's inner being.

They are convinced that their bodies belong to who they are. Their children do. So do their friends, their material possessions, their identity, and their honor. They feel this way about their good fortune, their love, their success, their comforts, their hope, and their ideals. They feel this way about everything that is part of their lives, belongs to their human associations, and adds luster to their existence.

But all of this still does not devastate their inner being.

They are definitely aware of all these things, as though they are clothed with them, festooned with them, and enriched by them. But they can all be taken from them without fundamentally touching their inner being.

Job's indescribable suffering in his soul, his deadly fright, and his hellish oppression existed on this deeper level. He was picked clean, like a chicken of its feathers. He was like a fish scraped of its scales. He was like an eel stripped of its skin that lies naked and squirming at the feet of the person who caught it.

Bit by bit, piece by piece, Satan had taken everything away from him. Removed it! Ripped it from his heart! Sucked the blood out of it! Job was left completely naked. Totally exposed! Satan couldn't find anything else to strip from him. Job had nothing left. Even his faith was gone. All that remained was that deeply implanted but now completely hidden capacity to believe. That was embedded in the only thing that still remained, namely, his inner being.

---

2. Kuyper adds this footnote: "We intentionally stay with the *Statenvertaling* at this point, even though it can be established on clear grounds that the translators erred in departing from the sense of *hushyāh*. What's remarkable is that the exegetical enterprise, after first rather arrogantly scoffing at using the expression 'inner being,' chose to use 'wisdom' or 'comfort' or whatever else. Eventually preferring to come back to this 'indefensible' rendition, it recognized that the basic idea of 'inner being' is appropriate. Tact in the form of sanctified good judgment caused our translators to realize that, even in the face of unjustified etymological judgment, only 'smelting my inner being' captures the depth of terrible suffering involved here."

But now it seemed as though the most terrible thing of all had come. It seemed as though his inner being itself was being threatened. It seemed to him as though he was lost and his very existence was at stake. It seemed as though his inner being was in a meltdown.

Oh, all of you who fear the living God, note this well. Even his inner being needed to be tested so that Job could not say later: "My inner being held firmly to the ability to believe!" But it had to be transparently clear to both devils and angels alike that even his inner being was melting. Nothing in Job himself kept his inner being unscathed except the inner workings of God's gracious, almighty power.

This is what the Lord in his freedom did with Job.

Wouldn't you feel the sting of bloodied hands and knees when scrambling down a rocky cliff in an attempt to save your life? And if you would risk your hands for that, might not God also put you, one in a million of his most insignificant creatures, at risk for the sake of his glory and honor? So hold your tongue, you who would complain. Doesn't he deal with his heavenly hosts and with the dwellers on earth according to his good pleasure?

Above all, hasn't God been considered righteous in the eyes of men for centuries already with respect to Job's suffering?

Or does the Lord God seem incapable of granting double honor for double suffering? Didn't Job in retrospect rejoice that he had been counted worthy of being the kind of instrument of God's honor that he was? Wasn't its fruit magnificent? For Job himself? For his now completely revitalized soul? But also for his brothers? For all the saints of former times? For the martyrs of the Nazarene? For all those who wrestle at the Jabbok? For all those who yearn for the only true, genuine faith that triumphs over death and the grave?

And for you as well, my sisters and brothers?

For you, in order to teach you to deny everything about yourself? Naked, exposed, stripped down to the core of your being, and even denied that on behalf of the Holy One!

But also to teach you to trust in him when everything is gone, all is dark, and nothing more is left! To teach you that when love leaves, faith evaporates, and hope sinks away, all is not yet lost! For he, the Lord, is still powerful enough to gather your life to himself and say: "Satan, you can never tear this person out of my hands!"

Yes, to comfort you when the waves and billows of suffering crash over your head! For then you bow low to him like bulrushes at the riverside. So does a child of God ever suffer for no reason or without purpose?

Can't you see in retrospect why suffering needs to be endured by you? I don't say that it's for the purpose of saving you. No, it's for the sake of his honor, of exalting him, and for his name's sake! Tell yourself, you who are driven by life's storms, shouldn't you be able to rejoice in your moaning like Job before you: "Do not forsake me, O Lord. But consume me, if I may only be an instrument of your sacred glory!"

47

VOLUME II

THE LAW WILL GO OUT FROM ZION

Come. Let us go up to the mountain of the Lord, to the house
of the God of Jacob, so that he may teach us his ways and
we may walk in his paths. For the law will go out from Zion
and the Word of the Lord from Jerusalem. Isaiah 2:3

The sins of God's people in our day consist mainly in redefining the boundaries God has set.

Simply put, God Almighty has determined in his majesty that his law went out from Zion, that it still does, and that it must keep on doing so until the end of all things.

This is not only his law for the ancient Jews, but also his law for the most up-to-date people living in our completely modern age when it seems like everything is being renewed.

It makes no difference if people say: "No! Zion's law is obsolete!" Their objection doesn't change a thing. That law remains in force. Because God will not allow himself to be dethroned, it continues going out from Zion. It is the standard and testimony by which all people will be measured. It applies to them from cradle to grave and is what will be used to judge them eternally.

It applies even if apostasy becomes even more widespread than it is today. It remains in force even if not so much as one king on earth bows down to God any longer. Even if not one judge still seeks God's counsel in rendering judgment! Even if not one priest prays to God anymore! Even if not one people or nation shines with divine glory! Even if not one single congregation in the whole wide world ever trembles at hearing God's Word or lives in his presence! Even if things become so terrible that actually no one at all ever thinks about Zion, everyone simply goes their own way, and Zion's God is treated as an outdated and dead object of worship! Then, even then, nothing in essence changes in the least little bit! Things remain in force exactly as they did in the most glorious period of faith on earth. Every living soul still stands under the law of Zion. They remain conscience bound to Zion's law. And on that great day of judgment that is definitely coming, they will be judged completely and exclusively according to the law that proceeds from Zion.

Once upon a time, in the days of Isaiah, no one realized any of this.

The entire Eastern world thought: "This Jehovah hardly matters at all! But Bel, Baal, Kamos, and Moloch ... now, those are powerful gods!" And the entire Western world sang the same tune: "Why should the god of the Jews matter to us? The Greeks' Zeus and the Romans' Jupiter are the mighty ones!" The Parthians from the north joined in the song, and the worshipers of Apis in Egypt to the south did as well with their equally audacious, God-provoking beliefs.

But God just laughed! He said simply: "But I've anointed my king over Zion, my holy mountain!"

And when no one put any stock in this, Zion stood waiting to be plundered, the heathens rose up to set fire to Jerusalem and watch it go up in smoke, and God came to Isaiah. He told his servant: "Isaiah, go to Jerusalem and prophesy that a time is coming when all these people will cry out: 'Come. Let us go up to the mountain of the Lord, for the law is going out from Zion!'"

The foreigner mocked this message. Even the men of Jerusalem did as well. But God wasn't the least bit perturbed by the mockery. He persisted. He followed his own counsel. His decree! What pleases him! And lo and behold, nine centuries later everything was reversed and turned out just as He Who Laughs said they would.

Then it came to pass that in the entire Eastern world no one thought about Bel, or Baal, or Kamos, or Moloch any longer. They all bowed down to Jehovah and listened to the proclamation from the Decalogue. Then it came to pass that in Egypt all worship of Apis was abandoned. In Greece, Zeus was forgotten. In Rome, so was Jupiter. But in all the churches in all those countries, praise and glory were lavished on the Lamb who was victorious.

Literally, it all came to pass.

All of Bashan's mountains were leveled. Only Zion was exalted. Among all the nations in every direction, there was but one quest, the quest for the law of our God!

But in our own day, things are reverting to the way they were before.

The ties have been cut, the cords tossed aside. "Away with Zion! Get rid of the law that's going out from Zion!" is once again the slogan that's dictating the mood. Zion represents an antiquated position that has been surpassed. It was good in its time, but it's useless today. People have gotten wiser. They know a lot more. And pay particular attention to the fact that people are much too civilized, too refined, and have become much more loving than to still submit to such a barbaric law as that of Zion. They're too gentle to defer to it. They know better now. People have advanced beyond it. They're above it. Bashan imagines that it has superseded the top of Mount Zion. It towers above it by quite a bit.

People once again look down on Zion in pity. Listen to them talking. Today men produce legislation far more suitable for the nation. Their laws are holier for guiding the people. They're also more merciful where punishment is involved. Understanding this, the philosopher says: "Listen to me, my good people. I will teach you more sensitive laws than the ones given by the God of Zion." And the sinful hearts of the people accept this as simply wonderful! "Just think what it will be like with Zion's law out of the way!" Won't life be delightfully liberated and unrestricted?

The misguided conscience is caressed by all of this and says: "Absolutely! You thoughtful men should guide me; your thinking is preferable to the law of Zion!"

And this is how everything becomes unhinged. Nothing is tied down anymore. As many petty-minded lawgivers can be found as there are people guided by their own judgment and sense of importance. Ultimately the family is affected by this, and every father thinks: "The law is what I say it is, not what goes out from Zion!" The country, the church, the family, and our own souls and the souls of our children all succumb to this way of thinking!

What a terrible situation!

Not because of God's eternal principles! These stand fast. No living soul can rip those loose! The law continues to go out from Zion and is the only thing that really matters. All other high places that issue laws will ultimately submit to the judgment of Mount Zion.

But it's a terrible situation for the church, for God's people, and with respect to the glory of his name.

What's so bad is that the people of the Lord do not resist this redrawing of the boundaries. The church participates in walking away from Zion. In fact, there are men with big names in the church who smooth over this creation of new, humanly determined standards for her life and who commend them as being Christian. Men simply state that now God is engraving them on the tablets of the heart!

This peddling of half-truth produces, without people really realizing it, putting first the human conscience and shortly thereafter humanity itself on the throne designated for Christ alone. Then all certainty is gone from Zion!

This is a situation even more terrible because our hearts desperately want it this way!

Oh, all of this is so soothing!

Bashan is back on top! Zion is at the bottom. What this means is that God as the measure of all things just stands aside and waits because people determine what's right.

What's even more frightful is that this tickles sins of the heart so delightfully! For people may not determine everything, but they still determine a very great deal!

Very simply stated, a mist descends over the conscience. That haze obscures how the boundaries are being reset. It also necessarily blurs the ability to evaluate what is happening!

48

VOLUME II

COVERED UP!

And the children of Israel had covered up things that were
not right but went against the Lord their God. 2 Kings 17:9

There's a good side to covering things up. But there's also a danger in doing so. The danger is so deadly that it completely eclipses the good side.

Take the cases of Jeroboam and Ahab.

Jeroboam was a man with a cloak. Ahab was a king without one!

Jeroboam was fundamentally an apostate and idol-loving man who hated Jehovah. He was not a whit better than Ahab. In fact, Ahab probably stands closer to us than Jeroboam does because Ahab was misled by Jezebel. What particularly shouldn't be forgotten is that when it came to a confrontation, Ahab humbled himself before the Lord, and on that basis the Lord temporarily withheld his judgment from Ahab's house.

But notice that while Ahab, who had been inflamed by Jezebel, shamelessly promoted the worship of Baal, built a counterpart to Zion's temple in Samaria for that purpose, and so openly proclaimed his hatred of Jehovah that everyone knew it, Jeroboam attempted to remain a spiritually pious person until the day he died.

Pay close attention to the fact that Jeroboam stayed faithful to the God of his fathers. He opposed all idolatry. He wanted nothing to do with the worship of graven images. Jeroboam wanted to maintain the worship of the only true God as the official religion of his kingdom. He donated money for the purpose of building churches and providing a generous income for the priests of Jehovah. And he came in person to worship Jehovah with his sacrifices. Oh, that Jeroboam! What a pious man!

Naturally neither he nor his people could go up to Jerusalem. That's just how it was. Judah was their enemy. So he had to erect alternative centers of worship in Bethel and Gilgal. They were not built with evil intent but in an effort to assist worship. They were at best a necessary evil.

He had no Levites, so he had to resort to appointing priests of his own. But he did this only out of necessity. That he placed several shining gold symbols next to these substitute altars was certainly not done with wicked intent. Just think about it! This was only done because the ark of the covenant with its cherubim stood in Jerusalem and the glory of the Lord shined only in Zion, not where he was located. In fact, Jeroboam really did nothing more than make a few adjustments on nonessential points because of the circumstances involved. Fundamentally, the situation was such that he couldn't do anything else!

When all is said and done, he spared neither trouble nor expense in his effort to maintain the pure worship of the only true God. He did what the situation he faced simply demanded.

So you'll appreciate the cloth out of which the cloak that Jeroboam was wearing was woven.

The cloak under which his angry heart was concealed and that covered up his inner hatred of God was dictated, quite simply, by circumstances.

These were circumstances that couldn't be changed.

They were circumstances beyond human power.

They were circumstances that made it impossible for him to do anything else.

They were circumstances that compelled him to do what he otherwise actually might not have done. Might not have done, but now definitely had to do because he couldn't do anything else!

Isn't Jeroboam's cloak still being worn today? Around you? Because of you? And within your own heart? Open your ears to those questions, my good people.

Or don't you recognize the explanations that others are so quick to give and to express in the hearing of others? These are the explanations that move from the ear to the heart and state that people naturally want to cling firmly to true Christianity and under no circumstances want to abandon their serving of the one true God, but ...

"The times impose their own special demands on us."

"People can't always keep on rowing against the stream."

"God simply doesn't demand of us that we continue flaunting our uniqueness."

"People find it impossible to keep their children on such a tight leash any longer."

"They definitely have to compromise a little."

"The circumstances have been sent by God, and it's not appropriate in days like ours to still be as exact and to take things as literally as in the days of our fathers!"

By continuing to sing those lullabies, people lull their consciences to sleep.

Naturally, people can't merely take the Bible at face value any longer. The mind has to be given its just due. Circumstances compel people to give in a little to what they feel is not completely pure but that can't be avoided because of scientific progress.

So the little ditty goes on!

It's perfectly obvious that people can't allow the old truths to stand as they once did. Everything has to be recast into new forms. Circumstances require revisions of even the most sacred convictions.

The tempter just keeps on singing the same tune.

It's just the nature of the case that people simply must break with the old customs. At one time these had their basis in Scripture, but now the Bible can no longer be taken as literally. Our century definitely compels us to break with the earlier narrow-mindedness. We have to be more open and temperate, and above all fresher.

And on that note of "freshness," the tempter casts his most powerful spell.

Consider for a moment how by "fresher" everything falls under that spell. People spread the word that "to cut yourself off" or "to box yourself in" doesn't apply anymore. They say that "those folks who reject Christ and his Word can't simply be pushed aside." They add that "going along with the world a little bit isn't actually so bad." In fact, circumstances are actually such that the best, most decent, and most constructive thing to do is act as though there is no real difference between you and the world, but then behind that cloak to keep on being a pious Christian quietly, secretly, and without calling attention to yourself!

Now, as we said, that kind of cover-up also has a good side. It did in the days of Jeroboam, and it does today as well.

That cloak is nevertheless a replica of the clothing that the Lord God fashioned out of animal skins for those who were tempted in Paradise. In Paradise they felt ashamed. That's why they covered themselves with fig leaves. But the Lord God let them know that covering their shame had to be seen as a lot more serious and important than that. So he gave them clothes of animal skins in place of their fig leaves. Being draped in such heavy cloaks indicated that they continued to feel their shame. They weren't yet free of it. The clothing indicated that they had to set things straight and that they actually had to become different.

Jeroboam added this: "I'm dealing with the living God!" What's important is that he expressed his shame before his people.

People in our own day feel the same way: "I'm dealing here with the Christ of God!" They express their shame before their fellow Christians.

This represents an enduring bridge over which people can still return. Sometimes one person or another who has wandered away into the world can return to us over that same bridge. And what we shouldn't discount in such cases is that the slandering of God's holy name becomes less horrible.

But what does this small benefit amount to in comparison with the deadly danger?

The danger is the hatred that we have in our hearts for God and his Word. Behind the cloak it has free reign. It grows rampant. In its most devious forms, it passes itself off as love for God. The consequences are that it kills the heart, or spreads poison in our surroundings, or destroys the entire future of our own descendants and other people.

The cloak of Jeroboam always covers up something disgraceful. But now you might desire that cover-up for two very different reasons. It might be so that people won't see what's shameful about you. Or it might be so that what's shameful can continue fermenting and growing behind that cloak!

The latter always accompanies the former!

A cover-up hides evil, but it also protects it.

The protection of it is what's so terrible.

Have a look at this in the case of Jeroboam.

Ahab, soon after the death of Solomon, had been less dangerous. But Jeroboam and his cloak were a lullaby for Israel, a sleeping potion, the magical song of the Tempter. And Jeroboam's people were put to sleep! They sank into a very deep sleep. And it wasn't Ahab but Jeroboam who according to God's Word was the man who occasioned God's judgment of damnation on Israel. It was Jeroboam, the son of Nebat, "who sinned and caused Israel to sin."

So when 2 Kings 17 describes God reckoning with apostate Israel in his holy wrath, he pronounced their doom because "the children of Israel had covered up things that were not right but went against the Lord their God." The man in the cloak brought it about!

Brothers and sisters, is he still at work? Also in our country? During our days? At your house? And in your own heart?

517

If so, reject him! Get rid of him, I pray of you in the name of God. He prevents you from acknowledging your guilt in the presence of God.

That cloak, that terrible cover-up, is a curse on God's people.

THEN YOUR PEACE WOULD HAVE FLOWED LIKE A RIVER!

*Oh, that you would have listened to my commandments.
Then your peace would have flowed like a river and your
righteousness like the waves of the ocean. Isaiah 48:18*

Peace in droplets! They provide just a little bit of cooling relief in the middle of our discomfort. Sometimes, rarely and only when it's plentiful, we empty a whole glassful of peace in long, satisfying drafts. But don't think about peace in terms of little drops or even by the glassful. Think of it in terms of a river, like a churning stream tumbling down from God's mountains. Think in terms of peace behind you and at your feet and ahead of you. Think in terms of an ocean of peace buoying the little ship of your soul. Think in terms of peace that you're able to drink every morning and again every evening without ever noticing that your supply is diminished. Peace like a river. You can bathe in it. Splash around in it! Have your whole being refreshed in it. Admit it, my brothers and sisters. Has your soul ever dreamed of anything more wonderful?

And don't you feel the sharp pain of bitter disappointment when the Lord comes along and says: "Oh, that you would have listened to my commandments. Then your peace would have flowed like a river and your righteousness like the waves of the ocean." You think to yourself: "And I could have had all that! I could have experienced the indescribable glory of being astonishingly transported in the depths of my heart! My soul could have been consumed by such glorious reflections!"

God said it himself. Peace like a river could have been my portion. My salvation! My sacred pleasure! I could have enjoyed righteousness like the waves of the ocean if, yes if, if only I hadn't been such a fool! If I had only been willing to follow the precious commandments of my God!

If only I had remained with my Father! If I had simply wanted to continue being his child! If my rebellious, defiant heart had not said: "I want to leave." And if in my soul I had not stated: "I really don't have any desire to obey that never-ending string of commandments!"

Oh, if I had only longed for Jehovah! Longed for Jehovah just as he is in his glorious, holy will and with his wonderful, blessed commandments!

But I didn't want any part of that. I found his commandments irritating, and afterwards I kicked against these pricks of the Lord. I looked for pleasure, joy, and peace in other places. What fool I was! I thought to myself: "If I just get rid of these annoying irritants, then I'll have some peace!" But of course, that peace never came. I only experienced deeper unrest, more fear, and greater depressing anxiety.

Then, watching what was going on, the Lord God sang me a song through the psalmist that touched my heart: "Oh, if my people had only followed my counsel, and if the seed of Israel had just steadfastly desired to pursue my good pleasure ... I would have fed you with the best wheat that grows and you would know that I satisfy you with honey that flows from the rock!"[1]

This faithful, merciful God is the everlasting and immeasurable depth of peace. He wants all his creatures and all his children to drink his sacred peace. He calls out in the words of his prophet: "Oh, that you would have listened to my commandments. Then your peace would have flowed like a river and your righteousness like the waves of the ocean."

Then, finally, the cry arises from the oppressed, desperate heart: "I will pick myself up and go to my Father. And I will tell him: 'Father, I have sinned

---

1. Kuyper is quoting Psalm 81:13 and 16. The latter verse provides the title for this collection of meditations.

against heaven and against you.' O my soul, there is enough abundance and wealth in my Father's house for everyone to enjoy. And I, poor soul that I am, am perishing from my hunger and dying in my thirst for peace."

So you kept your God's glorious commandments once again. He accomplished this in you because he loved you. He allowed you to keep them. You did this yourself, but it was really he who was at work in you. Things had just begun happening this way when it began. There was a rustling, a stream splashing around you and in front of you. It was this peace, flowing like a river. It was happening just as God's Word said it would.

But not long afterwards the comforting angel that goes around to encourage God's saints found your poor soul lying like a fish on dry land once again. The waters of marvelous grace that had been flowing had flowed away and were gone.

Terrible! But that's how it was.

So pay attention, brothers and sisters, to how profoundly detestable the godless source of unrighteousness churning in your own heart really is. It causes this to happen! But you had taken it much, much too lightly. You took to be a river of peace what actually was only a trickling brook. You stayed sitting in the gatehouse because you thought you had already entered the house of your Father. You imagined that you had already kept God's commandments, when at most you had only brushed them with your fingertips.

That's why you have to break through the sheet of ice again, fall in, and sink into the mud at the bottom of the stream.

But there is One who saw what was going on. There's One whose heart was saddened by the oppression you felt in your misery. So he came to you one more time, calling: "Oh, that you would have listened to my commandments. Then your peace would have flowed like a river and your righteousness like the waves of the ocean."

Then, with your anger aroused like Job's, you declare: "But my Lord and my God! Haven't I been keeping your commandments? Hasn't my peace actually been like a river?" But the Lord has something to say to that self-righteous heart of yours that couldn't be restrained from shamelessly asking: "Haven't I been keeping your commandments?" God in his exalted, everlasting love wants to teach you something; he wants you to track it, hear it, and take careful note of it: "You haven't touched even as much as the surface of my commandments. You've at most taken only a tiny sip of my peace!"

Then the doors that were closed to us fly open. We see immediately that the commands of God contain a labyrinth of hallways and rooms flooded with glorious light, while we thought they were plain and simple. Our souls are compelled to exclaim: "Your commands, O God, are immense!"

This is how Jehovah helps his limping, stumbling, and complaining saints here on earth.

Saints!

But don't shudder at that description!

Listen to how Satan taunts: "You? A proper saint? Really?"

Listen to what people whisper: "Now, if that's what you call a saint … !"

Listen to how down on yourself you sound when you say: "I'm a dirty, miserable person! What's holy about me? I'm contaminated from top to bottom!"

But in heaven, the Lord persists in saying: "You're a saint!"

Not gradually becoming a saint!

Not in the process of becoming a saint!

No, a saint without any conditions attached to weaken that status.

"O God, my God, I feel like I'm living under a curse." But God says: "You're a saint!"

Who is getting it right?

Simply listen to this, you who feel driven by the storms of life! He who is your God continues to maintain that he is a God who justifies the ungodly.

50
VOLUME II

DON'T WITHHOLD DISCIPLINE FROM A CHILD

Do not withhold discipline from a child, for if you strike him with a rod, he will not die. Proverbs 23:13

"Not with discipline, but with a soft touch! Above all, never strike a child, but win them with your love!" is what this world's experts assert. And that doesn't surprise us. But what definitely does astonish us is that so many Christians howl the same refrain right along with them, like a pack of wolves.

Christians in our country love their children. So, if they are genuinely Christian, they love them above all with a desire for their eternal well-being. They simply ask: "How can I save my child from going to hell?"

If a father should ask this with a heavy heart, the Lord God has an answer for him in his holy Word. You can simply read it in Proverbs 23:13: "You should strike him with a rod and save his soul from hell!"

But there could well be a father who doesn't agree with this.

God says what he does in his Word, but educational theory says something else. So that Christian father sets God's Word aside and lets the experts on child-rearing guide him. In that case, he himself needs to be disciplined for his scandalous rebellion against God. Then what God said in his Word happens: where discipline is gone, the child is lost.

This is how the father finds some peace of mind and the child receives respect.

What a dreadful state of affairs!

And yet that's a state of affairs that holds no promise whatever. But people settle for it without any pangs of conscience.

What did I just say? "Without any pangs of conscience"? No, let me put it this way: "in self-satisfaction!"

Just listen once to how people object when just one father, constrained by God's Word, picks up the rod again.

Above all, listen to how almost three-fourths of all preachers commend an approach that goes against God's Word!

But hanging the rod on a hook amounts to mutiny, rebellion, and open opposition to God.

Naturally, loving words, gentle warnings, and a friendly piece of advice can be offered by anyone and will be well received by almost everyone. You don't have to be a father to do this.

But a father has a status that carries something of God's majesty. He is consequently vested with authority over us, and he has the obligation to issue directives to us and to discipline us immediately when we overstep our boundaries. If necessary, he should do so by inflicting pain with the rod. And that's what so many categorically reject. They do so because this threatens freedom of the will and enforces submission. And forced submission is precisely what people don't want.

This is the ideal expressed for all authority throughout the entire world. A father must deal with his child as he would with an equal. The educator must do so with his students by modeling gracious obedience. The civil official must do so by confining the criminal as sensitively as possible, offering admonition in love and anticipating improvement.

Even on a warship discipline has to be curtailed.

Compliance with this approach applies to anyone in the whole world who has been given divine authority. It rests on no one more than on them. When they don't exercise it, the result is that they simply shove it aside. Then fools in their self-determined folly hold the reins and set the pace.

That's how souls are lost and how society implodes.

Or can the church still save the day?

My dear sisters and brothers, if you think so, before very long you'll hear how deeply enmity toward any form of discipline has penetrated to the very heart of Christ's church.

Discipline doesn't belong in the church, which should always be the proclaimer of everlasting love.

Discipline belongs in the Old Testament!

Phooey! Phooey on still wanting to exercise discipline over doctrine. Phooey on disciplining a preacher! How intolerable, how in conflict with the exalted position of a servant of the Word!

And talk about discipline of personal life! That would only produce resentment and hardening! If someone is reluctant to come to the Lord's Table, just extend a simple invitation to them to "Come!" But if someone wants to come and gets the message "Don't come," ... how unloving, how hard-hearted, and how unchristian that would be!

You know that the church has always been a huge hospital. Well then, admit those who are recovering as well as those who are chronically sick! And if someone should come who no longer believes but who is still a minister of the Word, let him in. Testify to them about unbelief. Admonish them and pray for them. But above all, don't discipline them. Don't use anything except moral influence. Use ethical measures.

So even in the church of Jesus Christ, people set aside the sure rule of God's Word and replace it with the rule of human insight.

That's what's called forbearance!

But sad to say, that contra-scriptural and fundamentally revolutionary wisdom forfeits all blessing. It incurs God's rejection. The vial of God's holy wrath is poured out on it.

In that spirit people build schools. They give instruction. They civilize. They shape culture.

That's how they produce highly educated and partially educated people. But it's not how they impart wisdom!

Wisdom is something different from being smart. Wisdom is not the ability to grasp an issue quickly and with conceptual clarity. Rather, it is to confront matters with one's entire being in a way that honors God's will.

Wisdom is not a profound lecture, but it flows through the channel of a person's will and into the depths of their emotions and impressions about life. In so doing, it leaves a stamp on their entire personality. That's the reason why a simple farmer is sometimes very wise while a well-educated natural scientist is quite stupid!

Consider the people of the Transvaal![1]

What a backward people! But they still practice discipline. They still use the rod! They don't really have a lot of education. But what do you think? Have they got wisdom? Wisdom about life? Wisdom about how to deal with matters? In that regard, aren't they a lot wiser than we are?

And don't bother saying: "By punishing the body I won't touch the soul!"

You know very well, don't you, that if the sinful soul wants to experience pleasure, it completely understands that the body is involved as well! Body and soul are one, and the one plays on the other! But what a bitter irony that when it comes to punishment, people suddenly believe that body and soul are two separate entities!

No, a person is not simply a soul housed in a lump of flesh, as Geulincx imagined.[2]

You are constituted as one being. We deal with the whole person in dealing with one another. That you blush when you get angry pretty well establishes that fact. Touch the body and you immediately and directly touch the soul!

But our generation keeps up a sustained appeal to abolish discipline and get rid of the rod!

And should the Lord God himself continue his work of chastising and disciplining, do you think he would withhold his rod?

Brothers and sisters, it's getting to the point that nations falling under God's disciplining hand no longer recognize that for what it is. They only recognize what they are experiencing as disturbances in nature and terrible catastrophes, but not as God's angry blows. These are blows that people definitely try to avoid, but not ones from which they pray to be delivered.

It's all so consistent!

They are passionate about free will. They want nothing to do anymore with submitting to authority. The rod has fallen out of the father's hand. In the home without discipline we have the nursery of an undisciplined society. The lack of discipline over men and women by a nondisciplining church is no longer protested. And finally, even the Lord's discipline itself is dismissed!

---

1. First published in *De Heraut*, no. 169 (March 20, 1881), this meditation appeared when the First Boer War (1880–81) between the British and the Afrikaners in South Africa was well under way. The war was followed closely in the Netherlands, which had very close, recent ties with this people group.

2. Arnold Geulincx (1624–1669) was a Flemish philosopher, disciple of Descartes, and later a convert to Calvinism who taught at the University of Leiden toward the end of his life. He espoused views disassociating body and soul. Kuyper's reference to him is interesting and curious.

That's when the appeal becomes: "Let's deal with this situation medically. Let's tackle the healing of wounded souls using an ethical approach!"

But from on high the Lord God Almighty shouts: "Cease and desist, you people! Whose breath is in your nostrils? The chastisements of my discipline are the way of life" (Prov 6:23).

So: "Do not withhold discipline from a child. If you strike him with a rod, you will save his soul from hell!"

He who has ears to hear, let him hear!

5 1

VOLUME II

A WORM AND
NOT A MAN

But I am a worm and not a man, reproached by
others and despised by the people. Psalm 22:6[1]

Man must become a worm and the worm a man! Doesn't that one profound thought capture the mystery of our precious, sacred gospel?

Passion Week is unfolding once again, and the church needs to give a responsible account of Jesus' cross as though things were happening in front of its very eyes. But what is preaching on Christ's sufferings except depicting step by step how the Man of Sorrows became a worm and finally crumpled in the dust of death?

The first mystery, namely that of Bethlehem's crib, portrays for you how he who was God became a man. The second one, in which the cross of Golgotha is the central feature, shows you how that man was lowered and humiliated in becoming a worm.

"After me is coming One," cried John the Baptist, "who was before me and whose shoelaces I am not worthy to stoop down and unloose." In doing so, he was alluding to the One at Peniel referred to in Genesis 32:24: "A Man wrestled with Jacob." And to the One in Joshua's vision of whom it is said: "He looked up and saw a Man standing in front of him" (Josh 5:13). And to "a Man

---

1. Psalm 22:7 in Dutch versions.

as though clothed in linen" seen by Ezekiel and Daniel! And to the same Man who "stood among the myrtle trees" before Zechariah (Zech 1:10)! And the One of whom it was prophesied that "this Man would be a shelter from the wind" (Isa 32:2)! And "a Man whose name would be 'the Branch'" (Zech 6:12)! And to the One of whom it would be said in that hour of terrible reckoning: "Awake, O sword, against the Man who is my companion" (13:7)! And he was alluding to the One whose deeply felt name for that reason would be "Man of Sorrows" (Isa 53:3)!

Power, strength, and majesty are conveyed in that Man. Together we all flee to him for comfort and protection—the weak, the helpless, and those in distress. And he, the Man of strength, protects us with his powerful arms and drives off our adversaries.

A Man! Yes, that's what he was when he caused the Devil to cower before him in the wilderness. That's what he was when he held thousands spellbound with his words. When he healed the sick and banished diseases! When he cast out devils and they slinked away! When he made the Pharisees shudder by the look in his eye! When he rebuked the storm and calmed the sea! And even more strongly, when he overpowered death and roused Lazarus from the grave! Yes, even in Gethsemane, when everyone shrunk back from him and his captors fell to the ground.

But could he remain that Man? As that Man, could he break through to what we needed? Could he help you and me by remaining a man? Could he triumph through power? Gain victory by his strength? Could his mighty arms gain the victory?

In response, God's holy Word says "no" and "no" yet again. Unless that Man became a worm, the little worm named Jacob was beyond help. Unless a grain of wheat falls to the earth from above, sinks into the soil, and dies, those who are lost gain nothing. It remains dormant and bears no fruit unto eternal salvation.

Consider this. We really aren't human any longer. All our strength has dried up like a potsherd. Human beings conceived and born in sin actually belong to the dust of the earth. They have become like worms.

Sin has stripped us naked. There is nothing whole left in us any longer. As Comré expressed it so very accurately, even our best deeds give God grief!

One of our glories gives him a little more, the next a little less!

They look good, but in essence they aren't.

We're rotten beams that creak and break under pressure.

We're hollowed out willow trunks in which the night owls build their nests and that are swayed by the wind.

Job fully understood this when he cried: "The stars are not pure in his eyes. How much less a man, who is a maggot and no more than a worm!" (Job 25:6).[2]

Oh, even if we wish this were not true, we see that it is. In God's eyes, we are like those poor little worms that crawl around in the dirt! But this is not what a rotting joist wants to hear! Not at all! It passes itself off as a sound beam and wants to be regarded as the kind of support that can hold up under the pressure of a house resting on it.

This is how a worm dreams in its arrogance. It dreams that it is really a man.

What a dreadful way of looking at yourself!

Then that infinitesimal speck of dust opens its mouth and weighs in against God. In its ungodliness, the mere worm begins murmuring against the Maker of heaven and earth.

This is precisely why Jesus had to be laid so low in the dust of death. For no other reason! What you in your proud heart were unwilling to do for your God, he in his mercy would do for you. In this he is the mighty hero! The man of glory in all his strength and power! The Lion of the tribe of Judah! And now this Lion allows his mane to fall to the ground. This Hero throws his quiver of arrows aside. This man bows his head. He crumples in the dust and lets the heavy load of God's anger fall on him. He buckles under it and succumbs to the dust of death. As One despised and rejected, he became like a worm creeping through the dust.

He was despised, and we did not esteem him! We didn't because whose heart ever trembles with holy indignation upon hearing this Man lament: "I am but a worm"?

So don't talk to me about how amazing the cross is. Don't come to me singing about the love of Jesus. All the superficial chatter about a descent into everlasting death is only a heavier crown of thorns that you push deeper into the bleeding brow of the Man of Sorrows. Those who talk this way don't understand. They are superficial. They miss it by a mile!

No, every individual who has not yet learned from the Father to fathom these unbearable sufferings at least to some extent smacks the Suffering Servant in the face all over again. They push that worm even deeper into the ground. They trample on his blood.

Not just several of them, but all of them!

You've done it too, and so have I!

---

2. This is said by Bildad, not Job. The quotation is from Job 25:5b–6.

But there is only one who no longer does this. It's the little worm of Jacob. And the little worm of Jacob, who might that be?

That's every man and every woman, every young person and every older one, everyone who has been set free and made serviceable. But previously they were intent on defending themselves and they thought: "This is great! Jesus is a worm, and I'm a real man." "I'm a real woman!" But then the Holy Spirit came. He battered their evil, arrogant hearts. He attacked and broke them until they finally learned to regard themselves as pathetic little worms. Then, lying humbled to the dust of the earth themselves, they yielded to their dear Savior. Then they cried out: "I by the grace of God am but a worm, but he and he only is the true Man."

5 2

VOLUME II

I AM POURED OUT LIKE WATER

I have been poured out like water, and all my bones are out of joint.
My heart is like wax and has melted in my inner parts. Psalm 22:14[1]

We know from the Old Testament what the New does not disclose, namely, Jesus' inner feelings as his struggle with death intensified. The evangelists certainly tell us what Jesus cried out on the cross. But they don't say what lay behind what he said. They don't explain what gave rise to those cries of anguish.

They couldn't report that because it wasn't obvious. It wasn't something that could be heard. And they had too much respect for their Lord's suffering to simply make something up!

But they really didn't have to say more than they did, because it had already been recorded.

The Messiah had already powerfully poured out the depths of his soul through the Holy Spirit. What he said came from the marrow of his bones. It was expressed in gripping language that was as deeply disturbing as it could be. He was not like one of us. He hadn't taken this suffering on without knowing what it would be like. He didn't go to the cross only half-knowing what was actually involved. And when he was crucified, he wasn't even partially

---

1. Psalm 22:15 in the Dutch versions.

dumbfounded by how terrible the suffering turned out to be. No, that would have been unworthy of his divine majesty. As the Son of God, he didn't take on something that he hadn't measured in all its depth beforehand. He had calculated its breadth and actually lived into and suffered every aspect of it ahead of time.

What was involved is captured by the Holy Spirit in the soul-wrenching lament on David's lips that we find in Psalm 22. It rose from the top of Judah's mountains: "My God, my God, why have you forsaken me? Why are you so far from helping me and so unresponsive to my groaning?"

So if you really want to know what Jesus was going through in his inner being and what he was ultimately struggling with on the cross, don't look for it in the Gospels. Go back to Isaiah 53 and Psalm 22. Then explain to me why we don't pay attention to these profound laments in our preaching on Christ's passion.

Well now, one of the features that we capture from this psalm of the cross is Jesus' inner meltdown and his emotional weakening and collapse. The Holy Spirit describes this very vividly in verses 15 and 16. He does so in a number of images and a flood of thoughts that make you realize how powerless our language really is to adequately describe this inner weakening of the Messiah.

While still living, the Lord felt like he was already dead and buried because he laments: "You lay me in the dust of death." Pouring out his soul had been cut off because "his tongue was cleaving to the roof of his mouth." He couldn't even voice his complaints. His tears refused to flow because he felt "as dried up as a potsherd." His heart was unable to resist any longer. He had lost all energy and even the will to live since "his heart was like wax and had melted within him." His body was totally powerless and it felt like he was falling apart because "all his bones were out of joint." In short, it felt to the Savior like his entire existence was caving in and ebbing away because he complained: "I'm being poured out like water!"

Where are those now who say that Jesus died as a martyr?

How do martyrs die?

Always upheld by grace! By power poured into their weakened hearts that gives them heroic courage! By an energized faith that keeps them strong and unwavering internally until their last gasp, despite the fact that externally everything is being destroyed.

But what do you see in the case of Jesus?

Exactly the opposite!

No grace, because he was forsaken by his God! No infused power, because drop by drop all his strength was sucked out of him. He was simply tapped out! No heroism whatsoever, because inside he was completely weakened even before that became evident on the outside!

Internally your Jesus had been broken, not strengthened.

But "broken" is not saying it strongly enough to capture the speed with which that emotional desolateness overcame him or how terrible it was. That's why the Holy Spirit reaches for a more powerful image. He doesn't say "broken," but "poured out." This doesn't convey "poured out" in the sense of oil slowly flowing from a jar, but in the sense of water rapidly gushing down the side of a mountain. "Poured out like water" is a forceful, powerful expression designed to help you grasp what Jesus' emotional weakening was really like.

"Poured out like water" intends to convey how one drop by falling pulls the next one after it. That one, in turn, pulls the next and so on with every drop that follows. Together all the water becomes one irresistible force that races and sloshes down as one mighty flood. That's how it was for Jesus. It began with the ebbing of his strength. That increased rapidly. It swelled and became more intense until all at once it seemed like he was totally in its grip. Suddenly he was poured out like a great river of water, drained of all strength for living, all spiritual courage, and all energy in his will.

This is an image that conveys indescribable weakness. It's a weakness capable of nothing, nothing at all. Incapable of opening the lips! Incapable of lifting the eyes! Incapable of inspiring the heart to stir the will! It conveys a weakening of the pulse. It's weakness that sucks all desire to pray out of the soul. It's the unspeakable weakness associated with fear and anxiety. It describes being so weak that even the thought of being weak takes too much effort for the completely despondent heart.

This is what the Holy Spirit wants you to see with complete clarity about the Jesus you profess. Crucifixion is not the most bitter of all deaths by far. That's not what this passage is all about. Countless people have suffered crucifixion. But no one except Jesus alone, hanging on his cross, has descended into the depths of hell. No one has ever shouldered the burden of God's wrath against the sins of all human beings. Furthermore, no one else by dying on a cross has ever been crucified in his soul, experiencing the unseen and painful weakness of dying a thousand deaths all at once.

Oh, to be Jesus! To be the Son of God! To possess power like that of the Lion of the tribe of Judah, the roar of his death cry was still frightening! And then out of sheer obedience and in tender mercy to be completely willing to descend into that terribly constricting and oppressive condition of total powerlessness and inner weakness! Can't you feel now, you who are so weak and powerless in yourself, what kind of indescribable torture Jesus your Savior felt in his soul? What a price he paid!

But what if he had not done this? What if he had resisted allowing his heart to melt like wax in his inner parts? What do you think? Could he have ever been your Savior? Or isn't your own weakness really not all that absolute and terrible compared with his? Or isn't it fitting that you have the kind of High Priest who descends so deep that he reaches the place where you are, lifts you in his arms, and carries you on high?

Oh, the wonderful mystery of divine grace!

You thought that you were too powerless yourself! But no, not powerless enough, you have to confess about yourself. You have to become totally powerless! Then Jesus will be with you.

Or, to turn this around, however powerless you may be and however close you may be to sinking into total despair, my brothers and sisters, never toss aside the staff of hope. He who once was the most powerless among all the powerless is now sitting on the right hand of power, at the throne of God.

53
VOLUME II

ELI, ELI, LAMMA SABACHTHANI!

My God, my God, why have you forsaken me? Why are you so far from saving me, from hearing my groaning? Psalm 22:1[1]

To say that our Lord and Savior, when dying on the cross in his dreadful fear and anguish, was thinking about Psalm 22 is basically to undercut Scripture. To think that he was consciously quoting its opening words when he cried *"Eli, Eli, lama sabachthani,"* is to diminish the person of our Mediator.

Or to come at it from the opposite direction, to suppose that God in his omniscience, because he already knew ahead of time what Jesus would say on the cross, had David write what he did, would be to impose external human standards on God! It would reduce the work of the Holy Spirit to a polished mechanical composition.

No, to retain Scripture as the divine work of the Holy Spirit, Christ as the eternal and faithful witness, and God as true God, all such artificial and superficial guesswork has to be swept aside. These words have to be understood in all of their exalted, godly character.

Christ understood the nature of his suffering from the outset. Not because someone explained this to him, but because of the nature of suffering itself! Death is not something capricious, but its terrible perverseness is determined

---

1. Psalm 22:2 in Dutch versions.

with exact precision by contrast with the very essence of life. What can also be determined are various levels of suffering in death. You can talk about experiencing it more deeply, less deeply, very deeply, or even sinking to the very bottom of its depths! What can be ascertained with great exactness and precision is how people experience death in proportion to the tenderness of their individual emotions, the strength of their respective awareness of life, and the degree of their own holiness. This is all determined not by some precise external measurement, but by the very nature of life, the character of destruction, the hellish depth of death's perversity, and the complete sensitivity and holiness of Jesus' totally sinless humanity.

Christ did not have to guess what was coming! He knew! He knew in the most exact and unique way possible. There was no uncertainty involved here whatsoever.

This is the Christ who was the inspiration of his church ever since the days of Paradise. This is the Christ who felt oppressed in all the oppressiveness that his people experienced. This is the Christ who from of old comforted his faithful as "the face of an angel."

This is the Christ, says the apostle Peter, who governed prophecy. In prophecy and through the Holy Spirit, he revealed himself, announced his own life, and predicted his own future. He even disclosed himself in the shadows so that the church of the old covenant could already be enlivened by the everlasting beauty of the Mediator and be justified by faith.

The Scriptures of the old covenant didn't merely announce him. He himself is the substance and content of the old covenant's Scriptures. He animated them. He brought them. He gave them to his church as a gift of his grace.

He gave her these Scriptures not as an external jewel, but as the avenue by which he came to her. He revealed himself to her in these Scriptures before he came to her in person, sending her images of his likeness, if we may put it that way. Abraham and Moses, David and Solomon, Job and Isaiah, and whoever else you might name are instruments whom he created to convey features of his likeness. It prepared the way for recognizing him when he came. And now, in retrospect, they describe for us all the fine points and tender features of his full work as our Mediator.

When the words *"Eli, Eli, lama sabachthani"* crossed David's lips, they amounted to the anticipated experience of Christ's frightful pain in his soul that was coming on Golgotha. This occurred by virtue of the definite qualities of human nature and their assured response to the depths of death that would inevitably come to expression then. What a terrible event that would be when the dreadfully frightening lament of "*Eli sabachthani*" would arise from Jesus' constricted throat as he made his last gasps.

Just as today we are sometimes given the privilege of bearing the scars of our Lord's suffering after Golgotha, so also a few of the elect under the old covenant were accorded the privilege of bearing the scars of the Lord's suffering before Golgotha. The Man of Sorrows is depicted beforehand in Jehovah's Suffering Servant. The entire body of believers already then was asked to bear to some extent a faint reflection of those scars of the cross. But only one man of God was assigned the honor of being set aside to bear them fully. That man was David.

Two things are noteworthy in the case of David. The first is that he had definitely been thrown into "the deepest pit that held no water." The second is that when he poured out his frightened lament about his own suffering, the Holy Spirit chose him as the instrument for revealing the Messiah's suffering. The tone of his complaining was immeasurably deepened when by inspiration his lips expressed total abandonment. The full reality of that abandonment then had to be conveyed by the lips of Jesus directly, not now through the work of inspiration.

This is how the experience of Golgotha lived ahead of time came to be expressed in the lament found in Psalm 22. The cry of hellish anguish arising from Christ's soul on Golgotha neither merely echoed it nor added anything to it. It was torn from his weakening soul at that moment and of necessity had to cross his lips. It conveyed how frightful his death was and the immeasurable depth of his emotions.

He, the eternal Word and the Son of God, was also human. He was flesh and blood. He was like us in every way, sin excepted. In the most intimate and tender way imaginable, he had united our human nature with his divine nature. Nothing whatever of his Godhead was diminished. How could it have been? And yet in his tender mercy, he arranged it that the human nature remained completely intact, which is completely unexplainable for us. This would make it possible for us to testify: "Yes, he truly does bear our flesh. He became one of us!"

And once he did, he entered into what is ours. Into our deep sorrows! Into our sinful and perverse lives! Into the shambles that make up our world! Into the catastrophe that we call human life! Walking on the appalling, subversive, and turbulent terrain beneath which hell's volcano lies concealed! From that hell, the thick smoke of death filled with the wrath of God rises. Heavy as lead, it settles across all of human life, which is cursed and doomed to destruction.

While everyone else avoided that and attempted to hide from it, he had to enter into it. While by God's marvelous grace they still had protections from it and could temporarily avoid its terrible, deadly destruction, the same was not true for him. He had to willingly go out looking for it. He had to concentrate on it completely. He couldn't rest until he had tasted the deepest and most bitter aspects of that death.

We're not talking here about death as we view it. We're talking about the death that lies even beneath that, death that culminates with falling into that deep, eternal pit with its hellish oppressiveness. That's where the wrath of God against all that is not holy clings to death.

We're talking about that death that is completely contrary to living. And God is Life. Death, therefore, is God's enemy. God pushes back against it. Sin is death. All sin is death. Because God is Life, he can do nothing else but pour out his everlasting anger against sin and death.

Even although you can never resolve or explain this matter, this much is sure. Either your Savior has tasted death or he has not. If he has not, where then is your hope, O you children of the kingdom? If he in fact has, then please tell me, you who call yourself one of the redeemed, which death has your Savior suffered for you? Merely the death of entering the grave? Or was it death in its deepest dimensions, with its hellish anguish, and where the wrath of God was fully poured out?

Then woe to you if you are not one of God's redeemed, for then you will have to bear this on your own! But that's impossible, isn't it? For then he's not your Savior!

But he bore it all for you! He experienced this essential death: death in its eternal depth, with all its hellish anguish, in the clutches of God's wrath!

Is it possible to actually experience that kind of death, and not just give the appearance of doing so, without feeling completely cut off from life for even one small moment?

So don't argue about a thing like this and desecrate something so sacred! Just believe it. Adore God for it. Thank him for such unrepeatable and match-less mercy!

This stands fast: the hellish anguish of the depths of death and God-forsakenness is either yours or his to bear.

This is when he said: "I did it for you, O my redeemed follower!"

This is when he was forsaken, and when God's angels heard it from his own lips: "*Lamma sabachthani!*"

For what reason?

So that you would never have to be forsaken by God but someday would dwell with him forever.

And this is by sheer mercy!

THE EFFORT OF HIS SOUL

He will see the effort of his soul and be satisfied. By his
knowledge, my servant, the righteous one, will justify many,
for he will bear all their unrighteousness. Isaiah 53:11

For what did Jesus hunger? For what was he yearning? What did he desire with a consuming passion in his soul when he broke out with the cry "*Eli lama*"?

Was it to be allowed to come down from the cross?

Would a spark of joy immediately light up his dying eyes if the Roman commander had ordered one of his soldiers to set a ladder against the cross? To remove the nails from his hands and feet? To give him back his clothes and remove the crown of thorns from his head? To allow him to return to his disciples as a free man?

Impossible!

If he would have returned to his disciples that way, Jesus wouldn't have been able to bring them a thing. Neither their hearts nor ours would ever have been able to experience the riches of our Lord Jesus. Yet, not three days later that's apparently exactly what happened. Jesus actually did return to his disciples. The crown of thorns was no longer on his head. His nakedness was covered with clothing provided by the hands of a friend. Ladders had stood against the cross, and he had been taken down.

Almost the same ... but with a big difference. Death had intervened. Jesus had been dead!

His coming back was a return from the dead. It was a triumph over death. It was the shining in sovereign majesty of regal, divine, inextinguishable life.

The way Jesus came back from death was like returning with a tamed dog on a leash walking behind him. Death, that monstrous death, which had recently been growling at him so fiercely that it filled him with deadly fear, was now trotting behind Jesus like a lamb. Even his thirst no longer overpowered and controlled him. He felt like a weak, shamed person who had been emasculated, abused, and broken but was now forever victorious.

No wonder Jesus' needy church always feels such unspeakable, indescribable joy every time Easter season comes around again.

When it comes right down to it, we are all terribly afraid of death. Actually, for nothing else except death! Believers and unbelievers alike! The first are always thinking about whether death is near. If not, we simply get on with living. If it is, then even the ungodly cringe at the prospect. Oh, death! Death in all its forms! With all of its appalling certainty! With all that accompanies it and all that comes after it! It fills the soul with such fear!

But at Easter, when Jesus draws very close to us once more with death tamed and trailing behind him on a leash, everything is wonderful again. Wonderful, at least, for those who can see it! For here's where the mystery lies. A godless individual doesn't even understand death when it grabs them by the throat and chokes them. A godless person doesn't understand Jesus until he casts them into outer darkness as their Judge. This is why a godless person doesn't comprehend the miracle of Easter. They don't grasp that death has been tamed, even when Jesus unleashes it and turns it loose on them to tear them to pieces.

Only believers understand this. They do not because they are any better than unbelievers. Oh, we're often more ungodly than the ungodly! No, they do because Jesus has done something for them and in them and with them. And he continues doing so. That's why they are different and are in the process of becoming different, although until the day they die they remain dreadful people. Oh, the depth of ungodliness!

But Jesus' work on their behalf and both with and within them continues. Jesus doesn't allow himself to be hampered by their continuing inner ungodliness. He quietly continues working. Then the scales fall off their eyes, and the light enters. Whether they want it or not, they see Jesus at work. They see that death has been tamed. They see the chains by which he restrains it. And they also understand what the Word says when it promises that he will never turn it loose on them again!

Sometimes Jesus even calls on one or two of his followers and hands them the chains restraining death. He does this so that they may walk in his presence with death subdued and walking along behind them. These people are known as the martyrs. And when his poor church witnesses this happening, they definitely and genuinely believe in him! Then a glorious joy springs to life in the church of Jesus. His people call out to each other: "What a glorious King our Jesus is!" They sing together a song that taunts and mocks death, now tamed: "Death, where is your sting? Where is your victory? Where is the pit into which you want to throw us?"

This is exactly what Jesus has passionately longed for in the depths of his soul. He has only one love, namely, his love for his Father. But because his Father has other children, this is a love that also extends to the elect of his Father. But he saw that these children, these elect of the Father, were living in constant fear, never free, but always deathly afraid. And that simply could not continue. Eternal peace would come only when it no longer did.

And behold; now it no longer does! Death is vanquished. Life has triumphed. Christ is King, God's own Son and the Prince of the kingdom of glory. By his own person he has determined the enduring reality that death is vanquished and life triumphs. Now there is jubilation among the children of his Father. Now the elect give thanks. Now love remains. Perfect love! And perfect love drives out fear.

This is what Jesus wanted to see happen! Only then would he be satisfied!

That's why the ancient prophecy stated: "He will see because of the effort of his soul and be satisfied. By his knowledge, my servant, the righteous one, will justify many, for he will bear all their unrighteousness."

This is what Jesus has now accomplished!

But before he died, he had to endure the curse of being forsaken by God. Before he could endure that curse, he had to wade through the river of our unrighteousness and ungodliness. Before he could vanquish our sins, he had to take on our flesh.

He did all of this only in order to grab death by the throat. But that grip couldn't be haphazard. It couldn't because hell was tied up with death. Sin and all unrighteousness and the most terrible curse were all bound to it. And so the Man of Sorrows endured all of this.

This took a lot of work on his part. It was work of the soul. Even God's angels were incapable of measuring its depth. All the redeemed will never be able, even together, to appreciate its everlasting beauty.

It was a work of the soul for him to become flesh. It was work of the soul to dwell in the flesh. It was work of the soul not to reject others who were in the flesh but to draw them to himself. It was work of the soul to bear sin, the curse, and the wrath of God. And finally, it was work of the soul to enter death, to tackle death from the inside, and ultimately to emerge from the kingdom of death with death tamed and chained and walking behind him as God's Conqueror. This is how Jesus appeared to his disciples, to the church, and to all who are in it. This is how he appeared to all who are sealed by the covenant.

Has he appeared like this to you? To me?

This is how he saw the work of his soul!

By accomplishing it, he justified many and was satisfied.

This is why we celebrate Easter, sisters and brothers.

Immanuel! God with us!

THE LORD OF HOSTS

*This is what the Lord of Hosts says: "Return to
me," says the Lord of Hosts, "and I will return to
you," says the Lord of Hosts. Zechariah 1:3*

Holy Scripture tells us to address our God with the solemn and impressive name "Lord of Hosts."

The name is not intended to convey that God is the head, commander, lord, or, if you prefer, the king of these hosts. Still, there it stands in the Hebrew: Jehovah of Hosts. "Lord" is God's sacred, covenant name in this context, therefore. "Lord of Hosts" is also designed to convey that we are not to think of our Jehovah, the All-Glorious and Greatly Exalted One, in any other way than as distinguished from his powerful hosts.

The beauty of this inspiring name of "Lord of Hosts" shines most brightly, therefore, in the hearts of those who feel abandoned.

It's when we feel insignificant and stop thinking highly of ourselves that this name offers us comfort. It does when we can't find meaning in this life anymore, but driven by all its storms we become so desolate and lonely that we quietly retreat into ourselves. It does when we no longer enjoy soul-stirring fellowship with others but everything seems to undercut it. It does when the wicked forces of sin, the Devil, and this world seize opportunities to oppress our anxious souls even more than they already do. It does when they drive us backwards and push us down under a flood of problems. Then, in such times, my sisters and brothers, our Most Holy God comes to you as the Lord of Hosts.

Then that powerful covenant name becomes a source of strength and comfort to your soul.

What is frightening to the soul in times like those is appealing to an impenetrable heaven that doesn't respond or to an unreachable God who gives no indication of wanting to be with us.

Then heaven is just as hollow and empty for us as our empty hearts. The All-Merciful Being whom we implore is just as isolated as the isolated, imploring souls within us.

As heaven exists in our souls mirrors what we think heaven actually is. The state of our souls determines how we in our foolishness imagine the Holy One actually is.

And that's precisely the reason why it's impossible for a sinful human being ever to find comfort in God by themselves.

No, consolation only comes when the living God himself comes to us, reveals himself to us, and permits us to see him as he is. He allows us to see him exactly as we need to see him at that moment.

For this reason, he comes as the All-Sufficient One who needs to be sufficient for you. He doesn't come just out of empathy for your weakness, but he comes surrounded with all his hosts. He appears before you when you're living with your sense of desolation, and he sweeps aside the curtain of heaven. He lets you see immediately life there in all its richness, fullness, and glory. He lets you see that while it is exalted far above you, it is also intimately close to you, sparkling and swirling with all the ranks of heaven, with the heavenly hosts in all their glory. He allows you to see all his cherubim and all his seraphim, with all his angels and all his archangels, with all his masses ten thousand and ten times ten thousand strong. And from the center of that indescribable, inexhaustible, and incalculably rich life that simply takes all your breath away, he cries out to you in a voice that reverberates through all those spheres. The Almighty, the All-Merciful, the Great Comforter says directly to you: "Behold, this is the kind of God of Glory that I am; the Lord of Hosts is my name!"

And now your soul drinks in what flows from that name.

The world that initially felt so immense and powerful compared with the weak, lonely soul within us now seems like nothing at all. It seems like a mere shriveled speck compared with the endless glory of that indescribable and unseen vitality surrounding the throne of our God.

This God himself—let's be honest enough to say so—had sunk so low and been so diminished in our unbelieving hearts that he seemed like little more than a mere footnote, only a name, and a mirage in our soul. But now as the

Lord of Hosts, this God has without notice reappeared to us in the full reality of his matchless power and incomprehensible majesty. He has reappeared as the One who can do anything and everything. He is the One whose broad grasp of strength and power has no beginning and no end. He is Jehovah of Hosts, our Almighty God!

Suffering and illness and misfortune—even worse, abuse suffered in the name of Jesus and taking up the cross laid on us all—little by little, all contributed to our lack of faith. Admit it, sisters and brothers, these all became forces alongside God and against us. It seemed to us in our foolishness that the power of such maladies was actually too strong for our God. So we doubted: "Would he ever be able to deliver us from it?" Then all the little forces began to emerge: suffering and oppression, anxiety and sickness, affliction and trials, cross and abuse. They were all assistants belonging to a much lower order and far subordinate rank to those of the hosts of our God and King.

Sin, the Devil, and death blunted your soul. In the sinful imaginings of your emotional dismay, they seemed like irresistible and unconquerable forces. They made you shudder. But now you see them as subdued and constrained forces for fulfilling, however unwillingly and with resistance, the counsels of the Lord of Hosts. They are being restrained by his hosts.

So the mouth can verbalize and the heart can hold good things again. We have space once more. We can breathe again. What loomed so large and frightened us so terribly now seems so small. It really amounts to nothing at all! And the One whom we allowed to become dim and powerless is once again the Only Powerful and All-Powerful God. He shines before us in all his power and majesty. This world has sunk to almost nothing. But heaven with its ten thousand times ten thousand hosts is what grips us. It exalts our soul. It blinds us with its light. We long to flee to it, to such divine majesty.

And if you permit the Only Powerful and the All-Powerful God to speak to you in his Word, then this Lord of Hosts says to you: " 'Return to me,' says the Lord of Hosts, 'and I will return to you,' says the Lord of Hosts." The last emphasis triumphs! For what initially seemed to be true, namely, that everything was stacked against you and you were all alone and simply driven by the storms of life, has now been turned completely around. Now what is against us actually doesn't matter at all! It turns out to be for us, to belong to us, to have been designed to help us!

He determines all things. He is the only One among all others who can help you. You are delivered for all eternity. The Lord of Hosts is his name!

RENEW A STEADFAST SPIRIT IN MY INMOST PARTS!

Create in me a clean heart, O God. And renew a steadfast spirit in my inmost parts. Psalm 51:10[1]

Not everyone knows about so-called spiritual conflict. And those who actually are involved with struggles of the soul have experienced for many years already that all this talk about "spiritual heavyheartedness" actually amounts to nothing more than pious fanaticism.

This situation can be explained by the fact that in the natural order of things, there is no inherent conflict between Satan and our hearts. If we begin with the fact that we are friends of Satan, how could we ever be his enemies? No, the conflict arises because God does what he promised in Genesis 3:15 that he would do: "I will put enmity between ... " If the conflict between us and Satan existed naturally, then God would not have had to promise that he would put enmity between the two of us. So now we are by nature friends of this world and enemies of God. Consequently, it's obvious that a real miracle has to occur

---

1. In the Dutch versions and the Kuyper meditation this verse is Psalm 51:12.

within us to turn this situation completely around! That miracle has to create a situation in our lives in which we become enemies of Satan and friends of God!

And when it once gets to that point in our lives, then the battle, the spiritual conflict, the wrestling of the soul becomes automatic. Not immediately at full strength! Not with equal strength for everyone! Here much depends on you personally, on your personal circumstances, and on your past. But once it does get to that point, everyone experiences this struggle. And once the battle begins, it doesn't stop until we enter our eternal rest. This is a battle not first of all against people whose thinking is different from our own or against worldly society. These actually have nothing to do with this spiritual struggle. But this is a battle that is fought in our inmost parts. In the hidden recesses of our hearts! Deep inside our souls, where no other person can detect what's going on there! On the distant horizons of our innermost emotional lives, where we discover our inner evil and corruption! Where our secret sins are found on which the Lord shines the light of his presence! On those concealed compromises that likely even our closest and dearest friends here on earth don't know about!

The battle rages between the Holy Spirit and Satan over us. As a result, it is also a battle between our own faith fostered by the Holy Spirit and our own wicked heart, behind which Satan hunkers down.

The faith in us is a new, sacred power that has been placed within us. It clings tightly to the Messiah, strives toward God, and does not abandon the Holy Spirit. Accordingly, it regularly and squarely opposes all the wicked, sinful, and godless desires that arise within us. Believing and yearning are the sharp instruments with which this battle is conducted. Originally everything was captured in a single desire. Then the law said: "You shall not covet!" But that didn't stop you! On the contrary! Desiring agitated you all the more intensely, adding fuel to the fires burning in your desires. And that's where things stayed until God created faith within you. And that faith, as you know, was something different, something contrary, and something that militated against your desiring. And that's how spiritual struggle began.

The battle did not consist of putting a stop to desiring and beginning to believe. Then no spiritual struggle would have occurred at all. No, desire continued. It even became stronger than it had been. And that's precisely what caused your inner wrestling, surprised you about your soul, and produced your heavyheartedness.

Now it wasn't Satan who was doing the yearning, but you were doing the coveting. Now it wasn't the Holy Spirit who was doing the believing in and for you, but you were doing the believing. It's true, the coveting did not originate with you, but Satan worked it in you. But it's also true that the fruit that this bore was that you yourself, personally, in your self-centeredness became a covetous person. And at the same time, faith did not originate with you either. The Holy Spirit worked it in you. But it's also true that its fruit was that you yourself, personally, in the core of your being became a believing person. Don't vacillate on this! Hold on to it resolutely. You are a being who yearns and one who believes. It's from the two of these that your inner spiritual struggle arises. This is a conflict not at the place you work. Not in the circles of people where you live and interact! Not even in your emotions! No, it's a conflict that occurs in that most deeply hidden part of you, deep inside you, in what David in Psalm 51 calls his "inmost parts" when he says: "Renew a steadfast spirit in my inmost parts." It happens in what we often refer to as our "ego." That's where the mystery is concealed. That ego is dead, because Paul states: "It is no longer I that live." And yet, that ego enters into the most glorious life imaginable, for the same apostle also says: "What lives in me is that I live through faith in the Son of God!"

What proceeds from that inmost core of our egos is a dynamic influence on every dimension of our soul's existence: on our imagination, on our emotions, and on our will. And what this dynamic influence on our ego produces in our imagination, emotions, and will is our spirit. It is the spirit of our humanity within us.

That spirit participates in the conflict going on within our inner selves. In the mysterious vacillation between longing and believing two frequently opposing dynamics are at work on this spirit of ours. If faith is busy working in the core of our being, well then, the strength of faith exerts a holy power on our imagination, our emotions, and our will so that they become instruments of righteousness. By the same token, if the force of longing is at work in us, then the power of sin exerts a sinful force on our spirit, and our imagination, our emotions, and our will become instruments of unrighteousness.

If that back-and-forth dynamic is exerting pressure so that now faith is working more powerfully and then it almost completely disappears and a powerful, terrible sense of yearning prevails, then the spiritual battle within us is at its most intense.

But God's long-suffering and his mercies toward us are great. Through his Holy Spirit he diverts and renders ineffective the depth of these powerful, natural desires. He causes our faith to work powerfully and consistently for a time. But then a moment comes once again when the dynamic is reversed and the power of yearning unexpectedly overwhelms us. It is turned loose and prevails. Then it enlists those parts of our being in the service of unrighteousness.

Then our soul mourns deeply, sadly.

And those dimensions of the ego thought: "Now I've arrived! Things have gone very well for so many days and weeks. Finally, after all this time, God in his mercy has heard me and broken the power of sin." But watch out! That's when you lose everything once again!

How can that happen? How else than because when things were finally going so well, you stopped being watchful. It happened when you actually began imagining that your faith is a sure thing! You no longer took it hour by hour, bit by bit. You no longer thought of it as a gift from the loving hand of your Father in heaven.

And that had to be punished. That's the reason, the only reason, that the Lord God turned you loose! He didn't fail you. That wasn't the cause of letting go of you. But it was for sinning with respect to your believing that he, the Holy God, was punishing you.

But he who punishes is also vigilant. He sees to it that the wounds that he had to inflict on you do not cause you to bleed to death!

And thus, while the punishment has not yet ended, the dynamic that turns you back to him begins working again. Faith begins functioning once more. A deep, soul-wrenching sorrow develops. Clinging to the all-sufficient blood of the Lamb is restored. A sense of your poor, naked, empty-handed dependence and smallness returns. You become meek and lowly once more, and God renews his grace to you.

Now the soul lives again, and prays again. But now it still doesn't pray with the same strength or earnestness or forcefulness that it had when it prayed: "Lord, create in me a steadfast spirit."

That vacillation now becomes the source of deep sadness where God is concerned. Initially a person didn't have much interest in this swinging back and forth. But now it has become a curse on the soul.

Initially it had the attitude: "Oh, if God would only sanctify my spirit, I'll see to it that it stays steadfast!" But that has changed. Languishing in the awareness of its own impotence, it now prays: "O Lord God, I'm not able to do this by myself! In your mercy, create in me a steadfast spirit."

57
VOLUME II

THEY TOUCH THE APPLE OF HIS EYE!

For whoever touches you, touches the apple of his eye. Zechariah 2:8

The strength of the Lord's love for his people is so huge and overwhelming that neither men nor angels will ever be able to fathom its source. His love is as wide as the ocean. It surges up from a bottomless depth. It is an everlasting, divine, all-powerful, and irresistible love that rises far above anything we ever dreamed possible. The highest ideals of our cold, hard hearts can never comprehend it.

A person can hardly grasp, therefore, how anyone who has ever experienced something that magnificent can still live in fear and worry or be discouraged. They should be able to testify in quiet simplicity: "In his all-sufficient grace, he moved me from darkness to light. In his tender mercy, he carried me from death to life. In his amazing pity, he pulled me from the fire when I was already being consumed like a piece of kindling." So how could they still be afraid?

Oh, I completely understand how a child of God can be sifted like wheat. I know how the source of faith can become clogged and stop flowing. I recognize how a person's soul can as a result be at such loose ends that the warmth of Christ's presence disappears from their life and they think: "Am I really still a child of God? Was I ever one? Or was I just fooling myself?" I don't begrudge contented and composed folks their quiet peace one bit! But I do know that far and away most of God's dear people swing back and forth like a pendulum. Now they're at heaven's door, then they're on the threshold of hell!

Being a child of God is such a big thing, therefore, that one can hardly believe even for a moment that they really are one. But that's when the Holy Spirit testifies to them that they are. He convinces them of this despite themselves, and he makes it possible for them to believe it.

Have all those who think that of course they are God's treasured children ever reflected on how completely censurable and damnable they are in God's eyes? Have they ever considered that there is no shape or comeliness in them and no glory in their souls that God should desire them? Have they ever measured God's matchless mercy, evident in how he loves a soul whose stench of sin repulses him or loves a person who pushes him away?

You have to be humbled deeply, to the dust, to experience what being shown grace is all about. For that, you need a sense of your soul's complete abandonment that makes it virtually impossible to believe that you really are a child of God.

That's why faith just doesn't operate unless God the Holy Spirit makes the impossible possible. I understand very well that you can be in circumstances where faith simply isn't at work and when you're left without hope or courage. Everyone who knows how things go experiences this. But this struggle in the soul of a person who knows God is for the sole purpose of receiving a faith that works once more. "Lord, increase our faith!" continues to be the prayer of every Christian.

But what is not acceptable is what someone often finds to be true. On the one hand people say: "Oh sure! I really believe, and I know that I am a child of God." But then on the other hand they add: "But my soul is so tired and dull. I'm so afraid in my heart. Do you think God really hears me?"

This is not permissible!

That's why, if you find yourself in that condition, you have to let go of your anxiety over secondary things and focus on the main thing. You have to be shaken to the core of your being until you ask: "Lord, am I alive or dead?" Ask it so that the Holy Spirit might enter you again and you start believing again. It's about faith and only faith!

How could the Lord God not love his child?

They are "the apple of his eye," says the Holy Spirit in Scripture. "The Lord loves his own as the apple of his eye!" Why should they be afraid?

"His people are the Lord's portion. Jacob is his heritage. He found them in desert places. He guided them and instructed them. He protected them as the apple of his eye!"

His people plead their cause on the promise contained in Psalm 17. They offer its prayer freely, encouraged to do so by the Holy Spirit. "Lord, protect us as the apple of your eye." And in Zechariah's prophecy, Christ appears again in the form of the Angel of the Covenant who encourages them not to be afraid of those who persecute them. The One who avenges them is the Lord of Hosts. "Those who touch you, touch the apple of my eye."

Your eyeball is the most sensitive part of your body. It's where the most sensitive nerves come together. No speck of dust, tiny fiber, or little flake of anything whatever blown by the wind or in the air, however small and insignificant it may be, ever touches your eyeball but that you immediately feel it. You sense it so strongly that your eyelid closes instantly in order to cover and protect your threatened eyeball. This is an image that communicated well, especially in the land where this man of God was living. This is a country whose air is full of the smallest particles of dust and little insects. The only protection a tender eye has there is a supersensitive eyelid.

It pleased the Lord God to convey his tender mercy for you by using this image.

No speck of dust can touch the outer membrane of the apple of his eye, namely, you, without immediately causing his protective love to spring into action. That happens instantly, immediately, automatically, without his deliberation or a calculated act of his will. That's how sensitive my soul is for you and about you and on your behalf, says the Lord, O you who have been purchased by the blood of the Lamb. Nothing can touch you or hurt you that I won't feel at that very moment. And before you even turn your thought toward me, my love is already being extended to you as gently as that highly responsive eyelid. I want to deter all evil from ever touching you.

This is what I am doing for you, my chosen people, says the Lord your God. If there is anyone who actually touches you, whether that's a wicked human being or one of Satan's demons, I will immediately lift my strong arm against them. If they attempt to extinguish your life, I will use my strength to repel this destroyer and turn this murderer of souls away from you. "For whoever touches you, touches the apple of my eye!" Whoever attacks a child of God, assaults God himself.

What unspeakably wonderful assurance!

This shouldn't be misunderstood as if to say: "I am God's child. Therefore, whoever misunderstands me or does anything against me can expect the wrath of God." This would be a misuse of words designed to give soul-rousing comfort and would reflect the worst possible kind of pride. Rather than sustain a person, those words would destroy them.

For the sake of your soul's salvation, my brothers and sisters, if such arrogant thinking sometimes creeps into your head, banish it! Get rid of it. Such thinking will kill you!

No, the reassurances of our God are for the lowly of heart who are able to say: "Just let them afflict and abuse me. I deserve a thousand times worse than that!" Reassurance is for those who in feeling oppressed don't try to get even with others. They are sad because God is not honored and because they too have violated that honor. They think to themselves: "It's all over for me. I'm dying and beyond hope." But it's precisely in the middle of that raging oppression of the soul that they are allowed to drink in the stirring reassurance of their God.

"Whatever you're up against," says the Lord, the All-Merciful, remember that "I love you as the apple of my eye. Whoever dares to touch you touches the apple of my eye!"

58
VOLUME II

A CLEAN TURBAN
ON HIS HEAD

Then I said to him: "Let them put a clean turban on his head."
So they placed a clean turban on his head and they dressed
him while the angel of the Lord stood by. Zechariah 3:5

Almighty God had severely afflicted his people while they were in Babylon. In his righteousness, he had punished them for their stubbornness and shameful unfaithfulness. But the hour of deliverance finally arrived even under such oppressive circumstances, and the Lord moved the high priest Joshua along with the leader Zerubbabel to make the journey to Jerusalem and rebuild the nation's capital.

But notice that then Satan intervenes. "Are you going to let this Joshua rebuild your temple? This unclean, sinful Israelite and unfaithful priest?" And yes, Joshua was something of a loser! The Lord himself said of him that he was "a burning branch snatched from the flames!"

Nevertheless, or to say it better, precisely for that reason, the Angel of the Covenant stepped up as his advocate and defender. "May the Lord curse you, Satan," he answered. "You are a thousand times worse! Moreover, aren't you the one who seduced my servant Joshua and motivated him to sin?" And immediately appealing to what pleases God, the Messiah based his plea on God's electing work. "Joshua wasn't designated for this sacred mission because of his personal excellence, but because the Lord chose Jerusalem!"

But look, there stood the miserable, deeply fallen Joshua clothed in all his dirty, stained, sin-soiled robes! But he also stood there shining in an everlasting, sovereign good pleasure that has the power to justify even that ungodly person and to purify that impure individual from all his unrighteousness. That's the source of the command given to God's angels, who are his ministering servants sent to preserve the inheritance of those being saved. They were commanded to strip Joshua of his dirty clothing and to clothe him with the garments of substitutionary righteousness woven on the cross. This is the clothing so nicely depicted here as the change of clothing the rescued Joshua now wore like a suit of armor incapable of being penetrated by Satan's arrows.

What a glorious and deeply comforting picture this is of the struggles that each of us constantly experiences in our own souls! First there is Satan's agitation inciting us to sin. And when we fall, Satan accuses us at the throne of God. This is followed by the High Priest, whom we profess gloriously and imploringly interceding for us, and by Satan being forced to retreat. We are pulled from the flames like burning branches. Then, deeply ashamed, we stand in the presence of Jesus. A blessed command is issued from heaven that we once again be served with saving grace. Our garments of sin are stripped off. We are then dressed in the new clothing of everlasting righteousness.

Isn't this the soul-stirring, spiritually reassuring experience of all God's children?

But now notice something else. Look at what follows.

Now the Messiah assigns the task of putting a perfectly clean turban on the head of this ungodly individual who has now been made righteous. This has remarkable significance for our own souls. That turban was the priestly cap or turban. It completed his attire, signifying that he had been clothed with grace. It added honor to the investiture and signified the capstone of the priestly consecration.

Only when the angel of God pressed the priestly turban on the guilty head of Joshua did he become a priest once again. Joshua had been greatly harmed by Satan, but he was now wonderfully rescued by the Messiah. Only now could he, reconciled and properly attired as a priest, convey the message of salvation and reconciliation to others.

And isn't that how the endearing works of salvation and reconciliation are always crowned?

Oh, that people would only realize this and understand that they are always influencing others. You and all other believers along with you definitely need to realize the extent to which you are priests and priestesses of the Son of God.

As long as and to the extent that you do not, you are actually priests and priestesses in the service of Satan even if you don't realize that you are.

Everything that you do has an impact on others. Your words do. So does a glance from you. Your personality, your character, your actions, your conduct, your emotional disposition, and whatever you're passionate about all do. In short, whatever others see in you influences them. If what they see in you is glistening with everlasting light, like heavy dew that captures the morning sunlight, then good. Then the Light from Above shimmers from every bit of your soul for the benefit of your sisters and brothers.

But if not, then you destroy and corrupt and disrupt everything around you. Then you spread the kingdom of Satan. You may not do this consciously or intentionally. But this happens nevertheless because everything has influence. Everything drags its consequences along behind it. A thoughtless word landing on the ears of a sinful person can be just enough to lead to everlasting destruction.

Lord, guard my lips! This is the church's prayer. Do you ever pray it sincerely?

But recognizing the danger involved here is not enough. You can't stay neutral and unengaged in the kingdom of heaven. If you don't want to continue being one of Satan's priests, you have to become a priest of Jesus. You need to wear a clean turban on your head!

The question of whether or not you are already wearing one I put to you quietly, seriously. This is a sacred, intimate question. I don't ask it in order to drive you out onto the streets. I'm not saying: "Quick. Get out of your house and into the alleys and behind the hedges and look for those who are lost." To be sure, there are those on whom the Lord our God lays this sacred honor. But woe to us if we covet that extraordinary work but neglect our ordinary responsibilities inside our own homes. Then we're not honoring Jesus but dishonoring him. This amounts to hypocrisy. It's passivity. It's self-seeking. But it is not serving the Lord!

No, to be completely truthful, if you want to apply yourself to what is extraordinary, you first have to embrace what is ordinary with passion and love and do so in the service of the Lord. Then and only then can you do the other. First things first!

This is why a clean turban first needs to be set on your head by God's angels if you would become a priest of priestess along with all other believers. Then the Lord needs to anoint your soul every morning, put the words of his Spirit on your lips, and guide you along his sacred paths. Then you will be an influence that blesses your husband or wife, your aged father and dear mother, your brothers and sisters, your older and younger children, and—yes—even your servants, guests, visitors, employees, and, in short, everyone else in the circles in which you move.

This is your sacred calling! It's not just about always preaching in your own home! Your preaching must mostly be in the form of a quiet reverence for the Word and allowing that pure and wonderful Word to speak for itself! No, it's about being an example of reconciliation and demonstrating a wonderful peace. It's to allow everyone to see in you what is written here about Joshua, namely, that "The angel of the Lord stood alongside him!"

That, and only that, is the secret of a wholesome soul!

As long as Jesus is standing alongside you and is seen at your right hand, then you are a blessing even though you might not say a word!

On the other hand, when Jesus leaves you and your faith is at loose ends, you can no longer function as a priest or priestess. Then you simply lower yourself once more to serving as a slave of him who accuses you in God's presence.

TONGUES AS OF FIRE

And tongues as of fire were seen resting on each of them. Acts 2:3

Monarchs wear crowns and princesses diadems. Men recognize geniuses with wreaths and laurels. And even when people don't descend from royalty or aren't geniuses, they struggle and contend for what here on earth is regarded as honor, glamor, and acclaim. Everyone reaches for a crown in their own setting. They feel their heart beating faster when they are accorded an honor.

Is that desire sinful? Is it forbidden? Does a child of God have to reject that kind of desire for recognition?

Jesus' holy apostle answered that question with an emphatic "No! Not in the least!" He frankly acknowledged that even he, after he began serving Jesus, expected a crown. He struggled with longing for a crown. He was energized by the thought of one day receiving a crown. But here's the difference! He didn't expect to receive a crown in the present age but at the consummation. He wasn't looking for one that would be placed on his head by the hand of some friend but by that of the righteous Judge. He also knew that that crown wouldn't just make him an apparent king but an actual king. "He has made us kings and priests of God, his Father!"

Understand that there are two kinds of light, two kinds of luster, and two sorts of radiance.

The first kind of radiance comes from below. It is stoked by the fires of passion in the heart. It flares up by imagining what honor is like. It is represented by gleaming metals and precious gems. This is radiance conveyed by the creativity of artists and with a glamor that will shortly be dimmed and disappear. It amounts to the flickering of a display that first flares up, but then is extinguished.

But there is a different kind of radiance. It doesn't come from below, but from above, from the Father of Lights. It emanates from the halls of everlasting glory. It streams over us from the depths of the being of One who is unseen and whose glory outshines the sun and is undiminished by an eternity of eternities.

The person whose eyes are fixed on the radiance from below sees nothing of this higher radiance. For them, that light from above simply doesn't exist. They can't get excited about it because they take no notice of it.

Conversely, for someone who was ungodly but who now has been justified, the nobler radiance is now the object of their desire. For them, the harsh light of earthly glory fades and diminishes. They turn away from it. Its sheen no longer has any appeal for them. What once had seductive appeal is now only faded and dim.

Pay strict attention! This isn't just imaginary. It's real.

You can't think about Christ in all his glory with a dull, expressionless face. And when you imagine him, you think of him as flooded with a wreath of soft, holy light, radiant with a shine brighter than diamonds. This is no mere fantasy. Not at all! It's an outpouring of his inner being. It's his sacred personality coming to external expression. And the aroma of his anointing envelops him.

Holy Scripture tells us that even Moses, the mediator of the old covenant, had a countenance that glowed when he came down from the mountain. The people couldn't bear to look at his face, and he had to cover it when he tried to speak to them face-to-face.

From ancient times, therefore, whenever the church of Jesus Christ wanted to portray the patriarchs or martyrs as well as the prophets and apostles, it did so with a sacred halo around their faces. It wanted us to recognize in this way that these people were pure in heart. They had ascended the mountain of God's holiness and they mirrored the glory of the everlasting God in their faces.

Sensitive, pious, and godly men and women who shine as lights in the life of a congregation have also often given the impression of something more exalted shining in their eyes and of having a holier expression on their faces. They seemed to be like angels, messengers from heaven who never appear here on earth without that greater glory radiating from their clothing and flashing like lightning.

And when it pleases the Lord God once again to take one of our own, their entrance into their eternal rest after having fought the good fight here on earth can often be seen on their faces. On their deathbed, they are surrounded by that greater radiance. It's so obvious from their appearance that it makes every bystander jealous. They are delighted by it.

Even what happened on Pentecost was similar. Then the Holy Spirit descended, and tongues of fire were seen resting separately on every individual present. What happened on that occasion was nothing short of every believer there being on their own Mount Tabor.

On Tabor the Lord had received his crown. He had blazed in the light of heavenly glory. On Pentecost, the believers that collectively constituted the church were baptized with the same glory. As princes and monarchs, they had heavenly diadems of light placed on their heads because they desired no mere human wreath or crown bought by Jesus.

The church of Christ is diminished if the laurels distributed to her come merely from human hands. But she increases in spiritual power when earthly radiance disappears and tongues of fire are obvious on believers as radiant crowns of spiritual light.

The cross of Jesus is powerless and his atoning blood is ineffective when people kneel at the foot of the cross still adorned and honored by all the decorations, wreaths, and crowns conferred by their fellow sinners. But that cross becomes a source of blessing only when they kneel there having removed those laurels and crowns. The heavenly blood does its pervasive work only when they throw them down before it.

So, my brothers and sisters, what glistens for you? What makes you radiant? What shines for you and around you? Is it still an earthly radiance? Then tremble in your hearts. Because then you're still accepting human honor and glory. Then you can't really believe and you'll perish. Then you're surrounded by harsh, wild flickering. Then the dew drops of the everlasting tomorrow are not yet glistening on your face.

Would you like to have a Pentecost blessing today?

If so, then let the tongues as if of fire be evident on your head. Let the heavenly glory radiate from your face. That's not a harsh light but a gentle one. It doesn't just flicker but shines powerfully.

Those tongues of fire on every one of us should be the most glorious proclamation possible of God's tender mercies. They are a blessed foretaste of you dying bathed in the light of blessed glory. They are the Tabor of your deathbed, experienced before your exit to the heavenly Jerusalem through the dark gateway of death.

60
VOLUME II

HE HIMSELF KNEW
WHAT WAS IN A MAN

He did not need someone else's testimony about man,
because he himself knew what was in a man. John 2:25

Every individual is ready to share a mouthful of what they know about themselves, others, and human nature generally!

That's natural, because of all the creatures and topics with which we have any contact, human beings are the most important. That's just the nature of the case. We depend on other people. We live with other people. We work with them and contend with them. And we are human beings ourselves.

It's no wonder, then, that people both in former times and in our own era have been fixated on understanding humanity. They continue to praise and listen to the perceptive experts who have contributed most to our understanding of human nature. And yet the experts have contributed precious little to what in this world passes for an understanding of it.

What people mean by an understanding of human nature is usually and almost entirely reserved for the ability to explain someone else's character traits. This involves making sense of their appearance, conduct, and unusual habits. It means learning to recognize their weaknesses. It means understanding how others should take them in order to get the desired response from them. In other words, it means detecting the unique nature of their character and studying it so thoroughly that a person can predict how that person will react in any given situation. Knowledge of human nature, therefore, is exclusively designed to serve craftiness, manipulation, and a kind of judicious caution. It has only human objectives in mind. It proceeds from no other motive than to develop the skill to lead someone else around at the end of a leash.

But that's not the knowledge of human nature that the Word of God is interested in or that is praised as helpful for knowing the way of salvation.

No, the knowledge of human nature given to us by God is completely different. No one but God and his Word can teach us what it is. This understanding of human nature differs totally from the earthly, worldly knowledge of it in both essence and intent.

This divine knowledge of human nature doesn't ask in the first place about what is unique about this or that individual. It inquires about what all people have in common. It's not interested in certain features in their face, the natural qualities they possess, or their character traits. It focuses on their inner being, their existence, and the basis of that existence. It addresses their nature and disposition as human beings. It considers their demeanor and their spiritual relationship to God Eternal.

So it goes deeper, much deeper. It goes to the heart of the matter. It isn't designed for fostering a good self-image or stimulating a sense of self-worth. Rather, it undercuts them.

What's unique about you makes you interesting. That's what people talk about. People find this noteworthy and sometimes nice even when it might not be commendable. And this sort of interest on the part of others grows on you. You certainly don't merely dismiss that sort of self-understanding!

But a godly knowledge of human nature that gets to the bottom of things simply isn't interested in all those things that other people find remarkable and interesting. So when God's Word exposes what you are as a human being, it finds nothing, nothing at all, that's interesting. It only sees inner brokenness, disappointment, and failure.

The knowledge of human nature that the Word of God teaches us from beginning to end rejects all mirages, dreamy delusions, illusions, beautiful fantasies, or pretentious ideals that we may have formed about human nature. All these are one long stream of soap bubbles that burst, one by one right after one another. All that's left for us is a sense of human nature's shattered greatness; chaotic and desolate ruin; emotional embers cold on a hearth; a spring flowing with evil, fermenting, roiling works of the flesh.

"Flesh" you have to understand not in the sense of "flesh and blood." You have to understand "flesh" as the expression of your entire human personhood that should have been spiritual but that has become carnal. It is degenerate in body, soul, and spirit. It has been shattered and bastardized. It has deteriorated and is sinful to the core. This is true not just physically but with respect to the spiritual capacities of your reason, will, and emotions. It is so extensive that even your spiritual activities have become sinful, despite the fact that you may have labeled them as virtues and expressions of piety. Despite the labels, whatever proceeds from you even in the best form possible is grossly inflated. It reflects a proud heart and thinks more highly of yourself than you ought to think. It amounts to hypocrisy.

Look here! There are really only two kinds of people.

The first kind hears this all very clearly. They can make no objection to it. But they won't accept it! They contrive a system for finding evidence that human nature is not that way at all but is totally different.

These people are the wise of the present age.

But thank God, there is also another kind of people. They find it terrible to have to admit: "That's how I am. That's my situation. It truly describes me to a T!" Convinced of this by God's Word and the light of the Spirit, they still live like this. The result is that they fully concur that human nature is like this and that they are as well. So everywhere and in every way possible they oppose and resist the false hope that human beings are different and in the process of becoming better.

According to the world, they are fools.

But aren't these last ones the ones who really get it right?

They're the ones walking in the light. They're living in the light of God's face. And that light exposes what they themselves have become. They are the upright who acknowledge how it is with them. They escape the frightening necessity of always having to embellish or hide something about themselves.

They have been weaned from all disappointment, because they have understood what human nature involves and expect nothing from it. They have placed no hope in this creature. They have always thought and understood that this creature would produce even worse things than it already has.

They know nothing of the temptation to vanity, for in their eyes everything is disposable clothing. Only the work of the Spirit within them is work that can stand in the presence of God.

They are discerning and alert, and they live in this world with their eyes wide open. They see what's behind all its screens and curtains and coverings. They discern clearly what's churning and operating in the hearts of others and is at work in the background. That's how they avoid a great deal of strife and difficulty and set their eyes on the things that are above, in the New Jerusalem, whose Maker and Builder is God.

Finally, each morning, noon, and evening they feel empty if the Holy Spirit is absent from them. When he no longer lives and works in them, they feel like a lamp without oil, a tree devoid of sap, and a machine lacking the steam that drives it. They know only one power and one driving force within them. It is to believe. It is to be joined to the working, energizing power of the Holy Spirit in their souls.

We only add this yet. They are the ones who don't experience much struggle at all when their King calls them from this world of sinful human beings to that realm of blessed saints dwelling around the throne of God! That's because they know that there they will find human beings who are different, better, and glorified. They also know that there, around the throne of grace with other sanctified human beings, they will be like him who is seated there in his pure, holy human nature.

He is the only One among all others who already understood while here on earth what human nature is. He did so without knowing any sin himself.

A GOD WHO SHOWS HIS WRATH EVERY DAY

God is a righteous judge; he shows his wrath every day. Psalm 7:11[1]

You believe in the love of God, don't you? At least you confess that the Lord is "merciful and gracious, slow to anger and filled with loving-kindness." A deeper, more unfathomable pity than the tender compassion of your heavenly Father is unthinkable. And it's well that you, who are capable of only stammering your praise, stand amazed at such love and worship him for his compassionate pity.

But, dearly beloved, why are your hearts troubled when the church of Jesus Christ whispers to you—yes, even drums it into your conscience—that this sensitive God becomes angry and even shows his anger daily? When you hear that, why do you turn away, plug your ears, and even beg us to keep quiet about it?

Are you wrong in doing this?

You are deluding yourself if you think God's wrath diminishes something of his eternal love. Or that it limits to some extent his divine pity! Yes, that it

---

1. Psalm 7:12 in the Dutch versions.

even clashes with his mercy to some extent! But are you seeing this clearly? Is this really the case? Are you right about this?

Suppose that the Lord our God never got angry or didn't show his wrath on a daily basis. Would that in fact still make his tender love for you tender?

You imagine that God's anger is a bad thing and a stain on the robes of his sacred compassion. But aren't you misguided in this? Isn't it just the opposite? Isn't the wrath of God one of the most tender features of his loving-kindness? Isn't it the font and source of many precious realities for you and all his other people? Without God's anger, what would the world around you actually become? Now the wrath of God is burning daily as an almost irresistible force in the hard, callous consciences of the children of the present age. It acts like a cauterizing iron on their hearts that sears and shrivels for a time all the boils and abscesses and pustules that are ready to burst and spread their unhealthy filth who knows how far. God's anger working in the consciences of worldly people is like a bit in the muzzle of wickedness. It restrains evil so that it doesn't destroy you, sweep you along in its wake, and poison and corrupt the air around you too much.

God's anger shown every day is the mighty force at work in your own home. It keeps the unconverted members of your household in check. It restrains them by putting a divine foot on the lids of their hearts. This suppresses the ungodliness that would otherwise come to the surface.

God's anger is the guardian of your loved ones when you leave them at home alone or send them off a little way into the world. It protects them when you can't watch over them so closely, set boundaries for them, or discipline them any longer. That's when God's anger does this for you. It takes over where you left off. It is a blessing in the lives of your children who would otherwise be lost.

Moreover, even when you're present with your children, other members of your household, or your friends and when you earnestly admonish them to put an end to some evil or wicked activity, God's anger is at work. You yourself can't do anything about it, and your words are ineffective, unless at the same time God's wrath makes an impact on their hearts and disturbs them spiritually.

To take this a little deeper, suppose that on some occasion or other you became intensely angry over the wicked behavior of your dearest children. You had the satisfying experience of venting your anger in a tender, holy, earnest, and passionate way. Then weren't you able to thank God that he let you share his anger and use you as his instrument? His anger was expressed in yours and gave it a flaming, penetrating power!

But I ask you to think about yourself for a minute. Aren't you indebted to God's anger yourself? Should you overlook what you've been benefiting from for your entire life and what's been yours because of God's anger? Simply allow me to lay out that matter a little further for you.

As you look back on it and remember, you really consider it quite a blessing, don't you, that the part of your life that preceded your conversion was not all that terribly tarnished. You weren't all that humiliated or stained by your sinfulness. You understand perfectly well that you're not a hair's breadth better than someone else who's fallen deeply. You recognize that nevertheless you deserved to be lost for eternity. But looking back, you realize that for you it's been relatively less agonizing or grievous. That's because you were dealt with charitably. That in itself is a gift! So how do you explain that charity now? Was it a gift granted because you were so careful about not being corrupted or humiliated? Admit it, my brothers and sisters. Wasn't it because the wrath of God had made such a sharp impression on your soul and the souls of your caretakers? It was so unrelenting in its opposition to ungodliness that even though you wanted to take a swim in the river of unrighteousness, you didn't dare to jump in. In fact, you really couldn't!

That's the first point I ask you to think about. Here's the second.

During your conversion, wasn't God's anger at work just as strategically as his sacred mercy? Both were instruments he used. In fact, if the Lord had not used his anger in this connection, would you ever have been converted?

I know very well that there are many people who think that it was only the enticing sound of the King's invitation that attracted them, like the soft and cool evening breezes after a hot day. But isn't that a delusion and self-deception? Wasn't the soft, cool breeze preceded by an earthquake and the earthquake by a powerful wind? Would that enticing invitation ever have attracted you if it had not been preceded by restlessness, some disturbance, or a convulsion in your soul? Would you ever have broken with the world if God had not first raged against the world in your own heart? Didn't you feel something for God's law at the time? And does that law ever work without anger? Would you ever have known what divine compassion is, to briefly summarize, if your terrible carelessness had not first been hounded by a sense of God's wrath?

And now the third point.

The big event has now occurred in your life! Everlasting praise and honor be given to God for this! The Spirit testifies with your spirit that there is now an "Abba, Father" to whom you can appeal. And for the rest of your life your resounding song can be: "I was lost. I was lost. I was lost, but now I've been purchased by my Lord!"

But now it might be asked of your soul how you're going to conduct yourself in that new status. Are you finished with the world, or are you still in it? Have you gotten rid of your sin, or do you still struggle with it? Is the battle won, or do you wage it every day? Have you grasped this, or do you still strive to do so?

And what does the experience of God's most precious children teach you in this regard?

It teaches that from the very first days after their conversion they've been kept busy with unmasking Satan. It teaches that from the beginning Satan's henchmen have been deliberately aiming their poisoned arrows at their hearts. It teaches that the world, like an adulterous woman, has been working from the outset to tempt their souls. You can safely add that God's children have learned that from the time Christ first laid his hands on them they've known that they still carry around an ungodly heart in their chests. They know that their souls are graves filled with dry bones. Be sure of this: when an unconverted person is exposed to Satan's temptations for as much as one moment, they cave in and their fall is tremendous. It's not the same for a child of God, who comes through it triumphantly.

If this is how it is, therefore, let me simply ask this. Who is your helper in all this frightening conflict? What power is available to help a child of God get through it triumphantly? Just admit it! Isn't it God's anger?

This is the anger of God that allows you no rest. It's an anger that visits half-hearted efforts with lashes of reproach and self-criticism. It's a holy indignation that afflicts you so deep in your loins that you crumple with pain. And when Satan numbs you half asleep, it's an anger that pierces your heart so intensely that you're shocked awake. Your head snaps back, and wide-eyed, you immediately see that you've reached the point of offending your God with your terrible wickedness.

Do you really want to wish away that kind of anger from God? Do you really prefer love without such anger?

Wipe such unholy language off your lips, brothers and sisters. It's much better that you pray with all God's people: "O Lord, my Lord and my God, please let your anger continue to bless me. Show me your anger every day, every day that I still feel afflicted by sin."

POURED UNDILUTED!

If anyone worships the beast and his image ... that person
will also drink the wine of God's wrath that has been poured
undiluted into the cup of his fury. Revelation 14:9–10

When during that terrible future the final judgment will have arrived and the day of grace will have passed, the wine of God's wrath will be poured out undiluted. Every single creature, whether man or woman or angel, that has thirsted for what opposes the Lord Jesus and has chosen for Satan instead will then drink from that undiluted cup!

I emphasize undiluted!

Note well what's in that cup because for now, before the final judgment and in our present age, the wine of God's wrath is never served up for any creature without containing a measure of his mercy and long-suffering grace. Mixed in, that softens the drink.

The wine of God's wrath has so far never bubbled up undiluted in the chalice of suffering or in the cup of chastisement. We've never held that kind of cup in our hands. It has never touched our lips.

And however frightened our spirits may have sometimes been, and also however much our harried and relentlessly hounded souls, trembling and frightened, may have hidden in the crevices of the rock, they have never tasted anything more than a delicate mixture of God's sacred anger. Just a few drops of his flaming fury, that's all it was! But at the same time they were flushed with quaffing full drafts of his divine mercy!

So the idea of God's undiluted wine that's coming makes us appreciate his tender, loving mercies now and makes us feel very guilty when we complain about today's barbs.

It's our own twisted reflection on them that makes it so hard for us to believe in God's pity on us. God guarantees that difficulty because his anger burns so fiercely in his afflictions visited on nations, the distresses experienced by our friends, and the wounds suffered by our own hearts.

In fact, the cloud of God's holy displeasure is often so dark for us that any semblance of his divine being seems to go into eclipse. Then we have to force our souls still to cry out, "Abba Father."

It's almost as though the Lord God in his power falls on us like a lion does on its prey, tearing it to pieces. That gives rise to the question "Is there no compassion at all with God?"

Still worse, sometimes it happens that the distresses and obstacles experienced from all sides are accompanied by a deadly emotional exhaustion, a frightful sense of spiritual abandonment, and a pronounced and paralyzing inner terror. Then we imagine that all of God's waves and billows come crashing over us. That's when our souls scream: "I can't stand this anymore!" That's also when a child of God realizes that they have finally hit bottom in an extraordinarily sinful situation. That's when they complain to others about seeking God and, wringing their hands, ask even the angels: "Has God forgotten to be gracious? Will he never show his mercy again? Has he in his anger cut off all compassion?"

But while our souls were guilty of such a God-forsaken notion and were in open rebellion against the Father of All Mercy, and while we obsessed about this or that affliction and groused with this or that complaint against the Almighty, what was our God doing?

What was our God doing then?

He was simply mixing something into all our afflictions that assured that we would not be totally consumed by them, as we would have been if he had left our cup undiluted. He was busy mixing into the cup of his wrath the water of his compassion. Meanwhile, we troubled ourselves with our weak and spineless complaining.

He was not the one who stirred up wrath. You and I did that all by ourselves through our sinning. So just think about this. While this was going on and the wrath we're talking about was deservedly moving closer toward us, our Father in heaven was busy with something else. The full wrath would have hardened us, flamed higher, and afflicted us even more intensely than it has. But, filled with divine compassion and tender patience, God was tempering every drop of that wrath by blending his mercy into it. That's how he softened it with his loving consolation.

You suppose that God shows anger so that you'll feel your pain more deeply. But God's idea is just the opposite. While you see his anger as a cloud of dust stirred up by your sinning and feel like it's choking you, God in his tender mercy makes it bearable so that you don't suffocate from it.

Our guilt is that we refused to acknowledge our sins, as though we were cut off and lying in a deep pit without any water. And when God who is holy confronted us with them, we pushed them aside. We refused to reflect on them deeply or face their complete lack of holiness. That explains why we don't experience an inner sense of condemnation. That's also why we don't have a sense of God's anger as a decay-preventing antiseptic designed to fight off the rot that lies on the soul like gangrene and needs to be stopped and cut out.

Unholy and superficial, we deflect our guilt onto our faithful Father. We claim that he is too harsh and lacking in compassion. We claim that his burning anger is too severe.

And so it comes down to this. We have no appreciation any longer for God's tender mercy. Therefore, precisely therefore—mark my words on this and test them in your soul—therefore, we forfeit any comfort from our God.

Still diluted for now! That thought casts a soft, quiet sheen on this world's suffering as well as on the suffering of God's children. Now we are still dealing with the white horse of Zechariah's vision! The black horse will follow! Even here we experience a wrath that simply drips down without being poured out in heavy streams. But into every one of those drops divine mercy is mixed as well as an antidote of most tender compassion.

But even that tempered mixture will eventually come to an end.

The hour is coming when mercy will no longer boast about tempering judgment.

Then in that terrible hour when the eternal destiny of all people will commence, the mixture of which we are speaking will end. Then no stream of mercy will be poured into the cup of wrath any longer. Then the wine of God's wrath will be undiluted!

Today people often speak about the terrible eternal condition that we call "hell." They say, "People shouldn't talk about that dreadful state of affairs. Terror doesn't compel men and women to turn to God!"

That's very true. Hiding death and hell behind a veil definitely doesn't do anything for dead wood, and green wood is simply too supple for it to have any effect.

But even though we are not in favor of hiding death and hell behind curtains, is it the most advisable thing to do to deal with hell's awful reality the way most preachers and believers do today? Is it really advisable to just keep quiet on the topic?

Our thought on the matter is that we should talk about it. We should think about it seriously. And we should talk about it in a timely fashion. This would be closest in spirit to the One who not infrequently—and let's be honest about this—talked about the worm that never dies and about the fire that never goes out.

That's the reason why these verses in Revelation consider with such profound seriousness the horrible, inexpressible oppressiveness that will be experienced in hell.

The most frightful, terrible suffering that has ever been experienced on earth, Gethsemane excepted, has always been mixed with mercy.

But when the hour comes when the realities of hell commence, the time of undiluted wrath will have arrived.

My dear sisters and brothers, may God be gracious to our souls and the souls of our children!

63
VOLUME II

DO NOT NEGLECT THE WORK OF YOUR HANDS

The Lord will complete what he began with me. Your mercy, O Lord, is everlasting. Do not neglect the work of your hands. Psalm 138:8

Nothing weighs on hearts or crushes and haunts us more than our weakness with respect to the work of our hands.

A farmer experiences this when he plows and harrows, sows and weeds, but then can do nothing at all about the growth. In order to reap a good harvest, he is deeply dependent on the rain that falls and the sun that shines on his field.

It requires faith and courage to plant a stand of oak trees. That's because you understand when you place acorns in the soil that they germinate very slowly and grow even more slowly! You don't even think that you yourself will ever enjoy a harvest from what you've planted.

The construction of huge cathedrals like those of Cologne or Strasbourg that went on for centuries wasn't undertaken by a generation so egocentric that in considering the success of their immediate task they thought their work was finished.

That same sense is of extended time is felt even more strongly by everyone who devotes themselves to the moral work of building the invisible temple of the Lord.

Simply consider the basic scope of rearing your children. How often don't you face this with a sense of powerlessness and embarrassment? Someone else puts much less of their best effort into this than you do. They hardly ever complain about it. They virtually permit their children to grow up wild, but amazingly they turn out well. But your children, on the other hand, for whom you pray every morning and every evening, seem so much less loving and appear to have almost no fear of the Lord whatsoever. They weigh heavily on your heart. You cherish them as the apple of your eye. You nurture them in the fear of the Lord with the greatest care. Despite this, they arouse your growing concern. But you persist and certainly never even think of letting go of them! You don't know why you react this way, but you don't ask about it. You can't do anything else. Nor do you want to! In fact, you must not. That quiet nurturing of your offspring is automatic and unconstrained.

Or have a look at our Christian schools. Isn't it discouraging when you sometimes see that a generation being nurtured in a secular school begins to inquire about God once again, while the results in our own schools can be so contrary? Yet, isn't it the case that even then you don't stop giving sacrificially for the school building? And you continue to testify, despite negative results, that it's only a school based on the Bible that's strong enough to protect our people.

And it's true that this is exactly how it goes with all spiritual effort in the kingdom of God. In one congregation after another, an invasion of unbelief and modernistic preaching has swept away the old mustiness. It has also created spiritual ferment and a remarkable return to a lively faith. Meanwhile, elsewhere congregations blessed with the steady preaching of the Word unfortunately simply sleep through it and grow deaf to it. Nevertheless, you don't hesitate for a moment to continue to preach the Word or battle unbelief.

Take whatever field of endeavor you like. It could be Sunday schools, young people's groups, or missions to people of other faiths, to Jews, or to merely nominal Christians. It could be attempts to restore the state's involvement with the church or struggles to have the country's government submit to the power of the Lord. But you'd always give up in discouragement if you relied only on yourself. You would as well if you only considered your weakness, continual disappointment, and meager results. But that's not what you do. You keep on working. Rather than complain about your own sluggishness, you always work with renewed courage, stronger energy, and holier zeal!

This even happens, doesn't it, when in the depths of your soul you're engaged in a restless struggle to find greater peace, inner fellowship with the Lord, and more evidence of the power of the Spirit? It happens when these are even further diminished and you raise the sad complaint that you lack spirituality but feel spiritual depression and emptiness. In times like those, you never think about the state of your soul so that you abandon inner struggle or concede the battle to Satan. Rather, in some mysterious way that you can't explain, you then experience a higher, holier, and more exalted condition in your heart—definitely not with respect to your always-accusing awareness, but definitely with respect to your standing with God.

So how do you explain such an unusual experience in the context of human effort?

How do you explain always swimming against the stream like this and still prevailing? Facing so much discouragement but always maintaining courage? Confronting what's against all odds but never giving up and continuing to plant acorns when you will never see the greening of the treetops?

My good reader, you only explain it in terms of faith!

It's faith that everything is exactly the opposite from what it seems to be! It's faith that it's not really the person doing the work but that the real Worker involved is the Lord God. It's faith that they are a much smaller and less significant instrument in the almighty hand of God at work than the chisel is in the hand of a sculptor.

This is the faith that all of our working and striving and effort is of no use and produces nothing unless it is guided by inspiration from above. It reflects holy intuition. It proceeds blindfolded, yet it is guided unnoticed by our God with invisible ties to his eternal wisdom and tender love.

Realize this! Only a person who has this disposition of soul quietly continues working without asking about the outcome. Such a person realizes: "The real worker is actually the Lord my God. It's not I who is raising my children, but God is doing it. It's not I who is doing the teaching at school, but the Lord is the educator. It's not I preaching, but the Lord himself causes his Word to go forth. It's not I who harbor tender desires for my people, but the Lord is the one keeping watch over them."

Then, if people are aware of this, the work is genuine. For God endures forever, and even if we sink away and disappear, his work always goes on. Then it doesn't really matter whether or not I see the results with my children if the Lord attends to them after I die. Then my work of bringing up my children is not in vain as long as it pleases God to cause the seed that I have sown to ripen in the next generation.

With that kind of faith, no effort is ever in vain. Then every endeavor comes to fruition quietly and peacefully. In that context, people pay attention to years rather than to days and to centuries rather than to years. Then at heart they consider people and conditions and momentary opportunities in terms of principles. Or, if you prefer, they see them in terms of him who is the Source of all things and who has the power to bring all things to completion.

A generation that lacks this kind of faith and this sense of eternity lives fast. Its work is driven at a feverish pitch. In just a few years, it magically causes half a city to appear on what was only bare ground. But you can push its houses over with your bare hands. On the other hand, the generation in which the work of God is going on is involved in building monuments that endure for ages. They reflect the praise and fame of their Chief Builder dwelling in the heavens, not that of the workers here on earth.

A sinner living without this kind of glorious faith struts around on the peak of their roof and in their pride exclaims: "Is this not the proud Babylon that I have built?" But for the sinner who is permitted to stand in blessed faith and does not ask about the outcome but keeps on working quietly in the service of their God, it is otherwise. They labor on behalf of their home, their country, and industriously for their school and the church of Christ. They always find strength and comfort in praying the prayer that was on the lips of David: "Lord, not my work, but your work be done. Complete the work of your hands."

64
VOLUME II

THIS PEOPLE SAYS, "THE TIME HAS NOT YET COME"

This people says, "The time has not yet come, the time for building the Lord's house." ... But is it time for you to be living in your own paneled houses, while this house lies in ruins? Haggai 1:2, 4

See to it that your soul isn't misleading or that you're not misled by the seemingly pious language of others.

Jerusalem was living in pain. The house of the Lord lay in ruins. People were bad-mouthing him. The sacred book that in his tender mercy he had given his wayward children they despised and defiled. In fact, things had gotten so despicable when God in his holiness surveyed them, that hardly one of his children burned with the anger of Elijah and, looking around, wondered whether there was anyone who would stand with them in condemning the devastation of God's house.

But that fire had been smothered.

It was extinguished by the expedient advice of knowledgeable people who urged him to keep such unholy fire off God's altar. They advised them not to rely on his own strength but simply to leave things to the work of Lord. And if that fire burning in him still threw off sparks, the last trace of warmth was cooled by quoting that sure word of the Lord: "Not by might or by power, but it will happen by the work of my Spirit."

The situation was this. Those sage and wise men who extinguished the fire of enthusiasm in young zealots had felt the same urge burning in their own hearts when they were young. But they had lacked the courage to be consumed by it. They didn't find the energy to act on it. So they became disobedient to that inner, holy urge. They couldn't stand it that the same fire was now burning in others. Their consciences were reproaching them!

What didn't work out for them mustn't be allowed to succeed with others. Because they were now too old to do anything about it, they thought the time had passed to honor God in this way. This is how they rationalized their own lack of spiritual vitality. This is, as a rule, how they wanted to construe their own lack of energy in dealing with others. Finally, it's how they found unholy delight in their determination to put a stumbling block in the path of others, despite all their pious blather.

What an unsettling situation!

God Almighty definitely loves his house! He is jealous about the honor of what is holy to him. And as long as the people of God were not energized by holy zeal for rebuilding his house, his full blessings would not be poured out on them. Until then, his curse would rest on all their endeavors.

It can be properly said that all renewal in an unredeemed situation needs to proceed from being deeply humbled, having a thoroughgoing sense of guilt, and being prostrated before our God with a broken spirit. We know of no other way of salvation than one that begins by a person completely humbling himself before our thrice-holy God.

But what we can't accept spiritually or identify with is when we think we are truly, deeply humbling ourselves when we do not straightforwardly confess our guilt for our lack of love for God Everlasting and our lack of zeal for his name. That's why every confession of guilt that is honest and has integrity absolutely must lead to striving seriously for better things. This is true not only with respect to our own souls and the spiritual welfare of our own homes. It's also true especially with respect to God's honor and the improved condition of the Lord's house.

Unless this is true, we will receive material things, to be sure. But as the Holy Spirit puts it in the words of Haggai, we receive them "in a sack with holes in it!" We've gained and amassed them. But they don't last. No blessings are attached to them.

You're searching for many things, the Lord tells us reprovingly, but behold, you're receiving very little. So when you bring it home, I breathe judgment on it. Why? Because my own house lies in ruins, says the Lord of Hosts, and because each one of you works on behalf of his own home!

This constitutes our own deep sinfulness.

When the talk is about paying attention to our personal affairs, to improving our own situation, and to building our own homes, these same sage, pious, wise leaders don't have any counsel about all this pious display and passive acceptance. But they become much too quick tempered and agitated when you admonish them to be more patient materially. They grumble when you say: "Seek first the kingdom of God and his righteousness, and all these things will be given to you!" Dissatisfied and unsettled by the Lord's deeply serious admonitions, they tell you with intense animation that "we still have to do what our hands require us to do!" "We may never sin by trusting in the Lord with a false sense of passivity," they say. "The use of means has also been ordained by him in whom all our confidence rests," they add.

Do you sense how profane such arid reasoning really is?

When it involves their own house, people know how to quickly and effectively, eloquently and persuasively defend themselves. But when it applies to God's house, they reveal the sinful attitude of imposing exactly the same arid reasoning on others as irrefutable proof of their position.

In and of itself that is shocking and terrible enough. But even worse is the spiritual offense people give by distorting God's holy Word when they know better. They continue living in their opposition to it, all the while trying to give their passivity the appearance of piety.

The saying found in Zechariah 4:6 is often cited: "Not by power or by might, but it will happen by my Spirit." But that certainly does not mean that people should just sit still and that things will happen by some divine miracle, apart from human effort. Just the opposite! It means that Joshua and Zerubbabel as two human beings would be the two instruments in the hands of the Lord. It means that their courage and leadership and their energy and passion for the sacred things of God would overcome the desecration.

The saying "Not by power or by might, but by my Spirit" is derived from the Lord's prophets with respect to Judah's return from captivity. And what was the spiritual condition of the returning people? Were they overly zealous? Did they demonstrate an excess of spiritual determination? Did the zealots among them have to be calmed down?

Quite the opposite! They demonstrated dullness, listlessness, and a sinful indifference worthy of punishment. And in those days, they hid behind this set of sinful excuses: "The time will certainly come when we have to put our hands to the plow. The time will arrive when we will have to turn our efforts to rebuilding. But now is not the time; now is the time for waiting!" That's when the Holy Spirit agitated the seer Haggai, who in the name of the Lord stated with piercing bitterness: "O people of Jehovah, you say 'It's still not time, the time has not yet come for the house of the Lord to be rebuilt!' But, I say to you in the name of Jehovah: 'The Lord also asks whether it is time for you to be living, then, in your paneled houses when for all this time my house has been lying in ruins?' Therefore, he is putting you under a curse and is withholding his blessing from you because 'you allow my house to lie in ruins, while you walk in and out of your own houses every day.' "

And that's our own situation as well: people will turn things around however they wish!

"This has to be looked at carefully!"

"Our own effort is useless; the Lord has to accomplish it by his Spirit!"

"The time will definitely come, but now the time is not right!"

Meanwhile, people appeal to doctors and medicines for help, so that they won't consider carefully whether they are sick.

Meanwhile, people work by day and even trouble themselves at night in building their own houses in the Lord's strength.

Meanwhile, out of self-interest people put their hand to the plow rather too late than too early.

This is exactly how you're sinning, O you pious, clever people who smother Elijah's fervor! You don't deal with your own houses the way you say you do. And meanwhile you don't do a lick of work on the house of the Lord.

Haggai is God's witness! In our day as well as his own!

He is testifying against you!

65
VOLUME II

MAY LOVE BE MULTIPLIED TO YOU

May mercy, peace, and love be multiplied to you. Jude 2

Is there anything that pours more sheer joy into the soul than the blessed, glorious sense of loving? Not loving in that forced, imagined sense that people feel compelled to express in their enthusiasm. Nor that display of loving that is so restless that it's always looking for some new altar on which to sacrifice itself. No, we're talking about that intimate, deep, tender, and genuine loving that is too full for words but that completely overwhelms the soul. It's loving that drives us to our knees in prayer. It produces an unspeakable, indescribable sense of joy, glorious bliss, and quiet amazement in us. It is loving captured in that one pregnant exclamation "I love God!"

"I love God!" is not something we say to let it be known that we are so pious and good-hearted, and that we want to favor our glorious and holy God with our love. It's not intended to say: "I once hated God in my heart, but now that I've been converted, that hatred has been replaced with love." Even less does it convey the cool judgment: "God is so great, so glorious, so completely the essence of love itself, that it's only logical to show God my love for him." Taken in any of these senses, "I love God!" is little more than a lie on our lips. I'm only hiding our own sinful pride and arrogance behind such expressions.

No, "I love God!" expresses the conviction of our heart when we have been powerfully, completely mastered, despite ourselves, by our love for this

Ever-Blessed Being. Only then is it authentic. Then it presses on us internally with such urgency that we can't hold it in. Then we become lovesick over the God of all mercy. Then it's fruitless for us to second-guess or to explain away how suddenly, unexpectedly, and overwhelmingly this sense of love for the Lord entered our cold, calculating hearts.

This is the pinnacle of blessedness that we can experience here on earth! Then we ask for nothing more. Then we have no more complaints. We are so focused, attentive, and dedicated to this gracious God that no sin or problem can ever separate us from him again. None can cause that tender, all-consuming, blessed love ever to slip from our souls once more. Now that they have been warmed by it, none of them can cause our souls' ardor to ever cool again. Now that our souls have been made alive, none can make them revert to being stone-cold. Oh, may we be so favored that no sin or problem prevents us from living in fellowship with him or from always being near to God. May that shameless, enrapturing love for our Father in heaven remain unbroken. May it satisfy us in ever-fuller measure!

But the Lord hardly ever grants those kinds of intense longings in his children.

When you ask why, you get no answer.

It's simply enough for you to know, either from Scripture or from the spiritual experience of the Lord's people, that he doesn't always give you that indescribably blessed love in the same sustained, complete measure.

It's undeniable that a few devout folks and sometimes rarely even a lone minister have been graciously favored with an infusion of that kind of tender love. This happened especially in the calmer days of a bygone era and in very unusual and amazing ways. But such "greatly sanctified" believers, as our faithful catechism calls these members of Christ's body crowned with an exceptional measure of grace, are a rare exception. They are not the rule. And not a single soul here on earth has ever achieved an uninterrupted fellowship of love with our fully blessed God.

Our hearts, our standing with God, and the standing of the entire church of Jesus is not even close! Everything possible militates against the kind of tender, sensitive love involved here.

But suppose once that for a few days or weeks you were to be favored with such a wonderful experience. Then Satan would immediately see to it that what happened to Job in ancient times would also happen to you. The difference between the actually sinful condition of your heart and the warm love that the Holy Spirit poured into you would be so lamentably dismal that you'd immediately lose part of that blessed love. Have you ever considered "how exceptionally great his power would have to be toward those that believe" to instill this blessed love into hearts as cold as ours? Even for a moment? In spite of Satan's influence?

It seems so obvious what this would take! And yet, who can calculate what an exertion of power this would require of divine compassion?

The church has slid so far from the faith of the apostles!

It occurs to us as being pretty obvious that all those converted to God experience his peace and mercy. Naturally, we never think about haggling about the adequacy of the completed work of the Lord. But to understand that it has been completed and to personally experience the grace, peace, mercy, and love that that affords is something else again. Jesus' holy apostles definitely realized this. That's the reason that they worked the hardest at the beginning of the church's life in Christ, and that they never addressed God's people without first praying that the experience of God's grace, peace, and mercy might be multiplied among them. They regarded these people as lying before them like parched fields and they prayed that the gentle drops of peace and salvation might fall on them. And when some serpent slithered into the bosom of the church and spewed its poison all around, Jude knew that those who were being tossed this way and that and being vexed in their hearts needed deeper grace and peace. That's why he included in his letter the prayer "May mercy, peace and love be multiplied to you!"

And now, is there any petition that the people of the Lord can pray in our own heart-wrenching days more than to implore God to taste his love more fully and richly? It's as though the refreshingly cool breezes have stopped blowing. Everything has gotten so cold and overcast in the courts of the Lord. You hear so little about the blessings of salvation anymore. You see even less spiritual fruit quietly ripening.

An active love that wants to bless may still be found. A professed love that wants to inspire is still present. But that tender, mystical, deeply private love that only the Holy Spirit can infuse into our souls, where is it still known?

The church still does a lot for God. It still talks a lot about God. But when does he himself come to us, he who alone can instill into our hearts a fully blessed love for him?

And yet, beloved, let no one deceive themselves! Without ever having experienced that love at some time, a person is not his child. Understand clearly, we're not saying: "who does not have that love and has never tasted it." That would only drive many souls to despair. No, but this is what we're saying: whoever does not now taste that love and is truly a child of God must now learn how to experience it. We assert that no one may think: "This is reserved for a select few who have received grace, but not for an ordinary child of God!" Let this be understood: to be a child of God is not ordinary. Rather, it's so indescribably amazing and glorious that you're not allowed to live with a cold, unloving heart. You're not permitted to experience peace if you live devoid of this love. Rather, to live with yourself personally, you first have to experience, by this greater grace, the sweet taste of such secret, deeply private love.

AND THE GOD OF PEACE WILL HIMSELF SANCTIFY YOU COMPLETELY

Refrain from all evil. And the God of peace will himself sanctify you completely. And your upright spirit and soul and body will be completely preserved, without blemish, at the coming of our Lord Jesus Christ. He who calls you is faithful, and he will do this. 1 Thessalonians 5:22–24

Is there any one prayer in our book of songs based on the Psalms that rises from the heart with as much intense feeling as the closing petition of Psalm 130?

> On hearing their fervent plea,
>> He will make all Israel free
> From their wicked misery.
>> This he will do as well for me![1]

---

1. This is the second half of the fourth stanza of the rhymed versification of Psalm 130 as found in the 1774 Dutch Reformed Psalm book. This portion is based on Psalm 130:8 and in Dutch reads:

Note especially the two connected petitions here. There's the prayer that God will not allow "me" to be overwhelmed by the battle with Satan. But there's also the related request that in his grace God will take pity on all those others trapped in their own frightening struggle.

Test your own soul accordingly. A child of God is not permitted to be self-centered, even when wrestling with their own unrighteousness. That's because a child of God is a loving being, and in the tenderness of their love they must be attentive to their brothers and sisters who are struggling with their own sinfulness. Their personal struggle with the sin that continuously surrounds them and frequently tempts them is not isolated. Satan is waging a single battle against all of God's children. That's the very reason that a person must reach out in tender compassion and deep sympathy to the many others who are struggling like they are. They must do so knowing the pain they are suffering in their own soul and understanding how ashamed and powerless and deadly oppressed they themselves feel in their own struggle. They realize that others are burdened by the same suffering they endure.

Despite our own sinfulness, we experience this sort of tender love. The psalm's petition says so incredibly much. He will set Israel free from their unrighteousness, and "this he will do as well for me!"

He does this! He has to do it. Only he can do it. Only he, God Almighty! For what can resist this detestably cunning, gigantically strong, virtually irresistible power of sin? What can our own hearts possibly do to resist it? Our own hearts have even consistently been Satan's partners in sin. When tested, they prove to be so weak, stripped of all strength, amount to nothing at all, and seemingly incapable of any good.

No, he has to do it. And that's why we pour out our souls in this prayer. It's an intense, intimate, almost heart-wrenching prayer. It's not just a prayer that sounds more like mumbling, but it's one that crashes the gates of heaven in our dreadful fright and forces its way to the throne of grace. If imaginable, it imposes itself with our tears of pain and sorrow on the God of mercy and compassion. It appeals to his heart of everlasting love.

And after that prayer comes a blessed response. I purposely don't say "through" or "because of," but "after" and "upon." How? In what form? This is

---

Hij maakt op hun gebeden
Gansch Israël eens vrij
Van ongerechtigheden;
Zoo doe Hij ook aan mij!

how: an enmity is set deep within our hearts. And when God's divine enmity is placed within us, then we've arrived.

What was the source of our misery? What caused our weakness and shame? It was this: that we experience no enmity and no bitter anger in our hearts against sin. We contend with sin, to be sure. But we do it like a young woman who resists the fondling of a young man in a way that really permits him to do what he's doing. So we really do contend, but not meaningfully. We do so half-heartedly! Not intensely! Without any power!

And only God can change that. Then we notice that enmity has arrived. It's enmity against sin. It's enmity always paired with and born out of love for God and for Jesus Christ, as well as for all his people and for his law.

So then what do we do?

Then we begin contesting our so-called sins of the heart. Far be it from us that we deny that there are such things as sins of the heart! Sin can take thousands of shapes and forms. Since every person is unique, it's obvious that sin will manifest itself more strongly in one person in this form and more strongly in another form in someone else. It's also natural that through a long life of sinning one form of sin will have developed more strongly in a person than some other form. Just as our right hand is usually stronger because we use it more often, so our dominant character sins are a stronger force for evil in our lives simply because we have fallen into them more often.

But be careful now, if you find that God has put the kind of enmity we're talking about into your heart. Don't start thinking: "Oh, if I simply contest this one main sin of my heart, repress it, and triumph over it, then I'll have arrived!" Don't do it.

Remember that our spiritual fathers often identified as a main feature of being a child of God that they realize that they only manifest a small part of perfect obedience. They always sense at work within them a strong desire and love for living not just according to some of God's commandments but according to all of them. That's the reason why the holy apostle prayed with such emphasis on behalf of believers: "May the God of peace sanctify you completely," that is, in every part of your existence. Not just in one dimension of your spiritual life, but in every dimension simultaneously! And then in the sense that you will contest and overcome all sins of the spirit, soul, and body at the same time! And may it be that they would all be seared out of you!

He was in fact praying that every struggling soul would pay attention to this.

Look, Satan's not at all opposed to having you lament your sins of the heart with hot tears for a while, or for that matter to earnestly resist them.

He understands the strategy of pulling back for a period of time. He simply uses your resistance to that one sin to create a false sense of self-satisfaction in your heart. That false sense becomes the pervasive leaven of sin slowly working within you. It feeds sin until it piles up a mountain of infidelity, self-ishness, self-righteousness, and impiety. Then that sin of the heart that has run for cover sees its chance and reemerges with heightened power to attack you, dominate you, and overwhelm you with despair. That's when it seems as if God is faithless and that your soul is beyond saving.

No, sin is never put to death by striving against one isolated kind of sin! That's not a valid position to take!

You might obstruct mainly the one sin that tempts you most. But to God in his holiness all your other sins are equally disgusting. So you should never fight against any one sin because it is a hindrance to you but because it is an obstruction in the sight of your holy God.

The only way of escape is that you immediately and without delay denounce your entire situation before God as soon as that one sin that brought you to repentance breaks out again in its overwhelming power. You open up about all the wounds in your soul without hesitating or wavering. You lay out all your sins in his holy presence, to their very foundation in your soul. You even expose the cornerstone on which that foundation rests. You directly expose how your sin is rooted in your unbelief, in your lack of love, in gratifying your-self, in being mired in what is merely visible, in your blindness to the glories of heaven, and in your deafness to the Word of God.

Then what's going to happen to that poisonous plant of the bosom sin rooted in your heart? Simply this! It's going to stop being fed. No life-giving sap will flow into it and nourish it any longer. Following the patterns established by God, it's going to shrivel and ultimately die.

That definitely is not going to happen if you have to sanctify yourself. For how a powerless force can ever achieve that in its powerlessness is more irra-tional than irrationality itself!

But whoever understands this and confesses and believes it will experi-ence this: He is doing it! God is sanctifying me! Paralyzing fear just doesn't exist for such a person. They do nothing apart from the Spirit's leading. The Spirit inspires them from the Word by holding before them that glorious, soul-inspiring promise: "He who calls you is faithful, and he will do it!"

GET BEHIND ME, SATAN!

Get behind me, Satan. You are not concerned about what
matters to God, but what matters to people. Mark 8:33

What do we understand at all about the powerful role that Satan plays in our lives? About the influence that he has on us? About the net he stretches across our path each evening or the pit he digs to trap us every morning? He and his angels laugh when we get tangled in his net or fall into his pit!

Our holy, glorious Savior had a great deal to do with Satan while he was here on earth. He met Satan everywhere. He often pointed out his obstacles. He battled Satan. He resisted him. Still more, he taught God's children to pray against his influence every morning and evening: "Lord, lead me not into temptation, but deliver us from the Evil One!"

This proves that our sensitive, perceptive Lord Jesus clearly understood how Satan would approach every child of God every day and put pressure on them and attack them. That's why he urged them to lift the shield of prayer against Satan daily.

It's terrible to admit this, but it has to be said: Satan possesses a bewitching power. It's a power that every man and woman enslaved to sin has discovered when they first fell into sin. The result is that the soul caves in to sinning. It falls under its spell. And ultimately it finds itself doing what at first it did not want to do.

That bewitching power has no name. But it's real. And it's deadly in the way it works. Knowing this, Jesus put in place another mystical power for opposing it when he said: "This is how you should pray: 'Deliver me from the Evil One.'" He didn't tell us to make the sign of the cross, like we were told to do by the religious leaders of the Middle Ages. And magically repeating the name of Jesus over and over doesn't help. No, the antidote against Satan's bewitching power is this simple, powerful, genuine prayer! This is a prayer that arises from the soul like a child's cry of desperation yelled to its mother to protect them from the wolf it sees coming! For the frightened cry of God's child is a prayer that his Fatherly heart can't ignore. It's a prayer that he simply has to hear. And he always does! It's also a prayer whose power Satan has learned to recognize through experience. When he hears it, he automatically gives up and leaves us alone for a while. He snorts a curse about "that damn praying that no power of hell can resist!"

But who prays like this? Where do you hear people caught up in this kind of praying against Satan? In God's house? In prayer meetings? In family circles? Among friends? Even when now and then you hear a prayer expressing some semblance of opposing Satan, does it convey trembling of the soul? Or real fear of Satan? If so, is it a fear of Satan that calls God to rise up against him?

But praise God, horror over sin may still be found in Christ's church. People couldn't be God's children or connected with the Lord's people if they didn't continue begging to be delivered from sin.

But sin is not the same thing as Satan!

Sin is the goblet of intoxicating wine that passively stands on the table in front of you. It won't do you any damage unless you reach for it and drink from it. But Satan is an overpowering person who with one hand pries open your mouth and with his other brings the goblet to your lips and forces you, despite your resistance, to drink the intoxicating wine from it.

This is why you still pray when you know no more than the idea of sin. But your praying won't be a cry of anguish. It will be no more than an expressed self-awareness and quiet conviction that you have to keep that intoxicating liquid off your lips. But when the scales fall off your eyes and you finally see that Satan is always behind that sin, your calm approach disappears. Praying becomes "crying out to God." It's as though the lips that you open in prayer have already tasted Satan's poison on them.

Now you've reached the turning point!

A child of God who is still only dealing with sin is still on the way to the battlefield. The one who has reached the battlefield immediately sees the actual enemy standing in front of them. They're overwhelmed with the fear that they're dealing with a life-and-death situation. For them at that moment Satan becomes a terribly living person. He's a mighty Goliath advancing toward them, and he's intent on "feeding their flesh to the birds of the heavens!"

That's when people first realize who Jesus actually is and how unbelievably powerful, even almighty, Jesus has to be in order to overpower this dreadful Satan. But that's also when the true joy of knowing that Jesus is our Jesus also appears. Every child of God realizes then that in the name of Jesus they can resist and overcome Satan. This doesn't happen by letting their arms hang limply at their sides, or by their knees buckling, or by their souls trembling in them like reeds in the wind. It happens through the all-powerful prayer of a child who can and must pray to their all-powerful Father.

Guard your soul carefully, so that you don't regard Satan as some monstrous being, for that's not how he ever approaches God's children. He only approached Jesus man-to-man. He never approaches us in any other way than as concealed in something or someone else. Satan will only be seen in all his horribleness when he is cast into the lake of fire. But now he almost always comes in some totally inoffensive and often in some completely lovable form.

That's how he once crept into the presence of Jesus in the person of Peter, his dear, faithful, and dedicated disciple. He caused this disciple to run to Jesus with words that were filled with heartfelt, tender, empathetic love. "No, Jesus! You must never be whipped and crucified!" Jesus mustn't be anticipating his death. His Lord and Master shouldn't be so determined to talk that way. Peter's heart, his love for Jesus, and his human emotions all totally resisted this.

When Peter said these things, he didn't appear to be at all devilish but tender and loving! You would have loved him for this more than you would the other disciples who remained silent. You could add that Peter appeared to be so far from being devilish that it appealed even to Jesus. But he began to feel a conflict in his soul over what Peter saw so clearly. Sensing that conflict, he realized that he was dealing with Satan. In order to break immediately with Peter's appealing proposal, he didn't want to look at him any longer, so he said: "Get behind me, Satan!"

Understand clearly, therefore, how Satan approaches you in your own life: through whom, in what way, and in what form. Sometimes he does it through something very loving and tender. Not infrequently it's through your dearest friends and family here on earth.

Brothers and sisters, never forget that Satan is very involved with you. He's engaged with everything and everyone that appeals to what you know to be unholy in you. He's present in everything and everyone that troubles your conscience and produces better, higher estimates of yourself than are healthy. Very often you meet him in the sweet lips and voices that appeal to your humanity and oppose what's godly.

Just realize that Jesus has given you what you need to stand firm: "Get behind me, Satan. You are not concerned about what matters to God but what matters to people."

And if it gets to the point that Satan talks to you in a friendly way, caresses you with his words, and converses with you warmheartedly, what should you do?

Allow yourself to be caressed? Soak up his warmhearted words like nectar? Or will you have the courage to plug your ears and to say: "Get out, you flatterer! Get behind me, Satan! You're inflaming my feelings against God!"

Let each person examine their own soul on this matter! Not just when Satan says: "Go ahead, take it," or "That's allowed!" Not just when he whispers in your ear: "You don't have to be that narrow!" Not just when your progress is compromised, or you exalt in your pride, or you're floundering in your dishonesty! No, but even more in the softer tissue of your soul that involves selfish inclinations, a slight character wrinkle, wanting to enjoy yourself, or being less loving and spiritual than you should be.

The kingdom of our God is peace and holiness and self-denial. That's where the tempter of your soul always opposes you in your own heart.

68
VOLUME II

IT COVERS ALL THINGS

Love is patient. ... It is not embittered. It keeps no record of
evils suffered. It covers all things. 1 Corinthians 13:4, 5, 7

To talk about love is not so difficult. It's easy to become enthused about it and to spread its sunshine all around. But what definitely is difficult is to maintain the love of God faithfully in your heart when you're trying to get through an intense conflict or overcome the world. Then it's hard not to shortchange the tender holiness of the Lord your God.

To love God above all, with all your strength and all your soul, and to love your neighbor as yourself sounds so beautiful and so devout. These are like two glorious, heavenly angels who are paired off, never to be separated. Unfortunately, in the realities of our everyday life that connection seems like an illusion. Our struggles in this world don't permit it. Time and again we face the painful temptation either of not loving our brother tenderly enough because of our zeal for God or of missing the target of truly loving God because we are afraid of our neighbors.

This happens daily in every home and in everyone's personal life. It happens with the mother who looks the other way when her child does something that the Lord does not condone. It happens with the husband who is inwardly conflicted about confronting the wife he loves so deeply, although he knows it's his obligation before God to do so. It happens with the well-intentioned young person who is compromised because he doesn't dare speak to his friend about the evil he sees in him, not because he lacks the courage to do so but because he doesn't want to hurt him. This is how love struggles, repeatedly and in a thousand ways. In order not to seem too harsh but loving, we let slide what our love for the Lord would otherwise definitely require.

Rationalizing doesn't help us one bit!

For you can keep on telling yourself that love without courage is blind and doesn't amount to true love. Or you can add that continuing to be godly will in the long run prove to be the most profitable for your child or wife or friend, and then it will become obvious that it is the true love that blesses and redeems. But neither of these passes the test. Our human hearts aren't all that influenced by reasoning. In the cold, practical realities of life, our brotherly love fades repeatedly in our zeal for God, and the glow of love for God just as often is extinguished by love for our neighbor. We are so limited; our souls are so petty! The recesses of our hearts are so constricted that they can't accommodate these two unbelievably beautiful realities living together peacefully: love for God and love for our neighbor.

It's just as obvious that harboring the one form of love and shutting out the other isn't the answer either. That's because—and you have to understand this clearly—a child of God who is zealous for God in ways that simply overwhelm you but whose love for neighbor has cooled off noticeably finds that ultimately their love for God also fades. Similarly, a person with a loving heart who can't do enough for their neighbor but whose love for God suffers ultimately finds that the first apparently tender love for neighbor was trafficking in concealed egoism. In our life of pain and sorrow and in this sick, dismal world, the two of them can't live together comfortably. And yet they have to! They belong together!

Now you might say: "But that's contradictory!" If you did, you would be totally correct, at least when considered apart from the Holy Spirit. But then, again, I don't know that there can ever be genuine love glowing and radiating from a human heart that has not been poured into it by the Holy Spirit. Note well that this is love not poured out just one time, at some given moment, so that you could live off that supply ever after. Rather, it's poured out from moment to moment, or it will soon go out like light poured onto a field by the sun is soon followed by darkness when the sun goes down.

This amazing Spirit understands your heart. He knows your struggles. He's aware of your circumstances. Thus, he's well aware that your love for God could be diminished by your love for your neighbor, or conversely, that your love for your brother could be in conflict with your zeal for the Lord. Understanding this, he assures you that the supply of this love poured into you does not depend on you but is controlled by him and depends on him working it in you.

This is precisely the mysterious working of the Holy Spirit. Whatever comes to expression in you is done by you. At the same time, it is worked within you and comes to expression through you. You show love, and you enjoy this enormously. It makes you happy. But you yourself are actually a hater. Rather, it is the Holy Spirit stirring the song of love in your heart with such overpowering beauty that it sweeps you along and fills you with love.

And then you have that overwhelmingly blessed experience that defies all your calculation, mocks your rationalizing, and makes the unthinkable certain and self-evident. Despite all strife and conflict, it causes you to love both God and your neighbor in the name of God.

The world doesn't understand this. But in the kingdom, God's dear children do, and they take grateful note of it.

They offer no excuses for this or try to even things out. For in the sacred work of loving it's loathsome to smooth over differences or compromise them. All they can do is turn matters over to the Holy Spirit. Then the stream of holy responses begins flowing automatically. Then the heart melts. Then the soul basks in the wonderful sunshine of God's eternal love. Then something of this beautiful, divine love is reflected in all you do in this demanding, often very painful life.

For then this blessed love covers all things. You could say that it causes everything to look different. Harsh colors disappear, and everything takes on softer, calming hues. What once impeded no longer obstructs. The clouds above that formerly appeared so dark and oppressive are now stunningly beautiful. Sunlight penetrates them and smothers their oppressiveness.

Love in the human soul is an incredible work of divine mercy. By it a child of God experiences that all that is painful and oppressive in this life is diminished and appears to take on a holy glow. Whoever is permitted to enjoy God's love finds that it covers everything in their life, and they become a follower of God. They themselves likewise blanket everything with that love. Not mechanically, so that they think: "I have to do this." But naturally! The love of God and the love that the Holy Spirit stirs in our souls for others is one and the same love. The result is that its active working is also one. What seemed contradictory is resolved in this blessed harmony.

If you should still experience conflict in this regard, realize that this is due to operating with an imitation of love rather than with the real thing. Then all your efforts to hold together two incompatible things are doomed to fail. Attempts to do so only make the cleavage between them wider, the conflict more intense, and your heart colder.

The only thing left for you to do in that case is to flee to the Holy Spirit again for refuge and to implore him to warm you in his sheltering presence. Do this until he pours love into your heart again and resolves the riddle of this tension.

Look, you can't help but notice a very great deal in the lives of your loved one as well as of those to whom you are less drawn. This is inevitable. And now you confront three possibilities.

The first possibility is that you see what's wrong in the lives of others but simply keep quiet about it.

The second approach is that you're not quiet about it but that you do talk about it and in doing so you wound and offend and embitter them.

But there is a third strategy. It's that you do address them, if need be even angrily, but that you speak to them in such a way that it has its desired effect and blesses them.

Isn't the last one the best one? But is the last one even thinkable unless the Holy Spirit is at work in your heart?

Whoever has received God's love through the Holy Spirit proceeds with great tenderness. If someone has anything against you that you would find it difficult to hear, it would never cross their lips by way of casual comment, much less in order to elevate themselves above you. If their love for God was working powerfully in them and they felt "I can't remain silent," then and then only would they speak. They would also if their love for you personally were so inwardly compelling that they wanted to embrace you with those cords of love.

Then the person being addressed would feel what you were saying. But how? Not weakly, but ideally with compelling seriousness. Yet, they would definitely sense the tone of the unconstrained love you were feeling toward them. Their response would be: "That's not said out of bitterness. It's not loose talk. They just can't do anything else!" And where that kind speaking is found, it could involve anything you could name since the blessed love of God covers everything. And it is the kind of speaking that also blesses everything it touches.

69
VOLUME II

IMPORTANT PEOPLE
ARE A LIE!

Common people are a mere puff of air and important
people are a lie. Weighed together on a scale, they
amount to less than a breath. Psalm 62:9[1]

Yes, there definitely are important people here on earth. It's playing games to think that all people here on earth are the same. The children of human parents just are not! Among one another, they are very unequal. At the same time, everyone has to agree that the distinctions among them are so endlessly varied that any attempt to classify them is really quite lame. Yet, the people in the world around us noticeably fall into either an immeasurable mix of common ones or a small class of important ones.

They are regarded as common or important according to the standards of measurement that have always been applied and are still used. Common people have very little wealth, but important people have a great deal. Common ones have very little power, while important ones have a lot of it. Commoners have limited intellectual capacities, but prominent folks possess a great deal of thinking ability. Little people hardly matter in society, while big shots control it. Energy and willpower are in short supply among common people, but important people have them in epic proportions. Dependence is the norm for

---

1. Psalm 62:10 in Dutch versions.

one, dominance for the other. Here a countless mass of the weak and vulnerable look at the limited number of important people in awe and amazement. They in return are scarcely inclined to even notice the ones to whom little has been given. The important and the common people represent the undeniable, enduring distinction that cuts through and divides all facets of human life.

The very few are the ones who accomplish something significant. They have the treasure and power, the talent and the drive, the influence and the control over the opportunities to do so. They make a name for themselves by doing so. They leave their footprints on the life of their community, city, country, and church. These people are surrounded by an ocean of what the psalmist calls "common people," who endlessly beat against them like the waves of the sea. These are the ordinary folks who are weaker and poorer. They are powerless and lack the genius and money of the others. They haven't been granted the same talent, resolve, and persistence. All they can do is huddle together as the masses, find solace in their numbers, and undertake in their strength what they realistically dare to do.

These important people are traveling in circumstances that are extremely dangerous for them. "It is easier for a camel to pass through the eye of a needle than for a rich man to enter the kingdom of God," said our Savior. But no one should think that this applies only to those who are rich in terms of money. Sadly, no! This is equally true, and perhaps even more frighteningly so, for those who are rich in genius, knowledge, determination, or social influence. Pay close attention to how few important people enter through the narrow gate. Also notice how many of those who give the appearance of entering actually remain behind. This even applies to preachers! In every century, they have been numbered among the important people in the church of Jesus Christ. They were the powerful. They had the authority. Yet how rarely hasn't there been a time when Chrysostom's complaint was echoed with his burning intensity: "Most shepherds are standing outside the sheepfold of Christ!"

It can't be any different! It's almost impossible even for ordinary, weak, and helpless people to discount themselves. How terribly more difficult, then, it must be for the very few who are celebrated, important, rich, powerful, and influential! They don't only have to deal with their own egos, but they also have to deny all the incense offered to them, all their influence, and their public image. With God all things are possible, but without it one of these prominent people could never enter God's glorious kingdom. It's like it is with the beauty of a woman! What a miracle of divine grace has to happen to cause a beautiful young daughter not to be held at bay from God by her beauty and not to be seduced by her vanity. Who wouldn't admit this?

There are so few important people here on earth who will also be great in the kingdom of heaven. They are inwardly so small. "They are a lie," says the psalmist. You could even say: "It's a lie that they are important." They definitely seem to be. But they really aren't. Those who are truly important possess inner depth. They are significant in the sight of God and will be so eternally. You will find them much more often among those who are poor. They are poor in terms of money, material goods, genius, and power. "Blessed are the poor in spirit, for theirs is the kingdom of heaven." "Unless you become like a little child, O you who are important here on earth, your portion in Jesus will disappear!"

But it's not only that the important people are traveling in circumstances that are dangerous for themselves. They are dragging common people into danger along with them. They have such enormous influence and power that people can't resist them. When the power of money or personality or reason are so ungodly that they only serve egoism, then that miserable influence becomes very oppressive and domineering for common people. Fear arises. Then fear becomes oppressiveness that gives way to cowardly flight or creeping bitterness. You can see in the life of a village how pernicious the power of an influential man can be on the lives of common people. If it comes to that kind of expression on the village level, how much worse it will be in the cities. Our world and our hearts are so sinful that every powerful person, who is no more than a sinner among sinners, is dangerous!

When a powerful person is not against you but is for you, they are especially dangerous. That's true if they help or bolster and support you. Just take a look around you in your surroundings. Notice the powerful people among you who pose a double danger. They cause you to depend too much on them. And they lean too heavily on your enthusiastic amazement regarding them. This is how the idols of this world appear. It's how their little altars are erected. It's how people then light incense to them. It's how honor for the Lord disappears and how powerful people are corrupted.

The spirit of the age nurtures this terrible evil very strongly. It does so even among Christians. It is intent on gaining ground on the false premise that important and powerful people attain personal recognition and make a name for themselves because of what they are in and of themselves.

This is why we need God's Word so much. It's the Word that also lays down a premise where important people are concerned. It's the theory that asserts exactly the opposite. It's the affirmation that is a source of comfort to the weak, of salvation for those who are important, and of honor to God. It endures century after century. It is the affirmation that the church of Christ continues to make: "Important people are not what you think they are; they are a lie!"

For if I'm a weak, common person and if I believe that the important people are a lie, then fear naturally subsides in my heart. Then I begin to live again. I dare to breathe and celebrate in my soul. One thing have I heard. The Lord told it to me twice, namely, that strength belongs to God; it is not lodged in powerful people.

This is what likewise saves those important folks. For something happens to an important person who knows and believes and comprehends that they "are a lie," that is, that it's simply not true that they are someone special. Then that temptation loses its appeal. Its power is broken. They accept the fact that they are no different from the least of all persons and that they are only an instrument in the service of the Lord God. They can humbly kneel before God again, creep toward him, and squeeze through the narrow gate.

This is how God reclaims his glory in the lives of powerful people. These important people are the works of his hands. He has fashioned them. They are his instruments. Just as a blacksmith wields a huge hammer to bend and shape the metal on his anvil, so God Almighty has several powerful hammers in addition to his more refined tools. They are available for him to use. But they lie idle and powerless in the corner until he extends his strong arm, grips them, and uses them to strike the red-hot metal he's shaping.

If the hammer would say: "I'm the blacksmith," it would be lying. But if that huge hammer remained a passive tool and recognized that God is the smith who's doing the work, it would be truthful. And that's the truth by which God is shaping his church.

And this explains how sometimes people of noble birth appear who are "important individuals" among the people but who are "very common men and women" in God's presence. That's to say, you can find children of God who are simultaneously powerful people in their generation here on earth and who are also great in the kingdom of heaven.

These would include the holy apostles, the martyrs, and the church's giants. They were important people who began by regarding themselves as "a lie," but who became the truth in him who "for our sakes became a worm and no man at all."

70
VOLUME II

WHEN YOU FASTED, WAS IT IN ANY WAY FOR ME?

Speak to all the people of this land and to all their priests,
saying: "When you fasted and mourned in the fifth and
seventh months for these seventy years now, was it in
any way for me that you fasted?" Zechariah 7:5

What is false about our spirituality is terribly abhorrent to the Lord our God.

Piety is wonderful. Nothing is more blessed than genuine, quiet devotion and vibrant, intimate godliness. The person with whom God has fellowship and who is allowed to live in his tent is richer than any king on earth.

But the sin that is found even in a person's devotion is so terribly destructive! What's hard to believe in that connection is that there has never been human piety here on earth, with the exception of Christ's, that has not been affected by sin. I'm not talking in the generally recognized sense that sin is always still found in the life of a pious person and continues to exist alongside and with their piety. No, I'm talking in the much more frightening sense that sin raises its head precisely within their spirituality. Time and again their spirituality itself appears to be sinful. The spirituality from which they derive satisfaction very often seems to be a stained, impure expression of the soul for which they need to ask for forgiveness through the blood of the Lamb of God.

This goes deep!

If we are definitely sinners but our piety is still without stain, then that piety in our judgment still naturally has value as something good. We can go to God with it as an offering that will make him rejoice.

By contrast and contradiction of this, if our piety is always stained and sinful in and of itself, it ceases to provide any basis for our celebration. Spirituality as it still may come to expression in our lives is nothing less than an expression of God's grace in us. It causes our poor souls to celebrate and makes us find our comfort and assurance in him.

Listen to how God intrudes into what Israel was imagining and peddling about her own piety.

Israel had dealt unfaithfully with God. God responded by punishing her in Babylon. Suffering under that chastisement, Israel thought: "Let me just be pious again and humble myself deeply, otherwise I'll never escape this!" This is why she fasted. It wasn't true of a Jew here and there! No, it was true of all the people. Throughout all those long years! On the prescribed feast days! And now that God in his good favor had brought them back to their own land, Israel imagined that in Babylon they had been very pious. They also imagined that, properly understood, their return from captivity had occurred due their own piety, especially to their fasting.

And what did the Lord God have to say about all that? Well, he cut deep and laid bare that sham spirituality in their hearts. "What kind of piety is this spirituality of yours? Do you think that your devotion made you suitable candidates for your deliverance? Do you dare to glory in your fasting, as though that kind of godliness ultimately helped deliver you from your oppressors? Rather, that very piety simply piled one sin on top of the other," said the Lord. "Yes, you fasted. But how? You said that it was for me, your God! Israel, simply let your own consciences bear witness! Did you fast for me, for me in any way at all?"

Now, take a good look. Apply this to yourselves. Then tell me whether it doesn't frighten your hearts.

If God were to come to us like this and say: "Yes, you prayed, but when you did were you praying to me, were you praying to me in any sense at all? You sang psalms and hymns, but when you sang, were you singing to me, singing to me in any sense at all? You studied the Scriptures, but while you were busy with the Word, were you doing so in any way for me?

"Scrutinize your giving for the poor, your kneeling, and your solemn assemblies. Examine them down to the pious expression on your faces and tell me what remains of all these devout outward appearances. Won't I, your God, brush aside and sweep into hell all that goes on apart from me? All that did not proceed from me? Everything that was intended for anything other than my honor?"

You pious men and women, if God were to approach you like this, what would be left of all your spirituality? Wouldn't all your spirituality dissolve immediately? Worse yet, wouldn't you immediately recognize that all your praying, and kneeling, and whatever else your memories might fondly caress, now rebuke you? They now accuse you of being unspiritual. They drive you to the ground in guilt before your God and compel you to confess in your silent pain: "O Lord, self-centeredness crept into my praying. It stole in because of my indifference. O God, my God, when in my praying was I ever focused on you and on you alone?"

At this point, let no one say: "Then the ungodly person is better off, for at least they don't sin in their praying since they don't pray!" That would be the stupid rationalizing of a suicidal person who removes the possibility of sinning in small ways by committing one colossal sin!

No, your counsel must be to keep on praying, to keep on kneeling, and to continue walking in godliness—but, in a different way. Now that you've been made aware of the terrible danger in which a pious person is living, you have to stay alert. Stay alert to the danger involved in your praying or singing a psalm. Remain alert and awake. Be less thoughtless and a whole lot less focused on yourself.

Should you do so in order to become unblemished in your spirituality over time? Should you do so in order to become sinless in your praying and singing? Not at all, my sisters and brothers! You'll never get to that point here on earth. All perfectionism and utopianism is misguided, particularly where your spirituality is concerned.

No, you should do so in order to learn by stumbling along to set aside the foolish delusion that you could ever be the one actually praying or actually singing God's praises. Or that you could ever be a truly pious person. Do so from now on to replace such foolish delusion with the clear, sober, glorious truth that the Holy Spirit is the only One who truly prays and that the godliness of the Mediator can become your godliness in God's presence. Do so always to keep these matters clearly in front of you. Bind them on your heart.

This is what brings peace.

This avoids the wearying search for a false sense of perfection.

This enables the child of God to dare to truly pray once more, knowing that they are only praying along with Someone else. It's a matter of accompaniment, as with singing! Tell a timid person sometime that he has to sing a solo on a special occasion. Then he simply can't. His voice gets stuck in his throat. Everything falls to pieces. But allow some maestro to lead the singing and encourage others to follow his lead and sing along with him. Then suggest to your timid friend that he sing along. He will open his lips naturally and sing better than he ever thought he could.

That's how praying happens easily and naturally when the Maestro of Prayer, the Holy Spirit himself, prays for us and with us. We hear him praying, and the entire congregation of God praying along with him, and when a friendly voice invites us to pray along with this choir, we do. Our own little prayer is only a drop in the bucket of many waters that flow and swell before the throne of God.

And should we rise to our feet after praying and think: "That was still so miserably cold!" the Holy Spirit has a word for us. He tells us that the atoning blood is always at work. It is at work for those who are spiritually upright. It is at work for the sins involved in our praying.

The Lord God is satisfied with just a little.

"Have you looked for me in any sense at all in your praying?" He asks it with such merciful tenderness. He speaks with us in such a human manner. But isn't it also tremendously unsettling that God has to talk this way with his people?

The people don't even have to be intensely spiritual to be seeking the living God in their prayers! Nor does my own soul along with those of others! They don't in order to be seeking the living God!

This still needs to be said: The Lord doesn't only speak these harsh words of Zechariah to the people. The Lord speaks them particularly to the priests. He adds: "Speak to all the people of this land and to all their priests."

Let all who labor in the service of the Lord take special notice of this. All who pray for others, whether that's in the church, the school, or the homes, are in double jeopardy.

It's already possible for you not to stay close to God when you drop to your knees in God's presence at your bedside. What must it be like, then, when you pray in churches, evangelistic meetings, various gatherings, or in schools and Sunday schools? Can't you understand, then, that our holy, tender God sometimes recoils in horror at those pious, long, beautiful prayers he hears? Do you preachers hear God appealing to your hearts when he asks: "When you stand there praying in the pulpit, in front of all those people, are you in any sense praying to me and for me?" Similarly, do you evangelists and teachers and others who lead in prayer hear what he is asking?

He's not asking this in harshness, but out of deep concern and heartfelt compassion.

To be permitted to pray, even compelled to pray, in public situations is a high spiritual privilege for which sinful human beings are almost never adequately qualified. They can hardly pray without becoming entangled in the lie that immediately intrudes, or in the vanity, emphasis on appearance, or the compromised heart that does.

Oh, there are so many leaders of large crowds that sin in their praying because they are so cold, spiritually parched and impoverished, and verbose. And the congregation takes little notice. It doesn't pray for its ministers. They still spoil them sometimes with halting praise for an inspiring prayer they have delivered. "You prayed so beautifully again!" is said so glibly that it's really a curse against true prayer.

This is how preachers shrivel. It's how spiritual sap stops flowing in congregations. And this passes for piety. But God abhors it.

WHO IS THE MAN WHO FEARS THE LORD?

Who is the man who fears the Lord? He will instruct
him in the way he should choose. Psalm 25:12

In our day people in more refined circles speak with a degree of fondness about "seriousness," "living seriously," "being serious," and "thinking seriously." People in both orthodox and modernistic circles do this. In orthodox circles, this means that someone has reached a point of being reflective about their situation. In a modernistic context, it means that a person is not a carouser, doesn't live a debauched lifestyle, and is not enslaved to sensuality but sets their sights on higher things.

In the vocabulary of our century, the word "serious" has gotten wide usage because of its many-sided meanings. It's a word that people use readily and with appreciation. It awakens better aspirations in our heart. Everyone tolerates its usage. It's not entirely misunderstood even in rather superficial circles where now and then it's employed to refer to the serious side of life. It's comparable to the younger children in our aristocratic families, where everyone thinks of them lovingly, like little Benjamins. Thus the tone struck in our era by the image of being serious is such that almost all speakers appeal to it. They think that by talking about being serious they evoke a feeling of warmth and kindle a fire in their listeners. And it's true that the thought of being serious inspires you to do better and is uplifting.

"Serious or fun loving" tells you enough about what being serious involves. People are serious when they no longer joke around about everything. Getting serious starts when all the vain, empty talk stops. The person is serious who hesitates going along with all the lighthearted frivolity of our age that mocks everything that is dear or painful. "Being serious" is the opposite of "being playful" and is in stark contrast with literally making a game of everything from early morning until late at night. Those who are serious mean what they say. They embrace life in its reality. They restrain empty-headedness. Life becomes meaningful for them.

This is all quite wonderful! But it's also a serious indictment on the miserable, dissipated spirit of our age. A person for whom things are meaningful is an exception. So is one for whom life is much more than a game. Let's be clear. You're an exception when you get sick to your stomach of all the empty jabber and unrestrained chatter of the children of our time. They simply laugh and snicker their lives away!

Theirs is the true French spirit whose revolutionary atmosphere has settled over a pathetic Christianity. The French Revolution with its intoxicating brew has made baptized people so woozy that they are ashamed to identify what's good as good any longer. And when they have some need, they blush beet red if anyone catches them in a brief prayer.

These are bad times. Many families, both parents and youngsters—take whichever you choose—are just as entertaining and just as offensive to watch as a cage full of playful, howling, grimacing chimpanzees at the zoo. How often don't you encounter devilish dishonesty? Hellish pleasure in the mocking, devilish delight with what is evil, brutish, or vicious?

In such circles, you are certain to find a serious person, even a devout one, who will speak "a serious word" that falls like a drop of dew on some worn-out soul. Their voice is a call to seriousness. It's an expression of courage, love, and higher purpose. We wholeheartedly celebrate their kind of seriousness. We're pleased when a break occurs in unbelieving circles with what's empty, stifling, and vain. We're enthusiastic when oppression of all that's holy is somewhat diminished.

But should we as Christians then adopt the way the unbelieving world thinks about seriousness, with its emphases? Just because seriousness has somewhat higher standing in these circles with such low standards, does it measure up to the much higher, more glorious ideals set for us by the cross of Jesus Christ?

Understand that the Word of God knows virtually nothing about that kind of "seriousness" and "living seriously." The expressions "with seriousness," "seriously," and "serious" do appear a few times in Scripture. But they do so with a completely different meaning from the way people presently talk about "being serious." "Give serious attention to" in Exodus 15:26 and other places says no more than "listen carefully" to something. To do something "seriously" in Jeremiah 22:4 means no more than "to tackle something with enthusiasm." But you never read in God's Word about a "seriousness" that stands independently, like a distinct virtue that is the mother of all other virtues.

Taken in that sense, "serious" first appeared among the followers of Cocceius.[1] The larger portion of them called themselves "serious Cocceians" to distinguish themselves from the lighthearted impieties of others in their circle. Since then usage of the term has increased to the extent that emphasis on the seriousness of life has decreased. The more that everything was seen as a game, the more obvious it became that people often had to make clear that they weren't "simply playing around." The word that came in handy in making that point was the word "serious."

Simply for that reason the enthusiasm for parrying with "being serious" has become less applicable in a Christian setting. That's just the nature of the situation. There the canvas on which the more ideal images should be alluringly displayed is already beginning to be tinted with this notion of "being serious."

If Scripture wants to get our attention and shake us out of our complacency, and where it wants us to reflect on eternity, it doesn't approach us with the weak directive "Be a little serious now!" It takes a completely different and incomparably deeper approach. It says: "Fear God!"

"The fear of God" is the biblical language for what in our time passes for "being serious." But pay careful attention to the much loftier and more glorious meaning that this conveys.

A "serious person" is someone who is self-satisfied. They resist the dishonesty and scoffing emptiness of their surroundings. They oppose it and pursue what's better and more meaningful in life. They consider carefully what they're doing. They calculate the consequences. They're mindful of what people don't observe. But all of this happens in their own strength and through their own

---

1. Johannes Cocceius (1603–1669) was a Reformed theologian who taught at the University of Utrecht, where he became a leading advocate of federal or covenant theology.

excellent qualities. In their own estimation, such people are part of a kind of moral aristocracy.

By contrast, "the fear of the Lord" cuts this Arminian thistle off at its roots. It humbles you to the dust along with all those scoffers. It makes you as guilty in the presence of the Holy One as all the mockers. It teaches you that all you do must be done meaningfully and evaluated meaningfully because God is secretly involved with all of it. You can never say about any of it: "This involves me alone, not God!"

The "serious person" sets the standards for their life and opposes everything that puts pressure on the rules they have made. But the God-fearing person bows before the law of God and moves forward with all God's people in the power of the atoning blood.

You can be "serious" and still essentially worship yourself. But "the fear of God" keeps on disturbing you until every idol in your life has been toppled.

A person can be "serious" even on their deathbed, from which they'll be carried off to hell. But "the fear of God" bears a person up on the glorious promise that shortly they will see "the secret things of God!"

So now you understand why people endeavor to be "serious" but avoid talking about "the fear of God."

Oh, all that chatter about "being serious" inflates the ego! It keeps alive the sense of self as we imagine it! But when the "fear of God" takes over, the entire creature is compelled to submit. The Lord lives and he alone is great.

The lesson to be learned from all of this is obvious.

We learn that "being serious" is an inferior concept. It does bear a nobler stamp when contrasted with the terribly harebrained approach to life in our age. And we also learn that Scripture talks to us not about "being serious" but about something much higher, holier, and more glorious. It uses the language of "fearing God." It obligates us Christians to recognize that fundamentally we are "not serious" and that we reject our Christian honor when we allow ourselves to be inspired by the spirit of the age rather than by God's Word. For then, in effect, we sever the nerve of "fearing God." What we're left with is merely "being serious!"

EVEN CHRIST DID NOT EXALT HIMSELF BY BECOMING A HIGH PRIEST

*No one takes honor for themselves, but they receive it when they
are called by God, just as was true with Aaron. Hebrews 5:4*

Christ is our prophet. This means that he addresses us. He steadily speaks
an enduring word to us. Whether it penetrates our hearts is another question. Even if it only drones on in our hearts, it's still there. It continues serving
us notice moment by moment. It's always the same word coming from the King
sitting on his throne of honor. It's a word with power. It calls us to distance
ourselves from all unrighteousness and to be reconciled to God.

That's why this word becomes so appalling. It crushes us. It smashes rocks
to smithereens. It kills. That's because it's like a two-edged sword that cuts to
the bone, even through the bone to the marrow. It slices to that hidden spot
where soul and spirit are bound together. Nothing withstands it. This word
from Christ the prophet lays you low, so low that you can't get up again.

That's the precise reason that Christ the prophet is now also Christ the priest. The prophet kills, crushes, and shatters. But the priest is like the good Samaritan who, upon finding the wounded man lying in the ditch, binds his wounds, pours oil on them, revives his spirit, lifts him up, and sets him on his own donkey, and leaving him behind at the inn, provides money to cover his expenses.

Christ the priest does not cause suffering but suffers himself. He does so first of all with you, then for you, and finally instead of you. Christ the priest is the divine heart filled with tender mercy and love. This is a love that, like the Word, penetrates to the marrow and the joining of soul and spirit. But at the exact spot where the Word caused death, it also brings healing and life. Everything lies exposed and open to him. But the eye of the priest isn't looking for nakedness in order to rip open a wound. He's looking to bind it up, remove the gangrene, and replace it with the warmth of a revived spirit.

Christ the priest finds a leper but doesn't push him away. He touches him. He embraces him. He holds him against his heart. He embraces him so completely that the leprosy is transferred to him and his own strength and health permeate the leper.

For him being a priest is to have such a passion for the suffering of the creature that it completely overwhelms his heart. It's to wrestle until he absorbs it to the very last drop as his own. It's never to be at peace until the ungodly person who is the object of his mercy becomes a paragon of God's glorious achievement! This is how he's a real priest! He's the only true priest!

This is amazingly divine, isn't it?

So now you might be inclined to say that it was unbelievably tender on Jesus' part to be willing to do all this. But that's not how Jesus himself thinks about it. Through the apostle he says to you: "No, this wasn't glory that I sought from the Father. Just the opposite! It was an honor that I received from the Father."

That I was permitted to love like this was my glory. That I was permitted to step forward as a priest was the Father's good pleasure regarding the Son. No, I didn't take on the privilege of being named a priest, but it was given, and I received it. For just as no one among the sons of men takes on that honor unless it is conferred on them by God, so Jesus the priest did not glorify himself by becoming a priest. But it was given to him by the One who said: "You are my Son, and today I honor you! You are a priest after the order of Melchizedek!"

And are you now able to plumb the depths of divine perfection that is unsurpassed in the lowly form of Christ the priest?

Realize that such love, such tender and deep love, cannot tolerate being mixed with anything that is not pure devotion, self-denial, sacrifice, and submission. Such love is all-consuming, which is to say that it is a complete sacrifice! It is perfectly true because it totally self-absorbing.

For that reason, can our hearts ever comprehend it? The priestly love of Christ toward us can be no less. It can be no different!

To be permitted to love! To be permitted to offer oneself and by that sacrifice of love to be permitted to save! These may not be undertaken in one's own power, but they are a privilege received by the One who is recognized by the Father.

But now turn your thoughts to your own love.

It makes you very ashamed, doesn't it?

Don't be in a hurry to love. Don't be in a hurry to aspire to that devoted, self-sacrificing, truly self-denying love. And once you get there a time or two, take note of your feeling of self-satisfaction. It's as though you've experienced something miraculous. The conviction registers in your heart that you've made it that far only by the help of God.

Now Jesus, your priest, comes and stands opposite you. By comparison with his eternal love, your deepest devotion sinks like a drop in the expanse of the ocean. Then Jesus says to you with such divine simplicity: "That I might be your priest is not something I took on myself; it is an honor that I was given by my God."

Where does that leave you with your self-denial and your creaturely compassion? Doesn't that make you realize how much sin still clings to our best works? Doesn't it make you feel in your depraved heart like a worm gnawing on beautiful fruit? Doesn't exalting yourself because of it completely spoil the beauty of that blossoming, sacred, priestly love?

It has also been granted to us to be priests and priestesses.

Also we need to take on suffering. Also our hearts need to glisten with a passion to disarm pain and suffering. Also we need to experience the oppressiveness of assuming other people's burdens. Also we need to help bear the load weighing so heavily on others. We need to bear it for them, even though they themselves may not entirely understand what it is they are bearing.

Everyone is willing to be a prophet or prophetess. That's so much easier! Confronting, admonishing, irritating, punishing all needs doing! It cuts to the soul.

But woe to you if you are not also willing to be a priest or a priestess. Woe to you if no love follows and heals after you've spoken a word that wounds. Woe to you if you never offer a prayer, never shed a tear, and never feel inner compassion. Woe to you if sacrifice never beckons you and if the altar is not a precious place here on earth for you.

Yet, even this is not enough.

It comes down to loving in the right way.

You're on the wrong path as long as you think: "I'm definitely willing to do this!" Rather, you need to be able to give thanks with your whole heart that you're permitted to do it. No priest or priestess enters God's house by their own willing decision. You have to be appointed, appointed by the Lord your God.

You have to show this awareness: he, the Lord, calls me to the ministry of compassion. He, my God, considers me worthy of it. He, the One who elects me, has selected and anointed me for this.

That's when the work of loving becomes tender. Then it is glorious. Then people don't run in all sorts of unusual directions, but they are content to serve as priests in ordinary places.

Blessed is the family where the mother is a priestess to her offspring, where the father is a priest to all those entrusted to him, and where the domestic help is intent on serving the husband, the wife, and the children in a priestly way. That household is blessed threefold. It is blessed where the parents involve the children in the work of self-denying love and make them fellow builders of the home as a quiet temple of peace. Then it is filled with the fragrant aroma of a higher life.

Life becomes a ministry of love. It's a ministry of love that never disappoints. But it involves a love concerning which every child of God testifies: "I didn't achieve this, but I received it. To God be the glory!"

73

VOLUME II

MAJESTIC LIKE
A HORSE

*The Lord of Hosts will attend his flock, the house of Judah, and
he will make them like a horse majestic in battle. Zechariah 10:3*

Look at how God Almighty glorifies his elect people.

They were scattered like sheep, says Zechariah (10:2). Like defenseless lambs, they were abandoned to the rage of their enemies. They were oppressed and harassed. And listen to this! That same naked, repressed people now receives the amazing promise "I, the Lord your God, will make you like a horse majestic in battle!"

When the battle begins and the trumpet sounds, what will become of that weak and gentle lamb? Won't it become terribly frightened? Won't it run from its own shadow? Won't it shrink back and dash off in fear?

Consider your own soul. It was just like a "sheep set for slaughter" and fled in fear and utter despair. But it will be "made like a horse majestic in battle," says the Lord God. God will make you like a steed with great bloodlines. The Lord himself sang about it to Job: "Will you give the horse its strength? Can you clothe its neck with thunder? ... It mocks fear, is disturbed by nothing, and does not veer away from the sword. The quiver of arrows rattles against its flank. ... At the full blast of the trumpet it shouts, 'Aha!' It smells the battle from afar. It celebrates at the thunderous commands of the princes!"

Oh, the lamb transformed into a horse! There's a full-blown change of mood for you! Fright turned to confidence! Timidity fleeing and transformed into unflinching engagement of the enemy!

When our souls are like the sheep, our spiritual enemies are hard on our heels, and we are driven before them as though by a raging storm. But when our souls are "like horses majestic in battle," then our spiritual enemies flee before us. We strike them down and return from the battle as more than conquerors.

And that's a source of considerable amazement!

That's because while that glorious transformation is fully under way in our souls, we really don't sense what's happening. But when others observe us in combat, they are impressed that we engage the battle with the fury of a war-horse, while we ourselves feel like a trembling lamb that bleats in fear and is sure it's going to perish.

And that's how it should be.

For the person who feels like they are "like a horse majestic in battle" will immediately become confused and will stumble and topple over. The secret to that shining display of courage is concealed precisely in our internal quaking like reeds in the wind.

The lamb conquered hell and all its powers with the courage of a lion. Today God's elect, who are lambs by their own estimation, like lions are proven to be unconquerable in battle.

They are like lambs, naked and defenseless, but they maintain the bearing of "a horse majestic in battle" when they engage in spiritual conflict.

By that conflict don't understand first and foremost the disputes and problems you have with your neighbor over what you confess to be the truths in God's holy Word.

No, our battle is not with flesh and blood, that is to say, not with our fellow human beings who stand before us in their flesh and blood. But first and foremost it's with those evil spiritual forces that are without flesh and blood. They have the capacity to find us anywhere and everywhere and to penetrate to the very depths of our hearts.

The battle is not against you, but against God and against you only insofar and as long as you cling firmly to God.

Therefore, the fight is with Satan. It is with his henchmen and emissaries. It is with all the spiritual forces in the spiritual realm. It is with all the instruments of the Evil One that lie armed and waiting in the world around you as well as within your own heart. It is the conflict with your own ego, for it is Satan's specifically selected servant and his highly trusted secret agent.

It's all about battling all these powers arrayed against your soul. And you have to realize that it's not about disputes with fellow human beings. It's about the spiritual struggles you have with these frightful powers. It's about meeting them with resistance so that they are the ones that flee and you are the one who hunts them down.

In your soul you know beyond a doubt how reversed the roles were. You were the one who was always fleeing. You were the one always losing ground. You were the one always afraid.

And when those powers pursued you once again, your soul lamented weakly: "O God, how will I ever get from under this?" In the end, you simply laid down like a lamb sometimes does and thought: "All my kicking doesn't do any good, and fleeing doesn't work anymore, so that's it. Satan, do with me what you want!"

What a terrible situation!

Yet, there are situations that a person enters, sometimes with a deadened heart and the impassivity born of despair, when they would almost rather die. But then they think, "There may still be a way out!"

It's then that a shaft of light penetrates the soul, penetrates into that frigid, cold-as-death situation. It says: "But God is still there!" This can happen in a moment of utter desperation. And that's when we turn the entire matter over to the God "who is always still there."

At that moment something amazing happens. Something happens to us, around us, within us, and we suddenly realize that we are no longer lying down like that lamb but that we are standing again! The pursuer is no longer pursuing us, but he's fleeing from us! And he's no longer taunting us, as though he were standing over a bloodied lamb. But it's as though we are mounted on a snorting steed. That's when there's victory. That's when our soul has been set free. That's when, after the victory has been won, we spend the night in the tent of our God.

How does this happen? What causes it?

Look here! The Holy Spirit doesn't promise us through the prophet Zechariah that we will stand like a majestic horse, but that we will be made like a horse in its majesty.

Glorious, to be sure, but made that way by God himself!

You have to take it this way. Just as a commander on the battlefield mounts his noble animal and grips it between his legs ... ; just as he guides it by the tilt of his body ... ; just as he turns it by moving the reins between his fingers ... ; just as he nudges it with the spurs on his boots ... ; just as he makes it run, or trot, or come to a complete stop by the tone of his voice ... ; yes, just as he so completely controls his mount that the horse is no longer its own but has simply become an extension of the person in the saddle, is the way the Lord of Hosts controls the person who clings to him.

A superb mount does not follow its own will or its own path in the heat of battle. It is one in obedience, attentiveness, and responsiveness to the slightest movements of its rider. It instinctively turns where his eyes do. It charges where his battle sword slashes in the fight.

Likewise, there can be no triumph for your soul or mine as long as we in an even more profound sense are not a complete extension[1] of our God. We must be willing to let him totally control or "ride" us. We need to allow the breath of his mouth to propel us. It is important that we desire deeply to know no other life force at work within ourselves than the one that advances the power with which God restrains Satan.

That reality is more glorious than the greatest glory on earth!

Here's "the horse majestic in battle!"

You are God's dear children, the chosen instruments through whom he wants to display his majesty before Satan even more than he wants to do that through his holy angels!

That's princely!

That's to be crowned with our crowns already here below!

The person who is permitted to participate in the contending skirmishes of God's activity is a person who knows, appreciates, and even samples already now the glory of Satan's fall.

---

1. Kuyper uses the term *aanhangsel* here ("appendix, appendage"), which in English misses the point of "total covenantal identity with God" that he intends to convey, as his horse and rider metaphor indicates.

ALTHOUGH THEY WERE DREADFUL SHEEP!

So I pastured the sheep designated for slaughter, although they were dreadful sheep! And I took two staffs. The one I called Loveliness and the other I called Uniter, and I pastured the sheep. Zechariah 11:7

"Comfort, comfort my people," says your God. And the Lord's people have a tremendous need for comfort in our day.

People are like sheep in a pasture. They need shepherds. They can't get along without them. Only shepherds make a number of individual sheep into a flock. And just as there can't be a shepherd without sheep in a pasture, there can't be a flock without a shepherd. That's true of people as well as animals! Without shepherds! And not in the limited sense of ministers of the Word, as though they should be the only shepherds of the sheep! That's not at all how Scripture looks at it. God's Word is never that narrow, restricted, or one-sided. That sacred Word always considers the sheep in terms of their entire existence, in all their needs, in their complete dependence. That's why God identifies as shepherds of the people all the heads, guardians, and caregivers in home and school, church and state. There are shepherds in the armed forces. Other shepherds provide leadership in society. Still other shepherds set the pace in the arts and the sciences. And then there are shepherds of the soul as well.

All these shepherds taken collectively have the calling to care for God's dear people. That's because God himself has placed them over his people. But like seed at the center of the fruit, that's not outwardly obvious to the people.

Christ is God's only begotten Son. He's the pivot on which everything turns. Thus, everything here on earth is for the sake of Christ's body, those he has purchased, his precious bride.

The shepherds, therefore, exist for only one reason. Whether they are kings, professors, or preachers, their purpose is to adorn the bride of Christ. Or to use another figure of speech, their purpose is to pasture the flock of the Lord so that it flourishes.

But what are these shepherds doing, these kings and professors and preachers? Instead of sacrificially using all their talents for this primary purpose, they're looking for personal profit at the expense of God's people. They sacrifice the flock for material gain. They fail to recognize that the flock doesn't exist for their benefit but that they exist for its benefit. They turn God's counsel and assignment on its head. In envy and bitterness, they exert their power and influence against God's flock. They basically exasperate and resist it in the context of human society at large.

Sometimes that's even done with pious language and while giving thanks to God Almighty!

Listen to what God says about this sort of thing through Zechariah: "The shepherds regard themselves as the owners," says the Lord. "They kill the sheep and go unpunished for doing so. And when they sell the sheep that they have slaughtered, they piously fall on their knees and say 'Blessed be the Lord, for he has made me rich!' " This isn't being done by just a few of them but by all of them. "They spare none of those that they pasture" (see 11:5)!

This doesn't happen just once in a while, but it's always going on. Without letup! One century after the other! The situation has gotten so terrible and the shape of the sinful world is so abysmal that the very best that the Lord created has been spoiled. Often it's turned directly against his intended purpose.

The Lord's dear people are being overwhelmed, and they can't do anything about it. It's coming at them from all angles: from shepherds in the aristocracy, society's shepherds, academic shepherds, and spiritual shepherds. First of all, they're working together to shear God's sheep! Then to kill them! Then to sell them off for a handsome profit! But that's when things get worse and become even more bitter. God's people are pushed into a corner. They're regarded as crazy. They're ridiculed. They're assaulted and violated. They're treated like doormats. Only then, for the first time, do the shepherds see them as needing their ministry.

You poor people! What's left of you? Well, you become "sacrifices." Now that's a name of honor that God himself gives you. You're given over as "sheep for the slaughter." How frightening! That's an identity stained by the tears and blood of the martyrs. Yet it's also a glorious identity because it immediately identifies you with the "the Lamb who carries away the sins of the world." He's "the Lamb that was led to the slaughter, and who like sheep stood before his shearers as dumb and opened not his mouth."

On Golgotha the shepherds were intent on cooling off their rage against the Lamb. The shepherd Pilate, the shepherd Caiaphas, and the shepherd Herod all attacked the Lamb. But Jesus the Lamb did not answer; he endured it all. He was bitterly, savagely murdered by his own shepherds!

God's beloved people need to figure on this. They should not think it strange when they're being oppressed. They should be amazed only the minute it stops. They should not complain in anguish and despair when their shepherds spin flax for the rope they'll use to strangle them. Rather, they should be amazed if they ever see faithful shepherds on the throne, in the lecture hall, or in the chancel again.

God's beloved people need to believe him when he says: "In this world, you will be persecuted." They should not always be thinking like a discouraged child: "True, but for me he will certainly make an exception. I want so badly to have it good first here on earth and then to have it good in heaven as well."

But that contradicts the Word, for then you apparently don't belong among the sacrificial sheep. Then you obviously hate the honorable identity that the Man of Sorrows attaches to you. Then you'd rather be a lamb on exhibit with a wreath of flowers around your neck, like the sacrificial animals that the priests of Ephesus paraded through the streets. The result of this will be that you may walk around here decorated with garlands, but you will very shortly die on an altar where the name of the Lord is unknown.

You'll be a happy, fortunate, successful, and celebrated person among the children of this age, but precisely for that reason your heart will deviate far from trusting in God. Listen carefully! What's the identity that God assigns to his deeply loved people? Doesn't he call them "my dreadful people"? Even right here in this beautiful prophecy about sheep for the slaughter, why should the Lord have compassion on his people? As the Holy Spirit's interpreter, Zechariah says: "So I pastured the sheep designated for slaughter, although they were dreadful sheep!"

The heart of your everlastingly compassionate God is made gracious toward them precisely because they were suffering so much and were so desperate and violated. Because no one else wanted to pasture them, he decided to do it.

Are you still dubious? Do you still think: "It really doesn't need to be that bad"? Well, then read verse 11 with open eyes to see how bad it was for the sheep that knew the Lord. Even the afflicted sheep that waited on him understood that this was a word used by the Lord.

Feeling dreadful! Giving up! Not seeing a solution or receiving counsel! Being driven, as though by a raging storm! Hunted like the deer on the mountains! Being obligated but unable to meet obligations! Flattered for your sin but badgered for being holy! Helpless! Defenseless! No longer standing but collapsed and fallen! And then to have those shepherds who should be pasturing you come to you holding their shearing scissors and strangling rope and scales for weighing their gold! Then feeling smothered when everything is blackest! Then retreating into yourself! Discovering there, inside your heart, a very angry spirit and all sorts of criminal desires churning! Feeling that you've been deceived! Discovering Satan at the door of your heart wanting to slip in!

Really, my dear friends, this is what can finally overwhelm us as well. We are among those dreadful sheep that are waiting for the Lord. Through bitter experience I learn that I'm one of them as well.

But then a new world begins. Then you discover something you never expected. You discover that those sheep that you thought had no shepherds really do have a Shepherd after all! And he's a glorious Shepherd! He's a Shepherd that feeds them with the sweetest grass, slakes their thirst with the coolest water, and pastures them with the fondest love imaginable.

The Shepherd's staff is called Loveliness.

This is the secret approach of the Spirit. It's the covert knowledge of eternal Wisdom. It's the clandestine preaching of the everlasting Preacher.

It will be well for the person who knows the mystical intimacy of such blessedness.

SO THEN NEITHER HE WHO PLANTS NOR HE WHO WATERS IS ANYTHING!

So then neither he who plants nor he who waters is anything,
but God who gives the increase. 1 Corinthians 3:7

The existence of God's people preserves a nation. Nothing should ever minimize this idea. Jesus' cooking uses salt in order to prevent spoilage. His people are a light in the national darkness. They are a city set on a hill and therefore the strength on which a nation's preservation depends.

This persists even when the church is at very low ebb and it becomes little more than a courier of salvation's treasure from one generation to the next.

Consider how this happened with Israel!

In the days when everyone bowed down to their idols in Jerusalem's homes and palaces, the messianic seed still lay dormant in Israel's soil. It was the hope of the nation. It was the will of the Father.

The same is true in our own time. That seed is present in the part of a nation where a faithful witness is maintained. That's where hope for the future and expectation of a country's preservation is sheltered.

What will save and sustain a nation and its people and give them a future is not something that you provide. Only the Lord's testimony accomplishes this. God's people maintain his honor even when they do no more than suffer indignities for the sake of that witness.

That's why there should never be a moment's hesitation in paying close attention to his people. Everyone sins when they minimize or hate God's witnessing people.

The value of love, loyalty, and nobility of spirit for the future of a country should definitely never be discounted. But when you compare what these qualities mean for its future with what the testimony of God's people means for it, they hardly deserve mention.

God saves. God preserves. God himself protects a nation. No single individual does this. No mere creature does. And because God himself addresses a nation in no other way than through his own testimony, everything is dependent on that witness!

Woe, woe to the people of the Lord if they ever want to be anything other than bearers of that witness. That testimony is the seed of life. The people of God are its sowers. They do the sowing and all the watering.

So Paul plants and Apollos waters. But then what? Then still nothing happens ... unless! For just as a germ of life never emerges from a small seed apart from the work of God's almighty power, so too no germ of eternal life sprouts from the seed of his people's witness apart from the fruit-bearing work of God the Holy Spirit.

This requires attentiveness to loving God's people.

You have to show love for them. The love you have for his people is the measure of the love that you have for the Father. John asks how anyone who does not love the child can possibly love the God about whose child they are embarrassed. That sad situation seals the fact that every soul, however pious and tinted with genius they might be, will go awry unless something changes. They need to extract the thorn from their heart that has irritated and inflamed them against God's people.

We maintain adamantly, therefore, that every child of God has to love God's beloved people with an undivided love. And we add this. All withering of the tender shoots springing up in God's garden can be blamed on the fact that connecting with God's people is avoided and love for them is not nurtured. It happens when the existing population in countries is not engaged by Jesus' more recent witnesses.

But your love for those people needs to be careful and tender. Don't minimize this.

I don't mean being careful in the sense of being careful about getting too involved with them.

For me it means that I devote myself wholeheartedly and without reservation to this people just as they exist here in our country, with all their illnesses and festering sores. It means nothing less than "being one with them and making common cause with them."

No, being careful is meant in the sense that you don't become careless in your love and fondness for them so that they waste away instead of being built up and strengthened.

This people must not be flattered but shaken awake. They need to be shaken awake not by haggling about something in their testimony, by criticizing the form it takes, or by condemning its simplicity. But because you are sick and leprous yourself, you need to dedicate yourself to that sick and leprous people of God. It means that you don't stop warning them and saying: "Brothers, don't hold back in giving the Lord of Lords the glory due to him."

And this is how you uphold the people of God in your heart.

They will turn on you like a lion if they sense that when God says to them: "*Lo ammi*, you are my people," you sarcastically dare to add: "But yet you are really aren't God's people!"

Yes, we add that they will resist you to your face, treat you like a whitewashed tomb, and angrily set you straight if you tamper with their witness or attack their confession of faith that was sealed with the blood of martyrs.

But if you don't, God's dear people will definitely not become angry with your soul-searching admonition. At least as long as it comes from your heart! Then that people will feel: "That man carries us in his heart." Then that people will even be well disposed to identify with the sins of Israel. Then they will hate a flattering tongue. Then they will long for the truth, even when that truth rolls over God's heirs in the form of a torrent of judgments.

This is what God's people need to discover about themselves.

They have to understand what it is that is so endlessly, endlessly far removed from what God's people must be in order to bring him honor.

They have to understand that their knowledge of the gospel's secret mysteries has sunk away like water from a dried-up summer brook. That their praying scarcely ever deserved the name of genuine sighing of the soul! That their idols again roosted on the pedestals of sin remaining in their hearts! That their generosity remained bound by ropes and chains, while their stinginess strolled openly down the streets! And worst of all, that because of these ulcers and festering sores that cover them and cause them pain, one member of the body cannot stand the sight of another. As a result, the tender, melting brotherly love passes over them like a cloud whisked across the morning sky and is as scarce as the gold of Ophir.

The people of God need to hear all this. They need to hear it from those who love them, not from those who hate them. They need to hear it primarily from those who preach the Word, for they are one with them and hold them in their hearts. They must be involved daily in the ministry of love and must carry it out before the Lord with enthusiasm and faithfulness. They need to do it with such faithfulness that the Word does not just serve to give birth to children in the kingdom of God, as has been true now for many years. But they must do so in a way that makes the Word a power that causes these children to become grown-ups in grace, makes them increase in holiness, and deepens them in the glorious mysteries of the divine covenant of grace.

And should you ask what measure ought to be used to assess the effectiveness of this Word in their lives, here's the answer. It needs to be one that measures just one thing, namely, their unending desire to honor God to the full extent that he deserves.

Stop trying to be something!

Not by wanting to do nothing and simply sitting still until mildew covers your soul like a parasite!

On the contrary! The Lord tells you that you need to plant. But not just that! You also need to water. You need to do this with unbounded energy and by devoting all your effort to it!

And the secret is concealed in this. When you plant and when you water, people of the Lord, you need to say: "Not to me, but to God be all the honor." Then also remind yourself that you mattered. That needs to be acknowledged.

The apostle puts it so clearly and forcefully: "Neither he who plants, nor he who waters is anything, but ... "

UNENDING PAIN
IN MY HEART!

I am telling the truth in Christ. I am not lying. ... I have great
sorrow and unending pain in my heart. Romans 9:1–2

The mystery of pain is that it hurts so much more than we are willing to admit.

We do feel pain. We're more than willing to admit it. Suffering is compulsory. No one escapes drinking the cup of suffering. But it's especially children of the kingdom who figure that pain and suffering are part of their kingdom inheritance.

But do you know how many of God's dear children usually think about this? They imagine that life will go on without any anguish. They think it will pass in quiet good fortune. They suppose that these favored days will continue, interrupted only now and then by painful interludes. Sunshine will be the rule. Skies will rarely be overcast, and even then they will hardly ever be accompanied by storms and bad weather. So, pain, yes! But in small doses and as brief interruptions! Pain comes, but then it also leaves again. It's a passing cloud.

Jesus' holy apostle talks differently. He acknowledges unending pain. It's pain without letup. It's not passing. It persists and endures. That the apostle felt the great depth of his pain is expressed in what he says here. Just listen: "I am telling the truth in Christ. I am not lying. My conscience is my witness by the power of the Holy Spirit. I have great sorrow and unending pain in my heart."

Isn't that a deeper, more profound way of putting it?

If the heart is really tender, do you think it will be able to discount pain quickly? If the soul is genuinely sensitive, do you think it will easily be able to forget the pain it endured?

A dear child gives you grief, and its lack of love for you greatly disturbs you. You suffer because of this. You suffer not because you're hurt, but because it's your child! But a week later the cloud has blown over and your pain is gone. You poor father! This is to respond as though the unloving act that caused you pain was not a poison that meanwhile has been spreading like cancer. It was only the initial expression of more to come! This is also to respond as though it were insensitive and unloving on your part to feel pain when you were wounded by what your child did. Rather, it should be the wound itself that disturbed you.

Or someone in your circles died, and you were flooded and overwhelmed by the pain caused by this bitter loss. You wept like your heart had been torn out. You could never, ever forget the one who died. And yet, why shouldn't it be said openly? How quickly and suddenly the pain felt in our hearts over such a loss often passes!

And that shouldn't happen, should it? The pain I feel over my child's sin or my loved one's departure should be unending. It should be continuous and unabated. It shouldn't be experienced so superficially in my life, but it should penetrate to the depths of my soul.

How do people talk about this passing experience?

Well, that experience is definitely a message sent by God that affords quiet comfort. For if the pain that so gripped and overwhelmed us in those initial moments had to continue unabated, life itself would become impossible. We couldn't stand it. It would kill us! But what does the passing of time produce? Does it blunt our emotions? Does it muffle our hearts? Does it replace memory with forgetfulness? Possibly, for the children of this world! But should it do the same for the people of God? Not at all! What the passing of time can and should produce is a calming of the nerves, an easing of the pain caused by our heartrending denial, and even the removal of the constricting heaviness that constant awareness of our loss produced. But it should not eliminate pain from our souls. Instead, it should be an experience that purifies and sanctifies pain through faith. Then we experience it on a deeper level in the hidden depths of our hearts. The quieted and calmed child of God should suffer like the angels do! They bear the pain burning in their soul with holy laughter and dry eyes. It makes them look upward to their merciful God.

This is how an entirely different reality falls over our lives in this world. The blanket of pain spread over our entire existence is not there to smoother us with a somber outlook on life. No, it's there to enthrall us with a mercifully enduring comfort that through faith exists just beneath that quilt.

A child of God cannot live here on earth without pain. "In this world you will endure persecution," says the Lord. "He who would follow me must deny himself, take up his cross, and follow me!"

For a child of God, the cross is a sacred symbol towering over all of life.

They may never be greater than their Master, and they never will be. And what was the life of their Lord Jesus other than a life of unending pain? Can you think of the Christ of God here on earth in any other way than as feeling pain? Can you imagine that your Jesus may have ever distanced himself from the sins of the world? Or that he ever forgot the horror of sin for as much as a moment?

Just seeing those thoughts written down hits you hard, doesn't it? It's difficult for you to think about Jesus that way. But the profound harmony of the Lord's life would be destroyed by any such cleavage in his soul or between his experiences. Discarding all such superficiality, confess again with greater appreciation what the catechism says: "That he, especially at the end of his life, but also during all the days of his existence in the flesh here on earth bore the wrath of God against the sin of the whole human race!"[1]

If this was true for your Lord Jesus, why would it be any different for you?

"If we suffer with him, it is in order that we might be glorified with him." We should "always be bearing the crucifixion of our Lord Jesus Christ in our bodies." Or as our form for baptism expresses it, "Our life is nothing but a constant death."

Doesn't it seem strange to you, then, that things are so totally different in your own soul? My brother and my sister, shouldn't your "absence of unending pain" make you think seriously about all of this?

For many long years, people have made fun of "long faces" and "sourpusses." And we certainly haven't equated a glum face with piety. "Anoint your head and wash your face," Jesus said. Somberness is not an indication of more refined spiritual emotion; it only suppresses it. So if it isn't, does the always jovial Christian reflect the marks of true spirituality? I don't know. But could that possibly be the case if unending pain is what's always cutting into the heart? Believe me when I say that the laughter of angels that shines through their

---

1. Here Kuyper is quoting the first half of the answer to question 37, Lord's Day 15 of the Heidelberg Catechism.

pain is hugely different from the superficial laughter that has never tasted unending pain.

And what must that unending pain be all about?

In answering that question, more than one person feels endless oppression falling over their heart. In everyday living and external matters, people sometimes do feel pain without letup. There are physical infirmities that persist. There are wounds in family life that never heal. There can be afflictions all around us, sometimes in the form of actual people who sour the cup of our meager joy. You'd be terribly unloving if you had neither eye or heart for that kind of enduring pain poured out every morning and again every evening.

But not everyone encounters that sort of pain. Not many people experience unending pain like that. But what needs to be added here is that the unending pain of someone like Paul is of an even higher, nobler, and more deeply penetrating nature.

The unending pain about which Paul is complaining as a child of God involved his kinsmen, rebellious Israel. It touched the deep apostasy of others.

That's why it's important to ask how far your antennae stretch toward the suffering of others. Do you experience suffering because of sin? Do you feel pain because of your own sin? Because of the righteousness being obliterated all around you? Is your soul in anguish over the transgressions of the ungodly?

Do you know the pain of people who are struggling? Do you have the feeling that you have to be holy but that time and again you're revolted by you own self-serving, proud, and impure attitudes?

Do you already know the pain caused by knowing what others are suffering? By the sick and the sorrowing? By those humiliated by the human miseries they have to endure?

Have you ever wept over God's church or over the pain behind Jerusalem's walls? Can the lamentable condition of God's people ever move you to weep in your soul?

What's your answer?

Shame on you, right? Shame on all God's children because we've been so hard and callous, so deplorably insensitive and seemingly stonehearted.

Is it any wonder that there is so little prayer and so little appeal to God above?

Prayer without ceasing—it can't come unless there's first the experience of unending pain!

I WILL SPIT YOU OUT OF MY MOUTH

So, because you are lukewarm and neither cold nor
hot, I will spit you out of my mouth. Revelation 3:16

Terrible things are said in the Bible about half-hearted people. God rages against the ungodly in his anger. He declares a curse of damnation against the Pharisees. But the lukewarm person who hobbles along as a half-hearted Christian is so disgusting and intolerable to God that in the book of Revelation he says: "You lukewarm and half-hearted person, I'm going to spit you out of my mouth!"

This is the same God talking who speaks in the Bible about his unfathomable compassion and immeasurable depth of comfort. He's the One who reveals to us that he justifies the ungodly. He's the God who rushes out to meet the prodigal son and to embrace him in his merciful arms as his father.

Even though your sins are as scarlet, do not be afraid; I will make them as white as snow. Even if your heart is as cold and hard as marble, don't despair; I will gather you like a hen gathers her chicks and shelter you under my wings. I only ask one thing: do not be half-hearted. Don't say "yes" and "no" at the same time. Don't be lukewarm in my presence.

For then as surely as God is God, he will spit you out of his mouth!

That's terrible, isn't it? It's terrible for God to talk this way. It's terrible that he neither can nor may talk differently. But what's even more terrible yet is that the world and especially the church of the living God are full to overflowing with just these kinds of lukewarm and half-hearted people. And the most terrible of all is that these half-hearted folk by the thousands are Bible readers who read their own condemnation in it: "Because you are lukewarm, I will spit you out of my mouth!" They read over this and think, to the extent that they do still think at all: "But this doesn't affect me!"

But it definitely does affect you! The curse of being lukewarm is so corrosive that a lukewarm person is too lukewarm and impassive to even feel the impact of a word like this in their heart.

Everything merely slides off a half-hearted person. Their soul is like a plow without a plowshare; it is dragged between the clods without slicing a furrow across the field. The words of Scripture splatter against their souls and roll off like drops of water off a slick surface. Even on their deathbed they may read or have someone else read these words to them: "Because you are lukewarm, I will spit you out of my mouth." But it still doesn't register on their crippled hearts or occur to them that they are the ones who are lukewarm. And this continues forever, at least until God does what he says in his Word and actually spits them out in his divine contempt and nauseous disgust.

Can it be any different?

They are half-hearted members of the church. They want to be counted as members and be regarded as religious, but not as strictly devout. They do contribute something. They are very opposed to thoroughgoing modernists. But to love God, to glow with enthusiasm for the Lord's work, and to cry out: "Lord, be merciful to me, a sinner!"—never! They might sing along with some hymn, but it only amounts to going along with the flow of everything else that slips and slides along so superficially in their lives. They are so very smart, these half-hearted folks. They are very careful to avoid being one-sided and they have an innate aversion to being extreme in anything.

So what would you do if you were in God's position? Would you think: "But there's still something very lovable about these peaceable people who speak well of each other among themselves, and that semblance of love I take to be real love"? No, I tell you! You should push them away and shove them aside, saying: "For your God, it has to be all or nothing!"

A mother may never be at peace in her home and display a kind of cool detachment when her child takes up with every stranger who comes along. A father may not simply let things slide if his son favors him with only an outward show of respect. "My son, give me your heart!" is the attitude with which every father is obligated to approach his son. If he's satisfied with anything less than that, it's unsuitable for his father heart.

The same is true for God. Because he is truly God, he can be at peace with nothing less than glowing love, love sparkling like a fire, love that's alive.

It is possible to be cold toward God. Coldness is a force that can be turned against the Lord. It amounts to kicking against the pricks. But what was once stone cold can in reaction begin to glow with powerful warmth. Behold, the prostitutes and tax collectors will enter the kingdom of heaven before you do!

But being lukewarm is where there is no movement at all. It's a morass. It's a pool over which no gentle breeze is blowing. It's unbounded self-satisfaction. "Sure, God is my heavenly Father, and I really do love him!" That kind of talk God doesn't bother cursing. He doesn't become angry with it any longer. He simply spits it out of his mouth.

Those who confess Jesus in our good country of the Netherlands need to hear those frightening words clearly. The character of the Netherlands bears a fearful similarity to that of Laodicea! The same kind of composure, the same kind of caution, the same kind of caginess! Always appealing, but not too strongly! Always sloughing along quietly in the middle of the road! We're nakedly exposed to all of it. The nature of our poor people, especially in the midsection of the country, displays the same kind of sinning that happened in Laodicea!

People always have to first think things over. Those reflections first have to marinate for a while, summer and winter. Then, if it seems good, rarely is the response made with a strong and resounding "Yes!" It usually comes with a sneer and lands somewhere between "yes" and "no."

That sort of composure and constant appeal not to "go too far" into spiritual matters is a national sin. This is sin that kills the bud before the flower has a chance to unfold. It's a sin that forfeits what could have been a blessing. It causes many a village and small city to creep from one year to the next half asleep, as though living in a fantasy world.

It shows a lack of willpower.

The will can't take on any more.

People do really want to make decisions, but their decisions yield nothing. Nothing comes of them.

This is offensive and resisted only as long as the conscience still struggles against it.

But even that comes to an end. Finally, the conscience stops pricking and is blunted. Then the worst possible thing happens. People become half-hearted. Lukewarmness is approved. It's even seen as a virtue. It's extolled as the greatest of human wisdom. Instead of the clear testimony of God's Word, another witness is put forward: "Oh, if you were only lukewarm! But because you are fervent, I will spit you out of my social circles!"

A person who dares to be definite is then called a "Pharisee"!

Every lukewarm person merely hobbling along has now become one of the wise on earth!

It's particularly among those who possess many material goods that you find lukewarm Christians in droves!

Sadly, why are they also found among Reformed people who confess the name of the Lord? And where are they hidden? They're right there talking and singing and praying along with all those about whom you would say: "Their hearts definitely have to be beating warmly!" But when it comes to denying the flesh and to loving God in his tender mercies, they are lukewarm in the depths of their souls—grimly lukewarm.

Lord, dispense your terrible judgment especially on these lukewarm people, even to deepest union of spirit and soul. Their condemnation should be that great!

78

VOLUME II

KEREN-HAPPUCH

He also had three daughters. … And he named … the
third one Keren-happuch. More beautiful women were
not found in the entire country. Job 42:13–15

Job was and is a mystifying figure that God Almighty used to silence Satan and to send his religiously know-it-all friends home with shame written all over their faces. God also uses Job to comfort his own dear children, not with syrupy sentimentalism but with dynamic and godly reassurance.

Whoever has worked their way through the magnificent book of Job feels closer to God. That's particularly true if they've done so feeling its anguish and pain flooding their own souls. They feel closer to God simply because the book of Job is so thoroughly human. It disdains any trace of exaggerated spirituality. It accepts the spiritually oppressed, struggling person just as they actually are.

The secret of why Job's words are so wonderfully comforting to us is that he says exactly what he thinks. His piety isn't superficial. It's simple and genuine. He doesn't hold anything back from God. What you see is who he really is. He's not satisfied until he's come to God, the source of all that satisfied him, and unloaded all his human needs and desires on him.

Pay special attention to this one point. Job had had children, and among them were his daughters. Wouldn't he unquestionably have taken special delight if they had been beautiful to look at? This is true of every father, and you can also safely add, of every mother. That was true of parents in the Eastern world; and it's still true of us in the Western world today. We consider it a special blessing when we receive a beautiful child from the hand of God, especially if it's a girl.

But note that Job's bitter disappointments included the loss of his dear children. He would never again see all the friendly, lively, beautiful traits of his children. Oh, the pain he must have experienced! These children were the delight of his eyes, the overflowing abundance in his heart. But when his happy home life collapsed, all this was totally washed away. People deal with such blessings so superficially! But consider, once, what it would have meant to Job as he sat on his heap of ashes, if one of those precious children could have come to him in his bitter pain and anguish and called out to him, even if only from far away: "O my dear, dear father, you're suffering so unbearably!" Just a tear in the child's eye would have been soothing ointment on his wounded heart. It would have been more effective than all the misguided displays of comfort from his friends.

But look at how it all ended. Look at the solution to the puzzle, when Job was back and everything had turned around. What do we see then? That the Lord caused Job to begin flourishing spiritually once again? Of course! But even more than that! He granted him both grace and glory. Job wasn't only blessed with grace spiritually, but he was also given the glory of honor and material wealth.

And wealth in what way?

Literally, wealthy in everything that the human heart could desire.

In that regard, Job received the riches of children again. He was given seven sons and three daughters. But these weren't ordinary daughters. They were unusually beautiful daughters. They were the most beautiful daughters in the entire country.

That's how it goes with wealth from God!

We could say: "What does it matter whether the girls that Job was given were beautiful or not, unless they were also godly?" But the Lord God would respond: "No, but while all of that is true, their beauty is also a source of glory. Having beautiful daughters is a source of glory for parents. And I'm clothing my servant Job with that glory as well!"

In fact, so much emphasis was placed on their beauty that we take it that the beauty of these girls wasn't simply the typical beauty of childhood. They didn't outgrow it! No, their full beauty only blossomed when they were mature women. Then there were no women to be found in the entire land that were as beautiful as these daughters of Job. Their beauty was found, in addition, in the harmony of their entire beings. This was captured in the names they were given. "Jemimah" conveys beauty like that of a dove. "Keziah" expresses beauty like that of an exquisite perfume. But "Keren-happuch" communicates the greatest beauty of them all. It is beauty that overwhelms others by its charm and unrestrained graciousness.

Praise for Keren-happuch seems out of place in our Christian world today. I'm afraid that parents who understand the damage it can cause almost never pray for a "beautiful child" anymore. They certainly don't dare to pray for a physically gorgeous daughter! Their prayer is much more likely to be: "Lord, just don't let my little girl be physically gorgeous externally. That might only cause irreparable damage internally to the glaze of your marvelous grace adorning her soul."

There's good reason for taking that approach.

Every spiritual observer will have to testify to the fact that the overlooked Leahs very often precede the Rachels into the kingdom of heaven. It's not primarily the Keren-happuchs who are attracted to the spiritual beauty of Jesus' cross, but those who have been short-changed when it comes to external beauty.

There are exceptions, to be sure.

It does happen that there are daughters covered with beauty and grace who hate and resist vanity in case they lose sight of God. But they are exceptions. Moreover, who can appreciate the enormous amount of grace working in their hearts it would require to unravel and cut the cords of vanity in their lives?

A beautiful woman who never lets herself be adored and is never moved by anything except her adoration of the Lord is an outstanding example of divine grace. To be in a position of being idolized, but then to have no other gods before you than God himself, demands enormous effort.

Most often these poor Keren-happuchs aren't able to withstand such overwhelming temptation. Vanity overpowers them. Self-centeredness reigns. They forget the soul and focus on the body. The robes of righteousness are replaced by the glitz of the latest fashions. It's not the corrosive effects of sin on their hearts that trouble them but their aging and blemished skin.

Worse yet is when these Keren-happuchs are born into lower social classes! God only knows how many beautiful daughters born to poorer parents are overwhelmed by scandal and bestiality when they lose their beauty!

It's terrible!

But then take a look at a plain, unattractive girl who may even have an unpleasant voice. She uses it to quietly praise God by singing the Psalms. Now don't you think, you parents, that beauty has really become more of a curse and that a very ordinary appearance that doesn't attract anyone's attention is a greater blessing from the Lord?

That's the way it's been through the ages!

Naamah was judged to be the first beautiful girl among the sons of men (Gen 4:22).[1] She was born to Lamech and Zillah. Her brothers were Jabal and Tubal-Cain. It was an ungodly generation.

Things are becoming more and more like that in our own day. The emphasis on emancipation has particularly transfixed beautiful women. God has not prevented this from becoming a disastrous curse. In our times, all of life has been turned inside out, and the beautiful woman is being idolized in nature and in art. It's especially true in our time that a young woman can spend every hour of every day thinking about the changes in season-appropriate clothing! It's nothing short of a maelstrom that sweeps everything along. Whoever is beautiful and popular is vulnerable to this frightful danger.

But the alternative is still possible.

Even Keren-happuchs can find Jesus! Provided they aren't coquettish about scared matters! Provided they're convinced "I can't ever get there by myself" and, defenseless, throw themselves into the arms of Jesus in order to be rescued! And especially provided that they are protected and battle against the worst that could happen, namely, blending adoration of self with adoration of the Lord!

Parents, above all, love your girls with a very special love. May God guard you against ever regarding them as little dolls provided for your parental vanity. See to it that you never incite them to evil through clothing or makeup. Help them flee from the Evil One. Lead them from externals to what is inside, namely, to a nobler and holier beauty that radiates from the treasures of their souls.

---

1. Kuyper's judgment is based on the name's meaning: "pleasant, sweet, delightful."

MINISTERING DAILY

Each priest stood, ministering daily. ... But he, having offered one
sacrifice ... , sat down at God's right hand. Hebrews 10:11–12

S till outside? Or already in the Redeemer? It makes an enormous difference
for us as spiritual beings. "Outside" is not meant here in the sense of the
ungodly, who in their blindness continue cursing the glorious Son of God. Nor
is it meant in the sense of those who are definitely searching but who have not
yet found. No, I'm thinking here only about the truly converted person. I have
in mind the children of God who are not only among the eternally elect but
who through conversion became so in time. These have really and truly passed
from death to life and have been transported from the kingdom of darkness
into the kingdom of the Son.

I have to tell you that among the converted there are those still outside
the Surety and those already grafted into the Surety. This represents no
misunderstanding!

That by the counsel of his electing grace God has joined every child of his
to the Mediator, his Son, from before the foundation of the world is certain
and sure. And it is equally sure that in their actual transformation, that is, at
the time they experienced a deep sense of well-being, they were by an act of
God actually grafted into the vine as branches. But, and this is the only point
on which all of this turns, just as they do not know when they were joined to
the Son of God in their eternal election, their being grafted into the Vine as
branches almost always occurs without their awareness.

All of this makes a third experience necessary, just as in the realm of natural life. What occurs first in natural life is the act of God by which he decided to give us to our parents. Then comes the second, the moment of our birth, when our parents receive the child designated for them. But a third event is necessary to complete the picture. The child designated for them and given to them must finally, when growing up, come to realize that they are their parents' child. Then, in that knowledge, they are able to address their parents heart to heart as child to parent.

That's how it is in the spiritual realm as well. The first thing that happens is the act of God in eternity by which an elect person is given to the Son. The second is the act in time by which God converts the soul and by drawing them there presents the individual to the Redeemer. ("No one comes to me unless the Father draws him there.") But then there is the third event. It occurs within the soul. Here the person given to Christ comes to know that they belong to the Son. They are crystal clear in knowing that they are in Christ.

The difference between these two conditions present among God's converted children is like the difference between the saints in Israel and the saints in the dispensation of the new covenant. The spiritual fathers in the former were definitely not unconverted people. They were no longer searching; they had definitely found! "Abraham longed to see my day; he did see it, and he was overjoyed." Far from putting the saints of Israel on a lower plane than ourselves, we readily admit that to the extent that it was possible for them, their most outstanding heroes of faith were accorded an exceptional measure of grace. Through it they drank deeply of the salvation and glorious satisfaction they had in the Messiah.

And yet, the common situation that all God's children in Israel shared was that they lacked something that is present now. They had the promises, to be sure. But they had not yet received what was promised, so that without us they would never have been made perfect.

Precisely that explains the ambivalent situation of every child of God still today who has been brought to the Savior but is not yet clearly aware that they have been grafted into their Head and Lord. They haven't experienced this for themselves on a personal, spiritual level. The most that their soul notices in this regard is whether they "are standing and ministering daily," but not whether they are already "seated with Jesus who is seated at the right hand of God."

The apostle says that in Israel an individual priest stood, ministering daily. But Jesus, having offered one sacrifice for all time, is now eternally at rest and gloriously seated at the right hand of God.

We're not dealing here with work righteousness, since the priest who was standing there ministering daily was a priest of the Most High. Day in and day out he was ministering according to God's ordinances.

Those among us who are standing and ministering on a daily basis have been made priests and priestesses. We are people who have been instructed and incorporated into the service of the Lord our God.

And look, this is exactly consistent with the situation of the child of God drawn to Jesus. That person died to self the moment they were joined to him for eternity. But they have not yet felt the dawn of blessed enjoyment and sacred peace associated with being engrafted into the Savior. That consciousness has not yet registered in their souls.

This is the situation that almost all children of God find themselves in immediately after their conversion. There are exceptions, I admit. There are a very few that immediately experience the full light of this event. The Lord God is completely free in exercising his power. One of his ways of doing things, however, may never be imposed as the standard for all the ways he does things. But these exceptions to the usual spiritual experience are very, very rare. They have to be seen as extremely scarce particularly in our own day. Far and away the majority of God's children find that shortly after their conversion they enter a phase of discontent and disappointment. Only when we begin to rise above this does love begin entering our hearts. To put it more pointedly, a person would perhaps need to say that while a complete peace accompanies the love felt at the time of conversion, it then cools off, and a sense of discouragement follows. But we can't stop with these more precise distinctions. The main point is the fact that people are first joined to Jesus without actually, consciously experiencing that they have been grafted into him. Only afterwards does a person become consciously aware in their soul of how tender and blessed that engrafting actually is.

Then people in retrospect feel the difference. They acknowledge that in that first phase that now lies behind them they really were priests, served in his temple, and were responsive to his voice. But they also acknowledge that the blessed, glorious peace in doing so still wasn't theirs. Theirs was still an exhausting, draining standing in ministry. It was a standing in ministry day in and day out. It was standing every day in order to serve by repeatedly offering the same sacrifices that would never be able to achieve atonement for sin. That is to say, it was the same as with Roman Catholicism, that wants to make offering Christ every day effective through what we do, whether that's an act of contrition, an act of devotion, or an act of supplication. There needs to be the recognition that Christ's sacrifice accomplishes this. But Christ's sacrifice must then be realized. And that's where I need to be involved. Something is required of me. I need to do a great deal here. Every day again I need to confess: "O God, I have sinned!" Every day again I need to repeat: "O God, I want to deny myself!" Every day again I need to plead: "O God, do not hold my sins against me." Troubled, therefore! Always hunted, like the roe on the mountains! Still not having received the eternal Sabbath here in this life! All this will continue for as long as it pleases the Lord God to bring us through the depths prior to making our hearts conscious of the fact that we have been grafted into Christ. Then, aware that we have been engrafted into him, we will also possess eternal peace and celebrate before our God. We will have arrived at a completely different place.

For now self is gone and only Jesus remains. Our entire soul is immersed in Jesus. I no longer ask what I have done but what he has done. And he once made one offering, a single sacrifice to atone for sin. That one offering was totally sufficient. Nothing more needs to be done. And now he sits in sacred majesty on his eternal throne, where he waits in quiet peace until all his enemies will become a footstool for his feet.

And that which is said here about Jesus is applied by the Holy Spirit to those who have been engrafted into him. That's because in that one act of Christ we are all made holy. By means of that one sacrifice, he has eternally perfected all those who come to God through him. Now they have peace, a wonderful peace in their Lord Jesus. They are no longer always striving, but they are waiting, waiting until all their deadly enemies will be placed before them as a footstool for their feet.

These are the ones who have gone behind the curtain.

The wings of the cherubim shade their souls from the brilliance of God's glory radiating off the mercy seat.

What is so sad is that so few at present reach the light of full awareness in their souls. Two abuses account for this.

The first is that people apply the condition of being conscious of being engrafted into Christ universally, to all those who are converted. By doing so, they willingly or unwillingly foster a limp, half-hearted, and tired passivity, inactivity, and even antinomianism.

The second and no less damaging is that people dismiss the deeper experience of this conscious awareness of being grafted into Christ.

This explains why in almost every way there is at present a lack of "fathers in Christ" and "mothers in Israel."

Underbrush is thick and exists all around us. But where can you still find a towering tree among the Lord's people, one with a broad canopy that provides wonderful shade?

80

VOLUME II

BUT I AM OF THE FLESH, SOLD INTO SIN'S BONDAGE!¹

For we know that the law is spiritual, but I am of the flesh, sold into sin's bondage. Romans 7:14

Anything, anything at all alongside the Lamb, and you no longer have a Lamb that carries your sins away.

The Lamb that bears the sins of the world is the one and only. He's everything; he's complete; he's lavish; he's more than sufficient. Whoever adds anything more rejects the Lamb.

It's either the Lamb or the mighty bull of Bashan. That's the choice.

The mighty bull of Bashan's power is evident in his horns, his thick neck muscles, and the unpredictable display of his strength. He eats grass, and this adds to its strength. He becomes even more powerful. He lives by his mighty horns.

---

1. Atypically, Kuyper adds a long footnote here on the history of interpretation of his chosen text. He argues with virtually all classical Reformed exegetes that this passage is referring to regenerate people, just as Kohlbrugge also does in reflecting on his own personal experience as well as on the context of this passage. Kohlbrugge was an earlier nineteenth-century religious leader whom Kuyper respected. We omit a translation of the note.

The Lamb is completely different. Tender, weak, and powerless, he trembles when he encounters the mighty bull of Bashan. He is dumb in the presence of one that lives by battering. Facing death, he looks to heaven.

What we see here are two approaches. They are entirely different, totally at variance, two completely divergent approaches.

The approach of the mighty bull is to become ever stronger, always greater in his goodness, piety, virtue, friendliness, and righteousness until he's finally seen almost as an angel by other people. Then, when he dies, he assumes that he'll automatically take his place where the angels live.

The approach of the Lamb, on the other hand, is to become ever weaker, needier, and more helpless. He affirms: "My strength is made perfect in weakness!" He believes: "My grace is sufficient for you!"

These are also two approaches that yield different outcomes. Head for head, the mighty bulls of Bashan perish and go to hell. But person for person, the followers of the Lamb escape and discover the path of Enoch and Elijah.

But what just never works at all is to live in part by taking the bull's approach and in part by taking the Lamb's approach. Yet, this seems to be innate with us. This is what our treacherous hearts want.

By not giving the Lamb first place in our lives! By wanting the benefits of the cross! By profiting from the sacrifice for sin! But ... as matters already achieved in the past! I was at one time such a sinner. Once there was that kind of Redeemer, and now that Redeemer helps me from becoming the kind of sinner I once was. But from now on, now that I've been healed, I'm living without the need of a healer. I'm healthy. My strength is back. Just look at my horns! Look how they've grown back! I've become so holy and godly and so much better than those others. I'm conscious of the fact that I almost never sin anymore. What I can still benefit from is someone who inspires me to holiness. I don't need someone any longer who lays a guilt trip on me. I no longer need an example of righteousness who is needed by those who recognize in their hearts how ungodly they are.

This is how people talk to each other. This is how the deceitful heart looks at itself. What an enormous fountain of spiritual treachery! This is how people never bad-mouth the cross but still keep self front and center.

But there is another type of person. They are no better, no more decent, and no godlier. It's not about that. But something has happened inside them. They have experienced pain in their relationships. They can't make progress in becoming more virtuous. They're becoming discouraged. They disappoint themselves increasingly with every passing day. They feel like debtors without money that face a growing mountain of debts. They are thoroughly disheart-ened. They feel so miserable and ungodly. Not because they've just been duped in a big way; no, not that! But they feel like this because they now see brightly illumined what they didn't see before. Earlier they had no sense of it. Now they do. That's why they cry out so bitterly in their souls. Their hearts are breaking, and their spirits are crushed.

But then their merciful Father showed them something.

And what was it?

He showed them the Lamb. The holy Lamb of God! The Lamb that takes away the sins of the world!

God asked them: "Do you want to be counted among the ungodly that are being completely justified, sanctified, and redeemed?"

Out of the depths of their hearts they responded: "For your name's sake, O Lord!" And that response "For your name's sake, O Lord!" was their faith crying out.

What did they receive, then, in the Lamb?

Everything!

In the Lamb, they approach God freely. In the Lamb, they stand before God as though they had never sinned, even as though they themselves had done everything that Christ did for them.

And when, at what moment, did they acquire this magnificent benefit?

Not a moment before, and not an hour later than the exact instant that they first felt: "I am completely ungodly. I am a leper from the top of my head to the soles of my feet." When they cried out: "Lord, I feel like I'm completely ungodly." Then the assurance followed immediately: "Therefore you're justified!"

This is how it is and how it will be with the Lamb!

Do you feel like you're completely ungodly? Alienated? Bruised and broken? Then you have instantly embraced the Lamb—fully, gloriously, bountifully. On the other hand, do you feel good about yourself in many respects, but not entirely? Then your Savior is not around. The Lamb is not there for you. The cross affords you no depth of divine comfort.

But for those people who experienced the former realities, who felt enslaved, and who trembled before the Lord but who then saw the Lamb and believed, it's different. They continue for their entire lives to struggle with their miser-able hearts, compromised souls, and ungodly egos.

They can handle this because of the wonderful work of being born again and renewed spiritually in the image of the Son. This happens despite the fact that they can find no unblemished virtue or source of holiness within themselves. Even their best works, time and again, are "always stained with sin." Their guilt only increases.

But along come the others who tell them: "Then things aren't right with you. If you were really a child of God, you would feel that you are now without spot or blemish!" That opinion then rages through their souls like a storm. That's because they want so very badly in their hearts to be God's children. But according to the opinions of the others, they are not. So they go around fearful and comfortless. "My God, am I then lost forever?" they ask.

This continues until they encounter the Word of God again! It's the word of a pious child of God or of the apostle who exclaims: "But I am of the flesh, sold into sin's bondage." "O miserable man that I am, who will deliver me?"

Then things are good again. The storm in their soul subsides. They are cordially reassured by their God once more.

Even Paul says: "O wretched man that I am! I am still so tied to the flesh and sold into sin's bondage!"

This is what they experience in their souls.

But this is also when they rejoice again.

The outcome is that they celebrate with the apostle: "I thank God through Jesus Christ, my Lord!"

81
VOLUME II

SO THAT GLORY MAY DWELL IN OUR LAND

Surely salvation is near to those who fear him, so
that glory may dwell in our land. Psalm 85:9[1]

Are the elect the only ones that matter? Aren't others affected as well? Is the ministry of God's Word intended only for the souls of some for eternity? Does the church on earth have no other calling than to awaken faith in those whom God calls through preaching? Shouldn't we be concerned about reaching the masses? Don't the state and society matter as well? Does it matter what becomes of Sodom and Gomorrah around us, just as long as the little creek that is the church stays pure and trickles along between its banks?

"No, not at all," exclaims the psalmist in response. "That's not the extent of things at all, not by a long way. That's part of the picture, to be sure, but it's not the heart of the matter. What it comes down to, and this is true for all generations, is that God receive his glory and that he be feared."

You may not push the elect to the foreground. The electing God is in the foreground, and he remains there eternally. He is the glorious, almighty, and living God, the spring and fountain of all that's good. He's the overflowing source of all that lives, whether in nature or by grace.

---

1. Psalm 85:10 in Dutch versions.

Do you suppose that it's enough if only the elect benefit and if those that aren't do not? If so, you'd be standing in the way of God receiving the glory that is rightfully his. Then you'd be not the least bit worried about what goes on outside the circle of the Lord's people.

But if you regain the right perspective and see that the elect have a subordinate importance, you'll give more weight to everything around you. You'll also come to appreciate once more that God is above all and that the honor of his name is the only measure of all things. Self-centeredness falls away rather automatically.

If I'm a Father, the Lord says through Malachi, where is the honor due to me? And if I'm the Lord, where am I feared? What father is not affected by his children's scandalous conduct or when his good name is discredited by the terrible way they live? And how can Almighty God look on with indifference when a country here and a group of people over there cause enormous damage and behave like animals? They are the most exceptional of all his creatures, yet they debase precisely what's exceptional about themselves!

God lives. He reigns. Moment by moment he is also the Almighty God who has called into existence every tribe, city, village, household, and person. He not only created them, but he also sustains them and allows them to go on living by his powerful Word.

He alone is the God who is generous, gracious, and favorably disposed. He feeds and sustains every city and village. He makes corn grow in the fields. He protects people by his laws and comes to them through the preaching of his Word.

Would it really matter, then, to such a God how things are going, what's happening, or whether honor or scandal prevails as long as the people of the Lord are doing well?

No, I tell you, that's getting it backwards. That amounts to saying God exists for the elect, when in fact his Word instructs us so clearly and firmly that both the elect and all his other creatures only exist for his sake.

Causing all other creatures to exist and upholding them in their existence, especially all peoples and nations, entire cities as well as hamlets and villages, serves a purpose. This is not only a future purpose but a present one. It's a purpose for today, for the time in which we are living. And what else could that purpose be than that the Lord God be glorified by all those cities and towns and villages?

If attention were focused only on the elect, you'd necessarily miss the life going on in the entire world. Then the entire world isn't needed for the preaching of the Word. Once impacted by it, the souls of those responding to it are never finished with him who is their Fountain of Salvation.

The world is still there with all its treasures, its rich flourishing of life, its natural beauty, and all its developments in human affairs. All of this is significant to the Lord. These are not simply toys with which the ungodly amuse themselves before having their last meal and leaving for hell. All of these are treasures given by God—the silver and gold as well as the rich flourishing of life in art and science. God created it all. It belongs to him. He is worthy of it. To regard all of this rich, full, shining reality apart from God is to hold a very impoverished view of who he is.

No, this is the same God who at one time paid special attention to Nineveh, that enormous city with many people and much livestock. The same God is still the owner because he formed all this. He possesses it because he upholds it. He rules it because he determines its destiny. He is this same God for every country and region, every people and nation, every city and village, every hamlet and neighborhood and settlement. Even in the remotest of places, no tenant farmer can be living in such isolation that this holy, glorious God does not claim his glory from that little patch of ground and the people living there.

Things need to be done properly. Light needs to shine in the darkness. Proper order and conditions need to govern human customs. Life's clockwork must run daily according to God's ordinances, and it must be properly rewound every evening through prayer and the confession of sins.

Passions erupt in every home. Sin churns in every village. Injustice erupts and rises to the top in every city. Ungodliness pulses through the veins of people's everyday living. But in these cases, here is where God's honor comes to expression. His name restrains those passions, reins in those sins, curtails injustice, and bridles ungodliness. It's to God's glory that the people in that house talk together again, that things are under control in that village, that justice is administered in that city, and that good laws are written for the country. This is a credit to him, strengthens his rights, and gives God victory over Satan's terribly unholy power. It's to his honor most of all that where he extends his blessing day and night, he is thanked in city and countryside for his great compassion.

This is how every father needs to see things in his own home. He shouldn't only be asking how his children can be converted. Above all, he should be asking how his entire home can give glory to God.

As king in his home, he needs to say with David: "I will walk through my home with an upright heart. Whoever practices deceit will not remain in my house. The crooked heart I will keep far from me; the wicked I will not acknowledge."

This is how the mayor of every city and town must be an aggressive enemy of all injustice and root out all ungodliness. A private home is not his responsibility. In the home, the father is the mayor. But on the streets and with respect to all things public, the mayor must contend for God's honor. He must do so whether the law requires this or whether it does not. God Almighty will require from him the honor of his city or town. All drunkenness, dishonesty, lewdness, scandal, bitterness, and outbursts of hellish anger must be excluded from public life by him, or he will answer for it.

Likewise the king stands before God. What the father is called to do in his home and the mayor is called to do in his city or town, the king is required to do for the entire country and all the people. He is God's minister, the servant God has designated to see that God is honored in his country and that glory rises to the living God from the hearts of his people.

This is what the biblical Word teaches us.

This is what the Reformers clearly grasped.

This is what is still laid on the hearts of all Reformed people.

That's why we tolerate no yielding on this matter by our fatherland or its people.

If this were about us, we could. Because it is about God's honor, we cannot!

82
VOLUME II

LAMBS AMONG WOLVES

Go out. I'm sending you as lambs among wolves. Luke 10:3

When do lambs enjoy wandering around? When do they pay no attention at all to repeated calls and stray even farther from their shepherd? Reader, they behave this way when there is no hint of danger.

But just let them get a scent of danger, let them become aware of trouble, let them see a wolf's eye glaring at them through a cleft in the rocks, then the shepherd doesn't have to call out to them or sound his horn. Then the lambs come running to him from all directions. They crowd around him, almost pushing him over.

Do we behave any differently toward our Shepherd?

We scramble to Jesus when our wolves appear. We swarm around him in fright when a wolf is on the hunt. Isn't that the story that repeats itself in the church of our Lord?

Christians fled to Jesus in the years when they were first persecuted. It was during the days of Nero's evil frenzy and when the rabble sang: "Christians drink blood!" They fled to him once again when another refrain was heard: "Christ's little lambs are being slaughtered by the Spanish wolves!"[1]

---

1. The reference here is to the sixteenth-century Spanish Inquisition against Protestants in the Lowlands.

They pressed around Jesus, hiding under the wings of his tender love. They implored: "Lord, protect us, or we'll perish!"

But after he had protected them and the wolves slinked away, they went right back to wandering off without thanking him and promptly forgot the wonderful, priceless, and precious Shepherd of our souls.

What about your soul? Doesn't it definitely understand what I'm saying?

When Jeshurun became fat, his soul withered; but when teeth are gnashed against us, a frightened person flees to the Lord.

"Then why is the Lord tempting us?" we might ask somewhat critically. To put it more appropriately, because the God tempts no one, why does God send the Tempter our way?

As though the answer hasn't always been obvious!

He does it in order to compel you to return to him. He does it in order to keep you close to him. He does it in order to make this true for you once more: "Those who dwell in the shelter of the Most High will sleep peacefully in the shadow of the Almighty!"

Doesn't a shepherd usually do his work with the help of a sheepdog? And what actually is a sheepdog to the lambs other than a wolf under the total control of the shepherd? A lamb facing the fierce mouth of the dog is as deadly frightened as if it were facing a wolf's muzzle. Watch how that poor little animal immediately flees from it in total shock and fright when that dog comes running toward it. The lamb literally races away.

If the shepherd could have a wolf that merely nips like the dog but does not bite and backs off when he whistles, the wolf would be better yet than a dog. Then a shepherd wouldn't pick a dog. The wolf would do a better job of keeping his sheep close to him than a dog does.

But that won't work!

Out in the fields, a shepherd has no control over a wolf. His lambs would be dragged off and his sheep murdered.

That's why the shepherd doesn't wait until the wolf approaches. He picks an in-between animal, an animal that takes the place of the wolf. He chooses a dog.

The Lord God is mightier than that shepherd in the field.

Satan is God's wolf. He is the murderer of souls from the beginning. He lusts after the blood of lambs. And this wolf that preys on souls the Lord God has under his total control, we might say in the most complete way imaginable.

Without the will of God, this carnivore can neither make a move nor disturb a thing.

Even if he stands directly in front of a lamb with his muzzle hanging open, and God doesn't permit it, he can't lay a claw on the fleece, let alone scratch the skin.

For our amazing and powerful God, this is not a game. It's serious work. The exalted Lord knows within a hair's breadth just how far things can go. He determines where Satan may be present and where he may not. And whenever Satan is restrained by divine command, he stands still as a statue with his feet nailed to the ground. He is powerless. And the apparently powerless lamb freely scampers around him. It's protected by nothing else than a word from the Lord. But that word covers it as its shield and buckler.

You have to understand that insight into these deeper matters doesn't come all at once.

We first gradually experience dangers to our souls to the extent that we are able to withstand them. To the extent that faith resists. Otherwise we don't.

We first learn to float a little boat in the pond behind the house. Then we learn how to row while traveling on bigger boats to other places. Next we gradually become capable of handling turbulent waves. Eventually we learn to cry out: "The breakers are overwhelming my soul, and God's waves are washing over me!"

This is faith being exercised. This is exercising faith in the sense that God is the one working faith within us and this enables us to exercise it.

This is how it works with the little lamb within us when we face the wolf. Not immediately.

No, first the Lord works with us using the dogs. "For dogs have surrounded me and a crowd of evildoers surrounds me," David cries out in Psalm 22:16.[2]

Then Satan doesn't confront us directly, man-to-man. Then it's still not yet with evil spiritual powers in the air. No, then it's still with flesh and blood, that is, with other human beings. These are people who have a desire to bite us and hurt us but who do not concentrate on devouring us. These are people who are like the shepherd's dogs that lie down alongside the sheep. They behave lovingly toward us and nestle down with us once again after they have wounded, scratched, and bruised us.

This is the first test of our faith. It's still not very deep and is barely spiritual. But it is nonetheless an exercise of faith. Even the bitterness of other people toward us teaches us to return to the Shepherd.

---

2. Psalm 22:17 in Kuyper's meditation and in his Dutch version.

Then things progress further. Much further! Until we finally confront the wolf of the soul and look directly into his bloodthirsty eyes. It's like looking into the depths of Satan himself.

That's dumbfounding!

Then the lamb can barely escape. It sinks to the ground. Its entire appeal is: "O Jesus! My Shepherd!" Then it's an entirely different level of pressing toward Jesus and clinging to him than when the sheepdog nipped at you. Then it wasn't even about experiencing pain; but now it's a matter of survival.

The wolf of the soul has murder on his mind. He gets drunk by slurping the blood of the soul. He's the murderer from the beginning.

But then the One who will crush the head of Satan is very close by. And that's finally how a child of the Lord finds peace and lies down at the den of the wolf—definitely quivering, but nevertheless comforted!

And if someone who doesn't completely understand all this should ask him: "How is it that you are so consoled?" Jesus' little lamb answers warmly and thankfully: "Because my Jesus is my only comfort in life and in death. He delivers me from all the power of the Wolf-Devil, and he so preserves and protects me that without the will of my Father in heaven, not a hair can fall from my head."[3]

But then things progress even further. Finally that Devil opposes us by taking the battle directly within human beings. This is the situation that Jesus' apostle is describing when he says: "Now, our battle is not against the flesh and blood of human beings, but against the devils in the air." Then human hearts are shaken, shaken to the core. Then they are sifted like wheat.

That's when the lambs are sent out among the wolves!

But the Lamb who is seated on the throne has all power. Therefore, they cannot be defeated.

O people of the Lord, be of good courage in him who is the Shepherd of your soul.

Afraid, yes! But you really need to be afraid of only one thing!

You need to be afraid that you will never notice the wolves around you. You need to be afraid if everything in the world around you seems good and remains friendly. You need to be afraid if all people speak well of you. Ask yourself: "Am I among those who have been sent out by Jesus? Am I truly sent out as a lamb among wolves?"

If you aren't, then you really need to tremble!

---

3. Here Kuyper is weaving together excerpts from the answer to the first question and answer in the Heidelberg Catechism.

ALL THAT GOD
HAS PREPARED

*Things that eye has not seen and ear has not heard, and that
have not occurred to the heart of man—all these things God
has prepared for those who love him. 1 Corinthians 2:9*

Let me suppose, if I may, that by a genuine faith you have been engrafted
into Christ. How do you stand today with the initial confession you made:
"I believe in God the Father, Almighty, Maker of heaven and earth"? Also in those
days when you were far from the Lord, could you still confess this opening
article? Then did you still acknowledge that Almighty God is the Creator of all
things? That's why I ask the question now of whether, after you've learned to
know the Lord, you still believe that article of faith.

Don't tell me that that should be obvious! The sad discovery made about so
many dear Christians teaches us otherwise.

So just think about it.

If God Almighty is the Creator of all things, then there is nothing and can
be nothing that God has not created. Then he's not only the Creator of the earth,
but also of the trees that grow on it. Not just of the water, but also of the fish
that swim in it! Also not merely of human beings, but also of all the power and
potential that shines so brilliantly in their hearts! In short, he creates all of it.
He creates not only what is base and course and material, but on a higher level
also what is cultured and refined and noble. Then there is the total range of

good things about you personally that you need to include in your confession. God Almighty is also the Creator of those good things.

You believe! Good! Amen! But that awareness of believing, the capacity to have a sense of believing, and the actual exercise of that capacity to sense that you believe—all of this comes from somewhere. It is present. It really exists. It's not imaginary, but it's a powerful reality. It's something good. It reflects the best that's in you. It's the only thing that saves you. Consequently, with respect to that faith you have to confess that it is God Almighty who created in you both that sense of believing, the capacity to believe, and the faith working in you. Or to put it more completely, he created these for you and gave them to you.

However difficult it may be for you to grasp this point, you feel in your heart that God hates and is inclined to be angry. And in total contrast, you play with the idea that God loves and that Satan hates intensely. Where does this come from? Where does the love or the hatred come from? They are real. You feel their compelling power inside you. They are sensitivities that move you. Once again, they aren't imaginary but are real forces. As a result, I ask whether you can confess this about your love and your hatred: "By my own volition, I neither possess them now nor ever did. I couldn't create them in the past and I can't do so now. I was and am powerless to cause their existence in me. I never set them in motion and I can't stop them from working in me. Moreover, no other creature has the capacity to do what I can't in this regard"? Can you also confess: "The only power that can produce these amazing capacities in me or cause them to crumple is God Almighty; he's poured them into my life"? And can you say, consequently, that he is the Creator and Giver of all the love you have for him? Can you say that he's the Source for all the hatred you feel toward Satan that so continuously stirs up anger in your heart?

So you do good works. They're good not because you've examined your motives that are always less than pure. Nor are they good when measured by the standard of divine perfection. But they're good because they proceed from faith and not sin. It's true that you taint them with your sinfulness. But aside from that, they are good because you forgive people rather than curse them when they hurt you. They are good when you decide to stay home and be attentive to your sick loved one rather than go out when enjoyable pleasures beckon. They are good works when you rein in the flesh during the times it wants you to cut loose. Time and again there is a force for good at work in you. This leads me to ask what you have to say or confess about this. Is this your work or God's work in you? Who works in you both to will and to work? Is it the Creator or you, the creature? Who is the Giver, and who the recipient? Who is the debtor, and who the claimant? Here's the answer: It's God Almighty who is the Creator in all of this, the Giver, and the Claimant. You are the creature, the recipient, and the debtor. Even in those good works it is God Almighty who wants to bring them to expression in you; he is working in your works. He is your Creator and Lord in them.

How does he do that? God Almighty created you with faith, better urges, and good works. He did this initially by his creative work outside you and in Christ. Then he created these realities in you through Christ. These glorious results imparted to you were alien to your nature and your sinful disposition. The upshot is that not only did you not create them but he did, but also that it would never have occurred to you that he had done so! Your ear would have never heard about this, nor would your eye have ever seen the beauty of it.

No, you even lacked the preparation for this that aspiration always brings. The One who did the preparing, planning, creating, introducing, infusing, maintaining, activating, and sustaining is Almighty God himself!

So do you understand now, child of God, what you are really saying when you confess: "I believe in God the Father, Almighty, Creator of everything that exists"?

Pay attention to how our own catechism and the catechisms of all other Christian churches teach that creating also involves maintaining. We aren't finished when we confess that faith is a gift, love has been lavished on us, and God is our salvation. For a creature it isn't sufficient to know that they've been created. They want to know that they'll be sustained as creatures—in everything, consistently, and for all eternity.

Adam knew that he was a creature, but he wanted to get from under the creaturely dependence that that involved. That was his sin. The curse on him grew out of it. "You will be like God!" whispered the tempter.

What about God's children? Don't we consistently stumble and fall with respect to this second point?

God is my salvation. All boasting is impossible. But now I've arrived. I have faith. I'm loved and love in return. I have been made righteous. And from this point on, I do the loving and the believing.

What a bitter miscalculation! It's a grievous misunderstanding of who God Almighty is as the Creator of everything that exists. It's the same nonsense that the deist professes when he says that God created the world but then leaves it to its own devices. It's exactly the same thing that the misled child of God believes in their heart with respect to the world. They hold that God created a better world in them but that he now leaves the rest up to their own devices.

That is totally false!

You are always dependent, not just until you die but throughout all eternity. There is never, never one disconnected moment, however quickly it may flash past you, when God Almighty is not involved in the faith of your believing, the love in your loving, or the capacity in your working. In all of it, he is your Sustainer, your Supporter, your Upholder, and your Inspirer.

Just as light disappears from the earth when the sun slips below the horizon, every ray of light will vanish from your soul if the Lord God is shut out of your life.

To have one beam of light in your heart that God Almighty himself is not continuing to pour into you is completely impossible. That he does is a miracle of miracles.

OUR REDEEMER FROM OF OLD IS YOUR NAME!

You are our Father, although Abraham does not know us
and Israel does not recognize us. You, O Lord, are our Father.
Our Redeemer from of old is your name. Isaiah 63:16

Put your hope in the Lord your God! He can do it. He can make it happen. He provides all that you need.

Poor, lost people enslaved to sin have lived here on earth for thousands and thousands of years already. They have groaned and struggled and prayed.

You are not the first ones to struggle or crumple in fear and sorrow. Nor are you the first almost immobilized by your desperate need! You would certainly be mistaken if you imagined that your suffering is something new under the sun. To be mired deep in misery has been common through the ages, and it's still very common today.

All you have to do is listen to the voices of history! Then you're sure to hear screaming protests in desperate preoccupation with a lack of bread. You'll also hear weak murmuring from virtually undisturbed waters. But the dominant emphasis you'll hear in every century is the note of deep disappointment. You'll hear cries of frightful oppression rising from people's hearts. They come from everywhere. You'll hear their appeals for help and deliverance.

That was the case in Paradise. It was true in the days of Noah and Abraham and during the centuries when David and Hezekiah were alive. It's the situation now as well. Your own tears often flow down as far as your lips. They convey astounding things and still record nothing but depressing realities. They prove that life here on earth is a struggle. That our hearts are sinful! That sheer, pure, sacred joy has vanished!

As a child you were weaned. As an adolescent you daydreamed without a care. Then, still smiling, you entered adulthood, but not without a sense of somberness. Now it's also true that your greatest hopes have been disappointed. You've realized through the struggles that have gone on in your own heart as well as all around you that life has a painful side. You've noted it all too sadly and bitterly. It's true that our sinful human condition can be so sad, somber, and deeply painful.

That's when the impression first hit you: "I haven't escaped this! I'm involved here! It's crushing me too!" That's how you felt for a while, but without actually being overwhelmed. Then you learned from the history of the suffering endured by earlier generations that many men and women were assaulted much harder than you, and they got through it. You heard their sighing about being as good as dead. You heard them complaining about all the waves and breakers of God crashing over their heads. But you also heard them still praising God and still singing joyful hymns of praise to him.

Our hearts are almost always overly worked up like this.

When our little boat is driven off course by wind and tide, we imagine that we've escaped all danger and merely laugh off the black thunderheads looming on the horizon, ignoring ancient wisdom tied to their appearance. Everything seems so gorgeous and happy that, like little children without a care in the world, we play on the dancing waves. We don't give a thought to the terrible abyss hidden beneath the waters.

Conversely, when the thunderheads starts churning, the thunder rattles, the waves whip up as high as mountains, and our little boat doesn't respond to our persistent pushing on the tiller, we lose all hope. We simply close our eyes, let the tiller do what it wants, and fall into the gaping abyss.

Now, think about this. In both scenarios, days of prosperity and times of adversity, our deceitful hearts are lying to us. You can't trust your heart. It sees everything in a false light. It lives on misrepresentation. And the person who wants to live according to how things really are in either good or bad times, and not according to how they seem, doesn't rely on their heart! They don't listen to the dishonest possibilities of their own creation. They rely solely on the Word! On the truth! On what is told them from the heart of God!

And if you start there, what do you hear then about your needs and fears and sense of being smothered? That they're only imaginary? That you simply have to work your way through them? That ignoring them is the best medicine?

Not in the least!

The Word makes them worse rather than better! It portrays them more pointedly rather than more weakly. That's because it depicts your sufferings as deeply rooted in spiritual realities. This makes you feel even more miserable because now you understand that you're also dealing with miseries of your own soul.

I realize that this isn't the case with glad-handing Christians who simply glide over everything superficially. But this is the case with those who've been instructed by the Word and taught by God. Both the men and the women among them who suffer dare to sink the knife into their wounds. They dare to expose to you how terribly destructive and ungodly the poison oozing out of them really is.

Consequently, the Word teaches them that they're not dealing with superficialities. It affirms that spiritually sensitive people throughout the ages have suffered through such things. It discloses that those who have been justified have suffered most deeply and fearfully in this regard. These are God's most precious children, the pious and godly worshipers of his holy name.

If you identify with their sense of being overwhelmed, the Word will be a glorious source of comfort to you as well. For then the entire host of those made righteous will testify to you on the basis of Scripture that God lives. The testimony rises from their souls like a blast from an organ: "Our Redeemer, you are our Redeemer. From of old is your name!"

He has been found to be a Redeemer throughout all ages.

From of old, even from before the days of the flood, God's elect people suffered. Already then they sang: "The Lord has been our Refuge!"

Noah and his family were ridiculed. They were frightened. But from the ark a song of deliverance was lifted up; it sounded across the waters.

From of old, in the days of Abraham and Jacob, there were life-threatening struggles. They happened at Peniel. Songs of lament were heard from those who saw Joseph's coat. Yet, in those days of patriarchal glory jubilant songs of deliverance were sung to the Lord: "Redeemer is his holy name!"

And however far you want to go back into the days of those who have been justified, you will always find the same, unchanging, and unending reality. They were oppressed, afflicted, and trapped to the point of death. Yet then the oil of gladness began to flow once more. Their sadness lifted. They were delivered from the bands of death.

The cycle never ends. It never varies. It is repeated and unchanging. The route leads through the depths of fear and a thousand deaths. But then deliverance comes. The song "Hammaäloth" is sung. "Our Redeemer from of old is his name."

Redeemer! He's our Redeemer whether he delivers us from the breakers and brings us to dry land, or whether he teaches us how to navigate through those breakers, or whether he preserves our lives underneath those waves, as he did with Jonah.

He's our Redeemer whether the outward urgency disappears, or whether—which is even more wonderful—the gap through which Satan usually creeps in is walled off.

But he's always our Redeemer, always our Savior, and always our compassionate God!

From of old!

But not any longer? Not for you, my sister and my brother?

O you of little faith!

YOU PRIESTS WHO DESPISE MY NAME

*"If I'm a father, where is my honor? If I'm a master, where
is my respect?" This is what the Lord of Hosts says to
you priests who despise his name. Malachi 1:6*

What is a priest?

A priest is a luxury for the Lord of Hosts, if I may put it like that. It's something he doesn't need. It's a part of his creation that he really doesn't require. It's the kind of person whom he created pretty much just because it pleased him to do it. He did it out of divine generosity. He did it because he thought it might be a good thing to do.

Being self-sufficient is an expression of the richness of his unfathomable and completely blessed being. He doesn't need a priest! For "he is not served by human hands, as though he needed anything. He himself has given life and breath to every living thing." Consequently, if he then creates a priest, that's a luxury. It's a luxury in the sense that all that God does can be seen as a luxury. This expresses his overflowing majesty. It doesn't indicate deficiency, which would be ungodlike. Nor does it indicate need, because that would diminish his name.

Remember, he is the Lord of Hosts. More precisely, he is Jehovah of Hosts. He is Jehovah in the sense of Being in and of itself. He is both the essence of being and the One who lends being to all else that possesses being. He is the

One and Only who is the Fountain and Source of his own existence. He is the Divine Spring from whom all things flow.

This Jehovah is Jehovah of Hosts. Therefore he is the Lord of every part of creation and of the entire firmament. He is Lord of all the powers of nature and all the heavenly forces. He is Lord of the hosts of angels, seraphim, and cherubim. Above all, he is Lord of everything on earth that is subject to the human gifts and powers he has granted to people as his subordinates, subjects, and instruments appointed to serve him.

Being a priest has never meant contributing anything to God being God. It doesn't mean that now, and it never will. Not in the least! That's an impossibility. It always will be!

To be permitted to be a priest is a conferred honor. It is an advancement granted by divine favor. It is a sacred crown placed on a person's head just because it pleased God to do so!

The young birds hatched by the lark in its nest sing to God in the morning. But they don't know they're singing to God. By contrast, you as his children know very well that you are. You determine to do so not just for the sake of warbling but in order to praise God. Those young larks with their pure, pitch-perfect singing are not priests. But you with your off-key singing definitely are priests, at least as long as you're consciously singing to God because he is God.

The young hind born high on the rocky cliffs yearns for the doe's milk. But it neither understands what it wants nor prays for it. And the mother prays even less for her fawn. Yet the hind's mother has milk to give, and the fawn has milk to suckle, although neither knows the One who provides it. But you, his children, understand this very well. Those who have become mothers might ask God for a full breast. Those who set a table might ask him to provide food. You pray: "Give us this day our daily bread." That single petition sets you apart, even if you receive no more than dry bread and water. That's less than the hind got. But your prayer makes you so much richer, places you so much higher, and exalts you beyond measure. That you pray and are permitted to give thanks is the basis for your being a priest of your God.

The stormy winds come completely at God's command. The field yields its appointed level of the corn by which God feeds his people. Both serve God without realizing that they are responding to him. But you, his children, understand this very well. For your service involves struggle and triumph over your sinful inclinations. What the soil of your soul yields is an offering. It is based on your desire and is presented to God. This is not mere service but priestly service. It's offered in praise to him.

The lamb suffers, suffers terribly, when it is crunched as a chunk of meat between a lion's jaws. But that pathetic animal has no knowledge that it is serving God's majesty through its suffering. It screeches its death scream without any hope. But that's not how it is with you who are his children. Sometimes you are the lamb in the lion's mouth. Sometimes your bones are crunched. But when you suffer, you do so submissively. You even do so as an offering given by your priestly impulse. It is suffering on behalf of God, even with your God!

Let me take this higher and even elevate it to the highest level possible. The person who is decent and respectable but remains far from God curbs their instincts. They blush over their passions and display a beautiful love. But they are still like the stormy winds and the productive field. They don't realize that their decency and respectability come from God, exist for God, or are intended by God. Their virtues reflect self-interest. You who have become children of God, on the other hand, have also been awakened to a life of virtue. You've been sensitized too, but for you it represents something different. It's for the sake of God. It's about him alone. All your praise and earthly virtue is priestly. It proceeds from God by virtue of his compassion and is returned to him who provided you with it.

At least this is how to explain it! But it's not exactly how it is!

Just the opposite, in fact! We sing like larks with great feeling and perfect pitch, but not to God. We regularly drink our milk like the young hind, but without heartfelt thanks to God. We blow like the stormy winds and pile up fruit from the field, but we do both mechanically and without him in mind. We still suffer continually and shriek like the lamb caught in the lion's jaws, but not sacrificially. We are also consistently decent and often do loving things, but we do it like the hen fighting to protect her chicks or like a dog that growls and bites to protect its master. We do all of it in our own strength and apart from God. At least, we have no intention of doing so for him. And this is what it means to be a priest or priestess who opposes his name.

"O you priests! You despise my name!" is what Malachi says about this. "This amounts to wanting to be priests and to be called priests, but not in any way associated with my name. Not identified with my name or attached to it! Not being priests as they need to be! This is to carry on as priests as though I am not God and my name is not Jehovah or the Lord of Hosts. This is being priests who may do a lot of good, but not for me, the fully blessed Being whose name is God. You're not priests to me, the Fountain of all that's good, the Source of all strength, and the Spring from whom all blessings flow. And this is exactly how you despise my name. It's how you despise my name as your God. This is how with your priestly pretenses you want to make something different of me than your God!

"You want to bring me something. But you can't add anything to who I am.

"You want to lay something on my altar, but you come with nothing that I have not first created and entrusted to you. You can't fashion as much as a pair of turtledoves. I first need to make them for you. And only when I give them to you can you then bring them back to me and place them on my altar. Then it's not as though I have to thank you for bringing them. But it's because you need to express your thanks to me by doing so."

You need to bring me your love in the same spirit that you need to bring those turtledoves. The same holds for your humility, your piety, your spiritual fruitfulness, and your virtuous intentions!

Do you create piety in your soul? Do you create love or humility in your heart? Are you ever able to create fruitful godliness or the desire for virtue within you?

You empty-handed people! What can you ever produce out of the thin air swirling around you except something that is empty, amounts to nothing, and is less than vanity itself?

Watch out if you think like this: "I've overcome that problem again. Because I have, I'm pious once more. To this point, I've behaved pretty lovingly." If you hope that God is going to be gracious because of this, you don't deserve to be wearing a priest's crown. God says: "You who would honor my name, you have become despisers of it!

"Do you want to be priests? Then let me be God.

"But woe to you if my name as your God means nothing to you."

Then you really aren't priests any longer.

Then the sacred anointing oil merely dries up on your forehead.

Then God will despise you because you dared to despise his ever-blessed name.

86
VOLUME II

HOW HAVE
WE DESPISED
YOUR NAME?

*"If I'm a father, where is my honor? If I'm a master, where
is my respect?" This is what the Lord of Hosts says to
you priests who despise his name. But you ask, "How
have we despised your name?" Malachi 1:6*

In God's new covenant, all his children are priests and priestesses. If that had
only been true in Israel! For long before the law was given on Sinai, Jehovah
said the following to all his covenant people: "And you will be to me a kingdom
of priests and a holy nation."

But Israel forfeited that high honor through its fall into sin. So the priesthood was conferred on Levi, and the rest of the people bought freedom from
that obligation for their firstborn sons at the price of a pair of young doves. This
was only a symbol, to be sure. But it was an inspiring symbol of what should
have been true in Israel and of what would once again be the case in spiritual
Israel: "All the people in all generations will be one holy priesthood of the Lord."

We are that spiritual Israel. There is one church. In former times it was
associated with Abraham and David and now with Christ and his apostles. In
the church of the New Testament, the priesthood has definitely included all of

God's children once again. What has become impossible is saying: "I definitely am one of God's chosen, but I'm not a priest! I'm one of his beloved children, but I am not a priestess!" Being a priest goes right along with being a child of God. The holy apostle says: "You also have become living stones, built into a spiritual house, a holy priesthood, to offer spiritual sacrifices that are pleasing to God through Jesus Christ." The secret of being a child of God and escaping all work righteousness, while at the same time "abounding in the work of the Lord," consists precisely in this. You "offer sacrifices that are well pleasing to God through Christ Jesus." This occurs not because you are human, much less because you are a sinner, but because you are a priest.

What follows is this. As many offices as there may be in the church, the anointing oil of the living God is not intended for them, but for the entire church. This explains why the apostle John says: "But you have an anointing from the Holy One, and you know all things." He also says: "The anointing you received from him remains in you, and you do not need anyone to teach you. But this same anointing teaches you everything you need to know. This is why it is true." This is exactly the same sense in which the apostle Paul wrote to the Corinthians: "But he who established us in Christ and who has anointed us is God himself. He has also sealed us and given us the Spirit in our hearts as our guarantee."

Specific gifts and ministries and duties are certainly associated with offices. But the anointing with the holy oil of priesthood under the loving dispensation of the full gospel is not only tied to special office bearers. But it's poured out on all the favored of the Lord. And it's only to the extent that an office bearer is one of those favored by the Lord that he bears a priestly privilege. It's not because he's an office bearer that he shares in this holy anointing or is part of that more glorious priesthood.

This truth of God was obscured by the darkening of truth that occurred under Rome. Then office bearers arose who told the people: "We are the priests. You are only the laity!" But when that darkness passed and light was restored on God's candlesticks, that falsehood once again receded. Then, as during more ancient and more sacred times, the universal priesthood of all believers was again emphasized.

The universal priesthood of all believers was a strong tower in which our spiritual fathers took refuge. That's where our almighty and gracious God protected them from tricks and deceptions.

We have to get back to that tower now that darkness and obscurity have fallen on the church once again. A kind of separate priesthood has emerged again, this time in the form of an "educated priesthood." It has emerged over an undiscerning church, a people who "knows not the law" and is disparaged. So for a second time, the priesthood of all believers has been corrupted.

That's unacceptable! It shouldn't happen!

The assurance of being set free has been impressed too deeply on the hearts of church members for that to happen. The Holy Spirit is at work, not human beings. He understandably refuses to anoint this educated priesthood and withdraws the honor of his favor and grace from it. In his opposition he simply proceeds by personally imprinting his holy marks on the whole church so that no special standing benefits. God overturns all aggrandizement of special offices. He does his work by calling all his children to serve at the altar and by calling back into existence the priesthood of all believers.

"They will no longer say, everyone to his neighbor, 'Know the Lord!' for they will all know me." This is what the prophetic Word of God says. So this is how it will be, and that Word will be broken by no one. That Word stands. It must stand, since the honor of God's name depends on it.

If all believers are not priests and priestesses, then one of two things happens. Either believers take a seat on the sidelines and see all work done as work righteousness and as therefore sinful. Or they get involved in working as sinners and presumptive saints producing impure fruit laid on the Lord's altar as an imagined offering.

Both of these alternatives are like spreading cancers. The first involves hanging the hands limply at a person's side. The second involves exalting the working hand. God excises both of them with this single affirmation: "You are priests of the Most High."

A priest never has any rest, and yet they never work. But they're always offering sacrifices. They're presenting offerings in the sense that Peter talks about it: "presenting offerings that are pleasing to God through Christ Jesus."

This is what the external Word tells us, and in it it's also what the Holy Spirit is telling us.

But now an internal Word comes to us. It's also a Word from the same Spirit. In it the Holy Spirit reproaches us for being deceptive priests and priestesses and for tarnishing the name of our God. That voice reprimanding us so severely is also loving, merciful, and gracious. It is a voice that lifts up the sinking priest and drowning priestess when both are being overwhelmed by a flood of sin. All his effort here is majestic. It's magnificent in the way it preserves them.

Our holy and glorious God—for he is a great King, the Lord of Hosts is his name—sees that we are defiling our priestly anointing. He sees that we are not conducting ourselves properly at his altar. He observes that we treat these holy and sensitive matters despicably. So he enters the situation and pierces our self-satisfied souls, shakes us awake, and sears our hearts unsparingly. "Get away from me, you profane priest (v. 12), you deceiver (v. 14), you despiser (v. 6), you defiler of my holy name (v. 7)."

What enters our hearts when we hear him talking like this?

Do we thank this faithful, compassionate God of ours because he is so persistent? Because he cut to the heart of the matter in coming to save us?

No, not at all, my brothers and sisters! The calluses on our hearts are too thick for that. At the first rustling that we hear about our personal sinfulness, or at the first hint of it that we discover, we say: "God has got to be wrong. We're not that bad!" Then in our self-righteousness we ask from the heart: "How are we despising you? How are we profaning your name?" (vv. 6 and 7).

This is when our unrighteousness has peaked. This is when we recall most pointedly the deeply seething corruption within. This is when we still want to play dumb with God. This is when we risk considering whether our lost cause isn't still worth talking about with God. Then we're still pretending not to understand! Even while our tender conscience is inwardly chastising us and making us uncomfortable, we give the appearance of not knowing what the problem is, of thinking things really aren't so bad, and of believing that our compassionate God is being overly sensitive and too severe in his judgment.

That's really despicable about our hostile, evil heart, isn't it?

Yet, that's how we try to cover things up. That's how we are. That deeply mired! That's how we approach things.

We're exactly like the world!

No, not that, praise God! There's a difference. It's not a difference in the outburst. What erupts in each individual is equally hostile in every one.

The unrighteous person takes pleasure in their outburst. They sound off against God and persist in doing so. They make excuses and are dug in. But it's completely different with God's pilgrims who have been delivered.

True, they begin with an initial outburst. Their first urge is to defend themselves. But then they get over it. Then the Holy Spirit starts working in them, and the capacities of their faith produce a different result. They shed tears of deeply felt shame. Their hearts condemn them for expressing themselves in such a terrible way toward the Lord God. God's beloved child then hates that initial outburst by which they wanted to hide their guilt. They cut the bandages covering their wounds. Naked and exposed, they approach God and stand before him. The result is that they are thankful. They are thankful that their compassionate God chastises them. They are thankful that while they condemn themselves, God speaks a word of pardon that sets them free.

87
VOLUME II

TROUBLE AND SORROW

The days of our years are seventy or eighty if we are strong.
But they are filled with trouble and sorrow. Psalm 90:10

In our new, up-to-date mental institutions, people amuse themselves at the expense of the impaired in all kinds of ways.[1] They do this particularly in the way they portray them comically. If possible, it should be pushed to the point that the impaired actually forget that they are mentally challenged. Yes, so far that it must seem to them that all their dreams, imagining, and fantasies accurately depict reality!

Well, we'll just leave that for what it is! As long as the church of Jesus Christ unlovingly thinks that it is completely free to leave dealing with the impaired in police hands, we will maintain our shameful silence about the atrocities that are part of life in mental institutions. When oh when will our diaconates wake up and promote a higher and nobler attitude about these things?

But where we won't leave matters is this: that our entire life here on earth betrays the same unholy attitude. It massages all our miseries. It characterizes

---

1. The terms referring to the impaired have been "sanitized" throughout this meditation to conform to twenty-first-century conventions and sensitivities. While Kuyper used terms like "insane" and "crazy" and "drunkard" in the context of this meditation, they did not have the offensive connotations for him that they do for readers today, as the tone of this devotional makes clear.

our most intense pressure, tension, indifference, and insensitivity as a vacu-
ous, make-believe display.

What the inebriated person does at their worst, we all do indirectly, step
for step, and each in our own way. The drink that numbs the senses drags the
inebriate out of the wretchedness of reality and magically transports them to
a world of enjoyment and release. And what do the vast majority of people do
besides close their eyes to the realities with which they live? They babble to
each other about a life based on mere appearance, lies, and wishful thinking.

You could even take this to a deeper level. Suicide is the intoxicated person's
escape at the ultimate level. A drinker sobers up eventually. The imaginary
world they enter through their drinking soon disappears, and sober reality
returns with double intensity. But, if there were some way to recapture that
escape and to stay there forever, how could they do it? That's the way people get
to the point of committing the shameful act and awful sin of suicide. The big
difference is this, of course. The drink at least provides a momentary escape
and release, while a person who commits suicide immediately stands in the
presence of the terrifying God of whom the Scripture says, "Our God is a consuming fire!" Our souls recoil at this. Yet ... that which is sacrilegious and that
which is terrifying increase in direct and sobering proportion to one another!
So where oh where can we go?

How does this all happen?

Very simply, it comes from the fact that suicide and drunken stupor are
nothing other than the most sharply defined manifestations of that same misguided desire for escape and for whatever promises more than it delivers. That's
definitely a misguided desire, but it increasingly characterizes our entire lives,
even among Christians.

God is exalted. He is long-suffering. His mercies are boundless. Merciful
is even his name.

The Lord provides everything for us!

He knows eternity. He understands how endless the eternity of eternities is.
And that's why he measures according to the full blessedness of his own divine
being. That's the standard he uses for the indescribable and unspeakable glory
that awaits the bride of Christ in his perfect heaven.

That's why God the All-Merciful makes every effort to draw us into his
blessedness.

The Lord God finds it terrible that a person in the mere sixty or seventy
years of their earthly existence would gamble away and discard eternity. In so
doing, they lose the everlasting glory and the blessedness beyond description

that will endure for a thousand times a thousand, and then times another thousand ages.

He, the Holy One, says: "My dear man, my dear woman, don't devote your existence to an empty life that is only so-so. But dedicate your entire existence to reaching my totally blessed and delightful eternity."

To be able to do that, rid yourself of all lies. Do away with false appearances. Represent things as they are. Challenge yourselves. Challenge others to face who and what they really are. You are miserable sinners. So are those around you. That's why misery clings to you all the days of your earthly existence. Your God is merciful. He is also the source of enjoyment in your life, and sometimes he even provides pure pleasure—that is, provided that you don't discount suffering and the serious side of life. For you wisdom is completely summarized in this one command: "Walk before my face. Pay attention to yourself in the same way that I, seated in my blessed heaven, see you as you really are. Recognize all the dark and unmentionable aspects of your life. Walk before my face with integrity!"

But people pay no attention to this. "You may not live that way," they exclaim! They wave a magic wand over their lives, as it were. It casts a deceptive glow about what is best and most beautiful for them. Life magically seems like heaven on earth. Enjoyment is everything. Life is about reveling in pleasure and staying excited without any memory of misery.

No time for prayer anymore. It's much too quiet at home. Get out into the streets! Go to the taverns! Take a walk in the park. Get tickets for the theater. Everything has to be seen in an aesthetic and light, even seductive clothing. Even hair on the head has to be stylized so that it no longer looks drab and ordinary.

And what about Christians? Oh, at first they struggle against these trends. They live separately. But do they go along with that deadened and deadening world? Sad to say, now they do. We know that there is a cross we must bear. But today we drape it with flowers, and it has become the cross covered with roses. Deep-seated seriousness has been wiped away by a love for lightheartedness. Even those who are presently preoccupied spiritually will soon succumb to the same thing. While for them this will be slightly different, essentially it will serve the same purpose. Keep quiet and stop preaching about the law. Don't talk about hell. I don't want to hear about my nakedness. Quit warning us about eternal damnation! People just don't want to hear any more about what they mock as "splashing around in mud puddles!" No, everything has to be about love, laughter, and enjoying luxuries. One person characterizes another as "a lovable guy," who in turn describes the first the same way. Pretty soon you have a whole circle of "really lovable fellows!" Naturally, in such a circle of angels on earth you find a lot of hearty laughing, even if it's about the real miseries and problems of life. Now we're dealing with something different stirring in the soul!

This is going to go on until the Lord intervenes.

He said in his Word: "The days of our years are seventy or eighty if we are strong. But they are filled with trouble and sorrow." And those of us who read this or even laugh about it succeed in making it come true. We do until we feel our own heavyheartedness and burst out: "God was certainly right about that. Trouble, trouble and sorrow, is the very best I've been able to find."

It's quite exceptional when God makes this happen.

Sometimes he allows people to go on living for years before they hear about a friend who passed away or about an acquaintance who had been unhappy and took their own life. But this person always simply thought: "Those are exceptions." Those reports were not enough to shake them out of their own fantasies.

They were told: "That's just how it is!" They had seen blow after blow fall on other people and simply thought: "Sometimes it happens like that!" But they never applied those situations to themselves.

Then one day the Lord God finally knocked on their doors. Then they had to pick up the heavy crosses laid at their feet. Then they were brokenhearted. Then God put the terribly serious question to them: "Did I, your God, have it right, or did the world?"

Not that this is what happens to everyone. Not at all. On a battlefield where thousands lie wounded, no one amputates an arm or leg of those who are already gone. And at most they will spend only an hour helping those who are still alive but in serious shock.

There are also people, on the other hand, who live in a dreamland from the cradle to the grave. They enter life numb to its realities and die the same way. That's terrible. It's also terrible if God never visits them. It's terrible when he walks past our doors and doesn't amputate our maimed limbs. For then we are bastards!

There's something else that people don't quite understand, namely, that there has never been a single soul that God has not at some time struck on the outside before he has also totally broken them on the inside. As a rule, however, for us that is a blessed sign that God has begun an important work in us that will have eternal significance. At least that's true if he takes along his bag of instruments and begins his work of amputating an arm or leg.

How terribly, terribly hard our hearts begin pounding in fear when he does!

Sometimes a person cannot contain themselves. They simply have to scream!

But God keeps on working. He does so with a steady hand. He works until the limb has been removed. He doesn't let up until his purpose has been achieved. He doesn't proceed by trial and error, and that's why he never makes a mistake. Once he puts his hand to it, he does a beautiful job. He also works through the fear of dying. Our God is the Great Physician. He heals.

This is what happens if the Holy Spirit is involved in this work.

There are also frightening operations that the Lord God performs simply to reveal his anger. God administers blows that only weaken people. They become hardened to them.

Who has not known such people? Look at Pharaoh and his circle. Consider the flood!

But let's leave this kind aside.

Suppose that the Holy Spirit mixes suffering with faith.

That bears fruit.

Here? On earth?

But I thought that all of that was reserved for what's above! Then what happens when the fruit is presented to God there, in eternity?

Look, that's when everything gets turned around. That's when we see things in retrospect and when we realize that for our entire lives we have really lived with an illusion. We saw value in things that had none.

That's when we'll realize that what we regarded as most important was filled with sorrow and trouble: our gold, our status, our influence, our physical health and strength, right down to our flesh-and-blood children and the "children" of our heart's desire. Everything on which we had pinned our hopes, we will then realize, gave us trouble externally and sorrow internally!

The only thing that will then be able to remove our trouble and quiet our sorrow is the Lord our God, whom we had forgotten so often and served so half-heartedly.

Then God, that God, will be most important of all!

The most important of all! That is exactly what he always wanted to be in our lives. But the root reality—the sinful root—has been that we have lived, sadly misled, in a spiritual fantasyland that could never be real!

MAINTAINING THAT HIS OWN STRENGTH IS HIS GOD

Then the spirit changes and a man shows his guilt, maintaining that his own strength is his God. Habakkuk 1:11

No, to deny flat-out that there is no God is not something that most people do. But there is still a sense of horror among the masses when a lowly human being, who is kept alive only by God's long-suffering grace, dares to open their big crude mouth and mock this God. People are amazed that such a person doesn't fall down dead, fool that they are, when they deny that such a tremendous God actually exists.

But I ask that you not imagine too quickly that you're completely free from such horrible sinning. That's how the natural person thinks. They put on a pretext of faith. But the child of God no longer thinks this way.

Earlier, when our souls were standing on the outside looking in, we could repeat with Scripture: "The fool has said in his heart: 'There is no God!'" Then we could cheerfully and confidently read the account of the Pharisee and say right along with him: "Lord, I thank you that I am not as ungodly as these fairweather believers and atheists!" That's when in our blindness we thought to ourselves: "Those fools that say in their hearts that there is no God are such miserable folks. I detest them! But I'm one of those who is wise enough to really pray to God."

This is how the unconverted talk. Such people are focused on what's going on outside their own hearts. It's always about someone else, never about themselves.

But when a greater, more wonderful spiritual light finally dawns and illumines the supposed wisdom of our darkened hearts, we discover something totally different about ourselves. We clearly recognize that we actually belong to the spiritual family of those miserable folks we formerly detested. We see that their angry disposition isn't as far removed from our own hearts as we once thought. This may not come so much to visible expression as it registers within. But we definitely do realize it.

So when Holy Scripture says: "The fool says in his heart: 'There is no God!' " a child of God confesses in quiet shame that in this case Scripture is actually talking about their own heart. It's saying that they have been this fool. And sadly, they still are!

You might ask how this is possible, since as one of God's children you pray to him daily. Your lips overflow with praises to him. The answer could well be to ask whether you are a stranger to struggles of the faith, or to Satan's whispering, or to angry impulses.

But I'm not going to dwell on that now. That's all true from time to time. But as rare exceptions! In moments of terrible spiritual struggle! Then, when the Lord appears, they melt away. But in reality they're still very close.

No, the foolish intentions of a sinful heart to break with God are actually quite common. They occur on a daily basis. So tell me whether even one sin could exist if you genuinely, actually believed at that very moment that there is a living God. Is it really possible that anyone could harbor two things in their heart at the same time? On the one hand that there is a living God who sees and hears them, and on the other hand that they're just going to keep on sinning anyway? If that's not possible, what is every sin, large or small, other than an affirmation of the fool in their heart: "There really isn't a God! So why should I refrain from doing this or that?"

But there's more.

Habakkuk provides us with the most wonderful word from the Lord imaginable. It's filled with comfort, warnings against sin, and reassurance for any person who trusts in the living God. His prophecy concludes with these inspiring words: "Although the fig tree does not bud … , and there are no more cattle in the stall, yet I will rejoice in the God who saves me!" But the prophecy earlier says that this same man is someone who "changes his spirit and shows his guilt, maintaining that his own strength is his God!"

But now the prophet puts this question to you directly. Does that sin sound familiar to you? I'll ask you this clearly, pointedly. Examine yourself as I do.

Imagine that there were a man who attempted many things and flourished in all he did. His head swelled, and he was very pleased with himself. He liked talking about his accomplishments with other people. So he said: "I accomplished all this, otherwise it never would have succeeded." His pride was showing. Others wished that he would shut his mouth. But what does this thoughtless fellow do? Now he acts righteous and says: "Consider how gracious God has been to me. He enabled me to do all this!" What he says may seem pious, but it is fundamentally nothing more than a shameful abuse of pious talk designed to let him brag to his heart's content.

This reveals our own God-denying heart as vividly as possible!

The natural man always lives by that fundamental emphasis. It describes the basic tone of his life. He makes reference to God, but his intent is to stress his own strength. He gives the appearance of praising God's care, but in fact he exalts his own cleverness and discernment. The words are there, but as Habakkuk says, his spirit has changed. Worship is essentially nothing more than praising himself by using pious language. It's a sham.

God's children know about such things. They recognize it in themselves. But they fight it. Yet, not nearly hard enough! Nevertheless, in their hearts the Spirit's power is working against sin. The unconverted person can be compared to an animal that yearns for blood and tears into its prey with its teeth. The converted person has a taste for blood as well, but, fearing that they might be ripped open in the process, they clench their teeth and press their lips together tightly because in their heart they hate this thirst for blood.

This is why God's true children recognize their own foolish tendency to emphasize their own strength instead of God's. That's true even with respect to the ordinary things in life. But they fight against this urge.

Consider this example. If a person has earned their daily bread for many years by playing the organ, but then becomes deaf, they foolishly start thinking: "Now I'm afraid I won't have enough to eat!" As though for all those years their organ playing rather than God were the source of their existence! But even though they castigate their foolishness, they persist in it. They never escape it.

People now have two workshops. The first is their ordinary life. It is a carryover from earlier. But then an inner workshop develops in God's children. It's the workshop of the soul. Earlier it was closed and sealed off. Nothing was happening in it. But now it's open. The lights have been turned on in it. Filing, drilling, and sanding are going on there now. The great danger that now faces God's children is that in the workshop of the soul their "spirit changes and they become guilty of maintaining that their own strength is their God."

The real Worker in the inner workshop is the Holy Spirit. He works in and through me, so that I am at work in him. All our capabilities are tools of the Holy Spirit. Has a project been completed? Has something been produced? Any praise or any virtue? Then it's the accomplishment of the Spirit, a work of divine beauty.

But that's putting it a little too crassly for our conceited hearts.

All our tools need to be used for one purpose. The workshop of our hearts needs to be devoted to one objective. In the end, we need to say simply: "It's not my doing, it's his!"

That's going to be demanding!

One person will say: "I'm closing up shop. There's no more work for me here." That's the sin of laziness.

Another person will say: "The Holy Spirit really helped me. He served me well. He was a good servant, but I was the real worker here." That's sheer self-righteousness.

The person who is protected from both of these sins and who allows God to be God in that workshop is granted a double portion of grace.

"Lord, pass the cup with the double portion of grace my way" has to be the prayer of everyone.

With that, spiritual sinning doesn't disappear, but it's under control.

THEN ALL THE ARROGANT WILL BE LIKE STUBBLE

Behold, the day is coming that will be like a burning oven.
Then all the arrogant will be like stubble. Malachi 4:1

What appallingly separates us from God is cherishing our proud hearts. Pride destroys souls. No soul suffocates in everlasting death unless they are choking on their own pride.

"Restrain your servant, O Lord," cries the psalmist, "from having a proud heart. For when it no longer rules my life, I will again live to your glory and be free from great sin."

No, it's not that one of us is a sinner and another one is not. We are all sinners. "There is no one who is righteous, no, not one!"

Then, when it's all said and done and the world has come to an end, all flesh will appear before the judgment seat of the Lord Jesus Christ. Some won't stand there as goats who are the sinners and others as the sheep who are not. But all of us, head for head and soul for soul, will be standing there and testifying to what's on our conscience. We will admit that we were sinners and continued being so until we gasped our last breath. It's only when a person belongs to Jesus that they escape sinning, when they draw their last breath and die.

Here's the only difference. While all of us are sinners, some of us are proud sinners, and some of us are humble sinners.

In the verse following our passage, Malachi contrasts the proud with those who fear the name of the Lord. Those who are proud do not fear his name. They only reverence their own names and refuse to bow to the name of God. They refuse to serve him unless Almighty God is willing to be worshiped and served by the proudhearted. Unless they are permitted to be themselves! Unless the Lord God assures them: "You are deeply perverted, but I'm still going to be merciful to you!" Unless their egos are free not to serve him! Unless they're not forced to come with broken hearts and as completely dispirited!

No, they're not actually turned off by heaven. They really do want to get there. Heaven truly does appeal to them. But all only as long as they can enter it with their chests sticking out and when "the narrow gate" has been torn down.

And that is exactly what the Lord God is unwilling to grant. He continues to demand: "That terribly proud ego of yours first has to be shattered!"

The Lord is resolute on that point simply because he's God. He won't be sidetracked. Not a jot or tittle can be changed. It has to be as he stated. Not a single soul will be saved whose ego has not been snapped like a twig.

It doesn't matter what the sins are for which you're indebted. All that matters is that you come with a heart that acknowledges with a sense of complete estrangement that it is full of all kinds of evil. Then you won't be lost! That's because the blood of Jesus cleanses you from all your sin. Everything actually depends on your coming with that arrogant, hardened, unbending ego of yours humbled. That needs to happen on the inside; lip service isn't enough. What people think on this score doesn't count; that God knows it has happened is what does.

In contrast, if you were as friendly as an angel, met your daily obligations loyally, and lived modestly, it wouldn't matter if you did it all with a proud heart. That's true even if you were to talk with the Lord daily and your orthodoxy didn't deviate by a hair's breadth. Even if you gave your body to be burned, you wouldn't be an inch closer to heaven unless your ego was crucified, died, was broken, and was crushed by the weight of the Word.

I understand the difference perfectly well. One person is inflexible by nature. It takes immense effort for them to speak as much as a single word that shows humility. Another person talks in language as sweet and calm as can be imagined. It makes no difference to God. He doesn't just ask that a person bear witness but that that witness is genuine. As the One who has fashioned every heart, he knows exactly how far the branch has to bend before it snaps.

There are supple branches that can bend flat to the ground without breaking and then spring back up when released without being broken. Then there are other branches that snap when they bend a little too far. It's not the overly supple heart but the shattered one that pleases God.

Clouds filled with grace often hover over the church and release their gentle, wonderful drops of mercy. The falling rain doesn't stay on the high mountains, but it simply runs off them. It stays down below, flowing in the humble river-beds found there.

As long as your heart is like a mountain holding its proud head high in God's presence, it will be impossible for it to soak up his penetrating grace. It all runs off, even if you're deluged with it.

But when that mountain in your heart finally sinks into the depths of the sea, it is replaced by a gentle incline, a hollowed-out riverbed. And then you can't live or even exist unless that grace streams down over you, fills you to the banks, and flows through you.

The law of gravity is so beautifully eloquent. It says in its own secret language that grace will never flow into us unless our egos are humbled and brought low.

People try so many things. They worship. They sing. They celebrate. How they slave and toil! That's also true with respect to the kingdom. But how little notice they take of the one thing that really matters!

We can be so unloving as to stroke and caress the proud egos of others, even among brothers and sisters in the faith.

People think it's so precious of each other when this happens. The have nothing but good words for one another. They think this is first-rate and superb. Meanwhile, it all only amounts to more sod growing on top of an already very high dike. The sod prevents the waters of God's grace from flowing over the top and flooding the fields.

Oh, those cajoling words are such a deadly exchange! One person praises another, who turns around and praises them in return. Think about what kind of spineless flattery such folks practice with each other. It's as though they don't each have a whole lot of hard work to do in breaking and snapping their own inflated egos.

Brothers and sisters, let's make sure we give a great deal of careful attention to ourselves and others here. Every one of us needs to do this before we die, or our deaths cannot and will not be a transition to the blessedness of heaven.

You can be the most agreeable person imaginable. You can be bighearted and absolutely pure in doctrine. It won't matter. Even if all others regard you as a child of God and there's a complete, solid report on your piety, it won't matter if your ego hasn't been shattered. Gone with pride, in with humility! It won't matter as long as you revere your own name and don't fear the name of the Lord.

So now you understand what Malachi, inspired by the Spirit, was prophesying about these two options. On that terrible day, a light will shine on both the proud and the humble.

For those of you whose egos have been broken the blessed light of the Sun of Righteousness will shine on you, says the Spirit, for you have feared my name. There will be healing for your soul and shelter under my wings.

But for those of you who die in their pride and without being broken, there will be a fiery furnace discharging its gray smoke. You will be thrown into the outer darkness, lighted only by the flames of its inextinguishable fire.

The proud will be the stubble. They'll be powerless! Sifted chaff sucked up and churned around in the whirlwind of God's wrath!

That's the result of striving against your God for your entire life!

A QUIET SPIRIT THAT IS PRECIOUS TO GOD

The hidden person of the heart, adorned with
the imperishable beauty of a gentle and quiet
spirit, is what is precious to God. 1 Peter 3:4

The cross of Jesus offers nothing to the eye, but it offers everything needed by the heart. It's not a matter of appearance but of essence. Externally nothing is more miserable. But nothing is more precious if you're judging by what can't be seen. Humans find it deplorable. But God regards it as precious!

This is how Isaiah's prophecy expressed it: "When we beheld him, he had no form or beauty that we should desire him. He was despised, the least worthy of all men. He was a Man of Sorrows and afflicted with suffering, someone from whom people hid their faces. He was despised, and we esteemed him not."

That prophesy was fulfilled in Gethsemane, before Caiaphas, in Gabbatha,[1] facing Herod, along the way to the cross, and on Golgotha. It was fulfilled when the sponge soaked in hyssop was lifted to his lips. It was fulfilled when the Man of Sorrows grimaced with pain in his deadly anguish.

It was so terrible that you'd want to turn your head the other way and curse it. It was a spectacle from hell, especially the shrill, crazed screaming of the

---

1. This is the name for Herod's courtyard.

unpriestly priests through all of it. It was a repulsive drama. So it was a good thing that God caused a veil of thick darkness to spread over it.

The actual hellishness involved slinked off under the cover of darkness.

But amid all that was detestable there and overshadowed by a curse, something inexpressibly and indescribably precious was going on. It was something that the prophet of old called "the work of his soul!"

Seen from this side, the cross was something ghastly. But seen from heaven's side, from God's side, the cross was the most majestically beautiful thing imaginable. It was the most beautiful thing God's angels had ever seen. They were watching the flowering bud of everlasting grace unfold.

This was the work of Jesus' soul. The work of his soul produced a treasure. That treasure was so precious and still is that not one of God's children anywhere is ever draped with a white robe over their filthy shame but that a special jewel is also hung around their neck. This is all made possible by that one work of Jesus. All its fruit was pressed from his bitter, deadly fear. It was squeezed from his cross on Golgotha.

All the living that God's people have done throughout the ages, and all the living that they will ever do, flows from that one divine winepress. And it continues to flow from it. It was and is made possible by the work that went on in Jesus' soul on Golgotha.

A child of God is a godless person who has been completely justified. Not partially! They receive their total sanctification in Jesus. Not just some of it! They are given full redemption as their inheritance. Not merely half of it! Their entire justification, sanctification, and redemption all flow from that one effort that went on in the soul of Jesus. He is its intimate source for those who are close to him.

That struggle in Jesus' soul is very, very precious to those who know him. It was also very costly for God. Its riches are inexhaustible. All other treasures have measurable value, but this one does not!

Golgotha lacks harmony. Golgotha is the complete absence of harmony. The cross of Jesus stands in stark contrast with beneficial harmony.

Harmony exists when the inner life and the external life mesh perfectly. It exists when appearance and essence flow as one, when the inhaling and exhaling of life are united, when nothing obstructs it.

Harmony exists in heaven. You can even say that harmony exists in hell! That's because in hell the internal and the external are one. There's one curse, one doom, and one frightening destruction.

On second thought, that's not true because that word is too positive. A blessed harmony enthralls us only in heaven. Being cleansed of all sin and resplendent in glory will be the sacred lot of all God's children only there.

This is why Golgotha offers us no final point of rest. At Golgotha everyone experiences that we are not done with the cross. There's still more to come. Things cannot remain as they are. In its demanding effort, the soul is calling, even crying, for that priceless crown of glory.

And that's still coming. For after Golgotha, the first thing witnessed was the overwhelming display of God's triumphant power in the resurrection of the crucified One. Then came the divine rending of the firmament when Jesus ascended. Now we have his glorious rule from on high over all things subject to him. Finally, when the Day of Judgment arrives and all things will come to an end, we will see the Son of Man returning on the clouds. Then all his enemies will bow down at his feet, including those antagonistic priests on Golgotha.

This is what was unfolding there, at Golgotha. But here on earth things are still unfinished and in process. This world continues to lie in the grip of evil. The visible still cries out against God. In this kind of world, there is still no harmony between it and the work going on in Jesus' soul. His spirit is compelled to struggle against the world, and he pours his soul into this effort. The cross testifies to the disconnect between what is visible in this world and what is invisible in Jesus' soul. They are locked in a life-and-death battle. The world must triumph, or he will!

But, praise be to God, the Lion of the tribe of Judah has won the victory!

For all those who want to belong to Jesus, this is decisive!

Formerly, even a believing child of God could be hesitant. But not now, not after the cross of Golgotha became a reality and dripped with the most sacred blood ever shed.

The cross finished matters for everyone who fears God, submits to his Word, and through faith is committed to the Surety who is "the Lord of our Righteousness." For now it all comes down to one single and all-determinative choice that cuts through and penetrates everything in our lives. It's the choice of whether we identify with the cross or oppose it. A third option doesn't exist.

To look for the harmony we've been talking about already in the here and now amounts to denying the cross of Christ. Here on earth you can't be adorned with the internal and the external at the same time. That's true for now, but someday it won't be. But harmony won't and can't happen before death. A child of God is radiant to the Father above, but here on earth they trudge along as pilgrims. Conflict, opposition, and finally total exclusion exist here on earth.

You need to exist for one of two things now. You need to live for, work for, and think only about one of these two: for the visible or the invisible, for mere appearance or the essence of things, for the external or the internal, for the present or the future, for what passes quickly and is gone or for what is substantial and enduring and never perishes.

For people who are living outside Christ, everything that is visible is precious. They are enthralled by what they can see. They are captivated by the clothing and jewelry that gain them more attention and improve their appearance, while they should be simply stripping them off! They are also more engrossed with making a good impression by their affected language and display of piety than with how their vain, hollow personalities are influencing others. They're always focused on who and what they are. And that's never enough. They always strive for more, whether that's through their clothing, their language, or their religious bearing. They're always out to make a better impression. And that simply continues until either their flaunting of clothing, speech, and piety is denied them or they die. Then death drags them beneath the ground along with all their finery and infatuation with who and what they are.

God turns matters completely around. For the Lord God all this flaunting of clothing and gold jewelry is a curse, not a blessing. So are this inflated self-interest and display of pretentious piety. They'll kill you! What has value for God and is precious to him is how you're clothed inside! How your soul is inwardly adorned! Whether the tone of your life is pure within! If your soul is yielding true piety in your inner self! "The hidden person of the heart, adorned with the imperishable beauty of a gentle and quiet spirit, is what is precious to God."

Nature shows you that in the autumn harvest. That's when our all-powerful God loads the colorful and carefully trained branches of the espalier with its fragrant fruit.

Just consider those beautiful peaches, for example. You simply want to pick and feast on such wonderful fruit. But do you always yearn for that beautifully rosy, velvety skin as well? I see that you're already quickly peeling it off and throwing it away. You're not doing this because the skin displays so many beautiful shades of color but because you want to get at the succulent fruit inside. That's what attracts you!

If you act like this, why shouldn't the Lord treat you the same way?

He discards the skin, the outside that has such a colorful appearance. What's precious to him is only what's hidden inside, the succulent inner fruit.

BE LIFTED UP, YOU
EVERLASTING
DOORS

Lift up your heads, you gates. Be lifted up, you everlasting doors,
so that the King of Glory may come in. Who is he, this King of
Glory? The Lord Almighty, he is the King of Glory. Psalm 24:9–10

David yearned with his whole soul to be permitted to build a temple for
the ark of the Lord. But coming to him, the prophet said: "That is not
what Jehovah wants. He wants Solomon your son to be the one who builds the
temple, not you." And when David was sure about this, he didn't grumble or
force the issue. He put the matter behind him, and from that point on he was
thoroughly excited that Solomon and not he would accomplish this.

What a glorious day that would be when God's ark would finally be carried
into the completed temple! It was as if that day had already dawned for him.
He envisioned it all, as though it had already happened right before his eyes.
The beautiful metals! The high, stately walls! The procession bearing the ark
of God, the seat of his majestic presence! It was as though David, looking down
on the ark and the temple, saw much farther. It was as though he were looking into the heart of that other David, the one for whom the fathers of Israel

were praying and of whom both the ark and the temple were no more than shadows and symbols.

Next he sees that ark of God processing up the holy mountain in all its glory until the procession stops before the wall of fortified Zion. In the wall are gateways, and in the gates there are doors. And it's possible for the ark to pass through them, to be sure, but they are too low and unimpressive. They are too restrictive for him whose glorious entrance was only being symbolized by the ark's procession. So, filled with the Spirit, David sings a psalm. Listen to what he cries out: "Be raised higher, O you gates. Be bigger, wider, broader, and higher, you entrances. Expand, you everlasting doors. Get regal! Don't hold back! For behold, he is coming to you. The King of Glory, the Prince of the heavenly hosts, my heart's inspiration and my soul's desire, is entering!"

This psalm is referring directly to the narrow gate in the wall of Zion's mountain fortress. Here is Jerusalem. Above her rises the temple. And there are the solid walls with their formidable gates and everlasting doors. This is why David sings his psalm of holy exaltation. The ark of the Lord bearing God's majesty is arriving.

> Lift up your heads, O you gates,
> > Be lifted up, you everlasting doors,
> So that the King of Glory may come in.

> Who is the King of Glory?
> > The Lord strong and mighty!
> The Lord mighty in battle.

Then once again:

> Lift up your heads, O you gates,
> > Yes, be lifted up, you everlasting doors,
> So that the King of Glory may come in.

> Who is the King of Glory?
> > The Lord of Hosts,
> He is the King of Glory!

But all of this wasn't real because Zion itself wasn't the reality. Jerusalem was only a shadow. The temple was a shadow. The ark standing in it was a shadow. Even the walls of Zion separating the temple and the city of Jerusalem were shadows. All of it was a display for instructional purposes. It was a representation of reality and an image of what is true. It all pointed to what is enduring and deals with what is real and eternal.

The wise according to the world don't get this. God's church does. And within that church, all God's dearly loved elect people do. That's exactly the reason that the church of all ages didn't engage in guesswork. It knew certainly, definitely, and solidly what it was singing in this song of David: the ark was a symbol of the actual ascension of Jesus into heaven!

In Jerusalem people were thirsting for the living God. But the Lord was living on Mount Zion, and those walls and everlasting doors couldn't be budged. They were causing a continuing separation. The people saw the temple there and knew that the ark was inside it. They realized that that's precisely where the presence of the Lord was dwelling. But then there were those massive walls, and those narrow gates, and those everlasting doors!

But be lifted up, my soul, and be exalted Jerusalem that languishes. A new day is dawning. Salvation is flowing. The King of Glory is coming. The walls are giving way. The massive gates are being lifted high. The everlasting doors are being raised because the Prince of heaven's powerful army is marching in. And you who have been longing for God's coming are singing and celebrating in victory!

What could those everlasting doors really be?

Everything that shuts Jerusalem off from the ark! Therefore everything that acts as a barrier between languishing hearts of unhappy people and the sacred glory of their God.

A door is anything that prevents you from entering. Because it's bolted and barred, it keeps you out. An everlasting door defies your entrance however much you knock and bang on it. It stays shut, as shut as a wall. It remains so tightly shut that it suggests to you that it will never be opened. It is an everlasting door. It will keep you out eternally.

But now the Messiah arrives. God has mercy on those who are miserable and sends them a Savior. How, then, could those everlasting doors possibly keep him out?

In answering that question, the Spirit prophesies through David: "No, and once again no. The bolts and bars will fall off those everlasting doors!" The doors will be flung open for him. The openings will even be widened and broadened for him. The doors will be lifted up so that the King of Glory may enter in all his glory.

But pay attention! The door is still there! It's the everlasting door of the flesh. You're stuck behind it. It won't admit you. The flesh is oppressive. But

Christ breaks through it by coming in the flesh. He comes to you through that everlasting door of the flesh. This brings him close to you. He is one with you. He has become like a brother to you.

But you're still not quite there yet. The Word made flesh is definitely your Messiah. But he is so in a way that, while you are with him and he is with you, you are still languishing and shut out of Zion. You are still barred from glory. The wall and the everlasting door are still obstructions for you.

This is why in the flesh you still have to keep working at making progress in the flesh. You have to climb the mountain. You have to climb from the flatness of this world to the heights of heaven. The glory isn't here, but it's up there. While weak here, the Messiah is mighty there and great in his majesty. That's where he is capable of saving you and blessing you.

This required his ascension! To heaven! To the place where weakness is glorified! Where all the power is! Where power and strength can go to work! So that's where your flesh goes, your Messiah in your flesh, in exactly the same flesh and blood that hung on the shameful wood of Golgotha.

Now, finally, those everlasting doors are completely raised and lifted up. Here, finally, the King of Glory enters in. This is your King, church of God. He possesses all the wealth needed to exalt you, justify you, sanctify you, and redeem you completely.

He enters through the everlasting doors into that expanded tabernacle that is not made with human hands. From there your King causes salvation and blessing to flow freely. From there his strength is expressed, and Satan slinks away because those who were ungodly have now been made righteous.

But this is still not the end of the matter.

One everlasting door still remains. It is the door of your own heart that Satan has bolted shut. It is the door of your own soul that he has slammed closed.

How many thousands of times haven't you banged your head against that everlasting door? This became so oppressive that your fearful heart could hardly stand it any longer. You wanted to escape and you pounded on that door, crying: "Open, open up! Show some mercy! Don't let me choke in desperation!"

But it didn't help. You got no response. The door of your sinful heart seemed like an everlasting door.

That is ... until he came! Right? Until the King of Glory came!

That's when from his throne of glory he sent his messengers. They came with the sledgehammer of his Word and beat on that door. Then you realized that where the Word of the King comes, it comes with power. For then the locks are broken. The bolts are shattered. The doors are lifted, and he enters. The King of Glory comes in. The Lord strong and mighty!

Hallelujah!

LOVE POURED INTO OUR HEARTS THROUGH THE HOLY SPIRIT

And hope does not put to shame, because the love of
God has been poured into our hearts through the Holy
Spirit, whom he has given to us. Romans 5:5

The Holy Spirit is the true and eternal God along with the Father and the Son.

Truly God!

He's not a third part of the divine being, only a portion of what belongs to it. No, but this Exalted Being is simultaneously Father, Son, and Holy Spirit. Each of the three persons fully possesses the same being, and together they share one essence.

God the Holy Spirit is therefore the always-present God. He is not God at a distance, but he's very near. He's not far from every single one of us. It can never be said and should never be said that the Holy Spirit is here, but he's not there.

Note well that God the Holy Spirit is everywhere. And he's everywhere in his entirety. God the Holy Spirit is present even in a place like hell, where he is a frightful, consuming fire in the consciences of those caught in their calamity.

But although the Holy Spirit is everywhere and everywhere at the same time, by no means does he disclose, reveal, or show himself everywhere and at all times. He can be somewhere—and he is—without our hearing his rustling footsteps. When his face is covered! When we're not hearing his voice! When it's just like he's not there at all!

Sometimes as soon as you've sinned you're suddenly surprised deep inside with the stifling sense that there's Someone there reproaching you. He doesn't give you a minute's peace. But this Someone didn't show up just then. No, this saintly Presence was there all along. But he was hidden from you. That Presence was the Holy Spirit.

So the Holy Spirit discloses his overwhelming presence according to the nature of the person to whom he's showing himself. It can be for good or ill, for the purpose of comforting or of judging.

The Holy Ghost is always the same God, who with the Father and the Son is the one, eternal, and true God. But sometimes he's hidden behind a thicker and sometimes behind a thinner veil. And sometimes he discloses his full presence. Then we see his wonderful, reassuring face.

This explains why Holy Scripture teaches and Christ's church knows by experience that there are people who have never taken any notice of the Holy Spirit. Both sources also disclose that there are other folks to whom the Holy Spirit has disclosed himself. They indicate, furthermore, that those who live by grace sometimes miss the Holy Spirit, but then they also have moments when they possess him with soul-stirring blessedness.

If the unconverted experience the Holy Spirit's presence, they discover that he is a consuming fire and they shrink back from him and try to push him away. This amounts to experiencing him without the benefit of the Mediator.

But if by God's good pleasure someone is born again through faith, that person also experiences the Spirit's presence, but as a Comforter. For them, the Spirit is gentle, loving, nurturing, and soul soothing. This amounts to experiencing the Holy Spirit as poured out through the Mediator. As reconciling and unbelievably inspiring! As beneficial!

The thick fog is then mercifully wiped away. Then the soul sees the same Holy Spirit that it formerly could not. And that is heavenly. Once alone, they now have their God with them. He is present with them in the depths of their hearts.

Sometimes the Holy Spirit can even disclose himself almost in the same way to the unconverted, even though they have not been born again. Why this is so we're not going to get into now. But Hebrews 6 teaches that this does happen. Not a few people remember that before their true conversion they received some light that amounted to a false conversion.

But this differs completely from the experience of those who are truly born again. Even so, the veil is lifted a little at the corner, only to immediately drop down once again. In genuine rebirth, however, the veil completely falls away, and the evidence of the Holy Spirit in us is striking. He is poured out. The Holy Spirit takes up residence in his temple. He enters us, lives in us, prays for us, comforts us, and moves us.

The eye of the soul can even be partially or completely closed in the case of someone who has been born again. Then it no longer sees clearly or not at all. That's the reason why the comforting presence of the Holy Spirit remains even then. He no longer leaves.

And what is it about that comforting presence that is so blessed? Just this, brothers and sisters: that in, with, and through the Holy Spirit the love of God is poured into your hearts.

Paul, the holy apostle, bears witness to this. The church of Jesus Christ adds its hearty amen to that testimony! Is this an amen echoed in your soul as well?

This should not be the lukewarm, limp, watered-down explanation that this makes better sense of the Holy Spirit, so that whoever has this better sense also automatically shows love because God is love.

Paul's witness doesn't give a hint of this. No, the love of God here is the tender, divine, merciful love of the Highest Being toward us. It flows to us like a flood over parched fields. The thirsty ground of our souls is refreshed by the Holy Spirit streaming into them.

You have no love on your own. Your heart lacks love. And what passes for love is one of three things. It could be instinctive love like that a hen has for her chicks. This has no value in the sight of God. Or it could be an expression of love that dies immediately when you are constrained to show it. Or it could be a love that is worked in your heart by a higher power. This alone is love in the true sense. It penetrates your cold heart because it is nurtured there from outside. It is a holy spark in your heart's embers spattered there from the warmth of eternal tenderness.

By nature, your heart believes that there is no love in God. Measuring him in terms of who you are, you thought that in the depths of his being the everlasting God was cold and lacking in warmth. You did say: "God is love. He's everyone's Father and forgives everything." But that was just so much talk, superficial chatter that had no depth or substance. Then, when you're needy, out of bread, separated from the love of your life, or your honor is attacked, see how much of God's love you think is still left.

That sort of despicable game playing with noises about God is deeply wicked. What does someone who talks about forgiveness that way ever note about the terrible guilt that they themselves need to have forgiven personally? This sort of talk means nothing.

Coldhearted yourself, you thought that your God is just as cold as your own dull, sluggish heart. That's how you rationalized, measuring him in terms of who you are.

But then, all at once, a searing fire shot through to the marrow of your bones and made you double over. God slammed you down. Your sense of your own wickedness flooded over you. At that exact moment, God exposed you. Your illusion became obvious. The true God confronted you as a mighty, consuming fire.

There and then the Holy Spirit finally penetrated your soul and came to dwell in the depths of your heart. He whispered to you so wonderfully and addressed you in indescribably blessed language. He looked after you in countless tender ways. In them, you experienced the reassuring face of your God!

That's when you felt his love. God's love! It was the warm, splendid glow of the Beloved living in you and of the Living God loving you. And this was food and drink that nourished your soul.

And this love of God—no, it can't be expressed! It was indescribably glorious! It flowed into you like a flood of great waters, and every single drop of it opened up an entire ocean of well-being and bliss within you.

Oh, the Holy Spirit is God himself. His being is never mixed or confused with yours. But he causes you to recognize and feel in the depths of your being a shared recognition and feeling of the divine blessedness that he enjoys and experiences. This sacred peace comes into your dreadful heart, and the Eternal Being overwhelms you with his divine compassion.

This is what the holy apostle of the Lord experienced when he wrote about "the love of God that has been poured into your hearts through the Holy Spirit." And he added, "who has been given to you."

Although perhaps not yet accepted.

The Holy Spirit has been given by sheer grace. And that obligates every single one of God's elect people to express everlasting gratitude.

BY THEIR BEHAVIOR, WITHOUT WORDS!

Likewise you wives, be submissive to your husbands so
that if any of them is disobedient they may be won over
without words by the behavior of their wives. 1 Peter 3:1

The old customs are increasingly being set aside. The Lord God has ordained that his church has to be gathered and souls converted by the Word. For centuries people have been of one mind that the first mark of the true church is the true preaching of the Word. Right up to our own day, our confessional heritage has emphasized the power of the Word rather than our personal influence, our good example, or our charisma. The Word is the hammer that crushes into little pieces hearts that are hard as stone. That's because the Word is the instrument of the Holy Spirit and not of our spirits. He is the one who makes it effective spiritually.

But today there is change in the wind. The Word has lost its grip. It makes people unsettled. People say that you can't depend on the Word any longer. The only thing that remains as a refuge for the soul is the influence of the Christian spirit. It is the soul's salvation.

According to this approach, Christ communicated a certain spirit to his apostles. That spirit has been passed along from them to their followers. And in that way circles of people emerged who also embodied it. Eventually those groups coalesced and united to form one large circle that became known as the church. Continuously maintained by Christ himself, circles of living Christians were found who manifested that expression of spirituality. They were moved by it as by the wind. It influenced them. They felt it. And eventually, the explanation goes, it is also taken up by you and me, who breathe the same air. It makes us receptive to new influences that modify our hearts and change our way of living so that we are delivered from sin and led into a glorious and holy existence.

Now, if that's how it is, then obviously people are less dependent on the Word.

If it's no longer the Word that has to change my heart but "the spirituality that pervades circles of Christians," then to a certain degree it doesn't matter to me what people do with the Word. Just let them give me space to quietly absorb that kind of spirituality.

If the conversion of the soul does not depend on the Word but on the influence of the Christian spirit, I totally understand why people vigorously oppose "standing for the truth" and being vigilant for purity of doctrine. For what does all that really matter, as long as my genuine, clean, and exemplary life has a different source and flows out of a "Christian spirit"?

If this is really the case, and if the Word is not God's ordained instrument for changing lives, I understand completely those incessant warnings in sermons "to avoid zealots for the truth" because "the purity of life" is of much greater value. The kingdom of God comes not by smooth talking but by genuine and sincere walking in the spirit that inspires our lives.

"Not the Word, but your exemplary life!" is the new refrain. And who among us would dare dispute it? Doesn't Scripture itself make the same point—literally? Isn't this the deeply moving, fundamental admonition repeated by no one less than the apostle Peter?

In this connection, it may actually be asked whether it doesn't sound a little strange to hear these opponents of the Word making their appeal to the very Word that they have just diminished!

One could ask, if the Word doesn't have definitive authority any more, why make your case by appealing to it?

Moreover, it's worth noting that whoever appeals to the Word should at least do so genuinely and should not play games with it.

What is Peter really saying? Is there any trace found in this context that he is creating space for that overly spiritualized and unhealthy human striving we have identified? Is he making room for giving the Word second place in favor of greater emphasis on our exemplary living?

Not in the least, sisters and brothers! For it is precisely the apostle Peter who made the moving and powerful affirmation "For we have been born again, not of perishable but of imperishable seed through the living and eternally abiding Word of God." And should anyone object that the expression "Word of God" in this context does not refer to Scripture, but that Peter is referring here to Christian spirituality, that wrongheaded notion is immediately dispelled by the apostle himself. He instantly follows his reference to "the living and eternally abiding Word of God" with this: "And this is the Word that was preached among you."

He also says that destruction comes to those "who trip over the Word and are disobedient, as they were destined to be." Conversely, he says that "the gospel is preached to the dead so that they might be judged according to men in the flesh but live according to God in the spirit" (4:6).

Therefore, don't doubt for a minute that Peter stood where all God's saints stand. He expected the conversion of souls on the basis of the Word.

But who brings that Word? Is that everyone's work? Is it everyone's responsibility?

Scripture itself answers those questions by saying that the Lord God has determined this. Among his other ordinances, he has given one that says that the husband has a different relationship to the wife than the wife has to the husband.

The husband is the head of the wife. The wife is not the head of the husband. The husband has a responsibility for the spiritual life of the wife. That cannot be ignored.

The result is that the wife is not called to minister the Word with authority to her husband. But it is definitely his role to do so with her.

She may counsel her husband. She may tenderly entice him and try to induce him to be responsive to the Word. She may attempt to bless him with the Word. But it is not her place to address her husband authoritatively from the Word.

Because many wives want to take that approach based on their conversion and consequently consider themselves to be above their husbands, the holy apostle takes the position that he does. He directed that in such situations a wife must live in silence and must be submissive to her husband. She will then receive a blessing by taking the quiet, submissive approach he advocates. In that way, without speaking a word, she will be able to accomplish good things for her husband.

There is nothing to recommend the pretentious approach some women take. Instead of discarding the old standards, people should maintain them unshakably. The Word is the God-given instrument whose proclamation he uses for gathering his elect. For this purpose he uses the servants whom he has called. He gathers his people by his irresistible grace working not through the spirituality of other Christians but by the breath of his Holy Spirit.

That's when respect is created for the use of his Word that God himself had determined.

The Word is majestic. No one not called to bring it should trifle with it.

Don't minimize something else. Since this Word is preeminently the Word when it is ministered to our hearts by God himself, every individual should take special care that in their zeal for the Word they never, ever undervalue their walk of life.

A walk of life can never replace the Word. There should be no doubt about that. But if anyone ever pretends that the Word still holds when their conduct is outside its bounds, what do you think? Wouldn't that be like praising the sun when you prefer groping around in darkness?

Where the sun shines, there is light. Similarly, where the Word glistens in full glory, there you'll find that walking in the Lord's ways is honored. The Word works in us not by our own effort.

This is why on the one hand, new-style Christians who are lulled to spiritual sleep by "Christian spirituality" are warned not to take the Word lightly and not to casually dismiss what God has put in place. On the other hand, those who are zealous for the Word are admonished not to minimize the importance of Christian living, because a Word that does not enliven Christian living amounts to the clanging of symbols that never becomes a living Word of God.

9 4

VOLUME II

FILLED WITH THE KNOWLEDGE OF HIS WILL

That's why, from the day that we heard about you, we have not stopped praying for you and desiring that you might be filled with the knowledge of his will in all wisdom and spiritual understanding. Colossians 1:9

God's children are usually far less troubled about what their faithful Father wants than they should be.

You often notice that in sensitive, loving families flesh-and-blood children act just the opposite. No matter what comes up, in that kind of family the children ask whether their father would approve of something or whether it would contradict his values. Sometimes that sensitive attachment lasts so long that even years after their father's death, people hear his children asking: "Would Father have approved of this?"

Naturally, every comparison between an earthly father and our heavenly one is highly unsatisfactory. That's true even if the former is the best father possible. The latter is the only One who truly deserves the wonderful, sacred name "Father." Everyone senses and feels this. This is true even of God's children who show less respect, loyalty, or attachment to their Father in heaven than a natural child might to their earthly father. This may be so even when the earthly father doesn't have much social standing, lacks good character, or is unaccountable either to God or others for his disrespectful treatment of the most holy and exalted Being of all.

Formerly this only happened very rarely among God's pious people.

People lived more carefully then. They couldn't just go along with things. People had no peace or patience if others knew that they were off course. By getting off course people didn't understand, as they do today, making easy concessions. It referred to something much deeper and more unusual.

People held to the solid conviction that the Lord God has determined the lot of every one of us. In his counsel, he has regulated every person's life. The course of our lives from cradle to grave was defined by the Lord God. On that basis, people wanted to stay on that path every step of the way. They desired protection from veering off on an alternative path chosen in their arrogance. If they were inwardly inflamed by their passions, they wanted to make sure that they were being reined in so that their feet stayed on the course determined by their faithful Father in heaven.

This is not to say that this approach has completely disappeared.

On the contrary! Concerning serious, life-determining decisions, one still hears about evaluation made through prayerful consideration. One also still hears heartfelt comments that betray serious wrestling of the soul. Such reflections indicate a complete desire and longing to know the Lord's will.

Yet, while this seems to reflect the same approach as earlier, it is not the same.

What people understand about this at present is far too often that they should suddenly receive a special message in some unusual way about what God has determined on the matter in his secret will. People do have to make choices. But they don't get a jolt to the soul! Their deliberation yields no clear direction! Their will receives no overwhelming strength! And they still have to decide: do they go right or left? Today they so badly want to know inwardly what would please God for them to do. They'd like him to beckon with his finger what direction they should take—right or left.

But this isn't what the Lord our God does. Yet because people ultimately want so badly to experience the peace of mind that comes from choosing what they think God has chosen, they resort to this: they talk openly about a deeply indescribable emotional experience that led to their decision. And they imagine that this was a work of the Holy Spirit.

This approach is highly dangerous. It's the approach taken by enthusiasts and fanatics who follow an inner light. Our spiritual fathers never chose that approach. Rather, they urged us to reject it. They always pointed us to Scripture.

Should you ask whether Scripture ever lays anything different on our hearts, then the answer is beyond doubt.

What the Holy Spirit admonishes in the words of the sacred apostle is definitely not to ask about God's will only now and then or at certain crucial points. He asks that we "be filled with the knowledge of his will in all wisdom and spiritual understanding" (Col 1:9).

He's talking about choosing and walking in the way that should be followed precisely. What this amounts to appears in what follows immediately: being filled with the knowledge of his will "so that you may live a life worthy of the Lord, bearing the fruit of good works and increasing in the knowledge of the Lord" (v. 10).

The obvious difference consists of this: that we can so easily live for days and weeks at a time without coming to a deeper understanding of God's will. But then on a few occasions when we face difficult circumstances, we start praying for a revelation from on high. Meanwhile, Scripture presses us to ask persistently what God's will is in order that we might walk in his ways. It's precisely through such steady fellowship with the Lord that we develop confidence in his ways. Then in life's difficult and threatening moments our wills will bow to his, and we will not lack inner certainty that our choice has been his choice.

This is what it means to "be filled with the knowledge of his will." It suggests a fertile field abundantly drenched and saturated with the water oozing from it. It does not suggest a dry, parched field on which a meager drop of rain happens to splash down once in a while. Being "filled with the knowledge of his will" is to be inwardly permeated with the principles and spirit of God's law. It is to live in constant fellowship with him, so that we follow him in our daily lives.

That explains why Scripture doesn't talk about emotions or states of mind but speaks about "all wisdom and spiritual understanding." We are not being forced to take this approach in order to silence our thinking and reflecting and so that we may be led by a torrent of vague, mystical feelings and sentiments. Just the opposite! We are directed to rely on wisdom, "all wisdom," and on spiritual insight and understanding in determining the nature and disposition of all future matters. Then the way we should proceed will be determined clearly, calmly, and in a way worthy of the Lord. Mature judgment and a genuine spirit will prevail.

So you can see, my brothers and sisters, how far removed this understanding of Scripture is from the sick mysticism in which many are caught up today.

Jesus' holy apostle prays without ceasing for the Colossians. He doesn't just pray for them in a few special circumstances. He prays that they will be filled with the knowledge of the Lord's will, not just given some hint of it. For him this matter is not about emotions or states of the mind but about crystal-clear wisdom and spiritual understanding.

Those whom this describes then follow the example of our spiritual fathers. They searched the Word. They examined it. Through their continuous engagement with the Word, they penetrated the mind of the Lord. From then on, their entire life was one steady walk with the Lord their God. In all things, large and however seemingly small, it consisted of inquiring about his will. By continuously living with the Word and in the Spirit like this, by grace spiritual discretion developed in their lives. So did mature judgment and a more highly refined insight and a clearer understanding. The working of God's Spirit brought this about in their yielded hearts. He caused them to choose with a steady hand, not with uncontrolled passion, what they knew, witnessed, and experienced the Lord's will to be in every situation they faced.

Which of these two do you choose?

The emotional path is the way of spiritual uncertainty and lack of progress. For those who follow it, there is no mining of the gold ore contained in the Word. They don't pay close attention to God in life's little details, unless it's to ask him to overlook their daily messes and slipups. For when the occasion warrants and a serious decision has to be made, then the Holy Spirit will once again bring some verse to their attention or stir up some feeling in their heart.

By contrast, the biblical path requires hard work and close attention. To be certain in the choices you make at crucial turning points in your life, and to be sure that you know what God's will is in making them, requires that you plunge into the Word every day of your life. Then what the Spirit means will penetrate your thinking. This will lead you in the Lord's ways with respect to even the most ordinary and smallest matters. Yet, your soul will never experience living a greatly restricted life when you live in God's presence.

If you select the emotional path, you can make a strong impression on the undiscerning of being very devout. In this respect, you can even impress yourself with the enormous progress you've made in your spirituality. You can tell a lot of stories about how the Lord showed you this or that and then again something else. But it could also be possible that in doing so you were taking the name of the Lord in vain. You could actually only be seeing the face of your own heart, like the false prophets in Israel who thought that they had received a revelation from God.

By contrast, in staying the course on the biblical path, you're going to have to live much more attentively. It will demand greater effort. It will smell a lot less like pretentious piety. It will have the sweet, satisfying, and enjoyable taste of walking with integrity in God's presence and holding all pretenses at arm's length. By grace, it will be to live "filled with the knowledge of his will."

CHRIST THE FIRSTFRUITS

Just as in Adam all died, so in Christ all will be made alive.
But each one in sequence: Christ the firstfruits, and after he
comes, those who belong to him. 1 Corinthians 15:22–23

Your soul echoes what Paul said, namely that the Lord's Anointed "was delivered for our transgressions and raised for our justification." That's the starting point. That's the root of the matter. Without that justification, your soul would gain nothing from Jesus' resurrection.

But does this amount to saying that Jesus being raised is meaningful only with respect to justification? Does it have any bearing on my own resurrection? What about the resurrection of my pious friends who died young and preceded me to the Jerusalem of God?

How could that be possible? Doesn't this same holy apostle also say: "But now Christ has been raised and become the firstfruits of those who have fallen asleep"? Firstfruits are always connected to others that follow them, as the holy apostle adds immediately: "They will all be made alive in Christ. But each one in sequence: Christ the firstfruits, and after he comes, those who belong to him."

Our excellent catechism summarizes this as one of the three benefits of Christ's resurrection: "And the third is that Christ's resurrection is a sure guarantee of our own blessed resurrection."

Yes, it's definitely true, my brothers and sisters. Your own resurrection depends on Immanuel being raised.

But how?

By telling you: "Now that Jesus came back from the realm of the dead, we have compelling, irrefutable proof that there really is life after death"?

Impossible! Because the unspiritual person who doesn't acknowledge that eternity exists beyond the grave renounces and denies that Jesus really arose.

Then perhaps by telling you that someday all people will be raised?

That can't be the explanation, either. For Jesus' resurrection is the reliable guarantee of the resurrection of those who are saved. But is that the whole picture? The holy apostle testifies: "Christ as the firstfruits, and after he comes, those who belong to him." But do all people who die belong to Christ?

No, there's no basis here for mournful sentimentality that wants to go around looking at gravestones.

The apostle is singing a song of triumph here. It's a song of victory, a prophetic song of blessing, a song of ascent sung by God's children as they journey up to the city of the living God.

Make careful note of this. Jesus' apostle doesn't utter one word about what comes immediately after death or what happens to us personally when we die. He speaks exclusively about what will happen to God's children at the end of days when the Lord returns on the clouds. He expresses this in the words "after he comes."

He presumes that we know what happens in death, both after it and through it. The existence of God's children doesn't only continue. For the first time and forever they are now set free from sin. And being set free from sin, they will then experience full spiritual fellowship with their Redeemer. This is the wonderful certainty that Paul elsewhere affirms when he says: "I have a desire to depart and to be with Christ."

That this fellowship with Jesus after our death will also be a fellowship with "the assembly of the elect" is obvious. One who resides with the Head cannot remain outside the body. And the body of Christ is that great congregation "that is the fullness of him who fills all things in every way."

There is nothing earthly or wicked about the sweet hope that a dear, pious child of God who has departed remains in spiritual fellowship with the gathering of the elect that still lingers here on earth. This means that they are also in fellowship with you, as long as you are bound to that gathering.

Provided that—and you must never lose sight of this condition—provided that everything about you is tied to Jesus! This means that you must never allow yourself to slip into some sick attempt to pursue earthly exchanges with your departed loved ones, for this is not of Christ and dishonors God.

With death come the rejection of sin, intimate communion with Jesus, and fellowship with the host that no one can number. Even though there is still no resurrection for you!

To continue living and to be raised from the dead are two very different things.

When Jesus died on the cross on Good Friday evening, he did not stop existing. He continued living that evening and for the entire day Saturday. He arose only on Sunday morning.

And that's how it is as well for a child of God who dies among us. They do not stop existing even though they are dead. They continue to live for the entire time that passes since the day they died. But they still have not been raised up.

The children of God will only be raised from the dead when the end of the world comes, Judgment Day arrives, and Jesus returns on the clouds of heaven.

"Each one in their turn: Christ the firstfruits, and after he comes, those who belong to him."

During all the time proceeding this day, they rest in their graves, wherever those graves may be. They might be in the depths of the earth, or in the bowels of the monstrous sea, or in the flames and smoke prepared for them.

Adam and Eve, Abel and Seth are all still not raised from the dead. David and Isaiah as well as Peter and John and all God's children who have already died, all of them wait for the day of their resurrection.

That day of resurrection will be a day of great glory!

And we will one day experience that day along with all God's children, that is, if we have been born of God.

Resurrection is to be raised visibly, with our body. It's not merely having a future existence. But it's finally, conclusively to see coming what the church of all ages has confessed as the resurrection of the flesh.

It's like one of our devout spiritual fathers who planted a lot of tulips once put it: "When I die, I'm a tulip that creeps back into its bulb. In the resurrection, I sprout out of that same bulb, but looking much more splendid than I did before."

Or preferably, who doesn't remember Paul's much more striking description of a naked seed that was sown in the physical body and then released from that seed as the much more glorious spiritual body?

This is a profound mystery! It's a hope with which we die, expecting its fulfillment perhaps only centuries later. The holy apostle, who prophesied so confidently and wonderfully to us about these things, has been lying in his own grave for more than eighteen centuries already, but his delayed hope endures.

In his soul, the apostle was on such intimate terms with that hope that he himself continuously lived into the day of Jesus' return!

And that's how things may stay for a while!

We cry out, we prophesy, and we restlessly celebrate: "Maranatha! The Lord is coming!" The bride never stops imploring: "Come, Lord Jesus. Yes, come quickly!" Only the soul that is hard and cold can think about that glorious day without already savoring its glory.

You should realize that Jesus' resurrection provides a solid guarantee for that beautiful, precious hope.

It's a solid guarantee not that with your death your soul will be free from sin or that your fellowship with Jesus and his elect people will be sweet and blessed. No, rather, it's a solid guarantee that should you die this week and be buried the next, you will come forth from the womb of the earth and reappear. This will happen even though after two years no more is left of you here than a skeleton. It will happen even if men were to dig up your coffin in ten years and move your poor bones to an ossuary so that people would say: "There's really not much left of him!" It will happen even if a wild animal were to rip you apart or your remains were to be burned or pulverized. It will happen even if it takes a hundred or perhaps even a thousand years for that day to come. Then you, the same person who once lived here on earth, will be raised. You will reappear by a mighty miracle of God, not with some other body, but in your own. But it will now be a glorified body.

Then Jesus will be there in his glorified body. He will be joined by all God's saints from the old and the new covenant, all the prophets and apostles, all the martyrs and witnesses, all fathers and mothers in Christ, all sincere children of God that we have known, and also our own precious loved ones if they belonged to Jesus. If things were any different from this, there would still be a resurrection, but it wouldn't be a blessed one!

But that day will be a great one for the blessed of the Lord.

It will be a great and illustrious day. For on it vengeance will be heaped on all the world's unbelief, mockery, and slander.

Throughout the ages, the mocking laughter of unbelief directed at the resurrection of the dead has persisted.

Even so, throughout those same ages, God's people have maintained their steadfast confession: "But there will in fact be a resurrection of the dead!"

For now the mocker appears to be right, for the Lord still tarries.

But then, in the end, the child of God will have gotten it right!

And that's the precious glory that Jesus' resurrection guarantees.

NOT ONLY IN WORDS, BUT ALSO WITH POWER

Knowing of your election by God ... , our gospel came to you not only in words, but also with power, in the Holy Spirit and with great conviction. 1 Thessalonians 1:4–5

Salvation does not come by works but through faith. This precious faith, in turn, is not by free will but through obedience. And this obedience that turns life around, again, does not consist of making a show of knowledge but is only in response to preaching. And finally, that preaching is only true preaching if it both intends and actually achieves making known, announcing, and instilling the Word of God.

This process is beyond comprehending. It's a mystery. It's a mystery in the sense that it pleased God to grant a secret blessing through preaching, to tie an inscrutable benefit to it, and to promote his work in the souls of those who sit under this preaching.

It could have been otherwise, but that doesn't deserve much attention. It simply pleased God to work as we've described and not otherwise. Everything flows from the foolishness of preaching. It's all in the preaching! Preaching cuts to the bone. It stirs the soul. It gets the spiritual juices flowing.

But how?

Is it enough to have a building? To put a chancel in it? To have a preacher in that chancel? To have sounds about that Word on the preacher's lips?

You know better than that!

Do you need to be reminded how often you sat in such a building, beneath such a chancel, listening to that kind of preacher? Do you remember how what he said was above your head? Slid into one ear and out the other? Do you recall how it never stirred your soul?

Doesn't everyone know pillar huggers in their neighborhood who come in with dead hearts to sit under the preaching of the Word and that leave more dead than when they entered?

Aren't there congregations that are more loyal to the church than any other, adhere to the truth with the best of them, live up to their reputations, but that are nevertheless so arid and lifeless that they're languishing?

Don't ever say that the job is done when you've got a preacher in the chancel with the Word on his lips. Work finished! End of discussion!

Whoever talks like that is dead wrong.

Listen! Just listen to the distinction that this apostle of the Lord Jesus is making.

He's writing to the hardy, newly flourishing congregation in Thessalonica, the capital city of Macedonia. He says to them: "Our gospel came to you not only in words, but also with power!" This is a stirring claim! It would have made no sense if it weren't true always and everywhere. It also shows that Paul was well aware of false preaching going on that lacked power and consisted of empty words. That kind was useless!

A telegraph operator can do all the excited ticking he wants. If the line is down and the electricity isn't working, his message doesn't get through. Likewise, the preacher can move his tongue and lips all he wants. It won't work at all unless there is spiritual fellowship between the congregation and its Head; they have to be connected! When they are, God's power flows instantly from Christ the Head into the congregation.

A building, a preacher, a Bible, and a congregation don't constitute a church or define preaching. A church and preaching exist only when God is present, Christ is working, and power is flowing from on high.

It's like an organist. They can't produce a sound with all the movement of their fingers, or feet, or strokes unless there is air in the bellows. But if it's sucked in and pressed out through the pipes, they make music. That's how it is with a preacher. He can't communicate with the congregation by merely using his brains, shaping words, or making gestures. A more exalted breath of air has to come from the throne above and be impressed on the consciences of those listening.

In the chancel nothing is going on except stroking the keys unless the effort and the music come from the Lord.

If the Lord withholds his effort, nothing happens either. Then you hear words, but they only sound like hailstones bouncing off a slate roof. They merely slide off your slippery soul. They don't penetrate. Nothing is aroused. Everything remains cold and unmoved—doomed, shriveled, sinful.

Everything depends completely on this power from on high. It comes to us from God and through Christ. Even the ten best preachers couldn't affect as much as a single person without it. But if it pleased the Lord to dispense that power through the humblest village shepherd, a thousand souls at once couldn't resist it.

Brothers and sisters, remember that it's not enough to have a church, a preacher, and orthodox preaching. You can't be without God in all of this. You can't for a second get along without the Fountain of irresistible grace. Your gas line may be in perfect condition and your lamp very fashionable. But if the valve to the kerosene tank is shut, you're still going to be sitting in pitch-black darkness. The pipes of your water line may have been laid as precisely as possible, and your faucets may be scrubbed until they glisten. But if the taps stay closed, you could die of thirst. Your church building may be lovely and your preacher ever so orthodox. But if they're shut off from the pipeline of light and life, you're going to be as unresponsive as stone to the purest and most beautiful preaching you hear.

Said better, then there is no preaching, only what looks like preaching.

What it takes to make talking from a chancel into preaching is the power of the Holy Spirit through what's said.

Where there's actual preaching of the Word, it's always effective. If it's not turned on, it's turned off. Like the well-sharpened blade of a plow, actual preaching slices through the soul's soil. Applied to good earth, it brings blessing. But when it hits a rock, it's dinged and turns up stones.

When the Word of God is preached like it should be and power is flowing from above, God's enemies can't stand it. It shocks them. It makes them shudder. They shrink back from it. Nothing testifies against a preacher more effectively than when God's enemies are never irritated by his preaching.

In a full and complete sense, it all depends on that power about which Paul is talking. It depends on the penetrating, impregnating work of the Holy Spirit. It depends on him imprinting absolute conviction on the listeners.

This is why the preaching of the Word is such sensitive, sacred work. It's why it's so terrible when the preacher shatters the beautiful harmony of reassurance because he botches the playing of his organ, the Word.

That's why it's also as essential as daily bread that the congregation is in prayer. They shouldn't be praying only for the preacher, as though he's someone special. Look, the field hand and factory worker need God's help just as much as the preacher does. They shouldn't be praying just for the preaching itself either, as though this work is so exceptionally difficult. People with limited or average gifts are often capable of handling it! No, the congregation ought to be praying that heavenly power will flow into the Word so that God will work in those who come in and sit down to hear it. It ought to be praying that the Holy Spirit will impregnate preaching.

Where the church is found, it's not enough to find a preacher at work with the Word. The congregation has to be found at work along with him by praying. Preacher and congregation have to be working side by side in the conviction "We're powerless and have nothing unless Almighty God descends on us with his power!" Only then will the waters of life flow to them. Only then will there be real preaching of the Word.

A barrier is created where this joint effort isn't happening.

Blessing, God's effective work, and the flow of his power are all impeded.

Then preaching isn't only ineffective. It does actual damage.

Words without power from above only feed a preacher's vanity and self-interest. They put the congregation in harm's way, sliding down the slippery slope of giving the appearance of godliness but without its power!

9 7

VOLUME II

AFTER I UNDERSTOOD MYSELF

Truly, after I repented, I was sorry; and after I understood myself, I beat my chest. Jeremiah 31:19

Punishment doesn't only follow sin. It isn't attached to sin. God doesn't add the punishment to the sin. Rather, the punishment inheres in the sin and in its own good time manifests itself. It's like a mine explosion that goes off when the fuse has burned to the end.

Pay careful attention to how sin lies! It bears the lie within itself. By lying we are tortured terribly.

When Eve stretched out her arm for the fruit of the tree in Paradise, at that very moment she sucked in Satan's lie. The Lord God had said: "Don't reach out your hand for it, or you'll become a child of death." And that's how it was. That was the truth. But Satan directly opposed the truth by stating a lie when he hissed: "Go ahead; reach for it. It will make you feel wonderful!" This was not true at all. It was concocted. It was a lie. And what did Eve do then? Look, if I'm standing alongside a powerful steam engine and the machinist says to me: "Be careful, or you'll get caught in the gears and be killed," I'll take a few steps back. So would you, out of your fear of dying. And if Eve had believed the truth, really believed that that tree would have caused her to die, she would have run away from it. People don't sample poison in order to determine whether it really is poison. They push it away. By extending her arm toward the tree, Eve showed that she believed Satan's lie much more than she believed God's truth. She believed the lie that eating the fruit of that tree would make her feel wonderful.

The sin is rooted in the lie.

God said: "This is how it is!" But then Satan dared to say: "No, that's not how it is!" Eve really heard both voices, God's and Satan's. And she chose all by herself not to take God at his word but Satan at his!

That was the fall, the fall into sin. It resulted in the loss of creation's glory and the beauty of Paradise. It was yielding to sin, death, and judgment.

There is no other way for you to escape this judgment than the way God provided in Paradise. You didn't think he was right then, but now you must. Then you said: "I don't take God at his Word. I do Satan at his!" Now you have to do exactly the opposite and confess: "Satan lied! Only God's Word is true!"

So it all comes down to the Word, not some personal feeling.

God discloses his majesty in his Word. His majesty can only be restored honorably through his Word.

Our fathers in the faith understood this. That's why they insisted on standing only on Scripture.

To let go of Scripture is to honor the sin of Eve.

But you haven't let go of Scripture. You believe it. You take God at his Word.

But now you ask what you still lack.

Well, by affirming what you just did, you come out from under the curse of sin and its "angel" in whom the lie resides. Admitting that God is right and Satan is wrong—nothing seems easier than this! Naturally it does, at least as long as you don't take it too seriously. As long as you only talk this way! As long as you only pay it lip service and what you say isn't coming from your heart!

But take it more seriously. Make it meaningful. Make a real effort to be upright. Then you'll see, feel, and experience how terrible it is to have a lying heart.

You could simply say: "That's right! I'm giving God the glory again. I believe him and not Satan." My lovable fellow, do you really think that Satan's lie is like a little spot that landed on your clothing? Don't you realize that Satan's lying is rust that eats through everything it touches? It's oil that soaks through to the deepest fibers of your clothing. It's cancer that spreads to the marrow of your bones. Do you actually think that the lying that's been going on for sixty centuries now is only a drop in the bucket that you can wipe up with one finger? Is it like a speck of dust that you can merely blow off a scale? Do you really think that a little pious talk is sandpaper that rubs out the deep lying that's been going on? Is the cancer like a small sliver that you easily remove? Can a little spot remover of good intentions quickly lift out sin's spots that have soaked in so deeply?

Don't fool yourself!

Oh, it is nothing other than the same sinful lie eating away at you if you imagine such things. Or if you even think they are possible! Or if God says: "You can do this by the grace that I give you, but not by yourself!" but Satan then whispers: "Yes, you can do it by yourself, if you only give it a try!" Then you are doing what Eve did sixty centuries ago. This is the lie eating away at you. And this is going on even when you think you believe! This whole sad scenario, if it applies, only emphasizes that you don't believe the Word of the Lord.

No truth exists among human beings or within any of them. It's not as though all of them intentionally misrepresent everything every day in ways they know are contrary to fact. No, sisters and brothers, every one of us knows better than that. We push that kind of crude, brash liar as far away as we can. We bar them from our circles. But this is not what's meant by saying that all people are liars.

But the depth of your misery is that you no longer really know how things are. What isn't so appears that it is. You accept this, then that, as being real. You walk around with what you think and imagine long enough until you finally get tangled up in your own ropes. That's when the severe punishment develops. Precisely what you maintained in your lying heart to be solid and sure turns out to be solidly and certainly untrue and imagined. It was pure invention and deceptive appearance.

Your suffering is not that you believed a lie thinking that it was a lie. If so, you'd put a stop to it tomorrow. But this is to your deep embarrassment and undoing, that you believed the lie thinking that it was the truth. So you worked for it and fought for it. You were mired so deep in it that you even did this in the name of the Lord and with a lot of very pious babble. You battled and worked for the lie as though it were the truth.

Appearance, fraud, self-deception! These are the terrible punishments tied to sin because they themselves are lies. Punishment is locked into sin. They come to expression all the days of our lives in order to battle us so painfully.

We wanted the lie. So God, who is righteous and just, ordained that the lie would snare us like a web does a fly. We're caught in the strands of illusion, deceit, and self-delusion that wrap themselves around us, where our life-giving blood is sucked out of us.

This is what the lie does to us for our entire lives. The most frightening and stifling thing is what it does to us personally and how it affects our own egos.

If each pathetic individual really knew who they are, point by point, how quickly Satan's kingdom would come to an end. Sadly, they're incapable of knowing themselves. Satan sees to that. From the time they're toddlers, Satan is busy painting a false picture for them of who they really are. It's not a picture that appears to be false. No way! Rather, it's a very lovely, friendly, and attractive image of themselves that he produces. He promotes it long enough that we fall in love with it. Then he whispers to us: "Do you know who this is? That dear person is no one other than you!" That flattery slides over us like soothing oil. Our inflated hearts, filled with imagined ideas about who we are, were ready to hear that. The gratification provided by being in love with ourselves followed easily. Naturally, God's Word had nothing to offer us any longer.

That's because God's Word tells ungodly people that they need to be converted. But I'm so precious, good, and exceptional just the way I am! That's the image we have of ourselves. That mistaken image has been internalized. We don't see ourselves any longer as we really are. We don't look at ourselves that way, but we're completely focused on the false image of who we think we are.

We bury our true self in forgetfulness. We disappear without a trace, and we can't find ourselves back again.

This is how the lie punishes you with a lie. You're all tangled up in it, and you can't escape the lie about yourself. You're dangling in Satan's web.

You can scream and shout and whine all you want, but it won't do you a bit of good. You simply can't find yourself any longer. No other person, whoever they are, can ever reveal to you who you are. Satan might be able to help you with this, but he won't.

All humanity is completely trapped in this frightful, terrible situation. Every person has lost sight of who they are. They can't recover the truth about themselves.

There's only one small circle of people in the entire world for whom this is different. In that circle, head for head, each individual has broken with that deadly lie and escaped Satan's web. That circle is the little group of God's elect people.

In that circle, you'll find one huge reality that's found nowhere else. People are singing in that enclave! They're singing: "After I repented, I was sorry; and after I understood myself, I beat my chest."

Do you want to know whether you belong there? Then ask yourself whether you've come to truly know yourself. Then and only then will you find victory!

GOD SEARCHES FOR WHAT HAS BEEN DRIVEN AWAY!

That which is has already been, and that which will
be also has already been. God searches for what
has been driven away. Ecclesiastes 3:15

"That which is has already been, and that which will be also has already been. God searches for what has been driven away," says the preacher. Do you understand these words?

This is what they intend to say. Now that it is summer, winter has been driven away. But while we've forgotten the winter, God searches for the winter that's been driven away, and he will bring it back at the end of the year. It will reappear.

When the signs of autumn, the sweet-smelling flowers and the colorful leaves, have been driven away, we shut ourselves off in our houses. But God searches for the flower and the leaf that have blown away. He longs to restore them back to the swaying stems and branches of spring.

That which has already been has now returned. And what will be has already been. Everything passes. It's carried out of our presence, as if borne by a flowing stream. But there is Someone who's searching again for what has been carried off. In his own good time, he will put it back in our laps renewed and refreshed.

Here everything is part of one restless stream flowing past us. It's the long morning shadow that shrinks by noon. But the Lord God is everlasting. He embraces what was and is and is to come in one eternal thought. And from that one eternal perspective of God, everything unwinds in very similar form as past, present, and future.

We see this happening in nature so obviously that even a child can tell us what's going on.

But have you ever thought about how it mirrors what's going on in our spiritual lives?

God also searches for what's been driven away in our spiritual lives. In that regard, what all hasn't been driven away and carried off on the stream of apparent forgetfulness?

Unfortunately, a great deal of all sorts of things that, when they were driven away and carried out of our sight, it was a great relief to our souls.

We ourselves constitute the stream of life. Every breath that crosses our lips distills into a droplet that is caught up in that stream and adds to it, then is carried off.

And who is there who can sum up for us all our sin and impurity and false-hood that is added to that broadening stream during the twenty, thirty, or forty years of our presence here below?

You can compare this to an assassin who drags the corpse of his victim to the shore and dumps it into the water. He feels an enormous sense of relief as he watches the swift current carry the bloodied body farther and farther into the distance. It gets smaller and smaller so that he can hardly see it. Finally, it disappears from view entirely. That's how it goes with us and our sins!

Every sin is in the deepest sense an act of murder. It's destroying something higher and better out of self-interest or from a baser motive. And our lives are so long and the numbers of opportunities we face are so endless. In each of those moments of opportunity, we did something. What we did had either a good or a bad influence.

Set aside for the moment the more refined sins in that tapestry of your sin-fulness. In a piece of fine needlework, you can hardly see the lay of each thread without the help of a magnifying glass. Similarly, without the prism of God's Word, it's extremely difficult to detect your more subtle sins.

So simply discern the more painful moments when your sinning broke out more flagrantly, and it now takes a considerable effort to quiet your conscience about them. But you sinned in such a way that at the moment you did, God's fearful displeasure struck your soul like a bolt of lightning. His foreboding clouds hung over you and robbed you of any sacred sense of freedom.

Am I stretching things? Or does this reflect pretty well your own spiritual history? At times weren't you quite happy that your sin could be thrown into that stream of forgetfulness and driven off? Weren't you pleased when it became smaller and smaller in the distance and finally disappeared from sight altogether?

So what do you think? Is there a living God who is searching for those sins that have been driven away?

Haven't you noticed that the Lord God is busy doing this? Or hasn't that ever happened to you? Maybe you haven't ever noticed the sins of long ago floating past you, so close that it's like you had just thrown them into the passing stream. You wanted to drive them away long ago. Maybe you haven't thought about them for weeks or even months. But there they are, right in front of you again.

And who was it who brought them back other than God himself? He's that holy God who's been searching for those sins that were driven away. He found them and brought them back to you. He did it to shock you about your own past. He did it to ask you whether you still haven't gone to Jesus with your soul.

Our conscience is such an amazing force. Suddenly each one of our past sins can pop up in front of us again. It's as though planted in our consciousness is something of the eternal awareness by which all things are ever-present for God.

Forgetting is drawing a curtain over the past. It prevents you from seeing what's there. But no matter how carefully you attempt to cover the past, it's always there, just beneath the surface, all your sins lined up in a row. And all that the Lord God has to do to bring them before you again is to lift the curtain. He could do it in a quiet, lonely moment or at a time of deep pain and sorrow. When he does, you see it all. All your sin! All that seemed to have been driven away!

It's useful to add that more than one person has seen that curtain lifted when they were on their deathbed. That proved to be shocking. It was so anxiety producing that the worm that gnaws and never dies really need amount to no more than us being eternally confronted with our own wickedness.

But don't let the thought of that get you down. The Lord is compassionate. His searching for the sins that you have driven away serves another purpose.

There are people who have the experience at some frightening moment of seeing all their sins at once. This can happen not just at the time they die, but it might occur in the middle of their lives. Then their soul breaks into a cold death-sweat. They're terrified. They feel like they could die. They're afraid for their lives. And it's all because they're allowed to see their sin as wicked intrigues against the living God.

It's the Lord who caused this to happen. He did it because he knew it would be effective. He searched for the sins that had been driven away. In the presence of these people, he shined the light of his law on those sins. He did it to crush their souls and bring them to sorrow and repentance. He did it to make them to flee to the foot of the cross.

This was the salvation of their souls. These were souls in which God did his terrible but also glorious work. He caused them to die a thousand deaths. But by dying, they found eternal life.

That sort of soul was once big and stood tall. Now it becomes small and humble like a child once again. And like a true child it is blessed by crying: "*Abba*, Father."

With people such as these, God always keeps on working by "searching for what has been driven away." This includes the sins that have been driven away.

He no longer does this for the purpose of frightening but for the purpose of bestowing grace. For now God takes out of the stream those sins that have been driven away, bundles them together, and throws them out—far away from you. He throws them so far away that no one can find them again, not even Satan. He throws them into the depths of the sea.

So is it the case that nothing of those sins remains any longer?

How could that be true, sisters and brothers? As though there could ever be anything in the way God deals with the mystery of sin that lacks purpose!

It's like this. If through self-discovery you detect something of your sin while still here on earth, it will ultimately be a blessing to you. You thought it would be for evil, but God intended it for good.

Still more!

Then God's angels will show you exactly how your sins reveal the power of Jesus' atoning blood.

This is how what was driven away comes back to you again.

But now it comes in glory! For the purpose of stripping off the sinful person! For the purpose of their justification by God in his righteousness!

99

THOSE WHO MOURN IN ZION!

To provide for those who mourn in Zion, adorning
them with jewels instead of ashes. Isaiah 61:3

Are you always hesitant to feel sympathy for those who mourn in Zion, or are there moments when you feel drawn to them?

At present it's not very fashionable among Christians to be mourning in Zion. Everything has to be happy, celebrative, and jubilant. The more the better! Being excited is best. To the point of being uproarious!

This doesn't betray much that's good.

Sometimes you hear the question raised among us whether this shouldn't be stretched to the level of covering an inner emptiness or hollowness in a person's faith. It would be similar to the way people today swamp the casket in wreaths and mask the grave by strewing flowers over it. That's how lavishly they spread flowers on the spiritual grave of the soul.

It's all about love. Whoever isn't put off by this goes along with it. God's glorious children almost seem dispensable if they appear to be the least bit serious. Others are gilded, pursued, actively cultivated. It appears that every member of the upper crust will be living together in the holy temple.

Then, naturally, people can't put up with those who mourn in Zion.

Get rid of mournful spirituality, gloomy religion, long faces, being straight faced, and plastered-on sobriety. The Christian life has to be one long celebration. One psalm of praise! A totally joyful noise! How could anyone stand to be with those moaners and groaners and complainers? They're always in the pits, preferably sitting in the muddy ones, or maybe in those without any water!

So this is how people are raising their youth in an uproarious faith. In a pleasant, enjoyable faith! In lyrical faith! Joyful to the point of jubilant! They teach them to hate the crepe hangers and those others who fool around with gloomy religion. There has to be laughter, not mourning! Jubilation, not weeping! And it sounds so Christian, then, when they say: "Children, don't pay one bit of attention to those hypocritical Pharisees!"

Yet, spiritually speaking, people always fall into different groups.

Just because every serious Christian needs to make a strong effort to oppose that gilded, excessively jovial Christianity with its forced liveliness, this doesn't make every glumly spiritual person one of those who mourn in Zion.

You can discern the difference between them in terms of how humans mourn.

On the one hand, you can find a widow who mourns by breaking out emotionally in her despair. But hardly a year later, she finds her mourning dress stifling, and while still in sorrow, she's talking about getting married again.

On the other hand, you can find a quite reserved woman who suffers her pain silently. Her tears are no more than a few precious pearls. Sometimes when breaking out with heavenly laughter on her lips, she's inwardly mourning deep in her soul over the husband she's lost. Then, ten years later, you find that that's still the case. There's always the same tender laughter of an angel, and always the same controlled sorrow. Both are mingled through each other.

You find the same sort of thing among the mourners of Zion.

Subdued temperament and melancholy by themselves lack spirituality. A pale appearance in itself is not sacred. And you'll seldom hear a trembling voice among God's true children.

They're not hired mourners paid to cry when expected. They don't do it to make an impression. They find doing so for effect is offensive. Only someone who knows them well discerns their pain. They don't show strangers what's really in their heart.

But the mourners in Zion will make the impression on ordinary folks of being appropriately decent and quietly contented people who exhibit a high level of sacred peace.

In their lives, their calmness can give way to jubilance on a religious holiday. But you'll also find bitter sorrow on days of repentance when they or their children experience the reproof of the Lord God, their Father in heaven.

But these two examples are exceptions. Their lives are ordinarily characterized by a calm, quiet, peaceful demeanor. They are not overly excited or giddy like the merry Christians or glum like the morbid complainers. They're pretty consistently like the controlled widow. The have a consistent sense of sadness with a trace of melancholy in which their laughter is evidence of holy reassurance.

And how does this happen?

Really, quite naturally!

You have to understand that a child of God is living two lives. To put it in the words of our beautiful confession: "There are two kinds of life. The one is physical and temporal. It comes about through our natural birth and is common to all people alike. The other is spiritual and heavenly. It proceeds from our second birth and is shared only by God's elect children."

Also understand that there can be both joy and sadness in each of these two lives.

A child of God might receive an unexpected inheritance of thousands of treasures. In their temporal life they feel happy and fortunate. But it's not always true that they're glad in their spiritual, heavenly life. It might even be that they anticipate the danger to their spiritual, heavenly life that having all that money brings. They fear the snares of Satan that come along with it. They sense that as his power increases, their soul might be the poorer for it.

Alternately, how does a faithful martyr respond when they hear people shouting: "Take that heretic to the wood pyre and burn him"? His soul rejoices that he is counted worthy of dying for the name of the Lord Jesus, even though his nerves are quivering, his flesh feels the pain, and his heart shrinks back in fear.

So you have to ask yourself whether someone who mourns in Zion is experiencing internal or external grief.

Then it becomes quite obvious that "someone who mourns in Zion" refers exclusively to a person who experiences sadness in their spiritual, heavenly life, even though they might be sailing along smoothly in their physical, temporal life.

God our Father has to know when a child of his is mourning because of Zion. God's other children, who themselves are suffering, are able to notice this too. But that kind of mourning is much too sacred for a person of this world to take any notice of it.

Above all, something needs to be added that those given to gloomy spirituality frequently forget.

True sorrow never comes without deep reassurance.

"Blessed are those who mourn, for they shall be comforted!"

The Lord's promise is unshakable: "I will provide for those who mourn in Zion, adorning them with jewels instead of ashes, the oil of gladness instead of mourning!"

A child of God who actually mourns over Zion in the depths of their soul is absolutely certain that they will be one of those comforted by the Lord.

It's not as though you could say: "First I'll mourn for half a year, a year, or maybe even two or three; then, suddenly, I'll be covered with jewels and the ashes will be gone. I'll stop wailing and start rejoicing."

It's not that mechanical for a child of God.

Occasionally they experience a huge wave in their lives; first they rise on its crest, then they sink deep into its trough. But most often their life is pretty ordinary.

It's ordinary in this sense. Mourning for Zion is buried deep in their heart. They only have clear knowledge, vivid awareness, and a strong sense of it now and then. Only on a few rare occasions will that mourning overwhelm them. Only then will Jeremiah's lamentations come to their lips.

Mingled with that mourning, the riches of complete comfort provided by their Surety and Savior are found deep in their heart. But it's a comfort of which they have had experiential knowledge also only now and then. That's why they have broken out in enraptured singing of the psalms of deliverance and praise to their God on only a few isolated occasions.

Because those two realities are present for them, both the mourning in Zion and the all-sufficient comfort, traces of sorrow and joy are always mingled when they speak.

They couldn't go along with those exuberant Christians, for then they'd forfeit their mourning in Zion. And they couldn't sit down with the sad-hearted ones either, for then they'd lose their comfort.

So look at yourself in the mirror, brothers and sisters. As you examine yourself, hold on to this.

Mourning in Zion is to be humbled in deep dismay about the terrible effects of sin and the ever-increasing flood of wickedness in our lives. It's to mourn about how intensely that sin rages against the Lord your God and his Anointed. So first of all, mourn about the inner betrayal of which you are often guilty in your own heart as a child of God. Mourn about the terrible sin that often calls you to oppose your God, your Savior, his church, and his kingdom. Mourn over the cherished yearning in your soul to hang on to whatever delights your eyes.

AN OX KNOWS
ITS OWNER!

The ox knows its owner and the donkey its master's manger. But
Israel has no knowledge; my people do not understand. Isaiah 1:3

The world of animals is a wonderful world. It was definitely created to feed us. It was also created to serve us. In part, it was created to invigorate us by its singing and its loyalty. But above and beyond all this, it was created to shame us.

It shames the mother who walks out and leaves her young darlings' nest under the watchful eye of a stranger. It shames the sluggard who avoids work and is condemned by the ants. It shames the unruly individual who refuses to be tamed by bit or bridle. It shames the anxious, who should learn from the birds of the air how to handle their concerns. It also shames the disloyal, who choose friends and then easily abandon them. Most of all, it shames the fool-hardiness of our ignorance that prevents us from ever noticing whether our God is far away from us or close by.

What's gripping is how Isaiah directs this last barb at our souls.

Is any animal more stupid than an ox or dumber than a donkey? With your exceptional abilities, what do you as a brilliant human being think when you see the witless ox lift its blunt, dumb head into its yoke? Or, better yet, when you see the ungainly donkey jerking and stumbling down the road? Yet that ox ranks much higher than you. And the donkey puts you to great shame. When that ox is eating grass in the pasture and you enter the field, it moves away from you. But if its master opens the gate and comes into the pasture, the ox walks toward him, lets him secure a rope around its horns, and is willingly led away. Likewise that dumb, ungainly donkey! On its way home, it might pass ten sheds with a full feeding trough in front of open doors, but it will walk past every one of them. Then it will stand quietly at its master's crib because it knows that this wooden manger belongs to its lord.

So "the ox knows its owner and the donkey its master's manger." The ox's dull brain and the donkey's long ears don't explain why they react the way they do. An animal is nothing. It's nothing more than a mixture of matter and energy. And all that vitality comes from the Lord of Hosts. The hen that struts in front of her chicks displays the Lord's love imprinted on her. The dog loyally languishing next to its master's headstone is a witness to its innate faithfulness, which reflects that of the Almighty. When the ox knows its owner and the donkey its master's manger, it's only and actually because the Lord God created the ox and formed the donkey like he did. The instincts and awareness they bear have been implanted, imprinted, and instilled in them by him.

But what does that matter? What difference does it make? Don't these words apply to you too: " 'Dust you are, and to dust you will return.' Do you possess anything that I have not given you?" Therefore, is there any knowledge or any understanding that has not been imprinted on you? Is there any capacity or talent that has not been created in you by the Lord God?

So does it nevertheless need to be said to you: "The ox knows its owner and the donkey smells its master's manger; but Israel has no knowledge and you, my people, lack understanding?" Isn't this rebuke deeply shameful? Doesn't it betray the shameful depth of your fall?

That you don't know your owner certainly can't be because the Lord withheld that instinctive knowledge from you like he did with a mollusk or shellfish.

Quite the opposite! Your Creator implanted that knowledge in you as a human being. He imprinted it on you in a way and to a degree that he did with no animal. Your knowledge of him excels theirs by far. In Paradise, Adam and Eve knew their owner instantly after their creation. They knew him immediately, clearly, and lucidly. No animal ever has that kind of knowledge of their master by pure instinct.

That awareness and innate consciousness of the Almighty was undistorted. Knowledge and understanding of him was pure from the outset. That the awareness sank and that the clarity was lost is not because your creation was deficient. That wasn't the cause of your soul becoming too dull to notice whether God is close by or far away, either. These are due entirely to the ravages suffered by your entire being. You now exist as a sinner. That's what you are and how you live. All true knowledge is gone. What is left is at best weak guesswork, lacks good judgment, and amounts to groping around in the dark.

The Lord God is present everywhere. He's in every person's blood. All creation tells of his glory. Day and night utter his speech. No one has to ascend to heaven any longer to acquire his Word because it has descended to us and is close by. Yet, the larger half of the four million souls living in our fatherland never even notice that the living God exists. Day after day they slog along, fret, and keep on sinning.

They roam around, get lost, and run here and there. All the while they're looking for something, sampling, and grasping at something they can't identify. Their lips are glued together by a feverish thirst in their souls. Like Hagar, they sit down close to a spring while their Ishmael lies dying next to them. Neither one of them notices the nearby brook flowing with wonderful water.

Without air and with sealed lungs, they gasp for breath. Devoid of air in their own vanity and emptiness, they neither notice nor detect the healthy air swirling and streaming off God's holy mountain when it's only two steps away from them.

They have to have God. And their God really is present. This is the God who upholds them and feeds them and protects them. This is the God who tenderly reaches his arms toward them and shows them compassion. But they hear nothing. They notice nothing. "The ox knows its owner and the donkey its master's manger. But prominent people have no knowledge and sinners do not understand."

If only it were only that!

But that's not how things stand.

No! It's Israel that has no knowledge. It's my people who lack understanding.

We are the ones, we who confess Jesus, we believers who are put to shame by the ox and reproached by the donkey. We have been pardoned. We no longer stand far off. We have been given knowledge of our God through tender compassion and frequently squandered grace. God created a bright light in our darkened hearts.

We are the ones whose souls have been pierced by his Word. We have a very different Owner from sinners and a very different Lord from the ungodly. We have One who purchased us with his own blood and made us his possession.

It becomes obvious, then, that we have an external knowledge of our Owner and the capacity to know him through faith planted in our hearts. Without this we would not be children of God. But it is of no benefit, and you would forfeit all comfort if you entirely lacked that external knowledge or innate capacity to believe.

But this is guilt you should acknowledge. That knowledge is like a drop of oil floating on the surface of the water and that never penetrates your inner existence. That precious capacity to believe frequently isn't working and shrivels inside instead of operating with power.

For the ox the question isn't whether the animal has some impression of what its owner looks like but whether it notices and responds to its owner when he comes to him. And for you, it's shameful when your God can be with you and near you moment by moment and you never notice his footsteps or respond to the rustle of his clothing.

If God's hand strikes you, those around you would hear you whining about your God even though God himself, whose hand hit you, is right there with you in person.

In dryness of soul, you cry out for a drop from the Fountain of all goodness, even though God is not a God who is far away but close, covering you with his wings.

Time and time again, lies and truth are scrambled together. But you lack the discernment and instinct and sensitivity to distinguish which are Satan's lies and which are the sacred truth of God directed at you.

Alongside your God's manger is Satan's trough. In the former lies the Savior whose flesh you are to eat and whose blood you are to drink to sustain you. In the other lies the poisoned fodder of the tempter of souls. But you lack the judgment to discern between them, so you take turns eating from one and then the other.

Could you distinguish, and should you then say: "I'll never again behave like that, beginning day after tomorrow!"—even that much you couldn't do. You're too dull even for that! You'll just get it wrong, time after time.

The only thing that can save you is to confess that the ox excels you in knowing its owner and the donkey in discerning his master's manger. It's to confess in your despair that from this time forward you will lean only on God's faithfulness for support, imploring: "Lord, lead me beyond my dullness and stupidity and into the glory and blessedness of knowing you!"

2018 DUTCH REFORMED TRANSLATION SOCIETY BOARD OF DIRECTORS

DR. JOEL R. BEEKE
President, Puritan Reformed
Theological Seminary
Grand Rapids, MI

PROF. GERALD M. BILKES
Professor of New Testament and
Biblical Theology
Puritan Reformed Theological
Seminary
Grand Rapids, MI

DR. JOHN BOLT
Professor of Systematic Theology,
emeritus
Calvin Theological Seminary
Grand Rapids, MI

PROF. RONALD CAMMENGA
Professor of Dogmatics and Old
Testament
Protestant Reformed Theological
Seminary
Grandville, MI

DR. JAMES A. DE JONG
President and Professor of
Historical Theology, emeritus
Calvin Theological Seminary
Grand Rapids, MI

DR. I. JOHN HESSELINK
President and Professor of Theology,
emeritus
Western Theological Seminary
Holland, MI

DR. EARL WILLIAM KENNEDY
Senior Research Fellow, A. C. Van
Raalte Institute
Hope College
Holland, MI

JAMES KINNEY
Executive Vice President of
Academic Publishing
Baker Publishing Group
Ada, MI

REV. MAARTEN KUIVENHOVEN
Pastor, Heritage Reformed
Congregation
Grand Rapids, MI

DR. RICHARD A. MULLER
P. J. Zondervan Professor of
Historical Theology, emeritus
Calvin Theological Seminary
Grand Rapids, MI

DR. ADRIAAN C. NEELE
Director of Doctoral Studies
Puritan Reformed Theological
Seminary
Grand Rapids, MI

DR. DONALD W. SINNEMA
Professor of Theology, emeritus
Trinity Christian College
Palos Heights, IL

MR. GISE VAN BAREN
Retired businessman
Crete, IL

MR. HENRY I. WITTE
Witte Travel and Tours, retired
Ada, MI

SUBJECT INDEX

SCRIPTURE INDEX

Old Testament